MW00640061

Rupp's
Insurance &
Risk Management
Glossary

By Richard V. Rupp, CPCU

NILS Publishing Company
Chatsworth, California

Rupp's Insurance & Risk Management Glossary
Copyright © 1991 by NILS Publishing Company

All rights reserved. No part of this publication may be reproduced or transmitted in any form or by any means, electronic or mechanical, including photocopy, recording, or any information storage or retrieval system, without permission in writing from NILS Publishing Company Inc., the publisher.

The information contained in this glossary is provided for reference uses only. NILS Publishing Company, by publishing this glossary, does not render advice of any sort. If expert assistance is required, the services of a competent professional should be sought. No representations are made to this glossary's completeness or accuracy, although NILS Publishing Company has made every effort to provide you with the most up-to-date and useful information possible. NILS hereby expressly excludes all warranties.

Printed in the United States of America.
International Standard Book Number: 0-89246-224-8
Library of Congress Catalog Number: 89-060224

Dedication

This effort at compiling and clarifying insurance and risk management terms is dedicated to The Society of Chartered Property and Casualty Underwriters, its members and staff, who have played an extremely important role in my life and my wife Coleen's life.

Rupp's
Insurance &
Risk Management
Glossary

Table Of Contents

ACKNOWLEDGMENTS

I have been fortunate for the contributions and assistance, as well as the wise counsel and amazing breadth of knowledge of numerous people in the development of this work. It would be impossible to thank everyone who gave me helpful direction, but the following people are owed a special debt of gratitude for their contribution to this book.

First, my loving wife Coleen, who, for a large part of the last three years, has seen only the top of my head sticking out over a stack of books, and who has spent countless hours reviewing my efforts and compiling all of the information on the associations included in this book; my son Matthew, who amazed me with his energetic research efforts, and who located hundreds of resource materials for my use; and to Sandra Ruffner, who had the unenviable task of entering the initial draft of this book into our word processing system; a contribution made with care, unceasing good humor and an interest that is seldom found today.

The breadth of knowledge and unselfish commitment of my friends and fellow CPCUs who are listed as reviewers never cease to amaze me. They are true professionals, dedicated to the growth, education and excellence within our industry.

Finally, I must thank Chuck Welch, Gary Yim and Jon Fish at NILS Publishing, who have become good friends, and deserve both my thanks and gratitude for their continual advice and the professional editing of my work.

The following reviewers, listed in alphabetical order, checked glossary terms for factual and technical accuracy in these categories:

- **French Terms:** Suzanne D. Bergeron, CPCU; assistant secretary, Munich American Reinsurance Company, San Francisco, California.

- **Insurer Operations and Regulation Terms:** Joseph P. Decaminada, J.D., CPCU, CLU, ChFC; executive vice president, The Atlantic Mutual Companies, New York, New York.

- **Boiler and Machinery Terms:** Russ H. Driscoll, CPCU; regional vice president, Hartford Steam Boiler Inspection, Universal City, California.

- **Reinsurance Terms:** Edward W. Frye, Jr., CPCU; Underwriting Consultant Service of Connecticut, Stamford, Connecticut.

- **Health and Life Insurance Terms:** Jerrol L. Harris, CPCU, CLU; executive vice president, California Casualty and Life Insurance Company, San Mateo, California.

- **Inland and Ocean Marine Insurance Terms:** Jim Hawkins, CPCU; Fireman's Fund Insurance Company, San Rafael, California.

- **German Insurance Terms:** Marcus Hildman, Chairman of the Board, President and CEO, Allianz Insurance Company, Los Angeles, California.

- **General Insurance Terms:** Donn P. McVeigh, CPCU; Creative Risks Concepts International, Oakland, California.

- **Spanish Insurance Terms:** Maria C. Miranda, manager, International Division, Seguros La Commercial, New York, New York.

- **Insurance Organizations, research and editing:** Coleen-Ann Mulhern, marketing manager, The Information Store, Inc., San Francisco, California.

- **Loss Prevention and Control and Workers' Compensation Terms:** Sharyn S. Simmons, CPCU, CSP; marketing vice president, CIGNA Property and Casualty Companies, Menlo Park, California.

- **International Insurance Terms:** Mary Sklarski, CPCU; manager, International Insurance Department, Chubb Group of Insurance Companies, San Francisco, California.

- **Agency and Insurance Organization Terms:** Roger L. Smith, CPCU; president, Insurance Education Association, San Francisco, California.

- **Employee Benefit and Casualty Insurance Terms:** Lawton Swan III, CPCU, CLU; Interisk Corporation, St. Petersburg, Florida.

- **Property Insurance Terms:** Ginny Talucci, CPCU; regional manager, Commercial Property Division, American Home Insurance Company, San Francisco, California.

- **Risk Management and Property Insurance Terms:** David Warren, CPCU; risk management consultant, Orinda, California.

Most of the foreign insurance terms listed herein were compiled by *Reinsurance Digest*, published by Reinsurance Communications Co., Inc., New York, New York. They are used here with their permission.

RICHARD V. RUPP

Richard V. Rupp, CPCU, is a nationally recognized author and lecturer on insurance and risk management. Beginning his insurance career with the Insurance Services Office in 1961, the author has been an officer of both Marsh & McLennan, Inc. and the Continental Insurance Companies, and a principal consultant with Warren, McVeigh & Griffin. Mr. Rupp is currently Director of Risk Management, Andreini & Company, San Francisco.

Mr. Rupp is an active member of the Society of Chartered Property and Casualty Underwriters (CPCU) and the Society of Insurance Research. He served on the CPCU Research Activities Committee for seven years, three of which were as the Committee Chairman and is currently serving on the Interest Sections Governing Committee. As a Member of the Self-Insurance Institute of America, Inc., Mr. Rupp also served on the Publications Committee. He has conducted seminars for the Society of CPCU, Risk and Insurance Management Society, Professional Insurance Agents, and the Self-Insurance Institute of America, Inc.

Dick and his wife Coleen reside in the Northern California community of Half Moon Bay.

USING THE GLOSSARY

Rupp's Insurance and Risk Management Glossary is a comprehensive reference which defines over 4,000 insurance-related and risk management terms. Most glossary entries include several features that enhance their informational value:

Subject Categories

Each term is categorized as belonging in one or more subject areas. This classification scheme provides information as to the context in which each term is used. The Subject Categories used in this edition of the Glossary are:

- Agency
- Automobile Insurance
- Aviation Insurance
- Casualty Insurance
- Crime Insurance
- Employee Benefits
- Financial Guarantee Insurance
- Financial Planning
- General
- Health Insurance
- Inland Marine Insurance
- Insurer Operations
- International Insurance
- Life Insurance
- Loss Prevention/Loss Control
- Mortgage Insurance
- Ocean Marine Insurance
- Organizations
- Property Insurance
- Regulation
- Reinsurance
- Risk Management
- Surety
- Title Insurance
- Workers' Compensation

Cross References

To give you a greater sense of a term's usage and context, we've added cross-references to most of the terms defined in this Glossary. These cross-references direct you to other terms in the Glossary; follow them to broaden your understanding of insurance and risk management concepts:

> **"syn"** (synonym) is used to indicate other terms that are used interchangeably with the defined term.

"compare" indicates terms that are the opposites (antonyms) of the defined term, or terms which are similar in meaning except for some distinguishing differences.

"see" references refer you to related terms; also, if a term is not defined in the Glossary, the instruction to "see" another term means that the first term is synonymous with the second term, which we have defined elsewhere.

Acronyms

When applicable, we've listed any acronym that is commonly used in place of the term. If you know the acronym, but not the term, a table of acronyms (listed in alphabetical order) is included at the end of the Glossary, starting on page 361.

Foreign Terms

The abbreviations **Fr**, **Gr**, and **Sp** are used in cross-references, to indicate French, German and Spanish equivalents to the defined English-language term. Beginning on page 371, there are three tables, listing (in alphabetical order) all foreign terms included in this Glossary, with their English-language equivalents.

By using these tools, we hope your understanding of insurance and risk management concepts is increased and enriched.

A

AAA
Organizations.
   see: American Automobile Association

AAA tenant
Financial Planning.
   see: triple A tenant

abandonment
General. The abdication of property into the hands of another, or into the possession of no one in particular (i.e., the state).

Ocean Marine. The relinquishing of property by its owner to an insurance company, in order to claim a total loss when, in fact, the loss is less than total. This is generally not allowed by property insurance policies, but under certain conditions it is allowed by ocean marine policies.
   see: abandonment clause

abandonment clause
Ocean Marine. A provision in some ocean marine policies, allowing the insured to abandon lost or damaged property to the insurance company and claim a total loss. The abandonment clause applies to two types of losses: actual total loss and constructive total loss.
   see: abandonment, actual total loss, constructive total loss, salvage

abatement
Ocean Marine. The refund of duties on damaged or imported goods. The goods may be damaged during importation or while in a bonded warehouse.
   see: bonded shipments, bonded warehouse, duty

able to earn
Workers' Compensation. In state workers' compensation laws, the phrase "able to earn" in reference to wages refers to a fair average of the weekly or monthly wages which an employee is able to earn, over a period of time sufficient to determine the employee's earning capacity.
   see: reduced earnings

abnormal use
Casualty. Use of a product in a manner, or for a purpose, other than its intended use. "Abnormal use" is a defense used sometimes in products liability cases where the use could not have been reasonably foreseen by the manufacturer or seller of a product or installation. *Example:* Using a hand-powered lawn mower to trim hedges, ultimately causing injury to the operator or an innocent bystander.

abortion clinics professional liability
Casualty. Insurance that protects abortion clinics from general and professional liability claims. Generally, coverage is written on a hospital liability form and is provided for the clinic, its employees and staff.

abortion coverage
Health. Coverage under health insurance policies for abortions that are involuntary or necessary to preserve the mother's health. Some policies also cover voluntary abortions by not specifically excluding them.

above-normal loss (ANL)
Insurer Operations. A loss enhanced by secondary conditions or circumstances, such as weather.
   see: probable maximum loss

abrogate
General. The act by an authority to cancel, repeal,

© 1991 NILS Publishing Company

1

abrogate — continued
abolish or declare a law, contract or other legal transaction or document null and void.

absolute assignment
Life. The transfer of all control and rights in a life insurance policy to another party, which cannot be reacquired except by action of the assignee. Such transfers cannot be made to the individual insured by the policy.
see: **assignment**

absolute beneficiary
Life.
see: **irrevocable beneficiary**

absolute liability
Casualty. Liability without fault, that generally arises from extremely dangerous operations. Some states impose absolute liability when an insured's actions are determined to be against public policy. *Examples:* Use of explosives by a blasting contractor or possession of poisonous snakes by an individual.
syn: **strict liability**

absolute ownership
Title. An unconditional, indisputable interest, or right of ownership that is totally free from any conditions, constraints or restrictions; so complete and perfect by itself that it cannot be claimed without permission.

absolve
General. The act by one party (or authority) to release another from obligation or responsibility.

absorption rate
Property. A rate once used by factory mutuals on their property insurance policies; after January 1, 1986, its use was abandoned. An initial premium deposit was charged, equal to three to five times the net annual premium. On an annual basis, an "absorption" — which equalled the annual premium — took place, which resulted in the premium deposit being reinstated for the following period.
see: **Factory Mutual System**

abstract
Title.
see: **abstract of title, title, title insurance**

abstract companies
Title. Companies which perform title searches or specialize in providing or assisting in abstract of bids, or abstract of records.
see: **abstract of title**

abstract of bids
Surety. An owner's summary of unit prices, allowing the owner to select a contractor by comparing the contractors' bids with the owner's unit price list.
see: **bid bond**

abstract of title
Title. A written, chronological summary of the title to land, including conveyances of the title (such as wills and deeds) and legal proceedings (such as liens). The abstract provides the names of all involved parties and their legal descriptions, as well as a description of the property and its location.
see: **chain of title, title**

abstractors professional liability insurance
Casualty/Title. Insurance that protects title abstractors against claims for negligent acts, errors or omissions. Coverage is often written in conjunction with title agents errors & omissions insurance.
see: **abstract companies**

abstract plats
Title. A summary of records showing the size, location and owner's name of each lot, parcel, or plot of land within a specified area.

abuse of minority stockholders
General. Decisions made by officers and directors for personal reasons, rather than for furthering the company's fortunes, which have the effect of treating minority stockholders unfavorably. *Examples:* Shares issued to insiders to gain greater control, or excessive remuneration paid to favored individuals.
see: **directors & officers liability insurance**

abuse of process
General. A legal term used to refer to a departure from reasonable use, contrary to orderly established usage; e.g., use of the criminal legal process for civil or noncriminal matters.

abutment
Loss Control. That part of a structure that directly receives thrust or pressure; the area or point where a supporting member touches or adjoins the member it supports.

accelerated benefits
Life.
see: **living benefits**

accelerated depreciation
Financial Planning. A method of accounting for depreciation, where greater amounts of depreciation are taken in the early life of an asset, and smaller amounts toward the end of its depreciation period. This form of depreciation has the effect of deferring taxes to later years.
see: **depreciation, straight line depreciation**

2

© 1991 NILS Publishing Company

accelerated option

Life. A life insurance policy provision allowing the policyholder to use accumulated policy dividends and cash value to create an endowment, or to pay off the policy premium.

see: **accelerative endowment**

accelerative endowment

Life. One of the accelerated options under a life insurance policy; the endowment elected under this option.

see: **accelerated option**

acceptance

General. An element needed to form a legal contract. It is the expressed agreement by one party to the offer of another party which concludes a contract and legally binds the parties. For insurance purposes, contractual acceptance occurs when an applicant receives a policy from the company and pays a premium.

syn: **mutual assent;** see: **contract**

Life. An agreement to an offer. Because the initial premium in life insurance is usually submitted along with the application, the insurer's issuance of a life insurance policy based on the application constitutes acceptance.

Insurer Operations. The acceptance of a risk by an underwriter or other person authorized to act on behalf of an insurer. The risk is accepted when the underwriter or other person expresses a willingness to issue an insurance policy. *Contractual acceptance* of the insurance contract occurs when the underwriter issues the policy and the insured pays the premium.

syn: **assume;** compare: **rejection;** see: **submitted business**

accepted bid

Surety. The quotation that an owner accepts as the basis for entering into a contract with the offeror (contractor) who submitted the bid.

see: **bid**

accession

General. The principle that an owner of property becomes entitled to all property which that property produces, whether the property is produced by skilled labor (e.g., manufactured goods), nature (e.g., growing timber), or artificially (e.g., cultivated crops). Conversely, the possessor of property may become entitled to it, as against the original owner, if the additions made by his or her skill and labor is of greater value than the property itself, or if it is impossible to restore the changed form to its original condition.

accessory

General. 1) Anything that, when added to another object, renders it more perfect, or which accompanies it, is incidentally connected to it, is subordinate to it, or belongs to or with the object.
2) In a legal context, one who, although not present, is connected in the commission of an offense, either before or after the performance of the offending act, is an accessory.

see: **accessory after the fact, accessory before the fact**

accessory after the fact

General. An individual who, with the knowledge that an illegal offense has been committed, receives, aids, assists or shelters the offender.

see: **accessory**

accessory before the fact

General. An individual who counsels, commands or otherwise causes another to commit an illegal offense.

see: **accessory**

access to health care

Health. A term used to describe the ability of an individual to receive medical care, either through employer-provided health benefit plans or through government programs.

accident

Casualty. A sudden, unplanned and unexpected event, not under the control of the insured, resulting in injury or damage.

compare: **occurrence;** see: **accidental occurrence, fortuitous event, industrial accident, injury;** Fr: **accident;** Gr: **Unfall;** Sp: **accidente**

accidental bodily injury

Health. An injury to the human body which results from a sudden, unplanned and unexpected event. Often there is a fine line between accidental bodily injury, which would be covered by an accident only insurance policy, and nonaccidental bodily injury, which would not be covered. *Example:* If an individual was injured while changing the tires of a car because the jack slipped, the injury would be accidental. However, if the jack did not slip, but instead, the individual strained his or her back while operating the jack, the injury would not be considered accidental.

see: **accident, accident only insurance**

accidental death

Life. A death caused by unexpected and unintended means.

see: **death**

accidental death and dismemberment (AD & D)

Health. Insurance coverage which pays either a specified amount, or a specified number of weekly disability benefit payments, when the insured dies, loses sight, or loses limbs as the result of an accident.

see: accident only insurance

accidental death benefit

Life. A provision added to a life policy that pays an additional benefit if a person is killed in a serious accident. An extra premium is often, but not always, charged.

syn: additional death benefit, double indemnity

accidental death insurance

Health/Life. An insurance policy which pays its benefit when an insured is killed in an accident. Most commonly combined with dismemberment insurance and offered as accidental death and dismemberment insurance.

see: accidental death and dismemberment, accident only insurance

accidental occurrence

Casualty. An event or series of events happening by chance or unexpectedly, and not in the usual course of affairs, that causes injury or damage. An occurrence can be the result of continuous or repeated exposure to conditions, with no single accidental event causing an injury. On the other hand, an "accident" is generally sudden and at a definite place in time and location.

see: accident, occurrence

accident analysis

Loss Control. The analysis of a specific accident by separating or breaking it down into segments, in order to determine its nature, proportion, function or relationship. From this analysis, a report is developed which identifies and evaluates the unsafe conditions and/or acts associated with the accident.

accident and health insurance (A & H)

Health. A class of insurance which pays benefits for losses caused by disease, accidental injury or accidental death.

see: group accident and health insurance, accident only insurance

accident and sickness insurance

Health.

see: health insurance

accident control

Loss Control. Steps taken or procedures implemented to reduce accident potential or to limit accident frequency or severity. Techniques employed often include premises and equipment inspection; education through safety meetings; personal protective equipment, and loss engineering.

see: loss control, loss prevention, loss reduction

accident experience

Loss Control. A loss experience report which relates a risk's frequency of accidents to selected units of measurement, thereby making the loss experience more meaningful to management. For example, the accident experience report may list such things as the rate of disabling injuries, number of lost work days due to accidents, or the number of first-aid cases.

see: loss experience, loss run

accident frequency

Loss Control. The rate at which accidents occur over a period of time. Generally expressed as the number of accidents per given amount of hours worked, it may also be expressed per employee days worked, per employee, or employee years.

Formula: "Accident frequency" = Number of Accidents x 1,000,000 hours/Total Hours Worked During the Year.

syn: accident rate; compare: accident severity, loss frequency, loss severity

accident insurance

Health. Insurance under which benefits are payable after a disabling accident. Benefits include lost earnings, medical expenses, and indemnity for death or loss of limbs or sight.

see: health insurance

accident only insurance

Health. Policies providing coverage for death or dismemberment caused by, or hospital and medical services necessitated because of an accident.

see: accident and health insurance, accidental death and dismemberment

accident prevention

Loss Control. A term which has largely been replaced by terms such as loss prevention or loss control. Accident prevention still is used frequently to refer to the loss prevention and control efforts of workers' compensation insurers.

see: loss control, loss prevention, loss reduction

accident rate

Loss Control.

see: accident frequency

accident report

General. 1) A report used to document an accident,

4

© 1991 NILS Publishing Company

completed by participants in an accident or by objective third parties. 2) A report prepared and issued by law enforcement officials following an accident.

see: **incident report, notice of loss**

accident severity

Loss Control. A measure of the severity or seriousness of loss caused by accidents. Generally expressed as days lost per thousand hours worked.
Formula: "Accident Severity" = Number of Days Lost x 1,000 Hours/Total Hours Worked During the Year.

compare: **accident frequency, loss frequency, loss severity**

accident year experience

Risk Management. A comparison of all losses (paid or reserved) during a twelve-month period, with all premiums earned for the same period. The losses included in the report are those which occurred during the period (regardless of when reported); premiums included in the report are those earned during the period (regardless of when written). Once calculated for a given period, accident year experience never changes. *Formula:* Accident Year Experience = Total value of all losses during a defined twelve month period/Earned premium for the same period.

see: **calendar year experience, policy year experience**

accident year statistics

Insurer Operations/Risk Management. Used by insurers and risk managers in predicting future losses, these statistics show incoming premium and outgoing losses for a 12-month period. Since these statistics show the percentage of the premium that is paid out, these statistics are also important in setting future premiums.

see: **loss ratio**

accommodation

General. An obligation offered or assumed as a favor to another. There is no consideration required or expected for the granting of an accommodation.

compare: **contract**

accommodation line

Agency/Insurer Operations. Insurance policies written for an agent or policyholder, covering risks which normally would be rejected based on normal underwriting criteria, but for which coverage is granted because the agent's or policyholder's other business is desirable.

accommodation party

Surety. A person or party signing a commercial document in any capacity (e.g., as a co-signer), for the purpose of lending his or her name to another party to the instrument.

accord and satisfaction

Insurer Operations. The process of adjusting a previously disputed amount, and paying that amount, to discharge a claim. *Accord* is the agreement to the adjustment; *satisfaction* is the performance and execution of that agreement.

accountability

General. The periodic obligation of a business' management to provide appropriately detailed and complete information to stockholders, bondholders, lenders, governmental agencies, or any party that could be affected by a contractual obligation.

accountant

General. A person skilled in the art or system of keeping financial records.

see: **Certified Public Accountant**

accountants' materiality test

Risk Management. A guideline used by accountants to determine the significance of an event's financial impact on a business. The amount most commonly used is 5% of net income before taxes from continuing operations; any event which has an impact of 5% or greater is considered "material." This test is sometimes used to determine a self-insured's risk retention level.

see: **retention**

accountants professional liability insurance

Casualty. Insurance protecting accountants and accounting partnerships against liability for negligent acts, errors or omissions of officers, partners or employees in performing professional accounting services. Coverage generally includes protection against loss caused by dishonesty, fraud and misrepresentation. Policies do not cover liability based upon intent to deceive by the insured or any partner. Coverage against liability imposed by the Securities Act of 1933 and its amendments may be added.

account current

Agency/Insurer Operations. A monthly financial statement between an agent and an insurer, indicating policy numbers, premiums, and applicable commissions on business produced by the agent.

see: **agent's balances**

account executive

Agency. An individual – employed by either an insurance agency or brokerage – who is directly responsible for servicing accounts. Often, an account executive will specialize in a particular type of coverage or insured, or will provide account service for a single large organization having numerous policies.
Reinsurance. An individual – employed by either the reinsurer or the reinsurance intermediary – who is

© 1991 NILS Publishing Company

account executive – continued
responsible for managing the reinsurance account of a particular insurer (the reinsured).

accounting
General. A system or method of recording financial transactions and reporting, verifying and analyzing the results. The surveying of pertinent data and subsequent preparation of statements representing the financial condition of an enterprise. The two most common accounting methods are cash basis and the accrual method.

see: accrual basis of accounting, cash basis of accounting, financial statement, Generally Accepted Accounting Principles, Statutory Accounting Principles

accounting cycle
General. The full sequence of procedures that occur during each accounting period; the recording and posting of transactions.

syn: accounting period

accounting depreciation
General.
see: depreciation

accounting period
General.
see: accounting cycle

accounting postulates
General. Theoretical assumptions on which modern accounting principles are based.

see: Generally Accepted Accounting Principles

accounting principles
General. The doctrine and principles which serve as an explanation of accounting practices.

see: Generally Accepted Accounting Principles, Statutory Accounting Principles

account premium modification plan
Property. An insurance rating plan for large commercial property accounts, which considers such factors as prior losses, maintenance, housekeeping and quality of management. Under this rating plan, credits or debits of up to 25 percent can be applied to the standard (manual) rates.

see: "A" rates, judgment rates

accounts receivable
General. The amounts that a customer owes a business on a current account for completed sales of goods or services. Deposit accruals and other items not arising out of everyday transactions are not considered accounts receivable.

see: accounts receivable insurance, receivables; Fr: effets à recevoir; Gr: Forderungen Aussenstände; Sp: cuentas por cobrar

accounts receivable insurance
Inland Marine. Insurance covering uncollectable sums, extra collection fees, and costs associated with the reconstruction of damaged or destroyed records, all caused by a destruction of accounts receivable records by an insured peril. The value of the blank media upon which the records were stored (records, disks or computer tapes) are usually not covered. The coverage includes interest on loans to offset collections, and additional expenses resulting from impaired or damaged records. Large-limit policies can be written on a monthly reporting basis.

see: accounts receivable

accretion
Loss Control. The gradual accumulation of land (including sand bars and deposits, delta land, etc.) by natural causes, such as alluvial deposits or the flow of rivers into seas. Accretion is of two kinds: alluvial (the deposit of soil), and dereliction (the sinking of water levels below normal).

see: alluvion, avulsion

Financial Planning. The added principal or interest accruing as a result of investment income.

accrual
General. Something which comes about as a natural growth, increase or advantage; that which accumulates or issues after a period of time. *Example:* Profits of mutual companies accrue to policyholders.

see: accumulation

accrual basis of accounting
General. A method of recording earnings and expenses as they occur or are incurred, without regard to the actual date of collection or payment.

compare: cash basis of accounting; see: accounting, accrued expense, accrued income, accrued interest

accrual of discount
Insurer Operations. Adjustments made to the original purchase price of bonds when those bonds were purchased for less than par value, in order to increase the book value to par at the maturity date.

accrue
Employee Benefits/Risk Management. Benefits under a pension plan which have been accumulated by an individual from years of prior service.

© 1991 NILS Publishing Company

accrued benefit cost method
Employee Benefits/Risk Management.
see: unit credit actuarial cost method

accrued expense
General. An expense which has been incurred but not yet paid.
see: accrual basis of accounting; compare: accrued income

accrued future service benefit
Employee Benefits. The portion of an employee benefit plan participant's retirement benefit which is attributable to service after the plan's effective date and prior to a specified current date.

accrued income
General. Income which has been earned but not yet received.
compare: accrued expense; see: accrual basis of accounting

accrued interest
General. Interest which has been earned but not yet received.
compare: accumulated interest; see: accrual basis of accounting

accumulated benefit cost method
Employee Benefits/Risk Management.
see: unit credit actuarial cost method

accumulated depreciation
General. The total amount of reduction in an asset's value as of a given date, as the result of depreciation.
see: depreciation

accumulated funding deficiency
Employee Benefits. A deficiency in a pension plan's funding standard account. This is caused by a failure to meet the minimum funding standards established by ERISA for pension plans.
see: funding standard account, minimum funding standard

accumulated interest
General. Interest payments which are past due and unpaid.
compare: accrued interest

accumulated plan benefit method
Employee Benefits.
see: unit credit actuarial cost method

accumulation
Life. Increases made to a life insurance policy's benefits – such as interest on accumulated dividends left with the company, or increased cash values. The

benefits are a reward to the insured for continuous renewal of the policy.
syn: accumulation benefits; see: accumulation period

accumulation benefits
Life.
see: accumulation

accumulation period
Life. The period of time during which the insured makes premium payments on a life insurance policy.
see: accumulation
Health. The period of time during which the insured accumulates covered expenses to satisfy the policy deductible.

accumulation value
Life. A value accumulated in a universal life insurance policy which is calculated by taking the sum of all premiums paid and interest credited to the account, less deductions for expenses, loans and surrenders.
see: level death benefit option, universal life insurance

acid and chemical damage policy
Property. Insurance covering losses to property caused by acids and chemicals.

acid-test ratio
Risk Management/Surety.
see: quick ratio

acknowledgment
General. To admit, confess, avow, affirm, declare, imply an obligation, or admit to a responsibility. Most states have adopted a uniform standard of acknowledgment, i.e., the Uniform Acknowledgment Act.

ACORD Corporation
Organizations. Members: Property and casualty insurance agent and broker associations, vendors of automatic systems and insurance-related services. *Objectives:* Promotes the interests of the American Agency System through improved agency-company operations and communications. *Founded:* Formed in 1983 by a merger of Agency Company Operations Research and Development Corporation founded in 1970, and Insurance Institute for Research founded in 1978. *Headquarters:* White Plains, NY.

ACORD forms
Agency/Insurer Operations. Industry-wide, standardized forms developed by insurance companies and agency groups for insurance applications, certificates of insurance, quotations, etc.
see: ACORD Corporation

acquiescence

General. The act of implying consent by remaining silent. When there has been an infringement of rights, either implied or specific, and the victim of the infringement agrees to continue as though nothing has occurred, the victim's acquiescence is considered his or her assent to the alleged infringement.

see: **estoppel, laches, reservation of rights, waiver**

acquired immune deficiency syndrome (AIDS)

Casualty/Health. A fatal, incurable virus transmitted by exchange of body fluids, such as blood and semen.

see: **blood bank professional liability insurance, communicable disease exclusion, dread disease policy, extra percentage tables, limited policy**

Life.

see: **living benefits**

acquisition cost

Insurer Operations. The expense incurred by an insurance company to solicit and underwrite new insurance policies. These expenses include advertising expenses, commissions paid to agents or brokers, inspection expenses, credit and motor vehicle report fees, medical examination fees, and rating and underwriting expenses.

see: **administration expenses**

Reinsurance. Those expenses (administrative, commissions, etc.) incurred by a reinsurer which are directly related to acquiring business from ceding companies.

see: **ceding commission**

acting insurer

Insurer Operations. An insurer performing duties for another, or performing temporary services.

see: **fronting**

acting representative

General. A person with authority to act on behalf of another person or organization while performing temporary service or holding temporary rank or position.

see: **agency**

action in deceit

General. A legal action or court proceeding under which damages may be collected as remedy for acts of fraud.

see: **deceit, fraud**

actions

Regulation. References in an insurance policy to "actions" are to legal proceedings in a court. Some actions – such as claims against an insuring company – are usually restricted by policy language with time limits on commencement of such an action. These time limits usually run one year from the date of the occurrence of the loss or damage, or one year after the cause of action begins.

see: **actions and proceedings, cause of action**

actions and proceedings

General. "Actions" in this context refers to filings made to and requests made of judicial or administrative authorities. "Proceedings" means any action or hearing, investigation or inquiry in which testimony can be required. In general, "actions and proceedings" means the orderly manner of conducting business before the court.

active life fund

Life. An unallocated fund which is maintained for active participants included under a deposit administration plan. As participants retire, individual annuities are purchased with money from this fund.

syn: **deposit account, deposit administration fund, deposit fund, purchase payment fund**; see: **deposit administration plan**

active life reserve

Health/Life.

see: **policy reserve**

active malfunction

Casualty. A products liability term referring to bodily injury or property damage caused by a product originally designed to benefit the user. Active malfunction claims are insured under products liability coverage. *Example:* An insecticide, intended to protect crops from pests, actually kills the crops.

see: **bench error, defective, hidden defect, latent defect**

active retention

Risk Management.

see: **retention, self-insurance**

active waste

General. An intentional, affirmative act that results in damage to another's property. *Example:* Cutting down a decorative hedge or row of shade trees.

act of God

General. A naturally-occurring event caused by conditions outside and beyond human agency, control or intervention, such as floods, earthquakes and hurricanes. "Acts of God" are excluded under most standard property forms, although they may be bought back at additional premium.

see: **commercial impracticability, force majeure coverage, vis major**

Casualty. Proof that an act of God is the direct or

8

© 1991 NILS Publishing Company

proximate cause of injury or damage is an affirmative defense in negligence cases, under the law of torts.

acts of independent contractors

Casualty. An independent contractor is free to do a job in his or her own way, in his or her own time, and subject to no other person's direction or control. Therefore, one who employs an independent contractor is generally not liable for the acts of the independent contractor.

compare: agency, contingent liability, respondeat superior; see: general contractor

actual authority

Agency/Insurer Operations. An insurance agent's authority that the insurer (the principal) intentionally confers on the agent in writing.

compare: expressed authority, implied authority; see: agency

actual cash value (ACV)

Automobile/Property. A valuation method where the value is set at the cost of repairing or replacing the damaged automobile or property with property of like kind and quality in the same physical condition. Usually, actual cash value equals the current replacement cost, less depreciation (based on age, condition at time of loss, time in use, and obsolescence). Other factors, such as the nature of the property and market value of the property, may be involved in determining the actual cash value of an individual loss. Actual cash value is the primary valuation method used to determine the amount of property or physical damage insurance to be purchased, when the policy limits are stated as actual cash value amounts.

syn: cash value; compare: depreciated value, fair market value, functional replacement cost, manufacturer's selling price, market value, market value clause, original cost, original cost new, replacement cost, reproduction cost, tax-appraised value; see: functional obsolescence, valuation of potential property loss

actual damage clause

Surety. A surety provision providing that an architect or engineer will arbitrate between the owner and contractor in determining damages from a proven breach of contract by the contractor.

see: arbitration

actual damages

General. Compensation that a court allows a plaintiff for actual injury or loss, as distinguished from potential or possible damage.

see: damages

Casualty. A type of damage award for which indemnity is allowed under liability insurance policies.

compare: punitive damages; see: damages

actual total loss

Ocean Marine/Property. Property that has been so badly damaged by fire, sinking, windstorm, collision, or that has mysteriously disappeared so that it is unrepairable or unrecoverable or there is so little left of a salvageable or repairable nature that it has no value. A total loss usually signifies the maximum settlement possible under the terms of a policy.

see: abandonment clause, constructive total loss, total loss, total loss only clause

actuarial

Insurer Operations. A term used to describe insurance statistical calculations that are usually performed by an actuary.

see: actuary, open group actuarial cost method, unfunded supplemental actuarial value, unit credit actuarial cost method

actuarial adjustment

Insurer Operations/Risk Management. A change (increase or decrease) in premiums, size of reserves, rates of reserve buildup and other calculations which reflect actual loss experience and expenses and expected, but unpaid benefits.

actuarial assumptions

Risk Management. The facts or suppositions utilized by an actuary to forecast uncertain future events. Assumptions on such subjects as future interest rates, claims costs, payrolls, etc. are indicated in the actuary's report.

actuarial benefit equivalence

Risk Management. A term used to describe the degree to which and whether benefits under varying coverages and plans can be compared.

see: actuarial equivalence tables

actuarial cost method

Risk Management. A method used to determine 1) a pension plan's future benefits based on current fixed contributions, or 2) the contributions required to reach some desired benefit level at a future point in time. Several different factors are considered in this calculation, such as mortality forecasts, expenses, interest, labor turnover, salary scales and retirement rates.

see: actuarial funding method, open group actuarial cost method, unit credit actuarial cost method

actuarial department

Insurer Operations. The employees and operations of an insurance company whose principal functions are developing premium rates and rating procedures, determining reserve adequacy, and assisting in the drafting of policy language.

© 1991 NILS Publishing Company

actuarial equivalence tables

Risk Management. Tables of numbers which provide factors to be assigned to various coverages for comparing the actuarial benefit equivalence across plans.
see: **actuarial benefit equivalence**

actuarial equivalent

Employee Benefits/Risk Management. Two or more benefits which are of equal actuarial present value. When two series of payments have equal present values, assuming a given interest rate and mortality according to a specified mortality table, they are actuarially equivalent.

actuarial funding method

Risk Management. A funding method selected by an actuary to determine the amount and timing of contributions needed to meet a specified financial obligation.
see: **actuarial cost method**

actuarial gains and losses

Employee Benefits/Risk Management. A comparison between a past event predicted by actuarial methods and the event that actually occurred. Actuarial gains result when the actual experience under the plan is better than the actuary's estimates. Actuarial losses result when the actual experience under the plan is worse than the actuary's estimates. In the case of a pension plan, this comparison is used to calculate funding needs.

actuarial liability

Risk Management.
see: **present value**

actuarial present value

Risk Management.
see: **present value**

actuarial report

Risk Management. A report prepared and signed by an actuary, indicating current conditions or future requirements of an insurer, self-insured or pension fund to meet its obligations.

actuarial science

Insurer Operations/Risk Management. The science which deals with the technical and mathematical aspects of insurance, including the determination of premium rates, premium and loss reserves, dividends and other management statistical studies.
see: **statistics**

actuarial soundness

Employee Benefits. A signed written report prepared by an actuary stating that, in the actuary's opinion,

reserves established to fund a pension plan are adequate to make projected benefit payments.
see: **actuarial cost method**
Risk Management. The degree of confidence that an actuary expresses in his or her opinion.

actuarial valuation

Risk Management. The determination by an actuary at a specific date of the value of an insurance company's or self-insured's reserves and/or liabilities.
Employee Benefits. The determination by an actuary as to whether or not pension plan contributions are being accumulated at a sufficient rate to fund promised pension benefits. The actuarial valuation indicates the plan's actuarial liabilities and identifies the plan assets available to meet such liabilities.
see: **actuarial cost method**

actuaries and pension consultants professional liability

Casualty. Errors & omissions insurance for actuaries and pension consultants. This coverage is generally designed to meet the requirements under the Employee Retirement Income Security Act of 1974 (ERISA), which created specific responsibilities for fiduciaries, and standards of competence for actuaries and pension consultants working with pension and employee benefit plans.

actuary

Insurer Operations/Risk Management. An individual (often holding a professional degree) who uses mathematical skills to define, analyze, and solve complex business and social problems involving insurance and employee benefit programs. An actuary's work involves the various contingencies which face humans: birth, marriage, sickness, accidents, loss of property, legal liability, retirement, death, and the financial effects that these and other contingencies have on various insurance and benefit programs. Many of these programs involve long-range financial obligations, for which actuarial forecasts are fundamental in maintaining a sound financial basis: rate-making, premium determination, loss reserves, investment valuation, pension benefits, and, of course, insurance statistics.
see: **Fellow of the Casualty Actuarial Society, Fellow of the Society of Actuaries, Fellow of the Society of Pension Actuaries**

actuary enrolled

Risk Management. An actuary who has been professionally certified by the Internal Revenue Service and the Department of Labor and is thereby authorized to sign actuarial reports mandated by Title II of the Employee Retirement Security Act of 1974.

addendum

General. An addition or a thing that is to be added; a

© 1991 NILS Publishing Company

list, paragraph, designation, or section consisting of added material.

Surety. A document issued prior to the opening of bids that clarifies, corrects, or changes bidding documents or contract documents.

additional coverage

Property.
   see: coverage extension

additional death benefit

Life. An amount of insurance payable in addition to the face amount of the policy, usually in a specified, agreed-upon amount. This life insurance provision is often called "double indemnity."

   syn: **accidental death benefit, double indemnity, multiple indemnity**

additional deposit privilege

Life. A clause in universal life insurance policies allowing the policyholder to make unscheduled premium payments at any time prior to the policy's maturity date.

additional expense insurance

Property.
   see: **additional living expense insurance, extra expense insurance**

additional extended coverage

Property. Coverage for property damage caused by such perils as vandalism and malicious mischief; water from ruptured plumbing and heating systems; glass breakage; ice, snow, and freezing; falling trees and collapse. These coverages are in addition to extended coverage, and are often provided in conjunction with a fire insurance or package policy.

   compare: **coverage extension, extended coverages**

additional insurance

General. A term used generally to describe additional coverages or increases in policy limits added to an existing policy.

additional insured

General. A person or entity, other than the named insured, who is protected by the policy, most often in regard to a specific interest.

   syn: **additional named insured**

Life. A person, other than the individual whose life the policy was originally intended to cover, who is added to a life insurance policy as an additional insured. *Example:* A child may be added to the policy of a parent. This method of providing life insurance is generally less expensive than the purchase of a separate policy.

   syn: **additional interest; see: family life policy**

additional interest

Property. The interest of another party or entity in an insurance policy, usually because that party has provided financing for an insured property or automobile. The additional interest is usually stated in an endorsement attached to, or a certificate issued under, the policy.

   see: **additional insured, insurable interest, loss payee**

Life.
   see: **additional insured**

additional living expense insurance

Property. Coverage included in residential property insurance policies (homeowners, condominium owners, renters) which provides payments when a property loss results in above-normal living expenses for the insured. Additional living expense coverage allows the insured's household to maintain its normal standard of living, covering such expenses as hotel rooms, restaurant meals and cleaning and laundry charges.

   syn: **additional expense insurance; compare: extra expense insurance**

additional medical

Workers' Compensation. An endorsement attached to a workers' compensation policy that provides medical benefits over and above those indicated by the workers' compensation law. In a small number of states, medical benefits are still subject to a statutory limit; this endorsement extends that limited coverage.

   see: **coverage A**

additional named insured

General.
   see: **additional insured**

additional perils

Ocean Marine.
   see: **inchmaree perils**

additional premium (AP)

Insurer Operations. The premium due to an insurer on an insurance policy in addition to the initial premium, as a result of increased coverage, increased rates, retrospective rate calculations, or a premium audit.

   compare: **initial premium, return premium; see: premium**

additional provisions

General. A clause added to the existing insuring and benefit provisions of a policy, or to the standard or uniform provisions, to further define, extend, or limit the coverages provided.

   syn: **general provisions**

© 1991 NILS Publishing Company

additur

General. The power of a trial court to increase an inadequate award made by a jury. The increased award can be used to deny a plaintiff's motion for a new trial. The defendant must consent to and accept the increase; otherwise, the defendant maintains its right to a new trial.

see: **superaddition**

add-on no-fault benefits

Automobile. A policy provision that adds no-fault benefits (where permitted) to automobile liability coverages, without restricting the right of the victim to sue the wrongdoer.

see: **no-fault insurance**

adequate

Regulation. A requirement of most state insurance department regulations which stipulates that an insurer's rates must be adequate to cover the cost of doing business, claims payments, and provide for a reasonable profit.

compare: **excessive**; see: **nondiscriminatory, rate making**

adhesion

Insurer Operations. A term used to describe a unilateral contract, drafted by one party and offered to another party on a take-it-or-leave-it basis. Insurance policies are considered contracts of "adhesion" since they are drafted by the insurer and offered to the insured without the possibility of material modifications. As a result, courts have come to rule that an ambiguity or misinterpretation in an insurance policy is construed in favor of the insured.

see: **ambiguity**

adit

Loss Control. A horizontal tunnel built into a hillside for mining, exploration or drainage.

see: **cross-cut, raise**

adjacent building

Loss Control/Property. A building situated so that it is very close to, but not in actual contact with another building.

compare: **adjoining building**; see: **exposure**

adjoining building

Loss Control/Property. A building situated so that it physically touches another building.

compare: **adjacent building**; see: **party wall**

adjudicate

General. To settle or decide a controversy through the presentation of evidence to a court or other legal proceeding.

see: **arbitration, litigation**

adjustable barrier guard

Loss Control. An enclosure attached to the frame of machinery or equipment with adjustable front and side sections, that protects workers using the machinery from injury.

see: **barrier guard**

adjustable life insurance

Life. A life insurance policy which allows the policyholder to change the face value, premiums, and certain other terms at his or her own discretion.

compare: **universal life insurance**

adjustable policy

Property. Policies which cover property with changing values or volumes of value, such as the inventory of retail stores. The insured reports the value of all items to be covered by the policy to the insurance company at stated periods. The adjustable policy premium is adjusted to reflect the increased or decreased value of the property.

adjustable premium

Health/Life. An insurer retains the right to change premium and rate structures on a class of insureds or business during the year, and apply the new rates to renewal policies.

see: **annualization**

adjustable rate mortgage (ARM)

Financial Planning.

see: **variable rate mortgage**

adjusted base cost

Property. The cost (per square foot of building space) which is subject to adjustment if alternative components are used.

adjusted earnings

Insurer Operations. An estimate of insurance company earnings which considers written premium, income growth and net earnings from operations.

adjusted net worth

Insurer Operations. An insurer's adjusted net worth is calculated by taking the total of the company's capital, surplus, voluntary reserves, estimated value of in-force policies, and unrealized capital gains, less any income tax due on the capital gains.

adjuster

Insurer Operations.

see: **claims adjuster**

adjuster errors & omissions insurance

Casualty. Insurance coverage for an individual adjuster or adjusting firm against claims for breach of duty by reason of any alleged negligent act, error or

12

© 1991 NILS Publishing Company

omission committed by the insurer or its employees in their capacity as adjusters.

adjustment

Insurer Operations.
see: claims adjustment

adjustment bureau

Organizations. An organization that provides adjustment services to insurers. These organizations are used by insurers to supplement staff adjusters and by insurers that do not employ their own staff adjusters.
see: claims adjuster

adjustment expenses

Insurer Operations. Expenses associated with adjusting an insurance claim, such as investigation and usual expenses, but excluding actual claim payments or adjustments.
see: claim expense

adjustment income

Life. Benefits payable to a surviving spouse or other beneficiary as a part of the life insurance policy when the primary wage earner dies. Such a payment is intended to provide for the beneficiary until the beneficiary becomes self-sufficient. Adjustment income is the amount and period of time over which such payments are made. This coverage can be purchased when the original policy is purchased, or it can be added for an extra premium at a later date.
see: readjustment income

administration bond

Surety. A form of fiduciary bond that guarantees the faithful performance and fidelity of an executor or administrator of a will, trust or estate.
see: fiduciary bond

administration expenses

Insurer Operations. Costs incurred in operating an insurance company, excluding loss adjusting expenses, acquisition costs, and investment expenses.
see: acquisition cost

administrative agent

Risk Management.
see: third-party administrator

administrative law

General. The body of law created by state or federal administrative (executive) agencies, with the consent of the respective legislatures. Administrative law usually takes the form of rules, regulations, orders, and decisions. Insurance department regulations are a form of administrative law.

administrative law judge

General. Formerly called "hearing examiner" or "hearing officer," an individual who presides at administrative hearings and has the power to administer oaths and affirmations, rule on questions of evidence, take testimony, and make agency determinations of fact.

administrative order

Regulation. A regulation issued by an administrative agency (such as an insurance department) which is designed to clarify or implement a law or policy, by interpreting the provisions of a statute.

administrative procedure

Regulation. Rules governing practice and procedure allowed before federal or state administrative agencies, as distinguished from the judicial procedure usually applied to courts.
see: Administrative Procedure Act, emergency rules and regulations

Administrative Procedure Act

Regulation. Federal. The law enacted in 1946 which governs practice and proceedings before federal administrative agencies.
State. Individual states have enacted variations of the Federal Act. Such acts govern practice and proceedings before state administrative agencies.
see: administrative procedure

administrative services arrangement (ASA)

Health/Life/Risk Management.
see: administrative services only

administrative services only (ASO)

Health/Life/Risk Management. An arrangement whereby an insurer agrees to provide certain services to a self-insured entity, such as providing printed claim forms, and the processing and auditing of claims. The insurer does not provide any insurance protection under an ASO arrangement.
syn: administrative services arrangement; see: deposit administration plan, third-party administrator

administrator

General. An individual legally vested with the right of controlling an estate.
Risk Management. An individual or firm appointed by a self-insured employer to administer its plan.
see: third-party administrator

administrator's deed

General. A legal instrument given by a court-appointed administrator. The administrator is charged with the responsibility to manage the assets and liabilities of an estate, especially the estate of a minor, an incompetent, or of a testator having no competent executor.

admiralty

Ocean Marine. A term referring to anything pertaining to navigable waters.

see: maritime

admiralty court

Ocean Marine. The court or system of courts having jurisdiction over maritime questions and offenses, including suits involving marine insurance policies and general average adjustments.

see: admiralty proceeding

admiralty liability

Ocean Marine. Liability that arises or results from any type of maritime activity.

see: Jones Act, seaman's remedies

admiralty proceeding

Ocean Marine. A proceeding involving questions of admiralty law, generally settled by an admiralty court. In the U.S., federal courts have jurisdiction over admiralty and maritime actions.

see: admiralty court

admission

General. In criminal law, an acknowledgement in a legal proceeding regarding the existence of certain matters of fact. Legally, admissions are insufficient to establish guilt. In civil law, it is a positive affirmation of fact or an allegation, usually made during a pretrial discovery proceeding.

admission certification

Health. A medical utilization review procedure for assessing an individual's physical and psychological condition and whether that condition requires admission to a hospital or other in-patient institution.

see: utilization review

admitted assets

Insurer Operations. Assets of an insurer that the state insurance department or other regulatory authority include in determining the insurer's financial condition.

compare: excluded assets, nonadmitted assets; see: annual statement, assets, legal list, Statutory Accounting Principles

admitted company

Insurer Operations.

see: admitted insurer

admitted insurer

Insurer Operations. An insurance company authorized to do business in a state by the state's insurance department. While the procedure may vary slightly from state to state, approval is usually granted when an insurer presents financial information demonstrating the insurer's financial stability over a period of time.

syn: admitted company, authorized insurer; compare: nonadmitted insurer

International. An insurance company authorized to do business in a given country by its being licensed or approved to conduct business within that country. Many countries require that local or admitted insurance companies be used to insure risks within their country.

admitted liability

Aviation. A term used in aviation insurance to describe those payments to an injured passenger made without the need of establishing liability.

Fr: responsabilité avouée; Gr: anerkannte Haftpflicht; Sp: responsabilidad admitida

admitted market

Insurer Operations. The market provided by insurers that are admitted to do business in a state or jurisdiction.

compare: nonadmitted market; see: admitted insurer

admitted reinsurance

Insurer Operations/Reinsurance. Reinsurance that is ceded to a reinsurer that is admitted to operate in the state of the primary insurer, and for which credit will be allowed on the insurer's annual statement.

compare: authorized reinsurance, nonadmitted reinsurance; see: reinsurance credit

adult day care

Health. Daytime services such as health, medical, psychological, social, nutritional or educational care which will allow an elderly adult individual to function in his or her own home, rather than having to be admitted to an in-patient institution.

ad valorem bill of lading

Ocean Marine.

see: valued bill of lading

advance

General. The movement of something forward in time or place. The payment or delivery of money or something other of value – such as goods, credit, loans, or other items of value – before such payment or delivery is due.

advance commitment

General. A promise or pledge made in advance.

advance discount for mortality

Employee Benefits/Life.

see: discounting for mortality

14

© 1991 NILS Publishing Company

advance discount for severance

Employee Benefits/Life.
see: discounting for severance

advance freight

Aviation/Inland Marine. The partial payment of a freight bill-of-lading prior to shipment. Typically, payment is made when the freight is accepted for shipment by the carrier.
compare: free on board; see: freight

advance payment

Insurer Operations. A term used to describe any amounts tendered with applications for coverage, or any premiums paid before the beginning of a policy period. Advance payment on some policies may result in a discount.

advance payment bond

Surety. A guarantee that a principal will repay or liquidate any money advanced to them that is related to construction, supply bonds, or other contracts.

advance premium

Insurer Operations.
see: deposit premium

adventure

Ocean Marine. The commercial enterprise in which a vessel and its cargo are subjected to the hazard of a loss at sea.
see: adventure clause, common venture, venture

adventure clause

Ocean Marine. An accurate description in the declarations of an insurance policy of a proposed trip or voyage, so that insurance may precisely cover the insured.
see: adventure

adverse possession

General. A method whereby someone other than the true legal owner of a property takes title to a property by possession for a statutorily prescribed period of time.
see: possession

adverse selection

Insurer Operations. The insuring of risks which are of a poorer class (more prone to losses) than the average risk. Poorer risks or less desirable insureds tend to seek or continue insurance to a greater extent than better risks.
compare: anti-selection; see: benefit of selection, ultimate mortality table

Reinsurance. A reinsurance term which recognizes that insurers often cede their poorer business to reinsurers and retain their better business.

adverse underwriting decision

Insurer Operations. An unfavorable decision regarding an individual insurance application. Includes refusal to accept a risk, termination or restriction of coverage, acceptance only at higher rate, or placement through an assigned risk or other risk-sharing plan.

advertisement to bid

Surety. Public notice of construction or demolition work to be undertaken, giving contractors an opportunity to bid for the work.
syn: invitation to bid, request for proposal

advertiser's liability

Casualty.
see: advertising injury coverage

advertising injury

Casualty. An oral or written publication of material that injures a person or organization or that person's or organization's goods, products or sources. The injurious oral or written material may be slanderous, libelous, or disparaging; in violation of the right of privacy; a misappropriation of ideas; or the infringement of copyright, trademark, service mark, title or slogan.
see: advertising injury coverage, commercial speech

advertising injury coverage

Casualty. Coverage for advertising injury resulting from the oral or written publication of material. Coverage is automatically included in the ISO commercial general liability form under Coverage Part B. It may also be purchased as a separate advertiser's liability policy.
syn: advertiser's liability; see: advertising injury, patent insurance, personal and advertising injury liability

advisory loss cost rating

Insurer Operations.
see: loss cost rating

advisory opinion

General. An informal decision that is often an interpretation – given in advance – on how a court or administrative agency would decide a legal question given a certain set of facts. In common law and in most states, advisory opinions are not given by courts, but are usually issued by administrative agencies. These opinions are not binding.

advisory organization

Organizations. An organization that provides support services to insurer rating bureaus or governmental agencies (e.g., rates, forms or statistics).
see: Insurance Services Office (ISO), rating bureau

© 1991 NILS Publishing Company

affidavit

General. A voluntary, sworn written statement of fact made under oath or affirmation, before an authorized official. The affiant (the person making the statement) is not questioned or interviewed in the document by attorneys; it is simply the affiant's statement.

compare: deposition

affidavit of claim

Insurer Operations. A statement containing the facts on which an insurance claim is based.

see: proof of loss

affiliated companies

Insurer Operations. Insurance companies that are closely tied to each other through common stock ownership or interlocking directorates.

see: fleet of companies, intercompany transaction, parent company, pup company, subsidiary company

affiliation of health providers

Health. Health care providers that are linked together under a formal or informal agreement to provide services to certain patients, either as a subcontractor or backup facility.

see: backup facility agreement

affirm

General. To re-assert, ratify, or repeat a solemn declaration of fact or trust; to agree with an earlier judgment; to agree that an affidavit is true.

see: attest, stipulation

affirmation

General. A solemn and formal declaration to tell the truth by persons who have religious principles against taking an oath (i.e., swearing on the Bible to tell the truth).

affirmative defense

General. Generally, a legal defense in a civil case, characterized by a denial of the charges and an offering of evidence to show it is the plaintiff who is guilty of actionable negligence or contributory negligence. Included often in affirmative defenses are accord and satisfaction, assumption of risk, duress, or estoppel.

see: accord and satisfaction, assumption of risk, duress, estoppel

affirmative warranty

Insurer Operations. An agreement by an insured that specific facts exist at the time an insurance policy is issued.

see: representation, warranties of insured

affreightment

Ocean Marine. A charter party or bill of lading contract to transport goods by an ocean vessel.

syn: contract of carriage; see: bill of lading, charter party

after-acquired property

Financial Planning. Property acquired after the date of a loan or mortgage, that becomes additional security for the loan.

aftercare

Health. A term used to describe a contact made with a patient following a surgical procedure or other health treatment process, to support and increase the gains made in the treatment.

aftercharge

Property. A premium charge added to a commercial fire insurance policy which can be deleted if the insured complies with certain fire prevention recommendations (e.g., providing fire extinguishers or smoke alarms).

compare: increased hazard; see: fault of management

age

General. For most legal documents, age is the whole number of years since birth, as determined by the most recent birthday. Automobile insurance applications and annuities use this method of determining age in their underwriting and rating formulas.

Life. For life insurance rating, two common age options are used: 1) Age closest to the individual's birthday, or 2) Age at the individual's last birthday.

see: age change, age discrimination, age limits, attained age, original age

age-adjustment clause

Life. A provision in life insurance policies that allows for the adjustment of the amount payable at the death of the insured, if it is shown that the age of the insured was misrepresented. Usually, the amount payable at death in such cases is the amount of coverage that the premium would have purchased for the applicant at his or her true age and sex when the insurance was taken out.

see: age, misstatement of age

age change

Life. For life insurance rating purposes, the date, halfway between natural birth dates, when the "age" of an individual changes to the next higher "age."

see: age

age discrimination

Regulation. Unfair discrimination in employment,

16

© 1991 NILS Publishing Company

credit, and other aspects of life is prohibited by the Age Discrimination Act of 1967 (amended in 1978).

Automobile. The use of age as a rating factor in automobile insurance, where drivers between 30 and 60 years of age are considered preferred risks; drivers under 30 and over 60 have a difficult time obtaining coverage and pay significantly higher premiums. The reason insurers treat different age groups preferentially or punitively is that statistics indicate that very young and very old drivers have a greater number of accidents than drivers in the middle years of life.

Health/Life. The use of age as a component affecting rates and premiums. Usually, premiums will increase as an individual's age increases. For some policies there is an upper limit on age, above which the insurer will not accept an application for insurance.

see: age limits, uniform premium

Casualty. Liability for claims alleging age discrimination may or may not be covered within the definition of personal injury in a liability policy. Some policies may cover age discrimination, in general, while others will specify the types of discrimination claims covered, which can include claims alleging discrimination based on age.

see: discrimination

Age Discrimination Act of 1967
Regulation.
see: age discrimination

age limits
Health/Life. Underwriting age limits established for life and health policies. Applicants can be declined because they are younger or older than specified age limits.

see: age, age discrimination

agency
General. A legal relationship between two parties who agree that one (the agent) is to act on behalf of the other (the principal), subject to the principal's control. When agency is assumed to exist, the principal is frequently held liable for the agent's actions.

compare: employee, independent contractor

Agency/Insurer Operations. A group of individuals working together to sell and service insurance policies based on agency agreements with certain insurance companies.

syn: insurance agency; see: actual authority, agency agreement, agent, agent's authority, agent's certificate of authority, agent's license, apparent agency, appointment, authorization, expressed authority, implied authority

agency agreement
Agency/Insurer Operations. The contract establishing the legal relationship between an insurance agent or agency and an insurer. The contract specifies the

degree of authority given to the agency; the types of insurance the agency may write for the insurer; what commission is to be paid; and the payment terms between the agency and insurer.

see: agency, agent's authority, agent's certificate of authority, ownership of expirations

agency by estoppel
Agency/Insurer Operations.
see: apparent agency

agency company
Agency/Insurer Operations. An insurance company that uses independent agents to solicit its insurance business.

compare: captive agent, exclusive agency system; see: independent agency system

agency plant
Insurer Operations. An insurance company's sales organization, usually meaning the total of all agents and marketing representatives working for or on behalf of the insurer.

agency reinsurance
Agency/Reinsurance. A contract of reinsurance between an insurer and a reinsurer that concerns or is confined to the business produced by a named agent of the ceding insurer, and administered with the reinsurer by the named agent with the permission of the ceding insurer.

agency superintendent
Insurer Operations. An officer of an insurer who supervises agents within a given territory or region.

see: agency

agency system
Agency.
see: captive agent, direct selling system, exclusive agency system, independent agency system

agent
Agency/Insurer Operations. An individual who represents the insurer in negotiating, servicing, or effecting insurance policies. An agent may be an independent contractor or employee of the insurer.

see: agency, agent of record, broker, captive agent, debit agent, exclusive agency system, general agent, independent agent, local agent, managing general agent, nonresident agent, policywriting agent, resident agent, recording agent, special agent, state agent, sub-agent

agent of record
Agency/Insurer Operations. An insurance agent who has the policyholder's approval to order an insurance policy from an insurer. Also, an agent designated in

agent of record – continued

writing by a policyholder to service certain policies on behalf of the policyholder with a company represented by the agent.

compare: broker of record

agent's authority

Agency/Insurer Operations. The authority granted to an agent by an insurer through a contract between the agent and the insurer. The courts have held that an agent's authority is that which the public may reasonably expect the agent to have, regardless of the provisions in the contract.

syn: agent's power; see: actual authority, agency agreement, delegation, expressed authority, implied authority, respondeat superior

agent's balances

Agency/Insurer Operations. The amount due to an insurance company from an agent, which is calculated by taking the premiums paid to the agent by policyholders, less the agent's commissions and policy fees. In some instances, the agent will also be responsible for uncollected premium from a policyholder. It is often required that these funds be held in a trust account until they are paid to the insurer.

see: account current, agent's trust

agent's certificate of authority

Agency/Insurer Operations. A document evidencing an agent's appointment to represent a specific insurer. Usually this document must be filed by the insurer with the insurance department of each state in which the agent transacts business.

see: agency agreement, agent's authority

agent's commission

Agency. An amount paid to an agent by an insurer for placing and servicing their policies. It is usually expressed as a percentage of premium. New commissions are those paid for the first policy year, and renewal commissions are those paid for subsequent policy years.

see: acquisition cost, expense allowance, first-year commission, flat commission, graded commission, lead fee, level commission, overriding commission, renewal commission, unlevel commission, vested commissions

agents errors & omissions insurance

Agency/Casualty. Insurance coverage for damages claimed against an insurance agent due to any act or omission of the agent (or of any other person for whose acts or omissions the agent is legally responsible), arising out of the performance of professional services as an insurance agent.

syn: insurance agents liability

agent's general lien

Surety. The right of an agent to retain possession of a principal's (insurer's) goods and papers until the entire balance of all accounts between the principal (insurer) and the agent are settled.

agent's license

Agency. A certificate of authority issued by the state, allowing an insurance agent to engage in the sale and servicing of insurance.

see: agent's qualification regulations

agent's power

Agency.

see: agent's authority

agent's qualification regulations

Agency. Laws or regulations in many states which require that an insurance agent or broker meet certain educational or experience requirements to be initially licensed or to renew a license.

agent's trust

Agency. Most states require that an insurance agent establish a trust account with a financial institution for the deposit of funds due insurers, but which are not yet remitted. Usually, agents are permitted to retain the interest earned on such accounts; however, such funds may not be used for any purpose except to pay insurers.

see: agent's balances, broker's float

age "rate up"

Life.

see: substandard life expectancy

aggregate benefits

Health. The aggregate policy amount payable to an insured or claimant under two or more policies or two or more coverages of a single policy. The maximum amount of benefits an insured or claimant may receive, under a policy regardless of the number of claims.

see: limit of liability

aggregate excess insurance

Casualty/Property. Coverage that responds when self-insured losses exceed a predetermined retention (self-insured or deductible) amount during an annual period. *Example:* An insured with a $100,000 property deductible may purchase aggregate excess coverage to limit the total of all property losses within the deductible during the year to $500,000.

see: aggregate excess workers' compensation insurance

aggregate excess of loss reinsurance

Reinsurance. A form of excess of loss treaty reinsurance, whereby the reinsurer responds when a ceding

© 1991 NILS Publishing Company

company incurs losses on a particular line or book of business during a specific period (usually 12 months) in excess of a stated dollar amount.

syn: excess aggregate reinsurance, nonproportional reinsurance, stop loss reinsurance; compare: excess loss-ratio reinsurance; see: treaty reinsurance

aggregate excess unemployment compensation coverage

Employee Benefits. Insurance coverage for nonprofit organizations that elect to self-insure their unemployment compensation losses. The coverage insures losses in excess of a specified, self-insured aggregate amount during an annual period. It places a cap on the maximum amount the insured will have to pay during a twelve-month period. Coverage can be written for unemployment losses caused by loss of a physical facility or for loss caused by an economic condition.

aggregate excess workers' compensation insurance

Workers' Compensation. Insurance coverage for organizations that self-insure their workers' compensation benefits. It indemnifies the insured for claims in excess of a specific annual aggregate retention. This coverage places a cap on the maximum amount the insured will have to pay during a twelve-month period. Coverage (who is covered, what accidents are covered, etc.) is based on the insurance provided by standard workers' compensation policies.

compare: specific excess workers' compensation insurance

aggregate indemnity

Health. The maximum amount which may be collected under a health insurance policy for any single disability, or for any period of disability.

aggregate limit

Casualty. The maximum limit of coverage available under a liability policy during a specified period of time – usually one policy year or the policy period – regardless of the number of separate accidents that may occur or the number of claims that may be made. Losses paid under coverages subject to aggregate limits reduce the amounts available for future losses. Aggregate limits may apply to a specific type of coverage, or they may apply to all losses under the policy.
The ISO commercial general liability coverage form contains two aggregate limits: a "general aggregate limit" and a "products-completed operations aggregate limit."
The ISO businessowners liability coverage form also has two aggregate limits. The first is for all injury or damage during the policy period from the products-completed operations coverage, and the second is an aggregate limit applying to all other injury or damage during the policy period except for legal liability losses.

compare: automatic reinstatement clause; see: commercial general liability form, general aggregate limit, limit of liability, products-completed operations aggregate limit
Insurer Operations. The maximum limit of coverage under a policy regardless of the number of claims.
see: limit of liability

aggregate operations liability limit

Casualty. The maximum limit of liability available to respond to claims for damages caused by the insured in the operation of a business. The aggregate limit usually applies only to property damage liability.
see: limit of liability

aggregate products liability limit

Casualty. The maximum limit of liability payable under a liability policy during the term of the policy or in any one policy year, for all products liability claims covered by the policy.
see: aggregate limit, commercial general liability form, limit of liability, products-completed operations aggregate limit

aggregate protection liability limit

Casualty. The maximum limit of liability available to respond to claims which arise from activities of independent contractors working for the insured.
see: aggregate limit, limit of liability

aggregate working excess reinsurance

Reinsurance. A form of treaty reinsurance under which the ceding insurer retains a portion of each risk as well as an aggregate amount of losses in excess of each retention.
see: aggregate excess of loss reinsurance

aggrieved party

General. A legal term used to refer to an individual or entity that has been injured, suffered a loss, or whose legal rights have been violated by the act of another.
see: claimant, injury, plaintiff

aging schedule

General. A report showing how long accounts receivable have been outstanding. It gives the percentage and amount of receivables not past due and the percentages and amounts of receivables that are past due for 30 days, 60 days, 90 or more days.

agrarian

General. Relating to, or pertaining to land or its ownership.

agreed amount

Property. An amount of coverage which the insurer

agreed amount – continued
and insured mutually agree represents a fair valuation for a property or properties at the time insurance is purchased.

see: agreed amount clause, agreed value, coinsurance clause, stated amount

agreed amount clause

Property. A provision in a property policy, under which the insurer agrees with the insured that the amount of insurance purchased will automatically satisfy the coinsurance, average, or contribution clause of the policy.

compare: coinsurance clause; see: agreed amount, statement of values

agreed amount endorsement

Property. An endorsement to a property insurance policy, in which the insurance company agrees that adequate amounts of insurance have been purchased and that the policy coinsurance or average clause requirements are waived.

syn: agreed value provision; see: statement of values, agreed amount

agreed value

Property. An agreement between the insurer and the insured, that the limit of insurance set out for a scheduled item of property is the property's worth. This value would be the amount paid by the insurer in the event of a total loss. For some items such as jewelry and fine arts, the insurer may require an appraisal.

see: agreed amount

agreed value clause

Property. A method of avoiding a coinsurance penalty in business interruption coverage, entailing a two-step procedure: 1) The insured completes a business income report/worksheet showing financial data for the previous twelve months and an estimate of financial condition for the next twelve months; 2) The agreed value is entered in the declarations and becomes part of the policy. The agreed value must at least equal the coinsurance percentage multiplied by the estimated net profit and operating expenses shown for the next twelve months on the worksheet.

see: coinsurance clause

agreed value provision

Property.

see: agreed amount endorsement

agreement

General. One of the elements required to form a legal contract. It is the mutual understanding which exists when an offer made by one party has been accepted by another party.

see: contract

agreement for sale

General. An obligation on the part of the purchasing party to purchase.

compare: agreement to sell

agreement to sell

General. An agreement obligating the vendor (seller) to complete the promise to sell. The purchasing party is not obligated to buy.

compare: agreement for sale

agricultural cooperative

General. An organization formed and collectively owned and operated for the mutual benefit of farmers, usually to sell and process their crops or to purchase seed. Many of these cooperatives formed mutual insurance companies to insure their members.

see: farmers mutual insurers

agricultural equipment insurance

Inland Marine. Coverage for mobile agricultural equipment and machinery, including apparatus such as saddles, straps, harnesses and liveries, against specified perils (usually fire, lightning, vandalism, malicious mischief and removal). Excludes aircraft, watercraft, crops and feed.

syn: agricultural machinery insurance

agricultural machinery insurance

Inland Marine.

see: agricultural equipment insurance

agricultural workers

Workers' Compensation. Broader in meaning than "farm labor," this term is understood to include those involved in farming in all its forms, such as horticulture, dairying, bee keeping, poultry and ranching.

AIA documents

Surety. Standard construction-related agreements developed by the American Institute of Architects (AIA) for separate performance and payment bonds (A311) and for bid bonds (A370).

see: American Institute of Architects

air bag

Automobile.

see: passive restraint systems

air bill

Aviation/Inland Marine.

see: air waybill

air cargo insurance

Aviation. A form of aviation insurance covering an air carrier's legal liability arising from damage, destruction, or loss of cargo during shipment.

© 1991 NILS Publishing Company

aircraft hull insurance

Aviation.

see: hull policy

aircraft insurance

Aviation. Aircraft insurance is a specialized segment of the insurance industry that covers both physical damage to the hull or parts of an aircraft and liability for bodily injury or property damage to others, arising out of the operation of the aircraft.

see: aviation insurance

aircraft nonowned coverage

Aviation.

see: nonowned aircraft liability insurance

aircraft passenger insurance

Aviation/Life.

see: air travel insurance

aircraft product liability insurance

Aviation. Product liability insurance for the manufacturers and dealers of aircraft and for fixed base operators that repair and maintain aircraft. Most insurance companies will not write aircraft products liability insurance because of the catastrophic potential in the event that the product does fail while an aircraft is in flight. This coverage is usually written by specialty aviation insurers or through specialized Lloyd's of London syndicates.

aircraft spare parts insurance

Aviation. "All-risks" insurance coverage on leased aircraft parts – including aircraft engines, spare parts, and equipment – while the property is on the ground or is being carried as cargo by air, land or waterborne transit.

air passenger insurance

Aviation/Life.

see: air travel insurance

airport owners and operators liability insurance

Aviation. Liability insurance which is based on the commercial general liability policy, but is tailored to the needs of airport owners and operators and is underwritten by aviation insurers.

see: fixed base liability, hangarkeepers legal liability insurance

air rights

General. Rights vested in real estate, allowing the owner to use all or a portion of the air space above his or her property. Airlines have a right to pass over land; however, an owner has a right to recover damages if airline flight paths interfere with that owner's use of such land.

air sampling

Loss Control. Scientific method of testing a representative sample of air to determine the quantities and types of atmospheric contaminants. The most frequently found atmospheric contaminants are chemicals divided into 1) particles which are mixtures or dispersions of solid or liquid particles in air and include dust, smoke, mist, and similar materials, and 2) gases or vapors.

air taxi

Aviation. An aircraft principally used in the business of carrying passengers or freight for hire or reward, but excluding aircraft used for instruction or rental to others. Also called charter aircraft, air taxis differ from airlines in that the entire aircraft is hired by a single individual or organization, instead of on a seat-by-seat basis.

syn: charter aircraft, charter

air transport insurance

Aviation.

see: aviation insurance

air travel insurance

Aviation/Life. A form of life insurance which may be purchased by passengers of scheduled airlines. The policy face value is paid to the named beneficiary in the event that death results from a particular flight.

syn: air passenger insurance, aircraft passenger insurance; compare: aviation passenger liability insurance; see: charter fare protection insurance, travel accident insurance

air waybill

Aviation/Inland Marine. A bill of lading issued by an airline, acknowledging receipt of merchandise and indicating conditions for carriage.

syn: air bill; see: waybill

alcohol bond

Surety. A bond that guarantees that the principal complies with federal or state laws or regulations administering the sale, manufacture, or warehousing of alcohol. If the alcohol is for beverages, the bond is frequently called a liquor bond, or intoxicating liquor bond.

syn: intoxicating liquor bond, liquor bond

alcoholic beverage liability insurance

Casualty. Insurance coverage that protects the owners of a business in which alcoholic beverages are sold or served, against liability arising out of accidents caused by intoxicated customers.

see: dram shop liability insurance, liquor legal liability coverage

alcoholic intoxication

Health. A state of limited or impaired physical or

alcoholic intoxication — continued
mental ability caused by ingesting alcohol. Coverage for claims is denied under some policies if an accident or sickness results from alcoholic intoxication.

alcoholism

Health. A pathological condition resulting from continued and excessive use of intoxicating liquors.
see: substance abuse

aleatory

General. Depending on luck, as in gambling. Dependent on an uncertain event or a contingency as to both profit and loss.
see: gambling

aleatory contract

General. The legal term for a contract where the monetary values of the consideration and the subject of the agreement are not equal.
see: contract

Insurer Operations. Most insurance policies are of unequal benefit to one party or the other. The insured pays a premium to the insurer, for which the insured may receive nothing, or the insured may receive monetary benefits in the form of claim payments that far exceed the premium amount. This is an excellent example of an aleatory contract.

alienate

Title. To convey or to transfer title to property by a specific act, either by will or voluntarily (as opposed to passing title by the operation of law).

alienated premises

Casualty. Property to which an insured no longer holds title. Generally, public liability policies insure against the liability of the insured arising out of conditions on premises alienated by them. They do not cover liability for damages to the premises themselves resulting from such conditions.

alienation clause

General. A provision in a document or other written instrument giving persons the right to transfer (or forbidding said right to transfer) property which is the subject of the document.
Mortgage Insurance. In mortgages, the alienation clause requires that the entire loan balance be paid upon the property's sale.
Property. In fire insurance policies, the alienation clause usually voids the insured's policy when the property is transferred to another owner.

alien carrier

Insurer Operations.
see: alien insurer

alien company

General.
see: alien insurer

alien insurer

Insurer Operations. An insurer or reinsurer domiciled or incorporated under the laws of a foreign country, but doing business in the United States. A U.S. company selling in a foreign country would be an alien insurer from that country's perspective.
syn: alien carrier, alien company, alien reinsurer; compare: foreign insurer, domestic insurer

alien reinsurer

Reinsurance.
see: alien insurer

all cause deductible

Health/Employee Benefits. A health insurance plan deductible that applies to all covered expenses incurred by a coverage participant as a result of the same or related causes within the accumulation period.
see: accumulation period

all causes maximum limit

Health/Employee Benefits. The maximum benefits payable under a health insurance plan for covered expenses incurred by covered plan participant(s) during a specific period of coverage.
see: maximum plan limits

allegation

General. An assertion regarded as unsupported; a statement which has yet to be proven.

allergy and susceptibility

Casualty. A defense sometimes used against products liability claims involving products for intimate body use (i.e., cosmetics, deodorants), where the manufacturer is not liable for injury caused by an individual's rare allergy or sensitivity to the product.
see: products-completed operations insurance

Alliance of American Insurers (AAI)

Organizations. Members: Property and casualty insurers. *Objectives:* Promote the interests of property and casualty insurers. Sponsors educational and research programs. *Founded:* 1922. *Headquarters:* Schaumburg, IL.

allied lines

Property. Coverages which are frequently written with property insurance. Allied lines include insurance for data processing, demolition, earthquake, increased cost of construction, radioactive contamination, sprinkler leakage, standing timber, vandalism and malicious mischief, and water damage.

© 1991 NILS Publishing Company

All-Industry Research Advisory Council (AIRAC)

Organizations. Members: Insurance companies. *Objectives:* Promote interests of property and casualty insurance companies. *Founded:* 1977. *Headquarters:* Oak Brook, IL.

allision

Ocean Marine. A term for a moving vessel striking against a stationary vessel or object.

all lines insurers

Insurer Operations. Insurers writing both life and health insurance and property-liability lines. Because of regulatory restrictions and various business realities, so-called "all lines insurers" rarely offer all such coverages.

All Nations

Organizations. Members: Cooperative insurance facilities. *Objectives:* Provide financial and technical assistance to new and developing cooperative insurance facilities. *Founded:* 1966. *Headquarters:* Columbus, OH.

allocate

General. To distribute or apportion for a specific purpose or to particular persons or things.

allocated benefits

Health. A health insurance policy provision that pays certain expenses (usually miscellaneous hospital and medical charges such as x-rays, dressings and drugs) according to rates set in a schedule in the policy. There is usually a maximum total that will be paid for all allocated expenses.

allocated claim expense

Insurer Operations. An expense assigned to and recorded with a specific claim. It includes such items as defense and investigation costs. Allocated claim expenses have more significance in liability insurance because of the legal costs involved in defending liability claims.

syn: allocated loss expense, paid expense; compare: unallocated claim expense; see: claim expense

allocated funding instrument

Employee Benefits.
see: group deferred annuity

allocated loss expense

Insurer Operations.
see: allocated claim expense

allocation

General. Distribution or apportionment for a specific purpose or to particular persons or things.

allotment

Title. Apportionment. Land divided into smaller parts and often sold without improvements; a subdivision.

allowed costs

Health. Fees for services, medicine or supplies furnished which qualify as covered expenses and for which the health care plan will pay in whole or in part.

all payers system

Health. A health care system where all public and private third-party payers are subject to the same rules and rates of reimbursing hospitals for services.

"all-risks" insurance

Inland Marine/Property. A term used to refer to any property or inland marine insuring form which insures against damage by "all risks" of loss, except those which are specifically excluded.

compare: open perils; see: broad form property insurance endorsement, named perils

all-states endorsement

Workers' Compensation. Coverage that is included in some workers' compensation policy forms, and which must be added by endorsement to other workers' compensation policies. It provides that the insurer will indemnify the insured if the insured 1) undertakes operations in any state not specifically designated in the policy, and 2) is required to pay a compensation loss under the law of such state. Coverage for monopolistic states is excluded.

compare: broad form all-states endorsement, extraterritoriality

alluvion

Loss Control. The wash or flow of water against a shore. The gradual accumulation of land by the addition of clay, silt, sand, gravel or similar material deposited by running water.

compare: avulsion; see: accretion

alteration

Crime. Changing or varying a thing from one form to another without changing its identity.

compare: amalgamation, amendment; see: spoliation

alteration bond

Surety. A bond which indemnifies the insured for loss sustained by reason of alterations to stated instruments, documents or securities. Alteration coverage is included in a forgery bond.

see: forgery bond, lost instrument bond

amalgamation

General. A union of different and diverse elements, to form a new body; consolidation; merger.

compare: alteration, amendment

© 1991 NILS Publishing Company

A.M. Best Rating
General.
   see: Best's Ratings

ambiguity
Insurer Operations. An uncertainty of meaning. A lack of clearness in an insurance policy's terms or words, allowing the policy to be interpreted in more than one way. Generally, the courts have construed ambiguity in a policy against the insurer and in favor of the insured.
   see: adhesion

ambiguous instrument
General. A negotiable instrument containing incomplete statements or omissions which render the exact intent of the instrument unclear. Such instruments are unenforceable; however, the holder has authority to complete the instrument as authorized and thus make it negotiable.

ambit
Ocean Marine. The geographic scope of a voyage, including time extensions.
   see: adventure, voyage

ambulance service malpractice insurance
Casualty. Insurance coverage for ambulance drivers and attendants which covers bodily injury or mental injury to or death of any patient caused by or alleged to have been caused by error, omission or negligence in professional services rendered or which should have been rendered by ambulance drivers or attendants in the course of their work.
   compare: paramedics professional liability

ambulatory care facility
Health. A health care facility that is freestanding or contained within a hospital that provides diagnostic or medical services including minor surgery on an outpatient basis where overnight confinement is not required.
   see: out-patient

ambulatory surgical centers
Health. Facilities designed to provide elective surgical care in which the patient is admitted and discharged within the same day.
   see: out-patient

amendment
General. Adding to or changing a thing, so that its basic identity remains intact, but certain details are changed, usually resulting in an improvement.
   compare: alteration, amalgamation
Insurer Operations. Provisions added to an original insurance policy that alter, modify, correct, improve, or change a policy's benefits and coverages.
   see: endorsement, rider

American Academy of Actuaries (AAA)
Organizations. Members: Actuaries. *Objectives:* Facilitate relations between actuaries and governmental bodies. Promulgate professional standards for actuaries. *Founded:* 1965. *Headquarters:* Washington, D.C.

American agency system
Agency.
   see: independent agency system

American Agents Association (AAA)
Organizations. Members: Insurance agents. *Objectives:* Promotes interests of insurance agents and compiles statistics. *Founded:* 1980. *Headquarters:* Indianapolis, IN.

American Annuitants Mortality Table
Life. A table comprised of statistics provided by twenty American insurance companies in 1918, comparing mortality rates for males and females.
   see: American Experience Table of Mortality, mortality table

American Arbitration Association (AAA)
Organizations. Members: Law firms, businesses, trade and educational associations, arbitrators, unions and other interested individuals. *Objectives:* Encourages arbitration as an alternative to litigation for purposes of resolving disputes. Recommends individuals to arbitrate or mediate certain controversies. Its accident and claims tribunal handles no-fault and automobile liability claims. *Founded:* 1926. *Headquarters:* New York, NY.

American Association of Crop Insurers (AACI)
Organizations. Members: Crop insurers and agencies selling multiple peril crop insurance. *Objectives:* Promotes interests of crop insurers. *Founded:* 1981. *Headquarters:* Washington, D.C.

American Association of Dental Consultants (AADC)
Organizations. Members: Dental insurance consultants and others concerned with dental insurance plans, from administrative and design perspectives. *Objectives:* Increasing knowledge in the area of dental insurance plans, including the interrelationships between insurers, the dental profession and the consumer. *Founded:* 1977. *Headquarters:* North Babylon, NY.

American Association of Insurance Management Consultants (AAIMC)
Organizations. Members: Insurers, agents, brokers,

© 1991 NILS Publishing Company

attorneys and others with advanced management degrees. *Objectives:* Promotes interests of insurance management consultants; offers a referral service and educational seminars. *Founded:* 1978. *Headquarters:* Estes Park, CO.

American Association of Insurance Services (AAIS)

Organizations. Members: Property and casualty insurers, mutual, stock and reciprocal insurers. *Objectives:* Develops rates, rules and forms for fire, multiple lines, inland marine and casualty insurance. *Founded:* 1936. *Headquarters:* Bensenville, IL. Formerly known as the Transportation Insurance Rating Bureau.

American Association of Managing General Agents (AAMGA)

Organizations. Members: Managing general agents. *Objectives:* Presents chairman awards, maintains speakers' bureau, offers educational programs and compiles statistics. *Founded: 1926. Headquarters:* Kansas City, MO.

American Automobile Association (AAA)

Organizations. Members: Individual members of associated automobile clubs throughout the United States. *Objectives:* Promotes traffic safety, better highways, more efficient and safer cars, energy conservation and improvement of motoring and travel conditions. *Founded:* 1902. *Headquarters:* Heathrow, FL.

syn: AAA, auto club, automobile club, Triple A

American Bar Association (ABA)

Organizations. Members: Attorneys in good standing, admitted to the bar of at least one state. *Objectives:* Fostering professional improvement; providing public services; improving the availability of legal services to the public; and bettering the administration of civil and criminal justice. *Founded:* 1878. *Headquarters:* Chicago, IL.

American Bureau of Shipping (ABS)

Organizations. Members: Shipowners, shipbuilders, naval architects, marine underwriters and others associated with the marine industry. *Objectives:* Classification society which surveys vessels and grants their "class" if the vessel meets the standards of construction, material and workmanship. *Founded:* 1862. *Headquarters:* Paramus, New Jersey.

see: American Bureau of Shipping Record

American Bureau of Shipping Record (ABS Record)

Ocean Marine. A register prepared by the American Bureau of Shipping of all United States ocean-going vessels in alphabetical order containing the complete description of each vessel.

see: American Bureau of Shipping, Lloyd's Register of Shipping

American Cargo War Risk Reinsurance Exchange (ACWRRE)

Organizations. Members: Ocean marine insurers. *Objectives:* Spread war risks through reinsurance on cargoes in ocean commerce. *Founded:* 1939. *Headquarters:* New York, NY.

American College

Organizations. The accrediting body for both the CLU (Chartered Life Underwriter) and the ChFC (Chartered Financial Consultant) designations. Formerly it was known as the American College of Life Underwriters.

see: American Society of Chartered Life Underwriters and Chartered Financial Consultants, Chartered Financial Consultant, Chartered Life Underwriter

American Corporate Counsel Institute (ACCI)

Organizations. Members: Attorneys in corporate legal departments. *Objectives:* Provides information on various issues, including an in-house legal department's liability exposure. *Founded:* 1984. *Headquarters:* Washington, D.C.

American Council of Life Insurance (ACLI)

Organizations. Members: Life insurers, including legal reserve life insurance companies. *Objectives:* Promotes interests of life insurers. Conducts economic and social research programs; compiles statistics. *Founded:* 1976. *Headquarters:* Washington, D.C.

American Depository Receipt (ADR)

Financial Planning/International. Most countries will not allow stock certificates issued there to leave their geographical confines. Therefore, to transfer these shares to a United States investor, a non-U.S. company will deposit shares of stock with a branch of a United States bank located in the country of issue. That bank will then issue an American Depository Receipt to represent these shares in the United States. Each ADR is equivalent to a specified number of shares. ADRs can be traded between investors.

syn: American Depository Shares

American Depository Shares (ADS)

Financial Planning/International.
see: American Depository Receipt

American Excess Insurance Association (AEIA)

Organizations. Members: Excess liability insurers. *Objectives:* Provide large United States companies with excess liability insurance. *Founded:* 1986. *Headquarters:* East Hughes, CT.

American Experience Table of Mortality

Life. A table published in 1868 by Shepard Homans, of

© 1991 NILS Publishing Company

American Experience Table of Mortality —
continued

expected mortality rates, based on data accumulated from twenty American insurance companies. This table was widely used by life insurers until the 1950s, to establish rates. It is superseded by the Commissioners Standard Ordinary Table.

see: **mortality table**

American Hull Insurance Syndicate (AHIS)

Organizations. Members: U.S. insurance firms and foreign countries, acting as a syndicate for writing coverage on ocean-going and Great Lakes vessels, foreign hulls and builders' risks. *Objectives:* Promotes the American Merchant Marine; offers protection to shipowners, shipbuilders and maritime interests worldwide. *Founded:* 1920. *Headquarters:* New York, NY. Until 1943, known as the American Marine Syndicate.

American Industrial Hygiene Association (AIHA)

Organizations. Members: Industrial hygienists. *Objectives:* Promotes the study and control of environmental factors affecting the health and well-being of industrial workers. *Founded:* 1983. *Headquarters:* New York, NY.

American Institute for Property and Liability Underwriters (AIPLU)

Organizations. Members: Insurance underwriters. *Objectives:* Conducts examinations and awards the Chartered Property and Casualty Underwriter (CPCU) professional designation. *Founded:* 1942. *Headquarters:* Malvern, PA.

see: **Chartered Property and Casualty Underwriter, Insurance Institute of America, Society of Chartered Property and Casualty Underwriters**

American Institute of Architects (AIA)

Organizations. Members: Architects. *Objectives:* Develops standard agreements, including insurance provisions, for construction contracts. *Founded:* 1857. *Headquarters:* Washington, D.C.

see: **AIA documents**

American Institute of Marine Underwriters (AIMU)

Organizations. Members: Marine insurers authorized to conduct business in one or more states of the United States. *Objectives:* Analyzes international conventions and agreements of marine insurance. Provides training and educational seminars and programs. *Founded:* 1898. *Headquarters:* New York, NY.

American Insurance Association (AIA)

Organizations. Members: Property, casualty and surety insurance companies. *Objectives:* Promotes the interests of participating companies. *Founded:* 1964. *Headquarters:* Washington, D.C. Formed by a merger of the National Board of Fire Underwriters, the Association of Casualty and Surety Companies and the earlier American Insurance Association.

see: **Association of Casualty and Surety Companies, Fire and Theft Index Bureau**

American Insurance Services Group (AISG)

Organizations. Members: Property and casualty insurers. *Objectives:* Assists in the proper resolution of property claims. Serves as a clearinghouse for insurance claims. Maintains an index of property and theft loss reports. *Founded:* 1984. *Headquarters:* New York, NY.

American Insurers Highway Safety Alliance (AIHSA)

Organizations. Members: Automobile insurance companies. *Objectives:* Conducts programs on accident prevention and traffic safety. Publishes safety leaflets, fleet safety materials and conducts community safety campaigns. *Founded:* 1920. *Headquarters:* Schaumburg, IL.

American Land Title Association Standard Loan Policy

Title. A policy issued to a mortgagee covering against loss of precedence for repaying the mortgage lien.

American Life Convention (ALC)

Organizations. A former association of life insurers; it is now part of the American Council of Life Insurance.

see: **American Council of Life Insurance**

American Lloyd's

Insurer Operations. A type of insurer consisting of a syndicate of individuals banding together to assume insurance risks. Though these groups are patterned after Lloyd's of London syndicates, they have no connection with that British institution. American Lloyd's are authorized to operate in a limited number of states.

compare: **insurance exchange, Lloyd's of London**

American Marine Insurance Clearinghouse (AMIC)

Organizations. Members: Ocean marine insurance underwriting groups. *Objectives:* Acts as a secretarial organization for providing risk-sharing arrangements. *Founded:* 1938. *Headquarters:* New York, NY.

American Marine Insurance Forum (AMIF)

Organizations. Members: Ocean marine insurance underwriters insuring hulls, cargos and similar risks. *Objectives:* Promotes education and friendship among ocean marine underwriters. *Founded:* 1955. *Headquarters:* New York, NY.

© 1991 NILS Publishing Company

amortization

American Men Table

Life. A mortality table that was never widely adopted, showing the experiences of major life insurers for the period 1900 to 1915. This table, published in 1918, was excellent in many respects, but suffered from too many legal technicalities to gain wide acceptance.

see: **mortality table**

American National Standards Institute (ANSI)

Organizations. Members: Engineers and safety design experts. Objectives: Promotes the use of approved standards for industry, engineering and safety design. Founded: 1918. Headquarters: New York, NY.

see: **ANSI Standard**

American Nuclear Insurers (ANI)

Organizations. Members: Liability and property insurance companies. Objectives: Provides property and liability coverage for the nuclear energy industry. Founded: 1957. Headquarters: Farmington, CT.

American Risk and Insurance Association (ARIA)

Organizations. Members: Insurance educators, and others interested in risk and insurance education and research. Objectives: Operates as a professional society; offers a placement service for academic positions. Founded: 1932. Headquarters: Orlando, FL.

American Society of Chartered Life Underwriters and Chartered Financial Consultants (ASCLU & ChFC)

Organizations. Members: Individuals who have been awarded the Chartered Life Underwriter (CLU) or the Chartered Financial Consultants (ChFC) designations. Objectives: Provides education programs for continued professional development. Founded: 1927. Headquarters: Bryn Mawr, PA.

see: **American College, Chartered Financial Consultant, Chartered Life Underwriter**

American Society of Industrial Security (ASIS)

Organizations. Members: Security managers. Objectives: Sponsors the Certified Protection Professional (CPP) examinations. Founded: 1955. Headquarters: Arlington, VA.

American Society of Mechanical Engineers, Inc. (ASME)

Organizations. Members: Mechanical engineers. Objectives: Promotes safety to prevent loss of life. Founded: 1880. Headquarters: New York, NY.

American Society of Pension Actuaries (ASPA)

Organizations. Members: Individuals involved in the consulting, administration, and design aspects of the employee benefit business. Objectives: Promotes high standards for pension actuaries. Awards designations to its members. Founded: 1966. Headquarters: Washington, D.C.

American Society of Safety Engineers (ASSE)

Organizations. Members: Safety engineers. Objectives: Promotes safety and health in the workplace. Sponsors conferences and continuing education seminars. Founded: 1911. Headquarters: Des Plaines, IL.

American Surety Association (ASA)

Organizations. Members: Surety agents, attorneys, consultants and firms operating in the surety field. Objectives: Improving the efficiency of surety bonding and reducing bonding costs. Founded: 1980. Headquarters: Washington, D.C.

American Tort Reform Association (ATRA)

Organizations. Members: Law firms, professional groups, business and trade associations and state legislators. Objectives: Promoting reform of the United States tort law system. Sponsors educational programs for reform of the civil justice system. Founded: 1986. Headquarters: Washington, D.C.

American Trust Fund

Insurer Operations. A trust fund established by Lloyd's of London and maintained in the United States to pay claims. Started in 1939, when there was concern about claims payments during World War II, the fund has been maintained to reduce the exchange problems between the U.S. dollar and English pound and to maintain the confidence of U.S. brokers. Initially funded for $40 million, today it is well in excess of $1 billion.

see: **guaranty funds, Lloyd's of London, Lloyd's Premium Trust Fund**

amicus curiae

General. Literally, this Latin term means "friend of the court." An individual or organization that is not a party to a particular litigation, but which is allowed by the court to provide its views on the case in question. Usually these views are presented in an "amicus curiae brief" (or "amicus brief," for short).

amortization

Risk Management. The liquidation of a debt on an installment basis; the gradual reduction of an interest-bearing liability by making periodic payments until the outstanding liability reaches zero; a technique used for the gradual retiring of a liability, deferred charge or a capital expenditure over a period of time. Examples: Depreciation, depletion, and write-off of intangibles.

see: **capital charges, depletion, depreciation**

© 1991 NILS Publishing Company

amortization period

Reinsurance. In the rating of per-occurrence excess coverages, the amortization period represents the number of years at a given premium level necessary to accumulate total premiums equal to the indemnity.

syn: payback period

amortized value

Insurer Operations. A method of valuing certain premium bonds carried on an insurance company's financial statement. The value of a bond under this method is the amount to which the purchase price of the bond has increased or decreased from its discount or premium price.

amotion

General. The common law procedure by which a director may be removed for cause by stockholders.

see: stockholder

amount at risk

Life. The amount of its own funds that a life insurance company has at risk on a whole life insurance policy; the difference between the policy's face value and cash value.

Casualty/Property. The policy limit or the probable maximum loss, whichever is less.

compare: amount subject, probable maximum loss

amount limit

Crime. The amount of insurance specified in an open stock burglary policy, beyond which the coinsurance percentage limit does not apply. This is not the same as the policy limit, which is usually greater.

amount of insurance

Insurer Operations.
see: limit of liability

amount subject

Loss Control/Property. The maximum amount which may be expected to be lost in any one fire or other casualty. Its determination depends on the protection and construction of the risk, and the distribution of values within the risk. Determining the amount subject is a major responsibility of loss prevention specialists and property underwriters.

see: amount at risk, fire division, probable maximum loss

analyst

Financial Planning.
see: securities analyst

analytic schedule

Property.
see: analytic system

analytic system

Property. A system for measuring the relative probability of fire loss to property, and of determining fire insurance rates. The analytic system was used for many years in the United States, but has been replaced, for the most part, by other rating methods used by the Insurance Services Office (ISO).

syn: analytic schedule

anchor tenant

Financial Planning. A retail merchant in a shopping mall or retail center that draws large numbers of consumers to the mall or area. Sears, Macy's or J.C. Penney are examples of retail stores which attract many customers who will often shop in adjacent stores as well.

see: triple A tenant

ancillary

General. A term used to describe a person, place or thing that is subordinate, supplementary or subsidiary to a primary person, place or thing. *Example:* A main factory and its ancillary locations.

ancillary benefits

Health. Benefits that pay for miscellaneous hospital charges, including ambulance service to and from a hospital, drugs, blood, operating room, medicines, bandages, X-rays, diagnostic tests, and anesthetics.

ancillary services

Health. Hospital departments that provide patient services such as radiology and laboratories. Excluded from ancillary services are routine services such as housekeeping, dietary needs, nursing and supplies.

animal insurance

Inland Marine. A broad term referring to insurance coverage for the health or life of animals and livestock.

see: animal mortality insurance, bloodstock insurance, livestock auction market form, livestock commercial feedlot reporting form, livestock floater, livestock mortality insurance, livestock transit insurance, pet insurance, poultry insurance

animal mortality insurance

Inland Marine. A form of life insurance written on domesticated animals which covers death from any cause, including voluntary destruction for humane reasons (when the necessity for such destruction is certified by a veterinarian).

see: animal insurance, livestock mortality insurance

anniversary date

Insurer Operations. The month and day of policy

© 1991 NILS Publishing Company

issue, renewal, and expiration, as shown in the policy declarations.

see: policy anniversary, policy period, renewal

annotation

General. A commentary written to explain the meaning of a text.

annual

General. Occurring every year; pertaining to a year (12 months' time) without regard to any particular point in time during that year.

see: calendar year, fiscal year

annual aggregate deductible

Insurer Operations. The maximum dollar amount for which an insured is responsible under a policy's deductible provisions during a twelve-month policy period. Once an insured has assumed claims up to the annual aggregate deductible amount, the insurer assumes all remaining claims for their full value, up to any policy limits.

annual bond

Surety. A bond that covers contracts or bids awarded or submitted during a twelve-month period, or during a period ending with a fiscal year-end.

annual financial statement

Insurer Operations/Regulation.
see: annual statement

annual implementation plan (AIP)

Health. A written plan prepared by a hospital or clinic, indicating the short-range objectives it needs to achieve during the next 12 months to accomplish the long-term goals indicated in the health systems plan (HSP) for its region of operation. The HSP is produced by a regional planning agency – a health systems agency (HSA) – under the National Health Planning and Resources Development Act of 1974. Directed by consumers and health care providers from within the health service area, HSAs assess health care needs within their region and monitor quality – all with the goal of preventing duplication of effort and maximizing the effectiveness of limited healthcare resources.

syn: health systems plan, National Health Planning and Resource Development Act of 1974

annualization

Insurer Operations. A policy provision which allows the insurer to adjust the annual premium of policies issued for more than one year to the rate prevailing at each anniversary date.

see: adjustable premium

annual payments annuity

Life. An annuity requiring annual premium payments to maintain the contract in force.

see: annuity

annual policy

Insurer Operations. A policy issued for a twelve-month period.

see: policy year

annual renewal agreement

Life. A policy clause in which an insurance company agrees to renew a given insurance policy under specified conditions.

see: renewal

annual renewal term

Life.
see: yearly renewable term

annual report

General. A formal financial statement issued annually by a corporation to its shareholders. This statement may include comments from management concerning events of the prior fiscal year and the events which may be expected during the next fiscal year.

see: financial statement, Generally Accepted Accounting Principles (GAAP)

annual statement

Insurer Operations/Regulation. A report of an insurance company's financial operations for a particular year, including a balance sheet supported by detailed exhibits and schedules, filed with the state insurance department of each jurisdiction in which the company is licensed to conduct business. The form used was developed by the National Association of Insurance Commissioners (NAIC).

syn: annual financial statement, blank, convention blank; see: financial statement, gain and loss exhibit, Schedule P, Statutory Accounting Principles

annual supply contract bond

Surety. A bond guaranteeing that a contractor will furnish contracted commodities during a twelve-month period.

see: manufacturer's penalty insurance

annual total return

Financial Planning/Risk Management. An investment banking term, defined as the capital gain or loss, plus the sum of dividend disbursements expected over the next three to five years, all divided by the recent stock price and expressed as an average annual rate of growth.

© 1991 NILS Publishing Company

annuitant

Life. A person who receives or owns an annuity.
see: annuity

annuity

Life. A contract that provides for periodic payments, starting after a stated period or on a contingent date, and continuing for a fixed period or for the remaining life of the annuitant.

syn: life annuity; see: annual payments annuity, annuity certain, annuity conversion rate, annuity due, annuity period, annuity purchase fund, annuity starting date, annuity table, Annuity Table for 1949, annuity with period certain, cash refund annuity, cost-of-living variable annuity plan, deferred annuity, deferred group annuity, equity variable annuity plan, fixed annuity, flexible premium annuity, group annuity, group deferred annuity, guaranteed annuity payments, immediate annuity, increasing annuity, insured variable annuity plan, investment annuity, joint and survivor annuity, joint life and survivor annuity, liquidation charge, liquidation period, modified refund annuity, normal annuity form, optional annuity form, pure annuity, refund annuity, retirement annuity, reverse-annuity mortgage, tax deferred annuity, temporary life annuity, temporary life annuity due, variable annuity

annuity certain

Life. An annuity contract under which the benefits are paid for a specific number of years, regardless of whether the annuitant lives or dies.

syn: installment refund annuity, payment certain; compare: annuity with period certain; see: annuity

annuity conversion rate

Life. A rate that usually varies by age and sex of the annuitant which is used to determine the amount an annuity will pay to the annuitant for each dollar of contribution accumulated to the date of retirement.
see: annuity

annuity due

Life. An annuity which disburses benefit payments at the start of the benefit period, rather than at the end.
see: annuity

annuity period

Life. The length of time between each benefit payment made under an annuity contract (i.e., monthly or quarterly).
see: annuity

annuity purchase fund

Life. A fund established under a deposit administration plan, to retain annuity purchase payments transferred from the unallocated active life fund.

syn: retired life fund; see: annuity, deposit administration plan

annuity starting date

Life. The first day of the first annuity period in which an annuity payment has been made.
see: annuity

annuity table

Life. Similar to mortality tables used in calculating life insurance risks and premiums, these are charts showing for a defined group of people (grouped by age, sex, etc.), the number living at the beginning of a particular year and the number dying during that year. The yearly probabilities derived from an annuity table are used to calculate annuity premium payments and future income payments.
compare: mortality table

Annuity Table for 1949

Life. A table, published by Jenkins and Lew, of projection factors that affect reductions in mortality rates.
see: annuity

annuity with period certain

Life. An annuity contract under which the benefits are payable for a specified period in any event, and after that period for as long as the annuitant lives.
compare: annuity certain; see: annuity

ANSI Standard

Loss Control. Specifications established by the American National Standards Institute as a guide to aid manufacturers, consumers and regulatory agencies.
see: American National Standards Institute

answer

General. The response by a defendant to a summons and/or complaint by a plaintiff. A defendant must file an answer to a summons or complaint within the time period prescribed by law. If the defendant does not file an answer, a default judgment may be entered.
see: complaint, counterclaim, default judgment, summons and complaint

antedate

General. Using a date prior to the date on which an undertaking or transaction was made. Dating a document before the date on which it actually was written or executed.
syn: backdate; compare: postdate; see: warranted no known or reported losses

© 1991 NILS Publishing Company

anti-arson application forms

Property. Property insurance application forms used in those areas with a high incidence of arson.

anti-coercion law

Regulation. A provision in most states' insurance statutes, prohibiting the use of coercion when selling an insurance policy. Normally, the provision is found in act entitled "Unfair Trade Practices," and the act also prohibits boycott and intimidation.

syn: unfair trade practices; see: twisting

anti-compact laws

Regulation. Anti-trust laws that prohibit or place limits on agreements that could prevent or restrict competition among businesses.

see: anti-trust laws, tying arrangement

anti-discrimination laws

Regulation. State laws prohibiting insurance companies from extending certain preferential terms or rates to certain policyholders or classes of insureds, when such preferential treatment is not warranted by the company's normal underwriting standards.

see: discrimination

anti-rebate law

Regulation. Statutory provisions found in most states that prohibit agents from offering or returning any portion of the commission they receive from insurance companies to policyholders, as an inducement to purchase insurance from that agent. In recent years, as insurance consumerism has grown more active, some states have modified their anti-rebate laws to allow partial rebates in certain lines of business.

see: rebate

anti-selection

Insurer Operations. The adverse impact upon insurers that occurs when insureds select insurance coverage for only those risks that are likely to generate losses.

see: adverse selection

anti-trust laws

Regulation. Federal and state statutes that protect trade and commerce from price fixing, price discrimination, monopolies and unlawful restraints. State acts are generally modifications of federal antitrust acts.

see: anti-compact laws, Clayton Act, McCarran-Ferguson Act, Sherman Antitrust Act

apparent agency

Agency/Insurer Operations. A legal doctrine applied in connection with estoppel which holds that an agent has whatever power or authority a reasonable person would assume they have. In the public's eyes, an individual acting under apparent agency binds the company (the principal) as fully as he or she would under actual authority.

syn: agency by estoppel; see: actual authority, agency, estoppel

apparent partner

General. A partnership, which permits an individual (not a *partner in fact*) to represent him or herself to a third party as being a partner, and is liable to the same extent for the actions of the *apparent partner* as it would be for the actions of an actual partner.

The apparent partner has the power to bind the partnership. If all partners consent to the apparent partner's representation, any of his or her transactions are considered acts or obligations of the partnership. If fewer than all partners consent, the act is a joint obligation between the partners who consent to the obligation, and not to the partnership itself.

see: partnership

appeal

General. Taking the decision of a lower court to a higher court for review of the lower court's decision. An appeal is generally reviewed by a panel of judges, who either affirm or reverse the ruling of the lower court. In certain situations, the court of appeal may ask the trial court to conduct a new trial or to reconsider its verdict.

see: appellate court, certiorari

appeal bond

Surety. A bond filed with a court that has made a decision, by a party against whom a judgment has been rendered. The bond stays the execution of the judgment, pending appeal to a higher court. An appeal bond guarantees that the appellant will pay the original judgment (sometimes with interest) if the appeal fails or is denied.

see: court bond, judicial bond

appellant

General. A person who appeals a lower court decision. An appeals action may be initiated by either the plaintiff or defendant.

compare: appellee

appellate court

General. A court of law having the power to hear appeals from, and review cases litigated in lower courts.

see: appeal

appellee

General. The party against whom an appeal is sought.

compare: appellant

Appleton Rule

Regulation. A provision of the New York Insurance Code requiring insurance companies licensed in that

Appleton Rule — continued
state to follow specific provisions in the New York Insurance Code, even when operating outside of the state. Violation of this regulation can result in the suspension or termination of the operations of a New York-licensed insurer.

applicability

General. The appropriateness or relevance of one thing to another. It is especially used in the law when discussing the relevance of laws, regulations, or case precedents to a current situation.

application

Insurer Operations. A printed form developed by an insurer which includes questions about a prospective insured and the desired insurance coverage and limits. It provides the insurer's underwriter with information for accepting or rejecting the prospective insured and rating the desired policy. Some policies — most often, life, health and professional liability insurance policies – make the application part of the policy, and misrepresentations in the application can void the policy.

see: **representation; Fr: proposition, soumission; Gr: Antrag; Sp: solicitud**

application for payment

Surety. A form which a contractor, requesting payment for work completed up to the date of application, issues to an owner. The application for payment includes documents required by the contract before payment will be made.

appointment

Agency. Authorization of an individual to act for or represent an insurance company. Such authorization is formalized by the signing of an agency agreement.

see: **agency agreement**

apportionment

Property. A provision in a property insurance policy that divides a property loss among all insurance policies that might be in force with respect to a covered property, in the same proportion as each policy's coverage limit bears to the total amount of insurance in force. Differences in coverage among the policies may operate to reduce an insured's recovery to something less than 100 percent of the loss. *Example:* Two $10,000 property insurance policies apply to a building, but only one of the policies covers the peril of windstorm. The insured would recover only $2,500 on a $5,000 windstorm loss – fifty percent of the loss.

see: **contribution clause, other insurance clause, pro rata liability clause**

Insurer Operations. A provision for dividing a loss among insurance policies when more than one policy is in force. It provides that a loss covered by several insurance policies shall be divided in the proportion that each policy's coverage bears the total coverage applicable to the loss. *Example:* Policy A = $10,000. Policy B = $20,000. Policy C = $70,000. Total coverage applicable = $100,000. Under the apportionment clause found in most policies, Policy A would pay 10% of any loss ($10,000/$100,000); Policy B would pay 20% of any loss ($20,000/$100,000), and Policy C would pay 70% of any loss ($70,000/$100,000).

see: **contribution by limits, contribution by share**

appraisal

Property. A report or document prepared and signed by a specialist, indicating his or her best estimate as to the value of property or of an ongoing business. An *insurance appraisal* is specifically designed to determine the appropriate amount of insurance to be purchased or the amount of a loss to be paid.

see: **actual cash value, appraisal clause, appraisal inventory, appraised value, appraiser, replacement cost; Fr: devis estimatif; Gr: Schätzung; Sp: avalúo, peritaje, tasación, valuación**

appraisal clause

Property. A property insurance policy provision which allows an insured and insurer who cannot reach an agreement on the amount of a loss settlement to each select their own appraiser. The appraisers then select a disinterested umpire. Disagreements between the appraisers are settled by the umpire whose decisions are usually binding on both parties.

see: **arbitration clause, umpire**

appraisal inventory

Property. A detailed record of individual items that constitute a property. An appraisal inventory is included in an appraisal report, and lists the values set by the appraiser.

appraised value

Property/Risk Management. A value assigned to a property after an appraisal of the property is completed. The appraised value is used to ascertain the appropriate amount of insurance to be purchased, or the amount of loss to be paid.

appraiser

Loss Control. A person who determines the value of property or the amount of a disputed loss.

compare: **claims adjuster**

appreciation

General. An increase in the conversion value of a specific property or medium of exchange, caused by

32

economic or related factors which may be either temporary or permanent.

compare: depreciation; see: inflation

Financial Planning. An increase in the price of a stock, which is the fundamental investment objective. A stock advancing from 30 to 50 dollars per share is said to have appreciated by 20 points.

appreciation rate

Financial Planning/Risk Management. A rate or index figure that is applied against the value of a property or investment at one date, to bring it up to its present or future value.

approach

Agency. The part of an agent's sales presentation which creates openings for further discussion with prospective insureds.

approved cargo

Inland Marine/Loss Control/Ocean Marine. A term used to describe goods transported by ship, rail, air, etc., indicating that the goods are not particularly suspectible to loss and/or damage due to their nature or packaging.

syn: approved merchandise

approved charges

Health. Charges for medical care that are partially paid (usually 80 percent) by supplemental medical insurance. The list of approved charges and their amounts are updated annually, based on an economic index formula that considers inflationary costs of medical practice and increased earnings levels.

see: diagnostic related group, reasonable and customary charge, schedule

approved merchandise

Inland Marine/Ocean Marine.

see: approved cargo

approved roof

Loss Control/Property. A roof that is constructed of fire-resistive materials, rather than more flammable wood. Tile, metal and asphalt shingles are all approved roofing materials.

see: construction

approved sprinkler system

Loss Control/Property. An automatic sprinkler system that has been installed in accordance with fire or building codes, that uses the proper automatic heads for the structure's occupancy and construction, that has an adequate and reliable supply of water, and that has been tested and shown to be in working order. Buildings protected by such systems usually qualify for discounts on their fire insurance premiums.

see: automatic sprinkler system, protection

appurtenant structures

Property. Incidental structures of lesser value – such as a garage – on the same premises as the main structure (i.e., the building that is the primary subject of the insurance). Some property insurance policies provide additional coverage for appurtenant structures, subject to limits that are percentages of the insured building's coverage amounts.

see: coverage extension

"A" rates

Insurer Operations. Rates that are established by judgment and do not have loss experience statistics as a foundation for their development. These rates are developed by the underwriter or company on an individual risk, based on what is believed equitable for the risk involved.

compare: manual rates; see: account premium modification plan, judgment rates, schedule rating

arbiter

General.

see: arbitrator

arbitrage

Financial Planning. The simultaneous purchase of securities in one market and the sale of them in another, in order to profit from price discrepancies between the two markets.

arbitration

General. A form of adjudication used in lieu of litigation, to render a decision when a matter is in dispute. The matter is submitted for judgment to a specified number of disinterested persons called "arbitrators," whose decision is called an "award," and is binding upon the parties.

compare: litigation; see: adjudicate, appraisal clause, arbitration award, arbitration clause, arbitrator, fact finding; Fr: arbitrage; Gr: Schiedsverfahren; Sp: arbitraje

arbitration agreement

General. The written document that specifies the terms and conditions of a settlement as the result of an arbitrator's decision.

arbitration award

General. The final decision of an arbitrator upon settling a dispute.

arbitration clause

General. A clause found in many contracts which requires the parties to the contract to settle any disputes by arbitration.

Reinsurance. A provision in reinsurance contracts in which the parties agree to submit any dispute or controversy to an official tribunal of their choosing, in

arbitration clause — continued
lieu of other proceedings (e.g., civil litigation) provided for by the law. Although wording of arbitration clauses may vary, it normally provides for an appointment of two arbitrators, one selected by each party, who in turn appoint an umpire. The decision of any two of the three is binding on the parties to the reinsurance treaty.

Property. A clause found in property insurance policies which provides that if the insured and the insurer cannot agree on an appropriate claims settlement, each will appoint an arbitrator, who in turn will then select an independent umpire. A decision by any two of the three prescribes a settlement. The arbitration clause binds both parties to this procedure, as well as to the final decision.

see: **appraisal clause, umpire**

arbitrator

General. An individual chosen or appointed to decide a controversy out of court.

syn: **arbiter, mediator, umpire; compare: referee**

architects professional liability insurance

Casualty. Provides coverage for an individual architect or an architectural firm for claims which the insured becomes legally obligated to pay as damages arising out of the performance of professional services including errors, omissions or negligent acts. Coverage is usually written on a claims-made basis.

see: **professional liability insurance**

area

Casualty/Property. The measure of a planar region or zone. Area is used as a rating basis for several types of liability insurance coverage (e.g., premises liability), and is also useful in verifying insurance-to-value calculations in property insurance. In rating formulas using square feet, the number of square feet is expressed in thousands of square feet of floor space (excluding open spaces such as mezzanines, courtyards, parking areas, and the non-public parts of buildings used for maintenance or for heating or air conditioning equipment).

see: **exposure unit**

arising out of and in the course of employment

Workers' Compensation. A phrase used in workers' compensation policy forms, to restrict coverage to individuals who are injured or who contract diseases in their roles as employees. The phrase expresses a two-part test: "arising out of employment" means that there must be a causal relationship between the employment and how the injury or disease occurred;

"in the course of employment" refers to the time, place and circumstances of the injury or disease.

see: **covered injury, employee, industrial accident, occupational accident, occupational disease, workers' compensation insurance**

arithmetic mean

Risk Management. The average value that is computed by dividing the sum of a set of terms by the total number of terms. *Example:* The arithmetic mean of set 13, 19, 11, 9, 8 is 12 (i.e., the sum 60 divided by 5).

see: **mean**

armored car and messenger service insurance

Inland Marine. Insurance against losses incurred during the transfer of money, securities, precious metals, and certain kinds of valuables by armored cars.

arm's-length transaction

General. A transaction involving unrelated parties, with no undue influence exercised by or imposed upon either party; the standard under which unrelated parties would carry out a particular transaction.

see: **fair market value**

Armstrong Investigation

Regulation. An investigation by New York State, conducted in 1905, of the life insurance industry, which resulted in the regulation by many states of life insurance policy forms and provisions. The regulations required life insurance companies to provide minimum benefit levels and to write policies in understandable language.

arrears

General. 1) The state of being overdue or behind schedule. 2) The payment of bills or debt.

Insurer Operations. A term used to describe an insurance policy with past-due premiums, but which is still within the grace period and hence not yet subject to cancellation for nonpayment of premium.

see: **bucking arrears**

arson

Property. An act of actual or attempted malicious and deliberate destruction of property by fire. If the person committing this crime (the arsonist) is not the insured, most property insurance policies will cover any damage that results. If it is proven that the arsonist is either the insured or someone operating at the insured's behalf, most property insurance policies are voided.

syn: **incendiarism; see: arson fraud**

arson fraud

Property. Arson committed by or at the behest of the insured is usually considered fraud. Property insurance policies generally do not exclude loss by arson,

© 1991 NILS Publishing Company

but public policy does not allow profit by wrongdoing. Homeowner's policy forms developed by the Insurance Services Office (ISO) now have specific exclusions dealing with intentional loss.

see: intentional loss

articles of association

Regulation.

see: articles of incorporation

articles of dissolution

Regulation. A document filed with the Secretary of State or other appropriate governmental agency, prior to dissolution of a partnership or corporation. The dissolution will not be approved until after provisions have been made for the distribution of assets, and after debts have been satisfied.

compare: articles of incorporation; see: distribution of assets

articles of incorporation

Regulation. An official document, filed with the Secretary of State or other appropriate governmental agency, which outlines a corporation's purpose and the rights and liabilities of shareholders and directors.

syn: articles of association; compare: articles of dissolution; see: bylaws, charter, corporation

articles of merger or consolidation

Regulation. Documents filed with the Secretary of State or other governmental agency that specify the terms and conditions of a merger or consolidation of corporations.

as if

Insurer Operations. The recalculation of prior loss experience, to show what underwriting results would have been if a particular program had been in force.

syn: what if

as interest may appear

Inland Marine/Ocean Marine/Property. A phrase used on a policy to describe the insurable interest in a property when it is unknown. It is avoided by most underwriters, because disputes can arise as to whom a claim should be paid.

compare: full interest admitted; see: insurable interest

asked price

Financial Planning.

see: asking price

asking price

Financial Planning. A commercial term indicating the formal price at which goods or services are offered.

This may not be the final price as the final price is often negotiable.

syn: asked price, offered price, offering price

as per

General. In accordance with; according to the terms of.

assailing thieves

Ocean Marine. Thieves (other than the officers or crew of a vessel) using violence or force to steal a ship or its cargo.

see: barratry, piracy

assault

Casualty. Any willful attempt to threaten or inflict injury, or any intentional display of such force that would give the victim reason to fear or expect bodily harm. Assault may be committed without actual contact or bodily harm to the victim.

compare: battery

assessable policies

Insurer Operations.

see: assessment insurance

assessable value

General. The value of real estate or personal property that is set by an appointed governmental entity (e.g., county or state tax assessor) to determine taxes.

assessment

General. Charges made to members of an association or other group, to fund losses, special projects, or ongoing operations.

see: deficiency assessment

Insurer Operations. An additional premium charge on policyholders by assessment companies to meet greater than anticipated losses.

see: assessment company

assessment company

General. An insurer with the right to assess policyholders additional amounts of premium to meet operational needs when a stipulated premium is not charged.

compare: legal reserve life insurance company; see: assessment insurance, reciprocal insurance exchange

assessment insurance

Insurer Operations. A type of insurance whereby the insurer can charge policyholders additional premiums if actual losses exceed those originally expected at policy issue. When specific premium payments are not fixed in the policy (as is often the case with fraternal

© 1991 NILS Publishing Company

organizations), an assessment from the insurer increases the total premiums paid by the insureds whenever necessary to meet claims.

syn: assessable policies

assessment mutual

Insurer Operations. A mutual insurer with the right to assess policyholders additional amounts of premium to meet operational needs.

see: assessment company, mutual insurance company

assessment rolls

General. A verified list of taxable property and persons constructed and maintained by cities or towns.

assessor

General. A public official who appraises and values properties for tax purposes.

asset

General. Property – real, personal, tangible, intangible – which belongs to a person, estate, corporation or association. Anything of commercial value.

see: assets

asset composition ratio

Risk Management. A financial ratio which considers the composition of an organization's total assets to evaluate solvency. *Formula:* Asset Composition Ratio = Total Current Assets/Total Assets. The higher the ratio, the greater the organization's ability to raise money to pay debt.

see: financial ratios, financial underwriting

assets

Risk Management. The total value of all properties (real or personal, tangible or intangible) which belong to a person, estate, corporation, or association that can be applied to the payment of its debts.

see: asset, balance sheet, book value, capital asset, cash assets, current assets, distribution of assets, excluded assets, fixed assets, good will, impaired asset, net quick assets, nonledger assets, quick assets, recapture of plan assets, tangible assets, trusteed assets, valuation of assets

Insurer Operations/Regulation. The assets of an insurance company include real estate holdings, stocks and bonds, securities and cash, mortgages, deferred and unpaid premiums. For statutory annual statement purposes, an insurer's assets would *exclude* accounts receivable which are over 90 days in arrears, and office equipment.

see: admitted assets, nonadmitted assets, Statutory Accounting Principles

asset share value

Life. The actual share of a life insurance company's assets represented by the policyholder's equity, based on the policyholder's contributions to assets (actual gross premiums minus actual costs, dividends and expenses related to the class of business involved).

Insurer Operations. The value that a class of insured business has to an insurance company.

assign

General. To transfer property, rights, or interests to another. To transfer to another for the benefit of creditors; to appoint or allot, select, or designate for a particular purpose. The person or entity to whom property, rights or interests have been assigned.

see: assignee, assignment, assignor

assigned risk

Insurer Operations. Risks insured through a pool of insurers and assigned to a company. Generally, these risks are deemed by underwriters to be "uninsurable," but because of state law or otherwise, they must be insured. Perhaps the best known of assigned risk programs are those that provide automobile insurance to drivers that cannot obtain such insurance through conventional means.

syn: automobile insurance plan; compare: Fair Access to Insurance Requirements; see: automobile shared market, Boston Plan, joint underwriting association, market assistance plans, residual markets

assignee

General. The individual or entity to whom property, rights or interests have been transferred.

compare: assignor; see: assign

assignment

General. The transfer of a legal right or interest in a contract (e.g., an insurance policy) to another, usually involving the sale of property.

Life. Most life insurance policies allow a policyholder to assign their benefits freely, to another or to an institution. Educational and non-profit institutions often ask donors for such assignments, although simply changing the beneficiary is usually the preferred method.

Financial institutions often ask to be assigned life insurance policies held by the debtor. If the insured dies before the loan has been repaid, the creditor receives benefits from the policy, up to the face amount. Any balance remaining would go to the beneficiary named in the policy.

syn: assignment of contract; compare: nonassignable; see: absolute assignment, assign, assignee, assignment and assumption, assignment of benefits, assignment of lease,

36

© 1991 NILS Publishing Company

assignment quota, assignor, collateral assignment

Casualty/Property. In property and casualty insurance, assignments of policies are usually valid only with the prior written consent of the insurer.

see: nonassignable

assignment and assumption

General. A transfer of some right, interest or obligation from one person or entity (the assignor) to another (the assignee) and the corresponding assumption of that right, interest or obligation by the assignee.

assignment fee

Life. An administrative fee, usually a nominal flat dollar charge on each assignable annuity policy, where the periodic payment option is assigned to a third party.

assignment of benefits

Health. A method by which the insured assigns health insurance policy benefits directly to a medical provider. The health insurer then pays the provider directly, less any deductible and/or coinsurance which are billed by the provider to the insured (e.g., amounts within the deductible, charges in excess of scheduled benefit amounts, charges for procedures, drugs or supplies not covered under the policy).

assignment of contract

General.

see: assignment

assignment of lease

General. The transfer by a tenant or lessee of all interest in a leasehold to another party. Such a transfer may require the landlord's approval.

assignment quota

Property. The sharing by insurers in losses by percentage (or "quota") with other insurance policies covering the same risk.

see: quota share

Reinsurance. An arrangement whereby a ceding company is reinsured for a fixed percentage of any loss expense.

assignor

General. The individual or entity who assigns or transfers a property, right, or interest to another.

compare: assignee; see: assign

Associated Aviation Underwriters

Aviation. An underwriting syndicate specializing in aircraft risks.

Associated Risk Managers International (ARMI)

Organizations. Members: Insurance agencies providing property and casualty insurance, risk management services and life and health insurance programs. *Objectives:* Serves as a marketing organization to develop and market specialized insurance and risk management services for trade associations, professional groups and other industry organizations. *Founded:* 1970. *Headquarters:* Austin, TX.

Associate in Risk Management (ARM)

Organizations/Risk Management. A professional designation earned after successfully completing three national examinations given by the Insurance Institute of America. The curriculum covers the risk management decision process as it applies to any organization.

see: Insurance Institute of America

Associate in Society of Actuaries (ASA)

Organizations. A designation awarded by the Society of Actuaries for individuals who pass a series of examinations.

see: Society of Actuaries

Associate of the Casualty Actuarial Society (ACAS)

Organizations. A designation awarded by the Casualty Actuarial Society for persons passing a series of examinations on actuarial mathematics.

see: Casualty Actuarial Society

association

General. A term used to designate a group, collection, or organization of persons who have united together for a common objective.

association captive insurance company

Risk Management. A captive insurance company established by members of an association to underwrite their own collective risks. An association captive usually will only insure members of the sponsoring association.

compare: group captive insurance company; see: captive insurance company

Association For Advanced Life Underwriting (AALU)

Organizations. Members: Advanced life underwriters specializing in estate analysis, business insurance, pension planning, employee benefit plans and other subjects relating to life insurance. *Objectives:* Promotes interests of members; lobbies legislatures for issues concerning life underwriters. *Founded:* 1957. *Headquarters:* Washington, D.C.

association group insurance

Health/Life. Group insurance that covers a trade or

© 1991 NILS Publishing Company

association group insurance — continued
business association and its members, rather than an employer or union providing the coverage.

see: group insurance

Association of Average Adjusters of the United States (AAA)

Organizations. Members: Marine insurance adjusters, marine insurers, admiralty lawyers and ship and cargo appraisers. *Objectives:* Maintains a library on marine insurance and bestows awards to marine insurance adjusters. Provides information to its members and produces publications. *Founded:* 1979. *Headquarters:* New York, NY.

Association of Casualty and Surety Companies (ACSC)

Organizations. An organization that was merged in 1964 with the National Board of Fire Underwriters to form the American Insurance Association.

see: American Insurance Association

Association of Defense Trial Attorneys (ADTA)

Organizations. Members: Attorneys who regularly represent insurance companies and companies that self-insure. *Objectives:* Gathering and distributing information to further insurer and self-insurer defense efforts. Continuing education of its members in matters pertaining to defense of claims involving insurance companies. *Founded:* 1941. *Headquarters:* Peoria, IL. Known until 1988 as the Association of Insurance Attorneys.

Association of Insurance Attorneys (AIA)

Organizations. Until 1988, the name for the Association of Defense Trial Attorneys.

see: Association of Defense Trial Attorneys

Association of Life Insurance Counsel (ALIC)

Organizations. Members: Legal counsel of life insurance companies. *Objectives:* Promoting interests of legal representatives of life insurance companies. *Founded:* 1913. *Headquarters:* New York, NY.

Association of Life Insurance Medical Directors of America (ALIMDA)

Organizations. Members: Medical directors of life insurance companies. *Objectives:* Advancing the science of medicine as applied to insurance. Continuing education of members and public relations. *Founded:* 1889. *Headquarters:* Springfield, MA.

Association of Mill and Elevator Mutual Insurance Companies (AMEMIC)

Organizations. Members: Mutual insurance companies. *Objectives:* Holds seminars and provides an exchange of information among its members concerning grain handling and grain processing plants. *Founded:* 1897. *Headquarters:* Itasca, IL. Also known as the Mill Mutuals.

Association of Professional Insurance Women (APIW)

Organizations. Members: Women in the insurance and reinsurance industry. *Objectives:* Provides professional networking and educational assistance. *Founded:* 1976. *Headquarters:* New York, NY.

association professional liability insurance

Casualty. Insurance coverage for non-profit associations that includes professional liability and directors & officers liability for all directors, officers, employees, committee chairpersons and members, and any other association member while acting on behalf of the association.

assume

General. To take up, to adopt as one's own, to receive or accept some right, responsibility, or position from another. To accept some premise as fact for the purposes of research, study, or prediction.

see: assignment and assumption, novation

Risk Management. The retention of some risk or exposure by an entity or individual.

Reinsurance. To accept (reinsure) all or a part of another insurer's (or self-insurer's or captive insurer's) risk.

compare: cede; see: assuming reinsurer, ceding company, reinsurer

assumed liability

General. Liability transferred or assumed in an agreement between people or organizations.

assumed liability policy

Insurer Operations. A policy providing business liability coverage for risks assumed or transferred by agreement or contract.

see: contractual liability insurance

assumed portfolio

Financial Planning. The collective assumption of all securities held by a person or an institution.

assumed reinsurance

Reinsurance.

see: reinsurance assumed

assuming reinsurer

Reinsurance. The reinsurer that accepts the transfer of risk through reinsurance from another insurer.

see: reinsurer

© 1991 NILS Publishing Company

assumption

Insurer Operations. An archaic term for gross line.
see: gross line

Reinsurance. The property value or liability limits accepted by a reinsurer.

assumption of risk

General. A common law defense, in use prior to the enactment of workers' compensation laws, that held that an employee implicitly assumes all of the ordinary and usual risks of a job when he or she accepts that job. Based on the common law view that an individual is free to contract with (i.e., work for) whomever he or she chooses at whatever price he or she desires.
see: common law defense, guest law, Priestly v. Fowler

Reinsurance.
see: assume

assurance

Insurer Operations. 1)A term used interchangeably with *insurance*, especially in European and British markets, although *insurance* is the preferred term in the United States.
2) A guarantee or declaration of full confidence.
see: insurance

assurance company

Insurer Operations.
see: insurance company

assured

Insurer Operations. Synonymous with insured; denotes the person or entity named in the policy which is insured against mentioned losses or perils.
see: insured

assurer

General. Synonymous with insurer; denotes the underwriter, insurer or indemnifier providing coverage against certain perils and dangers.
see: insurance company

asymmetrical curve

Risk Management.
see: skewed curve

atomic energy reinsurance

Casualty.
see: American Nuclear Insurers, MAERP Reinsurance Association

attachment

General. In law, the legal act of seizing property or the written document (a writ of attachment) which effects that seizure. Attachments usually require a court order.

Insurer Operations. An addition to a basic insurance policy which explains, adds or excludes coverages. It can also add or delete locations. An endorsement or rider which is added to an insurance policy.
see: endorsement, rider

attachment point

Reinsurance. The dollar amount under an excess of loss reinsurance contract at which a ceding (primary) insurer's retention requirements have been met, and the point at which the reinsurance will respond to a loss.
see: excess of loss reinsurance

attachment surety

Surety. An attachment occurs when a court or governmental agency takes the property of a defendant into custody before a trial, as security for paying any judgment.

attained age

Life. The insured's age at a specified point in time, often based on the the previous or next birthday, whichever is closer.
see: age, original age

attending physician's statement (APS)

Health. A statement made to an insurance company underwriter by a proposed insured's personal physician with the permission of the patient. Information obtained in this manner generally concerns illnesses and injuries that may have a bearing on the insurability of the proposed insured.

attest

General. To bear witness to a fact; to affirm to be genuine or true; to authenticate.
see: affirm

attestation clause

Insurer Operations. The final clause of an insurance contract where an officer or officers of an insurance company place their signature(s) to officially authenticate it as a binding contract.
see: insurance contract

attorney-in-fact

General. A person authorized by another (the principal) to act in the principal's place or stead, for a particular purpose. This authority is usually conferred through an instrument called "power of attorney."
see: power of attorney

Insurer Operations. An individual or organization that manages a reciprocal insurance exchange for the benefit of its members. Through a "subscriber's agreement," signed by each of the exchange members, the attorney-in-fact is given authority to conduct the day-

© 1991 NILS Publishing Company

attorney-in-fact — continued
to-day business of the exchange, including the exchange of insurance among the members.

see: **Lloyd's of London, reciprocal insurance exchange**

attractive nuisance doctrine

General. Individuals and organizations normally need not take particular care to safeguard trespassers upon their private property. The attractive nuisance doctrine states that there is a very special duty of care required with respect to artificial or uncommon conditions upon property which could attract children and which are inherently dangerous, such as sandpiles and empty trenches. Under this doctrine, children may be considered *invitees*, and persons or organizations allowing attractive nuisances on their land can be found absolutely liable for their injuries.

see: **absolute liability, invitee, negligence, trespasser**

auctioneers errors & omissions insurance

Casualty. Insurance coverage for auctioneers providing protection against claims caused by negligent acts, errors or omissions in the conduct of their business.

audible alarm

Loss Control.
see: **burglar alarm**

audit

General. To examine with intent to verify. A systematic inspection of accounting or other financial records.

Insurer Operations. Insurers commonly review the financial records of their commercial insureds, to determine premiums for business interruption, workers' compensation, manufacturing, contracting, product liability, and other risks, where premiums are based upon payroll, gross receipts, and other auditable factors.

Auditors (either employees of the insurer or independent contractors) survey insured businesses' records to determine premiums due, based upon expenses and conditions stated in the policy. Audits are usually performed annually, after the policy period in question has expired, and after the items to be audited can be considered final.

If the audit determines that an insured's initial premium was too low (i.e., the estimates for audited exposures were lower than actuals), the audit will result in an *additional premium*. If the audit shows that the initial premium was too high (i.e., exposures were over-estimated), the insured will receive a *return premium*.

see: **additional premium, audit policies, audit provision, initial premium, inspection, payroll audit, return premium**

Regulation.
see: **examination**

audit bureau

General. A central bureau where companies submit daily reports and copies of issued endorsements for auditing before transmittal to the insurance company. If errors are discovered, the originating office is informed and corrections are requested.

syn: **stamping office**; see: **examination bureau, rating bureau**

audited financial statements

General. Financial statements which have been prepared or reviewed by a Certified Public Accountant (CPA) and to which the CPA attaches an opinion letter that they conform to Generally Accepted Accounting Principles (GAAP). Occasionally, the opinion letter will indicate that there are some exceptions to GAAP or problems that exist with the organization's financial condition.

see: **Certified Public Accountant, financial statement, Generally Accepted Accounting Principles**

audit policies

Insurer Operations. Expired policies examined by an insurer, usually to determine the adequacy of premiums charged by its underwriters.

see: **audit**

audit provision

General. An insurance policy provision that explains the insurer's right to examine and audit the insured's books and records at any time during the policy period and within three years after expiration, insofar as such records relate to the policy. The calculation of the estimated and final premium are explained, as well as the determination of premium upon policy cancellation.

see: **audit**

authorization

Insurer Operations. Information and guidance given to agents by underwriters that specify the amounts and types of insurance that will be accepted on a risk of a given class or at a specific location.

see: **agency, agency agreement, agent's certificate of authority**

authorized insurer

Regulation.
see: **admitted insurer**

authorized reinsurance

Reinsurance. Reinsurance ceded to reinsurers that is acceptable to regulators, for the purpose of granting credit to the ceding insurer's account on the statutory annual statement. If the reinsurer is not acceptable to

© 1991 NILS Publishing Company

a state regulator, credit is not allowed unless ceded reserves are funded by cash or letters of credit.

compare: unauthorized reinsurance; see: admitted reinsurance, reinsurance credit

authorized shares

General. The maximum number of shares of stock that a corporation is permitted to issue, as stipulated in the corporation's state-approved charter.

syn: authorized stock; see: issued stock, share of stock, treasury stock

authorized stock

General.

see: authorized shares

auto club

Organizations.

see: American Automobile Association

auto dealers rating plan

Automobile.

see: dealer class plan

automatically convertible term life insurance

Life. Term life insurance policies designed to be converted to permanent insurance at a predetermined date without the expressed instructions of the insured at that time.

automatic cover

Casualty/Property. A provision permitting increases in coverages, changes in interests and newly-acquired property. The amount and duration of automatic coverage are usually limited; for continued and full protection, an insured must report increases and changes to the insurer, and obtain an amendment to the policy.

automatic increase in insurance endorsement

Property.

see: inflation guard endorsement

automatic premium loan

Life. A feature in life insurance policies that uses the cash value accumulated by the insurance policy to pay for past due premiums at the end of the grace period. This prevents a lapse of coverage.

automatic reinstatement clause

Casualty/Property. A provision in an insurance policy that reinstates the original limits of the policy after a covered loss has been paid. Not all coverages may be subject to automatic reinstatement of limits (e.g., those subject to aggregate limits).

syn: loss clause; compare: aggregate limit, first loss insurance, restoration premium

automatic reinsurance

Reinsurance. A reinsurance agreement under which the insurer cedes those portions of a specified class of risks that exceed the retention limits set by contract (treaty) with the reinsurer. The reinsurer must accept all risks ceded to it under the treaty with the insurer.

syn: automatic treaty; compare: facultative reinsurance; see: assume, cede, reinsurance, retention, treaty reinsurance

automatic retirement

Employee Benefits.

see: compulsory retirement

automatic sprinkler clause

Property. Clause in a property insurance policy (written on a building equipped with an automatic sprinkler system) that requires the insured to maintain the system in working order and to notify the insurer whenever the system is not operational, even when only briefly inoperative during maintenance. Coverage may be suspended if the insured fails to comply.

see: automatic sprinkler system, protective safeguards clause

automatic sprinkler system

Loss Control/Property. An automatic property protection device featuring sprinkler heads (usually mounted in ceilings) whose valves open at relatively low temperatures (the initial stages of a fire). Upon reaching those temperatures, the sprinkler heads release a spray of water to extinguish the fire and prevent its spread. Insurance underwriters typically require automatic sprinkler systems in certain types of buildings or occupancies, and sprinkler water systems usually must be independent of normal water service to the protected building. Periodic inspection and testing of sprinklers is required for them to be considered "approved." The existence of an approved sprinkler system normally reduces premiums for an insured.

see: approved sprinkler system, automatic sprinkler clause, deluge automatic sprinkler system, dry pipe automatic sprinkler system, fire extinguishing system, halon, preaction automatic sprinkler system, present value of sprinkler reduction, scuppers, sprinkler leakage coverage, sprinkler leakage legal liability insurance, wet pipe sprinkler system

automatic treaty

Reinsurance.

see: automatic reinsurance

automobile

Automobile. For business automobile and truckers' coverage, an "automobile" is defined as a four-wheel

41

automobile — continued
motor vehicle designed for use on public roads, and includes a land motor vehicle, trailer, or semitrailer. ("Mobile equipment" is not considered an automobile.) Under the personal automobile policy, an "automobile" is defined as a private passenger automobile, a pick-up truck, sedan, panel truck, or trailer, not used in any business or occupation.

see: automobile insurance; Fr: automobile; Gr: Kraftfahrzeug; Sp: automóvil

automobile club
Organizations.
see: American Automobile Association

automobile fleet
Automobile. A group of automobiles, owned and managed by the same owner. The economies for an insurer of covering a significant number of vehicles under a single policy allows a discounted premium to be offered on automobile fleet policies.

see: fleet policy

automobile insurance
Automobile. Insurance that provides coverage for physical damage to insured vehicles, and liability insurance against bodily injury and property damage arising out of the insured's operation of owned, non-owned, and/or hired vehicles.

see: assigned risk, automobile, automobile liability bonds, automobile liability insurance, automobile reinsurance facility, automobile shared market, basic standard auto policy, business auto coverage form, collision coverage, collision damage waiver, comprehensive coverage, family automobile endorsements, family automobile policy, good driver discount, good student discount, hired automobile, medical payments, Mexican automobile endorsement, Mexican automobile insurance, named nonowner endorsement, National Automobile Theft Bureau, nonowned automobile, nonowned automobile liability, personal automobile policy, physical damage, private passenger automobile, rental reimbursement coverage, special package automobile policy, temporary substitute automobile, uninsured motorists coverage

automobile insurance plan
Automobile.
see: assigned risk

automobile liability bonds
Automobile. Bonds maintained in lieu of automobile liability insurance to satisfy a state's financial responsibility or compulsory insurance law.

see: compulsory insurance laws, financial responsibility laws

automobile liability insurance
Automobile. A type of insurance that protects the insured against financial loss because of legal liability for automobile-related injuries to others or damage to their property.

automobile medical payments
Automobile.
see: medical payments

automobile nonowned coverage
Automobile.
see: nonowned automobile liability

automobile physical damage insurance
Automobile.
see: physical damage

automobile reinsurance facility
Automobile. One of several types of "automobile shared market" mechanisms, used to make automobile insurance available to persons who are unable to obtain such insurance in the regular market. Policies written under the plan are reinsured by a pool.

see: automobile shared market

automobile repossessors liability insurance
Casualty. Insurance for auto repossessors, consisting of general liability coverage, including personal injury coverage, towing and driveaway coverage (while repossessing a vehicle by the use of duplicate keys). Includes garagekeepers legal liability to insure against damage to vehicles while in the insured's care, custody or control.

automobile shared market
Automobile. Programs available in each state and the District of Columbia, in which all automobile insurers in that state participate, that make coverage available to car owners who are unable to obtain automobile insurance in the regular market. An exception is Maryland, which operates a state-funded mechanism whose losses are subsidized by private insurers. Each state uses one of three systems to guarantee the availability of automobile insurance: 1) an automobile insurance plan (also called an "assigned risk plan"); 2) a joint underwriting association or; 3) an automobile reinsurance facility.

see: assigned risk, automobile reinsurance facility, joint underwriting association

auxiliary fund
Employee Benefits.
see: conversion fund

© 1991 NILS Publishing Company

available seat miles (ASM)

Aviation. A measure of an airline's seating capacity available for sale. Each available seat mile is one seat flown one mile. This is one factor used by aviation underwriters to measure an airline's exposure to liability risks.

see: revenue passenger miles

average

Ocean Marine. Any loss or damage due to insured perils that is less than a total loss.

see: free of particular average, free of particular average American conditions, free of particular average English conditions, general average, general average bond, general average contribution, particular average

average adjuster

Ocean Marine.

see: general average adjuster

average agreement

Ocean Marine. A document signed by a cargo insurer, to allow release of the cargo after the occurrence of an average loss which is covered by the insurer. Prior to the release, the owner must post a bond or cash deposit for the amount of the assessment against the owner's shipment, or provide a guarantee from an acceptable insurance company.

see: general average bond, general average

average annual dividend yield

Financial Planning. The total common dividends declared per share, divided by the average stock price, for a given fiscal year. It is expressed as a percentage.

see: financial ratios

average annual price-earnings ratio (P/E)

Financial Planning. The average price of a share of stock for the year, divided by earnings per share (as reported by the company) for the year.

see: financial ratios

average blanket rate

Property. When property insurance is blanketed, this is the rate applied against all the property insured by the policy, and is the rate used to determine premiums on mid-term endorsements (e.g., increases in insured values). The rate is developed by determining premiums in the usual manner (i.e., multiplying each location's specific rate by the value at that location), totalling these premiums, and dividing this sum by the total of all values insured.

syn: average rate; compare: specific rate; see: blanket insurance

average clause

Property. When multiple properties are covered by a single policy, an average clause provides that each property shall be insured in the same proportion that its value bears to the total of all values insured. Used to prevent an insured from underinsuring one property (and thereby underpaying premium).

compare: coinsurance, coinsurance clause; see: insurance to value, pro rata distribution clause

average cost

Risk Management. A business inventory valuation method which develops an inventory value by dividing the total costs of goods available for sale throughout the year by the total quantity purchased.

compare: first in, first out; last in, first out

average daily census

Health. An average of the number of hospital in-patients which is calculated by dividing the number of patient days during a period by the number of calendar days in the period. An in-patient charged for occupying for a bed for one day constitutes one "patient day." Newborns are excluded from the calculation of this figure.

see: average length of stay, in-patient

average indexed monthly earnings (AIME)

Employee Benefits. A method whereby a worker's earnings are indexed (i.e., updated) according to changes in national average annual wages, so that retired workers maintain the same relative income level in their Social Security benefits.

see: average monthly wage

average length of stay (ALOS)

Health. The average number of in-patient days spent by patients in a hospital during a given period. It is used to measure health care facility utilization. Newborns are excluded from the calculation.

see: average daily census, in-patient

average monthly earnings

Employee Benefits.

see: average monthly wage

average monthly wage (AMW)

Employee Benefits. A weighted average of an individual's Social Security wages. *Formula:* 1) Determine the total number of years that the individual paid the Social Security tax, starting with the year beginning in their 21st birthday, subject to a maximum of 40 years; 2) Select the 35 years (420 months) of highest Social Security wage earnings; 3) Take the total wages subject to Social Security earned during those 35 years, and divide by 420 to calculate the average monthly wage (AMW).

The average monthly wage is then used when referring to a table published by the Social Security Administration (the Social Security Wage Index) to

© 1991 NILS Publishing Company

AMW — continued
find the corresponding primary insurance amount which will be paid.

syn: **average monthly earnings**; see: **average indexed monthly earnings, primary insurance amount, Social Security Wage Index**

average rate
Property.
see: **average blanket rate**

average risk
Insurer Operations.
see: **standard risk**

average weekly benefits
Workers' Compensation. A percentage of the average weekly wage, calculated or prescribed by state workers' compensation and disability benefits laws. It is subject to minimum and maximum amounts.

syn: **weekly compensation**; see: **average weekly wage**

average weekly wage
Workers' Compensation. The average rate of remuneration per week, computed or prescribed by state workers' compensation and disability benefits laws, and used for determining weekly workers' compensation or disability benefits.

syn: **weekly compensation**; see: **average weekly benefits**

aviation accident insurance
Life. Life insurance that protects passengers, pilots, or flight employees while on scheduled air flights against losses connected with airline accidents. Non-scheduled or foreign flight coverage generally requires higher premiums.

see: **aviation insurance**

aviation clause
Life. An exclusion found in many life insurance policies which denies coverage for a loss resulting from an aviation accident, unless the insured was a passenger on a regularly scheduled airline.

aviation hazard
Risk Management. The increased hazard of death or disability arising from travel on other-than-commercial aircraft.
Life. The increased life insurance risk associated with flight on other-than-commercial aircraft. Many life insurance policies exclude coverage for such risks, by use of the aviation clause.

see: **aviation clause**

aviation insurance
Aviation. A general label that describes insurance coverage products that protect an insured against losses arising out of the manufacture, use, or operation of aircraft. Such insurance is purchased by aviation-related businesses like airports, aircraft manufacturers, and airlines. Coverages purchased depend upon the insured's needs, and may cover bodily injury, property damage, medical payments, hull coverage, etc.

syn: **air transport insurance**; see: **air cargo insurance, aircraft insurance, aircraft product liability insurance, aircraft spare parts insurance, airport owners and operators liability insurance, air travel insurance, aviation passenger liability insurance, fixed base liability, hangar keepers legal liability insurance, hull policy**

Aviation Insurance Rating Bureau (AIRB)
Organizations. Members: Aviation insurers. *Objectives:* Promulgating rates for aircraft hulls, aircraft property damage liability and employers' aviation indemnity. Establishes and administers plans to secure statistical data for creating underwriting rules, classification of risks, rating plans, rates or premiums. *Founded:* 1948. *Headquarters:* New York, NY.

aviation passenger liability insurance
Aviation. Coverage for aircraft operators, in the event a passenger is injured, killed or disabled during an accident while aboard an insured aircraft. Aviation policies divide liability coverage into two parts — general liability (excluding passengers), and passenger liability.

compare: **air travel insurance**

avocations
Life.
see: **hobbies or avocations**

avoidable consequences
General. A legal term used to describe an adverse result that arises from a lack of care on the part of an individual, which result could have been avoided had the individual exercised proper care. Under this concept, a plaintiff cannot recover damages for events that are brought about by lack of reasonable care on his or her part.

see: **comparative negligence**

avoidance
Risk Management. A risk management technique that can be used by an organization to eliminate an exposure. The concept provides that the exposure to loss produced by a specific activity can be eliminated by avoiding the activity.

see: **diversification, insurance, retention, transfer of risk**

© 1991 NILS Publishing Company

avulsion

Loss Control. The sudden cutting off of land by flood, currents, or change in course of a body of water.

   compare: alluvion; see: accretion

© 1991 NILS Publishing Company

backdate

General.
see: antedate

backup facility agreement

Risk Management. A formal agreement between two businesses for one to provide the other with some form of assistance in the event of a breakdown of equipment or damage to property. *Example:* An agreement between two newspapers to print the other's paper in the event of a breakdown or loss.
see: disaster plan

Health. A formal or informal agreement between health care providers, to provide services to patients of one party in the second provider's facility or program. The agreement can involve either specific medical services or overflow patients. Such agreements may be between two similar health care providers (two hospitals or two clinics, for example) or two quite different health care facilities (a hospital for in-patient care, and a clinic for out-patient followup visits).

bad faith

General. Failure on the part of an insurer to perform under the terms of an insurance policy. Also used to describe assessments imposed by a court against an insurer which is found guilty of bad faith. Bad faith most often is found in first-party insurance when an insurer fails to promptly pay a legitimate claim after proof of loss has been submitted, or when they unreasonably refuse to pay a legitimate claim. In third-party insurance, bad faith is found when an insurer's refusal to accept the third party's offer to settle within a policy's limits ultimately exposes the insured or an excess insurer to a judgment in excess of the primary insurance coverage. Bad faith damages levied against an insurer are punitive in nature and are a penalty for

not acting in accord with the provisions of the insurance contract.
see: unfair claims practice

baggage coverage

Inland Marine. Coverage on the personal effects owned by and for the personal use, adornment or amusement of the insured (or a family member of the insured) while travelling. Coverage is written on an "all-risks" basis and applies anywhere in the world.

bail

General. A security given to a court guaranteeing the appearance of a prisoner in order to obtain his or her release from imprisonment.
see: bail bond

Surety. To deliver property in trust to another for a special purpose and for a limited period; to help from a predicament.

bail agents

Surety. Persons appointed by a surety to execute or countersign bail bonds.

bail bond

Surety. A bond provided to a court for the release of an individual (principal) who has been placed under arrest because of a civil action or criminal offense. The face value of the bond is forfeited if the principal fails to appear in court at an appointed time.

bailee

Inland Marine. An individual or business that has been given temporary custody of another's property. A bailee, such as a dry cleaner or appliance repair shop, will often provide a receipt when accepting a bailor's property. A bailee must exercise a high degree

© 1991 NILS Publishing Company

bailee – continued

of care in protecting property in their care, custody or control.

compare: bailor; see: bailment, fiduciary

bailee's customer insurance

Inland Marine. Insurance which protects a bailee for loss or damage to a customer's (bailor's) personal property while in the bailee's care, custody or control.

see: carriers legal liability

bailment

General. A temporary transfer of property from a bailor to a bailee. *Example:* A customer leaves a personal computer with a technician for repair. Most often a receipt signifying this temporary transfer of property is given by the bailee to the owner (bailor), although a receipt is not necessary for a bailment to exist.

see: bailee; bailor; care, custody or control

bailor

Inland Marine. The owner of property which has been temporarily entrusted to a bailee.

compare: bailee; see: bailment

balance

Risk Management. In accounting, the difference between credits and debits. If the balance is negative, it is a debit balance. If the balance is positive, it is a credit balance.

see: credit balance, debit balance

balance sheet

Risk Management. One of an organization's financial statements, it summarizes the nature and values of an organization's assets, liabilities and capital as of a specific date. In dollar amounts, it indicates what the organization owns, what is owed and the ownership interest in the business.

see: assets, financial statement, financial un-derwriting, liability

balance sheet reserves

Insurer Operations. Reserves for benefits owed to policyholders established by an insurer. They are shown as a liability on the insurer's balance sheet. Regulatory requirements that such claims reserves be adequate guarantee that an insurer will be able to pay the benefits for which it has received premiums.

see: loss reserve

Employee Benefits. A reserve, which may or not be funded, that is established as a liability on an employer's books so that it will be taken into account in determining the corporation's profits and stockholders' equity.

balloon loan

Financial Planning. A loan containing a repayment schedule of small periodic payments which alone are insufficient to fully amortize the loan within its time limit. At the end of the loan period, the balance of the loan becomes due. The balance – called a "balloon payment" – is usually paid through refinancing of the property.

see: amortization, balloon mortgage

balloon mortgage

Mortgage Insurance. A mortgage for a three-to-five-year period used in the belief that interest rates will drop during that period of time and a conventional mortgage can be arranged before the balloon payment becomes due.

see: balloon loan

bank burglary and robbery insurance

Crime. An insurance package that combines coverage for burglary, robbery, and vandalism or malicious mischief in a single policy. It is written on a primary basis for smaller banks, and on an excess basis for larger banks.

see: crime coverages

banker's blanket bond

Crime. A policy covering a bank or savings & loan for its fidelity exposures, inside and outside theft of property, and forgery.

syn: Financial Institution Bond Form 24; see: crime coverages, electronic and computer crime coverage

banking plan

Risk Management. A formalized self-insurance program where arrangements are made to obtain a policy with an insurer that spreads the cost of losses over a period of time and at the same time build a reserve fund to pay larger losses.

see: chronological stabilization plan, spread loss plan

bankrupt

General. A financial condition of an individual or business wherein the individual or business is unable to pay its debts, and is liable to be proceeded against by creditors. Under certain circumstances an individual or entity is entitled to seek court protection of certain financial or corporate assets.

bankruptcy

General. A court proceeding allowing for the distribution of the property of an insolvent individual or entity among its creditors. Although payment to some creditors is often made for less than their full value, the debtor is discharged of all liability to those creditors to which it makes payments. Bankruptcy is "voluntary" if the debtor initiates the petition seeking bankruptcy protection. It is "involuntary" if the debtor is forced

© 1991 NILS Publishing Company

into bankruptcy by the petition of a sufficient number of creditors.

compare: insolvency

bareboat charter

Ocean Marine. A charter arrangement under which the individual hiring the vessel provides his or her own crew.

syn: demise charter; compare: voyage charter; see: charter party

bargain

General. The process of coming to terms in a negotiation; a mutual undertaking; a contract between two parties, one agreeing to buy, the other agreeing to sell.

barge

Ocean Marine. A large, flat-bottomed open deck type vessel that usually is towed or pushed by a tug.

syn: lighter; see: lighter aboard ship

barratry

Ocean Marine. A fraudulent act or other breach of duty committed by a master or crew of a vessel which damages the vessel or its cargo.

see: assailing thieves, piracy

barrier guard

Loss Control. A shield which protects operators and other individuals from hazard points on machinery and equipment. Devices designed to prevent the accidental insertion of limbs or other appendages into the machinery or equipment.

see: adjustable barrier guard, fixed barrier guard, inrunning nip point, interlocked barrier guard, machine guard, machine tool, movable barrier guard, point of operation

baseline data

Risk Management. Benchmark statistics or data of expected losses. Actual losses and other pertinent data are then compared against this data.

base period

Employee Benefits. Generally, the 52-week or four-quarter period before a period of unemployment. It is used to limit benefits to workers currently or recently a part of the labor force. A period used to ascertain qualifying wages.

base premium

Reinsurance.

see: subject premium

base rate

Insurer Operations. The rate for a specific coverage indicated in a rating manual to which other factors are applied (i.e., exposure units, increased limits factor,

experience modification factors, etc.) to arrive at a final rate to be used in rating a policy.

see: exposure unit, experience modification, increased limits table, rate making

basic extended reporting period

Casualty. A provision found in most claims-made liability policy forms. Provides for a specified time following policy expiration, during which claims arising out of occurrences during the policy period may be made against the policy at no extra cost. The ISO commercial general liability claims-made form provides an additional 60 days to report claims.

see: claims-made form, extended reporting period, maxi tail, midi tail, supplemental extended reporting period, tail, tail coverage; syn: mini tail

basic form

Property. A coverage form that specifies the causes of loss which are insured. Causes of loss covered by this form include fire, lightning, explosion, windstorm or hail, smoke, aircraft or vehicles, riot or civil commotion, vandalism, sprinkler leakage, sinkhole collapse, and volcanic action – all subject to certain exclusions and restrictions.

compare: "all-risks" insurance, broad form, open perils

basic homeowner's policy

Property.

see: homeowner's policy form 1

basic limits

Casualty. The lowest limits of liability that can be purchased by a policyholder – often the same as the minimum amount of insurance required by law. The basic limits are the limits for which the base rate is developed. Higher limits of liability coverage may be requested by the insured, whereupon insurers will apply an increased limits factor to the base rate and other factors used to calculate the premium.

see: base rate, increased limits table

basic medical expense

Health. Coverage for hospital, surgical, and physician expenses. Usually provided on a "first dollar basis." Some policies now contain deductibles or coinsurance schedules or are subject to specified restrictions, limitations and exclusions.

compare: major medical insurance; see: corridor deductible

basic premium

Casualty/Life/Workers' Compensation. A factor used in retrospective premium calculations for casualty, workers' compensation and life insurance. It is a percentage of the standard premium and is used to provide the insurer with up-front money for agents'

© 1991 NILS Publishing Company

basic premium — continued
commissions, engineering service, administrative service and profit. An insurance charge for a stop loss or a maximum limitation can be included.

see: retrospective rating plan

basic protection insurance
Automobile.
see: Keeton-O'Connell Plan

basic standard auto policy
Automobile. A policy introduced in 1935 that was once widely used, but later replaced by the family automobile and business auto policies.

compare: business auto coverage form, family automobile endorsements, family automobile policy, personal automobile policy

basis point
Financial Planning/Risk Management. A term used by investment bankers when referring to interest rates. One basis point equals one-hundredth of one percentage point (0.01%).

battery
Casualty. The unlawful application of force upon another person which may result in bodily injury. An offensive touching without permission.

compare: assault

beachfront plans
Property. Assigned risk property insurance programs, established in response to heavy windstorm losses caused by hurricanes. Beachfront plans provide coverage for fire and windstorm, but generally exclude losses from high waves.

compare: beach plans; see: hurricane insurance

beach plans
Property/Regulation. FAIR plans specifically formed in the states of Alabama, Florida, Louisiana, Mississippi, North Carolina, South Carolina and Texas that require insurers to write homeowners coverage on homes located close to the coast where they are subject to high winds, flooding and wavewash.

compare: beachfront plans; see: Fair Access to Insurance Requirements

bear market
Financial Planning. A term used in the financial community by those who believe that stock market prices will generally decline in the near term.

compare: bull market

bell curve
Risk Management.
see: normal probability distribution

bell-shaped curve
Risk Management.
see: symmetrical curve

bench error
Casualty. A mistake made by a worker in the assembly of a product, or the incorrect measurement of materials being combined to manufacture the product, which causes a products liability loss. Bench errors are typically covered by products liability insurance.

see: active malfunction, defective, hidden defect, latent defect

benchmark
General. A historical condition, ranking or statistic used for future comparisons. The standard by which other things are measured.

see: standard risk

beneficial interest
General. A financial interest in the proceeds of an insurance policy, as distinct from the policyholder's legal ownership or control of the policy contract.

beneficiary
Life. A person, other than the insured, who is entitled to receive the proceeds on the death of the policyholder. Beneficiaries can be designated as primary or contingent, and irrevocable or revocable.

see: beneficiary change, beneficiary clause, beneficiary of trust, change of beneficiary provision, class beneficiary, contingent beneficiary, creditor beneficiary, irrevocable beneficiary, primary beneficiary, revocable beneficiary, second beneficiary, tertiary beneficiary, third-party beneficiary

beneficiary change
Employee Benefits/Life. Replacing the person eligible to receive benefits under a life insurance policy or employee benefit plan with another. Two conditions must be present. First, the policy must give the right to change the beneficiary to the policyholder, and second, the law must permit the change.

see: change of beneficiary provision, irrevocable beneficiary, revocable beneficiary

beneficiary clause
Life. A life insurance policy provision allowing the policyowner to name anyone as primary and contingent beneficiaries. It also allows the policyowner to change beneficiaries at any time by proper written notice to the insurance company.

see: beneficiary, change of beneficiary provision, contingent beneficiary, primary beneficiary, revocable beneficiary

beneficiary of trust
Life. The person who receives the benefits of a trust.

© 1991 NILS Publishing Company

Often the trust is created to prevent the dissipation of property or money left to minors or ill or disabled persons who may be unable to conduct business for themselves.

see: trust

benefit

Insurer Operations. The advantage, profit, gain or monetary sum payable or paid to a policyholder by an insurer in exchange for premiums paid by the insured. *Employee Benefits.* The rights of a pension plan participant to receive payments or services after meeting the plan's eligibility requirements.

benefit administration

Workers' Compensation. A division within a state's workers' compensation board or industrial commission that is responsible for administering laws and promulgating regulations concerning the settlement of claims for injured workers' benefits.

benefit formula

Employee Benefits. The actuarial method used to determine a pension plan participant's benefits.

syn: pension benefit formula, plan's benefit formula

benefit funds

Employee Benefits. Funds set aside by an employee benefit plan's sponsor (e.g., the employer or union) that are usually deposited with the plan's trustee or an insurance company.

benefit of selection

Insurer Operations. The business advantage gained by an insurance company, through the careful selection by its underwriters, to insure only those risks it feels are desirable and to decline those risks it considers as potentially adverse.

compare: adverse selection

benefit plan

Employee Benefits. A general term used to refer to any program established and maintained by an employer (or union) to provide its employers (or members) with one or several benefits, such as pension benefits, health insurance benefits, disability, profit-sharing, stock purchase programs, etc.

see: defined benefit plan, defined contribution plan, dental benefit plans, money purchase plan, target benefit plan

benefits manager

Employee Benefits. The person responsible for administering pension and employee benefit programs (life, accident and sickness, dental, etc.). Benefit managers may also assume responsibilities for a

501(c)(9) trust, 401(k) plan, savings and other related programs.

see: administrative services only, third-party administrator

benefits of survivorship

Life.

see: survivorship benefits

Bermuda Market

Insurer Operations. The insurance market in Bermuda, including captive insurers that will write non-related third-party business, and special insurers such as ACE Insurance Company Limited and X.L. Insurance Company, Limited. Similar markets have been established in Barbados, the Cayman Islands, and other offshore locations.

see: captive domicile

berth

Ocean Marine. The mooring place for a vessel.

Best's Ratings

General. An evaluation published by the A.M. Best Company of all life, property and casualty U.S.-domiciled insurers and U.S. branches of foreign property insurer groups which are active in the United States. These ratings are often used by agents, brokers and commercial insureds to determine the suitability, service record and financial stability of insurance companies.

syn: A.M. Best Rating

betterments

Property.

see: improvements and betterments

bicycle floater

Inland Marine. An "all-risks" inland marine policy used to insure expensive bicycles. It is often written through bicycle dealers who issue certificates to a master policy issued to them.

bid

General/Surety. An offer to perform a contract (usually expressed in monetary terms) for work, labor, goods, materials or coverage at a specific price.

syn: quote; see: abstract of bids; Fr: soumission; Gr: Angebot, Offerte; Sp: oferta

bid bond

Surety. A bond filed by contractors, guaranteeing that in the event a bid is accepted, the successful contractor will sign the contract and furnish a performance bond.

see: abstract of bids, performance bond

bilateral contract

General. A contract, such as a contract of sale, which

© 1991 NILS Publishing Company

bilateral contract − continued
includes the rights and duties from both contracting parties; an exchange of promises in which one party's promise is consideration in exchange for the promise of the other.

see: contract

bilateral mistake

General. Contracting parties making the same mistake of fact, usually voiding an agreement if the mutual mistake relates to a material fact.

bill of interpleader

General. A bill of equity to obtain a settlement when a disinterested third party (or stockholder) possesses property claimed by two other persons.

Insurer Operations. An interpleader is a legal device used by insurance companies when claims to the policy proceeds are made by different policies. Policy proceeds are deposited in court until proper ownership can be determined by the courts.

syn: interpleader

bill of lading

Inland Marine/Ocean Marine. A contract for the transport of goods between the shipper and the carrier. This document also specifies the carrier's duties and responsibilities for the property.

see: affreightment, bill of lading number, clean bill of lading, delivery receipt, dock receipt, endorsement in blank, manifest, on board bill of lading, order bill of lading, released bill of lading, short form bill of lading, valued bill of lading, waybill; Fr: connaissement; Gr: Konnossement; Sp: conocimiento de embarque

bill of lading number

Inland Marine/Ocean Marine. A unique number appearing on a bill of lading, used to identify the bill of lading and the shipment it represents.

bill of sale

General. A written agreement between a seller and a buyer, assigning the rights and interest in personal property to the buyer.

binder

Agency/Insurer Operations. An agreement issued, usually in writing, but occasionally orally, by an agent or an insurer providing temporary coverage until a policy can be issued. A binder should include a specified effective time limit, be in writing and clearly designate the company to which the agent is binding the coverage. The amount, the perils insured against, and the type of insurance must also be included.

Fr: couverture provisoire; Gr: Vorläufige Deckungszusage; Sp: cubierta provisional

Reinsurance. A temporary record of a reinsurance

agreement's provisions, used while the formal reinsurance contract is being drawn.

see: certificate of reinsurance

binding authority

Agency/Insurer Operations. The power of an insurance agent to bind one of his or her insurers to a risk.

see: actual authority, agency

binding receipt

Health/Life. A receipt issued by life and health agents, acknowledging the prospective insured's payment of the premium and providing evidence of a temporary contract. Such a receipt binds the company to the contract if the insurer accepts the risk and accompanying application.

syn: binding slip

binding slip

Health/Life.
see: binding receipt

birth rate

Life. The number of people born (expressed as a percentage of the total population) in any given period of time. It is usually expressed as births per 100,000 people in one year.

black lung disease

Workers' Compensation. A physical disability involving the lungs caused by excessive inhalation of coal dust. A disease in the pneumoconiosis family, black lung typically afflicts coal miners and causes total disability or death. Black lung disease is covered under a federal act which prescribes benefit payments to victims and survivors and dependents.

see: brown lung disease, byssinosis, occupational disease

blackout period

Life. A Social Security Act term which refers to the period during which benefit payments to a widow with children are suspended. The blackout period runs from the eighteenth birthday of the youngest child, until the widow's sixty-second birthday.

blank

Insurer Operations/Regulation.
see: annual statement

blanket basis

Property.
see: blanket insurance

blanket contract

Health. An accident or health insurance contract which provides benefits for all individuals designated in a special group that are not individually identified. *Example:* The purchase by an employer of a travel

© 1991 NILS Publishing Company

accident policy which covers all executive and sales staff employees while on business-related travel.

blanket coverage

Property.
   see: blanket insurance

blanket crime policy

Crime. A policy with the broadest coverage possible against crime hazards, written on a package basis under a single limit of liability. Covers the same hazards available on an optional basis under a comprehensive dishonesty, disappearance and destruction policy (e.g., employee dishonesty, loss inside and outside the premises, lost money orders and counterfeit paper currency and depositor's forgery).
   see: combination crime – single limit, crime coverages

blanket fidelity bond

Crime. A fidelity bond that covers loss of money, merchandise or other property owned by the insured, when such loss is due to employee dishonesty. The bond covers all employees unless any are specifically excluded.
   see: crime coverages

blanket group

Property. A method used in boiler and machinery policies, to insure objects by grouping them together by broad class of objects, rather than specifically naming each object.

blanket group policy

Health/Life. A policy that covers members of a natural group – such as employees of a particular business, members of a union or association – with no individual designation of the group's members. The insurance applies to the entire group.

blanket insurance

General. Any insurance policy that covers one or more broad classes of persons or property, without identifying the specific subjects of insurance in the contract.
Health. A broad medical expense policy which covers all medical expenses (except those which are specifically excluded), up to a maximum limit without any limitation on specific types of medical expenses.
Property. A single property insurance policy that can provide coverage for multiple classes of property at one location, or one or more classes of property at multiple locations. Coverage under this form is written for one total amount of insurance. No single item (building, machine) is assigned a specific amount of insurance, although different amounts may be shown

for buildings in general, equipment in general, and other items.
   syn: blanket basis, blanket coverage; compare: specific insurance; see: average blanket rate

blanket medical expense

Health. A policy which covers an individual for all covered, necessary and reasonable medical expenses up to a maximum limit established in the policy, without limitation for any specific procedure.

blanket position bond

Crime. A blanket fidelity bond insuring an employer against losses from dishonest acts by his or her employees, with the same amount of coverage applied separately to each position covered. The maximum amount of coverage is the per employee coverage limit, multiplied by the number of employees involved in the loss.
   see: commercial blanket bond, crime coverages

blank forms

Insurer Operations. Printed forms (applications, certificates of insurance, policy declarations, endorsements, etc.) used by insurers and agents – such as ACORD Forms or ISO Standard Forms – which contain spaces that have been left empty for entering specific information.

blasting and explosion exclusion

Casualty. An exclusion found in the 1973 ISO CGL rating program which was triggered when the rating classification for a particular risk was followed by an "X." For risks so designated, liability coverage for property damage arising from blasting or explosion was excluded by endorsement. If the policyholder needed coverage for these exposures, they could be bought back by paying a surcharged rate.
   see: collapse exclusion, underground exclusion, XCU exclusions

block

Property. An area of land surrounded on at least three sides by streets or avenues, usually within a metropolitan area.
   see: block limits

block cancellation

Insurer Operations. Cancellation and refusal to renew an entire class or line of insurance coverage by an insurer.

block limits

Property. A maximum amount of insurance that an insurance company will write within a specific city block, thereby limiting the company's risk of a large loss should a fire destroy the entire block.
   see: block, fire map

53

© 1991 NILS Publishing Company

block policy

Inland Marine. A single property insurance policy which covers all of an insured's property on an open perils basis. Coverage is generally extended to include property in transit and the property of others in the insured's care, custody, or control, *Examples:* Jewelers block, camera and musical instrument dealers block, and equipment dealers block.

blood bank professional liability insurance

Casualty. Coverage protecting the operators of blood banks, against claims for injury arising from alleged malpractice, error or mistake in the taking of blood donations, or the mishandling or misuse of or existence of any condition in any blood products handled or distributed by the insured. Most such policies include coverage for AIDS-related claims.

blood pressure

Health/Life. A factor used in evaluating the risk for health and life insurance coverage. High blood pressure may result in a higher incidence of illness and accident and lead to less favorable morbidity and mortality factors.

see: **sphygmomanometer**

bloodstock insurance

Inland Marine. A form of livestock mortality insurance designed specifically for thoroughbred, standardbred, quarterhorses, and prized show horses. The coverage is also available for stallions and for blood mares.

see: **animal insurance, breeder's policy**

blowout and cratering

Casualty/Property. An accident resulting from a penetration of a gas or oil reservoir during drilling operations under higher-than-calculated pressure. Blowouts are dangerous because of the risk they pose to workers and firefighters; blowouts can also be expensive, due to the cost of putting the fire out (it often burns for days), and the value of the oil or gas consumed while the fire burns. Cratering occurs when the circulation system (dug around the drilling rig to prevent blowouts) collapses. Often, the drilling rig itself is lost during a cratering incident.

see: **blowout prevention policy**

blowout prevention policy

Property. Covers drilling operations against losses associated with penetration of reservoirs containing high-pressure gas or oil.

see: **blowout and cratering**

Blue Cross and Blue Shield Association (BCBSA)

Health/Organizations. Members: An association of local Blue Cross and Blue Shield Plans. *Objectives:* Contracts with the federal government to act as the administrative agency for federal health programs. Promotes acceptance of voluntary, nonprofit prepayment of health services. *Founded:* 1982. *Headquarters:* Chicago, IL.

see: **Blue Cross Plan, Blue Shield Plan**

Blue Cross Plan

Health/Insurer Operations. An independent, non-profit, voluntary membership organization formed principally for the purpose of prepaying hospital medical care expenses for its members. Hospitals that participate in the Blue Cross Plan agree to accept payment based on a predetermined fee schedule and bill the plan directly for services provided to members.

syn: **Blue Plan, Blues; compare: Blue Shield Plan**

Blue Plan

Health.

see: **Blue Cross Plan, Blue Shield Plan, Blues**

Blues

Health. A generic reference to either Blue Cross or Blue Shield plans.

syn: **Blue Plan; see: Blue Cross Plan, Blue Shield Plan**

Blue Shield Plan

Health. An independent, non-profit, voluntary membership organization formed principally for the purpose of prepaying the physician and surgeon expenses for its members. Physicians and surgeons that participate in the Blue Cross Plan agree to accept payment based on a predetermined fee schedule and bill the plan directly for services provided to members.

syn: **Blue Plan, Blues; compare: Blue Cross Plan**

blue sky laws

Regulation. State statutes that limit and control the sale of new securities, to protect potential investors from securities fraud. Blue sky laws compel sellers of new stock issues or mutual funds to register their offerings and provide the minimum amount of detail required for investors, allowing them to make informed decisions.

board certified

Health/Casualty. A term used to describe physicians who passed an examination administered by a medical specialty board, indicating they have gained special knowledge or expertise in that field. Board certified specialists are often called on to provide expert witness testimony in court trials, as well as provide second opinions.

see: **expert witness, medical licensing boards**

© 1991 NILS Publishing Company

Board of Certified Safety Professionals of the Americas, Inc. (BCSP)

Organizations. Members: Safety engineers, industrial hygienists, safety managers, fire protection engineers and others who have received the Certified Safety Professional (CSP) designation by passing two exams and meeting other criteria set by the board. *Objectives:* Certifies the professional and technical competence of individuals in the safety field. *Founded:* 1969. *Headquarters:* Savoy, IL.

see: **Certified Safety Professional**

board of education liability insurance

Casualty. Insurance coverage protecting elected or appointed members of boards of education, administration staff, teachers and other employees of a school district from suit for wrongful acts.

board of trustees

General. The governing body of a voluntary and/or nonprofit organization.

bobtail

Automobile. A trucking term used to describe a tractor that is operated without its trailer and is not being driven for trucking purposes.

compare: **deadheading**

bobtail coverage

Automobile. Automobile liability insurance, purchased by tractor-trailer operators, which covers owned tractors returning empty from a trip and which therefore would no longer be insured by a contracting shipper's policy.

see: **bobtail**

bodily injury (BI)

Casualty. The injury of living tissue by an outside force; bodily harm, sickness or disease; includes resultant required care, loss of services and death.

see: **personal injury; Fr: blessure corporelle; Gr: Personenschaden, Verletzung; Sp: lesiones corporales**

bodily injury and property damage liability

Casualty. Coverage Part A of the ISO commercial general liability form which combines both bodily injury and property damage into a single insuring agreement and limit of liability.

see: **bodily injury, bodily injury liability, commercial general liability form, property damage liability coverage**

bodily injury liability

Casualty. Legal liability arising from physical trauma to a person or death arising from the negligent or purposeful acts and omissions by an insured. Includes sickness or disease contracted by the injured person as a result of an injury.

see: **bodily injury**

boiler and machinery

Property. Any refrigeration or air conditioning system; any piping and its accessory equipment; any compressor, pump, engine, turbine, motor, generator, gear set, fan or blower, including any shaft forming a part of the object, together with any coupling, clutch, wheel or bearing on that shaft; any transformer or electrical distribution equipment; and any other mechanical or electrical equipment used for maintenance or service of premises.

see: **boiler & machinery insurance**

boiler & machinery insurance (B&M)

Property. Coverage for the failure of boilers, machinery and electrical equipment. Such coverage can be extended to include consequential losses and business interruption losses. Insurance benefits are provided progressively, in order of the following listing, until the limit per accident is exhausted: 1) all property of the insured which has been directly damaged by the accident; 2) reasonable costs of temporary repairs and expediting expenses; and 3) liability for damage to property of others.

see: **boiler and machinery, covered boiler & machinery property, expediting expenses, object**

bona fide

General. In Latin, this term literally translates into "good faith." An act offered in good faith; without deceit or fraud; without fakery or pretense. A sincere effort made with earnest intent.

bond

Surety. A three-party agreement in which a party called the "surety" obligates itself to a second party – called the "obligee" – to answer for the default, acts or omissions of a third party, called the "principal." A bond can guarantee the performance of the principal under a contract with the obligee (i.e., a performance bond), or a bond can protect against the dishonesty of employees (i.e., a fidelity bond).

see: **administration bond, advance payment bond, alcohol bond, alteration bond, annual bond, annual supply contract bond, appeal bond, bail bond, banker's blanket bond, bid bond, blanket fidelity bond, blanket position bond, commercial blanket bond, contract bond, convertible bond, coupon bond, court bond, customs bond, defendant's bond to dissolve, depositor's forgery bond, depository bond, ejectment bond, family forgery bond,**

© 1991 NILS Publishing Company

bond — continued
federal bond, fidelity bond, fiduciary bond, financial bond, financial guarantee bond, forgery bond, general average bond, indemnity bond, industrial development bond insurance, injunction bond, judicial bond, labor and material bond, lender's bond, license bond, lost instrument bond, maintenance bond, movie completion bond, municipal bond insurance, name position bond, name schedule bond, partnership financial bond, payment bond, penalty, performance bond, permit bond, plaintiff's bond to secure, plaintiff's replevin bond, position schedule bond, probate bond, public official bond, registered bond, schedule bond, surety bond, warehousemen's bond

bonded shipments

Inland Marine/Ocean Marine. Shipments on which duty is payable, but which are permitted to travel to inland destinations before customs inspection is made and duty is actually paid. Until the duty is paid, such goods must be kept in a bonded warehouse.

see: abatement, customs bond, duty, federal bond

bonded warehouse

Inland Marine/Insurer Operations. A warehouse where bonded shipments are stored, pending customs inspection. Such warehouses must be secure, with dutiable goods segregated from nondutiable, and their operators must usually provide a customs bond.

see: federal bond

bonding

Surety. The act of issuing surety bonds.

see: bond

Loss Control. A method of preventing the accumulation and eventual discharge of static electricity, by connecting containers of hazardous materials or equipment with a grounded conductor that continuously drains the static charge.

see: electrical grounding; Fr: cautionnement; Gr: Garantieversicherung; Sp: bonding

bonds

Financial Planning. Long-term debt instruments secured by a lien on some or all of a corporation's property. Typically, a bond is either payable to the bearer and interest coupons, representing annual or semi-annual payments of interest are attached (these are called "coupon bonds"), or registered in the name of the owner as the principal only ("registered bonds").

The word "bonds" is sometimes used in a broader sense to signify unsecured debt instruments that take the form of a bond, but the interest obligation is limited or tied to the corporate earnings for the year. "Participating bonds" are another variation that take the form of typical debt instruments with the interest obligation arranged so that holders are entitled to receive additional amounts from excess earnings or from excess distributions, depending on the terms of the participating bond.

Bonds are often classified by their issuing body (U.S. government, state, county, town, etc.); the type of project financed (lighting district, reclamation development, etc.); the currency in which the bonds will be paid (dollars, gold, etc.); any special privileges (participatory or convertible); the types of liens which are the subject of the bond (junior, first or second mortgage); the bond's investment grade (savings bank) or the bond's maturity (short-term).

see: stock

bonus shares

Insurer Operations. Par value shares of stock usually issued in connection with preferred or senior securities or debt instruments; often issued without consideration. Bonus shares are considered a species of "watered" stock, and may impose a liability on the recipient equal to the amount of par value.

see: watered stock

book of business

Agency/Insurer Operations. The policies that an insurance agent or company has in force at a given point in time.

book value

General. When used narrowly, a term used to describe the value for an asset carried on an organization's balance sheet. (For many assets, this is the purchase cost less accumulated depreciation.) When used more broadly, to describe a company's book value, the formula is total assets (excluding intangible assets) minus current liabilities and minus any long-term liabilities and equity issues with prior claims.

see: assets

book value per share

Financial Planning/Risk Management. A business measure that places a company's value as its net worth, less the value of its preferred stock (at that stock's liquidation or redemption value), divided by the number of common shares outstanding.

bordereau

General. A detailed listing of accounts or documents.

see: marine insurance certificate

Reinsurance. A listing supplied by a ceding insurer that provides the loss and premium histories of all or certain types of risks ceded or proposed to be ceded to a reinsurer. It is used by the reinsurer in establishing

© 1991 NILS Publishing Company

terms of the reinsurance agreement and/or in monitoring the business ceded under an existing treaty, or in establishing the premium.

borderline risk

Insurer Operations. From an underwriting viewpoint, a risk of doubtful quality; bordering between acceptable and not acceptable.
  see: accommodation line

Boston Plan

Property. A plan first implemented by the city of Boston, in which insurers agreed not to reject property coverage in lower socioeconomic residential areas if property owners agreed to correct faults.
  see: assigned risk, Fair Access to Insurance Requirements

both to blame collision clause

Ocean Marine.
  see: running down clause

bottleneck

Property. A factor considered in underwriting business income insurance: A situation or condition that would extend the replacement period for buildings or equipment beyond the time that would normally be expected. *Example:* A multicolor printing press used to publish a major newspaper may take several years to replace.

bottomry

Ocean Marine. The oldest known form of transfer of risk. It was used by the ancient Greeks, and provided that a ship not returning to port is absolved of any debt, on the ship itself or on its cargo. Lloyd's of London refined this concept when it began insuring the shipment of goods across the Atlantic to the colonies. From this, modern property and casualty insurance evolved.
  see: insurance

branch manager

Insurer Operations. An individual responsible for managing an insurance company's branch office.
  see: branch office

branch office

Insurer Operations. A local business office supplying certain services and performing specified company functions, but which reports to a regional or home office.
  see: regional office

breach

General. The breaking or violating of a law, right, promise, obligation, duty, engagement or trust, either by omission or commission.

breach of trust

General. Violation of a trustee's duty to a beneficiary.

breach of warranty

Casualty. A legal term for the breaking or violation of an expressed or implied warranty. Used in proving negligence in a products liability case.

break bulk cargo

Ocean Marine. Loose cargo, such as cartons, stowed directly in a vessel's hold as opposed to containerized or bulk cargo.
  compare: bulk cargo, containerized cargo

break in service

Employee Benefits. Under a pension plan, an employee may lose benefits if a minimum number of hours (usually 500 hours) of service are not completed during a calendar year. Some pension plans contain a provision whereby an employee whose service has been interrupted can have such a break credited toward retirement.

breeder's policy

Inland Marine. A policy providing coverage on livestock owned by breeders from specified perils.
  see: animal insurance, bloodstock insurance, livestock mortality insurance

brick building

Property. A building of brick construction with a roof structure of combustible sheathing and/or combustible roof supports is a brick building for underwriting purposes.
  see: brick construction

brick construction

Property. A building or structure with 75% or more of the exterior walls constructed with some type of masonry materials – such as brick, stone, poured concrete, hollow masonry block, etc. – is considered to be of brick construction for underwriting purposes. Certain minimum wall thicknesses apply, depending upon the type of materials used.
  see: construction

brick veneer construction

Loss Control. A building with outside supporting walls constructed of combustible materials such as wood, and covered (faced) with a single layer of brick not exceeding a specified thickness is of brick veneer construction for underwriting purposes.
  see: construction

bridge insurance

Inland Marine. Coverage for damage and destruction to bridges. Normally it is written on an "all-risks" basis, subject to exclusions for war, wear and tear, inherent defect, and nuclear damages.

© 1991 NILS Publishing Company

broadcasters liability insurance

Casualty. An insurance policy that protects radio and television stations from errors & omissions in the production, use or dissemination of program or advertising material.

see: **professional liability insurance**

broad form

General. A general term designating policies that provide additional coverages beyond standard coverages. *(See: Specific types of broad form policies and endorsements, listed below.)*

see: **money and securities broad form insurance, storekeepers broad form**

Property. A coverage form that covers all causes of loss which are covered under the basic form plus breakage of glass, falling objects, weight of snow, ice or sleet, and water damage.

see: **basic form**

broad form all-states endorsement

Workers' Compensation. An endorsement that provides coverage similar to the all states endorsement, except that the broad form pays all claims on behalf of the insured employer, instead of indemnifying (reimbursing) the employer for claims payments already made. This form prevents penalties that can be imposed upon an employer for failure to have a workers' compensation policy in force in a particular state. If the standard all states endorsement is used, such penalties can be levied since the insurer would not respond to the claim directly, but only after the employer has paid any benefits.

compare: **all-states endorsement, extraterritoriality**

broad form comprehensive general liability endorsement (BFCGL)

Casualty.

see: **broad form liability endorsement**

broad form drive other car coverage

Automobile. An endorsement attached to commercial automobile policies, to protect employees who are furnished automobiles for their full-time use and who do not own and personally insure another automobile. A commercial auto policy only protects the employee while driving a company vehicle. This endorsement extends that coverage to other vehicles (not owned by the insured business) that the employee may drive.

syn: **drive other car coverage**

broad form liability endorsement

Casualty. An endorsement to the 1973 ISO comprehensive general liability form which added twelve broadening coverages: 1) blanket contractual; 2) personal and advertising injury; 3) medical payments;

4) host liquor liability; 5) fire legal liability; 6) broad form property damage liability; 7) incidental medical malpractice; 8) nonowned watercraft liability; 9) limited worldwide coverage; 10) additional persons insured; 11) extended bodily injury coverage; and, 12) automatic coverage on newly acquired locations. Most of these coverages have been incorporated into the 1986 ISO Commercial General Liability form.

syn: **broad form comprehensive general liability endorsement;** see: **comprehensive general liability policy**

broad form personal theft insurance

Crime. "All-risks" coverage for loss due to theft or mysterious disappearance of personal property. Also insures against damage to premises and property resulting from theft, and damage resulting from vandalism and malicious mischief to the interior of the premises. Sub-limits apply to property which is highly susceptible to theft (e.g., money, securities, paintings, coins, and jewelry).

syn: **personal theft insurance**

broad form products liability

Automobile. Coverage that can be endorsed to the garage coverage form, removing the "property damage to any of your products" exclusion and agreeing to insure damage-to-products claims (subject to a deductible of $250). This coverage does not guarantee the fitness or quality of a product, but rather covers property damage to a vehicle resulting from the defective product *(ISO Endorsement CA 25 01).*

see: **products-completed operations insurance**

broad form property damage (BFPD)

Casualty. Coverage that can be endorsed to the 1973 ISO comprehensive general liability policy and other older general liability forms, to reduce the restrictive scope of the "care, custody, or control" and "injury to work performed" exclusions contained in these contracts. The endorsement is needed by contractors, manufacturers, processors and service firms that work on the property of others. The 1986 ISO commercial general liability coverage form includes much of the coverage provided by the old broad form property damage endorsement.

see: **care, custody or control; care, custody or control exclusion; comprehensive general liability policy**

broad form property insurance endorsement

Property. An endorsement to a property insurance policy covering perils such as breakage of glass, falling objects, weight of snow, ice, sleet, or water damage, in addition to the basic perils.

see: **"all-risks" insurance, named perils**

© 1991 NILS Publishing Company

broad named insured definition endorsement

Casualty. An endorsement to a commercial liability policy, providing automatic coverage for all owned or controlled entities existing at policy inception or formed or acquired during the policy period.

see: named insured

broker

Agency/Insurer Operations. An individual or entity who represents the consumer in negotiating, servicing or effecting insurance policies with insurers. Many brokers are also agents of the companies with which they do business.

compare: agent; Fr: courtier; Gr: Makler; Sp: corredor

brokerage

Agency. A group of individuals working to sell and service insurance policies. Also used to describe the fee or commission received by a broker.

compare: agency

Financial Planning. The commission or fee charged by a broker-dealer for the execution of a securities transaction.

brokerage business

Agency/Insurer Operations. Insurance coverage placed by a broker with an insurance company as, opposed to business placed with the company by one of its agents.

see: broker

brokerage department

Insurer Operations. A division of an insurance company which negotiates with brokers in placing insurance coverage.

broker of record

Agency/Insurer Operations. The broker designated and authorized to conduct and handle specified insurance business on behalf of the policyholder.

compare: agent of record

broker's float

Agency. Premiums held by a broker until they are remitted to insurers, upon which the broker earns interest.

see: agent's trust

brown lung disease

Workers' Compensation. A physical disability involving the lungs and caused by excessive inhalation of dust connected with textile processing. It is a disease in the pneumoconiosis family, which frequently afflicts textile workers.

see: black lung disease, byssinosis, occupational disease

bucking arrears

Agency/Insurer Operations. A falsification of records and subsequent embezzlement of premiums, by an agent who applies advance payments of one policy to another policyholder's past due balance that is still within the grace period.

see: arrears, out of trust

buffer layer

Casualty. Coverage which lies between the upper limits of the primary insurer and the beginning of the umbrella or excess policy. *Example:* Total policy limits of $10,000,000 constructed as follows: Primary layer = $1,000,000; Buffer layer = $1,000,000 excess of $1,000,000; and Umbrella layer = $8,000,000 excess of $2,000,000.

syn: gap layer; compare: working cover; see: excess liability insurance, layering

builders risk hull insurance

Ocean Marine. A marine property insurance policy providing direct damage coverage on ships while they are under construction and until possession is transferred to the owners. Coverage is on an "all-risks" basis and includes protection during launch and sea trials. The policy may be written on a completed value (100% of final values) or reporting form (values reported as completed) basis.

builders risk insurance

Inland Marine/Property. A property insurance policy that provides direct damage coverage on buildings or structures while they are under construction. Also covers foundations, fixtures, machinery and equipment used to service the building, and materials and supplies used in the course of construction. Coverage may be written on a completed value (100% coinsurance) or reporting form (values reported as completed) basis, using either a property form (*Builders Risk Coverage Form CP 00 20*) or a broader inland marine form.

syn: course of construction insurance

building code

Loss Control. Municipal or governmental regulations, laws and ordinances concerning construction and maintenance standards within a specific jurisdictional area.

building ordinance or law coverage

Property.

see: ordinance or law coverage endorsement

building rate

Property. Fire insurance rates are usually developed separately for the building and/or structure and for the contents contained within them. The building rate is used to develop premiums for real property, tenants improvements and business income coverages.

© 1991 NILS Publishing Company

building rate — continued
Rates – whether for buildings or contents – usually apply per $100 of property values. Separate rates apply to fire, extended coverages, vandalism and malicious mischief, sprinkler leakage, earthquake and "all-risks" coverages.

compare: contents rate; see: buildings

buildings
Property. In commercial property insurance, those structures that are principally used for business or institutional purposes, including additions and extensions. Often the policy definition of "buildings" (for coverage purposes) is extended to include fixtures, machinery, and equipment used in servicing the building. In personal lines insurance, buildings include the primary residence structure and appurtenant structures (garages, sheds, etc.). In most property insurance policies – commercial or personal lines – separate coverage limits are provided for buildings and for contents.

Fr: bâtiment; Gr: Gebäude; Sp: edificio

building standards
Loss Control. Construction standards for buildings and structures.

see: building code, construction

bulk cargo
Ocean Marine. Unpackaged, loose cargo which is loaded directly into a vessel's hold.

compare: break bulk cargo, cargo, containerized cargo

bullion
Property. Precious metals, such as gold or silver, cast in ingots or bars.

bull market
Financial Planning. A term used in the financial community by those who believe that stock market prices will generally rise in the near term.

compare: bear market

bumbershoot
Ocean Marine. A marine umbrella liability insurance policy that provides coverage for ocean marine risks and can also include general liability, protection & indemnity, and Longshoremen's and Harbor Workers' Act coverages. The term "bumbershoot" is the British word for umbrella, and is used in this context to the broad, seemingly all-encompassing nature of this type of policy.

compare: parasol policy, umbrella liability insurance

burden of proof
General. A principle of law which states that a plaintiff is obligated to provide evidence proving his or her claim against a defendant.

bureau insurer
Insurer Operations. An insurance company that uses a rating bureau's rates and forms. Bureau insurers usually do not have a large enough data base or sufficient resources of their own to develop rates.

see: rating bureau

bureau rate
Insurer Operations. The rate developed on specific risks by a rating bureau for its member companies.

see: building rate, rate, rating bureau

burglar alarm
Loss Control. An audible or silent alarm, activated by unauthorized entry. Often, properties protected by burglar alarms can receive a discount on their property and crime insurance premiums.

burglary
Crime. The forced entry into the premises of another by a person or persons with felonious intent.

compare: theft; Fr: vol par effraction; Gr: Einbruchdiebstahl; Sp: hurto, robo con violencia

burglary divided coverage
General. Property insurance in which covered items are grouped by class, with a stipulated maximum payable for loss or damage for losses within each of the specified classes.

compare: divided coverage

burglary insurance
Crime. Coverage for property taken or destroyed by breaking and entering into an insured premises. The break-in must be made with felonious intent, and visible signs of forced entry should be present in order for the policy to pay.

see: burglary, crime coverages, theft

burn facility
Health. A specialized medical facility or center for treating burn injuries.

burning cost
Reinsurance.

see: pure loss cost

burning layer
Insurer Operations. The first layer of insurance in property and casualty coverage which will suffer initial losses. It is usually insurance above low deductibles, but providing less than catastrophe limits.

see: layering

burning ratio
Insurer Operations. The ratio of actual losses to the

© 1991 NILS Publishing Company

total amount of insurance in effect. The ratio of losses which could reasonably be expected to the amount of insurance in effect. By contrast, the loss ratio is the ratio between actual losses and earned premiums.

compare: loss ratio

business

General. A commercial activity, employment, occupation, profession, or enterprise carried on for gain or profit.

Fr: affaire; Gr: Geschäft; Sp: negocio, empresa

Insurer Operations. For property and casualty and health insurers, "business" usually refers to premium volume, and for life insurers, the face amount of life insurance written.

see: book of business

business and pleasure

Aviation. General aviation rating classification which applies when the aircraft operator is an individual, business or corporation owning and operating an aircraft for both business and pleasure, but not employing professional, full-time pilots.

compare: fixed base operators, flying clubs, industrial aid operators; see: general aviation

business auto coverage form

Employee Benefits. An ISO coverage form *(CA 00 01 01 87)* that provides selected liability and physical damage coverages on commercial vehicles. The form uses the simplified wording concept and must be combined with the appropriate declarations, conditions and endorsements to constitute a commercial auto policy. This form was introduced in 1977 to replace the basic standard automobile policy.

see: basic standard auto policy

business continuation insurance

Property.

see: business income coverage form

business income coverage form

Property. An Insurance Services Office (ISO) coverage form *(CP 00 30)* that pays for loss of earnings when normal business operations are temporarily suspended because of property loss caused by insured perils. Coverages usually provide for reimbursement of salaries, taxes, rents, net profits, and necessary continuing operating expenses within the time period of the policy for suspended or curtailed operations. This form replaced previous business interruption forms.

syn: business continuation insurance, business income insurance, loss of income insurance, loss of time insurance; see: business interruption insurance, chomage, contingent business

income coverage, continuing expenses, contributing location, extended period of indemnity, gross earnings, gross earnings form, maximum period of indemnity, monthly limit of indemnity, per diem business interruption coverage, period of restoration, taxation of business interruption loss payments, tuition and fees insurance, use and occupancy insurance

business income form dependent properties

Property.

see: contingent business income coverage

business income insurance

Property.

see: business income coverage form

business insurance

Insurer Operations. A term used generally to refer to insurance for commercial or business establishments, as opposed to "personal insurance" which is purchased for the protection of individuals; policies written for business purposes such as key employees, partnerships, and corporations.

see: commercial lines

business interruption insurance

Property. An insurance coverage form that was replaced in 1988 by the Insurance Services Office (ISO) business income coverage form.

see: business income coverage form

business interruption value

Property. The amount of business income insurance needed to cover a business' estimated business interruption loss. This amount is developed by completing a business income worksheet. The term also refers to the dollar amount of gross earnings to which the policy's contribution clause applies.

business judgment rule

Casualty. Officers and directors of corporations have a fiduciary duty to exercise a degree of care in making business decisions to protect fiduciaries. This exemption – the business judgment rule – holds a fiduciary not responsible for a loss resulting from prudent "business judgment."

business legal expense insurance

Casualty. An insurance policy for a business that provides coverage for legal consultation and defense costs when the insured is involved in a suit involving its business.

see: legal expense insurance

© 1991 NILS Publishing Company

business of insurance

Regulation. Mergers, securities regulation, and insurer contracts with health providers are not the "business of insurance." To be exempt from federal regulations and qualify for the "business of insurance" provisions of the McCarran-Ferguson Act, an insurer must meet the following criteria: 1) the practice must spread a policyholder's risk; 2) the practice must be an integral part of the relationship between the insurer and the insured; and 3) the practice must be limited to entities within the insurance business.

see: McCarran-Ferguson Act

business owners policy (BOP)

Property. A commercial insurance program that has been replaced by the business owners policy program. In a package policy, it provided broad property, liability, and business interruption coverage.

see: business owners policy program

business owners policy program

Casualty/Property. A package policy program designed for small and medium-sized businesses, such as retail stores, offices, apartments, and residential and office condominium associations. It includes both property and liability coverages and can be written on a basic or special perils basis.

business personal property

Property.

see: personal property

business risk

Risk Management. The basic risk inherent in a firm's operations. Business risk plus financial risk (resulting from a company's use of debt) equals total corporate risk.

see: **financial risk, loss of market, risk**

business use

Automobile. An automobile rating classification signifying that the driver uses the vehicle for occupational, business or professional purposes.

compare: **drive to or from work, farm use, pleasure use**

Butterfield v. Forrester

Workers' Compensation. An 1809 English court decision which first applied the common law defense of contributory negligence to a workers' compensation case. The defense of contributory negligence had been available for some time in personal injury cases outside of employment.

see: **common law defense, contributory negligence**

buy-and-sell agreement

General. An agreement among partners of a business (or key employees) that obligates a person withdrawing from the business (or their heirs) to sell their interest to the surviving owners (or key people) at a fixed price.

buy-back deductible

Insurer Operations. A deductible which can be deleted from a policy ("bought back") by paying an additional premium.

buyer's market

General. A market in which prices are in a downward trend, favoring the buyer rather than the seller.

compare: **hard market, tight market;** see: **soft market, underwriting cycle**

buying hedge

Financial Planning. A technique used in commodities trading, where commodities futures contracts are purchased to protect against possible future increases in the prices of the commodities.

syn: **long hedge**

bylaws

General. An organization's rules as adopted by its board of directors.

see: **charter**

byssinosis

Workers' Compensation. A physical disability involving the lungs that is caused by excessive inhalation of cotton, flax or hemp dust. It is an occupational respiratory disease afflicting mill workers and takes several years of exposure before manifestations are noticed. It can progress to chronic bronchitis and emphysema.

syn: **mill fever;** see: **black lung disease, brown lung disease, occupational disease**

62

C

cafeteria benefit plan

Employee Benefits. A benefit program under which employees of a company may choose the benefits program that best fits their needs, based on the individual's marital status, age, dependents, and income level. Normally, a firm allocates a stipulated amount of money and permits the individual within a given range to pick or tailor-make – cafeteria style – the program that best fits their needs. If the employee's allocation is not used up, the worker in some cases will receive the difference in cash. Such a program is similar to, but usually more limited than a flexible benefit plan.

compare: **flexible benefit plan**

caisson

Loss Control. A temporary watertight box or cofferdam used as a work chamber during construction of foundations, piers, and other structures below water.

calendar year

General. A defined, 12-month period of time, beginning on January 1 and running through December 31 (inclusive) containing 365 days. In a leap year – those years divisible by four – a calendar year contains 366 days.

compare: **fiscal year, policy year**

calendar year experience

Insurer Operations. An analysis of losses which matches incurred losses during a defined calendar year with premium earned during the same twelve-month period.

see: **annual, accident year experience, policy year experience**

callable

Financial Planning.
see: **call provision**

call option

Financial Planning. An order placed with a stock broker, to buy a specified number of shares of a stock at a specified price within a specific period of time. The option expires on the last day of the specified period if the number of shares ordered are not available at the requested price.

compare: **put option**; see: **option**

call provision

Financial Planning. A provision contained in a bond issue, allowing all or part of the issue to be redeemed prior to the maturity date under specific terms.

syn: **callable**

camera and musical instrument dealers coverage

Inland Marine. Insurance coverage designed for retail dealers of camera equipment (or musical instruments), to insure their merchandise on an "open perils" basis.

see: **commercial articles coverage**

camera floater

Inland Marine. A personal articles floater insuring most photographic equipment, including projection machines, portable sound and recording equipment, binoculars, and telescopes against direct loss on an "all-risks" basis. Each item must be individually described and valued.

Canadian Association of Accident and Sickness Insurers

Health/Organizations. Members: Accident and sickness insurers in Canada. *Objectives:* Fosters the development of voluntary insurance providing sound protection against loss of income and financial burdens resulting from accident and sickness. *Founded:* 1959.

© 1991 NILS Publishing Company

Canadian Council of Superintendents of Insurance

Organizations. Members: Superintendents of Insurance in the nine common-law Provinces of Canada (except the Quebec Province). *Objectives:* Promote uniformity in the regulation of insurance matters and the provision of a forum for consultation. *Founded:* 1917. *Headquarters:* Toronto, Canada. Formerly known as the Association of Superintendents of Insurance of the Provinces of Canada.

Canadian Federation of Insurance Agents and Brokers Association

Agency/Organizations. Members: Canadian insurance agents and brokers. *Objectives:* Encourages special educational qualifications for general insurance agents. Cooperates with provincial insurance departments, fire marshals and other organizations dedicated to conservation of life, limb and property by preventing disasters. *Founded:* 1921. *Headquarters:* Toronto, Ontario

Canadian Fraternal Association

Organizations. Members: Canadian fraternal benefit societies. *Objectives:* Promotes the interests of the fraternal benefit system in Canada. *Founded:* 1891. *Headquarters:* Ontario, Canada.

Canadian Home Office Life Underwriters Association

Organizations/Life. Members: Home office underwriters in Canada. *Objectives:* Holds informal discussions on issues facing underwriters. *Founded:* 1949. *Headquarters:* Toronto, Canada.

Canadian Institute of Actuaries

Organizations. Members: Canadian actuaries. *Objectives:* Advance and develop actuarial science in Canada. *Founded:* 1965. *Headquarters:* Ottawa, Canada.

Canadian Life Insurance Association, Inc.

Organizations/Life. Members: Life insurance companies in Canada. *Objectives:* Promotes the interests of life insurers. *Founded:* 1894. *Headquarters:* Toronto, Canada.

Canadian Life Insurance Medical Officers Association

Organizations/Life. Members: Life insurance medical officers in Canada. *Objectives:* Advance the science of medicine as applied to insurance. *Founded:* 1946. *Headquarters:* Toronto, Canada.

cancel

General. To strike or cross out; to obliterate; to destroy the effect of an agreement; to rescind, abandon, repeal, surrender, waive, terminate.

see: cancellation

cancellable policy

Insurer Operations. A contract of insurance that may be cancelled at any time by either the insured or the insurer upon notification to the other party and in accordance with the provisions within the contract.

cancellation

Insurer Operations. The termination of an in-force insurance contract by either the insured or the insurer. Termination may be voluntary, involuntary, or mutual in accordance with provisions contained in the contract.

see: block cancellation, cancellation notice, cut-off cancellation, evidence of cancellation, expiration date, flat cancellation, lapse, pro rata cancellation, run-off cancellation, short-rate cancellation; Fr: résiliation; Gr: Kündigung, Storno; Sp: cancelación

cancellation notice

Insurer Operations. By the insured: A written notice delivered to the insurance company requesting cancellation of the contract of insurance. Only the first named insured listed in the declarations may give notice of cancellation. *By the insurer:* The insurer must give notice of cancellation, in most cases, a minimum of ten days prior to the date of the cancellation's effect, for nonpayment of premiums. Generally, 30 days notice before the cancellation date is required for other reasons. The insurer's cancellation date can be renegotiated to a longer time frame (e.g., 60 days, 90 days, 120 days). Some states now require insurers to provide the cancelled policyholder with reasons for the cancellation.

syn: notice of cancellation; see: cancel, cancellable policy, expiration notice, flat cancellation, premium financing, pro rata cancellation, short-rate cancellation

cancer insurance

Health. A health insurance policy that specifically provides coverage for medical expenses resulting from cancer treatment.

see: dread disease policy, extra percentage tables

Life.

see: living benefits

capacity

Insurer Operations. 1) The total amount of insurance coverage available in the world market (or a smaller, sub-market) for a class of insurance or a single risk.

2) The maximum amount of insurance available from a single insurer (including that insurer's reinsurers) for a class of insurance or a single risk.

3) The maximum amount of insurance available from a

© 1991 NILS Publishing Company

single insurer excluding reinsurance (net line) for a class of insurance or a single risk.

see: **underwriting cycle**

capital

General. The accumulated assets of a business; an owner's equity in a business used for the production of profits and wealth.

see: **paid-in capital**

Insurer Operations. The aggregate par value of an insurance company's stock.

capital asset

General. An asset with a life of more than one year that is not bought and sold in the normal course of business.

see: **assets**

capital budgeting

General. The process of planning expenditures on assets whose returns are expected to extend beyond one year.

see: **cost of capital, cut-off point, internal financing**

capital charges

General. Charges against interest and amortization of monies invested in an enterprise.

see: **amortization**

capital expenditures

General. Amounts expended in acquiring, equipping and promoting an enterprise.

capital gains

General. Profits from the sale of capital assets, which are subject to special federal and state income tax provisions.

compare: **capital losses**

Insurer Operations. The excess of the sales price of an asset over that asset's book value. The total of all such amounts is shown on an insurance company's annual convention statement, and they are detailed in the statement's surplus account or in the summary of operations.

capitalization

General. The total amount received from the sale of all securities issued by a corporation. Preferred and common shares may be par or stated values.

capitalization rate

General. An assumed rate of return (interest rate) used by financial officers to determine the investment of available capital in a project.

capital losses

General. Losses on the sale of capital assets.

compare: **capital gains**

capital market line

General. A graphic representation of the relationship between risk and the required rate of return on an efficient investment portfolio.

capital markets

General. Financial market institutions which deal in instruments with maturities greater than a year.

capital rationing

General. A situation where a limit is placed on the total size of the capital investment a company may make during a particular period of time.

capital requirement

General. The investment necessary to equip, promote and operate an enterprise.

see: **organizational expenses**

capital stock

General. The sum of all outstanding shares of preferred and common stock that represent the total ownership interest in a corporation.

see: **stock**

capital stock insurance company

Insurer Operations.

see: **stock insurance company**

capital sum

Life. The maximum amount payable in one sum to the beneficiary in an accident policy in the event of accidental death or dismemberment of the insured.

see: **principal sum**

capital surplus

General. Surplus contributed by shareholders in excess of capital stock liability and not from normal business profits.

captive agent

Agency/Insurer Operations. An individual who represents only one insurance company and is restricted by agreement from submitting business to any other company unless it is first rejected by the agent's captive company. Captive agents, while not being employees of the company, usually receive financial assistance in the form of allowance for office expenses and some employee benefits.

compare: **broker, independent agency system;** see: **agent, exclusive agency system, marketing representative, policywriting agent**

captive domicile

Regulation. A term used to describe any state, foreign country or U.S. possession that allows (or, more likely,

© 1991 NILS Publishing Company

captive domicile — continued
encourages) the formation of captive insurance companies within its borders.

see: **Bermuda Market, captive insurance company**

Captive Insurance Companies Association (CICA)

Organizations. Members: Insurance companies originally formed for the purpose of providing insurance for their sponsoring corporations. *Objectives:* Promotes interests of captive insurance companies. *Founded:* 1973. *Headquarters:* New York, NY.

captive insurance company

Risk Management. A risk-financing method or form of self-insurance, involving the establishment by a corporation or association of a separate subsidiary insurance company legally organized to write insurance. Captives are domiciled either "off-shore" — in countries such as Bermuda or Barbados — or domestically in certain U.S. states. Captive insurance companies are formed to provide for the insurance needs of the parent organization, and to escape the highs and lows of insurance cycles found in the commercial insurance market. Captives owned by one parent (company) are generally referred to as single parent captives. Captives owned by two or more parents may be referred to as multiple-owned, group or association captives.

syn: **off-shore insurers**; see: **association captive insurance company, group captive insurance company, risk retention group, self-insurance, underwriting cycle**

carbon dioxide

Loss Control. A gas used in fire extinguishing systems which is nontoxic and nonpolluting. When directed at a burning flammable liquid or when used to flood an enclosure (oven or dip tank), it will snuff out a fire by depriving it of oxygen.

see: **fire extinguishing system**

carbon monoxide

Loss Control. A colorless, odorless, toxic gas generated by combustion of common fuels with an insufficient air supply or where combustion is incomplete. It causes poisoning in humans and animals due to the combination of carbon dioxide with the available hemoglobin.

carcinogen

Health/Loss Control. A substance or agent producing or inciting cancer.

CARE Alliance

Organizations.
see: **Concerned Alliance of Responsible Employers**

care, custody or control

Casualty. A term signifying the status of property in the possession of another individual or company (bailee). Use of the term confers, often by contract, the responsibility and liability for the safekeeping of the property on the bailee, pending its return to the owner (bailor). Insurance covering the value of the object being held may be purchased by the bailee. Liability policies usually exclude coverage for damage to property in the insured's care, custody or control, but the policies can be endorsed to afford protection. (Sometimes separate property or inland marine insurance policies are purchased, covering only property held under contract.)

see: **bailee; bailee's customer insurance; broad form property damage; care, custody or control exclusion; trust and commission clause**

care, custody or control exclusion

Casualty. A provision in most liability insurance policies which eliminates coverage for damage or destruction to property under the care, custody, or control of the insured.

see: **bailee, broad form property damage**

cargo

Inland Marine/Ocean Marine. Goods, merchandise or commodities of every description that may be carried by a vessel, train, truck or airplane. A vessel's stores or provisions are not included.

see: **break bulk cargo, bulk cargo, containerized cargo, deck cargo**

cargo insurance

Inland Marine/Ocean Marine. A general term used to describe marine insurance policies which cover goods being transported by ship, trucks, railroads, or airplanes. This coverage insures against most forms of loss to which the property may be subject.

syn: **cargo policy**; see: **cargo, officers protective policy, open cargo policy, special cargo policy, warehouse-to-warehouse coverage**

cargo legal liability

Inland Marine. A special insuring form covering a shipper's or handler's legal liability for loss or damage to cargo or baggage.

cargo policy

Inland Marine/Ocean Marine.
see: **cargo insurance**

Cargo Reinsurance Association (CRA)

Organizations. Members: Reinsurers of American cargo insurance companies. *Objectives:* Reinsures American cargo insurance companies. *Founded:* 1965. *Headquarters:* New York, NY.

© 1991 NILS Publishing Company

Carpenter Plan

Reinsurance. A concept developed by reinsurance executive Guy Carpenter where, under an excess of loss reinsurance contract, each year's final reinsurance premium is based on the ceding insurer's excess losses over a specified period of time. A type of retrospective rating formula is used to determine the policy's renewal premium, using losses from the previous three to five years.

syn: spread loss reinsurance

Carriage of Goods by Sea Act (COGSA)

Ocean Marine. Federal legislation that pertains to various phases of maritime ventures, particularly the rights and responsibilities of carriers, shippers and the bill of lading. This legislation encompasses the Harter Act and defines the liability and responsibility of vessels carrying cargo to and from United States ports. The act provides that a carrier's liability will be limited to $500 per shipping package and that the time limit for filing a claim against a carrier is one year.

see: Hague Rules, Harter Act

Carriage of Goods by Water Act (COGWA)

Ocean Marine. A Canadian act which is the equivalent of the Hague Rules (international agreement) concerning the shipment of cargo for which bills of lading are issued between Canada and foreign ports.

see: Hague Rules

carrier

Inland Marine/Ocean Marine. A business that transports merchandise from one point to another. The carrier can be a vessel's owner, manager, operator, an airline, a truck operator or a railroad.

see: common carrier, contract carrier, private carrier

Insurer Operations.

see: insurance company

carrier's form

Inland Marine.

see: motor truck cargo insurance

carriers legal liability

Inland Marine. An insurance coverage form that protects the insured carrier against the bailee liability that arises out of damage to property in the carrier's care, custody or control.

see: care, custody or control exclusion

Inland Marine/Ocean Marine.

see: Carriage of Goods by Sea Act, Hague Rules, Harter Act

carry-back

General. Financial losses (including casualty losses and insurance company losses) that can legally be carried backward to reduce federal income taxes.

carry-forward

General. Financial losses (including insurance losses) that can be legally be carried forward to reduce federal income taxes.

carrying charge

Financial Planning. A charge made by a creditor, in addition to interest, for providing installment credit.

see: interest

case law

General.

see: common law

cash assets

Risk Management/Surety. The sum of cash on hand, plus short-term demand certificates and securities (such as Treasury Bills), that can readily be converted into cash without disrupting normal operations. ("Cash assets" do not include marketable securities.)

see: assets, demand deposits

cash basis of accounting

General. An accounting method in which income is recognized only upon the receipt of a cash payment without considering the period for which payments are due. Also, expenses are accounted for only upon their cash payment. This accounting method is rarely applied to commercial businesses, but it may be used by professionals and small private enterprises. Government accounts are usually maintained on this basis.

compare: accrual basis of accounting;
see: accounting

cash budget

General. An estimate showing cash flows (receipts, disbursements, and net cash) for an organization over a specific period.

see: cash flow

cash cycle

General. The length of time between the purchase of raw materials and the collection of accounts receivable generated in the sale of the final product that is produced from those raw materials.

cash flow

General. Individual or aggregate infusions or expenditures of money traceable (through a "cash flow statement") from their first appearance in an organization's bank accounts, through their final disposition.

see: cash budget, negative cash flow, net net income

Risk Management. A term used to identify the money being held but not currently needed in a business' operation.

© 1991 NILS Publishing Company

cash flow program

Risk Management. An insurance program where premium payment is deferred over the policy term, or until losses are paid. This allows the insured to utilize or gain investment income on funds for a greater period of time.

see: cash flow, cash flow underwriting, paid loss retrospective rating plan

cash flow underwriting

Insurer Operations/Risk Management. A term used to describe an insurance underwriting practice, where coverage is provided for a premium level that is actuarially less than that which is necessary to pay claims and expenses. The insurer that engages in cash flow underwriting believes that it can make an adequate investment return on the premium paid up front to compensate for the underwriting loss and turn a profit.

see: financial underwriting, investment income, underwriting cycle

cashier's check

General. A check drawn by a bank on itself, giving the payee authorization to collect the amount represented on the check.

compare: certified check, draft

cash out

Employee Benefits. The act of withdrawing ("cashing out") from a pension plan by a participant through a lump sum distribution. Such withdrawals usually result in the forfeiture of any future benefits.

cash refund annuity

Life. A life annuity contract which agrees to pay a beneficiary, upon the death of the annuitant, a lump sum equal to the difference between the amount of premium paid for the annuity and the amount of installments already paid by the insurer to the annuitant. If the annuitant lives past the point where the income equals the premiums paid, the insurer will continue to make payments.

syn: lump sum refund annuity; see: lump sum

cash surrender value

Life. The amount of cash the policyowner is entitled to receive from the insurance company upon surrendering a life insurance policy with cash value. The sum is the cash value stated in the policy minus a surrender charge and any outstanding loan balances and interest thereon.

see: nonforfeiture cash surrender value benefit, policy loan

cash value

Life. The net proceeds that a life insurance or deferred annuity contract holder will receive after applicable charges have been deducted, upon termination or cancellation of a policy or annuity before its maturity or an insured event

see: excess interest, net cash value

Property.

see: actual cash value

casual sequence

Property.

see: concurrent causation

Casualty Actuarial Society (CAS)

Organizations. Members: Insurance actuaries. Objectives: Promotes actuarial and statistical science as applied to insurance problems, other than life insurance. Founded: 1914. Headquarters: New York, NY.

see: Associate of the Casualty Actuarial Society, Fellow of the Casualty Actuarial Society

casualty insurance

Casualty. A broad class of insurance which includes automobile and general liability, personal liability, employers' liability, plate glass insurance, professional liability, errors & omissions insurance, burglary, robbery and forgery insurance, boiler and machinery insurance, and aviation insurance. Sometimes workers' compensation insurance is included, and boiler and machinery insurance in recent years has instead been classified with property insurance. A common characteristic of casualty insurance is that it covers an insured against claims resulting from negligent acts, errors or omissions which cause bodily injury and/or property damage to third parties.

syn: liability insurance

catalyst

Loss Control. A substance that initiates or alters the speed of a chemical reaction without changing its own composition. It may accelerate or retard the reaction.

catastrophe

General. An event causing severe loss, injury or damage. Most often associated with natural disasters, the term usually is used when there is concentrated or widespread damage and extreme force. Also, "catastrophe" is now used to describe physical illnesses and losses occurring from these illnesses.

Property. A term applied to an incident or series of related incidents causing insured property losses totaling more than $5 million.

catastrophe hazard

Risk Management. A circumstance which increases the likelihood that a large loss affecting many insureds could occur. Example: The widespread loss that could result from a hurricane or tornado – either to property

© 1991 NILS Publishing Company

or human life – can be ascribed to the catastrophe hazards of a hurricane or tornado.

see: hazard

catastrophe loss

Risk Management. An exceptionally large loss which cannot accurately be predicted, and therefore should be transferred by an individual or organization to an insurer.

see: insurable risk

catastrophe number

Property. A number assigned by the National Board of Fire Underwriters (NBFU) to severe losses (i.e., those exceeding five million dollars), for insurance statistical purposes.

catastrophe plan

Loss Control.

see: disaster plan

catastrophe policy

Health. A designation previously used to signify a major medical insurance policy.

see: major medical insurance

catastrophe reinsurance

Reinsurance. A type of excess of loss treaty reinsurance which protects the ceding company against a loss or losses in excess of a specified retention, from an accumulation of losses resulting from a single catastrophic event or a series of events, subject to the reinsurance contract limit.

syn: catastrophe treaty; see: excess of loss reinsurance

catastrophe treaty

Reinsurance.

see: catastrophe reinsurance

catastrophic loss funds

Insurer Operations. Any special funds or reserves established and held for extraordinary or catastrophic losses (e.g., losses incurred by a fire insurer due to an extensive, general conflagration).

catastrophic peril

Property. A peril which has the potential to result in a major disaster (such as earthquakes, floods and nuclear accidents).

see: peril

causal sequence

Property.

see: concurrent causation

cause of action

General. A legally acceptable basis for filing a lawsuit.

see: actions

cause of loss

Property. The event that produces a loss that is covered by an insurance policy. Modern property forms have replaced the term "peril" when describing an event insured against, with the term "cause of loss." Usage within the insurance industry has maintained "peril" as the preferred term.

compare: exposure, hazard, risk; see: peril

caveat emptor

General. A maxim reminding a buyer to examine, judge, and test an item before buying it. Literally, the translation from the Latin is "let the buyer beware." However, the courts and statutes have substantially modified this maxim by giving consumers certain rights in the purchase of goods.

cease and desist

General. A court order, or the order of a governmental regulatory agency authorized and able to issue such an order, requiring the cessation of a potentially dangerous, injurious or fraudulent act. *Example:* The order that a business or industry halt disposal of toxic substances into the air, ground or bodies of water.

see: enjoin, injunctive relief

Regulation. A state insurance department may issue a cease and desist order to an insurance company under its jurisdiction, to halt activities which it considers illegal or improper, such as false advertising, redlining (bias in the selection of risks), or improper investment practices.

cede

Reinsurance. The act of transferring a risk from a primary insurer to a reinsuring company.

see: reinsurance

ceded reinsurance

Reinsurance. The dollar amount of insurance limits transferred from a primary insurer to a reinsurer.

cedent

Reinsurance.

see: ceding company

ceding commission

Reinsurance. The commission paid to a ceding company (primary insurer) by a reinsurer on reinsurance contracts, in order to obtain business.

syn: reinsurance commission; see: acquisition cost, management expense, sliding scale commission

ceding company

Reinsurance. The original or primary insurer which

© 1991 NILS Publishing Company

ceding company — continued
purchases the reinsurance; in so doing, the primary insurer "cedes" part of its business to the reinsurer.

syn: **cedent, primary insurance company, reassured, reinsured;** compare: **reinsurer;** see: **assume, ceding commission**

cemetery professional liability insurance

Casualty. Insurance protecting cemetery operators from third-party claims for bodily injury, sickness, disease or death (including mental anguish) made by any person, as a result of the professional actions of a cemetery, its owner, management or staff. Included is liability coverage for damage to property of others such as caskets, deceased human remains, urns and clothing which is in the insured's charge (care, custody or control) for use in burial or cremation.

center of influence

General. Also known as the "center of gravity," this term is used to refer to a legal concept used to resolve jurisdictional disputes where a conflict of law exists. The laws applied in tort cases are generally those of the state where the accident or injury occurred. Contract law considers where the parties reside, where the contract was signed and where the contract is to be performed. The laws of the state having the greatest influence or interest would apply over any other jurisdiction with an interest in the case.

see: **diversity jurisdiction**

central limit theorem

Risk Management. An actuarial theorem that states that if a series of samples is collected from a stable population, the distribution of the means (averages) of the samples will result in a normal distribution, where the mean approaches the population as the number of samples increase.

see: **mean**

central loss fund

Insurer Operations. A fund maintained in certain states by contributions from insurers used to pay claims for insolvent insurance companies, thus reassuring the insurance-buying public and safeguarding the integrity of the insurance business.

see: **guaranty funds**

certain defenses

Health.
see: **time limit**

certain payments

Life.
see: **guaranteed annuity payments**

certain period

Life. The predefined period over which an annuity's payments will be made, regardless of whether or not the annuitant is living. If the annuitant dies within the certain or guaranteed period, payments remaining in that certain period will be made as they come due to the estate of the annuitant.

syn: **guaranteed period**

certificate

General. A written authorization or official representation or assurance attesting to compliance with a legal formality.

see: **agent's certificate of authority, certificate of authority, certificate of convenience, certificate of deposit, certificate of insurance, certificate of occupancy, certificate of reinsurance, certificate of sale, certificate of title, group certificate, marine insurance certificate, renewal certificate**

certificate of authority

Agency. A document enumerating the powers granted by an insurance company to its agents.

see: **license**

Insurer Operations. A state-issued document empowering an insurance company to write contracts and perform certain business within its borders.

certificate of convenience

General. A certificate issued by an administrative agency (such as the I.C.C. or a Public Service Commission), granting operating authority for utilities and transportation companies.

Regulation. A license issued by a state insurance department on a temporary basis, which allows an individual to act as an insurance agent, even though they have not yet completed the normal licensing process. It usually is issued where a spouse or parent has died, has become disabled or has been called to serve in the military, and the spouse or children must step in to run an existing insurance agency.

see: **license, limited licenses**

certificate of deposit (CD)

General. A written acknowledgement by a chartered financial institution giving proof of a specific deposit amount with a promise to pay the amount indicated on the certificate to the order of the depositor, or to pay that amount to some other person.

certificate of insurance

Employee Benefits/Health/Life. Written evidence showing that an individual is a participant in a group life or health insurance program or employee benefit plan. In most group programs, only the employer or sponsoring organization receives a complete copy of

© 1991 NILS Publishing Company

the policy; members (employees, union members, etc.) receive only certificates of insurance.

syn: group certificate; compare: group contract, master insurance policy

Casualty/Property. Written evidence showing that an insurance policy or policies have been issued. The certificate indicates both the amounts and the types of insurance provided. Used by subcontractors to meet the requirements of general contractors or property owners, that the subcontractors provide proof of insurance. Sometimes requested by mortgage companies or other lenders, although such parties usually require loss payable clauses, because a certificate of insurance does not obligate the insurance company to the individual or organization to which the certificate is issued.

see: loss payable clause, master insurance policy, underlying insurance policies

Inland Marine/Ocean Marine.

see: marine insurance certificate

certificate of occupancy

General. A document issued by a municipality, certifying that a given premises complies with zoning and building ordinances and codes.

certificate of purchase

General.

see: certificate of sale

certificate of reinsurance

Reinsurance. An abbreviated documentation of a reinsurance transaction, usually incorporating standard terms and conditions by reference.

see: binder

certificate of sale

General. A document issued by a public official to the successful bidder at a judicial sale, which will entitle the bidder to a deed upon confirmation of the sale by the court.

syn: certificate of purchase

certificate of title

Title. The written document showing that an individual has legal possession to a specific plot of land.

see: paper title, title

certification forms

General. A preprinted form that confirms or attests to attaining some standard of compliance with a specified requirement.

certified check

General. A check that has been authorized by a bank, causing the bank to be liable to the holder of the check, in effect debiting the drawer's account and placing the sum in a separate account. Certified checks are often demanded because payment cannot be stopped.

compare: cashier's check, draft

Certified Employee Benefit Specialist (CEBS)

Organizations. A professional designation granted jointly by the International Foundation of Employee Benefit Plans and the Wharton School of the University of Pennsylvania. The designation requires the successful completion of ten college level courses and examinations in pension planning, Social Security, health insurance, economics, finance, labor relations, and group insurance and other employee benefit-related concepts.

see: International Foundation of Employee Benefit Plans

Certified Financial Planner (CFP)

Organizations. A professional designation granted by the College for Financial Planning. The designation requires the successful completion of a series of examinations in financial planning, insurance, investment, taxation, employee benefit plans and estate planning.

Certified Public Accountant (CPA)

General. An accountant who has met the accountant licensing requirements of a state. Usually, states require a college degree with accounting and auditing courses and qualifying experience. The CPA examinations require passage of the Uniform CPA Examination which covers accounting theory and practice, auditing and business law. Generally, an organization's annual report will be certified by a CPA.

see: accountant, audited financial statements

Certified Safety Professional (CSP)

Loss Control/Organizations. A professional designation awarded by the Board of Certified Safety Professionals of the Americas, Inc. which certifies an individual as having achieved professional competence by remaining abreast of technical, administrative, and regulatory developments in the safety fields.

see: Board of Certified Safety Professionals of the Americas, Inc.

certiorari

General. A Latin term meaning "to be informed of." A writ issued by a superior court to a lower court, requesting a certified record of a particular case that the superior court has decided to review and determine any possibilities of irregularities or mistakes in law. Also used to refer to the judicial proceeding wherein a party to the case requests such a writ.

see: appeal

cession

Reinsurance. The insurance coverage transferred to a

cession — continued

reinsurer by a ceding company. It corresponds with policy units of an insurance company. A cession may be all or a portion of a single risk, a group of defined policies, or defined portions of a policy.

syn: **reinsurance ceded; see: ceding company, reinsurance, reinsurance assumed**

cession number

Reinsurance. An assigned number used to identify reinsurance premium transactions.

cestui que vie

Life. The person whose life is the subject of a life insurance policy. The insured in a life insurance policy is the person who applies and pays for the policy, and they may or may not be the cestui que vie, the beneficiary, or a disinterested party.

chain

Title. A land measurement used by surveyors that is equal to 66 feet, or 100 links, or 4 rods. (An engineer's chain is equal to 100 feet)

chain of title

Title. The successive conveyances which affect a particular parcel of land, from an accepted starting point to where the present holder of real property derives his or her title.

see: **abstract of title**

chainstores multiple location policy

Property. A type of business insurance coverage packaged for stores under the same ownership with central management and selling uniform merchandise at multiple locations.

change in conditions insurance

Property.

see: **difference in conditions insurance**

change in occupancy or use

Casualty/Property. A term used to refer to a provision that appears in many property and casualty policies, whereby a change of occupancy, purpose, or use of a premises can void an insurance policy if these changes increase the hazards. The insurer may cancel the policy outright or charge additional premium to cover these additional hazards.

see: **increased hazard, occupancy permit**

change of beneficiary provision

Life. The provision in a life insurance policy which permits the policyholder to change beneficiaries at will, unless a beneficiary has been designated as irrevocable in the policy.

see: **beneficiary change, beneficiary clause**

change of occupation provision

Health. Provisions contained in health insurance policies which state that if the insured changes to a more hazardous occupation, benefits will automatically be reduced to those which could be purchased by the premium paid by an individual in the more hazardous occupation. If the change is to a less hazardous occupation, the premium will be reduced at the insured's request.

chaplain or priest professional liability

Casualty.

see: **clergy professional liability**

charge

General. A bill or invoice; a claim against property; the imposition of a burden; a debt or obligation to pay.

chargeable offense

Automobile. An action or offense committed while driving a motor vehicle for which it is proper for insurers to charge an additional premium, or because of which they may deny, terminate, or refuse to renew coverage. Parking tickets are not chargeable against a driving record.

see: **safe driver plan**

charitable annuities

Life. Annuities payable by a charitable, religious, benevolent or educational institution to a transferor of property.

charitable immunity

Casualty. A principle — somewhat eroded in recent years — stating that charitable organizations, in the normal performance of their duties, are immune from suit in tort.

see: **governmental immunity**

charter

General. A term synonymous with "articles of incorporation," a charter is a document describing the rights granted by a state or federal government to a business organization to conduct and transact certain business.

see: **articles of incorporation, bylaws, intra vires, ultra vires**

Ocean Marine. The mercantile lease of a ship or some principal part of it.

see: **charter party**

Aviation.

see: **air taxi**

charter aircraft

Aviation.

see: **air taxi**

© 1991 NILS Publishing Company

Chartered Financial Consultant (ChFC)

Organizations. A professional designation granted by the American College. The designation requires the successful completion of national examinations in financial planning, insurance, investments, taxation, employee benefits, estate planning, accounting and management.

see: **American College, American Society of Chartered Life Underwriters and Chartered Financial Consultants**

Chartered Life Underwriter (CLU)

Life/Organizations. A professional designation granted by the American College. Those seeking the designation must successfully complete ten college-level courses and examinations in insurance, investments, taxation, employee benefits, estate planning, accounting, management and economics.·

see: **American College, American Society of Chartered Life Underwriters and Chartered Financial Consultants**

Chartered Property and Casualty Underwriter (CPCU)

Organizations. A professional designation granted by the American Institute for Property and Liability Underwriters. Successful candidates are those who complete ten college-level courses and examinations in insurance, risk management, economics, finance, management, accounting and law.

see: **American Institute for Property and Liability Underwriters**

charterers liability insurance

Ocean Marine. Coverage which insures against the liability of a person who leases a vessel from another. The lessor may assume full responsibility for the vessel and crew (as in a bareboat charter), or limit insurable interest to partial responsibility (as in a time charter) and leave most insurance requirements for the vessel owner to handle.

see: **bareboat charter, charter party, time charter**

charter fare protection insurance

Health. A special form of accident and health insurance that reimburses an insured individual for the cost of a tour if the insured is unable to participate due to a covered accident or sickness. Coverage extends if the insured is unable to make a return flight on a scheduled date because of illness. In this case, the insured is reimbursed for the specific cost of a later return flight.

syn: **trip cancellation insurance**; see: **air travel insurance, travel accident insurance**

charter party

Ocean Marine. A written document between the individual, group, or company chartering a ship and the owner of the vessel, stating the terms and conditions of the charter.

see: **affreightment, bareboat charter, charterer's liability insurance, time charter, voyage charter**

chattel

General. An article of personal property – as opposed to real property. (A leasehold in land is known as a real chattel.) Generally, a chattel is moveable and may be animate (e.g., livestock) or inanimate.

see: **real chattel**

chattel mortgage

Mortgage Insurance. A mortgage whose collateral is personal (moveable) property, as opposed to a mortgage whose collateral is real property.

chattel mortgage nonfiling insurance

Mortgage Insurance. Insurance coverage that protects banks, credit unions and other lending institutions, against their financial loss due to the inability of the institution to obtain possession of property represented by a chattel mortgage or similar security instrument in the granting of the loan. Also, insures against the inability of the lending institution to enforce its rights under the instrument due to the intentional nonfiling of the instrument with the proper public official.

check alteration and forgery insurance

Crime.

see: **forgery bond**

chief executive officer (CEO)

General. The highest ranking executive of a business enterprise. CEO is the preferred and useful designation because official titles (chairman, president, managing director, etc.) vary widely from organization to organization.

compare: **chief financial officer, chief operating officer**

chief financial officer (CFO)

General. The highest ranking financial executive of a business enterprise or institution. CFO is the preferred and useful designation because official titles (vice president – finance, treasurer, controller) vary widely from organization to organization.

compare: **controller, treasurer**

chief operating officer (COO)

General. Usually the second highest ranking executive or an executive that shares responsibility with the chief executive officer of a business enterprise. COO is the preferred and useful designation because official titles (president, executive vice president, managing

© 1991 NILS Publishing Company

COO — *continued*

director, etc.) vary widely from corporation to corporation. The COO's responsibilities are usually limited to internal procedures, production and control.

compare: chief executive officer

childbirth

Health. The bringing forth, labor, or the bearing of a child. Childbirth coverage has historically been excluded in accident and sickness policies written on females, but is commonly covered by hospitalization insurance and employee health insurance benefit policies.

see: maternity benefit

child's benefit

Health. A benefit provided under Social Security, payable to the child of a disabled, deceased, or retired worker. In order to receive these benefits, the child must be under 18 years of age, or be a full-time student between 18 and 22 years of age, or must be disabled and have suffered the disability prior to 22 years of age.

chiropodists professional liability

Casualty. Insurance coverage that protects chiropodists against claims for personal injury arising from alleged malpractice, error or mistake in rendering professional services.

chomage

Property. An early form of business interruption insurance which based the insured's business interruption recovery on a percentage of the fire damage loss to a building or contents. *Example:* If the fire loss was $50,000, the chomage amount might be 20 percent or an additional $10,000.

see: business income coverage form

chose in action

General. "Chose" (pronounced "shows") means "thing." A chose in action is a type of ownership right which gives its holder a right to recover by action in law. It is not tangible, nor can it be destroyed by physical means. "Chose in action" is a right to sue. A written contract is evidence of a chose in action, because the destruction of the writing does not destroy the contract right. Claims, debts, insurance policies, negotiable instruments, contract rights, copyrights, and bills of lading are all "choses in action."

compare: chattel, chose in possession

chose in possession

General. An ownership right that contrasts with "chose in action." "Chose" (pronounced "shows") means "thing." A chose in possession is an ownership right involving a tangible, physical object.

compare: chose in action

chronological stabilization plan

Risk Management. An insurance program, the primary purpose of which is loss leveling or cost stabilizing, similar to some reinsurance plans or retrospective rating plans. The plan minimizes cost and maximizes stability. Losses are actuarially projected, to arrive at a premium figure which includes a small loading factor. Claims paid for the five-to-fifteen-year term of the plan will approach 85% to 95% of paid premium (depending on the terms and type of coverage). If the amount of payable losses falls short of actuarial expectations, a retrospective refund of the excess premium is paid. If losses exceed the calculated amount, an upward adjustment is made.

see: banking plan, spread loss plan

circulating main

Loss Control. A water main or piping used for fire protection that is fed from two directions.

see: deadend main

civil authority clause

Property. Coverage included in most business income forms. If access to an insured's premises is denied as the direct result of damage or destruction of neighboring or adjacent property belonging to others, and such damage or destruction is due to an insured peril, then the insured's loss of income is covered for up to two weeks.

syn: ingress/egress clause; see: governmental action exclusion, ordinance or law exclusion

civil commotion

General. A legal term for an uprising of people creating a prolonged disturbance that often results in damage or destruction of public and private property.

see: disturbance, riot, uprising; Fr: mouvement populaire; Gr: innere Unruhen; Sp: conmoción civil

civil commotion exclusion

Property. Property insurance policy clause which excludes coverage for losses caused by uprisings, riots, and civil commotion.

see: civil commotion, riot, uprising

civil commotion policy

Property. Property insurance coverage protecting the insured against losses caused by uprisings, riots, and civil commotion.

see: civil commotion

civil damages

General. The money awarded by a court to a plaintiff, in a civil lawsuit, which must be paid by a losing defendant.

see: damages

© 1991 NILS Publishing Company

civil law

General. That part of the law, based on common law and statutory acts, which is employed by injured parties to seek redress for private wrongs.

compare: criminal law; see: common law, contract law

civil liability

General. Negligent acts and/or omissions (other than breach of contract) normally independent of moral obligations, for which a remedy can be provided in a court of law. *Example:* A person injured in someone's home can bring suit under civil liability law.

compare: criminal law; see: contract law

claim

Insurer Operations. A demand by an insured or another party for payment for a loss under an insurance contract or bond; "claim" is also used to refer to the actual or estimated amount of a loss.

see: notice of loss, proof of loss; Fr: réclamation; Gr: Anspruch; Sp: reclamación

claim agent

Ocean Marine. A claims representative of an ocean marine insurer, located in ports and cities throughout the world, whom a claimant can contact in the event of a loss or damage to an insured shipment.

see: claims adjuster

claimant

Insurer Operations. One who claims or asserts a loss and his or her right to demand payment of compensation or benefits.

see: insured, plaintiff

claim expense

Insurer Operations. Expenses related to the adjusting and settlement of a claim, excluding any claim payment. Claims expenses include both allocated and unallocated claim expenses.

see: adjustment expenses, allocated claim expense, defense costs, economic loss, ex gratia payment, legal expenses, loss adjustment expense, loss development, paid claim count, paid expense, trending, unallocated claim expense

claim number

Insurer Operations. A reference number that is assigned by an insurance company or third-party administrator to each claim.

claims adjuster

Insurer Operations. An individual acting on behalf of, or employed by, an insurance company to settle claims.

syn: adjuster, claims representative; compare: public adjuster; see: adjustment bureau, claim

agent, general average, independent adjuster, staff adjuster, third-party administrator

claims adjustment

Insurer Operations. The process used by an insurer to evaluate and settle (adjust) a claim. This process includes determining the cause of loss; whether it was a covered loss; the value of the loss; and proportion of loss attributed to the policy covering the risk.

syn: adjustment

claims administration

Risk Management. The management of claims that have occurred. This includes certifying a claimant's eligibility; monitoring adjusters, attorneys and medical service providers; and preparing reports.

see: third-party administrator

claims deductible workers' compensation plan

Workers' Compensation. A form of deductible workers' compensation coverage where the policy deductible applies to both medical and indemnity benefits.

see: deductible workers' compensation plans

claims department

Insurer Operations. The division of an insurance company that administers the handling and payment of claims.

claims frequency

Risk Management.
see: loss frequency

claims-made form

Casualty. A liability policy that provides coverage for a claim for injury or damage if the claim is first reported or filed against the insured during the policy period. This is in contrast to the more broadly worded occurrence policy forms which provide coverage for injury or damage that occurs during the policy period, regardless of when the claim for injury or damage is first made. Generally, medical malpractice, professional liability, and high hazard products liability policies are written on a claims-made basis.

compare: occurrence coverage; see: commercial general liability form, extended reporting period, immature policies, laser endorsement, mature policies, maxi tail, midi tail, mini tail, prior acts coverage, retroactive date, tail

claims-made trigger

Casualty. Under a claims-made policy, coverage is activated upon the filing of a claim. The claims-made trigger is the first notification of a claim against the insured during the policy period and after the retroactive date.

compare: occurrence trigger; see: claims-made form

© 1991 NILS Publishing Company

claims management

Workers' Compensation. A process or system of reviewing and handling claims for benefits, designed to control hospital costs, provide the best medical care, and produce early return-to-work dates.

claims processing

Insurer Operations. Activities routinely involved in administering claims, from first receiving notice of loss to final settlement.

claims report

Agency/Insurer Operations.
see: loss run

claims representative

Insurer Operations.
see: claims adjuster

claims reserve

Insurer Operations.
see: loss reserve

claims run

Insurer Operations/Risk Management.
see: loss run

claims severity

Risk Management.
see: loss severity

class

Insurer Operations.
see: classification
Property.
see: protection class

class action suit

General. The joining together of many individual plaintiffs into a single liability lawsuit against a company or individual.

class A fire

Loss Control. One of four categories of fires. Class A fires involve solid combustibles (such as wood or paper), which are best extinguished by water or dry chemicals. A portable fire extinguisher using water or dry chemicals is called a "class A extinguisher."
see: class B fire, class C fire, class D fire, fire extinguisher

class beneficiary

Life. A specific, unnamed individual or member of a group receiving the proceeds of an insurance policy, such as "children of the insured."

class B fire

Loss Control. One of four categories of fires. Class B fires involve flammable liquids, which are best extinguished by foam, carbon dioxide or dry chemicals. Portable extinguishers using these agents are called "class B extinguishers."
see: class A fire, class C fire, class D fire, fire extinguisher, foam

class C fire

Loss Control. One of four categories of fires. Class C fires involve live electrical equipment which must be extinguished by a nonconductive extinguishing agent such as carbon dioxide or dry chemicals. An extinguisher using either of these agents is called a "class C extinguisher."
see: class A fire, class B fire, class D fire, fire extinguisher

class code

Workers' Compensation.
see: classification code

class D fire

Loss Control. One of four categories of fire. Class D fires involve combustible metals such as magnesium or titanium, which must be extinguished by special dry chemical extinguishers. Extinguishers designed to extinguish such fires are called "class D extinguishers."
see: class A fire, class B fire, class C fire, fire extinguisher

classification

Insurer Operations. Categorization on the basis of established criteria for rating risks, establishing premiums and tabulating statistical experience.
syn: class; see: classification code, homogeneity, rating class, risk classification, underwriting

classification code

Insurer Operations. A code used in commercial lines rating to determine a specific rate. The Commercial Lines Manual (CLM) published by ISO includes a classification table listing more than 1,000 types of operations with each assigned an individual class code.
see: class rate, classification
Workers' Compensation. A specific industry classification published in a workers' compensation rate manual. Such classifications are used to identify the activity(ies) of insureds and place them into underwriting and rating groups. Class codes are tied to premium rates based on underwriting experience for the class. Insureds may be rated using more than one class code, if their activities fall into more than one category.
syn: class code; see: class rate, governing classification

76

© 1991 NILS Publishing Company

classification endorsements

Insurer Operations. Endorsements that either restrict or expand coverages under a liability policy to meet the specific needs of special classes of business, or a specific insured.

see: XCU exclusions

classified insurance

Health/Life. A term for the writing of life or health insurance on substandard risks.

see: impaired risk

class rate

Insurer Operations. The rate assigned to similar risks or a class of risks, based on its class code.

see: classification, classification code, governing classification

clause

Life. A provision added to a life insurance policy, usually requiring an additional premium. Typical clauses include the waiver of premium clause, the disability income clause, the accidental death clause, and the policy purchase option.

Insurer Operations. A section or segment of an insurance policy describing its terms and conditions, such as the insuring agreement, exclusions, insured locations, insured's duties and cancellation.

Clayton Act

Regulation. Federal legislation enacted in 1914 which amended the Sherman Antitrust Act to prohibit price-fixing conspiracies in interstate commerce.

see: anti-trust laws, McCarran-Ferguson Act, Sherman Antitrust Act

clean bill of lading

Inland Marine/Ocean Marine. A bill of lading with indication of any problems with the cargo's condition when it was accepted for carriage.

compare: clean receipt; see: bill of lading

clean receipt

Inland Marine/Ocean Marine. A delivery receipt with no exceptions from damage or shortage noted by the party receiving the merchandise.

compare: clean bill of lading

cleanup fund

General. A term used to describe any insurance provision that pays for expenses associated with the occurrence of an insured event. *Examples:* A life insurance provision that pays funeral expenses; extra expense coverage in a property insurance policy.

clergy professional liability

Casualty. Professional liability coverage that protects clergy (priests, chaplains, ministers, rabbis, etc.) for claims arising out of their professional duties, such as counseling. Lawsuits have arisen for causing emotional or physical suffering as the result of giving allegedly wrong or inadequate advice.

syn: chaplain or priest professional liability

cliff vesting

Employee Benefits.

see: ten year vesting

close corporations

General. A corporation with relatively few shareholders and no regular markets for their shares. Close corporations usually have made no public offering of shares, and the shares themselves are usually subject to restrictions on transfer.

syn: closely held corporations

closed-end mutual fund

Financial Planning. A mutual fund whose charter limits the number of shares issued. The value of the shares are determined by trading on a major stock exchange or over-the-counter.

compare: open-end mutual fund; see: mutual fund

closed panel

Health. A requirement by a health maintenance organization (HMO) that a subscriber must receive medical treatment only from physicians associated with or approved by the HMO.

see: health maintenance organization

closely held corporations

General.

see: close corporations

closure and post-closure insurance

Casualty. Insurance coverage purchased by operators of hazardous waste treatment, storage and disposal facilities (TSDFs) to meet the requirements of the Resource Conservation and Recovery Act of 1976 governing proof of financial responsibilities for the closure and post-closure of waste and disposal sites. The regulations require hazardous waste site owners to provide the federal Environmental Protection Agency (EPA) with evidence that they will be able to close and then monitor the site, usually for a period of 30 years.

see: hazardous waste site, Resource Conservation and Recovery Act of 1976

coinsurance

Insurer Operations. An agreement between the insured and the insurer to share in the settlement of any covered losses in a proportion agreed upon in advance.

Fr: coassurance; Gr: Mitversicherung; Sp: coaseguro

coinsurance — continued

Property.

see: agreed amount clause, coinsurance clause

Health. The insured's share of covered health insurance benefits. Coinsurance has become common as costs to insurers have risen, and it is considered both a cost-sharing and cost-containment technique. *Example:* In some policies the insurer pays 80 percent of the covered medical expenses, and the insured pays the remainder.

coinsurance clause

Property. A provision contained in most property and inland marine policies which requires that property be insured to some specified percentage of its full value (usually 80 percent, 90 percent or 100 percent), in exchange for a rate credit. If at the time of a loss it is determined that the insured carried inadequate limits, the loss recovery will be a percentage of the total loss amount, calculated by dividing the insured amount by the amount of insurance required. *Example:* A building valued at $100,000 has a 90 percent coinsurance clause and is insured for $45,000. It suffers a $20,000 loss. The insured would recover $45,000/(.90 x 100,000) x 20,000 = $10,000 (less any deductible).

syn: average clause, coinsurance, contribution clause; see: agreed amount clause, agreed value clause, foundation exclusion clause

coinsurance deficiency coverage

Property. Insurance coverage that indemnifies the insured against financial loss sustained through the unintentional failure of the insured to purchase adequate insurance to comply with the provisions of a coinsurance clause in a property insurance policy.

see: agreed amount, coinsurance clause

coinsurance penalty

Property. A provision in property insurance policies that provides that if an insured had not purchased adequate insurance to value at the time of a partial loss, the loss payment is determined by the following formula: Loss Payment = (Amount of insurance carried/Amount of insurance required) x Loss, less the deductible amount (if any).

see: coinsurance clause

cold call

Agency. Solicitation of a prospective insurance buyer without a prior appointment.

syn: cold canvassing

cold canvassing

Agency.

see: cold call

collapse

Property. To fall down or inward. Collapse of a building is excluded from most property policies, except for losses where the collapse of a building is due to an insured peril. Collapse does not include settling, cracking, shrinkage, bulging or expansion.

see: fallen building clause

collapse exclusion

Casualty. An exclusion found in the 1973 ISO comprehensive general liability rating program which was triggered when the rating classification for a particular risk was followed by a "C". For risks so designated, liability coverage for property damage arising from collapse claims was excluded by endorsement. Insureds could purchase coverage for this hazard for an additional charge.

see: blasting and explosion exclusion, underground exclusion, XCU exclusions

collateral

General. Assets that are used to secure a loan.

see: chattel, chattel mortgage, mortgage, real chattel, real estate

collateral assignment

Life/Property. The transfer of benefits or payments, from a life or property insurance policy to a creditor, as part of the security for a loan. The creditor would recover only that portion of the policy's proceeds equal to the creditor's remaining interest or value in the loan.

see: assignment, credit life insurance, mortgage insurance

collateral estoppel

General. A doctrine based on the theory that once an issue has been litigated, the same parties should not be permitted to litigate the same issue again. When an issue has been litigated, the determination is binding when the same issue arises in subsequent suits involving the same parties.

collateral protection insurance

Property. Insurance coverage for financial institutions, providing physical damage coverage on collateral held by the lender to support a loan. Collateral covered can include automobiles, trucks, vans, motorcycles, campers, motor homes, boats, etc. Coverage includes reimbursement for mechanical liens and repossession expense.

collateral source rule

General. A rule used in judicial proceedings which prohibits any reduction in a money award of damages to a plaintiff, merely because the plaintiff has other financial sources (health insurance, disability income insurance) to pay such benefits.

compare: indemnification

collect freight

Inland Marine/Ocean Marine. Freight for which the

© 1991 NILS Publishing Company

charges are not payable to the carrier unless and until the merchandise arrives at the port of discharge named in the bill of lading.

compare: prepaid freight; see: freight

collection guaranteed endorsement

General. The endorser of a note which contains the words "collection guaranteed" agrees to pay only after the note holder is unable to collect on a judgement, or after the maker or acceptor has become insolvent.

collective bargaining

Employee Benefits. Bargaining or negotiations between an employer and an employee's union which are held in good faith to resolve issues of mutual interest.

see: collectively bargained contribution plan, collectively bargained plan

collective bargaining agreement

Employee Benefits.

see: collective bargaining contract

collective bargaining contract

Employee Benefits/General. A contractual agreement between an employer(s) and union(s) over wages, benefits, hours and conditions of employment.

syn: collective bargaining agreement; see: collective bargaining, collectively bargained contribution plan, collectively bargained plan

collectively bargained contribution plan

Employee Benefits. A defined contribution pension plan under which the employer contributions have been established by a collective bargaining agreement, usually involving a union. Generally, such a plan covers the employees of several firms and is administered by a board of trustees made up of employer and union representatives.

see: negotiated contribution plan

collectively bargained plan

Employee Benefits. An agreement reached through collective bargaining that is approved by the United States Secretary of Labor.

compare: nonqualified plan

College of Insurance

Organizations. A fully-accredited educational institution in New York City which specializes in insurance education. It offers the following degrees: Master of Business Administration (MBA), Bachelor of Business Administration (BBA), Bachelor of Science (BS) and Associate in Occupational Studies (AOS). It also offers certificate courses in insurance and financial services.

see: Insurance Society of New York

collision

Automobile. The upset of a vehicle, or its impact with another vehicle or object. *Examples:* An auto hitting another vehicle, a tree, a telephone pole or a building; loss of driver control that results in an upset; or collision damage to unattended vehicles in parking lots.

collision clause

Ocean Marine.

see: running down clause

collision coverage

Automobile. An automobile physical damage coverage which insures against damage to the insured vehicle, caused by collision with another vehicle or object, or overturn of the vehicle.

compare: comprehensive coverage; see: collision, physical damage

collision damage waiver (CDW)

Automobile. A provision found in many auto rental contracts which allows the individual renting a vehicle to pay a fee in exchange for the rental company waiving its right to recover physical damage losses from the renter.

syn: limited damage waiver

color code

Loss Control. A system of coding by which piping, wiring and equipment are identified by various colors.

combination crime – separate limits

Crime. A crime coverage plan developed under the 1986 ISO crime program which is similar to a dishonesty, disappearance and destruction policy and uses a combination of crime forms A through J.

syn: crime plan 1; see: dishonesty, disappearance and destruction policy

combination crime – single limit

Crime. A crime coverage form developed under the 1986 ISO crime program which provides coverage similar to a blanket crime policy. Crime coverage Forms A, B, C and D are used with a single unit applying.

see: blanket crime policy

combined ratio

Insurer Operations. A formula used by insurance companies to relate income to claims, administration and dividend expenses. *Formula:* Combined Ratio = Loss Ratio + Expense Ratio + Dividend Ratio. The combined ratio measures the amount that an insurer must pay to cover claims and expenses per dollar of premium. *Examples:* A ratio of .98 means that an insurer has made two cents of underwriting profit. A ratio of 1.17 means an insurer has an underwriting loss of 17 cents for each dollar of premium received.

see: dividend ratio, expense ratio, loss ratio

© 1991 NILS Publishing Company

combined single limit (CSL)

Automobile/Casualty. A single dollar limit of liability applying to the total of damages for bodily injury and property damage, combined, resulting from one accident or occurrence.

syn: single limit; compare: split limits

combined stock and mutual insurer

Insurer Operations. An insurers who has issued capital stock, but which are controlled by the votes of both shareholders and participating policyholders.

combustible

Loss Control. A material or structure which will burn. It is a relative term, as many materials which will burn under one set of conditions will not burn in other situations.

compare: fire resistive; see: construction, fireproof

commercial aircraft

Aviation. Aircraft used principally in an insured's business, including student instruction, carrying passengers or freight, carrying for hire or reward, and rental to others.

compare: air taxi

commercial articles coverage

Inland Marine. Coverage on an open perils basis, designed for cameras and musical instruments owned by, or in the care, custody, or control of a commercial insured.

see: camera and musical instruments dealers coverage

commercial blanket bond

Crime. A bond providing a single amount of coverage for any one loss caused by dishonest acts of employees, regardless of the number of employees involved in the embezzlement or other activity.

see: blanket position bond

commercial domiciles

Insurer Operations. A term used to describe jurisdictions in which a foreign insurer writes more business than in its state of domicile.

compare: domiciliary state

commercial general liability form (CGL)

Casualty. A form introduced by ISO in 1986 to replace the comprehensive general liability policy. There are two basic coverage forms available under the new CGL program: An occurrence form *(ISO Form CG 00 01)* patterned after the 1973 CGL form, and a claims-made form *(ISO Form CG 00 02)*designed for risks having long-tail exposures. This latter form automatically includes the following coverages: (Coverage A) bodily injury and property damage liability; (Coverage B) personal and advertising injury liability and (Coverage C) medical payments. The new forms provide coverage that is not as broad as the old CGL, in that the new forms contain a nearly absolute pollution exclusion and a general aggregate limit.

see: aggregate limit, bodily injury and property damage liability, claims-made form, comprehensive general liability policy, faulty workmanship exclusion, fire damage legal liability, general aggregate limit, laser endorsement, medical payments, personal and advertising injury liability, products-completed operations insurance

commercial impracticability

General. A legitimate excuse for nonperformance, or breach of a sales contract. The "impracticability" excusing a seller of goods from performance must be caused by an unexpected contingency that affects or creates conditions that neither party assumed would continue, such as a natural disaster, unexpected war, or shortage of materials caused by an embargo.

see: act of God, force majeure coverage

commercial inland marine conditions

Inland Marine. A form attached to a commercial inland marine policy that adds general conditions concerning claims reporting and losses.

see: standard provisions

commercial invoice

Inland Marine/Ocean Marine. An invoice issued by the seller to the buyer which clearly specifies the merchandise being sold, its packaging, number of units shipped, its per-unit cost, and the total cost. Generally, it also contains the names of the seller and the buyer.

commercial lines

Insurer Operations. A general term used to refer to any type of insurance (property, casualty, health, life, etc.) purchased by businesses, organizations, institutions, governmental agencies or other commercial establishments to protect risks associated with their operations.

compare: personal lines; see: business insurance

commercial lines manual

Insurer Operations. A manual developed and maintained by the Insurance Services Office that contains rating divisions for most commercial insurance coverages (excluding workers' compensation and some specialty lines of insurance).

see: Insurance Services Office (ISO)

commercial package policy (CPP)

Insurer Operations. A package insurance plan that includes a wide range of essential coverages for a commercial enterprise. The package policy usually

© 1991 NILS Publishing Company

features common policy conditions, common declarations and two or more coverage sections.

commercial paper

General. Unsecured, short-term promissory notes of large firms, usually issued in denominations of $1 million or more. The rate of interest on commercial paper is typically somewhat below the prime rate of interest.

commercial speech

General. A term used to describe any communication issued or sponsored by a commercial business. Certain liability damages may be awarded in cases of comparative advertising (e.g., when it contains untrue or misleading statements) or product disparagement (trade libel).

see: **advertising injury, advertising injury coverage**

commission

Agency.
see: **agent's commission**
Reinsurance.
see: **ceding commission**

commissioner

Regulation.
see: **insurance commissioner**

Commissioners Standard Ordinary Table (CSO Table)

Life. A mortality table prepared for the National Association of Insurance Commissioners in the years 1938 to 1941. Most states have adopted it as the minimum standard for calculating nonforfeiture values and policy reserves.

see: **American Experience Table of Mortality**

commitment fee

General. The fee paid by a borrower to a lender for a formal line of credit.

see: **line of credit**

Committee for National Health Insurance (CNHI)

Organizations. Members: Representatives from the health care field, government, labor, academic, business, economic and citizen organizations. *Objectives:* Conduct research and promote education regarding the health care system in the United States. Promotes reform measures by enactment of a comprehensive national health insurance program. *Founded:* 1969. *Headquarters:* Washington, D.C.

Committee of Lloyd's

Insurer Operations. A committee established by Lloyd's of London, to assure that Lloyd's is properly run and that its reputation for integrity is maintained.

Comprised of sixteen members who are elected by Lloyd's underwriters and brokers, no member may be on the Committee for more than four years. A chairman and two deputy chairmen are elected to office, usually for two years each.

see: **Lloyd's of London**

common area

Property. Areas under the control of a landlord or condominium association, which serve the community or the public (such as shopping center parking areas, greenbelts, walkways, etc).

see: **condominium**

common carrier

Automobile/Inland Marine. An airline, railroad, or trucking company that furnishes transportation to the general public or carries property. Common carriers are regulated by the Interstate Commerce Commission or by state public utilities commissions, and are liable to shippers for the safe delivery of freight entrusted to them (except for losses arising from certain named perils).

compare: **contract carrier, private carrier;** see: **carrier**

common equity

Financial Planning/Risk Management. The sum of the value of common stock at par, the surplus of capital received (over par) from the sale of common (i.e., capital surplus), and retained earnings (i.e., earned surplus). "Retained earnings," as used in this context, equals net profits earned in all years, less dividends paid in all years.

see: **retained earnings**

common equity ratio

Financial Planning/Risk Management. Common equity divided by total capital. "Total capital" as used in this context includes long-term debt, preferred equity, and common equity.

see: **financial ratios**

common law

General. That part of the law which is subordinate to constitutional law and statutory law, comprised of appellate court decisions and that part of post-Renaissance English law reflecting local public policy. Common law is "unwritten" in that it has never been enacted into statute, although court decisions are often published.

syn: **case law;** see: **civil law**

common law defense

Workers' Compensation. Before workers' compensation laws were enacted, employers being sued by employees often defended themselves by claiming that the employee contributed to the accident; that the risk of injury was assumed by the employee when

81

common law defense — continued
he or she agreed to the employment; and that fellow workers were responsible. Such "common law defenses" are no longer available, because workers' compensation laws made state-mandated benefits the so-called "exclusive remedy" of injured workers, except in cases where an employer's gross negligence, criminal behavior or other aggravating factor can be shown.

see: **assumption of risk, contributory negligence, exclusive remedy, fellow servant rule**

common law liability

General. The liability of one party to another party that is not imposed by a specific statute, but rather which is imposed upon a party based on custom and usage established by the courts.

common law system

General. The basis of American and English law which began as unwritten customs recognized and enforced by local law enforcement bodies (courts); the foundation for the U.S. Constitution.

compare: **civil law**

common name statutes

General. Partnerships using a common or fictitious name (a name other than the surnames of all the partners) must register the name in a public office.

see: **partnership**

common policy conditions

Insurer Operations. A common conditions section under an Insurance Services Office commercial rating program applying to various coverage sections attached to the policy.

common shares outstanding

Financial Planning/Risk Management. The number of shares of common stock actually outstanding at the end of the calendar (or fiscal) year, excluding any shares held in the company's treasury. The figures for common shares outstanding in previous years are fully adjusted for all subsequent stock splits and stock dividends.

common stock to surplus

Insurer Operations. The market value of the common stock held in the insurance company's investment portfolio divided by statutory net worth.

common stock to total investment

Insurer Operations. The market value of the common stock portion of an insurance company's investment portfolio divided by the reported value of the total portfolio, expressed as a percentage.

common venture

Ocean Marine. The combination of a vessel and its cargo involved in an adventure.

see: **adventure, venture**

common wall

Loss Control.

see: **party wall**

communicable disease exclusion

Property. An endorsement added to homeowner's policies, providing that the "personal liability" and "medical payments to others" coverages do not apply to bodily injury or property damage arising from the transmission of communicable disease by an insured.

see: **acquired immune deficiency syndrome**

comparative negligence

General. The apportionment of damages when both the plaintiff and the defendant are at fault. Recovery by the plaintiff is lessened or increased, depending upon the degree of each party's negligence.

compare: **sine qua non rule**; see: **avoidable consequences, contributory negligence, negligence**

comparison statement

Agency. A document which compares benefits of an existing policy to those of a proposed new policy.

compensating balance

General. A required minimum noninterest-paying bank account balance that an organization must maintain with a commercial bank in order to obtain a loan or line of credit. The required bank balance is generally equal to 15 to 20 percent of the amount of loans outstanding. Compensating balances can raise the effective rate of interest on bank loans.

compensation agreement

Agency/Insurer Operations. An agreement between an employer and employee, insurer and agent, etc., fixing the rate of compensation to be paid.

compensatory damages

General. A form of money damages in a liability suit which compensate a plaintiff for such things as disability, disfigurement, and pain and suffering.

see: **damages**

competitive state funds

Workers' Compensation. Several states operate state funds in direct competition with private insurance companies. Employers in these states may purchase workers' compensation insurance from either a private insurer or the state fund.

compare: **monopolistic state fund**; see: **state fund**

© 1991 NILS Publishing Company

complaint

General. A document initiating a lawsuit that is filed by the plaintiff, stating his or her version of the facts, the defendant's alleged wrongdoing, and the amount of recovery sought.

see: **answer, counterclaim, petition, summons, summons and complaint**

completed operations coverage

Casualty. Liability insurance for injury or damage resulting from real or alleged faults in work completed by the insured. Completed operations insurance is purchased by commercial insureds who provide services (e.g., plumbers, painters, carpenters, etc.), whereas manufacturers require products liability insurance. In most insurance policy forms, products and completed operations coverages are combined.

see: **products-completed operations insurance, turnkey insurance**

completion bond

Surety.

see: **lender's bond**

compounding

Financial Planning. The mathematical process of determining the final value of a payment or series of payments after all interest has been applied.

compare: **discounting;** see: **continuous compounding, interest, present value**

compound interest

Financial Planning. An interest rate that is applicable when interest in succeeding periods is earned not only on the initial principal but also on the accumulated interest of prior periods.

compare: **simple interest;** see: **interest**

comprehensive coverage

Automobile. An automobile physical damage coverage on an "all-risks" basis, for damage to an insured vehicle by causes other than collision or and overturn – which are insured separately under collision coverage.

syn: **other-than-collision coverage;** compare: **collision coverage;** see: **physical damage**

Comprehensive Environmental Response, Compensation and Liability Act (CERCLA)

Casualty. Federal legislation enacted in 1980 which created a federal emergency authority to clean up spills and other releases of hazardous substances into the environment. Funds are raised through taxes on chemical and petroleum companies. The act has been interpreted to impose strict liability on generators, transporters, treaters and disposers of hazardous wastes, including all costs of removal or remedial action, any other necessary response expense, and damages to natural resources, with maximum liabilities of up to $50 million. This federal "superfund" act created a cradle-to-grave liability for hazardous waste, and established severe criminal penalties for illegal activities (such as dumping). The liability for cleanup expenses is joint and several on all parties in the chain of handling the substance.

syn: **Superfund;** see: **environmental impairment liability, pollutant, pollution exclusion**

comprehensive general liability policy (CGL)

Casualty. The Comprehensive General Liability Policy Form was initially developed by the Insurance Services Office (ISO) in 1940 and revised in 1943, 1955, 1966 and 1973. It was the first commercial liability form to combine several coverages under a single contract. Coverage included bodily injury and property damage liability insurance for operations at (or emanating from) all described premises. Any new locations or operations added during the policy year were automatically insured. Although some insurers still use this form, it has been largely replaced by the Commercial General Liability Form introduced by ISO in 1986.

compare: **commercial general liability form**

comprehensive glass insurance

Property. A policy which provides coverage on windows and plate glass, for breakage from any cause except war and fire.

see: **glass coverage form, glass insurance, glass insurance 50/50 basis**

comprehensive medical expense policy

Health. Medical expense coverage which combines hospital-surgical expense coverage and major medical coverage. These plans are usually provided on a group basis with a relatively small deductible, and they usually contain some coinsurance provision.

see: **hospital-surgical expense insurance, major medical insurance, coinsurance**

comprehensive personal liability insurance (CPL)

Casualty. Broad coverage for an individual's or family's liability for bodily injury or property damage. It is usually included within a homeowner's policy, but it can be written as a separate policy.

see: **homeowner's policy, personal umbrella**

compulsory insurance

General. Insurance in any form which is required by law.

compare: **voluntary insurance**

compulsory insurance laws

Automobile. Laws implemented in several states which require a vehicle owner or an operator of a vehicle to carry automobile liability insurance at least

© 1991 NILS Publishing Company

compulsory insurance laws — *continued*
equal to certain minimum limits before the vehicle can be registered or licensed.

compare: **financial responsibility laws**

compulsory retirement

Employee Benefits. Prior to the mid-1980s, many organizations required an employee to retire upon reaching a specified age. Such a practice has now been found to constitute age discrimination and is illegal.

syn: **automatic retirement, mandatory retirement**

computer fraud

Crime. The use of computerized systems and equipment to illegally transfer money, securities or other property.

see: **computer fraud coverage form, electronic and computer crime coverage**

computer fraud coverage form

Crime. A crime coverage form which provides coverage for loss of — and loss from damage to — money, securities and other property by computer fraud.

syn: **crime coverage form F; see: computer fraud, crime coverages, electronic and computer crime coverage**

concealment

General. A legal term for the intentional withholding of information of a material fact which is crucial in making a decision.

Insurer Operations. The intentional withholding of information that will result in an imprecise underwriting decision. Concealment of e.g. an existing medical condition by an insured when applying for insurance can be grounds for an insurer to void or reduce the benefits of an insurance policy.

see: **contribute-to-the-loss statute, election to avoid a policy, material misrepresentation**

Concerned Alliance of Responsible Employers (CARE)

Organizations. Members: Companies and trade associations interested in employee benefits. *Objectives:* Lobbies against mandated health insurance and parental leave legislation. *Founded:* 1987. *Headquarters:* Washington, D.C.

syn: **CARE Alliance**

concurrent causation

Property. California courts have held that under certain circumstances, property policies should cover losses in conjunction with an excluded peril (such as an earthquake or flood) when an insured peril (e.g., fire) ensues almost simultaneously. Most policies now explicitly exclude such coverage.

syn: **causal sequence; see: proximate cause**

concurrent insurance

Casualty. A term used to describe insurance coverage provided under two or more policies, all of which are identical except that they may vary in amount or policy periods.

compare: **nonconcurrency; see: layering, other insurance**

condition

Insurer Operations. An insurance policy provision specifying the rights and obligations of the insured or the insurer as respects the policy.

see: **policy conditions**

conditional delivery

Life. A condition making it clear that no coverage exists until the terms of that condition have been met. *Example:* Mailing a policy with an accompanying letter stating the policy will become effective when the applicant pays a stated policy fee to the agent.

compare: **conditional receipt**

conditional receipt

Health/Life. A written acknowledgement that a completed application and initial premium payment has been received for life or health insurance, and that coverage is provided until the company issues a policy or declines coverage.

compare: **conditional delivery**

conditional vesting

Employee Benefits. A pension plan participant's right to receive benefits from a contributory pension plan may have limitations as to when and to what extent an employee is vested. The participant's receipt of benefits will be based on these conditions.

see: **vesting**

condition precedent

General. An event that must occur before a duty of performance becomes binding. For example, an insured need not file a claim for a loss, but the insurer is not obligated to pay unless the insured gives proper notice and proof of the loss.

compare: **condition subsequent**

condition subsequent

General. A future event that may or may not occur after a contract becomes legally enforceable. The condition terminates certain rights under provisions of the contract.

compare: **condition precedent**

condominium

General. A form of real property ownership wherein there exists individual unit ownership in a multi-unit structure. Also used to refer to the building itself — a single structure or group of structures housing several residences or businesses, which share common walls,

84

© 1991 NILS Publishing Company

ceilings/floors, etc. Each condominium owner controls the interior of his or her unit, and owns a share interest in "common areas," while control of the common areas rests with the association.

compare: cooperative; see: common area

condominium association coverage

Property. An insurance policy designed to protect condominium association property held in common (such as the buildings) or personal property used to maintain or furnish common areas. Excludes coverage for personal property or improvements owned or used by, or in the care, custody, or control of an individual unit owner.

see: common area

condominium commercial unit owner's coverage

Property. An insurance form designed to protect the owner of a business or commercial condominium unit against loss or damage to furniture, fixtures, stock, improvements and alterations owned by the insured.

see: loss assessment coverage

condominium forms

Property. Special coverage forms, differing from forms, used for buildings and personal property, that contain specialized language to account for the unique legal characteristics of condominiums.

see: condominium commercial unit owner's coverage, condominium unit owner's form

condominium unit owner's form

Casualty/Property. An insurance policy designed to protect condominium unit owners, combining broad coverage on personal property (including coverage for damage to additions and/or alterations made by the insured inside the unit) with broad personal liability coverage. The policy provides that its coverage is in excess of any insurance purchased by the condominium association.

syn: homeowner's policy form 6; see: condominium commercial unit owner's coverage

Conference of Actuaries in Public Practice (CAPP)

Organizations. Members: Consulting actuaries, governmental actuaries. *Objectives:* To advance the knowledge of actuarial science, to promote and maintain high professional and ethical standards among its members, and to keep the public informed of the professional actuary in public practice. *Founded:* 1950. *Headquarters:* Itasca, IL. CAPP is affiliated with the American Academy of Actuaries and the Society of Actuaries.

Conference of Casualty Insurance Companies (CCIC)

Organizations. Members: Casualty insurance companies. *Objectives:* Sponsors educational programs for executives of member firms. *Founded:* 1930. *Headquarters:* Indianapolis, IN.

confidence level

Risk Management. An actuarial term for the degree of certainty about a forecast or calculation. *Example:* A 95 percent confidence level indicates that changes are 95 in 100 that the forecast will fall within a stipulated range.

conflagration

Property. A fire which destroys properties which in the aggregate represent extremely high values. A fire which spreads across streets or open spaces, or which is of such size that it is beyond the capacity of available fire fighting equipment.

conflict of laws

General. A legal term used to describe jurisdictional questions which arise as to the operation of state or federal laws in a given case.

see: center of influence, diversity jurisdiction

conformity with statute clause

Insurer Operations. A clause in many policies which broadly states that any terms of the policy which are not in conformity with local statutes are amended to conform, thereby enabling the insurer to use a standard, countrywide form.

consensual relationship

General. A relationship in which both parties agree. A person may want to give another person certain rights, but the other person is free to accept or reject the offered rights.

consent order

General. A court order banning an alleged unlawful trade practice that is issued before a hearing is held. The party receiving the order may accept the entry of the order, waiving the right to appeal, and the effect is the same as if it had been issued after a formal hearing.

see: enjoin

consequential damage

Property. Damage to or destruction of property from a peril that is not the immediate cause of loss. *Example:* A burglar destroys records of accounts receivable during the burglary, causing a loss because the accounts cannot be collected. An indirect loss (i.e., a business interruption loss, extra expense, lost rent, etc.) arising out of an insured's inability to use property damaged by another peril.

syn: indirect damage, indirect loss, special damage; compare: direct loss

85

© 1991 NILS Publishing Company

consideration

consideration

General. One of the elements needed to form a contract. The exchange of something of value for a promise of performance.

see: contract, past consideration

Insurer Operations. For purposes of the insurance transaction, the consideration is the premium paid by the insured to the insurer for the insurer's promise to pay claims in accordance with the terms of the policy provisions.

consignee

Inland Marine/Ocean Marine. The party that is to receive the goods listed on a bill of lading.

compare: consignor

consignment

Property. The entrusting of goods by an individual or company to another for care or sale.

consignment insurance

Inland Marine.

see: in-trust policy

consignor

Inland Marine/Ocean Marine. The party that initiates the shipment of the goods listed on a bill of lading.

syn: shipper; compare: consignee

Consolidated Omnibus Budget Reconciliation Act of 1985 (COBRA)

Health. Federal legislation – a major part of which addressed health insurance – adopted in 1985 which applies to firms with more than 20 employees. COBRA provided that 1) Employees are allowed to remain covered under their group medical plan for 18 months after leaving their job. Employees must pay their own premium, but the rates will remain the same as for others in the group; 2) A group medical plan cannot require Medicare to be the primary provider for participants 70 years of age and over, and 3) Medicare was expanded to include state and local government employees.

consolidated tax return

Financial Planning. An income tax return that combines the income statements of several affiliated firms.

consolidation condition

Property. In a unification or merger of properties, this provision in a property insurance policy extends coverage automatically to the new premises, provided the insured notifies the insurer of the acquisition within thirty days and pays the additional premium.

consolidation endorsement

Ocean Marine. An endorsement to an open cargo policy which provides coverage on merchandise while in transit to, and while at a common consolidation point for the purpose of preparing or consolidating the merchandise for transit.

see: open cargo policy

consolidation of plans

General.

see: merger of plans

construction

Property. In fire underwriting, the types of materials used in the building and roof of the structure owned or occupied by the insured. Construction types include fire resistive, semi-fire resistive and combustible, and depend on whether steel, concrete, masonry or wood materials were used. Other construction factors which the fire underwriter will consider include the number of fire divisions in the building; the adequacy of electrical circuits for the occupancy; the number of stories; the age of the building; the type of heating system and fuel; etc.

compare: exposure, occupancy, protection; see: brick construction, brick veneer construction, fire resistive construction, frame construction, joisted masonry construction, masonry noncombustible construction, mill construction, modified fireresistive construction, ordinary construction

constructive receipt

Regulation/Risk Management. Under IRS rules, the constructive receipt of money occurs when an individual or entity has control over the disposition of money, when the present value of money is specifically set aside for use of the individual or entity, or when the funds are available to the individual or entity. When a structured settlement is used in settlement of a claim, periodic payments made to a claimant under IRS Code section 104 (a)(2) can be excluded from the claimant's gross income so long as the plaintiff has neither actual nor constructive receipt of the sum spent to fund those future payments.

see: structured settlement

constructive total loss

Ocean Marine. A constructive total loss occurs when the damage or destruction of the cargo is not total, but the cost of salvaging the cargo would be greater than the cargo's remaining value.

see: actual total loss, total loss, total loss only clause

consular invoice

Inland Marine/International/Ocean Marine. A special invoice that is required by some countries to control imported merchandise that must be notarized or validated by the country's consulate prior to shipment.

Consumer and Professional Relations

© 1991 NILS Publishing Company

Division of Health Insurance Association of America

Organizations. Members: Health insurance companies. *Objectives:* Provide information and technical assistance to hospitals, physicians and allied health care groups. *Founded:* 1946. *Headquarters:* Washington, D.C.

consumer credit compliance insurance

Financial Guarantee Insurance. Insurance for banks and savings and loans, which pays judgments, defense costs, and plaintiff's attorney fees from class or individual actions brought against the financial institution for alleged non-compliance with the Federal Consumer Credit Regulations, Truth in Lending Act, Fair Credit Billing Act, Equal Credit Opportunity Act, or Electronic Fund Transfer requirements.

Consumer Credit Insurance Association (CCIA)

Organizations. Members: Insurers underwriting consumer credit insurance in areas of life, accident and health and property insurance. *Objectives:* Bestowing the Arthur J. Morris Award for outstanding contributions to the consumer credit insurance industry. *Founded:* 1951. *Headquarters:* Chicago, IL.

container

Inland Marine/Ocean Marine. Large boxes made of steel, aluminum or fiberglass-reinforced plywood in which merchandise is shipped. They are made of standard lengths of 8, 20, 25, 35, 40, and 45 feet; each container has an individual identifying number assigned to it.

containerized cargo

Ocean Marine. Cargo shipped in large containers up to 45 feet long which can be easily on-and off-loaded on trucks, trains and ships.

compare: **break bulk cargo, bulk cargo;** see: **container**

container seal

Inland Marine/Ocean Marine. A steel, aluminum or plastic device affixed to the locking mechanism of a shipping container door, to protect against unauthorized opening. The seal, which is designed to readily show signs of tampering, is attached by the party packing the container.

container seal number

Inland Marine/Ocean Marine. Each container seal has a unique identifying number assigned to it which should be noted on all documents issued in conjunction with a shipment. In addition, the container number to which the seal is attached is noted.

contents rate

Property. Fire insurance rates are usually developed separately for contents contained in buildings, and the buildings and/or structures themselves. The contents rate is used to develop rates for stock, furniture and fixtures, equipment, electronic data procesing equipment and accounts receivable. Rates usually apply per 100 dollars of insurance value. Separate rates apply to fire, extended coverages, vandalism and malicious mischief, sprinkler leakage, earthquake, earthquake sprinkler leakage and "all-risks" coverage.

see: **building rate**

contested case

General. Under the Federal Administrative Procedure Act (FAPA), every party in a contested case has the right to appear in person or be represented by counsel at proceedings before federal agencies.

see: **Administrative Procedure Act**

contingent beneficiary

Life. The individual entitled to the proceeds of a life insurance policy if the primary beneficiary does not survive the insured.

syn: **second beneficiary, secondary beneficiary;** see: **beneficiary clause, irrevocable beneficiary, primary beneficiary, revocable beneficiary**

contingent business income coverage

Property. A form of business income insurance covering an insured's loss of income caused by a loss at a specific, nonowned location on which the insured depends for operating his or her business. The loss must have been caused by an insured peril. *Example:* A key supplier (or customer) suffers a major fire, making it impossible for the insured to continue to manufacture (or sell) its products at previous levels.

syn: **business income form dependent properties;** see: **business income coverage form, dependent property, power interruption insurance, tax interruption policy**

contingent fee agreement

General. A contract between a client and attorney by which the attorney is paid a fee only if there is a recovery by judgment or settlement. Nearly all personal injury cases are handled in this way. The fee is usually a percentage of the recovery, most commonly one-third of the award.

see: **defense costs, retainer**

contingent liability

Casualty. Liability incurred because of the negligence of a person or independent contractor engaged by the insured to perform work. The insured can be found liable for negligent acts by the individual or by the

© 1991 NILS Publishing Company

contingent liability — *continued*

contractor to the extent that the insured gave direction to either the individual or contractor.

syn: imputed liability, vicarious liability; compare: acts of independent contractors; see: agency, respondeat superior

contingent liability from operation of building laws endorsement

Property. An optional endorsement to a property policy covering a building, to insure against loss caused by the enforcement of building laws. When rebuilding a damaged structure, laws may require the demolition of all or part of the undamaged portions of an insured building; repairing, remodeling or rebuilding to conform with codes that have changed since the building was first constructed which now require more expensive materials or installation. The insurable value of the undamaged portions of the property is covered by this endorsement. Under the ISO Commercial Property Program this coverage has been incorporated into the ordinance or law coverage endorsement (*ISO Form CP 04 05*).

see: ordinance or law coverage endorsement

continuing care facilities

Health.

see: life care facilities

continuing expenses

Property. Expenses that continue during a business interruption, such as insurance, taxes, payroll of key employees, and debt service.

see: business income coverage form

continuous compounding

Financial Planning. Interest that is added continuously (daily) rather than at specific points in time.

see: compound interest, discounting, interest

continuum of care services

Health. Comprehensive programs of home and inpatient care which meet the physical, psychological, spiritual and social needs of families and patients during the final stages of an illness.

contract

General. A legally enforceable promise formed by a mutual agreement between two or more parties creating a specific obligation to perform an obligation. Elements to form a contract are the need for a legal consideration, competent parties, a formal offer, acceptance of the offer within a reasonable time, and a legal purpose.

compare: accommodation; see: acceptance, adhesion, agreement, aleatory contract, bilateral contract, blanket contract, chose in action, collective bargaining contract, consideration, consensual relationship, contract law, contract of

adhesion, discharge of contracts, doctrine of unconscionability, executed contract, executory contract, genuine assent, group contract, guaranteed investment contract, implied contract, incidental contract, individual contract, insurance contract, land contract, modification of contract, novation, offer, optionally renewable contract, personal contract, privity of contract, quasi-contract, unconscionable contract, unilateral contract, valid contract; Fr: contrat; Gr: Vertrag; Sp: contrato

contract bond

Surety. A surety bond which guarantees the faithful performance of a contract, including the payment for all labor and material involved with completing the contract. In some instances, two bonds are used, one to cover performances and the other to cover payment of labor and material.

compare: payment bond, performance bond; see: lender's bond

contract carrier

Automobile/Inland Marine. A shipping firm that enters into specific written agreements with one or more parties to carry their goods, and generally does not accept business from other parties.

compare: common carrier, private carrier; see: carrier

contract law

General. A form of civil law which involves written or oral agreements between two or more parties for some specific promise or action.

see: civil law, common law, contract, criminal law

contract of adhesion

General. A contract drawn by one party with the other party assenting to the terms and conditions with little opportunity to alter the agreement's words or terms.

see: contract, strict construction

Insurer Operations. An insurance contract is a contract of adhesion as it is drafted by the insurer without input from the other party.

compare: manuscript policy, modification of contract; see: adhesion, unilateral contract

contract of carriage

Inland Marine/Ocean Marine.

see: affreightment

contractors equipment

Inland Marine. Mobile equipment, tools and implements of a building, road or bridge contractor, including excavating and grading machinery, cranes, hoists and derricks.

see: mobile equipment

© 1991 NILS Publishing Company

contractors equipment floater

Inland Marine. An inland marine form covering contractors equipment on an "all-risks" or specified perils basis. Loss or damage due to wear and tear, use of the equipment, and for war and nuclear damage is excluded.

see: contractors equipment, mobile equipment

contractual liability insurance

Casualty. Policies covering losses incurred by the insured's express or implied assumption of liability under a contract.

see: assumed liability policy, broad form liability endorsement, incidental contract

contribute-to-the-loss statute

Regulation. When misstatements of fact or breaches of warranty are material contributions to a loss, some states permit insurance companies to deny payment of claims resulting from the insured's loss.

see: concealment, material misrepresentation, misrepresentation

contributing location

Property. A business that furnishes materials or services upon which an insured depends to conduct business. Coverage for the exposure can be purchased under a contingent business income form.

syn: contributing property; compare: dependent property; see: contingent business income coverage

contributing property

Property.

see: contributing location

contribution by limits

Insurer Operations. When two or more insurers' policies cover at the same level (primary or excess), under this concept each insurer pays the same proportion of the loss that its limit bears to the total of all applicable insurance. Paid losses will never exceed the insurer's limit of insurance.

compare: contribution by share; see: limit of liability rule

contribution by share

Insurer Operations. Under this concept, when two or more insurers' policies cover at the same level (primary or excess), each insurer contributes an equal amount to the loss settlement until the loss is paid, or until each insurer has exhausted its limits of insurance, whichever comes first.

compare: contribution by limits

contribution clause

Property. An insurance clause providing that when more than one policy covers a loss, insurers will share the loss proportionally. The clause is most often associated with business income forms.

syn: other insurance clause; see: contribution by limits, contribution by share

contributory group insurance

Employee Benefits. A group insurance plan requiring employees to contribute toward the cost of coverage. Statutes vary from state to state, but generally a minimum of 75% of eligible employees are required to participate in this type of plan.

compare: noncontributory group insurance, split dollar insurance

contributory negligence

General. A plaintiff's conduct which falls below the standard to which he or she should conform for their own protection and which is a legally contributing factor with the defendant's negligence in causing the plaintiff's injury.

Workers' Compensation. An early common law defense that originated in England, holding that one who negligently harms another cannot be found liable if the injured party was in the slightest degree negligent. Eventually, this defense was used to defend employers in suits brought by injured workers, where it could be shown that the employee's own negligence contributed to a work accident and resulting injury. Predates workers' compensation laws.

see: Butterfield v. Forrester, common law defense, doctrine of last clear chance, negligence, sine qua non rule

contributory value

Ocean Marine. The value of property saved as the result of a general average act during an ocean voyage which forms the basis for determining each party's general average contribution.

see: general average

controller

General. The chief accounting officer of a business enterprise or institution, who usually reports to the chief financial officer.

compare: chief financial officer, treasurer

convention blank

Insurer Operations/Regulation.

see: annual statement

conversion

General. The intentional, unlawful use of property to the detriment of the person entitled to the property.

Health/Life. The privilege of changing from one policy form to another (e.g., from group health to individual health), usually without evidence of insurability or without a medical examination.

© 1991 NILS Publishing Company

conversion, embezzlement, or secretion exclusion

Automobile. An older version of the current "false pretense" exclusion, found in commercial auto coverage forms.

see: trick and device exclusion

conversion fund

Employee Benefits. An unallocated employee benefit plan fund maintained by an employer trustee or an insurance company to purchase annuities which supplement annuities purchased through individual insurance contracts.

syn: auxiliary fund

converted losses

Automobile/Casualty/Workers' Compensation. A loss factor used in retrospective rating and retention plans which is developed by multiplying incurred losses by a loss conversion factor. *Formula:* Converted Losses = Incurred Losses X Loss Conversion Factor (LCF). *Example:* $100,000 (Incurred Losses) X 1.20 (LCF) = $120,000 (Converted Losses).

see: incurred losses, loss conversion factor

convertible bond

Financial Planning. A bond that, under the terms of the contract, may be exchanged for equity securities – usually from the same company.

see: bonds

cooperative

Property. An apartment building owned by a group of individuals (who are usually residents), each of whom do not own their individual units, but who have ownership interest in the corporation, or cooperative association that owns all of the units. Members of the cooperative are ensured a right to a perpetual lease to occupy a specific unit.

compare: condominium

coordination of benefits (COB)

Health. A provision contained in group health insurance policies which provides that the insurer will not pay benefits covered by other policies, or that coverage will be provided in a specific sequence when more than one policy covers the claim.

see: nonduplication of benefits, other insurance clause, proration of benefits

co-payment

Health. Under a health maintenance organization (HMO) or preferred provider organization (PPO) program, the payment that a member must pay in addition to their premiums. *Example:* A $3 flat fee for each visit regardless of how expensive the services rendered may be. Or a $2 fee for each prescription, regardless of the actual cost.

compare: percentage participation

corporate officers

Casualty. A term used to refer to the directors and executive officers of a corporation.

see: chief executive officer, chief financial officer, chief operating officer, directors & officers liability insurance, inside directors, treasurer

corporate risk

Risk Management.

see: business risk

corporation

General. A legal entity chartered by a government grant to act as a single enterprise although constituted by one or more persons and endowed with various rights and duties including the capacity of succession. This entity has three distinctive characteristics: limited liability, easily transferred ownership rights and continuing existence.

see: articles of incorporation, bylaws, charter, close corporations, de facto corporation, intra vires, perpetual succession, person, ultra vires

correlation

Risk Management. An actuarial term for the degree of interaction between two or more attributes of a group of elements.

corridor deductible

Health. A major medical policy deductible applied in the transitional area between basic coverage and the major medical expense coverage. Benefits are paid by the basic health policy first; when these benefits are exhausted, the corridor deductible is applied before benefits under the major medical plan are paid. The corridor deductible is usually a fixed dollar amount per loss.

see: basic medical expense, major medical insurance

cosmetic surgery

Health. Plastic surgery undertaken with the primary purpose of improving an individual's appearance, usually on an elective basis. Cosmetic surgery is generally excluded from health insurance policies, except when it is necessary due to an accident or to correct a congenital anomaly.

see: elective surgery

cost of capital

Risk Management. The discount rate that is used in the capital budgeting process. The cost, to a business,

90

of their funds (i.e., prime rate, interest rate on corporate bonds, etc.).

see: **capital budgeting**

cost of goods sold

Risk Management. The section of a financial statement which includes all the purchasing or production costs and expenses, both direct and indirect, of the merchandise sold during that period. These expenses include: raw materials, direct and indirect labor costs, plant costs (such as depreciation), electricity, water and shipping costs. *Formula:* Cost of Goods Sold = (All Goods Bought + Goods in Inventory at Beginning of the Period) - Goods in Inventory at the End of the Period.

cost-of-living variable annuity plan

Life. A variable annuity where the plan's benefits are tied to a specific index, such as the Consumer Price Index.

see: **variable annuity**

Council on Employee Benefits (CEB)

Organizations. Members: Employers interested in employee benefits. *Objectives:* Exchanges ideas, information and statistics on employee benefits. *Founded:* 1946. *Headquarters:* Akron, OH.

counterclaim

General. A defendant wishing to file a cause of action against the plaintiff answers the plaintiff's claims with a "counterclaim."

see: **answer, complaint**

countersignature

Agency/Insurer Operations. The signature of a licensed agent or broker, required to validate an insurance contract.

see: **countersignature law, nonresident agent, resident agent**

countersignature law

Agency/Insurer Operations. A law found in most states, requiring that all insurance policies covering persons or property in their state be countersigned by a licensed agent, broker or other resident representative of the insurer.

see: **countersignature, nonresident agent**

county clerks and recorders errors & omissions insurance

Casualty. Insurance coverage which indemnifies county clerks and recorders against claims from breach of official duties made against the insured by reason of negligent acts, errors or omissions committed or alleged to have been committed by the insured or members of the insured's staff. The coverage is required by legislation in some states.

see: **public entity insurance**

coupon bond

Financial Planning. A bond containing detachable coupons to be given to the issuer or agent when payments of principal or interest are due.

see: **bonds**

course of construction insurance (COC)

Property.

see: **builders risk insurance**

court bond

Surety. A bond required of a party in a lawsuit (litigant), as a condition of enabling the litigant to pursue his or her rights in court.

syn: **litigation bond;** see: **judicial bond**

court of equity

General. A term used to refer to a trial court with jurisdiction in cases of equity, as distinguished from a trial court having jurisdiction in the common law. Generally, common law and equity courts have merged into a single form of "civil court" using rules of civil procedure.

covenant

General. A protective clause contained in an agreement, designed to protect the interests of one or the other party. In loan agreements, covenants may protect the lender's interests by imposing limits on total indebtedness, restrictions on dividends, minimum current ratio, restrictions on self-insurance or requirements to purchase certain types of insurance.

covenant of good faith and fair dealing

General.

see: **good faith**

coverage

Insurer Operations. The protection afforded by insurance.

coverage A

Property.

see: **homeowner's policy – property coverage**

Casualty.

see: **commercial general liability form, homeowner's policy**

Workers' Compensation. The portion of a workers' compensation policy providing benefits required by the workers' compensation laws of an employer's state.

see: **additional medical, workers' compensation insurance**

coverage B

Workers' Compensation. That portion of a workers' compensation policy that provides employers liability coverage.

see: **employers liability insurance**

91

© 1991 NILS Publishing Company

coverage B – continued
Property.
   see: homeowner's policy – property coverage
Casualty.
   see: commercial general liability form, home-owner's policy

coverage C
Casualty.
   see: commercial general liability form
Property.
   see: homeowner's policy – property coverage

coverage D
Property.
   see: homeowner's policy – property coverage

coverage E
Casualty.
   see: homeowner's policy – liability coverage

coverage extension
Property. An extension of the coverage provided by a policy that may be applied to a specific type of loss, which is in addition to the amount indicated in the policy declarations. Some extensions – such as providing limited extra expense coverage in addition to a fire loss – increase the total amount of insurance. *Example:* Many commercial property forms add an off-premises extension of up to two percent of the amount of insurance applicable to each item of insurance – but not exceeding $5,000 – to be applied to each item. Other additional coverage provisions extend a percentage of the main structure limit to appurtenant structures and fences. Such additional coverage usually does not increase the total amount of insurance provided by the policy.
   syn: additional coverage; compare: additional extended coverage, extended coverages; see: appurtenant structures, debris removal clause, off-premises coverage

coverage F
Casualty.
   see: homeowner's policy – liability coverage

coverage form
Insurer Operations. Those portions of an insurance policy in which the insuring agreement and exclusions are contained.
   see: basic form, coverage part

coverage G
Casualty.
   see: homeowner's policy – liability coverage

coverage part
Property. That portion of an insurance policy (including endorsements) that indicates the types of perils and property that are insured.
   see: coverage form

coverage territory
Insurer Operations.
   see: geographical limitation

coverage trigger
Casualty. The event that activates coverage under a liability policy. The trigger varies between an occurrence and claims-made policy.
   see: claims-made trigger, Keene Doctrine, occurrence trigger

covered boiler & machinery property
Property. Any property that is owned by the named insured, or that is in the named insured's care, custody, or control and for which the named insured is legally liable. Boiler and machinery insurance is intended to cover damage to any property of the named insured as long as a "covered cause of loss" is responsible.
   see: object

covered injury
Workers' Compensation. An injury or disease covered under a workers' compensation policy and therefore eligible for benefits.
   see: arising out of and in the course of employment

covered instruments
Crime. A term used in crime insurance policies to describe any written promise or order requiring the insured to pay a certain sum such as a check, promissory note, bill of exchange, or similar document. Coverage applies to losses caused by forgery of a payee's name, falsifying documents and altering documents.

cratering
Casualty/Property.
   see: blowout and cratering

credibility
Risk Management. An actuarial term for the input data used in a calculation. High credibility indicates sufficient input data is available and that the dispersion of data from the mean of the distribution falls within a narrow range.
   see: dispersion, distribution curve, mean

credit balance
General. An amount of money owed to an individual

© 1991 NILS Publishing Company

or organization due to overpayment on an invoice, refund, or other adjustment.

compare: debit balance; see: balance

credit bureaus errors & omissions insurance

Casualty. Insurance coverage that protects credit bureaus against third party claims alleging "personal injury" arising from errors or omissions in the conduct of their operations. Covered acts would include wrongly assigning a bad credit rating to an individual.

credit health insurance

Health. Disability or health insurance sold by a lender to cover payment of a debt or an installment loan, in the event the debtor is disabled.

syn: credit insurance; see: credit life insurance, creditor beneficiary, mortgage insurance

credit insurance

Financial Guarantee Insurance. A guarantee to manufacturers, wholesalers and service organizations that they will be paid for goods shipped or services rendered. It applies to that part of working capital which is represented by accounts receivable.

see: lease payment insurance

Health/Life.

see: credit health insurance, credit life insurance

credit life insurance

Life. Life insurance coverage on a borrower designed to repay the balance of a loan in the event the borrower dies before the loan is repaid.

syn: creditor life insurance; see: collateral assignment, credit health insurance, creditor beneficiary, group credit life insurance, mortgage insurance

credit line

Risk Management.

see: line of credit

creditor

General. An individual or organization owed money from others (debtors).

compare: debtor

creditor beneficiary

Health/Life. In credit health and life insurance, the creditor is named as beneficiary, and will receive the balance due on a loan in the event of death or disability.

see: credit health insurance, credit life insurance, group credit life insurance

creditor life insurance

Life.

see: credit life insurance

credit report

Insurer Operations.

see: retail credit report

crime

Crime. A violation of law or an offense against the government. "Crime" and "misdemeanor" are synonymous terms; however, "crime" usually denotes a more serious offense.

see: felony, misdemeanor

crime coverage form A

Crime.

see: employee dishonesty crime form

crime coverage form B

Crime.

see: forgery or alteration coverage form

crime coverage form C

Crime.

see: money and securities broad form insurance, theft

crime coverage form D

Crime.

see: robbery and safe burglary form

crime coverage form E

Crime.

see: premises burglary coverage form

crime coverage form F

Crime.

see: computer fraud coverage form

crime coverage form G

Crime.

see: extortion coverage form

crime coverage form H

Crime.

see: premises theft and outside robbery coverage form

crime coverage form I

Crime.

see: lessees of safe deposit boxes coverage form

crime coverage form J

Crime.

see: securities deposited with others coverage form

crime coverage form K

Crime.

see: liability for guests' property – safe deposit coverage form

© 1991 NILS Publishing Company

crime coverage form L

Crime.
see: liability for guests' property – premises coverage form

crime coverage form M

Crime.
see: safe depository liability coverage form

crime coverage form N

Crime.
see: safe depository direct loss coverage form

crime coverages

Crime. A broad term which applies to insurance for losses involving the taking of money, securities and other property by an individual(s). Included within this term are employee dishonesty, forgery, theft, robbery, burglary and fraud insurance coverages.

see: bank burglary and robbery insurance, blanket crime policy, blanket fidelity bond, blanket position bond, computer fraud coverage form, crime coverage forms A, B, C, D, E, F, G, H, I, J, K, L, M and N, depositor's forgery bond, employee dishonesty crime form, extortion coverage form, forgery or alteration coverage form, hotel safe deposit box liability, innkeepers legal liability, lessees of safe deposit boxes coverage form, liability for guests' property – premises coverage form, liability for guests' property – safe deposit coverage form, mercantile open-stock burglary insurance, mercantile robbery insurance, mercantile safe burglary insurance, money, premises burglary coverage form, premises theft and outside robbery coverage form, property other than money and securities, robbery and safe burglary form, safe depository direct loss coverage form, safe depository liability coverage form, securities, securities deposited with others coverage form, storekeepers broad form, storekeepers burglary and robbery, theft, disappearance and destruction of money and securities coverage form

crime plan 1

Crime.
see: combination crime – separate limits

crime plan 2

Crime. A single limit, combination crime coverage plan withdrawn by ISO in 1988.

crime plan 3

Crime.
see: storekeepers broad form

crime plan 4

Crime.
see: storekeepers burglary and robbery

crime plan 5

Crime.
see: office burglary and robbery insurance

crime plan 6

Crime.
see: guests' property – safe deposit box

criminal law

General. Laws enacted to prevent harm to society. Under criminal law, the government initiates the legal proceedings and seeks redress on behalf of the public, while under civil law, an individual seeks his or her own redress through legal proceedings.

compare: civil law, civil liability, common law, contract law

Cromie rule

Insurer Operations. A guide used to apportion losses among nonconcurrent policies.

see: nonconcurrency, nonconcurrent apportionment rules

crop-hail insurance

Property. Specialized property insurance coverage underwritten by National Crop Insurance Services for farmers. While hail damage to crops is the basic peril covered, the coverage may be written for perils ranging from basic named perils to open perils, depending on the crop and the state in which it is grown.

syn: hail insurance; see: crop insurance, hail, National Crop Insurance Services

Crop-Hail Insurance Actuarial Association (CHIAA)

Organizations. Members: Insurers covering agricultural crops against hail damage. *Objectives:* Serves as a statistical and rating organization and statistical agents. *Founded:* 1947. *Headquarters:* Chicago, IL.

crop insurance

Property. Growing crops are subject to numerous perils, such as unfavorable weather conditions, hail, fire, floods, insects, and disease. Policies are written covering one or more of these perils, either through the Federal Crop Insurance Corporation or private insurers. Generally, coverage is effective 24 hours after an application is received by a company. When the crop is harvested, the insurance terminates; coverage is reduced pro rata as harvesting progresses.

see: American Association of Crop Insurers, crop-hail insurance, Crop-Hail Insurance Actuarial Association, Crop Insurance Research Bureau, Federal Crop Insurance Corporation,

© 1991 NILS Publishing Company

hail, multi-peril crop insurance, National Association of Crop Insurance Agents, National Crop Insurance Association, National Crop Insurance Services, open perils crop insurance

Crop Insurance Research Bureau (CIRB)

Organizations. Members: Crop insurance companies and other organizations related to the crop insurance field. *Objectives:* Supports research through joint sponsorship of programs. Increases the accuracy of hail loss settlements. Monitors the Federal Crop Insurance Corporation. *Founded:* 1964. *Headquarters:* Indianapolis, IN.

cross-cut

Loss Control. A mining tunnel, generally running horizontally and at right angles to a vertical shaft.

see: adit, raise

cross purchase plan

Life. A plan where each partner or stockholder in a closely held corporation purchases life insurance policies on each of the other partners or stockholders, in amounts sufficient to purchase the partners' or stockholders' interests in the concern in the event of their death.

see: key employee insurance, partnership insurance

cryogenics

Loss Control. The science that deals with the production of very low temperatures and their effect on the properties of matter.

cumulative dividend

Financial Planning. A preferred stock dividend that if not paid, accrues as an obligation which must be paid before dividends to common stockholders can be declared.

see: dividend, preferred stock

cumulative voting

General. A method of shareholder voting whereby each shareholder has the right to vote with all of his or her shares multiplied by the number of corporate directors when choosing a single director or group of directors. *Example:* A shareholder with 500 shares of a corporation that is electing three directors can cast 1,500 votes for one director or split the 1,500 votes among two or three directors.

see: proxy, share of stock

cure

Ocean Marine. Medical expenses paid by a shipowner to a seaman disabled by illness or injury. Such payments are made until recovery, or until the individual's condition has stabilized.

see: cure, Jones Act, maintenance, seaman's remedies, wages, maintenance and cure

current assets

General. Cash or other assets that are expected to be (or could be) converted into cash or consumed within twelve months or within an organization's normal operating cycle. Current assets include marketable securities, notes receivable, accounts receivable, inventory and prepaid items.

syn: quick assets; see: accounts receivable, assets, current ratio, prepaid expense

current liabilities

General. Liabilities that must be satisfied within the next 12 months. Current liabilities include trade accounts payable, taxes, wage accruals, current installments on long-term debt, and notes payable.

see: current ratio, liability

currently insured status

Employee Benefits. A Social Security provision which provides that the dependents of a deceased individual who has not reached fully insured status can obtain survivor benefits.

see: fully insured status

current ratio

Risk Management. A financial analysis ratio which indicates the liquidity or ability of an organization to pay current bills. *Formula:* Current Ratio = Total Current Assets/Total Current Liabilities. The higher the current ratio, the better an organization's debt paying ability.

see: current assets, current liabilities, financial ratios, financial underwriting

curtain wall

Loss Control/Property. An exterior non-bearing wall more than one story in height, usually supported by the structural frame, which protects from weather, sound or fire.

see: construction, panel wall

custodian

Crime. In crime policies, a "custodian" can be the named insured or any partner or employee of the named insured who has custody of insured property. However, a watchperson retained by the named insured and whose only duties are to have custody of the property inside the premises is excluded from the definition.

customs bond

Surety. A bond which guarantees the payment of import duties and taxes and also guarantees compliance with regulations governing the import of merchandise into the United States from countries.

syn: customs house bond; see: bonded shipments, bonded warehouse, federal bond

© 1991 NILS Publishing Company

customs broker

Inland Marine/Ocean Marine. A firm that specializes in the clearance of imported merchandise and that arranges subsequent inland transit, documentation and payment of all related charges.

see: freight forwarder

customs brokers and freight forwarders errors & omissions insurance

Casualty. Insurance coverage for customs brokers which protects them against suits arising out of negligence in arranging for the clearance and forwarding of imports on behalf of the importer.

customs entry form

Inland Marine/Ocean Marine. A U.S. customs form required for all merchandise entering the country indicating the country of origin, a description of the merchandise, and the estimated duty.

see: customs bond, import

customs house bond

Surety.

see: customs bond

cut-off

Loss Control. Masonry or brick division walls – which may or may not have doors or openings – that are designed to limit the area exposed to a fire.

see: fire division, fire wall

cut-off cancellation

Reinsurance. A reinsurance contract termination provision, stipulating that the reinsurer shall not be liable for a loss resulting from occurrences after the termination date.

compare: run-off cancellation;
see: cancellation

cut-off point

General. In the capital budgeting process, the rate of return established by business management as the minimum rate that will be accepted on investment opportunities.

see: capital budgeting

cut-through clause

Reinsurance. A clause in a reinsurance contract, stipulating that if the ceding (primary) company becomes insolvent, the reinsurer will be liable for its share of the loss directly to the policyholder, rather than to a liquidator.

compare: insolvency clause; see: cut-through endorsement

cut-through endorsement

Insurer Operations/Reinsurance. An endorsement attached to a primary insurer's policy, making a reinsurer liable for its share of loss directly to the policyholder should the ceding (primary) company become insolvent.

see: cut-through clause

cyclone

Property.

see: hurricane

© 1991 NILS Publishing Company

D

daily report (DR)

Agency/Insurer Operations. A written document which includes important information on a specific insurance policy in a shortened form, for use by an insurer, agent or broker.

damage from strikers insurance

Property. A form of commercial insurance coverage which indemnifies employers against loss due to sabotage by strikers.

damages

General. A court-awarded amount, claimed or awarded as compensation, for injuries sustained or property damaged by a wrongful act or negligence.

see: actual damages, civil damages, compensatory damages, consequential damage, incidental damages, money damages, nominal damages, post-judgment interest, prejudgment interest, punitive damages, special damages

damper control

Loss Control. An adjustable metal plate which controls airflow in furnaces and fireplaces.

database

General. A collection of information or data that is electronically stored and accessible by computer.

database system

General. A system for organizing, selecting and entering data into a computer system, so that that information can be searched, retrieved and manipulated by computer.

data processing

General. The use of a computer to capture, store, manipulate, and retrieve information.

data processing coverage

Property. A type of property insurance (usually an "all-risks" form) covering data processing equipment, magnetic tapes and disks, and extra expenses incurred while restoring the system to its normal condition.

data processors errors & omissions insurance

Casualty. Coverage for organizations that perform data processing services for others, against claims arising out of a negligent act, error or omission. Generally, coverage is available for organizations that process financial data as opposed to those doing scientific, engineering or mathematical calculations.

date of grace

Insurer Operations. The period of time between a premium due date and cancellation date; a policy will remain in force so long as premiums are paid sometime within this period.

see: grace period

date of issue

Insurer Operations. The date that a contract was issued by the insurer, which may be different from the effective date.

syn: issuance date; see: effective date

deadend main

Loss Control. A water main or piping used for fire protection that terminates and is fed from only one direction.

see: circulating main

deadheading

Automobile. Operating a tractor or trailer without a load.

compare: bobtail

97

© 1991 NILS Publishing Company

dealer class plan

Automobile. A specific rating plan developed for auto dealers under the ISO commercial auto insurance program, garage coverage section.

syn: auto dealers rating plan; see: floor plan insurance, garage coverage form, lemon aid insurance, limited coverage for customers

Dean Analytic Schedule

Property. An obsolete commercial fire insurance rating method that was developed by A.F. Dean in 1902. It was the first comprehensive rating method to consider the numerous physical factors that can affect a fire exposure.

death

Life. Being dead; the termination of life. For a life insurance policy benefit to be paid, an insurance company must receive a death certificate.

see: accidental death, decedent, living; Fr: décès, mort; Gr: Tod; Sp: muerte; syn: demise

death benefits

Employee Benefits. A payment made upon the death of a plan participant of the participant's share in benefit plans, such as investment plans and life insurance.

Life. A payment of benefits under a life insurance policy that is made when the insured dies. The benefit is the policy's face amount plus amounts due because of riders, less outstanding loans and their interest.

see: double indemnity

death rate

Life.
see: mortality, mortality assumption

death waiver

Life.
see: payor disability

debenture

Financial Planning. Loans to companies issued on general credit with no specific pledged collateral. A certificate of obligation and promise to pay (debenture) is issued, bearing a fixed rate of interest and a principal repayment schedule.

syn: unsecured bond

debit

General. An accounting and financial term, used to describe any item of debt recorded in an account.

Fr: débit; Gr: Debit (Soll); Sp: débito, cargo

Life. A term used to refer to the premium for an industrial life insurance policy.

see: industrial life insurance

debit agent

Life. An agent who sells industrial life insurance policies.

see: industrial life insurance

debit balance

General. An amount of money owed to an organization for merchandise or service they have supplied.

compare: credit balance; see: balance

debit insurance

Life.
see: industrial life insurance

debit system

Life. A system established by industrial life insurers to have agents or collectors personally collect policy premiums on a weekly or monthly basis.

see: industrial life insurance

debris removal clause

Property. Insurance coverage for the expense involved in removing the debris that results from a loss covered by the policy from the site of loss, if the limit of insurance purchased is insufficient to cover both the amount of loss and the added cleanup costs. Many property policies provide an additional $5,000 for each insured location. Higher limits must be purchased separately.

see: coverage extension, demolition clause

debt adjuster

Financial Planning. An individual or firm that provides a service by assisting in the valuation of debt, often in bankruptcy proceedings. Debt adjusters receive periodic payments from debtors, which are then distributed among creditors.

see: bankruptcy

debt cancellation contract

Financial Planning. An agreement whereby a debt is cancelled upon the death of the borrower.

debtor

General. An individual or organization owing money to others (creditors).

compare: creditor

debt securities

Financial Planning. Bonds, notes, or debentures issued by corporations to borrow money. Holders of debt securities have priority in the secured assets over unsecured debts held by the general creditors.

see: bonds, debenture, note

debt service

Financial Planning. The amount of money needed on a periodic basis to repay an organization's outstanding debt and interest; the funds needed on a monthly,

© 1991 NILS Publishing Company

quarterly, or annual basis, to pay the principal and interest on debt.

debt-to-equity ratio
Risk Management. A ratio used to measure the relative amount of funds provided from investors and from lenders. *Formula:* Debt-to-equity = total liabilities/total equity. The smaller the ratio, the greater the organization's long-term solvency.
see: **financial ratios, financial underwriting**

decedent
General. A person that is dead.
see: **death**

deceit
General. A term interchangeable with fraud and misrepresentation, practiced to induce another to part with a legal right or property, and which ultimately accomplishes the desired result.
see: **action in deceit, fraud**

decentralization
Insurer Operations. The dispersion of functions and control from a central authority to regional and local authority. *Example:* An insurance company can control all underwriting from the home office, or give authority to local branches.

decibel (dB)
Loss Control. A measure of sound expressed as the logarithmic ratio of two amounts of pressure, power, or intensity, between a measured quantity and a reference quantity. The two most frequent applications of decibel involve the measurement of sound intensity level and sound pressure level.
see: **hearing level, noise level**

decision tree
Risk Management. A device for graphically showing the relationships between decisions and chance events.

deck cargo
Ocean Marine. Cargo carried outside (on the deck) rather than within the enclosed cargo spaces of a vessel. Typically, cargo carried outside a ship's holds are more exposed to both the risk of foul weather and being lost overboard. It is less expensive to ship goods as deck cargo.
syn: **on-deck cargo**; see: **cargo**

declarations
Casualty.
see: **policy declarations**
Inland Marine/Ocean Marine. A form provided by an insurance company to insureds for reporting payments under an open cargo policy when no marine insurance certificates are issued.
see: **marine insurance certificate**

declaratory judgment
General. A legal term used to refer to a ruling or opinion of the court only as respects to a point of law and that does not order anything to be done.
see: **judgment**

declination
Insurer Operations. An insurance company's rejection of an application for insurance.

decreasing term life insurance
Life. A term life insurance policy where the face amount declines by a stipulated amount on a periodic basis. *Example:* A $250,000 policy may decrease by $10,000 annually so that after 10 years the face amount will be $150,000.
see: **term life insurance**

decree
General. A judgment issued by a court of equity.
see: **judgment**

decrement
General. The amount (of quality or quantity) lost by waste.
see: **depletion, depreciation**

dedicate
Title. To set aside private property for a public use. *Example:* The setting aside of private property for a public sidewalk or street.
compare: **eminent domain**; see: **easement, public easement**

deductible
Insurer Operations. The amount of an insured loss for which the insured is financially responsible before an insurance policy provides coverage.
see: **all cause deductible, annual aggregate deductible, buy-back deductible, claims deductible workers' compensation plan, corridor deductible, deductible average, deductible clause, deductible liability insurance, deductible workers' compensation plans, disappearing deductible, family deductible, first dollar, flat deductible, franchise deductible, indemnity deductible workers' compensation plan, medical deductible workers' compensation plan, memorandum clause, percentage of loss deductible, percentage of value deductible, retention limit, split deductible; Fr: franchise, déductible; Gr: Selbstbeteiligung; Sp: deducible**

deductible average

Ocean Marine. An ocean marine deductible that is either a percentage of the insured value of a shipment, or a specified dollar amount.

deductible clause

Insurer Operations. A provision in an insurance policy that indicates a specified deductible amount, and states how the deductible applies in the event of a loss.

see: deductible

deductible liability insurance

Casualty. Liability insurance where the policy contains a deductible that applies to each claim. Under this method, the insurer settles the claims and charges back to the insured the amount of each settlement up to the deductible amount. Occasionally, the insurer will require the insured to establish a claims trust account or a letter of credit to guarantee payment of claims within the deductible.

see: deductible

deductible workers' compensation plans

Workers' Compensation. A form of workers' compensation insurance introduced in 1990 and approved for use in some states. Under a deductible workers' compensation policy, the employer/policy-holder pays a reduced premium, but is required to reimburse the insurer for claims that fall within the deductible amount. There are three types of deductible workers' compensation plans: indemnity deductible plans, medical deductible plans and claims deductible plans.

see: claims deductible workers' compensation plan, indemnity deductible workers' compensation plan, medical deductible workers' compensation plan, workers' compensation insurance

deed

Title. A formal document used to transfer title of real estate from one party to another party.

see: administrator's deed, quit claim deed, trust deed, warranty deed

deed of trust

General.
see: trust deed

de facto corporation

Regulation. A corporation formed in good faith in a reasonable attempt to comply with the law, but, which fails to meet a minor requirement, is a corporation de facto (in fact) and is valid against everyone except the state.

see: corporation

defalcation

Surety. An archaic term for the embezzlement of money.

see: embezzlement

defamation of character

General. The intentional misrepresentation of an individual's or an organization's reputation to another party.

see: personal injury

default

General. The failure of a party to a legal proceeding to file an answer to a summons and complaint, or the failure to appear in court at a specified time. This failure to act can result in a default judgment.

see: default judgment

default judgment

General. A final court decision resulting from a failure to file an answer to a summons and complaint or failure to appear in court at a specified time.

see: answer, default, summons and complaint

defective

Casualty. Regarding products liability insurance, a term used to denote the lack of an essential element or an incomplete, deficient or faulty element within an insured product.

see: active malfunction, bench error, faulty workmanship exclusion, hidden defect, latent defect

defective product

Casualty. Three major areas of product defects are faulty manufacture or assembly; defective design; and failure to give warning. A strict liability exists for those engaged in manufacturing, installing, marketing or selling known defective products.

see: products-completed operations insurance

defendant

General. A legal term for the party in a civil suit who is accused by the other party (the plaintiff) of causing a civil wrong.

compare: plaintiff

defendant's bond to dissolve

Surety. One of two forms of injunction bonds. As the result of a judicial process, an order dissolving an injunction may be issued conditioned upon the defendant providing a bond of this type, guaranteeing to pay such damages as the plaintiff may sustain as a result of the performance of the act or acts originally enjoined.

compare: plaintiff's bond to secure; see: enjoin, injunction bond, judicial bond

100

© 1991 NILS Publishing Company

defense clause

Casualty. A liability insurance policy provision that the insurer will have the right and duty to defend any suit against the insured, even if the suit is false or fraudulent. In most policies the expense for defense is covered in addition to policy limits; however, some recent policies include this expense in their limit, effectively reducing the amounts available for damages by the costs of defense.

see: **duty to defend**

defense costs

Casualty. Legal expenses incurred by the insurer to defend suits brought against a policyholder for covered claims.

see: **claim expense, defense clause, duty to defend, legal expenses**

deferred annuity

Life. An annuity whose benefits begin after a given number of years or at optional ages specified in the contract. The contract may be purchased with a single premium or periodic premiums.

see: **annuity**

deferred dividend policy

Life. An old form of whole life insurance, where the dividends were postponed for several years. If the insured died or coverage was cancelled before the dividend date, dividends were then forfeited.

see: **life insurance**

deferred group annuity

Life. A funding method for insured pension plans, where the benefits are funded by the purchase of a single premium deferred annuity for each plan participant, for an amount equal to each year's accrued benefit for that participant.

see: **annuity**

deferred life insurance

Life. Policies providing higher death benefits after a period of vesting.

see: **life insurance**

deferred premium

Life. Life insurance policy premiums which are not currently due, such as monthly or quarterly payments of an annual premium.

see: **premium**

deferred premium payment plan (DPP)

Insurer Operations. Initially this concept was developed for multi-year (three- or five-year) policies, where the premium could be paid in annual installments. As policy premiums increased, this concept was expanded to include annual policies, where the premium payment is made over the course of the year in quarterly or monthly payments.

see: **premium financing**

deferred retirement

Employee Benefits. A term used to describe a pension plan participant who elects to work beyond the normal retirement age. Such deferral may or may not result in an increase of benefits.

see: **retirement age**

deferred vesting

Employee Benefits. A pension plan participant's right to receive benefits from a plan which requires a minimum age and a minimum number of service years before the participant is vested in the benefits.

see: **vesting**

deficiency assessment

Regulation. An assessment levied on insureds under an assessable policy when policy losses exceed those originally expected.

see: **assessment, assessment insurance**

deficiency judgment

General. A judgment against a borrower obtained by a lender, in an amount equal to the difference between the funds received from a court sale of property and the balance owing on a loan.

see: **judgment**

deficiency reserve

Life/Regulation. A reserve that must be maintained by life insurers when the gross premium charged on a class of policies is less than the net level premium reserve or modified reserve.

see: **valuation premium**

deficit

General. The amount by which liabilities exceed assets.

compare: **profit**; see: **deficit carried back, deficit carried forward**

deficit carried back

General. Transferring a debit balance from the current accounting period to a past accounting period.

compare: **deficit carried forward**; see: **deficit**

deficit carried forward

General. Transferring a debit balance from the current accounting period to a future accounting period.

compare: **deficit carried back**; see: **deficit**

defined benefit plan

Employee Benefits. Any benefit plan other than an individual account plan. Primarily a means of funding for retirement, a defined benefit plan uses a definite

© 1991 NILS Publishing Company

defined contribution plan

defined benefit plan – continued

formula to determine the exact benefit amount. Employer contributions to these plans are actuarially determined.

compare: defined contribution plan; see: target benefit plan

defined contribution plan

Employee Benefits. An employee benefit plan under which each participant's benefits are based solely on the contributions made to the participant's account. Income or gains will be credited to the account and expenses, losses or forfeitures assigned to a participant's account will be deducted from the account.

syn: individual account plan; compare: defined benefit plan; see: benefit plan, money purchase plan

degree of care

General. A concept used in the determination of legal negligence where, based on the circumstances involved and the relationship of the parties involved, the degree of care that an individual should have exercised can range from slight, prudent, due, reasonable, ordinary, great, extraordinary to utmost care.

see: attractive nuisance doctrine, degree of negligence, duty to warn, gross negligence, invitee, licensee, negligence, reasonable care, trespasser, wanton disregard

degree of negligence

General. A concept that conduct which causes harm ranges from: 1) slight negligence (failure to use great care); 2) negligence (failure to use ordinary care); 3) gross negligence (failure to use slight care); 4) reckless misconduct, and 5) intentional misconduct.

see: degree of care, negligence

degree of risk

Risk Management. The amount of uncertainty that can arise from a given set of circumstances. The probability that actual experience will differ from what is anticipated.

see: law of large numbers, odds, probability, risk

delay clause

Life. A life insurance policy provision which allows the insurer to delay policy loans or payments of the cash surrender values for a stated period (usually six months). Intended to protect life insurers from losses that might result from a "run" on cash reserves built up in life insurance during tough economic times.

see: policy loan

Ocean Marine. An exclusion found in ocean marine contracts, which denies coverage for liability for loss of markets caused by delayed voyages.

delayed payment clause

Life. A life insurance policy clause designed to handle a disaster where both the insured and the primary beneficiary die in the same accident. The clause provides that the beneficiary must survive the insured's death by a specified period of time to receive the benefits, and that payment will be deferred for that length of time. Or, the provision may state that in the event the beneficiary is likely to die as the result of the accident, the insurer will defer the payment of benefits for a specified period of time. Should the primary beneficiary die before that period of time has elapsed, the benefits will be paid to contingent beneficiaries or the insured's estate.

see: uniform simultaneous death act

delayed retirement credit

Employee Benefits. A gradual increase in retirement credits given to those who attain age sixty-five, to encourage working beyond age sixty-five.

see: retirement age

delegation

Agency/Insurer Operations. The transfer of one party's duty to another party. The responsibility for the duty remains with the transferor.

see: agency, agent's authority

delinquency charge

Financial Planning. A charge imposed for the late payment of a loan or credit transaction.

see: interest

delivered business

Life. Life insurance policies that have been issued and delivered by the insurer, but for which no premium has yet been collected.

compare: examined business, issued business, paid business, placed business, written business; see: conditional delivery, not taken

delivery

Life. The physical transfer of a life insurance policy from the insurer or its agent to the policyowner.

see: conditional delivery, conditional receipt

delivery receipt

Inland Marine/Ocean Marine. A receipt used by carriers to prove delivery of merchandise to the intended party. Occasionally, it is a copy of the bill of lading or waybill, with the recipient's signature.

compare: dock receipt; see: bill of lading

deluge automatic sprinkler system

Loss Control. An automatic sprinkler system where all the sprinkler heads are open and the water is held back at a main (deluge) valve. When the valve is triggered by the actuating device, water is delivered

102

© 1991 NILS Publishing Company

and discharged from all the sprinkler heads simultaneously. The triggering device is usually a smoke detector. This type of system is used where it is necessary to wet down a large area quickly, such as an airplane hangar or explosives factory.

see: **automatic sprinkler system**

demand deposits

General. Deposits (usually not interest-bearing) that a depositor may withdraw from an account at a bank or savings & loan association by writing a check.

see: **cash assets**

demise

General. The death of a person.

see: **death**

demise charter

Ocean Marine.

see: **bareboat charter**

demographics

General. The study of characteristics of a given population for such factors as age, sex, birth date, buying habits, etc.

demolition clause

Property. A clause contained in property insurance policies which excludes coverage for any costs involved in demolishing undamaged property as the result of a loss covered by the policy. This clause is necessary because some building codes require that a structure must be demolished in its entirety if it sustains more than a specified percentage of damage.

see: **debris removal clause, ordinance or law coverage endorsement**

demolition cost endorsement

Property. An endorsement once used in conjunction with the "contingent liability from operation of building laws" endorsement, to provide coverage (and a separate amount of insurance) for the costs associated with demolishing undamaged portions of a building. Now, under the ISO Commercial Property Program, the coverage has been incorporated into the "ordinance or law coverage" endorsement *(ISO Form CP 04 05).*

see: **ordinance or law coverage endorsement**

demonstrative evidence

General. In a legal proceeding, demonstrative evidence is that physical evidence that illustrates facts in a controversy.

see: **documentary evidence**

demurrage

Ocean Marine. The additional port charges that result from the act of detaining a vessel in port beyond the time needed for loading or unloading; ocean marine

coverage for the additional port costs that can be incurred when a ship is detained in port for reasons beyond the insureds' control, including delays in loading or unloading.

see: **embargo**

demurrer

General. A legal pleading which states that a prior pleading does not state a cause of action.

see: **pleadings**

demutualization

Insurer Operations. A term used to refer to the process of converting a mutual insurance company to a stock insurance company. A mutual insurer is owned by its policyholders with no outstanding stock. A mutual insurer may convert to a stock insurer with the approval of the insurance department of its domiciliary state, and in compliance with the appropriate laws. In the conversion process, a mutual insurer offers policyholders cash and/or stock in the new insurer. The company may then also sell stock to the general public.

compare: **mutualization**; see: **mutual insurance company, stock insurance company**

dental benefit plans

Health. Plans operated by dental plan organizations which directly provide dental services.

see: **benefit plan, dental plan organizations**

dental insurance

Health. Coverage of dental services provided under an employee benefit plan or as part of an individual health policy or a separate dental policy. Most often it contains a coinsurance provision and may stress preventative care (e.g., paying for cleanings as often as twice to four times a year).

dental plan organizations

Health. Organizations conducting one or more dental benefit plans, under which dental services are provided directly or are arranged for or administered directly on a prepaid basis.

compare: **dental service plans**; see: **dental benefit plans**

dental service plans

Health. Plans in which dental services are provided at the expense of the plan, by participating dentists or other health care personnel, in consideration for periodic payments by the participating members or subscribers.

compare: **dental plan organizations**

dentists professional liability insurance

Casualty. Coverage for dentists against claims for

© 1991 NILS Publishing Company

dentists professional liability insurance — continued

personal injury arising from alleged malpractice, error or mistake in rendering professional services.

see: physicians, surgeons, and dentists professional liability insurance

Department of Transportation (DOT)

Regulation. A federal regulatory department whose responsibilities include automobile safety standards and, along with the Interstate Commerce Commission, the regulation of truckers. DOT sets the truckers liability insurance standards for bodily injury, property damage and environmental impairment.

dependency period

Financial Planning. The period of time during which children are growing up and are dependent on their parents. The period ranges from the birth of the oldest child until the youngest child reaches maturity. The dependency period is used in financial planning to determine when a family will need money for such things as children's support and education.

dependent

Employee Benefits/Health. Most employee benefit plans define covered dependents as the spouse and unmarried children under age 18 (or sometimes age 21) of a plan participant who are not employed on a full-time basis, or who are full-time students at an accredited college to age 21 or 22. The term "spouse" is undergoing expansion, and in some cases, will include lifetime partners or others.

see: child's benefit, dependent adults, dependent coverage, spouse's benefit; Fr: dépendant; Gr: Angehörigen; Sp: dependientes

dependent adults

Health. Adults incapable of self-sustaining employment because of mental or physical handicaps.

dependent coverage

Employee Benefits/Health. Coverage under an employee benefit plan which extends to a plan participant's dependents. Frequently, the plan participant has the option to include the spouse and unmarried children.

see: dependent

dependent property

Property. Property owned or operated by a single supplier or customer of an insured. If the supplier's or customer's operations were damaged or destroyed, and it would cause substantial business interruption to the insured, that property can be considered a "dependent property." Such losses can be insured against using contingent business income coverage.

see: contingent business income coverage, recipient property

depletion

Risk Management. To lessen markedly in quantity, content, power or value.

see: amortization, decrement, depreciation

deponent

General. A legal term used to refer to an individual who gives evidence or testimony in a legal proceeding.

see: deposition

depose

General. To take or obtain a deposition.

see: deposition

deposit account

Life.

see: active life fund

deposit administration contract

Life.

see: deposit administration plan

deposit administration fund

Life.

see: active life fund

deposit administration plan (DAP)

Health/Life. A pension plan administered by a life insurance company where pension funds accumulate in a master group annuity policy until a participant retires. As plan members retire, individual annuity policies are purchased with money from the fund.

syn: deposit administration contract, group deposit administration annuity; see: administrative services only, annuity purchase fund, third-party administrator

deposit fund

Life. Provisions under individual life or annuity contracts in which amounts are paid, in addition to premiums, to accumulate interest.

see: active life fund

deposition

General. Sworn testimony of a witness or other party, used as a discovery device in judicial proceedings. The deponent or deposed (the person being questioned) may be interrogated by attorneys for both parties to the suit or proceeding.

see: deponent, depose, discovery

depositor's forgery bond

Crime. Insurance issued to individuals (not lending institutions), protecting them against financial loss due to alteration or forgery of checks, drafts, promissory notes and the like.

see: crime coverages

104

© 1991 NILS Publishing Company

depository bank

General. A bank which accepts money to be withdrawn at the will of the depositor or under agreed-upon rules and regulations.

see: demand deposits

depository bond

Surety. A bond which guarantees payment of funds to depositors in accordance with the terms of a deposit in a bank.

compare: Federal Deposit Insurance Corporation

deposit premium

Reinsurance. An amount paid by a ceding company to a reinsurer which represents a partial or total payment of premiums expected to be earned under the contract. The premium is then adjusted at the end of the contract term (or periodically within a multi-year term) to reflect actual premiums earned at the rates charged for the coverage.

Insurer Operations. A partial payment of premium to an insurer which may later be adjusted up or down. Or an initial premium, determined to be as close to the final premium as possible, but which can be modified later (after the close of the policy year) by an audit of the insured's records.

syn: advance premium; see: audit, estimated annual premium, initial premium, provisional premium

depreciated value

Property. The original cost of real or personal property less tax or accounting depreciation.

compare: actual cash value, fair market value, functional replacement cost, market value, replacement cost, reproduction cost, tax-appraised value; see: valuation of potential property loss

depreciation

Financial Planning/Risk Management. Two principal forms of depreciation exist: 1) physical depreciation, and 2) tax or accounting depreciation. Physical depreciation is the decline in economic value of a property over time because of wear and tear and obsolescence. Tax or accounting depreciation is based on an accounting schedule, which depreciates the property over a specific period of time (i.e. five years, ten years). In calculating insurable actual cash value, the physical depreciation method is used.

compare: appreciation, depletion; see: accelerated depreciation, accumulated depreciation, amortization, depreciation rate, deterioration, straight line depreciation; Fr: dépréciation; Gr: Abschreibung (Herabsetzung); Sp: depreciación

depreciation Insurance

Property. Coverage in case of a loss for the difference between the actual cash value of the property insured and the cost of replacement for comparable size and construction.

see: actual cash value, replacement cost insurance

depreciation rate

Financial Planning. The total amount of depreciation, depletion, and amortization charged to income during the year, expressed as a percentage of the gross plant (i.e., total plant and equipment, including land, at original cost as reported by the company) at the end of a year.

see: depreciation

deprivation

General. Confiscation or removal of property without just compensation.

derelict

Ocean Marine. The wreck of a ship, lying on the ocean floor.

compare: flotsam, lagan; see: jetsam

derivative insured

General. An individual or entity, such as an executor of an estate or an heir, who is entitled to receive insurance proceeds on behalf of the insured.

see: insured

dermatitis

Health/Loss Control. Inflammation of the skin, frequently caused by contact with harmful or allergic materials.

descent

General. Real estate that is passed to heirs of the owner, upon the owner's death.

design errors & omissions

Casualty.

see: architects professional liability insurance, efficacy coverage, engineers professional liability insurance, errors & omissions insurance, turnkey insurance

design load

Loss Control. The planned amount of authorized work to be performed; the weight to be carried by a device for a specific function or purpose.

destruction

Crime. One of the insured perils of a dishonesty, disappearance, and destruction (3D) policy. It is a covered peril under most money and securities policies, as well. Destruction is deemed to have occurred when the insured property is useless for its intended

105

© 1991 NILS Publishing Company

destruction – continued

purpose, even though the property may not be entirely destroyed.

see: dishonesty, disappearance and destruction policy

detached structures

Property. A structure not sharing any wall with another building on the same property. Under a homeowner's policy, a detached structure is any structure connected to the insured dwelling by a fence or utility line. Most homeowner's and commercial property insurance policies provide coverage for detached structures on the same premises.

compare: adjoining building; see: adjacent building, appurtenant structures

deterioration

Property. The natural and expected decline in the usefulness and value of property from wear and tear, disintegration, use, and action of the weather and sunlight. Deterioration results in depreciation.

compare: inherent vice; see: decrement, depreciation, wear and tear exclusion

deviated rate

Insurer Operations. Rates that are usually lower than the indicated manual or bureau rates. In most states, insurers must file justification for rate deviations with the insurance department.

see: deviation insurer, rate

deviation

Ocean Marine. A voluntary departure by a vessel from the usual course between a port of departure and a port of destination.

see: deviation clause

Insurer Operations. A rate for coverage that differs from a manual or bureau rate.

deviation clause

Ocean Marine. A provision found in ocean marine insurance policies allowing a vessel to deviate from the routes indicated in the policy for reasons beyond the insured's control.

see: deviation

deviation insurer

Insurer Operations. An insurance company that writes the majority of its business at deviated (usually lower-than-bureau) rates.

see: deviated rate

devise

General. A gift of real property by the last will and testament of the donor; property so given.

compare: escheat

diagnostic coverage

Health. A term used to refer to that coverage included in health insurance policies for diagnostic expenses such as laboratory tests and radiology.

diagnostic related group (DRG)

Health. A medical claims reimbursement system implemented by Medicare for hospitals, where predetermined payment amounts are developed for categories of procedures, for each episode of care. Recently, DRGs have been utilized by employers and insurers as a cost containment technique.

see: approved charges, reasonable and customary charge, schedule

die

Property. A form made of rigid metal or plastic, for shaping material to a desired shape.

see: dies insurance

dies insurance

Property. Insurance that specifically covers a manufacturer's dies, which may have exceptionally high replacement values; usually, such coverage is endorsed to a property policy, but it can be provided by a separate inland marine policy.

see: die, pattern and die floater

difference in conditions insurance (DIC)

Property. A property insurance policy, usually written on large risks, to supplement a named perils property policy. It provides "all-risks" coverage (often including coverage for flood and earthquake), but excludes the named perils provided by a standard fire insurance policy. The policy will be written for a specific limit (e.g., $5,000,000, $10,000,000) without a coinsurance provision.

syn: change in conditions insurance

International. An insurance policy issued by the international department of an insurer or Lloyd's of London, which provides relatively uniform worldwide coverages for an insured with operations in foreign countries. Such insurance supplements coverage purchased in a foreign country, by providing coverage for additional perils or higher limits of liability.

dike

Loss Control. A bank of earth or a masonry wall, constructed around storage tanks to prevent the leakage of their contents from spreading to other areas.

direct action statute

Regulation. A statute found in some states allowing an injured party to take direct legal action against the insurer of the other party. Usually, a direct action against an insurer cannot be taken without first obtaining a judgment against the insured.

© 1991 NILS Publishing Company

direct bill

Agency/Insurer Operations. The billing of insurance policy premiums directly by an insurer to a policyholder. This is in contrast to an insurance agent billing the policyholder and paying the company after receiving the premium.

see: premium

direct cause

General. A legal term which refers to the first action or cause that sets in motion a series of connected events which brings about a result without the intervention of any other action or force. The cause of an accident.

compare: concurrent causation; see: proximate cause

direct damage

Property.

see: direct loss

directed verdict

General. A jury verdict in a court case where the trial judge has ordered (directed) the outcome of the verdict. In effect, it takes the determination of the verdict away from the jury.

see: judgment, verdict

direct excess policy

Casualty. A liability policy that is issued for the sole purpose of providing excess insurance. *Examples:* A following form excess policy or an umbrella policy.

see: following form excess liability insurance, umbrella liability insurance

direct health care corporation

Health. A corporation providing direct health care services to its members and subscribers through contracts with licensed health service personnel and health service institutions, but not paying any cash indemnity benefits.

see: health indemnity plan, health maintenance organization, preferred provider organization

direct loss

Property. Property damage or destruction caused directly by an insured peril, as opposed to indirect or consequential loss (e.g., loss of rents, business interruption, etc.)

syn: direct damage; compare: consequential damage

direct marketing

Insurer Operations.

see: direct selling system

Direct Marketing Insurance Council (DMIC)

Organizations. Members: Direct response marketing divisions of insurers and service companies. *Objectives:* Holds educational seminars and awards the Direct Marketing Insurance Man of the Year Award. *Founded:* 1917. *Headquarters:* New York, NY.

director of insurance

Regulation.

see: insurance commissioner

directors & officers liability insurance (D & O)

Casualty. A specialized form of liability insurance covering legal expenses and damages to shareholders, members, bondholders, creditors, or others, for the personal legal liability of directors and officers of a corporation or nonprofit organization because of errors, omissions, negligence or other wrongful acts in the course of performing their official duties for the entity.

see: abuse of minority stockholders, accountability, amotion, business judgment rule, inside directors, intercompany transaction, intra vires, outside directors, ultra vires

direct placement

Financial Planning. The purchase of an issue of securities directly from the issuer, bypassing a stock broker or investment banker. Insurance companies and other institutional investors frequently purchase securities on a direct placement basis.

direct response marketing

Insurer Operations.

see: direct selling system

direct selling system

Insurer Operations. An insurance marketing system used by insurers, where company employees directly contact prospects by telephone or mail.

syn: direct marketing, direct response marketing; compare: exclusive agency system, independent agency system

direct writer

Insurer Operations. An insurer that markets its policies directly through salaried employees or captive agents, rather than through independent agents or brokers.

compare: independent agency system; see: captive agent

Reinsurance. A reinsurer that markets directly to insurance companies, rather than through a reinsurance intermediary.

see: intermediary

direct written premium

Insurer Operations. The amount of an insurer's

© 1991 NILS Publishing Company

direct written premium — continued
recorded originated premiums (other than reinsurance) issued during the year, whether collected or not.

see: premium

disability

Health/Workers' Compensation. A physiological or psychological condition which prevents an insured individual from doing one or more job duties.

see: disability income insurance, income policy, nondisabling injury, nonoccupational disability, partial disability, permanent partial disability, permanent total disability, presumptive disability, recurrent disability, short-term disability, temporary partial disability, temporary total disability, total disability, workers' compensation insurance; Fr: invalidité, incapacité; Gr: Invalidität; Sp: incapacidad

disability benefit

Employee Benefits. Insurance that provides payments on a periodic basis (usually monthly), to replace lost income because of a total or partial disability caused by illness, injury or disease which prevents the insured from working. Disabilities resulting from an injury covered by workers' compensation are excluded by a disability benefits policy.

see: temporary disability benefits

disability benefit law

Regulation. A law requiring employers to pay weekly benefits to employees who have nonoccupational accidents or who become ill outside of employment.

compare: workers' compensation law

disability income insurance

Life. A rider that can be added to an ordinary life insurance policy that pays the insured one percent of the face value of the policy each month, if the insured is disabled more than six months. Policy premiums are waived for the period that disability payments are paid.

Health. Coverage designed to replace lost income because of a total or partial disability caused by a work-related injury.

see: disability benefit, elective benefits, group disability insurance, lifetime disability benefit, long-term disability insurance, maximum disability income policy, partial disability insurance, payor disability, pilot and crew occupational disability insurance, quarantine benefit, residual disability income policy, short-term disability insurance, statutory disability income, temporary nonoccupational disability plan, unemployment compensation disability insurance

Disability Insurance Training Council (DITC)

Organizations/Health. The education division of the National Association of Health Underwriters (NAHU). The DITC provides seminars on disability income and health insurance, as well as marketing and underwriting clinics.

see: National Association of Health Underwriters

disappearance

Crime/Inland Marine. A crime insurance peril that encompasses losses from a known location at a known time, resulting from a theft or burglary. If a loss occurs without knowledge about the location or time of loss, it would be a mysterious disappearance, which is often excluded from coverage.

see: dishonesty, disappearance and destruction coverage form; mysterious disappearance

Aviation. An aircraft missing and not reported for a specified time (usually 60 days) after commencing a flight.

disappearance and destruction coverage form

Crime.
see: money and securities broad form insurance

disappearing deductible

Insurer Operations. A deductible which decreases in amount as the amount of a loss increases. When the loss equals or exceeds a specified amount, the deductible no longer applies or, in effect, disappears. For losses less than the deductible, an increasing proportion of the loss is paid. *Example:* For a $1,000 deductible, the insured would receive 125% of losses exceeding $1,000, 150% of losses exceeding $2,000, and at $3,000 the deductible disappears.

see: deductible

disaster plan

Risk Management. A detailed plan to transfer business operations to another location, or to utilize other equipment, if an existing facility is damaged; a plan to minimize the consequences of loss at a single location.

syn: catastrophe plan; see: backup facility agreement

disbursement

General. The act of paying out money.

discharge of contracts

General. Contracts may be discharged by: 1) contractual obligations ending through completed performance by both parties; 2) substitution of new agreements; 3) the impossibility of performance; or 4) the operation of law.

see: contract

© 1991 NILS Publishing Company

disclaimer

Casualty. The denial of an obligation or a claim. As respects products liability, a disclaimer may be a statement by the seller that the product is not warranted or has a warranty only for specific consequences or costs.

compare: express warranty, implied warranty; see: fitness for a particular purpose

disclosure authorization form

General. A form which authorizes the disclosure of information to a third party

disclosure form

General. A form which is used to report required information.

discounted cash flow techniques (DCF)

Risk Management. Methods of evaluating the return on a capital investment, by calculating the present value of the income flow. The analysis of the discounted cash flow is valuable when selecting from competing investments, by taking into account the time value of money.

see: cost of capital, discounting, internal rate of return, present value

discounted premium

Life. A lump sum advance premium paid in lieu of the frequency of payments specified in the policy. Such payments may be discounted by the insurer, based upon an agreed upon rate of interest.

see: premium

discount factor

Risk Management. A number which is multiplied by a dollar value to bring the value up to present-day dollars.

see: discounting, present value

discounting

Risk Management. The process of funding the present value of a series of future cash flows.

compare: compounding; see: continuous compounding, discounted cash flow techniques, discount factor, present value, risk-adjusted discount rate

discounting for mortality

Employee Benefits/Life. The discounting of pension plan contribution rates or benefit costs, under the assumption that a specified percentage of participants will die prior to qualifying for benefits.

syn: advance discount for mortality; see: mortality table

discounting for severance

Employee Benefits/Life. The discounting of pension plan contribution rates or benefit costs, under the assumption that a specified percentage of participants will stop working for the employer prior to qualifying for benefits.

syn: advance discount for severance

discovery

General. A legal term for the right of a party to litigation to determine any matter of consequence, by questioning under oath another party to the action. This right includes the review of any documents in the other party's possession.

see: deposition

discovery period

Surety. A provision in a fidelity bond that allows the insured to report a loss to the surety company for a specified period, usually one year, after the bond has been cancelled. The loss must have occurred while the bond was in force.

discretionary groups

Regulation. In group insurance, groups not included in standard group classifications, but which are permissible if approved by the insurance commissioner.

compare: fictitious group; see: minimum group, true group insurance

discrimination

Casualty. Some liability policies provide coverage against claims alleging discrimination, under the personal injury coverage section. Coverage may be for claims involving discrimination such as racial, religious, sex or age.

see: age discrimination, sex discrimination, sexual harassment, sexual harassment defense coverage

Regulation. To treat individuals or organizations differently, or to favor one over the other. State insurance laws prohibit insurers from unfairly discriminating against consumers who present similar risks.

see: equity, nondiscriminatory, rate making, unfair discrimination

dishonesty, disappearance and destruction policy (DDD)

Crime/Surety. A crime insurance policy which combines fidelity insurance with crime insurance. The form contains five insuring agreements: 1) employee dishonesty; 2) premises, money, and securities coverage; 3) off-premises money and securities coverage; 4) counterfeit currency or money order coverage; and 5) depositors forgery coverage. This policy has been replaced by the 1986 Commercial Crime Program.

syn: three-D ("3-D") policy; see: depositor's forgery bond, destruction, disappearance, employee dishonesty crime form, money and securities broad form insurance

© 1991 NILS Publishing Company

dismemberment

Health/Life. The loss by an individual of an arm or leg, finger or toe, or eyesight in one or both eyes.

dismemberment benefit

Health/Workers' Compensation. Insurance benefits for dismemberment.

see: dismemberment

dismissal

General. The ending of a particular court proceeding. It is not necessarily the final judgment. The dismissal may be "with prejudice," meaning it is based on the claim's merits (or lack thereof) and bars the right to bring or maintain action on the same claim. Or the dismissal may be "without prejudice," meaning the case is dismissed without reference to the case's merits, which allows a subsequent suit on the same claim.

see: judgment

disparagement of goods

Casualty. Untrue or misleading criticism of a firm's merchandise offered for sale, in an attempt to influence the public not to purchase it.

see: commercial speech, personal injury

dispersion

Risk Management. An actuarial term for the measurement of variability of data from the mean, median or mode in a projection. The farther losses occur from the point being measured, the lower their reliability.

see: mean, median, mode

dispossess

General. A legal term used to describe the action of depriving a party from the use of real estate.

see: ejectment bond

distress

General. A legal term for the seizure of the goods of another as a pledge, or to obtain satisfaction of a claim by selling the seized goods.

distribution clause

Property.

see: pro rata distribution clause

distribution curve

Risk Management. An actuarial term for the scattering of data around the mean. The normal distribution curve is a symmetrical bell-shaped pattern.

see: lognormal distribution, Poisson distribution, skewed curve, symmetrical curve

distribution of assets

General. When an organization is being dissolved or is in bankruptcy, assets are distributed in a specified order. Solvent assets or the proceeds from such assets are distributed in the following order, unless a partnership agreement provides otherwise: 1) creditors; 2) partner's advances; 3) each partner's capital and 4) remaining surplus to partners.

compare: articles of dissolution, liquidation distribution; see: assets, partnership

disturbance

General. Any act of annoyance, agitation, or disruption, or any act that prevents a person from enjoying his or her property.

see: civil commotion

diversification

Risk Management. A risk management technique that can be used to avoid a catastrophic loss, by spreading an organization's risk geographically, by type of risk, or by type of coverage. Diversification makes it less likely that a single event will adversely affect a significant percentage of an organization's operations or business.

see: avoidance, insurance, retention, transfer of risk

diversity jurisdiction

General. A term used to describe the jurisdiction of the federal courts concerned with cases involving claims for $10,000 or more, cases whose claims arise under the Constitution, between citizens of different states, or between citizens of one state and an alien state.

see: center of influence, conflict of laws

divided coverage

General. Insurance normally covered by one company, which is instead divided between two or more companies.

compare: burglary divided coverage; see: layering

dividend

General. The payment by a corporation to its stockholders of a portion of its net earnings.

see: cumulative dividend, ex-dividend date, nimble dividend, stock dividend

Insurer Operations. A percentage of premiums paid that is refunded by an insurance company to all or a segment of its participating policyholders.

see: dividend ratio, participating policy, policy dividend

dividend accumulation

Life. A participating life insurance policy option allowing dividends to be left on deposit with the insurer, to accumulate at an agreed-upon interest rate.

see: taxation of interest on life insurance dividends

© 1991 NILS Publishing Company

dividend addition

Life. An option allowing the insured to use dividends to purchase additional single premium life insurance.

see: **optional life insurance settlement modes**

dividend option

Life. A term used to refer to any of the alternative methods by which dividends paid under participating life insurance policies can be used by a policyholder.

see: **optional life insurance settlement modes**

dividend ratio

Insurer Operations. A formula used by insurance companies to relate income to policyholder dividends. Frequently, policyholder dividends are included in the expense ratio. *Formula:* Dividend Ratio = Policyholder Dividends/Earned Premiums.

see: **combined ratio, expense ratio, loss ratio**

dividend reinvestment plan

Financial Planning. A plan where the dividends paid on securities are automatically used to purchase additional shares of the same security.

dividend yield

Financial Planning. The year-ahead estimated dividend yield is the estimated total of cash dividends to be declared over the next twelve months per-share, divided by the recent stock price. The trailing dividend yield is the sum of the dividends declared over the last 12 months, divided by the recent stock price.

see: **trailing dividend yield**

divisible contract clause

Property. A policy provision that a violation of policy conditions at one insured location will not void coverage at other locations.

dock receipt

Inland Marine/Ocean Marine. A receipt used by carriers as evidence that merchandise was, in fact, received by the carrier for shipment.

syn: **received for shipment bill of lading;** compare: **delivery receipt;** see: **bill of lading**

doctrine of election

General. The voluntary act of choosing between two or more alternative rights or privileges.

doctrine of last clear chance

General. A contributory negligence rule asserting that one who has the "last clear chance" to avoid an injury and fails to do so is solely responsible for its happening and is therefore considered the proximate cause of the accident.

see: **contributory negligence**

doctrine of proximate cause

General.

see: **proximate cause**

doctrine of respondeat superior

General.

see: **respondeat superior**

doctrine of unconscionability

General. Contracts which are written so as to give one party an unfair advantage over another because they had superior bargaining power at the time the contract was entered into. Such contracts may not be enforced by the courts.

see: **contract, contract of adhesion**

doctrine of waiver

General.

see: **waiver**

documentary evidence

General. Evidence in written form or any inanimate object admissible as evidence in a court of law, as distinguished from oral evidence.

see: **affidavit, demonstrative evidence, deposition, evidence**

documentary stamp

Regulation. A revenue stamp for paying tax required by federal or state law – affixed to documents such as deeds, wills, checks – before the documents can be recorded. Federal Revenue Stamps were abolished in 1968.

domestic

Workers' Compensation. A household servant performing part-time or full-time services.

see: **employee, residence employee**

domestication agreement

Insurer Operations. An agreement by which an affiliated domestic insurer assumes the assets and liabilities of the United States branch of an alien insurer.

see: **affiliated companies, alien insurer, domestic insurer**

domestic carrier

Insurer Operations.

see: **domestic insurer**

domestic goods in transit

Inland Marine. Domestic shipments exposed to loss while in transit by rail, motor truck, aircraft, or while in the custody of the U.S. Postal Service. (Imports and exports – nondomestic goods – are not within the scope of inland marine insurance.)

see: **transit insurance, transportation insurance**

© 1991 NILS Publishing Company

domestic insurer

Insurer Operations. An insurer or reinsurer incorporated under the laws of a state of the United States, in which it is authorized to do the business of insurance.

syn: domestic carrier; compare: alien insurer, assurer, foreign insurer, insurance company

domicile

Insurer Operations.
see: domiciliary state

domiciled company

Insurer Operations. A company with legal jurisdiction and authority to conduct business in the state where the company's principal operations reside.
see: domestic insurer

domiciliary state

Insurer Operations. The state in which an insurance company has its true, fixed and permanent legal residence.
syn: domicile; compare: commercial domiciles

domino theory

Loss Control. An accident causation theory proposed in 1931, which observes that an accident is the result of a series of factors. Each factor is dependent on the previous factor, and if any factor can be prevented, an injury will not occur. The theory was developed by H.W. Heinrich, who said, "heredity and environment cause personal shortcomings; personal shortcomings cause negligent acts or omissions; individual's negligent acts or omissions, or a faulty machine, causes an accident; and accident causes an injury."
compare: energy-release theory

donee

General. The recipient of a gift.
compare: donor

donor

General. A person who gives a gift.
compare: donee

do not solicit list

Insurer Operations.
see: prohibited list

door to door coverage

Inland Marine/Ocean Marine. A term used to denote insurance which covers a shipment of merchandise from the original point of manufacture to its final destination.
syn: house to house coverage; see: warehouse-to-warehouse coverage

dosimeter

Loss Control. An instrument for measuring doses of x-rays or of radioactivity.

double compensation

Workers' Compensation. A legal doctrine which allows a minor who is injured in an industrial accident double the regular compensation benefits if, at the time of the accident, the minor was illegally employed. The minor does not have the right to sue the employer as long as the injury was job-related.
see: illegal employment

double indemnity (DI)

Life. A life insurance policy provision, contained in some policies, under which the face amount payable on death will be doubled if the death is the result of an accident.
syn: accidental death benefit, multiple indemnity

double insurance

General. Duplicated or redundant coverage on the same risk.
compare: dual coverage

double protection life insurance

Life. A form of life insurance combining equal amounts of whole life and term insurance, with the term insurance expiring at a stated future date. The limit on the term insurance is either equal to the whole life limit "double protection" – or twice the whole life limit – "triple protection." These policies are designed for younger insureds who cannot afford high-limit whole life insurance, but still want to build some cash value.
compare: split life insurance

dower

General. The legal right of a widow to the interest in real estate of a deceased husband.

draft

General. A negotiable instrument written by one party, instructing a second party to pay a third party. In insurance, the "draft" is the written claim instructing the insurer to pay the beneficiary.
compare: cashier's check, certified check; see: drawee, drawer

dram shop act

Regulation. A term used in reference to laws enacted by those states that hold taverns and bars liable for damages and injuries caused by intoxicated persons, who were served intoxicating beverages by the tavern or bar.
syn: liquor control laws; see: liquor liability law

© 1991 NILS Publishing Company

dram shop liability insurance

Casualty. A form of liquor liability coverage that responds to claims arising from dram shop acts.

see: **liquor liability laws, liquor legal liability coverage**

"D" ratio

Workers' Compensation. A ratio used in calculating a workers' compensation experience rating plan. It is the ratio of primary expected losses (those losses under $2,000 which an employer is expected to control), plus a discounted value of large losses, divided by the total expected losses.

see: **experience modification, experience rating plan**

drawee

General. The person on whom a draft is drawn, and who is thereby ordered to pay.

compare: **drawer**; see: **draft**

drawer

General. The person who initially draws or creates and signs a draft.

compare: **drawee**; see: **draft**

dread disease policy

Health. A health insurance policy with maximum limits, covering medical expenses for a specific disease (such as AIDS or cancer).

see: **acquired immune deficiency syndrome, cancer insurance, extra percentage tables**

Life.

see: **living benefits**

driveaway collision

Automobile. An endorsement to the garage policy, providing collision coverage on an auto dealer's vehicles driven or transported more than fifty miles from the point of purchase or distribution to their destination. Driveaway collision coverage is excluded from a dealer's garage insurance policy without this endorsement.

see: **garage coverage form, limited coverage for customers**

drive other car coverage

Automobile.

see: **broad form drive other car coverage**

driver training credit

Automobile. Credits (premium discounts) given by insurance companies to drivers who have completed an approved driver education course. Such a credit assumes that proper driving education will reduce accidents.

see: **good student discount**

drive to or from work

Automobile. An automobile rating classification used when a principal driver uses the insured vehicle only for personal use and to drive to or from work (i.e., the principal driver does not drive the car in business, nor strictly for pleasure use). Usually, the classification is divided into two categories: "to or from work less than 15 miles" and "to or from work more than 15 miles." (The miles are measured one way, not round trip).

compare: **business use, farm use, pleasure use**

drop-down provision

Casualty. A provision contained in umbrella liability policies, where the policy will provide primary coverage in the event that the underlying (primary) aggregate limits of liability are exhausted or reduced. This is one of the items that distinguishes an umbrella policy from an excess policy.

see: **umbrella liability insurance**

druggists liability coverage

Casualty. Liability protection against claims for bodily injury or property damage which arise out of drugs or other products sold by a retail drug store. The pharmacist owning the drug store is automatically protected by this policy, but employed pharmacists must be specifically added to the policy.

compare: **pharmacists professional liability**

dry chemicals

Loss Control. A combination of fine powders used in fire extinguishing systems which can be directed at a burning flammable liquid or flood an area (such as a restaurant cooking area) and snuff out a fire by depriving it of oxygen.

see: **class A fire, class B fire, class C fire, class D fire, fire extinguishing system**

dry pipe automatic sprinkler system

Loss Control. An automatic sprinkler system where all piping contains air under pressure. When a sprinkler head opens, the air is released and water flows into the system and to any open sprinkler heads. This type of system is used in areas where the sprinkler heads and the immediately adjacent piping can be exposed to freezing conditions.

compare: **wet pipe sprinkler system**; see: **automatic sprinkler system, dry valve**

dry season charge

Property.

see: **standing timber insurance**

dry valve

Loss Control. An automatic sprinkler valve under air pressure, designed to allow air to escape prior to the

© 1991 NILS Publishing Company

dry valve — *continued*
release of water. The air prevents freezing and bursting of pipes.

see: **dry pipe automatic sprinkler system**

dual capacity doctrine
Casualty/Workers' Compensation. A legal doctrine, stating that an employer who is normally immune from tort actions brought by employees (because of the workers' compensation laws) may be held liable for additional damages as a party who has committed a wrongful act outside of its normal role as an employer. *Example:* An employee of an aerosol shaving cream manufacturer is injured by an exploding can while stocking a merchant's shelves. The manufacturer must respond under workers' compensation laws to their employee, but may also be held responsible as the product manufacturer of a can that injured the employee, who could be considered a member of the general public.

see: **common law defense, exclusive remedy**

dual coverage
Casualty. A legal claim adjustment concept applying equal liability for a loss, when the loss is caused jointly by a covered occurrence in one insurance policy and an excluded occurrence in a separate policy. Typically, such a loss will include an automobile and personal or general liability policy. *Example:* An insured has a homeowner's policy which excludes liability "arising out of the use of an automobile" and an automobile policy which provides coverage for losses "arising out of the use of an automobile." The insured shoots at a deer from a moving automobile and hits another hunter. Since the homeowner's policy, which usually would provide coverage in this situation, except for the auto exclusion, and since the automobile policy could be said to provide coverage (although this type of loss is not normally contemplated by automobile coverage), a question of dual coverage is created which must be further litigated based on the specific facts of the incident.

see: **loading or unloading, overinsurance, pyramiding of limits, stacking of limits**

dual life stock company
Life. A life insurer formed as a stock company, which issues both participating and nonparticipating life insurance policies.

dual valuation clause
Ocean Marine. Hull insurance policies covering older vessels sometimes will contain this clause, which provides for a lower valuation for the vessel in the event of a total loss. A higher value applies to all other (i.e., partial loss) claims.

see: **hull policy**

due process of law
General. The regular, equal, fair administration of justice. A concept in U.S. law which states that a law shall not be unreasonable, arbitrary, or capricious; that all parties to an action shall be given the opportunity to be heard, to be aware of the matter pending, and to defend themselves in an orderly proceeding.

dunnage
Inland Marine/Loss Control/Ocean Marine. Loose packing material, placed in shipping containers to prevent damage to the items being shipped.

duplex
Property. A term used to describe a two-family dwelling, whether or not the accommodations of the two units are identical. The units may share walls with one another, or they may be on different floors of a multi-story building.

duration of risk
Insurer Operations. The extent, limit, or time specifically stated in a policy for which the risk is to run; the policy period.

see: **claims-made trigger, occurrence trigger, policy period**

duress
General. Compulsion by threat; forcible restraint under which a person acts, or is coerced by the will of another to act, contrary to his or her free will.

see: **rescission**

duties provision
Insurer Operations.

see: **evidence and duties provision**

duty
Ocean Marine. A governmental tax levied on imported items.

see: **abatement**

duty to defend
Casualty. A provision contained in a liability policy's insuring agreement, establishing the insurance company's obligation to defend the insured. For covered occurrences, defense must be provided even if a suit is found to be false, groundless or fraudulent.

see: **defense clause, separation of insureds**

duty to warn
Casualty. A duty to warn consumers that is required of manufacturers marketing products where there is knowledge of a danger or foreseeability of dangerous use.

see: **degree of care**

© 1991 NILS Publishing Company

dwelling

Property. A private structure in which people reside. A residence building.

   see: **condominium, duplex**

dwelling, buildings and contents form (DB & C)

Property. A property insurance policy designed specifically for private residences and other properties where people live. It provides, on a limited basis, some of the property coverages included in a homeowner's form.

   compare: **homeowner's policy**; see: **homeowner's policy – property coverage**

dynamo clause

Property.

   see: **electrical apparatus exclusion**

© 1991 NILS Publishing Company

E

early retirement

Employee Benefits. Voluntary and planned termination of employment before the normal retirement date or before a specified age. When an individual elects "early retirement," benefits are usually less than normal retirement benefits.

see: normal retirement age, retirement age

earned premium

Insurer Operations. That portion of an insurance policy's premium which represents coverage already provided. For each day a one-year policy is in force, an insurer earns 1/365th of the annual premium. For an insurer's accounting purposes, "earned premium" is the total of all premiums written during a period, plus the unearned premiums at the beginning of the period, less the unearned premiums at the end of the period.

compare: unearned premium, unearned premium reserve; see: premium

earned reinsurance premium

Insurer Operations/Regulation. That portion of premium earned on policies issued by a primary (ceding) company which is paid to a reinsurer. A part of the reinsurance premium, that is calculated on a periodic basis (monthly, quarterly, annually) and retained by the reinsurer if the coverage is cancelled.

compare: unearned reinsurance premium; see: premium

earnings

General. An accounting term used to refer to the sum of net profits; payroll expenses, taxes, rents and all other operating expenses of a business.

earnings insurance form

Property. Business interruption forms designed for small businesses. They are similar to gross earnings forms, except there is no coinsurance clause, and there is a maximum limit on the amount of loss payment during any 30-day period.

compare: business income coverage form, gross earnings form, simplified earnings form

earnings per share

Financial Planning/Risk Management. A financial term meaning the per-share earnings as originally reported by a company, but adjusted for all subsequent stock splits and stock dividends. This figure may be based on actual year-end shares outstanding, or on average shares outstanding, or on average shares outstanding plus common stock equivalents (in other words, "primary earnings per share"), or on actual year-end or average shares outstanding plus all shares reserved for conversion of convertible senior securities, and exercise of all warrants and options (termed "fully-diluted earnings per share").

see: estimated constant dollar earnings per share

earnings retained

Financial Planning.
see: retained earnings

earnings yield

Financial Planning. A financial ratio used to evaluate stock. A stock's annual earnings are divided by its current market price.

see: financial ratios

earthquake

Property. A trembling or shaking of the earth which is volcanic or tectonic (seismic) in origin, often resulting in severe damage.

see: volcanic action; Fr: tremblement de terre; Gr: Erdbeben; Sp: terremoto

© 1991 NILS Publishing Company

earthquake – *continued*
Ocean Marine. An earthquake under the ocean or the sea is a "peril of the seas" under an ocean marine policy.

earthquake insurance

Property. Property insurance coverage for damage caused by the perils of earthquake or volcanic action. The coverage is limited to direct damage caused by an earthquake, and excludes any loss which results from another peril – even if it is triggered by the earthquake, such as a fire, explosion, flood or tidal wave. Any earthquake – following an initial occurrence ("aftershock") for a 72-hour period is considered as the same event for the purpose of claims filing.
see: **earthquake, percentage of value deductible, volcanic action**

easement

Title. An irrevocable right given by a land owner to others for the limited use of land.
see: **dedicate**

Eastern Claims Conference (ECC)

Health/Life/Organizations. Members: Disability examiners, including life, health and group claims personnel of insurance companies. *Objectives:* Provides education and training to examiners, managers and officers who review medical and disability claims. *Founded:* 1977. *Headquarters:* New York, NY.

easy read

Insurer Operations. A term for simplified language policies, which are not written in the traditional legal contract form, but rather use commonly understood words.
see: **Flesch Test, plain language laws, policy**

economic loss

General. The estimated total cost – both insured and uninsured – of mishaps such as motor vehicle accidents, work accidents and fires. "Economic loss" includes costs such as property damage, medical, hospital and legal costs, funeral expenses, wage loss; and insurance administrative costs.
compare: **noneconomic loss**

economic perils

Property. One of three categories of perils, the others being "human perils" and "natural perils." Economic perils include those things that relate to the production, distribution, and consumption of goods and services. These perils would include loss of income, financial loss, and devaluation of property or goods.
see: **human perils, natural perils, peril**

economic value

Property. A method used to determine a building's value, which is based on the structure's earnings potential, as opposed to its depreciated or replacement value. Occasionally, an insurer will insure on the basis of economic values.
compare: **actual cash value, functional replacement cost, replacement cost, reproduction cost**

economic value of an individual life

Casualty/Life.
see: **human life value**

educational fund

Life. A life insurance policy that is designed to fund a child's education if the insured (the family's provider) dies.
compare: **emergency fund**

educators professional liability insurance

Casualty. Professional liability insurance that protects a school district from suits brought against the school board members, faculty, staff, student teachers, and volunteers, for acts, errors or omissions. Coverage is usually included for claims alleging bodily injury due to corporal punishment.

effective date

Insurer Operations. The date on which coverage under an insurance policy or bond begins.
see: **date of issue, expiration date, policy period**

efficacy coverage

Financial Guarantee Insurance. A form of financial guarantee insurance that is available for large industrial construction projects. Coverage guarantees that an installation (e.g., chemical plant, manufacturing facility) will perform efficiently (as represented or warranted). Coverage usually guarantees the loans used to finance the project, the repayment of which are contingent on the project meeting certain minimum production requirements.
see: **products warranty inefficacy insurance;** syn: **inefficacy coverage**

efficiency of a vessel

Ocean Marine. An ocean marine policy provision that pays for repairing damage caused by an insured peril.

ejectment bond

Surety. A bond that may be required of a plaintiff (property owner, landlord) before a law enforcement agency will dispossess a person of property they do not want to surrender. The plaintiff in the action must furnish the agency with the bond to protect them against a suit filed by the defendant in the event of wrongful dispossession.
see: **dispossess**

© 1991 NILS Publishing Company

election to avoid a policy

Insurer Operations. An insurer's right to not fulfill a policy's obligations if the insured misrepresents or conceals certain facts or activities. The right must be exercised with reasonable promptness, and the insurer cannot remain silent, or the right to avoid the policy will be lost (estopped).

see: estoppel, misrepresentation, concealment

elective benefits

Health. An option allowing an insured under a disability policy to receive a lump sum benefit payment for certain injuries (fractures, dislocations), rather than receiving periodic payments.

syn: optional benefits

elective surgery

Health. A surgical procedure or operation undertaken to treat or correct a condition that is not considered life-threatening.

electrical apparatus exclusion

Property. A property policy provision that excludes coverage for loss or damage caused by artificially generated electric current, including electric arcing that disturbs electrical devices, appliances or wires. However, if fire results, coverage is provided for the resulting fire damage.

syn: dynamo clause, electrical exemption clause; see: electrical disturbance coverage

electrical disturbance coverage

Property. Coverage designed to delete the apparatus exclusion in fire insurance policies.

see: electrical apparatus exclusion

electrical exemption clause

Property.

see: electrical apparatus exclusion

electrical grounding

Loss Control. An electrical connection between a conductive body and the earth, which eliminates any difference in potential between the object and the ground. A proper electrical ground will discharge a charged conductive body.

see: bonding, ground fault circuit interrupter

electronic and computer crime coverage

Crime. Coverage designed to complement insurance available under a banker's blanket bond (Financial Institution Form 24). Coverage is for fraudulent input of electronic data or computer instructions to the insured's computer, by unauthorized access to a terminal or a bank's communications lines, or by the fraudulent preparation of tapes or computer programs.

see: banker's blanket bond, computer fraud, computer fraud coverage form

electronic funds transfer plan (EFT)

General/Life.

see: preauthorized check plan

electrostatic precipitator

Loss Control. Equipment that removes dust or fume particles from the air. An electrostatic precipitator ionizes the particles and collects them on negatively-charged plates.

elevator collision insurance

Casualty/Property.

see: elevator liability insurance

elevator liability insurance

Casualty. An old form of liability insurance that was designed specifically for elevators, escalators or other hoisting devices. It provided coverage for claims brought because of bodily injury or property damage caused by the device, as well as damage to the device itself. In modern times, losses have been infrequent and the ISO commercial general liability (CGL) form does not address (exclude) this exposure.

syn: elevator collision insurance

eligibility period

Employee Benefits. A period of time (usually the first 30 days of employment) during which an employee may elect to participate in an employee benefit plan without proving insurability (by taking a physical examination).

eligibility requirements

Employee Benefits. Conditions such as a minimum employment period which employees must meet to qualify for benefits.

elimination period

Health.

see: waiting period

embargo

Ocean Marine. A government order prohibiting the departure of ships or the shipment of goods from some or all of the ports under its authority.

see: demurrage

embezzlement

Surety. Depriving an individual of his or her money or property by breaking a trust relationship.

see: defalcation

emergencies

Insurer Operations/Risk Management. Large-scale situations that have the potential to adversely affect the processing of claims and premium payments. "Emergencies" include war, economic depression, major earthquakes, hurricanes, etc.

see: disaster plan

© 1991 NILS Publishing Company

emergency exposure limit (EEL)

Loss Control. The maximum period of time an individual can be exposed to a toxic agent during an emergency situation and still be physically safe.

emergency fund

Life. A term used to describe the use of a life insurance policy with a small face amount which is specifically maintained to provide funds to cover emergency expenses after the death of the principal breadwinner in a family.

see: readjustment income; compare: educational fund

Emergency National Flood Insurance Program

Loss Control. One of two National Flood Insurance Programs available to communities. This program provides coverage until the requirements for the Regular National Flood Insurance Program can be met. The amounts of coverage available under this program are: 1) Single family dwellings: $35,000 on the structure and $10,000 on contents; 2) Small business: $100,000 on the structure and $100,000 on the contents.

compare: Regular National Flood Insurance Program; see: National Flood Insurance Program

emergency rules and regulations

Regulation. A term used to describe administrative rules or regulations adopted without prior notice and hearing, or after only an abbreviated notice period and cursory hearing.

see: administrative procedure

emergency service organization liability

Casualty. Liability coverage for volunteer fire departments and other emergency service organizations, that incorporates professional and general liability coverages.

eminent domain

General. A term used to refer to the power of governmental subdivisions to appropriate private land for public use without the owner's consent and requiring that the owner be fairly compensated.

see: inverse condemnation; compare: dedicate

emotional distress

Casualty.
see: mental distress

empirical rate calculation

Insurer Operations. A judgment-or experience-based rate loading that is added to the "burning cost" for expected increases in the number and sizes of

losses, IBNR, inflation, expenses, profits and contingencies.

see: rate making

employee

Casualty/Workers' Compensation. An individual who performs services for another under an expressed or implied contract, for wages or other valuable consideration, and who acts under the direction of that party.

compare: employer, independent contractor; see: arising out of and in the course of employment, domestic, leased employee, master servant rule, respondeat superior

employee benefit liability

Casualty/Employee Benefits.
see: employee benefit plans liability

employee benefit plan

Employee Benefits. A plan created or maintained by an employer or employee organization, providing benefits such as life insurance, health insurance, disability income insurance or dental insurance. The plan's cost can be completely paid by the employer or shared by the employer and employees. Such a plan can also provide advantages or benefits to employees whether or not they are insured, including sick leave, disability or profit-sharing.

see: Employee Retirement Income Security Act of 1974, Welfare and Pension Plans Disclosure Act

employee benefit plans liability

Casualty/Employee Benefits. Insurance coverage for employers against any claims made by employees or former employees caused by a negligent act, error or omission in the administration of the insured's employee benefit programs.

syn: employee benefit liability

Employee Benefit Research Institute (EBRI)

Organizations. Members: Any individual or organization with an interest in employee benefit plans. *Objectives:* Promotes development of effective and responsible public policy through research, publications, educational programs and seminars on employee benefits. *Founded:* 1978. *Headquarters:* Washington, D.C.

employee contributions

Employee Benefits. Payments made by an employee to an employee benefit plan, either to obtain coverage under contributory plans, or on a voluntary basis under a noncontributory plan to increase benefits.

employee dishonesty crime form

Crime. A crime coverage form which provides coverage for loss of, and loss from damage to, money,

© 1991 NILS Publishing Company

securities and property other than money and securities caused directly by employee dishonesty.

syn: crime coverage form A; see: crime coverages, money, property other than money and securities, securities

employee leasing

Workers' Compensation. A term used to refer to an arrangement whereby an employment service company provides full-time employees to other employers for a fee. Some leasing companies will assume or hire the employees of an existing organization, and lease them back to that organization. The employee leasing firm handles payroll and tax reports and obtains workers' compensation and employee benefit coverages for the leased employees. Such arrangements have been entered into by some employers to avoid application of a high workers' compensation experience modification factor. Rating bureaus have, in turn, adopted rules designed to discourage this practice.

see: employee, leased employee

Employee Retirement Income Security Act of 1974 (ERISA)

Employee Benefits. Federal legislation passed by Congress in 1974 (and subsequent amendments), imposing a fiduciary responsibility on individuals who administer, supervise and manage private pension plans. The act regulates plan funding, participation, vesting, termination, disclosure and federal tax treatment. Under ERISA, an insurance program has been established to guarantee that employees will receive their pension benefits in the event that a defined pension plan is terminated.

see: Pension Benefit Guaranty Corporation, self-administered plan

employee stock ownership plan (ESOP)

Employee Benefits. A form of employee benefit plan, where stock of a corporation is distributed to employees. Usually the distribution is based on a formula tied to wages and is not dependent on the corporation's profitability. It can be a qualified stock bonus plan or a qualified stock bonus and money purchase plan. Such plans are often used as a financing method for a corporation where funds are loaned to the ESOP, which are used to buy corporate treasury shares thereby increasing the corporation's capital. The stock is pledged to support the loan, and a corporate guarantee is given for its repayment. Tax benefits accrue to both the corporation and the employees under this plan.

employer

Casualty/Workers' Compensation. One who hires an employee. An individual, firm, partnership, association, corporation, legal representative of a deceased employer, or the receiver or trustee of a person, partnership, association, or corporation who uses or engages the services of another under a contract for hire.

compare: employee, independent contractor; see: respondeat superior

employer credits

Employee Benefits. Credits which apply against future contributions required under an employer's accounting and administration of a pension plan. These credits accumulate when an employee leaves prior to being fully vested or works beyond the normal retirement age. Exceptions to this requirement arise in those circumstances where the IRS requires "cash basis" accounting.

Employers Council on Flexible Compensation (ECFC)

Organizations. Members: Employers currently using or considering a flexible compensation plan. *Objectives:* Promotes and improves flexible compensation plans. *Founded:* 1981. *Headquarters:* Washington, D.C.

employers liability coverage

Casualty/Workers' Compensation. Insurance that provides coverage against an employer's common law liability for bodily injury to employees occurring within the scope of their employment when that liability is not covered by workers' compensation. Primary coverage is provided under coverage Section B of a workers' compensation policy. Excess coverage can be provided under most umbrella and excess liability policies.

syn: coverage B; see: workers' compensation insurance

employers mutual liability insurance association

Insurer Operations. Any corporation, association or other entity formed by employers to mutually insure against employer's liability claims.

employers nonownership liability

Automobile.

see: nonowned automobile liability

enact

Regulation. To develop and establish new laws; to pass through legislative and executive action.

compare: promulgate

encumbrance

Title. A legal term for a documented claim against property, such as a mortgage.

see: lien, mortgage

endorsement

Insurer Operations. A written amendment, added to and made part of an insurance policy, which modifies

© 1991 NILS Publishing Company

endorsement in blank

endorsement – continued

the policy. An endorsement supersedes the printed policy text. In the event that two endorsements contradict each other, the one with the latest effective date (or issue) prevails.

compare: rider; see: attachment, date of issue, effective date, insurance contract, interline endorsement; Fr: avenant; Gr: Nachtrag; Sp: endoso

endorsement in blank

Inland Marine/Ocean Marine. A term used to refer to the process whereby an insured may assign his or her rights to insurance on a special cargo policy for an order bill of lading, by endorsing the reverse side of a certificate issued by the insurer to provide the evidence of insurance.

see: bill of lading, open cargo policy, order bill of lading

endothermic process

Loss Control. A process in which heat is absorbed.

compare: exothermic process

endowment policy

Life. A form of life insurance which pays the insured the face value on the maturity date stated in the contract. If the insured dies before the maturity date, a beneficiary receives the policy's face value.

compare: term life insurance, whole life insurance

enemy alien

Regulation. An insurer domiciled in a country at war with the insured's nation, or an individual residing in a country at war with the insurer's country of domicile. It is against public policy for insurance to be transacted with enemy aliens at a time of war.

enemy goods

Ocean Marine. "Enemy goods" are those items of cargo carried on a vessel that are shipped from or to an opponent in war. A provision of the 1856 Treaty of Paris states that cargo, excluding contraband of war, is free of capture when it is carried on a neutral ship. Contraband of war (weapons, ammunition, etc.) are open to seizure, while other enemy goods are not.

see: free of capture and seizure

enemy property insurance

Ocean Marine. Property insurance for goods covered by a license granted by the insurer's country to an enemy for trading goods.

energy-release theory

Loss Control. An early loss control theory developed by Dr. William Haddon, Jr. It holds that accidents are caused by the transfer of energy with sufficient force to cause bodily injury or property damage, and if this transfer of energy can be interrupted or suppressed, the chain of events leading to the accident will be broken.

compare: domino theory

engineer

Loss Control.

see: loss control specialist

engineering approach

Loss Control. A loss control approach that concentrates on the physical characteristics of the risk to reduce accidents and injuries. The approach emphasizes the use of safeguards on equipment, air bags in autos, etc.

see: loss control

engineers professional liability insurance

Casualty. Provides coverage for an individual engineer or an engineering firm. Provides coverage for claims which the insured becomes legally obligated to pay as damages arising out of the performance of professional services including errors, omissions, or negligent acts. Coverage is usually written on a claims-made basis.

see: professional liability insurance

enjoin

General. An order by a court for an individual or entity to perform, desist, refrain, or abstain from a specific act.

see: cease and desist, injunctive relief

Enrolled Actuary (EA)

Organizations. An individual who is enrolled with the federal Joint Board for the Enrollment of Actuaries.

enrollment card

Employee Benefits. An application (in the form of a card) that an employee completes to enroll in an employee benefit plan.

entertainment insurance

Casualty. A broad term used to refer to any insurance that protects against loss of revenues suffered by promoters, film companies, concert facilities, distributors, etc., resulting from the interruption, cancellation or postponement of theatrical, musical, television, motion picture or other entertainment productions, including sporting events.

see: hole-in-one coverage, prize indemnification insurance, television closed circuit breakdown insurance

entire contract provision

Insurer Operations. A policy provision stating that the written policy contains all of the contractual agreements between the insured and insurer. This provision eliminates the possibility of either party

© 1991 NILS Publishing Company

utilizing outside evidence to modify the contract, such as an oral agreement. The policy terms can be amended or waived only by an endorsement issued by the insurer.

see: insurance contract

entire contract statute

Regulation. A statute enacted in some states which makes an insurance policy and its application the entire contract between the parties. Generally, an "entire contract" statute precludes an oral misrepresentation from being used as a defense by an insurer against claim payment.

environmental impairment liability

Casualty. Coverage against third-party claims brought because of damage to the environment caused by an insured. Such insurance usually will also cover the costs involved in the clean-up of pollution events. Intentional acts are excluded.

syn: pollution legal liability; see: pollutant; pollution exclusion; Comprehensive Environmental Response, Compensation and Liability Act

equipment

Property. For insurance purposes, a broad term applying to mobile property, including anything used to equip a person, organization or thing that is not a building or machinery.

compare: machinery; see: equipment floater

equipment dealers floater

Inland Marine. An inland marine policy form that provides coverage for dealers in agriculture implements and contractors equipment, such as bulldozers, reapers, harvesters, plows, tractors, air compressors and road scrapers. Coverage is usually written on an "open perils" basis and includes the dealer's stock in trade, and similar property of others in the care, custody or control of the dealer.

equipment floater

Inland Marine. A broad term applied to any of a number of inland marine forms for mobile property, including coverage forms for contractors equipment, equipment dealers, film, floor plans, jewelers, and physicians and surgeons equipment.

see: bicycle floater, camera floater, contractors equipment floater, equipment dealers floater, fine arts floater, floater policy, fur floater, installation floater, jewelry floater, livestock floater, pattern and die floater, personal articles floater, personal property floater, physicians and surgeons floater, salesmen's samples floater, sign floater, unscheduled property floater, wedding presents floater

equipment value insurance

Financial Guarantee Insurance. A policy covering leased equipment, guaranteeing its value on a specific date (usually, but not necessarily, the lease's termination date). If the equipment's fair market value is less than the value stated in the policy on the agreed date, the insurer would pay the difference.

see: residual value, residual value insurance

equity

General.

see: owner's equity

Insurer Operations. State laws require that insurance rates be nondiscriminatory for all consumers. Equity in rates is accomplished by setting policy rates according to the expected losses for a specific group of similar insureds. Thus, all insureds having these loss characteristics will be assigned to the same underwriting classification.

see: discrimination, rate making

equity variable annuity plan

Life. A variable annuity where the plan's benefit units or accumulation units are tied to the value of a specific portfolio of stocks or bonds.

see: accumulation, annuity, variable annuity

ERISA Industry Committee (ERIC)

Organizations. Members: Corporations that sponsor major employee pension and benefit plans. *Objectives:* Represents employers regarding policy, legislation, judicial, and regulatory matters involving the administration of private pension and benefit plans. *Founded:* 1977. *Headquarters:* Washington, D.C.

error

Casualty. A peril insured under some liability policies, an "error" is a departure from what is true, right or proper; a deviation from an established standard or guide.

see: errors & omissions insurance, omission

errors & omissions clause

Reinsurance. A provision included in some obligatory treaty reinsurance contracts, which provides that if an error or omission is made in describing a risk that falls within the contract, it shall not invalidate the reinsurer's liability for that risk.

see: obligatory reinsurance treaty

errors & omissions insurance (E & O)

Casualty. Coverage that protects the insured for damages arising out of the insured's acts, errors or omissions when performing duties for another party. This coverage often has a deductible in excess of $1,000, and unlike professional liability coverage, usually does not require the insured's consent to

© 1991 NILS Publishing Company

E & O — continued

settle claims. *Examples:* Advertising E&O broadcasters E&O, management consultants E&O, travel agents E&O, and real estate agents E&O.

see: adjuster errors & omissions insurance, agents errors & omissions insurance, auctioneers errors & omissions insurance, county clerks and recorders errors & omissions insurance, credit bureaus errors & omissions insurance, customs brokers and freight forwarders errors & omissions insurance, data processors errors & omissions insurance, error, errors & omissions clause, oil landmen and lease brokers errors & omissions insurance, omission, premium finance company errors & omissions insurance, professional liability insurance, real estate agents errors & omissions insurance, registered mutual fund representative errors & omissions insurance, seedmens errors & omissions insurance, tax preparers errors & omissions insurance, testing and research laboratory errors & omissions insurance, transfer agents errors & omissions insurance, trust departments errors & omissions insurance, trustees and fiduciaries errors and omissions insurance

escheat

General. A legal term for the reversion of property to the state when an individual dies without heirs, or when an individual fails to carry out an action. Bank accounts often are claimed by government when left inactive for an extended period of time.

compare: devise

estate planning

Financial Planning. The systematic review of an individual's or family's wealth, to enhance its value, to protect or conserve it, and to distribute it over an extended period of time.

estate tax

Financial Planning/Life. Tax paid to the federal government based on an estate's value after the owner dies.

see: federal estate tax; syn: inheritance tax

estimated annual premium (EAP)

Workers' Compensation. The amount of premium that an employer pays at the beginning of a policy period. EAP is determined by multiplying estimated payrolls by the rates which correspond to their classifications, and by the experience rating modification factor. At the end of the policy period, additional or return premiums will be calculated using the final payrolls.

see: deposit premium, initial premium, provisional premium; compare: additional premium, return premium

estimated constant dollar earnings per share

Property/Risk Management. An estimate of the impact of changes in the Consumer Price Index (CPI) on the cost of replacing – at today's prices – previously purchased property that was depreciated at rates sufficient only to recover the original costs. This estimate also adjusts earnings per share for the impact on cost of sales and inventories.

see: earnings per share

estimated premium

Insurer Operations.

see: deposit premium, estimated annual premium, initial premium, provisional premium

estoppel

General. A legal principle stating that when an individual represents a material fact to another individual, who materially changes position in reasonable reliance on the representation, the first individual is "estopped" (prohibited) from denying that the condition exists. *Examples:* An insurer may be estopped from denying a claim which occurs after a policy expired, if the insurer acted as though the policy had been or would be renewed.

see: acquiescence, election to avoid a policy, laches, nonwaiver agreement, reservation of rights, waiver

Eurodollars

International. United States currency deposited in foreign banks or other foreign financial institutions, used to settle international transactions.

see: money

evidence

General. Testimony, documents or physical articles legally submitted to a legal tribunal to determine the truth of a matter.

see: demonstrative evidence, documentary evidence, expert witness, hearsay evidence

evidence and duties provision

Insurer Operations. A provision in insurance policies requiring the insured to cooperate with the insurer in the investigation, settlement or defense of a claim or suit.

syn: duties provision, evidence provision

evidence of cancellation

Insurer Operations. When a cancellation notice is

© 1991 NILS Publishing Company

mailed, the insurance company generally is not required to show proof that the policyholder received the notice. The company need only prove that the notice was mailed.

see: cancellation, cancellation notice, first named insured

evidence of insurability

Health/Life. A statement on an insurance application, or in a medical examination report, that provides proof of an individual's occupation or physical condition, which helps determine that individual's acceptability for insurance.

compare: guaranteed insurability

evidence provision

Insurer Operations.
see: evidence and duties provision

examination

Regulation. The audit and review by a state insurance department of an insurance company's operations, records and books of account.

syn: audit; see: insurance examiner
Life/Health.
see: medical examination

examination bureau

Regulation. Organizations licensed to examine policies, renewal certificates, endorsements and other forms to ensure that appropriate rates are being charged, and forms are being used.

see: audit bureau, bureau insurer, rating bureau

examined business

Insurer Operations. Life or health insurance, where an applicant has applied for coverage and has passed a required physical examination, but has not yet paid the initial premium to allow issuance of the policy.

compare: delivered business, issued business, not taken, paid business, placed business, written business; see: medical examination

examiner

Regulation.
see: insurance examiner

excess aggregate reinsurance

Reinsurance.
see: aggregate excess of loss reinsurance

excess and surplus lines broker (E & S)

Agency. A speciality insurance broker who obtains coverage on difficult-to-place, unique or large risks through an insurance company that is not licensed to do business in the broker's state of domicile. These brokers come under special licensing provisions and usually act as wholesale brokers to agents.

syn: excess line broker; see: excess lines, non-admitted market, surplus lines, surplus lines broker

excess insurance

Insurer Operations. Coverage that is provided above a primary policy or a self-insured retention which includes the initial range of losses.

excess interest

Life. In a whole life policy, that portion of the interest credited to the policy's cash values that is in excess of the guaranteed minimum interest rate.

excessive

Regulation. Referring to a provision found in most state insurance departments' regulations, prohibiting an insurer from charging rates that generate an unfair amount of profit.

compare: adequate; see: equity, rate making

excess liability insurance

Casualty. Insurance coverage that is written in excess of primary insurance. It is designed to increase the limits of liability, thereby providing catastrophe coverage. Excess liability coverage does not respond to a loss until the amount of the loss exceeds (or exhausts) any existing primary policy limits. *Example:* A primary $500,000 liability policy is written, and excess insurance is written for $2,000,000 excess of the primary. The primary policy would pay all losses within $500,000 and the excess policy would pay losses in excess of the primary coverage, up to the excess policy limit of $2,000,000.

compare: umbrella liability insurance; see: aggregate excess insurance, buffer layer, direct excess policy, following form excess liability insurance, layering

excess line broker

Agency.
see: excess and surplus lines broker

excess line reinsurance

Reinsurance. An excess of loss reinsurance contract, where the limit and deductible are expressed as "each and every loss, each and every risk."

excess lines

Agency. A term used to describe insurance purchased to cover risks for which coverage is not available through normal channels, but which may be insured in the excess and surplus lines market.

compare: unauthorized insurance; see: excess and surplus lines broker, surplus lines

excess loss premium factor

Casualty/Workers' Compensation. A retrospective rating factor used when a specific loss limitation is included in the plan. A rate or flat charge is included in the plan, to limit the amount of any one loss that is to be included in the rating formula. *Example:* A plan with a $250,000 loss limitation would include only the first $250,000 of each occurrence in the plan's losses when the final premium is calculated.

see: **retrospective rating plan**

excess loss-ratio reinsurance

Reinsurance. A form of nonproportional treaty reinsurance, whereby the reinsurer responds when a ceding company's losses during a specified period (usually 12 months) on a specific line or book of business exceed a stated loss ratio – usually the ceding insurer's overall loss ratio – for the same period.

compare: **nonproportional automatic reinsurance**; see: **aggregate excess of loss reinsurance**

excess of loss insurance

General. Coverage for that portion of a loss which exceeds a certain amount retained by the insured or covered by other insurance, and then only for liability in excess of that figure.

see: **excess liability insurance, excess property insurance, layering, umbrella liability insurance**

excess of loss reinsurance

Reinsurance. A form of nonproportional reinsurance which indemnifies the ceding company for that portion of each loss occurrence which is in excess of a stipulated primary (ceding) company retention. This form of reinsurance is usually used with casualty risks.

see: **attachment point, net retained lines clause, nonproportional reinsurance, retention and limits clause, treaty reinsurance, workers' compensation catastrophe policy, working cover**

excess property insurance

Property. A property insurance program for large commercial accounts that is layered, with a primary policy that has a stop-loss limit designed to cover most losses, after which a separate excess policy will provide coverage for catastrophic losses. *Example:* A primary property policy written on an "all-risks" basis for $5,000,000, and an excess property policy written on a "named perils" basis for $20,000,000 excess of the primary policy's $5,000,000.

see: **layering**

exchange

General.

see: **insurance exchange, reciprocal insurance exchange**

exchange rate

International. The rate at which the currency cof one country can be exchanged for that of another.

see: **Eurodollars, money**

exchange transfer insurance

International. Exporters of goods are indemnified for a specified percentage (usually 80 percent) of their net loss if the government of the buyer's country prevents the transfer of payment by law, order, decree or regulation. Coverage can be extended to include financial losses resulting from the revocation of import and export licenses.

see: **export credit insurance**

excise tax

Insurer Operations/Reinsurance. A federal tax which applies to some types of insurance placed with non-U.S. domiciled insurers or reinsurers.

excluded assets

Insurer Operations/Regulation. Assets of an insurer which are not included in financial statements prepared under statutory accounting principles, but which would be assets for financial statements prepared under generally accepted accounting principles. *Examples:* Accounts receivable more than 90 days in arrears, or office equipment.

see: **Generally Accepted Accounting Principles, nonadmitted assets, Statutory Accounting Principles**

excluded period

Health.

see: **probationary period**

exclusion

Insurer Operations. An insurance policy or bond provision that denies (excludes) coverage for specified hazards, perils, persons, property, or locations.

see: **blasting and explosion exclusion, care, custody or control exclusion, civil commotion exclusion, collapse exclusion, communicable disease exclusion, conversion, embezzlement or secretion exclusion, electrical apparatus exclusion, face, family exclusion, faulty workmanship exclusion, foundation exclusion clause, governmental action exclusion, impairment exclusion rider, insects, birds, rodents or other animals exclusion, insurance contract, insuring agreement, limitations, military service exclusion, named driver exclusion, nuclear hazard exclusion, ordinance or law exclusion, ordinary payroll exclusion endorsement, passenger hazard exclusion, policy conditions, policy declarations, pollution exclusion, products recall exclusion, quarantine exclusion, strikes, riots and civil commotions exclusion,**

126

© 1991 NILS Publishing Company

temperature extremes exclusion, testing exclusion, trick and device exclusion, underground exclusion, water exclusion clause, watercraft exclusion, wear and tear exclusion; Fr: exclusion; Gr: Ausschlüsse; Sp: exclusión

exclusive agency system

Agency/Insurer Operations. An insurance distribution system within which individual agents or agencies have contracts with a single insurer. Such contracts limit the agents' or agencies' sales and service to policies of the insurer to whom they are contracted. The exclusive representation agreement between the insurer and exclusive agent also specifies that the ownership, use and control of policy records and expiration dates belong to the insurer.

compare: independent agency system; see: captive agent, direct selling system

exclusive remedy

Workers' Compensation. State workers' compensation statutes gave employees a definite remedy for injuries and diseases arising out of or suffered in the course of their employment. In exchange for this, an employee's remedy against his or her employer was made exclusive; that is, with just a few exceptions, a worker's right of recovery against his or her employer is limited to the benefits provided by the workers' compensation law. The employee may not sue. Exceptions include cases in which the employer had displayed gross negligence, has assaulted the employee, or where the injury has been caused through the employer's activities in some capacity other than as employer (e.g., as the manufacturer of machinery which is sold to others, but which is also used by the employer – and, by extension, by the employee – in the manufacturing process).

see: common law defense, dual capacity doctrine

ex-dividend date

Financial Planning. The date by which an investor must have purchased a stock in order to receive announced dividends or stock distributions.

see: dividend

executed contract

General. A contract under which all obligations of the parties have been performed.

compare: executory contract; see: contract

executor

General. An individual who is appointed or specified in a legally valid will, to execute the provisions of the will.

see: executrix

executory contract

General. A contract under which all obligations of the parties have not yet been performed.

compare: executed contract; see: contract

executrix

General. A female executor.

see: executor

exemplary damages

General.

see: punitive damages

exemption

General. A provision allowing an individual or organization to be free or excluded from certain duties.

Example: Tax exemptions, reporting exemptions.

see: tax planning

ex gratia payment

Insurer Operations. A payment made by an insurer to an insured or claimant, even if a valid claim does not exist. The payment is made because the insurer believes a mistake or a misunderstanding exists, but desires to maintain goodwill. The term "ex gratia" is Latin and means "from favor."

see: claim expense, nuisance value

exhibition policy

Inland Marine. A trip transit policy that covers property during transit, from the original location to the place of exhibit, while the property is on exhibition, and during the return trip to the original location. Coverage is usually written on an "all-risks" basis.

see: trip transit insurance

ex mod

Casualty/Workers' Compensation.

see: experience modification

exoneration

Surety.

see: right of exoneration

exothermic process

Loss Control. A process in which heat is produced.

compare: endothermic process

ex parte communications

General. Communications about any matter subject to a pending legal proceeding, occurring between one party to the proceeding and the presiding officer, in the absence of and without the knowledge of the other party.

expatriate

International. An individual that lives and works in a country other than his or her homeland.

© 1991 NILS Publishing Company

expected expense ratio

Insurer Operations. A formula used by an insurer to relate expected income to expected incurred expenses. *Formula:* Expected Expense Ratio = Expected Incurred Expenses/Expected Written Premiums.

see: expected expenses, expense ratio

expected expenses

Insurer Operations. Expense projections for a future period of time, developed by an insurer, generally through the budgeting process. "Expected expenses" does not include claims and claims adjusting expense figures.

see: expected expense ratio

expected losses

Insurer Operations. Loss and claim expense projections, based on actuarially developed probability calculations. An insurer will use such projections in their budgeting process.

see: expected loss ratio, incurred but not reported

expected loss ratio

Insurer Operations. A formula used by insurance companies to relate expected income to expected losses. *Formula:* Expected Loss Ratio = (Expected Incurred Losses + Expected Loss Adjusting Expense)/Expected Earned Premiums.

see: expected losses, loss ratio

expected morbidity

Health. The anticipated number of individuals within a given group who will become ill or injured within a specified period of time as indicated on a morbidity table.

see: morbidity rate; compare: expected mortality

expected mortality

Life. The anticipated number of individuals within a given group who will die within a specified period of time as indicated on a mortality table.

see: mortality rate; compare: expected morbidity

expected rate of return

Financial Planning. The rate of return an organization expects to realize from an investment.

see: return on investment

Risk Management.

see: rate of return

expected return

Risk Management. The expected return is the mean value of the probability distribution of the possible returns.

see: expected rate of return

expediting expenses

Property. Coverage included in business income and boiler and machinery policies, which pays for the extra expenses required to speed the repair of damaged property and thus resume operations more quickly.

see: extra expense insurance

expense allowance

Agency/Insurer Operations. An allowance paid to an insurance agent, in addition to commissions, to encourage the placing of business with an insurer.

see: agent's commission

expense constant

Insurer Operations. An expense factor (usually a flat dollar amount) that is added to the premium charged for a class of policies, which policies would otherwise produce insufficient premium to cover the cost of issuing and servicing them.

see: rate making

expense funds

Life. Funds maintained by nonlegal reserve insurers.

see: legal reserve life insurance company

expense loading

Insurer Operations. Insurance company administrative and sales expenses (e.g., commissions, taxes, advertising), which are added to the insurer's pure or basic premium to develop a final premium.

see: field expenses, general and insurance expenses, pure premium, rate making

expense-only claim

Casualty. A claim for which the insurer pays claims expenses, but no indemnity payments.

see: claim

expense ratio

Insurer Operations. A formula used by insurance companies to relate income to administrative expenses (e.g., commissions, taxes, acquisition advertising and administration expenses). *Formula:* Expenses (excluding losses, loss adjusting expenses and policyholder dividends)/Earned premiums.

compare: combined ratio, dividend ratio, expected expense ratio, loss ratio; see: underwriting margin

expense reserve

Insurer Operations. A reserve established for liabilities, resulting from incurred but unpaid expenses.

see: reserve

expenses

Insurer Operations. All expenses associated with the cost of doing business. Insurance companies divide

© 1991 NILS Publishing Company

expenses into two major categories: administrative expenses and loss expenses.

see: expense ratio, loss ratio; Fr: frais; Gr: Aufwendungen; Sp: gastos

experience

Insurer Operations.
see: loss experience

experience modification

Workers' Compensation. A factor (expressed as a percentage) that is developed by a rating bureau for workers' compensation insurance. The calculations relate an employer's losses, payrolls, and premiums, segregated according to classifications of operations, all as reported to the bureau by the employer's insurance company.

syn: ex mod; see: experience rating plan

Casualty. A factor that attempts to reflect an insured's actual losses in relation to the same insured's premium. This factor will either increase or decrease the insured's premium, based on the outcome of an experience rating calculation. A *retrospective plan* modifies the premium after the policy period or after most of the policy period, while a *prospective plan* will examine prior periods, such as the last three years, to produce a premium.

syn: ex mod; see: experience rating plan, prospective rating plan, retrospective rating plan

experience rating form

Workers' Compensation. A document produced on an annual basis that indicates an employer's premium, loss experience and experience modification factor.

see: experience modification

experience rating plan

Casualty/Workers' Compensation. Rating plans that consider the past loss experience of the insured to develop current policy rates. Usually, the past three to five years of loss experience are used to develop an experience credit or debit that is applied to the manual rates for the specific risk being rated.

see: "D" ratio, experience modification, rate making, retrospective rating plan

experience refund

Casualty/Workers' Compensation. The return of a portion of the premium paid by an insured because of a favorable loss ratio under a retention or retrospectively rated plan.

Reinsurance. A predetermined percentage of the net reinsurance profit which the reinsurer returns to the ceding company as a form of profit sharing at year's end.

expert witness

General. A witness who has been qualified in a judicial proceeding as an expert on a particular subject, and who will be allowed to give opinion testimony. Usually expert witnesses assist the judge or the jury in understanding technical subjects.

see: board certified, evidence

expiration card

Agency/Insurer Operations. A card maintained by an agent or insurer, which records the date on which a policy terminates. It is used to prompt the agent or insurer to solicit renewal of the policy.

see: expiration file, tickler

expiration date

Insurer Operations. The date on which an insurance policy or bond terminates or ceases to provide coverage.

see: cancellation, effective date, expiration notice, policy period, renewal

expiration file

Agency/Insurer Operations. A listing, often maintained on a data base by an agent and insurer, of the inception and expiration dates of all policies they have written. An expiration file has the same purpose as a collection of expiration cards.

see: expiration card, tickler

expiration notice

Insurer Operations. A written notice mailed to an insured, prior to the expiration date of an insurance policy.

compare: cancellation notice

explosion

Loss Control. A violent bursting, accompanied by a sudden burning, so that there is a violent expansion of hot gases with a great disruptive force and a loud noise. As respects insurance, the term includes the explosion of accumulated gases or unconsumed fuel which pass through flues or passages.

see: blasting and explosion exclusion, explosion-proof, explosive atmosphere, firebox explosion, furnace explosion, inherent explosion; Fr: explosion; Gr: Explosion; Sp: explosión

explosion, collapse, and underground exclusions

Casualty.
see: XCU exclusions

explosion-proof

Loss Control. A term used to describe electrical fixtures and devices which have been designed to prevent them from becoming a source of ignition for gases or dust located near the fixture or device.

see: fireproof

© 1991 NILS Publishing Company

explosive atmosphere
Loss Control. An atmosphere containing a mixture of vapor or gas which is within the explosive or flammable range.

explosive level
Loss Control.
see: flammable limits

export
International. To carry or send merchandise from one country to another country.
compare: import; see: customs broker

export bond
Surety.
see: federal bond

export credit insurance
International. Insurance that protects a domestic exporter against loss resulting from their inability to collect on credit that the exporter extends to its commercial customers in other countries. Coverage is divided into *commercial perils* and *political perils.* Commercial perils include insolvency of the debtor, inability or unwillingness of the debtor to pay. Political perils include war, blocked currencies, and other governmental actions that make payment impossible. Most export credit coverage is provided by government-supported programs, but some private insurers are involved.
see: exchange transfer insurance, Export-Import Bank, Foreign Credit Insurance Association

Export-Import Bank (EXIM Bank)
International. A joint venture between the United States government and the Foreign Credit Insurance Association, an association formed by major U.S. insurers to encourage export of American goods. It was formed in 1934 to insure U.S. business ventures in foreign countries, for losses resulting from uncollectible foreign accounts and investments, or goods lost through war, insurrection, confiscation and currency devaluation.
see: export credit insurance, Foreign Credit Insurance Association

exposure
Casualty. The extent of exposure to loss, as measured by an exposure base, such as payroll, receipts, area, or units produced.
Fr: risque; Gr: Gefahrenumstand; Sp: riesgo
Property. In fire underwriting, the chance of a fire spreading to an insured risk from adjacent structures.
see: adjacent building; compare: construction, occupancy, protection
Loss Control. A hazardous condition brought about by the nature of an insured's operations or the operations or activities of others.

exposure and manifestation theory
Casualty. A liability insurance policy coverage concept which evolved from the asbestos case *Keene Corp. v. Insurance Company of North America.* This theory provides that any occurrence policy in force between the time of an initial exposure to asbestos and the manifestation of injury must respond to a claim.
see: Keene Doctrine

exposure base
Casualty.
see: exposure unit

exposure in residence theory
Casualty.
see: Keene Doctrine

exposure unit
Insurer Operations. The unit of measure (e.g., area, gross receipts, payroll) used to determine an insurance policy's premium. Also, often used to refer to an individual's risk or location.
syn: exposure base; see: base rate, experience modification, increased limits table, rate making

expressed authority
Agency/Insurer Operations. Authority given by an insurance company to an agent that is distinctly and plainly expressed, either orally or in writing. The written authority is granted in an agency agreement which usually allows the agent to countersign, issue, and deliver policies and binders, cancel policies and obligations, provide all usual and customary services of an insurance agent on all contracts of insurance accepted by the insurer from the agent, and collect policy premiums.
compare: actual authority, implied authority; see: agency, agency agreement, countersign

express warranty
Casualty. A provision within a sales contract, guaranteeing that the item sold is of a certain quality or condition.
syn: guarantee; compare: disclaimer, extended warranty agreement, implied warranty

expropriation insurance
International. Coverage against the taking of a business, property or assets by a foreign government. Coverage is written by the Overseas Private Investment Corporation, private insurers or Lloyd's of London.
see: political risk insurance

© 1991 NILS Publishing Company

expulsion

General. Involuntary ejection or removal from membership of an organization.

extended care facility (ECF)

Health. A health care facility that is intended to offer care, including skilled nursing care, rehabilitation and convalescent care over a long period of time. Such a facility does not provide acute care.

extended coverages (EC)

Property. Coverage for property damage caused by windstorm, hail, smoke, explosion, riot, riot attending a strike, civil commotion, vehicle and aircraft collision. This coverage is usually provided by endorsement to a basic policy (e.g., in conjunction with the standard fire insurance policy and various "package" policies).

compare: **additional extended coverage, coverage extension**

extended health insurance

Health. Health insurance for persons 65 years or older, usually provided through a joint underwriting association.

syn: over-age insurance; see: **joint underwriting association**

extended period of indemnity

Property. An endorsement to a loss of earnings (business income) policy, that reimburses the insured for reduced earnings after the premises have been restored and business has been resumed. The coverage provides protection against a delay in a business' return to full activity. *ISO Form: CP 00 30.*

see: **business income coverage form**

extended reporting period (ERP)

Casualty. A provision contained in most claims-made policies, which provides coverage under an expired claims-made policy for claims first made after the policy has expired. The period of time allowed to report claims may be limited (i.e., 60 days) or there may be no limit on the extended reporting period. Some policies will require an additional premium to extend the reporting period.

syn: tail coverage; see: **basic extended reporting period, claims-made form, maxi tail, mini tail, supplemental extended reporting period**

extended term life insurance

Life. A nonforfeiture option contained in most whole life insurance policies, providing term life coverage for the face amount of the existing policy for as long as the whole life policy's cash value lasts to pay the term life premiums.

see: **nonforfeiture extended term benefit, term life insurance**

extended wait

Reinsurance. Reinsurance of disability insurance contracts, wherein the reinsurer makes the monthly benefit payments after the ceding insurer has paid a specified number of monthly payments.

extended warranty agreement

Financial Guarantee Insurance. A contract or agreement under which someone other than the manufacturer assumes the cost of repair or replacement of a product due to mechanical breakdown, wear and tear, deterioration or other reasons. Extended warranties are sold on such items as automobiles and other motor vehicles, major appliances, etc. In some states, an extended warranty agreement is considered an insurance contract.

see: **expressed warranty**

exterminator liability insurance

Casualty. Liability coverage for exterminators who use poisonous chemicals to eliminate termites, rodents and other pests.

extortion

Crime. To obtain money or other valuable property from a person or an organization by force, ingenuity or illegal action.

see: **extortion coverage form, extortion insurance, kidnap insurance, kidnap-ransom-extortion insurance**

extortion coverage form

Crime. A crime coverage form which provides coverage against loss of money, securities, and property other than money and securities, which results directly from extortion.

syn: crime coverage form G; see: **crime coverages, extortion, money, property other than money and securities, securities**

extortion insurance

Crime. Coverage for money surrendered in response to a threat to harm persons or damage property.

see: **kidnap insurance, kidnap-ransom-extortion insurance**

extra expense insurance

Property. Property insurance coverage for the necessary additional expense of continuing business operations after damage to an insured premises, caused by a covered cause of loss.

compare: **additional living expense insurance, expediting expenses**

extra percentage tables

Health/Life. Mortality and morbidity tables which are used to determine, as a percentage of standard table premium, the additional premium required to insure

© 1991 NILS Publishing Company

extra percentage tables — continued
persons impaired by serious health conditions such as cancer or AIDS.

see: **acquired immune deficiency syndrome, cancer insurance, dread disease policy**

extraterritoriality

Workers' Compensation. A workers' compensation policy provision which extends coverage to pay the benefit level of a state other than the state where an employee is hired, in the event that the employee files a claim based on the benefit level of another state because the injury occurred in that state.

compare: **all-states endorsement, broad form all-states endorsement**

© 1991 NILS Publishing Company

F

face

Insurer Operations. The first page of an insurance policy, which usually includes the policy declarations.

see: exclusion, insurance contract, insuring agreement, policy conditions, policy declarations

face amount

Life. The death benefit of a life insurance policy.

see: limit of liability

Insurer Operations. The amount of insurance provided by the terms of an insurance policy, usually found on the policy's face or declarations.

see: limit of liability

facility-of-payment clause

Life. A provision contained in group life and industrial insurance policies which is designed to simplify benefit payments when there is doubt as to the policy beneficiary. It provides that the insurer may pay the benefits to any relative or person who has physical possession of the policy and who appears equitably entitled to its benefits.

see: group life insurance, industrial life insurance

fact finding

General. A form of arbitration whereby an individual, or small group of individuals, conducts a hearing to resolve a dispute. During the hearing, each involved party is allowed to present its viewpoint as to the issues involved, supporting evidence, rebuttals, and a proposed solution. After the hearing, the fact finder(s) prepares a written opinion which includes a nonbinding solution which may be accepted or which may lead to further negotiation.

see: arbitration

Factory Insurance Association (FIA)

Insurer Operations/Property.

see: Industrial Risk Insurers

Factory Mutual System (FM)

Property. The Factory Mutual System – once comprised of as many as 40 individual mutual companies – has experienced consolidations and mergers over the years, resulting in just three member organizations today: Allendale Mutual Insurance Company, Arkwright Mutual Insurance Company, and Protection Mutual Insurance Company. The companies specialize in property coverages and loss prevention services for large industrial and institutional properties worldwide. Jointly, they own the Factory Mutual Engineering Corporation, Factory Mutual Engineering Association, Factory Mutual Research Corporation, and Factory Mutual Service Bureau.

compare: Industrial Risk Insurers; see: absorption rate

facultative obligatory reinsurance treaty

Reinsurance. A hybrid reinsurance agreement comprised of the facultative and treaty approaches. The reinsurer must accept all risks ceded to it under the treaty, but the primary (ceding) insurer need not cede every risk of the type covered by the treaty.

compare: facultative semi-obligatory reinsurance treaty, obligatory reinsurance treaty; see: open cover

facultative reinsurance

Reinsurance. A formal reinsurance arrangement by which individual risks are offered by a ceding insurer to the reinsurer, who has the right (faculty) to accept or reject it.

syn: specific reinsurance; compare: treaty reinsurance; see: non-proportional reinsurance

© 1991 NILS Publishing Company

facultative semi-obligatory reinsurance treaty

Reinsurance. A facultative obligation treaty whereby the ceding company may select which risks it will cede to the reinsurer who has the right to reject the risk within a certain time frame; otherwise the reinsurer is obligated to accept the risk.

compare: facultative obligatory reinsurance treaty, obligatory reinsurance treaty

fail-safe

Loss Control. Design of a guard, device, mechanism, or other equipment in such a manner that, when it fails or becomes inoperative it will do so in a safe position or condition.

Fair Access to Insurance Requirements (FAIR plans)

Property/Regulation. State-established programs (often called FAIR Plans) that require insurers writing property insurance to accept risks from economically depressed areas in the same proportion as their other property writings bear to the total property insurance market. In most states, the laws also provide for a facility that distributes risks among the participating insurers.

compare: assigned risk; see: automobile shared market, Boston Plan, extended health insurance, joint underwriting association, market assistance plans, residual markets

Fair Credit Reporting Act

Agency/Insurer Operations. Federal legislation requiring an insurance applicant to be informed of the purpose of a requested credit report. When insurance is subsequently declined because of information contained in the credit report, the insurer must give the credit company's name and address to the applicant.

syn: Public Law 91-508

fair market value (FMV)

Property. A property valuation method established as the price that a willing buyer would pay, and that a willing seller would accept, during an arm's length transaction.

compare: actual cash value, depreciated value, functional replacement cost, market value, market value clause, real estate values, replacement cost, reproduction cost, tax-appraised value; see: arm's-length transaction, valuation of potential property loss

fallen building clause

Property. A provision contained in some fire insurance policies which voids coverage in the event that the building collapses from a cause other than a fire or explosion.

see: collapse

false imprisonment

Casualty. The intentional restraint of another's freedom of movement, by physical action or the threat of force.

false pretense coverage

Automobile. A garage policy endorsement extending coverage for autos that the insured voluntarily parts with because of a trick, scheme, or false pretense, or acquires from a seller not possessing legal title to the vehicle. The trick and devise exclusion to the garage policy must be deleted.

see: conversion, embezzlement, or secretion exclusion; trick and device exclusion

false pretense exclusion

Automobile.
see: trick and device exclusion

family automobile endorsements

Automobile. Endorsements to the basic automobile policy which broadens the definition of persons insured and drive-other-car coverage.

see: basic standard auto policy

family automobile policy (FAP)

Automobile. A standard automobile policy used through the 1980s that has since been replaced by the personal automobile policy. The family auto policy was the first form to incorporate both auto liability and physical damage into a single form. Prior to its development, the basic standard automobile policy was the standard form.

compare: basic standard auto policy, personal automobile policy

family deductible

Health. A deductible on a health insurance plan which is satisfied or eliminated by the combined expenses of all covered family members. *Example:* A plan with a $150 individual deductible may limit its application to a maximum of three deductibles ($450) for the family, without regard to the number of family members.

family exclusion

Automobile/Casualty. An exclusion found in most personal automobile and general liability policies that denies coverage for bodily injury to or damage to property of family members.

see: family members, intra-family immunity

family expense insurance

Health. A type of health insurance which extends the medical coverage to all members of a insured's household.

syn: family health policy

family forgery bond

Crime. A bond that covers all members of a family for

© 1991 NILS Publishing Company

nonbusiness financial transactions against loss by: 1) forgery of outgoing instruments; 2) accepting forged documents; or 3) accepting counterfeit U.S. currency.

family health policy

Health. Health insurance covering all members of a family.

syn: **family expense insurance**

family income life insurance

Life. A life insurance policy which combines whole life with decreasing term insurance. In the event of the insured's death prior to a specified date, the beneficiary is paid a monthly income benefit. If the insured lives beyond the specified date, the full face amount of the policy is paid to the beneficiary. This policy is designed to protect a family with young children.

see: **family maintenance life insurance**

family life policy

Life. Life insurance combining whole life with term insurance to cover family members in a single policy. Coverage for the principal is whole life, while the spouse and children are insured on a term basis for a lesser amount.

see: **additional insured**

family maintenance life insurance

Life. Life insurance based on a family income policy which combines whole life with level term insurance to provide a beneficiary with income over a specified period of time (10, 20 years) if the insured dies during that period of time. Should the insured survive the specified period, the beneficiary would receive the policy face amount.

see: **family income life insurance**

family members

Insurer Operations. For insurance coverage purposes, individuals related to the insured by blood, marriage, or adoption, including a ward or foster child who is a member of the household.

see: **dependent, family exclusion, spouse's benefit**

family protection endorsement

Automobile.

see: **uninsured motorists coverage**

farm credit system associations

Organizations. Associations comprised of the major lenders to farmers, including the federal land bank associations, the federal intermediate credit associations and the production credit associations.

farmers comprehensive personal liability (FCPL)

Casualty. Similar to the comprehensive personal liability policy, but adapted to cover liability exposures peculiar to farming, such as damage caused by grazing animals, farm employees engaged in farm business, and the sale of farm products.

farmers mutual insurers

Insurer Operations. Domestic mutuals formed by farmers to insure fire, hail and other casualty losses to farm property, stock and rural buildings.

see: **agricultural cooperative**

farmowners and ranchowners policy

Casualty/Property. A package policy designed for family-owned ranches and farms patterned after a homeowner's policy. Coverages include farm dwellings (and their contents), barns, stables and other farm structures.

farmowners personal liability form

Casualty. A personal liability endorsement covering a farmer's liability arising out of a collision between covered animals and a motor vehicle not owned or operated by the insured or an employee of the insured. The collision must have occurred on a public highway or road and not while the animal was being transported.

see: **animal insurance, ranchowners personal liability form**

farm use

Automobile. An automobile rating classification used when a vehicle is principally garaged on a farm or ranch, and not used in any business other than farming or ranching.

see: **business use, drive to or from work, pleasure use**

fault of management

Property. A term used in the schedule rating of commercial property risks to describe hazards which exist due to the fault of management, and to which rating penalties are applied. These additional premium charges can be removed when the condition is eliminated. Such hazards include poor housekeeping, general disrepair, and improper or unsafe storage – all conditions which can be attributed to management carelessness, indifference, or neglect.

compare: **increased hazard**; see: **aftercharge**

faulty workmanship exclusion

Casualty. An exclusion in products-completed operations insurance that prevents an insured from recovering for a loss to his or her own work due to the insured's poor craftsmanship. However, the exclusion does not apply to damage to other property caused by the insured's faulty work or defective product.

see: **defective, maintenance bond**

© 1991 NILS Publishing Company

favored institution

General. Nonprofit organizations classed by the Internal Revenue Service (IRS) as including (but not limited to) private educational institutions, religious organizations and charitable institutions. Such organizations may be excluded from paying income tax or have special tax advantages.

see: nonprofit organization

feasibility study

Risk Management. A study or research project undertaken to determine whether a given plan of action will succeed. In risk management, such studies are undertaken to determine whether a business should self-insure, form a captive insurance company, or join with other businesses in a risk sharing pool.

see: risk management process

federal agencies

General. Agencies of the United States government.

Federal Aviation Administration (FAA)

Aviation/Regulation. The U.S. federal agency charged with regulating air commerce, foster aviation safety, promote civil aviation and maintain a national system of airports, achieve efficient use of navigable airspace and develop and operate a common system of air traffic control.

see: Federal Aviation Regulations

Federal Aviation Regulations (FAR)

Aviation/Regulation. Rules and regulations administered by the Federal Aviation Administration, to control and maintain safety in airspace over the United States.

federal bond

Surety. A bond guaranteeing that specific acts will be performed or that obligations will be met with respect to the federal government and its laws and regulations. Typical federal bonds include Internal Revenue Service bonds (for alcohol and tobacco taxes), export bonds, alien bonds (guaranteeing the departure of foreign students upon completion of studies in the United States), and customs bonds (also called customs house bonds (covering the temporary importation of normally dutied goods to be sold in "duty-free" shops)).

see: bonds, customs bond

federal crime insurance program

Crime. A crime insurance program that protects personal property of homeowners, tenants and small businesses located in high crime areas against burglary and/or robbery. The program is administered by the Federal Insurance Administration.

see: Federal Insurance Administration, National Insurance Development Corporation, Urban Development Act of 1970

Federal Crop Insurance Corporation (FCIC)

Property. A federal agency which is part of the United States Department of Agriculture. It provides crop coverage for farmers.

see: crop insurance

Federal Deposit Insurance Corporation (FDIC)

Regulation. A federal agency formed by Congress to insure the deposits of federally chartered banks. The insurance is financed through premiums charged the financial institution, and each insured account is covered up to a maximum of $100,000.

see: Federal Savings and Loan Insurance Corporation, Securities Investor Protection Corporation

Federal Employees' Compensation Act

Workers' Compensation. A type of workers' compensation plan for federal employees which makes payments for death or disability sustained when performing job duties.

see: workers' compensation insurance

Federal Employers Liability Act (FELA)

Workers' Compensation. A federal statute that provides benefits to injured federal employees (and other employees engaged in interstate commerce), which are substantially greater than those afforded by state workers' compensation laws. In the private sector, its application primarily affects railroad employees, who are exempt from state workers' compensation laws. Unlike state workers' compensation laws, FELA provisions do not limit an injured employee's recoveries to scheduled benefits, and it allows an employee to sue under tort liability.

see: workers' compensation insurance

federal estate tax

Financial Planning/Life. A federal tax paid from the estate of a deceased individual. Special provisions apply to the proceeds from life insurance benefits, and these vary by the type of life insurance policy providing the benefits.

see: estate tax

Federal Insurance Administration (FIA)

Regulation. An agency of the federal government headed by an appointed administrator which oversees the administration of the National Flood Insurance Program and the Federal Crime Insurance Program. The Administration is part of the Department of Housing and Urban Development. It has no involvement in the regulation of the insurance industry.

see: federal crime insurance program, National Flood Insurance Program

© 1991 NILS Publishing Company

Federal Insurance Contributions Act (FICA)

Regulation. A federal statute that established a payroll tax to assist in the funding of Social Security benefits.

see: Social Security

Federal Motor Carrier Act

Regulation. Federal legislation passed in 1935 and subsequently amended in 1980 which prescribes the legal liability of organizations engaged in transporting goods for hire.

see: motor truck cargo insurance

federal official bond

Surety.

see: public official bond

Federal Savings and Loan Insurance Corporation (FSLIC)

Regulation. A federal agency formed by Congress to insure the deposits of federally chartered savings and loans institutions (S&Ls). The insurance is financed through premiums charged each S&L, with each insured account covered up to a maximum of $100,000.

see: Federal Deposit Insurance Corporation, Securities Investor Protection Corporation

Federal Trade Commission (FTC)

Regulation. A federal agency that has conducted numerous investigations of the insurance industry but exercises no regulatory powers save enforcement of the Fair Credit Reporting Act, which requires insurers to notify an applicant for insurance that a credit report is required.

see: Fair Credit Reporting Act, McCarran-Ferguson Act

Federation of Insurance and Corporate Counsel (FICC)

Organizations. Members: Attorneys involved in the legal aspects of the insurance industry, insurance company executives and corporate counsels involved in the defense of claims. *Objectives:* Conducting research through the Federation of Insurance and Corporate Counsel Foundation. Sponsoring essay competitions for students at accredited law schools and bestowing awards. *Founded:* 1936. *Headquarters:* Marblehead, MA.

fee for service

Health. A billing method for health services where the provider charges separately for each service rendered. Most physicians and clinics bill on this basis.

fee schedule

Workers' Compensation. Most states publish schedules of maximum fees that a medical provider can receive for a procedure covered by workers' compensation insurance.

Health.

see: schedule

fee simple

Financial Planning/Title. A legal term for a form of property ownership indicating the property is owned completely and can be sold or transferred unconditionally. Upon the death of a fee simple property owner, the title passes to the owner's estate.

compare: fee tail; see: freehold, title

fee tail

Financial Planning/Title. An estate inherited by the donor's direct descendants.

compare: fee simple; see: freehold

Fellow of the Casualty Actuarial Society (FCAS)

Organizations. A professional designation acquired by the Casualty Actuarial Society after passing twelve examinations on actuarial science, insurance mathematics, statistics, accounting and finance.

see: Casualty Actuarial Society

Fellow of the Life Management Institute (FLMI)

Health/Life/Organizations. A professional designation awarded to individuals who successfully complete ten life and health insurance examinations, in such areas as finance, marketing, law, accounting, management and personnel, employee benefits, and information (computer) systems. The courses and examinations are administered by the Life Office Management Association (LOMA).

see: Life Management Institute, Life Office Management Association

Fellow of the Society of Actuaries (FSA)

Health/Life/Risk Management. A professional designation earned by passing ten examinations on the mathematics of life and health insurance, actuarial science, accounting, and finance. In addition, successful candidates must meet other educational and experience requirements. Exams and courses are administered by the Society of Actuaries.

see: Society of Actuaries

Fellow of the Society of Pension Actuaries (FSPA)

Organizations. An advanced designation awarded to Members of the Society of Pension Actuaries who successfully complete two examinations on pensions and actuarial practice.

fellow servant rule

Workers' Compensation. Prior to the passage of workers' compensation laws, this was a common law

© 1991 NILS Publishing Company

fellow servant rule — continued
defense used by employers defending suits brought by employees. The rule specified that if an employee were injured by a fellow employee, that individual was responsible, not the employer.

see: **common law defense, Priestly v. Fowler**

felony

Crime. A grave crime, expressly declared to be a felony by common law or by statute. A crime punishable by extended imprisonment.

compare: **misdemeanor; see: common law, crime**

fictitious group

Regulation. A group organized mainly to purchase insurance at a reduced rate. Many states have laws which prohibit the formation of fictitious groups.

compare: **discretionary groups, true group insurance; see: group insurance**

fidelity bond

Surety. A bond covering an employer for a loss resulting from an employee's dishonest acts.

syn: **individual fidelity bond; see: blanket position bond, name position bond, position schedule bond**

fiduciary

General. A person occupying a position of special trust and confidence, usually one holding the funds or items of value of another under personal care, custody, or control.

see: **bailee**

Reinsurance. A ceding insurer's fiduciary obligation with respect to a reinsurer's interests, was affirmed in *American Reinsurance Company v. MGIC Investment Corporation*, (Circuit Court of Cook County, Illinois County Department, Chancery Division, No.77 Ch 1457). Because the ceding insurer in a treaty reinsurance arrangement accepts risks on behalf of the reinsurer, and thereby controls the fortunes of the reinsurer, the court determined that a ceding insurer owes the reinsurance company the same duty as any other fiduciary.

see: **follow the fortunes, utmost good faith**

Regulation. Insurance, by its very nature, establishes a fiduciary relationship between insurer (the fiduciary) and the insured. Insurers hold the funds of many and are entrusted to manage those funds prudently, so that monies will be available in the event of an insured loss. Because of this, oversight and control in the form of regulation is necessary to protect the public interest.

fiduciary bond

Surety. A type of judicial bond which guarantees the faithful performance of a fiduciary (e.g., an executor, guardian, or a trustee) as directed by the court.

compare: **court bond; see: judicial bond, probate bond**

field

Agency/Insurer Operations. A term no longer in frequent use, referring to a geographical area or territory covered by an agent, special agent, agency or insurer.

Insurer Operations. A type or line of insurance, as "in the life insurance field."

field expenses

Insurer Operations. Commissions, training allowances, agency and local office salaries and rent, and all other expenses incurred in agency supervision and the production of new business.

see: **expense loading, field**

field force

Agency/Insurer Operations. Employees of an insurance company or agency that work away from the home or principal office.

see: **field**

field representative

Agency/Insurer Operations.
see: **marketing representative**

field service representative

Insurer Operations. An employee of an insurer or managing general agent who assists agents or solicitors in the soliciting or negotiating of insurance.

see: **field, managing general agent**

file-and-use rating

Regulation. A method of insurance rate regulation used by some states which allows insurers to adopt new rates without the prior approval of insurance regulators.

compare: **modified prior approval rating, open competition rating, prior approval rating; see: rate making, rate regulation**

filing requirements

Regulation. The specific information and documents that are required to be filed by an insurance company with a state department of insurance in order to write certain kinds of business or to obtain approval for new rates or coverage forms.

see: **rate making**

film coverage insurance

Inland Marine. A form which provides coverage on an "all-risks" basis for exposed motion picture and magnetic or video tapes, including sound tracks and records. (*ISO Form CM 0045.*)

© 1991 NILS Publishing Company

fine print

financed premium

Insurer Operations. Payment of insurance premiums, in whole or in part, with funds borrowed from a financial institution. This term does not apply to payment of premiums with funds borrowed from a policy's cash value.

see: premium financing

Financial Accounting Standards Board (FASB)

General. A professional standards board created by accountants to establish Generally Accepted Accounting Principles (GAAP) which are the national accounting standards used by U.S. accountants. The GAAP standard reporting method makes it possible for investors and regulatory authorities to more accurately determine an organization's financial results. A previous name for this Board is the Accounting Principles Board.

see: Generally Accepted Accounting Principles, Governmental Accounting Standards Board

financial bond

General. A corporate or government security that pays interest and obligates the issuer to pay the promised interest at the end of specific time intervals and to pay the principal at maturity of the security.

see: bonds

financial guarantee bond

Surety. Judicial bond forms which guarantee the payment of money such as an appeal bond, bail bond, plaintiff review bond or sales tax bond.

see: court bond, judicial bond

Financial Institution Bond Form 24

Crime.

see: banker's blanket bond

financial lease

General. A lease that does not provide for maintenance services, is not cancellable, and is fully amortized over its lifetime.

financial ratios

Risk Management. Ratios developed from an organization's financial statements that are used in analyzing its financial position or stability.

see: asset composition ratio, common equity ratio, cost of goods sold, current ratio, debt-to-equity ratio, earnings yield, financial statement, financial underwriting, net income, net worth ratio, operating ratio, quick ratio, return on investment

financial responsibility laws

Automobile. Laws enacted in many states requiring an operator to furnish evidence of the ability to pay for automobile-related injuries or damage. An automobile

liability insurance policy will usually suffice as evidence of financial responsibility, although in some states, a bond can usually be posted instead.

compare: compulsory insurance laws; see: automobile liability bonds

financial risk

General. A portion of total corporate risk, over and above basic business risk, that results from using debt.

see: business risk, risk

Financial Planning. The risk that is associated with making a financial or a speculative investment which can result in a financial gain or loss.

syn: investment risk

financial statement

General. A written report summarizing the financial status of an organization for a stated period of time. A financial statement describes the organization's activities and resulting profit or loss, the flow of resources and the distribution or retention of profits.

see: annual report, audited financial statements, balance sheet, balance sheet reserves, financial underwriting, Generally Accepted Accounting Principles, income statement, retained earnings, statement of changes in financial position, statement of opinion

financial structure

General. The complete right-hand side of the balance sheet which details the way in which an organization is financed.

see: balance sheet

financial underwriting

Insurer Operations/Risk Management. The review of an organization's financial statements and related background with the belief that this will indicate the quality of its management. This financial analysis can reveal the moral and morale hazards present in an organization and the potential of the organization for growth, as well as confirm that exposures to risk exist and indicate its ability to pay premiums and comply with financial obligations or guarantees.

see: cash flow underwriting, cash flow program, financial ratios, financial statements, paid loss retrospective rating plan

fine arts floater

Inland Marine. An inland marine form that provides coverage for fine arts (paintings, statues, sculptures or antiques) on an "all-risks" basis. Usually, items to be covered are scheduled on the form for a specified stated amount.

fine print

Regulation. A reference to an earlier period in the insurance business (pre-1920), when policy benefits were presented in larger print, while small type was

© 1991 NILS Publishing Company

fire

fine print — continued
used to present exclusions, reductions, exemptions, and limitations of coverage. Most state laws now specify a minimum type size for use in explaining both benefits and exclusions. In some cases, exclusions must be printed in type that is actually *larger* than that used to illustrate benefits.

see: **insurance contract**

fire

Property. A rapid, persistent chemical reaction that releases heat and light. For the purpose of fire insurance coverage, a fire must be a hostile fire rather than a friendly fire.

see: **explosion, friendly fire, hostile fire; Fr: incendie; Gr: Feuer; Sp: incendio**

Fire and Theft Index Bureau

Organizations. A department of the American Insurance Association which compiles and shares fire and theft claims information with Association members in an attempt to identify and prevent fraudulent claims.

see: **American Insurance Association, Insurance Crime Prevention Institute, Insurance Services Office, interinsurer claim service organization, Medical Information Bureau, National Automobile Theft Bureau, Property Insurance Loss Register**

firebox explosion

Property. The extended coverage provisions of a property insurance policy include coverage for explosion of accumulated gases or unconsumed fuel within the firebox, flues, or passages of any fired vessel. This provision can duplicate coverage provided by a boiler and machinery policy.

see: **explosion, joint loss agreement**

fire brigade

Property.
see: **underwriters fire patrol**

fire damage legal liability

Casualty. Coverage protecting an insured against legal liability incurred for negligent acts resulting in fire damage to a premises rented by or loaned to the insured. This coverage is included in the ISO commercial general liability coverage form, usually for a limit of $50,000, with higher limits available for an additional premium. Occasionally, this coverage is added to fire insurance policies.

syn: **fire legal liability**; see: **commercial general liability form, fire damage limit**

fire damage limit

Casualty. The highest amount an insured can recover under the ISO commercial general liability coverage form for claims arising out of the legal liability for any one fire, usually $50,000.

see: **commercial general liability form, fire damage legal liability**

fire department service clause

Property. A provision in most fire insurance policies which indemnifies the insured for fees charged by a fire department for responding to a fire alarm at the insured location. The provision applies to insured property located outside a fire district where an alarm will be answered only for a fee.

fire detection systems

Loss Control. A system or apparatus designed to discover or determine the existence of a fire within a building or structure, then sounding or sending an alarm. Such systems include smoke detectors, heat detectors and fusible link monitors.

fire division

Loss Control/Property. A section of a structure formed by fire walls, including fire doors designed to stop a fire from spreading beyond or into its confines.

see: **cut-off, fire door, fire stop, fire wall, parapet**

fire door

Loss Control/Property. A door constructed of noncombustible materials that has been tested and rated for its resistance to fire. Fire doors may be used in horizontal openings (ceilings and floors) or vertical openings (walls), and usually must remain closed under normal circumstances. They must be equipped to shut automatically in the presence of fire.

see: **fire division**

fired pressure vessel

Property.
see: **pressure vessel**

fire extinguisher

Loss Control. A portable or wheeled apparatus for putting out small fires by ejecting fire-extinguishing chemicals. Fire extinguishers are classified by a letter or group of letters to indicate the type(s) of fires they are designed to extinguish.

see: **carbon dioxide, class A fire, class B fire, class C fire, class D fire, dry chemicals, foam, halon**

fire extinguishing system

Loss Control. An apparatus or system designed to cause a fire to cease burning or to quench it. Such systems include water spray, carbon dioxide, dry

© 1991 NILS Publishing Company

chemicals, halon and foam, portable or fixed fire extinguishing systems.

see: **automatic sprinkler system, carbon dioxide, dry chemicals, fire extinguisher, foam, halon**

fire insurance

Property. A general term used to describe coverage that insures against losses to real or personal property caused by the peril of fire.

see: **New York standard fire policy**

fire legal liability

Casualty.

see: **fire damage legal liability**

fire load

Loss Control. The amount of combustibles present in a given situation, usually expressed in terms of weight of combustible material per square foot.

fire map

Loss Control/Property. Diagrams that represent an individual property, industrial complex or properties within a specific area. Fire maps usually distinguish between different types of construction (i.e. frame, reinforced concrete, etc.) and indicate the proximity of fire hydrants and stations. Today, fire maps are principally used to present large accounts to underwriters and for loss control purposes. Historically, they were used by fire insurers, to plot insured properties for the purpose of avoiding catastrophic losses.

see: **block limits; map; map clerk; Sanborn Map Company, Inc.**

fire mark

Property. A metal plaque or medallion that was attached to the front of buildings to indicate which fire brigade was to extinguish a fire in that building. Each insurer had its own fire brigade and would compete for business on the brigade's ability to extinguish a fire. The original fire marks are valuable collectors items today.

see: **underwriters fire patrol**

fire marshal

Loss Control. A state, county or municipal official that is responsible for fire prevention and public fire safety in a specified geographical area.

Fire Office Committee Forms (FOC)

International. Uniform international property insurance forms developed by the Fire Office Committee in London, England.

fire prevention

Loss Control. Measures taken to avoid a fire.

see: **fire protection, loss prevention**

fireproof

Loss Control. A term historically used to describe a material or structure capable of withstanding damage by fire. It is misleading because no material or structure is totally safe from fire. The preferred term is fire resistive.

syn: **flameproof**; compare: **fire resistive**; see: **explosion-proof**

fire protection

Loss Control. Methods of providing for fire control or fire extinguishment. Also, the prevention, detection, and extinguishment of fire.

see: **fire extinguishing system, fire map, loss control specialist, protection**

fire protection funds

Loss Control. Any funds collected, assessed or appropriated to support local fire departments.

fire resistance

Loss Control. A relative term, used with numerical rating or modifying adjectives to indicate the extent to which a material or structure resists the effect of fire. *Example:* Fire resistance of two hours.

fire resistive

Loss Control. Properties, material or equipment designed to resist fire.

compare: **fireproof**; see: **fire retardant, flame retardant**

fire resistive construction

Loss Control. A building or structure constructed of fire resistive materials to reduce the severity of a potential fire. Lower fire insurance rates apply to fire resistive construction.

compare: **fireproof**; see: **construction**

fire retardant

Loss Control. Chemicals (such as boric acid, ammonium sulfate, and calcium chloride) used to treat materials or property for the purpose of reducing or delaying their flammability.

see: **flame retardant**

fire stop

Loss Control. A barrier of thick wood, or noncombustible material used to limit the rapid spread of fire in hollow walls, floors, other concealed air spaces, and under long continuous work tables.

see: **fire division**

fire wall

Loss Control/Property. A structural feature (wall) separating a building into parts, designed to prevent fire from spreading, thereby minimizing loss. Fire walls, along with fire doors, create fire divisions.

see: **cut-off, fire division, fire door, parapet**

© 1991 NILS Publishing Company

first dollar

General. The primary amount of loss for which the insured is financially responsible.

see: deductible

first dollar coverage

Employee Benefits. An employee benefit plan that reimburses benefits from the first dollar without applying a deductible.

Insurer Operations. An insurance coverage providing payment of claims without applying a deductible.

see: deductible

first dollar defense

Casualty. Coverage under some umbrella or professional liability policies that indemnifies the policyholder for the cost of defending against claims, even when the claim falls within the policy's self-insured retention.

first in, first out (FIFO)

General. An accounting method used to value inventory, where sales are considered to be made against the earliest-purchased merchandise or inventory. During times of increasing prices, the FIFO method tends to overstate profits. FIFO, LIFO (last in, first out) and average cost are of importance to insurers, since inventory valuation methods are used in estimating business income losses.

compare: average cost; last in, first out

first loss earthquake insurance

Property. A separate earthquake insurance policy which has a limit significantly less than the insured property's value. (No coinsurance applies.) It is designed to insure a portion of the 5-to-15% deductibles contained in standard earthquake insurance policies. First loss policies usually have a flat dollar deductible.

see: percentage of value deductible

first loss insurance

Property. Frequently used in property insurance, an insurance policy which covers a single loss during the policy period. Also describes property insurance policies whose limits are reduced (and not reinstated) by loss payments, or policies covering multiple locations that insure only the first loss occurring at each location during the policy period.

compare: automatic reinstatement clause; see: restoration premium, stop loss

first loss retention

Reinsurance.

see: net retention

first loss scale

Property.

see: Lloyd's property first loss scale

first named insured

Insurer Operations. The individual or entity whose name appears first in the declarations of a commercial policy. Recent policy forms allow an insurer to satisfy contractual duties by giving notice (of cancellation, for example) to the first named insured, rather than requiring notice to all named insureds.

compare: additional insured, insured, named insured; see: evidence of cancellation

first-party insurance

Health/Life/Property. Insurance on the policyholder's or insured's own property (i.e., building, contents, automobile) or person (i.e., life, health).

compare: third-party liability

first surplus reinsurance treaty

Reinsurance. The first layer of reinsurance in excess of the ceding company's net retention shared by the reinsurer and ceding company on a pro rata basis. Their respective shares can be fixed or variable, depending on the class of risk and the net retentions, which the ceding company retains.

see: second surplus treaty, surplus reinsurance treaty

first-year commission

Agency/Insurer Operations. The commission an insurance company pays to an insurance agent on a policy's first-year premium. In most lines of business, first-year commissions are paid at a higher rate than commissions for subsequent years.

compare: renewal commission; see: agent's commission, graded commission, unlevel commission

fiscal year

General. A twelve-month period used by an organization for financial (fiscal) planning and reporting. A fiscal year may or may not correspond to a calendar year (January 1 through December 31).

compare: calendar year; see: annual

fitness for a particular purpose

Casualty. A phrase used in product warranties affirming the product's fitness for use when the seller is aware of the intended use and sanctions this use to the buyer. Usually, language that disclaims fitness for a particular purpose appears in product warnings and warranties.

see: disclaimer

five-percent rule

Property. A clause in a property insurance policy, stating that covered losses lower than $10,000 and less than 5 percent of the total amount insured need not be appraised or inventoried by the insurer.

see: coinsurance

© 1991 NILS Publishing Company

five-year vesting

Employee Benefits.
 see: ten year vesting

fixed amount option

Life. An option which a life insurance beneficiary may select as a settlement where the policy proceeds are paid through periodic fixed amount installments until the principal and interest are exhausted.

 compare: fixed period option, interest option, life income option, life income with period certain option; see: optional life insurance settlement modes

fixed annuity

Life. An annuity offering guaranteed or fixed benefit payments to the annuitant for the annuity term.

fixed assets

Risk Management. Generally permanent assets which are required for use in the continuing operations of a business over a number of years, and are not subject to sale.

 see: assets

fixed barrier guard

Loss Control. A barrier guard located at a point of operation. An enclosure attached to the machine or equipment.

 see: barrier guard

fixed base liability

Aviation. Aircraft liability insurance specifically designed for fixed base operators such as aircraft dealers, charters, and flight instructors.

 see: fixed base operators

fixed base operators

Aviation. General aviation rating classification applying to businesses which are located (based) on the premises of airports and which own, operate, buy, sell, rent, or lease aircraft. They also may perform such services as fueling, repairs or flight instruction.

 compare: business and pleasure, flying clubs, industrial aid operators; see: fixed base liability, general aviation

fixed benefit

Life. A benefit from a life or annuity policy that does not vary in amount and is paid on a regular periodic basis.

fixed charges

General. Costs that do not vary with the level of output, especially fixed financial costs such as interest, lease payments, and sinking fund payments.

fixed machinery

Property. Machinery which is permanently affixed to real property, including its hangings.

fixed period option

Life. An option which a life insurance beneficiary may select as a settlement where the policy proceeds are left on deposit with the insurer to accrue interest which is paid to the beneficiary in equal payments for a specific number of years.

 compare: fixed amount option, interest option, life income option, life income with period certain option; see: optional life insurance settlement modes

fixture

Property. An object attached to a building or structure as a permanent appendage, apparatus or appliance. At one time, fixtures were considered "personal property," but now they are generally considered part of "real property." An insurable interest can exist with both the building owner and a tenant who has installed the fixtures.

 see: improvements and betterments

flameproof

Loss Control. A term historically used to describe a material capable of withstanding ignition by a flame. It is a misnomer in that no material is totally flameproof. The preferred term is flame retardant.

 compare: fire resistive; syn: fireproof; see: flame retardant

flame resistant

Loss Control.
 see: flame retardant

flame retardant

Loss Control. Materials which have been chemically treated or have inherent properties so that they will not ignite readily or propagate flames under a small to moderate fire exposure.

 syn: flame resistant; see: fire resistance, fire resistive, fire retardant

flammable

Loss Control. A term used to describe any material or substance that is easily ignited or that will burn.

 syn: inflammable

flammable limits

Loss Control. Gases and flammable liquid vapors that can form flammable mixtures with air or oxygen have upper and lower limits to the concentrations that will provide ignitable mixtures. The lower flammable or explosive level (LEL) is the lowest percentage of vapor in air that will burn. The upper flammable or explosive level (UEL) is the maximum percentage that will burn.

© 1991 NILS Publishing Company

flashover

Loss Control. A term used to describe the result of a process whereby a slowly developing fire (or radiant heat source) produces radiant energy at wall and ceiling surfaces; the radiant feedback from those surfaces gradually heats the contents of the fire area, and when all combustibles in the space have become heated to their ignition temperature, simultaneous ignition occurs.

flash point

Loss Control. The lowest temperature at which a flammable mixture is formed between the vapor of a liquid and the surrounding air.

see: ignition temperature

flat amount benefit formula

Employee Benefits. A benefit formula which bases each participant's benefits on a fixed amount per year of service. *Example:* For each year of service, a participant is credited with $50 of monthly retirement income. If a person worked for eleven years the monthly benefit would be $550.

syn: flat benefit plan

flat amount pension plan

Employee Benefits. A pension plan under which all of the plan participants receive the same benefit amount on retirement. This usually requires each participant to attain a minimum number of service years and a minimum age. Upon achieving these requirements all participants receive the same dollar amount as a retirement benefit regardless of income, position, or additional years of service.

syn: flat schedule

flat amount unit benefit formula

Employee Benefits. A method for determining the amount of pension benefits due an individual. *Formula:* Per-year Benefits Amount x the Years of Service Completed = Pension Benefit.

flat benefit

Health. A specified amount for certain medical expenses payable under certain circumstances, such as a $75 daily payment made only while a person is confined to a hospital.

see: flat maternity benefit

flat benefit plan

Employee Benefits.
see: flat amount benefit formula

flat cancellation

Insurer Operations. Cancellation of an insurance policy on its effective date as if it had never been issued. No coverage was provided and no premium is due.

compare: fully earned premium; see: cancellation, rescind, return premium

flat commission

Agency/Insurer Operations. A commission percentage rate that does not vary with the type of policy written, whether the policy is new or a renewal.

syn: level commission; compare: graded commission; see: agent's commission

flat deductible

Property. A specific dollar amount that is deducted from each loss or claim, regardless of the size of the loss or claim.

compare: franchise deductible, percentage of value deductible; see: deductible

flat dollar benefit formula

Employee Benefits.
see: flat amount pension plan

flat maternity benefit

Health. A maternity benefit of a specific dollar amount, rather than one based on actual medical or hospital expenses.

see: flat benefit, maternity benefit

flat percentage benefit formula

Employee Benefits. A pension plan whereby all eligible retirees receive the same percentage of annual wage as a retirement income.

flat rate

Reinsurance. 1) A reinsurance contract rate which is not subject to subsequent adjustment on the basis of loss experience or size of risk.
2) A reinsurance premium rate based on the entire premium income received by the ceding company from business ceded to the reinsurer, as distinguished from a rate applicable only to the excess limits premium.

Insurer Operations. An insurance rate that is not subsequently adjusted even if an insured risk suffers unexpectedly high losses.

see: rate making

Property. A property insurance rate used when no coinsurance clause appears in the policy. Usually higher than the coinsurance rate, the actual cost of a flat rated policy may be less because the insured values do not have to meet a coinsurance requirement and losses cannot be reduced by a coinsurance clause.

see: coinsurance

flat schedule

Employee Benefits.
see: flat amount pension plan

144

fleet automatic

Automobile. Business or commercial automobile coverage that provides automatic coverage on all automobiles owned by the insured during the policy period. Premium for this blanket, automatic coverage is determined on a reporting or audit basis.

compare: nonfleet automatic; see: automobile fleet, fleet policy, newly acquired

fleet of companies

Insurer Operations. Insurance companies which are under common ownership and, frequently, common management.

see: affiliated companies

fleet policy

Ocean Marine. A single ocean marine insurance policy that covers all ships of a single owner. A fleet policy is advantageous because older ships, which are less attractive from an underwriter's perspective, can be written at the lower average fleet rate.

Automobile. A single automobile insurance contract that applies to a number of vehicles, usually five or more, under common ownership. Coverage may be written for specifically scheduled vehicles (nonfleet automatic, for example), or it may apply to all vehicles of the insured on a reporting or audit basis (fleet automatic).

see: automobile fleet, fleet automatic, nonfleet automatic

Flesch Test

Insurer Operations. A test adopted by many insurance departments that determines the understandability of an insurance contract. The Flesch Test is designed to rate a contract on a scale where the standard is a document easily understood by someone with an eighth-grade education. The test limits the number of words that can be used in a sentence, and the number of letters and syllables that a word can contain. The ISO simplified policy forms are designed to comply with this test.

see: easy read, insurance contract, plain language laws

flexible benefit plan

Employee Benefits. A benefit program which complies with Section 125 of the Internal Revenue Code, that allows employees to choose between permissible taxable benefits (including cash), and nontaxable health and welfare benefits (such as life and health insurance, child care, retirement plans and vacation pay). Dollar allocations are determined by the employee from the total amount provided by the employer.

syn: flexible compensation; compare: cafeteria benefit plan

flexible compensation

Employee Benefits.
see: flexible benefit plan

flexible premium adjustable life insurance

Life.
see: universal life insurance

flexible premium annuity

Life. An annuity which allows the amount of each premium payment to be determined by the policyowner. This type of annuity is used principally to fund Individual Retirement Accounts and Keogh Plans where payments are tied to an individual's earnings.

see: annuity

flexible premium life insurance

Life. A form of variable life insurance where after the payment of an initial premium, the amount and timing of each additional premium payment is determined by the policyowner. A minimum death benefit is guaranteed with a higher benefit payable based on the actual premiums paid and the investment performance of the plan.

flight coverage

Aviation. Coverage on a fixed wing aircraft from the craft's actual take-off run and continuing until it has completed its landing roll. For a rotorcraft, coverage commences when the rotors start to revolve under power for the purpose of flight until they cease to revolve.

compare: ground coverage; see: in motion

float

General. Interest earned by a bank in the time between deposit of a check, and the earliest date when the bank allows the depositor to use those funds. With the advent of electronic funds transfers, many states are enacting laws shortening this period during which banks have, customarily, been using this "float" as an interest-free loan.

floater policy

Inland Marine. An inland marine policy designed to cover movable property, wherever it may be located. May be written on an "all-risks," open perils or named perils form.

see: bicycle floater, camera floater, contractors equipment floater, equipment dealers floater, equipment floater, fine arts floater, fur floater, installation floater, jewelry floater, livestock floater, pattern and die floater, personal articles floater, personal property floater, physicians and surgeons floater, salesmen's samples floater, sign floater, unscheduled property floater, wedding presents floater

© 1991 NILS Publishing Company

flood

Property. The rising and overflowing of a body of water onto normally dry land or the excessive level of inland or tidal waters.

Fr: inondation; Gr: Ueberschwemmung;
Sp: inundación

Flood Disaster Protection Act of 1973

Property. Federal legislation which amended the National Flood Insurance Act of 1968. Major changes included making the new program mandatory for flood-prone communities and increasing the amount of coverage available.

see: National Flood Insurance Program

Flood Hazard Boundary Map

Loss Control. A flood map published by the Federal Insurance Administration for a specific community which indicates areas within the community that are subject to severe flooding. These maps are the basis for requiring a community to join the National Flood Insurance Program. If a community does not join the program, it may lose federal disaster relief in the event of flooding. Each community map is assigned an identification number which must be used when applying for flood insurance in that community.

see: National Flood Insurance Program

flood insurance

Property. Insurance that reimburses the policyholder for damage to property caused by the peril of flood.

Flood Insurance Manual

Property. A manual published by the National Flood Insurance Program which includes the program's eligibility and policy writing rules, as well as rating information.

see: National Flood Insurance Program

flood insurance rate map (FIRM)

Property. A flood map published by the Federal Insurance Administration which is developed from a community flood study and is used to produce actuarial rates. Once this map is complete, a community is eligible for the regular National Flood Insurance Program. Rates developed from this map are termed *pre-FIRM* or *post-FIRM* depending on when a building is constructed.

see: National Flood Insurance Program, post-FIRM rates, pre-FIRM rates

floodplain

Property. A relatively level area alongside a river that is periodically subject to flooding.

floor plan insurance

Inland Marine. Inland marine insurance that provides coverage to a lending institution for merchandise that has been financed through the institution and is held for sale by a dealer or vendor. Coverage is usually provided on an "open perils" basis. *ISO Form M 00 52.*

Florida Insurance Exchange

Insurer Operations.

see: Insurance Exchange of the Americas, Inc.

flotage

Ocean Marine.

see: flotsam

flotsam

Ocean Marine. The floating wreckage of a ship or its cargo, including all cargo found on the shore between the high- and low-water lines. Ocean marine insurers today pay for *flotsam, jetsam, lagan,* and *derelict* without distinction.

syn: flotage; compare: derelict, jetsam;
see: lagan

flying clubs

Aviation. General aviation rating classification denoting a nonprofit organization comprised of at least three individuals who jointly own and operate an aircraft for pleasure use only.

compare: business and pleasure, fixed base operators, industrial aid operators; see: general aviation

foam

Loss Control. A fire extinguishing agent that is created by mixing a form of detergent with water. It is used to snuff out the fire by depriving it of oxygen and cooling it down with water. It is most effective on petroleum or flammable liquid fires.

see: class B fire, fire extinguisher, fire extinguishing system

following form excess liability insurance

Casualty. An excess liability policy that provides coverage identical to that provided by a specified primary liability policy. This term may also be applied to an umbrella policy that has been endorsed to provide coverage at least as broad as that provided by a specified primary policy.

compare: nonconcurrency; see: excess liability insurance, layering, umbrella liability insurance

following form excess property insurance

Property. An excess fire insurance policy that follows the terms and provisions of a specified primary fire insurance policy. *Example:* A fire insurance policy or other form written under exactly the same terms as a property insurance policy and providing the same coverage as other insurance on the same property.

compare: nonconcurrency; see: layering

© 1991 NILS Publishing Company

follow the fortunes

Reinsurance. A reinsurance contract provision stating that once a risk has been ceded, the reinsurer is bound by the same fate as that of the ceding insurer.

see: **fiduciary, utmost good faith**

Food and Drug Administration (FDA)

Regulation. A federal agency within the Department of Health, Education and Welfare, established to set safety and quality standards for food, drugs, cosmetics, and other household substances sold as consumer products.

food rejection insurance

Ocean Marine. A form of ocean marine insurance that provides coverage against the risk of rejection of food at a port of entry by government authorities.

force majeure coverage

Casualty. Insurance which provides protection to an insured – most often involving, but not limited to – a construction contract. Covers financial loss caused when commitments cannot be honored because of an unexpected or uncontrollable event, such as governmental intervention, war, or acts of God.

see: **act of God, commercial impracticability**

International. Political risk insurance covering out-of-pocket expenses resulting from the loss of a contract in a foreign country resulting from force majeure perils such as war, revolution, flood or epidemic.

Foreign Credit Insurance Association (FCIA)

International/Organizations. Members: Marine, property and casualty insurance companies. *Objectives:* Provides export credit insurance policies for overseas sales of products and services and lessors of U.S. equipment. In cooperation with the Export-Import Bank of the United States (Eximbank), it insures exporters against the risk of nonpayment by foreign buyers for commercial and/or political reasons. *Founded:* 1962. *Headquarters:* New York, NY.

see: **export credit insurance**

foreign direct investment (FDI)

International. An investment made to establish a business or to purchase the assets of an existing business in a foreign country.

foreign/home insurance

International. A term referring to the insuring of businesses or properties in a foreign country owned by United States organizations. Many insurance companies have established special international departments to handle this business.

see: **reverse flow business**

foreign insurer

Insurer Operations. An insurer or reinsurer domiciled or incorporated under the laws of one state of the United States, but doing business in another state. It is considered a domestic insurer in its own state, but a foreign insurer in all other states where it operates.

compare: **alien insurer, domestic insurer**

foreign securities

International. Securities issued by a company which is incorporated in a foreign country and produces most of its business in a foreign country, or through a security issued by a foreign government.

forgery

Crime. Producing a written document or altering an existing written document, resulting in a counterfeit or fraudulent document.

see: **alteration**

forgery bond

Surety. Insurance against loss due to alteration or forgery of negotiable instruments, checks, or other documents.

syn: **check alteration and forgery insurance;**
see: **alteration bond, lost instrument bond**

forgery or alteration coverage form

Crime. A crime coverage form covering loss involving checks, drafts, promissory notes, bills of exchange and similar documents resulting from forgery or alteration of any covered instrument.

syn: **crime coverage form B; see: crime coverages, forgery bond**

form

Insurer Operations. A written document that is used to complete or make up a section of an insurance policy (i.e. vendor's block coverage form, garage coverage form).

see: **ACORD forms, application, insurance contract**

forthwith payment

General. A cash payment at the time of settlement to cover attorney's fees, costs, outstanding liens, and/or a payment to the plaintiff.

see: **release**

fortuitous event

General. An event subject to chance, an unforeseen event or an unintentional happening that does not imply suddenness. Insurance is protection against events of a fortuitous nature, not against events that are intended.

see: **accident, insurable risk, occurrence**

foundation exclusion clause

Property. A provision in a fire insurance policy that excludes the value of a building's foundation when

© 1991 NILS Publishing Company

foundation exclusion clause — *continued*

determining the proper amount of insurance under a coinsurance clause.

see: coinsurance clause

foundering

Ocean Marine. The sinking of a disabled vessel below the surface of a navigable waterway.

frame construction

Loss Control. Buildings with outside support walls, roof and floors of combustible construction. The exterior walls may be covered with stucco or brick veneer and the interior walls with lath and plaster.

see: construction

franchise deductible

General. A deductible once popular in personal automobile and homeowner's policies. The deductible applies in smaller losses, but gradually is reduced as the size of loss increases so that in a large loss the insurer provides first dollar coverage.

compare: flat deductible, percentage of value deductible; see: deductible

franchise insurance

Health/Life. A group insurance plan under which individual policies are issued to the employees of a common employer or the members of an association. Plan premiums are collected by the employer or association and remitted to the insurer. These plans are designed for small groups that would not qualify for true group coverage.

syn: wholesale group insurance; see: group insurance

fraternal benefit society

Health/Life. A life or health insurance company formed to provide insurance for members of an affiliated lodge, religious or fraternal organization. Such companies are regulated less strictly than life insurance companies which offer coverage to the public at large.

see: insurance company

Fraternal Field Managers Association (FFMA)

Organizations. Members: Sales managers for fraternal life insurance societies. *Objectives:* Sponsors the designation of Fraternal Insurance Counselor (FIC) for representatives meeting education and production standards. *Founded:* 1935. *Headquarters:* Downers Grove, IL.

fraternal insurance

Health/Life. Life or health coverage developed for members of a lodge or fraternal order.

Fraternal Insurance Counselor (FIC)

Organizations. A designation awarded by the Fraternal Field Managers Association after passing specified educational and production requirements.

see: Fraternal Field Managers Association

fraud

General. The intentional misrepresentation of a material fact, made to induce another party to make, or to refrain from making, a contract or to deceive or cheat a party.

see: deceit, rescission

fraudulent delivery

Inland Marine. Coverage for a loss resulting from the fraudulent delivery of goods is included under inland marine coverage forms. The delivery or surrendering of goods to a party posing as an agent for the receiver is considered an invalid delivery and coverage applies under an inland marine form.

free along side (FAS)

Ocean Marine. A term of sale providing that the shipper will place the goods to be shipped along side a specific vessel or at a designated shipping point. The goods are the shipper's responsibility until they are along side, at which time the responsibility passes to the consignee.

syn: free alongside ship, free alongside vessel; compare: free on board

free alongside ship

Ocean Marine.

see: free along side

free alongside vessel

Ocean Marine.

see: free along side

free and clear

General. A term used to refer to property that is not mortgaged or otherwise encumbered.

freedom of the seas

International/Ocean Marine. A doctrine in international law stating that the ships of any nation may travel through international waters without hindrance. Also, the right of ships of noncombatant nations to trade at will during wartime, except where blockades have been established.

free examination period

Health/Life.

see: free look period

freehold

Financial Planning/Title. A tenure of real property

© 1991 NILS Publishing Company

which holds an estate of inheritance in fee simple or fee tail or for life.

see: fee simple, fee tail

free look period

Health/Life. A period during which a consumer may cancel a life or health insurance policy and receive a full refund of all premiums paid. In most cases, the free-look period extends for ten days after delivery of the policy.

syn: free examination period, free trial period

free of capture and seizure (FC&S)

Ocean Marine. An exclusion in ocean marine policies for loss to a vessel from capture or seizure or loss to a vessel's cargo from pirates or assailing thieves.

see: assailing thieves, enemy goods, piracy

free of particular average (FPA)

Ocean Marine. An ocean marine policy provision where coverage is provided only if a total loss of the insured property occurs from an insured peril.

see: average, Janson clause, particular average

free of particular average American conditions (FPAAC)

Ocean Marine. Coverage for a partial loss resulting from stranding, sinking, burning or collision with another vessel.

see: average, free of particular average

free of particular average English conditions (FPAEC)

Ocean Marine. A broader form of ocean marine free of particular average coverage (FPA). In addition to the FPA coverages, insurance is provided for a partial loss to the insured property if at any time during the voyage the vessel is stranded, sunk, burned, on fire or in a collision with another vessel.

see: average, free of particular average

free on board (FOB)

Inland Marine/Ocean Marine. A term of sale which provides that the shipper will place the goods on board a vessel, freight car, truck, or other means of transport, at which time the responsibility passes to the consignee. Indicates that delivery charges are not included in a quoted sales price.

compare: free along side, free on board destination

free on board destination (FOB Destination)

Inland Marine/Ocean Marine. A provision in the term of sale which provides that the shipper will be responsible for the goods until the consignee accepts them.

compare: free on board

free trade zone

Insurer Operations. A facility through which insurers can negotiate insurance policies with insureds without paying tariffs or taxes.

see: insurance exchange

free trial period

Health/Insurer Operations/Life.
see: free look period

freight

General. Goods carried by a vessel or vehicle. Goods transported as cargo by a commercial carrier, in contrast to mail, baggage and express.

syn: lading

Inland Marine/Ocean Marine. The charge a carrier makes for transporting goods.

see: advance freight, collect freight, guaranteed freight, prepaid freight

freight forwarder

Inland Marine/Ocean Marine. A firm that specializes in arranging the transportation of merchandise and completing the documentation needed for its orderly transportation. Some forwarders will pack or consolidate merchandise with other cargo for export to the same country.

see: customs broker, customs broker and freight forwarders errors & omissions insurance, house waybill

frequency

Insurer Operations/Risk Management. The number of times an event occurs in a given period of time. *Frequency* is one factor used to evaluate and underwrite risks; another factor is *severity*. A series of low severity losses that occur at a relatively high frequency can be just as costly to an insurer (or to a self-insurer) as a single, severe loss, because of the loss administration expenses necessary to resolve each claim.

see: probability

frequency distribution

Risk Management. An actuarial term for the arrangement of statistical data that exhibits the frequency of the occurrence of the values of a variable; the number of times losses occur and their severity.

see: standard deviation, variable

friendly fire

Property. A fire started and remaining in a place where it was intended to be confined. Insurance does not cover losses caused by a friendly fire. If events conspired to accidentally spread the fire to the structure or structures around the fire, this fortuitous event would then be covered by any insurance in force.

compare: hostile fire; see: fire

fringe benefits

Employee Benefits. Benefits or compensation provided by an employer in addition to normal payroll compensation.

see: benefit plan

frontage

Casualty. The length of the side of a plot of land that fronts on a street or road. It is sometimes used as a rating base for casualty insurance.

front-end load

Life.

see: premium load

fronting

Insurer Operations. An agreement by an insurer to issue a policy on behalf of a reinsurer, captive insurer, self-insurer or another insurer. This *fronting* insurer assumes little or no loss exposure; instead, financial arrangements are made to guarantee claims administration and payments. The fronting insurer is usually paid a percentage of the premium. Fronting is done for a number of reasons, but is increasingly disfavored by regulators who contend fronting is not true risk-shifting.

see: acting insurer, fronting companies

fronting companies

Insurer Operations. Authorized insurers or associations that transfer most of their risks by reinsurance or other means to unauthorized insurers or associations.

see: fronting

frustration clause

Ocean Marine. An ocean marine provision that applies when war perils are insured, which states that a loss doesn't exist simply because of the termination (frustration) of a voyage due to an outbreak of hostilities. For a loss to exist, the goods must have suffered actual physical damage.

see: force majeure coverage

full coverage

Insurer Operations. A term which indicates that the insurance coverage involved will pay all insured losses in full. While this may be the intent of many coverages, it frequently is impossible to restore a party to "exactly" where they were before a loss occurs.

see: indemnification

Full Disclosures Act

Regulation.

see: Securities Act of 1933

full interest admitted (FIA)

Ocean Marine. A phrase found in ocean marine policies whereby the insurer agrees that the insured has the sole right to loss payments. A concession by the insurer that the insured is the only party with an insurable interest.

compare: as interest may appear; see: insurable interest

full reporting clause

Property. A provision in commercial property policies written with a reporting form, which requires the insured to report the full value of insured property – even if this value exceeds the policy limit. While this endorsement can provide a premium savings, if, at the time of a loss it is determined that the full value had not been reported, a severe penalty will be applied in the loss adjustment.

syn: honesty clause

full tail

Casualty.

see: maxi tail

full value declared (FVD)

Inland Marine/Ocean Marine. A provision in a marine contract requiring that the shipper declare the full value of the merchandise to the carrier, at the time of shipment.

fully earned premium

Insurer Operations. A provision in some policies stipulating that all or a portion (10 percent, 25 percent) of the premium is fully earned by the insurer when the policy is issued. Usually found only in excess and surplus lines policies, this stipulation states that even if a policy were cancelled, e.g., on its second day of coverage, the insurer would retain that portion of the premium indicated under this provision.

compare: flat cancellation; see: premium

fully funded

Employee Benefits. A pension plan is considered to be fully funded when there are sufficient assets to make all payments that are due at specific times. A fully funded pension plan provides assurance to the plan participants that they will receive their benefits even if the employer ceases business.

fully insured status

Employee Benefits. A term used to describe an individual who has met the Social Security requirements to obtain full retirement benefits which are 10 years (40 quarters) of covered employment.

see: currently insured status

fully paid policy

Life. A life insurance policy with limited benefit payments where all benefits have been paid to the beneficiary.

functional obsolescence

Property/Risk Management. A plant, building or

© 1991 NILS Publishing Company

facility that has outlived it useful value because of antiquated equipment or impractical or outmoded design.

see: actual cash value, functional replacement cost, replacement cost, reproduction cost

functional replacement cost

Property. Occasionally, a property insurance policy will provide for loss adjustment on the basis of functional replacement cost, which is the cost to replace damaged property with less expensive and more modern construction or equipment. *Example:* A brick warehouse building may be replaced with a concrete tilt-up warehouse building that is just as functional and less expensive.

compare: actual cash value, depreciated value, fair market value, market value, replacement cost, reproduction cost, tax-appraised value; see: functional obsolescence, valuation of potential property loss

funded spread loss plan

Risk Management.
see: spread loss plan

funding instrument

Employee Benefits. A trust agreement or an insurance contract, stating the conditions under which the funding agency performs. Specifies the terms under which the funding agency will accumulate, administer, and disburse plan assets.

funding of reserves

Reinsurance. A method of providing security to a ceding company when reinsurance is obtained through an nonadmitted reinsurer. Under this procedure, the ceding company retains the reinsurer's funds in an amount equal to the outstanding loss reserves and/or unearned premium reserves.

syn: outstanding claims account; see: unearned premium reserve

funding standard account (FSA)

Employee Benefits. An ERISA requirement that a bookkeeping account be maintained in which credits and debits are used to determine a balance. The credits and debits are determined from actuarial valuations of the plan's actual experience for the period. The objective is to identify funding deficiencies, which occur whenever the sum of negative entry amounts exceed the sum of positive entry amounts

see: accumulated funding deficiency, minimum funding standard

fund states coverage

Workers' Compensation. In certain states, workers' compensation insurance must be purchased as a separate policy through state-owned insurance funds. These are referred to as monopolistic state "funds."

The monopolistic states are Nevada, North Dakota, Ohio, Washington, West Virginia, and Wyoming. (The Commonwealth of Puerto Rico also operates a monopolistic fund for workers' compensation.) Fund states coverage provides this coverage, and can be added as part of an all states endorsement.

see: all-states endorsement, monopolistic state fund

fur floater

Inland Marine. Personal furs insured on an "all-risks" basis, under a personal articles floater or a scheduled personal property endorsement to a homeowner's policy.

compare: furriers' customers insurance; see: personal articles floater, scheduled personal property endorsement

furnace explosion

Property. An explosion resulting from the accumulation of gases or unconsumed fuel within the combustion chamber of a fired vessel. Such an explosion is covered under a fire insurance policy rather than a boiler and machinery policy.

syn: firebox explosion; see: explosion

furriers' customers insurance

Inland Marine. An inland marine form which provides "all-risks" coverage on furs and garments trimmed with fur. The coverage is purchased by furriers, department stores, warehouses, and laundries and cleaners that accept such items for storage. Coverage for a declared value is provided for customers' property left with the insured, for which customers are provided with receipts.

compare: fur floater

fusible link

Loss Control. Two pieces of metal fused (linked) together, usually by bismuth, tin, lead or antimony. The link is designed to melt at a prescribed temperature, thereby allowing a sprinkler head or fire door to automatically operate.

151

© 1991 NILS Publishing Company

G

gain and loss exhibit

Insurer Operations. An insurance company annual statement exhibit section that indicates the company's gains, losses and policyholder surplus for the year.

see: annual statement

gambling

General. A risk which involves an uncertain outcome. Therefore, a chance of either a gain or loss exists. Insurance differs from gambling because it presents no chance for gain on the part of the insured, and it eliminates or reduces an accidental or fortuitous loss.

compare: insurance, indemnification; see: aleatory

gap layer

Casualty.

see: buffer layer

garage coverage form

Automobile/Casualty. An ISO coverage form *(CA 00 05 01 87)* written to provide such coverages as garage liability, medical payments and auto physical damage in a single contract for auto dealers, service stations, auto repair shops and parking lots. The initial form for this coverage was developed in 1935.

see: dealer class plan, driveaway collision, garagekeepers insurance, lemon aid insurance, limited coverage for customers

garagekeepers extra legal liability

Automobile. An endorsement that extends a garagekeepers legal liability insurance policy to provide coverage for any legal liability, regardless of the insured's legal liability as respects vehicles in the care, custody or control of the insured.

see: garagekeepers legal liability insurance

garagekeepers insurance

Automobile. Covers garage operators against direct damage or legal liability for damage to vehicles in the insured's care, custody, or control. This coverage is included as part of the garage coverage form or as a separate endorsement to other policies.

see: garage coverage form, garagekeepers legal liability insurance, garagekeepers extra legal liability

garagekeepers legal liability insurance (GKLL)

Automobile. An obsolete form of insurance for a garage operator, protecting him or her against legal liability for damage to vehicles caused by specific acts while in the insured's care, custody, or control. This form has been replaced by the garagekeepers coverage form.

compare: garagekeepers insurance; see: garagekeepers coverage form, garagekeepers extra legal liability

gate guard

Loss Control.

see: movable barrier guard

gender rating

Insurer Operations. A distinction used in developing rates that assumes that life expectancy, health costs and frequency of accidents differ between males and females. For example, women usually live longer than men, and young women are usually better drivers than young men. Recently however, women claim they have not in the past, nor do they now, receive the benefits these statistics suggest.

see: sex discrimination, uniform premium, unisex legislation

© 1991 NILS Publishing Company

general agency system

Insurer Operations. An insurance distribution system where an insurer appoints a general agent to service the agents within a specified geographical area, rather than opening an insurance company branch office.

compare: direct writer; see: agent, general agent

general agent (GA)

Agency. An individual or entity appointed by an insurance company to operate on its behalf in a particular geographic area. The agent provides all the services (sales, policy issuance and service, and agency appointments) usually provided by an insurance company branch office.

compare: managing general agent; see: agent, policywriting agent

General Agents and Managers Conference of National Association of Life Underwriters (GAMC-NALU)

Organizations. Members: Insurance general agents and managers. *Objectives:* Improving the management capabilities and the ability to sell life insurance products through research, education and a code of ethical practices. *Founded:* 1951. *Headquarters:* Washington, D.C.

general aggregate limit

Insurer Operations. The maximum limit payable for claims that occur under specified coverages during the entire policy period.

Casualty. The highest amount an insured can recover under the ISO commercial general liability coverage forms for Coverages A, B, and C. Excludes claims falling under the "products-completed operations hazard" provision.

see: aggregate limit

general and insurance expenses

Insurer Operations. An insurance company annual statement exhibit section which indicates expenses of the insurer, except for commissions and taxes.

syn: general operating expense; see: expense loading

general average (GA)

Ocean Marine. An ocean marine loss which occurs through the voluntary sacrifice of any part of the vessel or cargo, or an expenditure, to safeguard the vessel and its cargo from a common peril. When such a loss occurs, all interests at risk contribute to it based on their respective saved values. A party can insure their portion of such a loss under an ocean marine policy.

compare: particular average; see: average, contributory value, general average bond, general average contribution, general average deposit,

general average guarantee, general average percentage, York Antwerp Rules; Fr: avarie commune; Gr: grosse Havarie; Sp: avería gruesa

general average adjuster

Ocean Marine. A marine specialist responsible for adjusting and providing the general average statement. Usually this individual is appointed by the shipowner or insurer and collects the general average deposit average deposit or obtains a general average guarantee from each party to the general average loss and authorizes release of cargo to the owners when the cargo is fully secured.

syn: average adjuster; see: general average, general average contribution, general average deposit, general average guarantee, particular average

general average bond

Ocean Marine. A bond prepared by the general average adjuster binding the owner of the goods to pay a proportion of the general average.

see: average agreement, bond, general average

general average contribution

Ocean Marine. The amount that each party to a general average loss must contribute. This is determined by applying the general average percentage to each party's contributory value.

compare: general average deposit, general average guarantee; see: average agreement, general average

general average deposit

Ocean Marine. A cash deposit required by a general average adjuster from the owners of goods, to secure the payment of a proportion of the general average. The amount of the deposit is usually based on a percentage of the general average, and it is required in addition to the general average bond.

compare: general average, general average contribution, general average guarantee; see: general average adjuster, general average bond

general average guarantee

Ocean Marine. An insurer's written guarantee to a general average adjuster, guaranteeing payment of the proportion of general average finally assessed against the goods insured. This guarantee is usually accepted by the adjuster in lieu of a cash deposit and is additional security to a general average bond.

compare: general average contribution, general average deposit; see: average agreement, general average, general average adjuster

general average percentage

Ocean Marine. A percentage arrived at by dividing the total amount of a loss and expenses incurred as the

© 1991 NILS Publishing Company

result of a general average, by the total amount saved as a result of general average.

see: **average agreement, general average**

general aviation

Aviation. A term which includes all aviation except commercial airlines and military aviation. This would include operations such as pleasure aircraft, business (corporate) aircraft, air taxi operators, crop dusting, highway patrol aircraft, sports and instructional flying.

see: **business and pleasure, fixed base operators, flying clubs, industrial aid operators**

general contractor

General. An independent contractor who arranges, through sub-contractors, for the completion of work under a contract with the property owner.

see: **independent contractor**

general cover form

Property. An obsolete term used to identify a reporting form policy.

see: **reporting form**

Generally Accepted Accounting Principles (GAAP)

General. A set of uniform accounting rules for the recording and reporting of financial data, so that that data may be considered a fair representation of an organization's financial condition. These standards are endorsed by the Financial Accounting Standards Board (FASB), and the use of these principles are required by the Securities and Exchange Commission (SEC) for all corporations under its jurisdiction.

compare: **Statutory Accounting Principles;** see: **accounting, Financial Accounting Standards Board, financial statement**

Insurer Operations. Stock insurers and some mutual insurers will issue annual reports based on Generally Accepted Accounting Principles (GAAP) to report to their stockholders or policyholders, but use Statutory Accounting Principles (SAP) developed by the National Association of Insurance Commissioners (NAIC), when reporting to state insurance departments.

see: **Statutory Accounting Principles**

general operating expense

Insurer Operations.
see: **general and insurance expenses**

general partnership

General.
see: **partnership**

general provisions

General.
see: **additional provisions**

genuine assent

General. An element needed for an enforceable contract. It requires that the contracting parties must be real or "genuine" for a valid contract to exist. Genuine assent is missing if one party to the contract deceives the other, or if one or both parties acts on a mistaken assumption.

see: **contract**

geographical limitation

Insurer Operations. An insurance policy provision that designates its area of geographical coverage; e.g., limited to occurrences happening or claims made in a specific state (for a workers' compensation policy), the United States and its territories (for a property insurance policy) or worldwide (for a liability insurance policy).

syn: **coverage territory, territorial limitation;** see: **worldwide coverage**

glass coverage form

Property. A commercial property form which covers the costs of both replacement and incidental costs of building glass due to breakage or the accidental or malicious application of chemicals to the glass. For glass, including its lettering, frame and ornamentation to be covered, it must be specifically listed in the declarations. Excluded from coverage under this form are stained glass, memorial windows, art glass, mosaic art, lenses, halftone screens and rotogravure screens. *ISO Form CP 00 15.*

syn: **plate glass insurance;** see: **comprehensive glass insurance**

glass insurance

Property. Protection for loss of or damage to glass and its accessories.

see: **comprehensive glass insurance, glass coverage form, glass insurance 50/50 basis**

glass insurance 50/50 basis

Property. An endorsement to a comprehensive glass policy which provides a 50 percent reduction in premium; however, in the event of a loss, the insured must bear losses up to an amount equal to the premium paid. The insurer pays any further loss.

see: **comprehensive glass insurance, glass insurance**

golden parachute legal expense

Employee Benefits. Insurance coverage for corporate executives that provides them with reimbursement for their legal expenses in contesting denials of "golden parachute" employment contracts following the takeover of a corporation.

good driver discount

Automobile. A premium discount granted on a personal automobile insurance policy for a good driving

© 1991 NILS Publishing Company

good driver discount — continued

record. In order to obtain the discount, a driver's record must be clear of moving violations and/or accidents for a period of time (usually three to five years).

    see: chargeable offense, good student discount, safe driver plan

good faith

General. A term used to refer to conduct which is to be expected in any other commercial transaction; that is, all parties to a transaction are expected to have honest motives, to fully intend to perform their obligations under the terms set forth in the relationship, and to abstain from defrauding or taking unfair advantage of the other party. In many legal relationships (e.g., the employment relationship, an insurance contract, etc.), there is an "implied covenant of good faith and fair dealing" which requires both parties to treat the other party fairly and to give at least as much consideration to the other party's welfare as it gives to its own.

good student discount

Automobile. A premium discount granted on a personal automobile insurance policy for students with good academic records. Some statistical studies indicate that good students have fewer automobile accidents.

    see: driver training credit

good will

General. An intangible asset maintained on the balance sheet of a business which is expected to generate substantial future profits. *Example:* A famous brand name or a good business reputation.

    see: assets

governing classification

Workers' Compensation. The workers' compensation rating classification that applies to the majority of an employer's payroll, and which generally describes the insured employer's business. Except for employees that qualify for one of the standard exceptions, all employees' payroll will be rated using the governing classification.

    see: classification code, class rate, rate making

Governmental Accounting Standards Board (GASB)

General. An accounting standards board formed to specifically develop accounting standards for governmental entities. It is patterned after the Financial Accounting Standards Board, which develops accounting standards for private entities. Public risk financing began in the mid-70s and GASB was formed to develop consistent methods for preparing public entity financial statements.

    see: Financial Accounting Standards Board

governmental action exclusion

Property. An exclusion found in most property insurance policies, denying coverage for losses occasioned by governmental seizure or destruction of property, except for acts of destruction taken to prevent the spread of fire.

    see: civil authority clause

governmental immunity

Casualty. Generally, public entities (municipal, state or federal government) cannot be held liable for their actions for the overall public good. However, court decisions and legislation have acted to significantly reduce this immunity.

    see: charitable immunity

government insurance

General. A term referring to insurance programs sponsored or provided by federal or state governments, such as social security, unemployment insurance, workers' compensation funds or FAIR plans.

    compare: public entity insurance; see: social insurance

grace period

Health/Life. A specified period (usually 30 days) after a policy premium payment is due, in which the insured may make such payment, and the policy remains in force.

    see: cancellation notice, lapse

graded commission

Agency. An agent's commission scale where the commission percentage rate varies by class of business and premium volume written.

    syn: unlevel commission; compare: flat commission; see: agent's commission, first-year commission, renewal commission

graded death benefit

Life. A provision usually found in juvenile life insurance policies where the benefits in the early years are less than the face amount of the policy and increase over time until they reach the face amount.

    compare: jumping juvenile life insurance, lien plan; see: juvenile insurance

graded premium

Life. A provision found in some whole life insurance policies where the premiums are lower in the early years and increase over time to a point where they become level for the remainder of the policy.

grading schedule

Property. A schedule used by the Insurance Services Office for grading the fire protection provided by cities, towns and other fire districts. The schedule has ten grades or "protection classes," with "1" being the

© 1991 NILS Publishing Company

highest degree of protection and "10" meaning unprotected. In using the schedule, such factors as locations of fire stations, firefighter training, water supplies and building codes are considered.

see: protection, protection class

graduated life table

Life. A mortality table that reflects such irregularities as an insufficient data base, use of a nonhomogeneous data base, or statistics weighted too heavily toward particular years.

see: mortality table

gross combination weight (GCW)

Automobile. The maximum loaded weight for a truck-tractor and the semi-trailer(s) for which the truck-tractor was designed (as specified by the manufacturer).

compare: gross vehicle weight

gross earnings

Property. A coverage amount developed for business interruption insurance which essentially is calculated by subtracting the cost of goods sold from total sales. (With the development of the business income coverage program, this concept was abandoned).

see: business income coverage form, gross earnings form

gross earnings form

Property. A property insurance loss of earnings form that was widely used until the business income coverage program was developed. Under the gross earnings form, the amount of insurance was based on the coinsurance percentage selected (50%, 60%, 70%, or 80%), which in turn reflected the expected length of time (part of a year) a business would be out of operation after a loss.

see: business income coverage form, earnings insurance form, gross earnings

gross line

Insurer Operations. An amount of coverage written by an insurer on a single risk, including the insurer's net line and ceded reinsurance.

syn: assumption, maximum line; compare: net line

gross negligence

General. A legal term for negligence which involves reckless, willful and wanton acts taken without regard to another's life, limb or property. The failure to use ordinary care.

see: degree of care, negligence, wanton disregard

gross premium

Insurer Operations. The entire premium charged by

an insurer to a policyholder which includes all of the insurer's expenses, estimated loss costs and profits.

see: premium

gross vehicle weight (GVW)

Automobile. The maximum loaded weight for which a single vehicle is designed, as specified by the manufacturer.

compare: gross combination weight

ground coverage

Aviation. Physical damage insurance coverage on an aircraft hull, that applies when the aircraft is not in flight.

compare: flight coverage; see: in motion

ground fault circuit interrupter (GFCI)

Loss Control. A fast-acting circuit breaker that is sensitive to very low levels of current leakage to the ground. The interrupter is designed to limit electric shocks to a specified current and time duration value, to prevent serious injury.

see: electrical grounding

group accident and health insurance

Health. An insurance plan designed for a natural group, such as employees of a single employer, or union members and their dependents. Insurance is provided under a single policy issued to the employer or union, with individual certificates issued to each participant or family unit.

see: accident and health insurance, group insurance

group annuity

Life. A master annuity contract issued in conjunction with an employee benefit plan, which provides that individual annuity contracts will be issued to plan participants on their retirement.

see: annuity

group captive insurance company

Risk Management. A captive insurance company established and owned by a group of companies engaging in similar businesses, to underwrite their own collective risks. A group captive usually insures only its owners.

compare: association captive insurance company; see: captive insurance company, risk retention group

group certificate

Health/Life. An insurance coverage summary provided to participants of an employee benefit plan which indicates they are included in the plan. The certificate confirms that a master policy has been issued to the employer which may be reviewed by the employee.

syn: certificate of insurance; compare: group contract, master insurance policy

157

© 1991 NILS Publishing Company

group contract

Health/Life. A master insurance contract issued to an employer or other entity which provides life or health coverage to a plan's qualifying participants. Individual group certificates are issued based on the group contract to indicate that the individual is covered.

syn: master insurance policy; compare: certificate of insurance, group certificate

group credit life insurance

Life. Credit life insurance coverage which protects a lender (bank, credit union, credit card company) in the event that a debtor dies before repaying the loan's balance. Coverage is written on all of a lender's debtors and recovery is limited to the outstanding loan balance. The premium for this coverage is paid by the lender.

see: credit life insurance, creditor beneficiary

group deferred annuity

Employee Benefits. A group annuity program where a series of single premium paid-up annuities are issued to provide retirement benefits for each plan participant.

syn: allocated funding instrument

group deposit administration annuity

Health/Life.

see: deposit administration plan

group disability insurance

Health. An employee or association group insurance program that provides individual disability insurance coverage to each qualifying employee by issuing a certificate to a master plan contract. The coverage provided consists of the payment of a percentage (50%, 60%) of the plan participant's lost wages due to an illness or accident, subject to a maximum monthly payment.

see: disability

group health insurance

Health. An employee or association group insurance program that provides each qualifying plan participant with medical insurance coverage by issuing a certificate to a master plan contract. Generally, each employee is responsible for an annual deductible and some coinsurance portions of medical costs incurred, unless the plan uses a health maintenance organization or preferred provider organization.

see: coordination of benefits, group certificate, group contract, health maintenance organization, preferred provider organization, schedule, true group insurance

group I rates

Property. A classification for property insurance rates under the 1986 ISO Commercial Lines Program, for

the perils of fire, lightning, explosion, sprinkler coverage and vandalism.

see: group II rates

group II rates

Property. A classification for property insurance rates under the 1986 ISO Commercial Lines Program, for the perils of windstorm, hail, smoke, riot or civil commotion, aircraft, vehicles, sinkhole collapse, and volcanic action.

see: group I rates

group insurance

Employee Benefits. Insurance provided by an employer, association or other natural group (as opposed to a fictitious group, formed just for the purpose of purchasing insurance) to its employees or members by arranging a master insurance contract to which individual certificates are issued, to cover plan participants, and generally, their dependents. The cost of insurance under a group plan is usually lower than for individual policies because of lower acquisition and administrative expenses.

see: association group insurance, deposit administration plan, fictitious group, franchise insurance, group annuity, group certificate, group contract, group credit life insurance, group deferred annuity, group disability insurance, group health insurance, group life insurance, group permanent insurance, group property and liability insurance, guaranteed issue, master insurance policy

group life insurance

Life. An employee or association group insurance program that provides each qualifying plan participant with life insurance by issuing a certificate to a master plan contract. Usually, yearly renewable term policies are issued, but some plans provide permanent life insurance policies.

syn: group term life insurance; compare: group permanent insurance; see: facility-of-payment clause

group permanent insurance

Life. A group life insurance plan where plan participants may choose permanent life insurance coverage. They usually are allowed to select from one of several forms of permanent insurance policies.

compare: group life insurance

group property and liability insurance

Casualty/Property. An employee or association group insurance program that provides each qualifying participant with homeowner's or automobile insurance provided for members of a group. It is most often an elective employee benefit, fully paid for by

© 1991 NILS Publishing Company

the employee. The cost is usually lower than purchasing individual policies, since the insurer can save on certain administrative expenses.

see: cafeteria benefit plan

group term life insurance
Life.
see: group life insurance

guarantee
General.
see: express warranty

guaranteed annuity payments
Life. Annuity payments that are not contingent upon how long the annuitant lives. If the annuitant dies, these payments will be made to the decedent's estate as they become due.

syn: certain payments

guaranteed continuable
Health/Life.
see: guaranteed renewable

guaranteed cost
Casualty. A term used to refer to any insurance policy where a fixed premium is paid, based on the policyholder's exposures, and no additional premium can be charged because of adverse loss experience.

compare: experience rating plan, prospective rating plan, retrospective rating plan

guaranteed freight
Inland Marine/Ocean Marine. Freight which is not prepaid, but which is payable whether or not the merchandise arrives at the final port or destination.

see: freight

guaranteed insurability
Health. An insurance policy option which at inception allows the insured the right to purchase additional benefits at a future date, such as additional disability income or higher medical expense benefit limits, without providing additional or updated evidence of insurability.

compare: evidence of insurability; see: guaranteed renewable

Life. A life insurance policy option which may be purchased at inception that allows the insured to purchase additional amounts of life insurance without taking a physical examination or having to provide evidence of insurability. Generally, the provision requires the insured to increase the amount of insurance at a stated time (i.e., specified anniversary dates, upon the birth of a child).

see: guaranteed issue

guaranteed investment contract (GIC)
Life. An investment contract offered by a life insurance company which guarantees the repayment of principal and a compound interest return. It is frequently used to fund qualified pension plans.

guaranteed issue
Health/Life. A group insurance plan where the insurer does not require individual employees to provide evidence of insurability to obtain coverage. The amount of coverage provided is sometimes determined by group sizes and distribution of ages.

see: guaranteed insurability, guaranteed renewable

guaranteed payout
Life. The sum of certain payments, i.e., guaranteed lump sums, annuities certain, and the payments generated during the certain period of a life-contingent annuity.

see: certain period

guaranteed period
Life.
see: certain period

guaranteed renewable
Health/Life. An insurance policy which provides that the insured has the right to continue the policy in force until the insured reaches a specified age. The insured must make the premium payments in a timely manner, and the insurer cannot unilaterally change the policy except for rate increases which apply to all policyholders in that class of coverage.

syn: guaranteed continuable; compare: optionally renewable contract; see: guaranteed insurability, guaranteed issue, lifetime policy, noncancellable policy

guarantor
Surety. The party who guarantees the actions or debts of another party. Under a surety bond, the surety is the guarantor.

see: surety

guaranty funds
Regulation. Funds created by statute in most states, which guarantee the claim payments of state-domiciled insurance companies that become insolvent. The funds are created with assessments made against the other insurers operating in that state. Most state guaranty funds operate on a post-insolvency basis; that is, the assessments are made following an insolvency. New York is the exception; their guaranty fund is prefunded by assessments made to maintain the fund at a certain level.

syn: insolvency funds; see: American Trust

© 1991 NILS Publishing Company

guaranty funds — continued
Fund, central loss fund, insolvency, liquidation, Lloyd's Premium Trust Fund, rehabilitation

guardian

General. An individual legally entrusted with the custody and/or the property of another party (most often a minor or an incompetent).

guardian ad litem

General. A person appointed by the court during the course of litigation who protects the interest of a minor or an incompetent who is a party to the suit. The appointment automatically ends when the case is resolved.

guardian of the estate

General. A person to whom the court has entrusted the custody and control of funds (e.g., periodic payments in a claims settlement) going to a minor (during minority) or an incompetent (while he or she is incapacitated).

Guertin Laws

Life. Laws dealing with life insurance which are named after Alfred Guertin, former actuary for the New Jersey Insurance Department. The laws, initiated in 1947, apply to the valuation and nonforfeiture of life insurance policies and protect the insured's ability to recover from a life policy and obtain any equity built in the policy.

see: nonforfeiture benefit, nonforfeiture cash surrender value benefit

guest law

Automobile. Generally, a passenger in an automobile has the right to bring suit against the driver for ordinary negligence in the event of an automobile accident. However, some states have enacted statutes which prohibit the passenger from filing such a suit unless willful and wanton negligence is involved.

syn: guest statute; see: assumption of risk, passenger hazard exclusion

guests' property — safe deposit box

Crime. A crime coverage plan developed under the 1986 ISO crime program which provides coverage similar to the hotel safe deposit box liability form. Coverage Form K is used in this plan.

syn: crime plan 6; see: hotel safe deposit box liability

guest statute

Automobile.

see: guest law

guideline premium

Life. A premium defined in universal life insurance policies as the maximum premium payable that will qualify the policy as life insurance for federal income tax purposes.

160

© 1991 NILS Publishing Company

H

Hague Rules

Ocean Marine. A set of rules resulting from a 1921 conference at The Hague in Holland, concerning bills of lading for the carriage of goods by sea. In 1922, the rules were adopted by most countries to cover the carriage of goods by sea.

see: **Carriage of Goods by Sea Act, Carriage of Goods by Water Act**

hail

General. Precipitation that takes the form of small pellets of ice that occasionally are of sufficient size to cause severe property damage.

see: **crop-hail insurance; Fr: grêle; Gr: Hagel; Sp: granizo**

hail insurance

Property.

see: **crop-hail insurance**

halon

Loss Control. A nontoxic, vaporizing liquid used in fixed fire extinguishing systems for protecting enclosures. The vapor is injected into the enclosure, snuffing out the fire by depriving it of oxygen. Most often used in computer and laboratory rooms, where foam or water extinguishing systems might do more damage than good.

see: **fire extinguishing system**

hangarkeepers legal liability insurance

Aviation. Coverage for the owner or operator of an aircraft hangar, for damage to or destruction of the aircraft of others while in the insured's custody for storage, repair or safekeeping.

see: **airport owners and operators liability insurance**

hard market

Insurer Operations. A term used to refer to that period of time during the underwriting cycle when insurance coverage is difficult for some insureds to obtain and pricing is high. Some coverages, such as products or professional liability may not be available for some insureds during a hard market. Generally, "hard" markets are caused by heavy underwriting losses and extreme price cutting, whereas a "tight" market is caused by a lack of capacity, such as when money is invested in places other than insurance companies.

compare: **buyer's market, soft market, tight market; see: underwriting cycle**

Harter Act

Ocean Marine. A federal statute adopted in 1893 concerning maritime ventures to and from United States ports which limits the responsibility of vessel owners for damage or loss due to navigational error if the vessel was properly equipped and manned and was a seaworthy vessel.

see: **Carriage of Goods By Sea Act**

hazard

Property. A condition or situation which creates or increases the probability of or extent of a probable loss from a peril such as poor housekeeping, slippery floors, wood shingle roofs or congested traffic.

compare: **exposure, peril, risk; see: moral hazard, morale hazard, physical hazard**

hazardous waste `

Casualty. Chemical or other products specifically listed as hazardous waste by the Comprehensive Environmental Response, Compensation and Liability Act (CERCLA) of 1980. The materials are categorized

161

© 1991 NILS Publishing Company

hazardous waste — continued

according to their ignitability, corrosivity, reactivity and toxicity.

see: closure and post-closure insurance; Comprehensive Environmental Response, Compensation and Liability Act; pollutant

hazardous waste site

Casualty. A site that is contaminated by or used for the disposal of hazardous waste.

see: hazardous waste

head office

Insurer Operations.

see: home office

health indemnity plan

Health. A form of health insurance — usually group health insurance — in which the insured is reimbursed by the insurer after paying his or her own medical expenses. The insured is then reimbursed for such expenses less any deductible and/or co-payment.

syn: hospital indemnity insurance; compare: health maintenance organization, preferred provider organization; see: indemnification

health insurance (HI)

Health. Coverage for hospital and medical expenses resulting from illness or injury. Also includes coverage for the accidental loss of life, limb or sight.

syn: accident and sickness insurance, sickness insurance; see: accident insurance, accidental death insurance, disability income insurance, dismemberment benefit, medical expense insurance

Health Insurance Association of America (HIAA)

Organizations. Members: Accident and health insurance companies. *Objectives:* Promotes interests of accident and health insurers. *Founded:* 1956. *Headquarters:* Washington, D.C. Formed by a merger of the Bureau of Accident and Health Underwriters and the Health and Accident Underwriters Conference.

see: Health Insurance Institute

Health Insurance Institute (HII)

Health/Organizations. Members: Representatives from the health insurance industry; usually members of the Health Insurance Association of America (HIAA). *Objectives:* Acts as the public relations arm of the HIAA. Relays health insurance information to consumers. *Founded:* 1956. *Headquarters:* Washington, D.C.

see: Health Insurance Association of America

health maintenance organization (HMO)

Health. A prepaid medical, group practice plan that

acts as both an insurer and health care provider. Group participants are entitled to services from participating physicians, clinics and hospitals for a flat monthly or quarterly fee.

compare: direct health care corporation, health indemnity plan, preferred provider organization; see: in-area emergency services, managing physician

health service area

Health.

see: annual implementation plan

health systems agency (HSA)

General.

see: annual implementation plan

health systems plan (HSP)

General.

see: annual implementation plan

hearing level

Health/Loss Control. The deviation in decibels of an individual's hearing threshold from the zero reference of an audiometer.

see: decibel, noise level

hearing loss

Health/Loss Control.

see: hearing level

hearsay evidence

General. Evidence in a legal proceeding that is not based on a witness's personal knowledge, but rather on matters told to the witness by another person. Usually, this form of evidence is not admissible in a court of law.

see: evidence

hidden defect

Casualty. A concealed deficiency or fault in a product which may cause it to fail when used.

see: active malfunction, bench error, defective, latent defect

highly protected risk (HPR)

Property. A property insurance program for larger commercial properties that are protected with automatic sprinkler systems and superior construction. Insureds that qualify for an HPR Plan will pay significantly lower premiums.

see: Factory Mutual System, Industrial Risk Insurers

high pressure steam

Loss Control. Steam that is at a pressure in excess of 15 pounds per square inch.

compare: low pressure steam

© 1991 NILS Publishing Company

Highway Loss Data Institute (HLDI)

Organizations. Members: Motor vehicle property and casualty insurers. *Objectives:* Provide consumers with insurance industry data about human and economic losses resulting from highway accidents. *Founded:* 1972. *Headquarters:* Washington, D.C.

hired automobile

Automobile. An auto leased, rented or borrowed by the insured.

compare: nonowned automobile

hobbies or avocations

Life. A life insurance underwriter will consider an applicant's hobbies and avocations in rating individual life policies. Such hobbies as auto racing or skydiving may necessitate higher life insurance premiums.

see: impaired risk, occupational hazard

holder in due course

Financial Planning. The individual or entity that has obtained a bill of exchange (such as a check, stock or bond) in a bona fide way for value. The bill of exchange is taken free of previous defects in title.

see: holder in due course insurance, lender's holder in due course insurance, personal defense

holder in due course insurance

Financial Guarantee Insurance. Coverage developed as the result of a 1976 Fair Trade Commission ruling which removed a lending institution's defense that as a holder in due course they were immune from disputes involving products for which they had arranged financing. The coverage protects a lender when a dealer refuses to correct an inherent defect in a product and the debtor refuses to repay a loan.

compare: lender's holder in due course insurance

hold harmless agreement

Casualty. A provision contained in many contracts which provides that one party to the contract will assume whatever liability arises under or because of the contract for the other. Such agreements are frequently found in leases, sidetrack agreements and easements. There are three major types of such agreements: 1) clarification type – both parties provide that each shall assume their own legal responsibility or make only a small or reasonable transfer of responsibility from one party to the other; 2) moderate type – one party assumes all legal liability except that arising out of the negligence of the other. This form is usually considered the "standard" agreement; and 3) severe type – one party assumes all legal liability without regard to fault or negligence.

syn: indemnity agreement

holding company

General. A business that confines its activities to owning stock in and supervising the management of other companies.

see: parent company

holdup

Crime. Robbery at gunpoint.

see: robbery

hole-in-one coverage

Inland Marine. A form of prize indemnification insurance which covers the insured (usually a tournament sponsor) should a hole-in-one be made on a specified hole on a golf course during a specified tournament. The policy warrants that certification of a hole-in-one must be made by at least two tournament officials prior to payment of a claim against the policy.

see: prize indemnification insurance

home office

Insurer Operations. The headquarters or principal office of an insurance company, where the chief executive officer and the senior executive staff are located.

syn: head office

Home Office Life Underwriters Association (HOLUA)

Organizations. Members: Underwriters of legal reserve life insurance companies. *Objectives:* Offer education programs through the Academy of Life Underwriting for professional home office life underwriters. *Founded:* 1930. *Headquarters:* St. Paul, MN.

homeowner's policy

Casualty/Property. An insurance policy designed to protect a homeowner, which combines broad property insurance coverage for the structure and personal property, with broad personal liability coverage. Numerous versions of homeowner's policies exist, but most insurers use or base their coverage on ISO forms. The ISO policy provides personal liability coverage for the homeowner, and extends coverage to include the spouse, children and relatives residing in the home. Numerous endorsements can be added to the homeowner's policy, such as a personal articles floater for highly valued jewelry or furs, or an inflation guard endorsement. All forms, except Form 4, have the following structure: Section I – Coverage:
A – Applies to the dwelling.
B – Applies to appurtenant structures
C – Applies to unscheduled personal property
D – Applies to additional living expense
Section II – Coverage:

© 1991 NILS Publishing Company

homeowner's policy — continued
A – Applies to personal liability
B – Applies to medical payments to others

see: **condominium unit owner's form, dwelling, buildings and contents form, homeowner's policy form 1, homeowner's policy form 2, homeowner's policy form 3, homeowner's policy – liability coverage, homeowner's policy – property coverage, mobile home policy, renter's insurance, residence employee**

homeowner's policy form 1

Property. A homeowner's policy where the perils insured under the property coverage section are fire, lightning, windstorm, hail, explosion, smoke, theft, vandalism, malicious mischief, riot, civil commotion, glass breakage, vehicles and aircraft.

syn: **basic homeowner's policy, standard homeowner's policy**; compare: **homeowner's policy form 2, homeowner's policy form 3**

homeowner's policy form 2

Property. A homeowner's policy where the perils insured under the property coverage section are the same as Policy Form 1, with additional coverage for sudden and accidental damage from smoke; falling objects; weight of ice, snow or sleet; collapse of building or any part thereof; accidental discharges, leakage or overflow of water or steam; sudden and accidental tearing asunder, cracking, burning or bulging of appliances for heating water; breakage of glass; freezing of plumbing; heating and air conditioning systems and domestic appliances and smoke; and accidental injury from artificially generated electrical currents to electrical appliances, devices, fixtures and wiring.

compare: **homeowner's policy form 1, homeowner's policy form 3**; see: **condominium unit owner's form, renter's insurance**

homeowner's policy form 3

Property. A homeowner's policy where the perils insured under the property coverage sections are "all risks" of physical loss, subject to certain exclusions. This is the broadest homeowner's form available.

syn: **special homeowner's policy**; compare: **homeowner's policy form 1, homeowner's policy form 2**

homeowner's policy form 4

Casualty/Property.
see: **renter's insurance**

homeowner's policy form 5

Casualty/Property. An obsolete form homeowner's form which provided "all risks" coverage for dwellings and personal property. This is now accomplished by attaching Special Personal Property Coverage Endorsement (ISO-HO-15) to Special Form HO-3.

homeowner's policy form 6

Property.
see: **condominium unit owner's form**

homeowner's policy form B

Property. A homeowner's policy designed for older homes which insures the property for actual cash value, rather than replacement cost.

homeowner's policy – liability coverage

Casualty. Most homeowner's policies provide the liability coverage in Section II of the policy, which contains three separate coverage sections. Under the ISO policy form these sections are:
Coverage E – provides coverage in the event that a suit is brought against the insured homeowner or spouse, relatives of either and others under 21 in the care of the homeowner, because of bodily injury and/or property damage for which the insured is legally liable.
Coverage F – covers reimbursement of reasonable medical expenses for injuries sustained by a third party as a result of the insured's activities, whether or not the insured is legally liable.
Coverage G – covers reimbursement up to $250 for property damage sustained by a third party as a result of activities of the insured whether or not the insured is legally liable.

homeowner's policy – property coverage

Property. Most homeowner's policies provide property insurance coverage in Section I of the policy, which itself contains four separate coverage sections. Under the ISO policy form these sections are:
Coverage A – provides coverage on the structure of the home for an indicated amount of insurance. Coverage is usually written on a replacement cost basis with a small (e.g., $100 or $250) deductible. The remaining three property coverage sections provide limits based on a percentage of the structure value.
Coverage B – provides coverage on the garage or other appurtenant private structures not attached to or part of the home, usually for 10 percent of the structure's value.
Coverage C – covers the homeowner's personal property within the home (40 to 50 percent of the structure's value) and away from the premises (10 percent of the in-home personal property limit).
Coverage D – provides additional living expense coverage, if the home is damaged, for 10 to 20 percent of the structure's amount.

see: **condominium unit owner's form, homeowner's policy form 1, homeowner's policy form 2, homeowner's policy form 3, renter's insurance**

© 1991 NILS Publishing Company

home service insurance
Life.
see: industrial life insurance

homestead
Property/Title. The right to land created by the construction of a home on a plot of land and the filing of a homestead with the appropriate local jurisdiction. An insurable interest is created by a homestead.

homogeneity
General. The quality of sameness or similarity among members of a group or class. In insurance, identification as one of a large group of homogeneous exposure units – allowing proper classification and rating of the risk, as well as spread of risk – is a condition that must be met before most insurers will provide coverage for a given risk.
see: insurable risk, spread of risk

homogeneous exposure units
Insurer Operations. Units which are alike in size, value, use, or other relevant characteristics, and so are similarly exposed to loss. Insurance underwriters evaluate a risk's characteristics, and place risks into classifications representing large numbers of similarly situated risks.
see: classification, insurable risk, rating class

honesty clause
Property.
see: full reporting clause

hospice
Health. A health care facility that provides care for terminally ill individuals in a home-like setting. Usually the stay begins a few months prior to their anticipated date of death, and includes medical care and counseling.

hospital benefits
Health. Benefits provided under an insurance policy for hospital charges which the insured has incurred because of a covered illness or injury.

hospital confinement insurance
Health. A limited form of health insurance that pays a stipulated daily, weekly or monthly benefit while an insured is confined to a hospital. The benefit is payable on an unallocated basis, without regard to the amount of actual hospital expense incurred.
syn: hospital income insurance

hospital expense insurance
Health.
see: hospital-surgical expense insurance

hospital income insurance
Health.
see: hospital confinement insurance

hospital indemnity insurance
Health.
see: health indemnity plan

hospitalization insurance
Health.
see: hospital-surgical expense insurance

hospital malpractice insurance
Casualty.
see: hospital professional liability insurance

hospital professional liability insurance
Casualty. Coverage for a hospital against claims for personal injury arising out of medical malpractice, error or mistake in rendering professional services.
syn: hospital malpractice insurance

hospital-surgical expense insurance
Health. A limited form of health insurance which reimburses the insured for expenses directly related to hospitalization. This includes room charges, nursing, and surgical expenses resulting from the illness or injury of the insured.
syn: hospital expense insurance, hospitalization insurance

hostile fire
Property. A fire occurring in a place where a fire is not intended. Property insurance contracts protect against damage from hostile fires, but not from damage from friendly fires. Insurance is designed to cover *fortuitous losses*, such as hostile fires.
compare: friendly fire; see: fire, fortuitous event

host liquor liability
Casualty. A special liability form which provides coverage to individuals or organizations that entertain guests, employees or organizations at events where liquor is served. Coverage is provided should a person that has been served liquor cause injury or damage because of his or her intoxication. Host liquor liability is covered under a homeowner's policy and the 1986 ISO Commercial General Liability form.
compare: dram shop liability insurance

hotel safe deposit box liability
Crime. Coverage for an innkeeper from loss or damage to a guest's property kept in safe deposit boxes on the premises. Coverage is provided for the insured's legal liability, defense and supplementary payments.
compare: innkeepers legal liability; see: guests' property – safe deposit box, liability

© 1991 NILS Publishing Company

hotel safe deposit box liability – continued
for guest's property – safe deposit coverage
form, safe depository direct loss coverage
form

house confinement

Health. A health insurance contract provision requiring the insured to be confined to his or her residence in order to collect loss of income benefits.

compare: nonconfining sickness

household and personal property

Property.

see: condominium unit owner's form, homeowner's policy, personal property floater, renter's insurance

housekeeping

Loss Control/Property. A hazard that creates or increases the probability of a loss. It is the general care, cleanliness and maintenance of a property.

house to house coverage

Inland Marine.

see: door to door coverage

house waybill

Aviation/Inland Marine. A waybill issued by a freight forwarder for air or truck shipments.

compare: master air waybill; see: freight forwarder, waybill

HR-10 plan

Employee Benefits.

see: Keogh Plan

Huebner Foundation for Insurance Education (HFIE)

Organizations. Members: Appointed trustees. *Objectives:* To strengthen the teaching of risk management and insurance at the collegiate level by providing pre-doctoral and post-doctoral fellowships at the Wharton Business School of the University of Pennsylvania and through publication of doctoral dissertations, research papers and sponsored lectures. *Founded:* 1940. *Headquarters:* Philadelphia, PA.

hull

Aviation. The fuselage, wings, tail, rudders, and other major structural features of an aircraft.

Ocean Marine. The frame or body of the ship, exclusive of masts, yards, sails, and rigging.

Fr: coque; Gr: Kasko; Sp: casco

hull policy

Aviation. An aviation contract that indemnifies the insured for damage to or loss of the hull of an aircraft.

syn: aircraft hull insurance; see: aircraft insurance, hull

Ocean Marine. An ocean marine contract that indemnifies the insured for damage to or loss of the hull of a ship, including most of the machinery attached to it.

see: hull

hull syndicates

Ocean Marine. An association or group of ocean marine underwriters who have joined together to underwrite oceangoing vessels.

human approach

Loss Control. A loss control technique that concentrates on modifying the habits of people in order to reduce loss frequency and severity. *Examples:* Driver safety programs and seat belt usage campaigns.

see: human factors engineering, job safety analysis

human factors engineering

Loss Control. A loss prevention technique that concentrates on the physical movements, working attitudes and physical condition of a work area.

see: human approach, job safety analysis

human life value (HLV)

Casualty/Life. The monetary value of a human life, measured by determining the net present value of benefits that others (the decedent's spouse, dependents, partners, employers) might reasonably expect to receive from the future efforts of the individual whose life is being valued. This amount is used to calculate the benefit amount needed to replace lost future earnings of a wage earner, to set the amount of life insurance needed or the amount of a liability award or settlement.

syn: economic value of an individual life

human perils

Property. One of three categories of perils, the others being "natural perils" and "economic perils." Human perils include such things as acts by men or women against each other or damage to property. These perils include bodily injury, products liability, crime and fidelity.

see: economic perils, natural perils, peril

Hunter Disability Tables

Health. Actuarial disability tables which indicate the rate of disability in a specific population; the rate of mortality among disabled people and the probability of total and permanent disability.

see: mortality table

hurricane

Property. A severe tropical storm with winds exceeding 75 miles per hour, and accompanied by rain, thunder and lightning.

syn: cyclone, typhoon; compare: tornado; Fr: ouragan; Gr: Orkan; Sp: huracan

© 1991 NILS Publishing Company

hurricane insurance

Property. Coverage against physical damage caused by the peril of wind produced by a hurricane. Usually part of a group of property coverages (e.g., added to a homeowner's or commercial property policy).

see: **beachfront plans**

hypothecate

Ocean Marine. To pledge a vessel by a bottomry bond.

© 1991 NILS Publishing Company

Identification

Risk Management. The first of the five steps in the risk management process, in which potential sources of loss are identified by conducting complete examinations of possible events that could occur by negligence, oversight or accident.

see: risk management process

Ignition temperature

Loss Control. The lowest temperature at which a flammable material will ignite.

see: flash point.

Illegal employment

Workers' Compensation. The employment of persons in jobs which are inherently dangerous or injurious to their health or morals. Employment in violation of child labor laws or other legal proscriptions. *Example:* Minors employed as bartenders.

see: double compensation

Illinois Insurance Exchange (IIE)

Organizations. An insurance exchange created as a not-for-profit corporation by the Illinois Legislature on September 24, 1979. Opened for trading on November 20, 1981, it is the only one active of the three exchanges that operated in the U.S. during the mid-1980s. (The other two exchanges were located in New York and Florida)

see: insurance exchange

Immature policies

Casualty. A liability policy written on a claims-made basis, which has been in effect on a continuous basis for less than five years. The rates applied to immature policies are less than those applied to mature policies, because their period of claims exposure is less.

compare: mature policies; see: claims-made form

Immediate annuity

Life. An annuity contract that commences periodic benefit payments immediately after the last regular premium payment is paid.

Immediate vesting

Employee Benefits. A pension plan participant's right to receive full benefits from a plan without a waiting period; an immediate, 100 percent vesting in a pension plan.

see: vesting

Impaired asset

General. An asset that is specifically pledged to secure liabilities and is not available to meet general obligations.

see: assets

Impaired property

Casualty. Property which has lost useful or monetary value because it contains a product or work which is defective or inadequate. Property impairment is the basis for liability claims and litigation, brought by the property owner against the supplier of the product or work causing the impairment.

Impaired risk

Health/Life. An applicant for life or health insurance having a substandard physical condition or a hazardous occupation or hobby. While many insurers avoid

© 1991 NILS Publishing Company

impaired risk – continued
such risks, some insurers specialize in insuring substandard, or impaired, risks.

syn: **substandard risk**; see: **hobbies or avocations, occupational hazard, qualified impairment insurance**

impairment exclusion rider

Health. A rider attached to a health insurance policy that excludes losses arising from certain preexisting causes; e.g., prior heart attack(s) often necessitate an exclusion for subsequent heart attack(s).

see: **preexisting condition, qualified impairment insurance**

impairment of capital

Insurer Operations. The depletion of a stock insurer's surplus account, forcing it to use its capital funds to meet liabilities. Some states allow a specific percentage of capital funds to be so used by insurers.

see: **surplus**

implied authority

Agency/Insurer Operations. Authority given by an insurance company to an agent, that is not actually expressed or otherwise communicated. This method of granting an agent the authority to act for the insurance company allows the agent to perform all the usual and necessary tasks to sell and service an insurance policy and to exercise the agent's authority.

compare: **actual authority, agency agreement, expressed authority**; see: **agency**

implied contract

General. A contractual relationship in which the promise or promises are implied by conduct rather than expressed in writing.

see: **contract**

implied covenant of good faith and fair dealing

General.

see: **good faith**

implied seaworthiness

Ocean Marine. The application for and acceptance of an ocean marine policy communicates an implied warranty that the insured vessel's condition, its crew, and its equipment are prepared to make the voyage covered by the policy.

implied warranty

Casualty. Courts have sometimes ruled that a warranty is passed to another even though the warranty is not explicitly stated in writing. *Example:* For the purposes of an ocean marine contract, a vessel is implicitly assumed to be seaworthy.

compare: **disclaimer, express warranty**; see: **implied seaworthiness**

import

International. To bring merchandise or services into a country from another country.

compare: **export**; see: **customs entry form, duty**

imprest account

Risk Management. An account – usually established by a self-insurer or in a deductible liability plan – to fund the low-severity, high frequency losses. It is generally used to pay such losses as they occur. As the account is depleted, new money is deposited from the self-insurer's operating account.

see: **sinking fund**

improvements and betterments

Property. A term describing additions made to premises by a tenant, which improve the rented property, but which also become part of the realty and revert to the building owner upon termination of the lease. A tenant may purchase insurance to cover loss or damage to the improvements and betterments.

syn: **betterments**; compare: **personal property, real estate**; see: **fixture, improvements and betterments insurance, loss of use – value in improvements and betterments**

improvements and betterments insurance

Property. Property insurance purchased by a building tenant to protect its interest in improvements and betterments it has made to the building. Many commercial property and renter policies automatically provide some limited coverage (10 percent of the policy limit) for improvements and betterments.

see: **loss of use – value in improvements and betterments**

imputed liability

Casualty.

see: **contingent liability**

inactive insurers

Insurer Operations. Insurers not actively engaged in the business of insurance, but whose charter still exists. This term excludes liquidated and insolvent insurers.

inactive risks

Insurer Operations. Risks not currently being exposed to the hazards against which they are insured.

in-area emergency services

Health. An HMO coverage provision that allows treatment of a critically injured HMO enrollee on an emergency basis at the nearest medical facility, rather than at a more distant HMO-authorized hospital.

© 1991 NILS Publishing Company

incendiarism
Property.
see: arson

inception date
Insurer Operations.
see: effective date

inchmaree clause
Ocean Marine.
see: inchmaree perils

inchmaree perils
Ocean Marine. An ocean marine clause originated as the result of a lawsuit in 1887 involving the vessel "Inchmaree." The clause now is captioned "additional perils" and covers loss or damage to the property of the insured caused by bursting of boilers, breakage of shafts, or through any latent defect in the hull or machinery of the vessel. This clause also includes coverage for accidents in handling cargo, repairer's negligence and crew negligence as long as the damage is not a result of want of due diligence by the vessel owner.

syn: additional perils, inchmaree clause

incidental contract
Casualty. A term used in older commercial general liability forms to refer to contracts and agreements for which coverage was automatically included, such as 1) easement agreements, except in connection with grade crossings; 2) agreements required by municipal ordinance, except in connection with work for the municipality; 3) lease of premises agreements; 4) sidetrack agreements; and 5) elevator maintenance agreements. All other (i.e., "non-incidental") contracts required special contractual liability coverage.

see: contractual liability insurance

incidental damages
General. A form of money damages in a liability suit which compensates the non-breaching party in contractual litigation for expenses reasonably incurred as a result of the other party's breach.

see: damages

incidental medical malpractice liability
Casualty. Coverage for injury arising out of the rendering of (or failure to render) certain types of medical professional services, provided that the insured is not in the health care business. For example, this coverage can apply to a first aid facility operated by an employer. This coverage, once added to the Comprehensive General Liability policy by the broad form liability endorsement, is now included in the 1986 ISO Commercial General Liability form.

incident report
General. A report prepared and issued by law enforcement officials following an automobile accident or crime.

accident report

Risk Management. A report prepared by an insured or their agent when an action or occurrence is likely to lead to a claim being filed.

see: notice of loss

income
Financial Planning. Revenue received from all sources by an individual or organization.

income averaging
Employee Benefits. The calculation of an employee benefit plan participant's income over a period of time (e.g., the three most recent years), to calculate the participant's plan benefits.

income replacement
Employee Benefits. A disability insurance policy benefit which provides an ill or injured insured a monthly income payment.

see: disability income insurance

income statement
Risk Management. The section of a financial statement that provides information on an organization's revenues, expenses and income. This statement traces an organization's profits or losses, usually for a period of one year, and indicates the efficiency of its financial management during the reporting period.

syn: profit and loss statement; see: financial statement

incompetent
General. An individual who the courts determine is unable to manage his or her own affairs.

incontestable clause
Health/Life. A clause found in life and health insurance policies, stating that once a policy has been in effect for a specified period of time (two or more years), an insurer can no longer contest statements in the policy application in order to deny claims or void coverage.

incorporeal interest
Property. A right that does not physically exist, but that issues out of property. *Example:* The right obtained by a secured creditor in property that has been pledged to secure a loan. An incorporeal interest provides the basis for an insurable interest.

see: insurable interest, loss payee, mortgagee clause

171

© 1991 NILS Publishing Company

increased cost of construction endorsement

Property. An endorsement that can be added to a property policy to cover any increased cost of repairs or construction resulting from the enforcement of any building, zoning or land use laws following damage by an insured peril. Under the ISO Commercial Property Program, this coverage has been incorporated into the Ordinance or Law Coverage Endorsement *ISO Form CP 04 05).*

see: **ordinance or law coverage endorsement**

increased hazard

Property. A provision found in property insurance policies, releasing an insurer from its obligations under its policy if a loss is caused by a hazard increased by any means within the insured's control or knowledge. Such increased hazards must be materially greater than those contemplated when the insurer originally agreed to provide coverage. *Example:* A moving and storage company that begins using its warehouse to store paints, explosives, and resins.

compare: **aftercharge; see: change in occupancy or use, hazard, occupancy permit**

increased limits table

Casualty. An actuarially developed table of factors expressed in percentages, used by underwriters to increase rates for basic limits of liability to rates for higher limits.

see: **base rate, basic limits, exposure unit, rate making**

increasing annuity

Life. An annuity policy featuring payments which increase at a predetermined rate over the life of the contract. *Example:* An annuity which increases its monthly payment at an annual compound rate of three percent.

see: **annuity**

increased but not reported (IBNR)

Risk Management. A term used to refer to losses occurring over a specified period that have not been reported to the insurer. IBNR losses are often calculated as a percentage of claims paid and claims outstanding and are reported in an insurer's annual report. Reinsurers establish IBNR reserves on their business as a part of their rating plans under a facultative reinsurance treaty, lest an overly optimistic view of its treaty results lead to further under-rating on a book of business. *Example:* Product liability losses are seldom reported during a policy year. This "tail" of claims will upset any rating plan, unless an IBNR reserve is established and factored into the profit picture.

see: **expected losses, loss development factor**

incurred losses

Risk Management. Both paid and known reserved losses occurring within a specific period of time.

compare: **incurred but not reported, loss reserve, paid losses; see: loss conversion factor, loss development factor**

incurred loss ratio

Insurer Operations/Risk Management. The portion of an earned premium dollar that is spent on incurred losses.

see: **incurred losses**

indemnification

General. A principal of insurance which specifies that an insured should be restored to the same position as they were before they suffered a loss or damage. Insurance should not allow the insured to make a profit, but rather to make the insured whole for the loss or damage suffered.

compare: **collateral source rule, gambling; see: full coverage, pure risk**

indemnify

Casualty. Some casualty insurance policies provide that the insurer will indemnify or reimburse the insured for those sums that the insured becomes legally obligated to pay, as opposed to making direct payment on behalf of the insured. Under this form of coverage, the insured must first make payment and then is reimbursed by the insurer.

compare: **pay on behalf of; see: pure risk, reimbursement**

indemnitee

General. A party receiving compensation from an indemnitor.

compare: **indemnitor**

indemnitor

General. The party paying compensation to an indemnitee.

compare: **indemnitee**

Surety. A party entering into an agreement with a surety, that should a principal on whose behalf a surety bond has been issued default, the indemnitor will assume the principal's obligations.

indemnity

General. Compensation for an incurred injury, loss or damage.

Fr: **indemnité;** Gr: **Entschädigung;** Sp: **indemnización**

172

© 1991 NILS Publishing Company

indemnity agreement

General.
see: **hold harmless agreement**

Insurer Operations. An insurance contract; an agreement to restore a party to its original financial position following an incurred injury, loss or damage.
compare: **valued policy**; see: **indemnification, insurance contract, nonvalued policy**

indemnity bond

Surety. A bond compensating an obligee if a principal fails to perform to the standards mutually agreed upon by the obligee and principal.

indemnity deductible workers' compensation plan

Workers' Compensation. A form of deductible workers' compensation coverage under which the policy deductible applies only to workers' compensation indemnity benefits.
compare: **medical deductible workers' compensation plan**; see: **deductible workers' compensation plans**

independent adjuster

General. An organization or a professional who charges a fee for settling claims for insurers.
compare: **public adjuster**; see: **claims adjuster**

independent agency system

Agency/Insurer Operations. An insurance marketing system where independent agents sell and service insurance for one or more insurance companies. The agents are independent contractors who are compensated by commissions and/or fees and own the records and expirations of the policies issued through them.
syn: **American agency system**; compare: **captive agent, direct writer**; see: **agency company, broker, exclusive agency system, independent agent, Independent Insurance Agents of America, Professional Insurance Agents**

independent agent

Agency/Insurer Operations. An independent contractor (individual or entity) selling insurance on behalf of (or representing) usually more than one insurance company under the independent agency system. Independent agents operate their own business, own the records of the policies sold through them, and are compensated on the basis of commissions and/or fees.
see: **agent, independent agency system**

independent contractor

Workers' Compensation. An individual or entity that agrees to perform specific work for another party and is responsible for completing the work, but is not subject to the direction of the party who contracted for their services. An independent contractor is not an employee of the party who retained them. Independent contractors are not covered under an employer's workers' compensation policy.
see: **acts of independent contractors, employee, general contractor**

independent contractors insurance

Casualty.
see: **owners and contractors protective liability**

independent filing

Insurer Operations/Regulation. Application for an insurance rate and/or form submitted by an insurer to a state insurance department and not filed on its behalf by a rating organization.
see: **rate making**

Independent Insurance Agents of America (IIAA)

Organizations. Members: Sales agencies handling fire, casualty and surety insurance. *Objectives:* Promotes and represents the common business interests of independent insurance agents within the industry, and before government and the public consistent with the best interests of the insurance buying public. *Founded:* 1896. *Headquarters:* Alexandria, VA. Until 1976, known as the National Association of Insurance Agents.

independent insurance company

Insurer Operations. An insurance company that is not associated with or owned by another insurer or an insurance holding company. Such insurers are generally special insurers or serve a limited geographical area.
see: **fleet of companies, pup company**

indexed life insurance

Life. A life insurance policy, similar to a whole life policy, except that its face value varies according to a prescribed index of prices. The index can be applied automatically or the policyowner can retain control of the index application for an extra premium. As with most other whole life policies, a physical exam is not required.
see: **whole life insurance**

indirect damage

Property.
see: **consequential damage**

indirect loss

Property.
see: **consequential damage**

individual account plan

Employee Benefits.
see: **benefit plan, defined contribution plan**

individual contract

Life. A life insurance policy covering one person as opposed to a group of people. Such a contract can include specified members of the insured's family.

syn: individual life insurance; compare: group life insurance

Health. A health insurance policy covering one person, as opposed to a group of people. It can include specified members of the insured's family.

syn: individual health insurance; compare: group health insurance

individual fidelity bond

Surety.
see: fidelity bond

individual health insurance

Health.
see: individual contract

individual level cost method

Employee Benefits. A method used to project individual employee pension plan benefits upon reaching retirement age. Based on the projections, costs can be allocated on a level basis over a specified funding period.

individual life insurance

Life.
see: individual contract

individual retirement account (IRA)

Employee Benefits. A federally approved tax deferred savings plan for individuals. The individual selects a plan administrator (bank, savings and loan, approved investment advisor) that establishes the plan on behalf of the individual, who may make payments to it up to $2,000 annually. Funds withdrawn from the plan are penalized until the individual achieves the age of 59-1/2 years old. Limitations apply to the establishment of the IRA when an individual is covered by an approved employer pension plan.

see: registered retirement saving plan, rollover individual retirement account

individual risk premium modification rating plan (IRPM)

Casualty/Property. A large account rating plan where factors such as size of premium, spread of risk, superior construction, and quality of management are considered in determining the premium.

see: rate making

Health/Life. A group insurance rating plan under which individual participants' premiums are lowered, based on the size of the group and premiums generated. The premium reduction is based on lower acquisition and administrative expenses resulting when a large number of participants are combined into a single contract.

industrial accident

Loss Control/Workers' Compensation. An accident arising out of one's employment.

see: accident, arising out of and in the course of employment, occupational accident, workers' compensation insurance

industrial aid operators

Aviation. General aviation rating classification which applies to corporations which own aircraft and employ full-time professional pilots.

compare: business and pleasure, fixed based operators, flying clubs; see: general aviation

industrial development bond insurance

Financial Guarantee Insurance. Financial insurance coverage for public entities that guarantees the prompt payment of principal and interest on industrial development bonds should a bond issue default. The insurer's financial rating affords the bonds a high-grade investment rating – often higher than the issuing party's rating – all of which makes the bond more marketable and provides financing at a reduced cost.

industrial health insurance

Health. Low-valued health insurance policies where the premium is collected by the salesperson directly at the home of the insured on a weekly or monthly basis.

see: industrial life insurance

industrial insurance

Life.
see: industrial life insurance

industrial insureds

Risk Management. Companies who buy their own insurance through an insurance manager, risk manager or full-time insurance consultant. Such insureds have minimum annual nonlife and health premiums of $25,000 per year and employ at least 25 persons on a full-time basis.

industrial life insurance

Life. Low-valued life insurance policies with the premium collected by the salesperson directly at the home of the insured on a weekly or monthly basis.

syn: debit insurance, home service insurance, industrial insurance, weekly premium insurance; see: debit, debit system, industrial health insurance, register

industrial property policy program

Property. A property insurance program that preceded the special multi-peril (SMP) policy program. It was designed to insure manufacturers with two or more

© 1991 NILS Publishing Company

locations and could include coverage for buildings, stock, machinery and equipment. As an option, an insured could also cover improvements and betterments at leased locations.

see: special multi-peril program

Industrial Risk Insurers (IRI)

Insurer Operations/Property. A pool originally formed in 1890 by the major stock insurance companies, to compete with the Factory Mutual System on large industrial accounts which are protected by automatic sprinklers and which meet certain other minimum protection requirements. The operation's name was changed to Industrial Risk Insurers in 1975, by the merger of the Factory Insurance Association (FIA) and Oil Insurance Association (OIL).

compare: Factory Mutual System; see: highly protected risk

Inefficacy coverage

Casualty.
see: efficacy coverage

Inflammable

Loss Control.
see: flammable

Inflation

General. A generalized rise in the prices of goods and services which results from demand for such good and services outstripping their supply (demand-pull inflation), or from the increase in the costs of resources (raw materials, component parts, labor, etc.) needed to produce goods and services (cost-push inflation).

see: appreciation

Inflation factor

Insurer Operations/Risk Management. A loading added during the development of insurance rates, to provide for increased claims costs because of anticipated medical service, construction, or vehicle repair cost increases.

see: rate making

Inflation guard endorsement

Property. An endorsement to property policies that automatically increases the amount of insurance on buildings by a specific percentage (usually one or two percent per quarter). Specifically designed to offset the increased costs of replacing a building due to inflation.

syn: automatic increase in insurance endorsement

In-force business

Health/Life. The total dollar amount of paid-up policies, and those policies currently being paid on, which a life or health insurer carries on its books. A life insurance company's in-force business is measured by the total of all policy face values in its portfolio; a health insurer by its total premium volume.

syn: life insurance in force

Ingestion

Aviation. Under an aircraft policy, coverage for damage resulting from taking into its engine or power units foreign objects or substances (e.g., birds) which immediately disable the plane with enough severity to require immediate repair before further use.

Ingress/egress clause

Property.
see: civil authority clause

Inherent explosion

Loss Control/Property. An explosion arising out of inherent (existing in and natural to) characteristics of an insured risk. *Example:* A dust explosion in a flour mill. Inherent explosion risks may be covered or not, depending on the coverage forms used.

see: explosion

Inherent vice

Inland Marine/Property. A quality within an object, material or property that results in its tending to deteriorate or destroy itself. Inherent vice is excluded by most property insurance policies. *Example:* The spoilage of fruit being stored or shipped would be excluded from a property policy. The destruction of unspoiled fruit by a fire would, on the other hand, be covered.

compare: deterioration

Inheritance tax

Financial Planning/Life.
see: estate tax

In-hospital medical expense

Health. A provision in some hospital insurance policies that extends coverage to pay for hospital physicians' services, such as hospital calls. This coverage is provided only while the physician is in the hospital and often excludes the physician's expenses for surgical procedures.

Initial premium

Insurer Operations. The amount of premium charged at the time a policy is issued. This amount is subject to adjustment – up or down – during the policy term due to changes in coverage, additional underwriting information, etc. Or, in a participating policy, it is subject to a dividend.

compare: additional premium, return premium; see: deposit premium, estimated annual premium, net premium, participating policy, policy dividend, provisional premium

© 1991 NILS Publishing Company

initial reserve

Life. A life insurance reserve which is established at the inception of each life policy year.

compare: mean reserve, terminal reserve

Insurer Operations. The first reserve established ("put up") by a claims adjuster when a covered claim has been reported.

injunction bond

Surety. A bond written as the result of an injunction issued by a court requiring a party to refrain from performing a particular act. There are two bond forms: Plaintiff's bond to secure and a defendant's bond to dissolve.

see: defendant's bond to dissolve, judicial bond, plaintiff's bond to secure

injunctive relief

General. A court order that restricts or prohibits the performance of an act.

see: cease and desist, enjoin, judgment

injury

General. Impairment to a part of the body as the result of an accident or hazardous condition such as amputation, laceration, bruise, scratch, poisoning, asphyxiation, or suffocation. Also, sometimes used to describe, in legal terms, a nonphysical event resulting in loss of income or reputation, such as a slanderous statement resulting in an injury to one's standing in the community.

see: accident, bodily injury, intentional injury, personal injury; Fr: blessure, lésion; Gr: Verletzung; Sp: lesión

injury independent of all other means

Health. A health insurance policy provision covering an injury apart from any previous injury which would be excluded.

see: preexisting condition

in kind

Property. A term used in many property insurance policies, giving an insurer the option to replace damaged or stolen articles with new or equivalent ("in kind") replacements, instead of paying cash to the insured.

see: indemnification

inland marine

Inland Marine. Transit of goods over land and generally, the insurance of such goods. The term now includes any goods in transit – anywhere – except on the ocean. The essential condition is that the insured property be movable or is included in the nationwide definition of marine insurance. Bridges and tunnels are also considered proper subjects for inland marine insurance, because they act as instruments of transportation.

see: domestic goods in transit, Nationwide Marine Insurance Definition; Fr: transport; Gr: Binnentransport; Sp: seguro terrestre, terrestre

inland marine insurance

Inland Marine. Coverage for property which involves an element of transportation. Either the property is actually in transit; held by a bailee; at a fixed location which is an important instrument of transportation, or is a movable type of goods which is often at different locations.

see: domestic goods in transit, inland marine, marine insurance

Inland Marine Underwriters Association (IMUA)

Organizations. Members: Insurers transacting inland marine insurance within the United States. *Objectives:* Promoting interests of the inland marine industry. *Founded:* 1930. *Headquarters:* New York, NY.

inland waybill

Inland Marine.

see: waybill

in motion

Aviation. A term used in aviation hull insurance policies, stating that an aircraft is moving when it is under it own power or momentum generated therefrom, including while in flight. The aircraft is considered "not in motion" at any other time.

see: flight coverage, ground coverage

innkeepers legal liability

Casualty. Legal liability imposed on operators of inns, hotels and motels for safekeeping guests' property. Coverage for this exposure is available through an innkeeper's legal liability policy which usually provides a limit equal to the limit of liability imposed by the state's innkeeper's statute.

see: liability for guests' property – premises coverage form, liability for guests property – safe deposit coverage form

in-patient

Health. The status denoting a patient that is admitted to a hospital who receives lodging and food as well as treatment. Health insurance policies have always covered most costs incurred during in-patient hospital stays, but it hasn't been until recently that most policies covered out-patient services, as well.

compare: out-patient

in rem

Ocean Marine. The admiralty court-granted authority to take or keep in custody a ship or other property

© 1991 NILS Publishing Company

until a claim has been decided or acceptable security has been substituted.

"in rem" endorsement

Ocean Marine. An endorsement on a marine policy, making the vessel owner an additional insured under the policy.

inrunning nip point

Loss Control. A dangerous rotating machine part or assembly that can seize and wind loose clothing, belts, hair, body parts, etc. It exists when two or more shafts or rolls rotate parallel to one another in opposite directions.

syn: nip point; see: barrier guard, machine tool, point of operation

Insects, birds, rodents or other animals exclusion

Property. A special cause of loss exclusion contained in "all-risks" or special form property policies, which excludes damage or destruction of property caused by insects, birds, rodents or other animals.

inside directors

Casualty. Directors of a publicly held corporation who hold executive positions with management. The number of inside and outside directors in a corporation is of concern to a directors & officers liability underwriter.

compare: outside directors; see: directors & officers liability insurance

inside limits

Health. Limits for specific benefits of a health insurance policy which are less than the maximum policy benefits or which modify the policy benefits to some extent. *Example:* Hospital room benefits may be limited to a semi-private room for 90 days.

syn: sublimits

insolvency

General. An organization's inability to pay maturing debt obligations. Insolvency frequently results in bankruptcy.

compare: bankruptcy; see: guaranty funds, liquidation, negative cash flow, rehabilitation

insolvency clause

Reinsurance. A provision contained in a reinsurance contract which holds the reinsurer liable for losses assumed under a treaty when the primary company has become insolvent.

compare: cut-through clause

insolvency funds

Insurer Operations.
see: guaranty funds

inspection

Loss Control. The in-person confirmation of an individual risk to determine whether it meets acceptable or established standards and to gather pertinent underwriting information. Inspections may be performed by an agent for the insurer, or by a loss control specialist employed by the insurer. The inspection may result in recommendations which will improve the risk.

Workers' Compensation. A workers' compensation insurer's verification of a payroll record. Workers' compensation premiums are based on the business's gross payroll, making this procedure the basis for the premium charged. The product of this investigation is called an inspection report.

see: audit

Casualty/Property. In property and casualty insurance, the insurance company retains the right, but not the obligation, to make inspections and surveys that relate to the insurability of the risk and the premiums charged; at any time such inspections seek to uncover inherent structural defects and other hidden hazards, as well as providing the insurer the opportunity to develop and recommend a loss prevention program for the insured.

see: audit

Life. The verification of statements by a life insurance applicant, along with a summarization of the applicant's financial, moral, physical condition and any other relevant information, often obtained by an independent source, but also by insurance investigators or agency personnel. The product of this investigation is called an inspection report.

inspection bureau

Organizations.
see: rating bureau

inspection report

Life/Workers' Compensation.
see: inspection

installation floater

Inland Marine. Inland marine policy written to cover machinery and equipment of all kinds during transit, installation, and testing at the purchaser's premises.

installment refund annuity

Life.
see: annuity certain

Institute of Home Office Underwriters (IHOU)

Organizations. Members: Home office life insurance underwriters. *Objectives:* Provides educational programs, such as examinations leading to the Fellowship in Academy of Life Underwriting. *Founded:* 1937. *Headquarters:* Atlanta, GA.

Institute of Life Insurance

Organizations. Formerly an organization supported by the life insurance business, responsible for building the image of life insurance through a variety of programs. It is now a division of the American Council of Life Insurance.

see: **American Council of Life Insurance**

institutional investors

Insurer Operations. Large investors, such as mutual funds, pension funds, insurance companies, and others who invest the money they hold in trust. Recently, this group of investors has accounted for an increasing portion of all public securities being traded and are major holders of insurance company stocks.

institutional property

Property.

see: **public and institutional property**

instrumentalities of transportation and communication

Inland Marine. Part of the nationwide marine definition, which describes "means of communication" as bridges, tunnels, and other similar instrumentalities, including auxiliary facilities and equipment attendant thereto. Other such properties included are piers, wharves, docks, slips, dry docks and marine railways; pipelines; power transmission and telephone and telegraph lines; radio and television communication equipment; and outdoor cranes, loading bridges and similar equipment.

see: **Nationwide Marine Insurance Definition**

insurability

General. The ability of an individual or entity to be insured.

see: **insurable risk**

insurable interest

Life. The interest for financial loss which must be proven when a life insurance policy is purchased. Once a life insurance policy has been issued, the insurer must pay the policy benefit, whether or not an insurable interest exists.

Insurer Operations. Any interest an insured may have in property that is the subject of insurance (e.g., a home or warehouse), so that damage or destruction of that property would cause the insured financial loss. The possibility that financial loss to a property may occur that can be insured against and from which benefits may be recovered from a property or casualty insurance policy. Generally, an insurable interest must be demonstrated when a policy is issued and (with the exception of life insurance) it must always exist at the time of a loss. An insurable interest in property is not created solely by the ownership of a property. *Examples:* Ownership of property; custody or control and vendors and mortgagees for the remaining balance due on property sold to others.

see: **additional interest, as interest may appear, full interest admitted, incorporeal interest, loss payee**

insurable risk

Insurer Operations. The following seven criteria are needed for a risk to be insurable: 1) An insured loss must have a definite time and place; 2) The insured event must be accidental; 3) The loss must cause an economic hardship on the insured; 4) The insured risks must belong to a sufficiently large enough group of homogeneous exposure units to make losses predictable; 5) The risk must not be subject to a catastrophic loss where a large number of exposure units can be damaged or destroyed in a single event; 6) The coverage must be provided at a reasonable cost; 7) The chance of loss must be calculable.

compare: **noninsurable risk**; see: **catastrophe loss, fortuitous event, homogeneous exposure units, insurability, spread of risk**

insurance

Insurer Operations. A contract where one party (insurer) agrees to indemnify or guarantee another party (insured) against loss by a specified future contingency or peril in return for the present payment of premium.

syn: **assurance**; see: **aleatory contract, avoidance, bottomry, diversification, fiduciary, gambling, retention, Thaisoi, tontine, transfer of risk**

Insurance Accounting and Systems Association (IASA)

Organizations. Members: Insurers, independent public accountants, actuarial consultants, management consultants, statisticians, statistical organization and other groups. *Objectives:* Promotes the research and development of insurance theory, practice and procedures, as applied to insurance accounting and statistics. *Founded:* 1928. *Headquarters:* Durham, NC.

insurance agency

Agency.

see: **agency**

insurance agent

Agency/Insurer Operations. The representative of an insurance company responsible for soliciting (selling) insurance products and providing services to policyholders. As such, the agent acts in place of the insurance company. Over the years the courts have issued decisions, laws have been enacted and regulators have promulgated regulations placing legal responsibility on the agent in areas such as acceptance

© 1991 NILS Publishing Company

and binding of risks, notice, and other situations where the agent acts as the insurance company.

see: agency, agent, captive agent, independent agent

Insurance agents liability
Casualty.
see: agents errors & omissions insurance

Insurance appraisal
Property.
see: appraisal

Insurance broker
Agency/Insurer Operations.
see: broker

Insurance Bureau of Canada (IBC)
Organizations. Members: Insurance companies in Canada. *Objectives:* Provides a forum for discussion on all matters in the field of general insurance by its member insurance companies. Collects, analyzes and disseminates actuarial and statistical information. Studies legislation and engages in research and public relations activities. *Founded:* 1979. *Headquarters:* Toronto, Ontario

Insurance carrier
General.
see: insurance company

Insurance commissioner
Regulation. The principal or senior executive of a state's department of insurance or other insurance regulatory agency.

syn: commissioner, director of insurance, superintendent of insurance; see: insurance department, insurance examiner

Insurance company
Insurer Operations. An organization which has been chartered by a governmental entity to transact the business of insurance.

syn: assurance company, assurer, carrier, insurance carrier, insurer; see: alien insurer, domestication agreement, domestic insurer, domiciled company, domiciliary state, enemy alien, fleet of companies, foreign insurer, fraternal benefit society, insurance, legal expense insurers, medical liability indemnity associations, mutual insurance company, old line company, parent company, primary insurance company, quasi-insurance institutions, reciprocal insurance exchange, stock insurance company; Fr: compagnie d'assurances; Gr: Versicherungsgesellschaft; Sp: compañía de seguros

Insurance Company Education Directors Society (ICEDS)
Organizations. The former name for the Society of Insurance Trainers and Educators.

see: Society of Insurance Trainers and Educators

Insurance Conference Planners (ICP)
Organizations. Members: Insurance personnel involved in planning insurance conventions. *Objectives:* Sharing concepts and ideas on planning meetings to promote professionalism in the insurance industry. *Founded:* 1958. *Headquarters:* St Paul, MN.

Insurance Conference Planners Association (ICPA)
Organizations. Members: Canadian insurance personnel involved in planning insurance conventions. *Objectives:* Sharing concepts and ideas on planning meetings to promote professionalism in the insurance industry. *Founded:* 1958. *Headquarters:* North Vancouver, British Columbia, Canada.

Insurance consultation services
Risk Management. Survey inspection or advisory services performed by insurers, agents or service contractors to reduce the likelihood of injury or loss.

see: inspection, loss prevention services

Insurance contract
Insurer Operations. A unilateral aleatory contract between an insured and an insurer which agrees to indemnify the insured for loss caused by specified events. The consideration for an insurance contract is the premium paid.

syn: insurance policy; see: aleatory contract, application, attestation clause, contract, contract of adhesion, declarations, easy read, endorsement, entire contract provision, entire contract statute, evidence and duties provision, face, face amount, filing requirements, fine print, Flesch Test, form, indemnity agreement, insuring agreement, jacket, manuscript policy, modification of contract, noncancellable policy, nonvalued policy, plain language laws, policy conditions, utmost good faith

Insurance Crime Prevention Bureau
Organizations. Members: Canadian insurance companies and underwriters. *Objectives:* Provides assistance to police and fire authorities in the detection, investigation and prosecution of insurance-related crimes. *Founded:* 1923. *Headquarters:* Toronto, Ontario, Canada.

see: Fire and Theft Index Bureau, Insurance Services Office, interinsurer claim service organization, Medical Information Bureau, National Automobile Theft Bureau, Property Insurance Loss Register

179

© 1991 NILS Publishing Company

Insurance Crime Prevention Institute (ICPI)

Organizations. *Members:* Insurance companies. *Objective:* Investigates and seeks prosecution of fraud involving property and casualty insurance claims. *Founded:* 1970. *Headquarters:* Westport, CT.

see: interinsurer claim service organization

Insurance department

Regulation. A state agency that is responsible for administering the laws regulating insurance, including the licensing of insurance companies, agents, and brokers.

see: insurance commissioner, insurance examiner

Insurance Educational Association (IEA)

Organizations. *Members:* Insurance organizations. *Objectives:* Sponsors educational programs for insurance, risk management and financial services. *Founded:* 1876. *Headquarters:* San Francisco, CA.

Insurance examiner

Regulation. The insurance department representative assigned to audit the books or the market conduct of an insurance company.

see: examination, insurance commissioner, insurance department

Insurance exchange

Insurer Operations. Insurance centers or organizations patterned after Lloyd's of London, formed during the 1980s in New York (NYC), Florida (Miami), and Illinois (Chicago). Exchanges were originally formed to write large or unique risks, generally on a surplus lines basis, or to write reinsurance business. Both the New York and Florida exchanges have suspended operations.

see: Illinois Insurance Exchange; Insurance Exchange of the Americas, Inc.; New York Insurance Exchange

Insurance Exchange of the Americas, Inc.

Organizations. An insurance exchange created as a not-for-profit corporation in Miami, Florida on October 1, 1979, and which began trading on April 4, 1983. In February 1987, the exchange's management suspended all underwriting activity, and on March 18, 1988, the Florida Department of Insurance was appointed receiver of the exchange.

syn: Florida Insurance Exchange; see: insurance exchange

Insurance Hall of Fame

Organizations. *Members:* Elected board of directors from the international insurance industry. *Objectives:* To recognize outstanding persons for their vision, integrity, innovation, enterprise and leadership in the insurance field. *Founded:* 1957. *Headquarters:* Columbus, OH.

see: International Insurance Society

Insurance Industry Meetings Association (IIMA)

Organizations. *Members:* State and regional insurance company communication representatives. *Objectives:* Conducts seminars on insurance business techniques, sales practices and claims processing. *Founded:* 1980. *Headquarters:* St. Louis, MO.

Insurance in force

Life.

see: in-force business

Insurance Information Institute (III)

Organizations. *Members:* Property and casualty insurance companies. *Objectives:* Promotes interests of insurance companies by providing information and educational services. *Founded:* 1959. *Headquarters:* New York, NY.

Insurance Institute for Highway Safety (IIHS)

Organizations. *Members:* Casualty insurance companies and trade associations. *Objectives:* Conducts research on highway accidents to reduce deaths, injuries and property damage. *Founded:* 1959. *Headquarters:* Washington, D.C.

Insurance Institute of America (IIA)

Organizations. The educational division for the American Institute for Property and Liability Underwriters.

see: American Institute for Property and Liability Underwriters, Associate in Risk Management

Insurance Institute of Canada (IIC)

Organizations. *Members:* Canadian insurance companies. *Objectives:* Maintains a uniform insurance educational program throughout Canada. This organization administers the examinations for the AIIC and FIIC designations in Canada. *Founded:* 1952. *Headquarters:* Toronto, Ontario, Canada.

Insurance Loss Control Association (ILCA)

Organizations. *Members:* Loss prevention specialists for fire and casualty insurers. *Objectives:* Providing educational programs for loss prevention techniques. *Founded:* 1932. *Headquarters:* Indianapolis. IN.

Insurance management

Risk Management. In contrast to risk management, insurance management is security-oriented management that deals with loss exposures almost exclusively through the use of insurance.

compare: risk management

© 1991 NILS Publishing Company

Insurance Marketing Communications Association (IMCA)

Organizations. Members: Advertising, marketing, public relations and sales promotion executives of insurance companies. *Objectives:* Sponsors competition among members and presents annual awards for advertising excellence. *Founded:* 1923. *Headquarters:* Wellesley, MA. Known as the Insurance Advertising Conference until 1984.

Insurance policy

Insurer Operations.

see: insurance contract

Insurance Premium Finance Association (IPFA)

Organizations. Members: Companies licensed to finance premiums for automobile and other liability coverage on an installment basis. *Objectives:* Promotes the exchange of information between members. *Founded:* 1961. *Headquarters:* Buffalo, NY.

Insurance Regulatory Examiners Society (IRES)

Organizations. Members: Insurance department personnel. *Objectives:* Awards the Accredited Insurance Examiner (AIE) and Certified Insurance Examiner (CIE) designations. Sponsors educational seminars for regulators. *Founded:* 1987. *Headquarters:* Overland Park, KS.

Insurance Regulatory Information System (IRIS)

Regulation. A system of ratios designed to monitor an insurance company's financial condition developed by the National Association of Insurance Commissioners (NAIC). The system is designed to provide regulators with a warning that an insurer is having financial difficulties by applying a series of financial tests which would determine, for example, a large increase or decrease in net written premiums or the ratio of net written premiums to adjusted policyholders' surplus. Different tests apply to property and casualty insurance companies and life and health insurers.

Insurance representative

Agency/Insurer Operations. Producers and field representatives serving as agents, brokers, consultants, solicitors or adjusters. Also, sometimes used to refer to third-party administrators.

see: agent, broker, claims adjuster, third-party administrator

Insurance Services Office (ISO)

Organizations. Members: Rating bureaus, actuarial associations and other insurance research groups. *Objectives:* Provides statistical and actuarial information, policy forms and other related services to insurers. Functions as an insurance advisory organization and statistical agent. Publishes rate manuals, plans, policy forms and endorsements and other materials. *Founded:* 1971. *Headquarters:* New York, NY.

see: commercial lines manual, intercompany data

Insurance Society of New York (ISNY)

Organizations. Members: Insurance companies and brokers. *Objectives:* Serves as the parent organization of the College of Insurance. *Founded:* 1901. *Headquarters:* New York, New York.

see: College of Insurance

Insurance Testing Institute (ITI)

Organizations. Members: Insurance companies. *Objectives:* Provide testing services for insurance agents and brokers. *Founded:* 1984. *Headquarters:* Malvern, PA.

Insurance to value

Property. Insurance coverage written at or near the value of the insured property. Or, the ratio that the amount of the insurance purchased bears to the value of the insured property.

see: agreed amount, coinsurance

Insurance Value Added Network Services (IVANS)

Organizations. Members: Property and casualty, life and reinsurance insurance companies. *Objectives:* Provides low cost, efficient electronic communications services between independent agencies and the insurance companies which they represent. IVANS provides a high speed, easy-to-use interface. *Founded:* 1983. *Headquarters:* Greenwich, CT.

Insured

Insurer Operations. The term preferred over other terms such as "policyholder" or "policyowner," to describe the party protected under an insurance contract, to whom the insurer reimburses losses, pays benefits or provides services.

syn: assured; see: additional insured, derivative insured, first named insured, insurable interest, named insured; Fr: assuré; Gr: Versicherungsnehmer; Sp: asegurado

Insured loss ratio

Reinsurance. The ratio that a reinsurer's percentage of losses incurred bears to premiums earned.

see: loss ratio

Insured peril

Property. The danger to a property against which it is insured. A cause of loss. *Example:* The perils of fire, explosion, wind and vandalism are insured against under a property insurance policy.

compare: exposure, hazard, peril, risk

insured variable annuity plan

Life. A variable annuity where the plan's units are tied to the investment results of a specific investment account managed by an insurance company.

see: variable annuity

insurer

Insurer Operations.

see: insurance company

Insurers' Advisory Organization of Canada (IAO)

Organizations. Members: Canadian property and casualty insurance companies. *Objectives:* Provides rating, statistical, actuarial, policy form information and loss control engineering services on an advisory basis. *Founded:* 1883. *Headquarters:* Toronto, Ontario.

insuring agreement

Insurer Operations. The section of an insurance contract outlining the parties to the contract; terms of the policy; premiums and due dates; limits of coverage; property or persons (and its location) to be insured; the perils insured against and the period of the contract.

syn: insuring clause; see: exclusion, face, insurance contract, policy conditions, policy declarations

insuring clause

Insurer Operations.

see: insuring agreement

intangible personal property

Casualty. Those rights or possessions which belong to an insured, but which are of an abstract (non-physical) nature. An abstract right insured against would best be illustrated by libel; whereas an intangible property would be a patent, a copyright, a trademark or the goodwill of the community or public.

see: personal property

Integration with Social Security

Employee Benefits. Employee pension plans are usually coordinated with Social Security benefits in compliance with provisions developed by the IRS. The offset method of integration is restricted to defined benefit plans. It allows the employer to subtract a set percentage of the monthly retirement benefit payable to an employee. The integration method can be used with both a defined benefit plan or a defined contribution plan, which allows an employer to establish a basic level of compensation which must be funded. Actual benefits can be greater or less than this level, depending on the Social Security benefit level during the term of retirement.

see: Social Security

intentional injury

Health. A self-inflicted or personally-caused injury. Such injuries are generally not covered by insurance policies.

syn: willful injury; see: injury

intentional loss

Insurer Operations. Willful destruction of property, with intent to defraud an insurer, excluding arson fraud.

see: arson fraud

intentional tort

General. The deliberate commission or omission of an act (e.g., assault, battery, invasion of privacy, libel and slander). With the exception of libel and slander, intentional torts are generally not insurable.

see: public policy, tort

interchange insurance

Automobile. Insurance coverage for truckers frequently trading trailers with other truckers under an agreement which makes truckers responsible for damage to the trailers in their care, custody or control. The insurance covers an insured's legal liability for damage to trailers not their own.

syn: trailer interchange insurance; see: trailer interchange agreement

intercompany arbitration

Insurer Operations. An arbitration between two or more insurers as the result of a dispute over the responsibilities of each in the settlement of a specific loss. Each company is bound by the arbitration decision.

see: arbitration

intercompany data

Insurer Operations. Internal insurance company statistics shared by individual insurers through a bureau or rating organization.

see: Fire and Theft Index Bureau, Insurance Crime Prevention Institute, Insurance Services Office, interinsurer claim service organization, Medical Information Bureau, National Automobile Theft Bureau, Property Insurance Loss Register

intercompany transaction

Risk Management. Any financial transaction among affiliated companies, including contributions to the reserve fund of a subsidiary by its parents.

see: affiliated companies

interest

Financial Planning. The charge or fee paid by a borrower to a lender for a loan of money, usually a

© 1991 NILS Publishing Company

percentage of the amount loaned or the unpaid balance.

see: carrying charge, compound interest, compounding, continuous compounding, delinquency charge, net interest earned, prime rate, service charges, simple interest

interest adjusted cost

Financial Planning/Life. A method of comparing the cost of life insurance to other investments, using the time value of money. Several different interest adjusted cost comparison methods are used, including the Linton Yield Method.

see: Linton Yield Method, time value of money

interest assumption

Employee Benefits. The expected rate of return on an employee benefit plan's assets.
Life. A minimum rate of return guaranteed on a life insurance policy which is used in calculating the policy's benefits.

interest free loan

Life. A policy loan option available under some universal life insurance policies for which no interest is charged.

see: universal life insurance

interest option

Life. An option which a life insurance beneficiary may select as a settlement, where the policy proceeds are left on deposit with the insurer to accrue interest which is paid to the beneficiary annually. Subject to restrictions established by the policyowner, the beneficiary may withdraw all or part of the principal.

compare: fixed amount option, fixed period option, life income option, life income with period certain option; see: optional life insurance settlement modes

interest-sensitive life insurance

Life. Life insurance policies that credit the policyholder with interest, based upon the investment return earned by the insurance company on all of the policies in a particular group.

interinsurance exchange

Insurer Operations.
see: reciprocal insurance exchange

interinsurer claim service organization

Insurer Operations. An organization established by insurers to compile and share information on fraudulent claims and disseminate claims information to the public.

see: Fire and Theft Index Bureau, Insurance Crime Prevention Institute, Insurance Services Office, Medical Information Bureau, National Automobile Theft Bureau, Property Insurance Loss Register

interior robbery policy

Crime. A crime insurance policy which insures only against robberies within an insured's premises. Covered losses include loss of money, securities, personal property, and damage or destruction of real or personal property due to a robbery or attempted robbery.

interline endorsement

Insurer Operations. A policy endorsement applying to more than one coverage part of a multiple line package policy.

see: endorsement

interlock

Loss Control. A device which interacts with another device or mechanism to govern succeeding operations. *Example:* Interlocked guards prevent machines from operating unless the guard has been moved to its proper place.

see: interlocked barrier guards

interlocked barrier guard

Loss Control. A barrier guard on machinery, such as a power press or drill, that is framed and interlocked with the power switch so that the operating cycle cannot be started unless the guard is in its proper position.

see: barrier guard, interlock

intermediary

Reinsurance. An individual or firm that negotiates reinsurance contracts with reinsurers on behalf of an insurance company.

syn: reinsurance broker; see: direct writer

intermediate

Automobile. A commercial automobile rating classification for vehicles that customarily operate within a radius of between 51 and 200 miles of the vehicle's garage location.

compare: local, long haul, radius of operation

intermediate disability

Loss Control/Workers' Compensation.
see: permanent partial disability, temporary partial disability

internal financing

Risk Management. Funds that are made available for capital budgeting and working capital expansion through the normal operations of the firm; internal financing is approximately equal to retained earnings plus depreciation.

see: capital budgeting, working capital

© 1991 NILS Publishing Company

Internal rate of return (IRR)

Risk Management. The rate of return on an asset investment. The internal rate of return is calculated by finding the discount rate that is equal to the present value of future cash flows to the cost of the investment.

see: asset, discounted cash flow techniques, return on investment

Internal Revenue Code

Regulation. The federal tax statutes, many of which have a material effect on insurance companies, insurance policies, self-insurance, captive insurance and employee benefit plans.

Internal Revenue Code: Section 79

Life/Regulation. A section of the Internal Revenue Code which extends to employees tax benefits on the value of group whole life insurance policies provided by the employer. The benefit is provided by dividing the term and cash value elements of each policy, thereby taking advantage of the tax exemption on a specified amount of group term insurance plans and the special tax rate on the premium for insurance in excess of that amount.

Internal Revenue Code: Section 125

Regulation.
see: flexible benefit plan

Internal Revenue Code: Section 303

Regulation. A federal tax code section concerned with stock redemption plans which specifies the procedure by which a corporation cancels or redeems its stock with funds from earnings or profits.

Internal Revenue Code: Section 401(k)

Employee Benefits/Regulation. A section of the Internal Revenue Code which provides the rules and regulations to establish an employer-sponsored retirement savings plan, allowing employees to invest pretax dollars which an employer can match on a proportional basis.

Internal Revenue Code: Section 403(g)

Employee Benefits/Regulation. A section of the Internal Revenue Code which extends tax deferral to employees of tax-exempt organizations, such as public school districts, to pay for retirement annuity policies.

Internal Revenue Code: Section 461(h)

Regulation. Federal tax statute section which affects the way self-insureds treat their long-term structured obligations. Prior to the enactment of this section, some self-insureds accrued the total of the future payouts and claimed that amount as a deduction in the tax year in which the settlement was concluded. This statute allows deductions only when economic performance occurs (i.e., each time a payment is made to the plaintiff).

Internal Revenue Code: Section 501(c)

Regulation/Risk Management. A federal tax code section specifying which organizations are considered nonprofit corporations, funds, and foundations, and therefore exempt from federal income tax.

Internal Revenue Service bonds

Surety.
see: federal bond

International Association for Insurance Law – United States Chapter

Organizations. Members: Insurance company executives, professors, attorneys, state insurance regulators and others interested in international and comparative aspects of insurance law. *Objectives:* Promote international collaboration in insurance law. *Founded:* 1963. *Headquarters:* Chicago, IL.

International Association of Defense Counsel (IADC)

Organizations. Members: Attorneys practicing defense trial law. *Objectives:* Sponsors research projects and annual legal writing competitions. Awards the Yancey Memorial Award for best article in its journal. Sponsors the Defense Counsel Trial Academy. *Founded:* 1920. *Headquarters:* Chicago, IL.

International Association of Health Underwriters

Organizations. The former name of the National Association of Health Underwriters.

see: National Association of Health Underwriters

International Claim Association (ICA)

Organizations. Members: Claims executives and administrators of life, health and accident insurance companies. *Objectives:* Education of and exchange of information between professionals in the claim settlement business. *Founded:* 1909. *Headquarters:* Rock Island, IL.

international development bank bonds

International. Bonds, notes, or other obligations issued by international development banks, such as the International Bank for Reconstruction and Development and the Asian Development Bank. Such bonds typically cover loans and grants to third-world countries, encourage those governments to raise their standards of living, increase import and export levels, and foster increased activity in world commerce.

International Foundation of Employee Benefit Plans (IFEBP)

Organizations. Members: Public and privately sponsored employee benefit plans, administrators, labor

184

© 1991 NILS Publishing Company

organizations, employer associations, benefit consultants, investment counselors and insurance consultants. *Objectives:* Maintains liaison with medical and hospital associations. Lobbies state and federal governments. Cosponsors the Certified Employee Benefit Specialist program. *Founded:* 1954. *Headquarters:* Brookfield, WI. Until 1973, known as the National Foundation of Health, Welfare and Pension Plans.

see: **Certified Employee Benefit Specialist**

International Insurance Advisory Council (IIAC)

Organizations. Former name of the International Insurance Council.

see: **International Insurance Council**

International Insurance Council (IIC)

Organizations. Members: Companies and U.S.-licensed trade associations that are risk-bearing companies or insurers. *Objectives:* Promotes the business of international insurance. Acts as a trade policy advocate representing U.S. life or nonlife insurers and reinsurers. *Founded:* 1946. *Headquarters:* Washington, D.C. Until 1988, known as the International Insurance Advisory Council.

International Insurance Seminars, Inc. (IIS)

Organizations. The name of the International Insurance Society prior to 1987.

see: **International Insurance Society**

International Insurance Society (IIS)

Organizations. Members: Professors of insurance of major universities and others in the insurance field. *Objectives:* Offers annual seminars to facilitate international economic development. *Founded:* 1959. *Headquarters:* University, AL.

International market categories

International. A categorization of insurance markets, primarily located in developing countries. Categories are: *Monopolistic markets:* countries with a small number of insurers or a single state-controlled insurer. *Pluralistic markets:* monopolistic state intervention in a country, usually taking place in reinsurance. *Other markets:* state-controlled insurers and reinsurers that insure portions of domestic markets.

International Society of Certified Employee Benefit Specialists (ISCEBS)

Organizations. Members: Graduates of the Certified Employee Benefit Specialist program. *Objectives:* Promotes continuing education and professional development in the employee benefit field. *Founded:* 1981. *Headquarters:* Brookfield, WI.

see: **Certified Employee Benefit Specialist**

Interpleader

Insurer Operations.

see: **bill of interpleader**

Interstate carrier

Automobile. A trucking company that operates across state lines and is regulated by the Interstate Commerce Commission.

compare: **intrastate carrier**; see: **Interstate Commerce Commission**

Interstate Commerce Commission (ICC)

Regulation. A federal agency that regulates commerce between states – which includes the activities of trucking firms that transport goods across state lines. Regulation of interstate trucking includes establishing standards of liability on truckers for cargo damage, requiring that they demonstrate an ability to meet these standards through evidence of insurance or the posting of letters of credit or bonds.

see: **interstate carrier**

Interstate Commerce Commission endorsement

Inland Marine. A provision endorsed to a motor truck cargo or traveler's legal liability policy which guarantees that all losses to cargo will be paid by the insurer regardless of the perils insured by the policy. For losses not covered by the policy, but which are paid by the insurer pursuant to this endorsement, the common carrier must reimburse the insurer.

Inter-vivos trust

Financial Planning. A general type of trust that is established by individuals while they are living, to organize the distribution of their assets after their death. *Examples:* Living trust, personal trust, and testamentary trust.

see: **living trust, personal trust, testamentary trust, trust**

Intestate

Financial Planning. A legal term used to describe an individual who has died without leaving a legal will.

Intoxicating liquor bond

Surety.

see: **alcohol bond**

Intra-family immunity

General. A legal doctrine which states that a family member is "immune" to a suit by another member of the same household. The validity of this doctrine has been reduced by the courts over time.

see: **family exclusion**

© 1991 NILS Publishing Company

intrastate carrier
Automobile. A trucking firm that operates within a single state.
compare: interstate carrier

intra vires
General. Meaning to act within the powers or stated purposes of a corporation.
compare: ultra vires

in-trust policy
Inland Marine. An inland marine policy that insures specific items of property without regard to the insured item's location or in whose care, custody or control the insured items rest. In effect, the insurance follows the property.
syn: consignment insurance, on-consignment policy

invalidity
Health. A sickness or illness.

inverse condemnation
General. The taking of or reduction in the value of land by a governmental agency through the power of eminent domain without just compensation. *Example:* The acquisition of land for a new airport which results in the use and value of adjacent property being materially diminished.

investment annuity
Life. An annuity plan developed in conjunction with a bank or trust company using an irrevocable agreement with the institution to fund monthly retirement annuity income payments.
see: annuity

investment club
Financial Planning. An organization in which the members pool their funds to build up an investment portfolio larger than individual members could afford by themselves.

investment company
Financial Planning.
see: mutual fund

investment department
Insurer Operations. The employees and operations of an insurance company that handle the investments of company funds, including premium and claim reserves.

investment income
Insurer Operations. An insurance company's earnings from its investment portfolio, including interest, stock dividends and capital gains and rent from real estate and equipment.
see: cash flow underwriting, investment year method of allocating investment income, net interest earned

investment reserve
Insurer Operations. An insurance company balance sheet item that establishes a reserve to compensate for the reduced value of stocks, bonds or real estate held by the company in its investment portfolio. Most insurers do not establish this form of reserve.
syn: investment valuation reserves; see: mandatory securities valuation reserve, securities valuation

investment return insurance
Financial Guarantee Insurance. Insurance against the risk of loss for the value of the redeemable securities of an insured investor.

investment risk
Financial Planning.
see: financial risk

investment tax credit
General. A specified percentage of the dollar amount of new investments in each of certain categories of assets that business firms can deduct as a credit against their income taxes.

investment valuation reserve
Insurer Operations. A reserve established by an insurer to protect against sudden, large fluctuations in the value of certain types of assets (stocks, bonds) so that the policyholders' surplus remains within certain parameters.
syn: investment reserve; see: mandatory securities valuation reserve, securities valuation

investment year method of allocating investment income
Insurer Operations. A method by which a life insurance company matches or allocates investment income to each of its policies, based on the date the premium was received for the policy.

invitation to bid
Surety.
see: advertisement to bid

invitee
General. A legal term for an individual that has been requested or induced to come onto the premises of an inviter. Customers of a business who go onto the business' premises to purchase merchandise are considered invitees. An inviter has an obligation to maintain his or her property in a safe condition for an invitee.
compare: licensee, trespasser; see: attractive nuisance doctrine, degree of care

© 1991 NILS Publishing Company

invoice

Inland Marine/Ocean Marine.
see: commercial invoice

iron safe clause

Inland Marine. A provision in some inland marine policies that requires the insured to keep all valuable papers and records in a safe when not in use. This is an archaic term, since safes are not necessarily made of iron today.

irrevocable beneficiary

Life. A life insurance policy provision by which the beneficiary cannot be changed unless the insured obtains the beneficiary's approval.

syn: absolute beneficiary; compare: revocable beneficiary; see: beneficiary, trust

irrevocable trust

Financial Planning. A trust that, once created, cannot be revoked or done away with by the individual who created the trust.

see: short-term reversionary trust

issuance date

Insurer Operations.
see: date of issue

issued business

Insurer Operations. Life insurance policies that have been sold and on which the premium has been paid, but which have not yet been delivered to the policyholder.

compare: delivered business, examined business, not taken, paid business, placed business, written business

issued stock

General. Shares of stock that a corporation has actually issued and has not cancelled. Issued shares should be contrasted with authorized shares. Issued shares that have been reacquired by the corporation are called treasury shares.

see: authorized shares, share of stock, treasury stock

itemized premium charges

Insurer Operations. Separately identified charges for insurance coverages in a multi-peril policy, or where premiums are included in the overall purchase price or financing of real or personal property.

© 1991 NILS Publishing Company

Jacket

Insurer Operations. The outer covering of an insurance policy that often contains common provisions of the policy.

see: **face, insurance contract**

Janson clause

Ocean Marine. A clause occasionally added to ocean marine hull policies which provides that the insurance is free of particular average if the amount of a partial loss is equal to, or exceeds, three percent of the insured value of the property covered, or should the vessel be stranded. The insured warrants that they will remain uninsured for this three percent.

see: **free of particular average, particular average**

Jetsam

Ocean Marine. Goods purposely thrown overboard or jettisoned, either to lighten (and thereby save) a ship, or to keep the goods from sinking with a foundering ship. Technically, such cargo must then be brought ashore and above the high-water line; otherwise the cargo remains *flotsam.*

compare: **flotsam, lagan;** see: **derelict**

Jettison

Ocean Marine. A peril covered by an ocean marine policy which is the voluntary dumping overboard of a vessel's cargo or gear to lighten its load in an effort to save it from imminent peril.

Jewelers block insurance

Inland Marine. An inland marine form providing coverage specifically tailored to the needs of wholesale and retail jewelers. Coverage is written on an "open perils" basis for the insured's entire stock of pearls, precious and semi-precious stones, jewels; jewelry, watches and watch movements; gold, silver,

platinum, other precious metals, alloys; and the other stock common to the business of a jeweler, including items held in custody for others.

Jewelers package policy

Inland Marine. A policy that is broader than the standard jewelers block, and that includes "all-risks" coverage on all stock, property of others, furniture and fixtures and improvements and betterments. Coverage for a building and business interruption can be included.

Jewelry floater

Inland Marine. A form of personal articles floater covering individual items of jewelry that are scheduled in the policy on an "open-perils" basis.

see: **personal articles floater, scheduled personal property endorsement**

Job safety analysis

Loss Control. A procedure of analyzing a job by its component parts to determine the hazards connected with it and the requirements or qualifications of those who perform it. This includes identifying hazards or potential accidents associated with each step or task and to develop recommendations that will eliminate, nullify, or prevent such hazards or accidents.

see: **human approach, human factors engineering**

Joint and several liability

General. Liability arising from a contract, where both joint liability (that of several people) and several liability (each individual) promise the performance indicated in the contract. This allows the other party to the contract the ability to seek a remedy in either way.

see: **joint liability, several liability**

© 1991 NILS Publishing Company

joint and survivor annuity

Life. An annuity contract which provides periodic payments during the lifetime of two individuals. The amount of this periodic payment may decrease when the first individual dies. Joint and survivor contracts are usually written on a husband and wife.

syn: reversionary annuity, survivorship annuity

joint and survivorship option

Life. A life insurance policy benefit option which allows the policy cash value to be converted into a joint and survivor annuity.

see: joint and survivor annuity

joint control

Surety. When an estate is controlled jointly by a surety and fiduciary (estate administrator or executor), funds are maintained in accounts that require the signatures of both the surety and fiduciary. The joint control concept is used to reduce fraud when large estates are involved.

joint insurance

Life.

see: joint life insurance

joint insured

Life. An individual insured under a joint life insurance policy.

see: joint life insurance

joint liability

General. A legal term for liability or an obligation that is shared by two or more parties.

compare: several liability; see: joint and several liability

joint life and survivor annuity

Life. Life insurance coverage which converts to an annuity contract for two or more individuals (usually husband and wife) where the annuity benefits continue until the death of the last insured.

joint life and survivor insurance

Life. Life insurance coverage for two or more individuals where the death benefit is payable when the last surviving insured dies. Premiums on this type of policy are much lower than individual life policies because the period of time before the final benefit payment is longer.

compare: joint life insurance; see: second death insurance, tontine

joint life insurance

Life. Life insurance coverage for two or more individuals where the death benefit is payable upon the death of the first insured individual. Premiums on this type of policy are significantly higher than individual life policies because of the greater chance that one of two individuals will die.

syn: joint insurance; compare: joint life and survivor insurance, second death insurance

joint loss agreement

Property. An endorsement to a boiler and machinery policy that prorates the policy limits with other property policies when both policies provide coverage on a similar basis.

see: firebox explosion, other insurance clause

joint tenancy

General. A legal term for the ownership of property by two or more individuals where ownership passes to the remaining individual(s) upon the death of one of the owners.

see: tenancy

joint underwriting association (JUA)

Insurer Operations. An organization of insurance companies formed with statutory approval to provide a particular form of insurance to the public. JUAs are usually formed because voluntary market availability is lacking. They are generally allowed by regulators to establish their own rates and develop their own policy forms.

see: automobile shared market, extended health insurance, Fair Access to Insurance Requirements

joint venture

General. An association of two or more parties as co-owners to engage in a limited business transaction for a profit. Generally, profits and losses are shared upon some preagreed formula.

joisted masonry construction

Loss Control. Buildings with outside support walls constructed of noncombustible masonry materials (concrete, brick, hollow concrete block, stone or tile) and roof and floor made of combustible materials such as wood.

see: construction

Jones Act

Ocean Marine/Workers' Compensation. Section 33 of the Merchant Marine Act of 1920 is commonly referred to as the Jones Act. A federal act which covers ships' crews with the same remedy available to railroad workers; that is, seamen may sue the employer/shipowner for injuries sustained through their fault or negligence. The act applies to navigable waters used for international or interstate commerce.

see: cure, Longshoremen's and Harbor Workers' Compensation Act, seaman's remedies

© 1991 NILS Publishing Company

judgment

General. The final decision of a lawsuit by a court.

see: declaratory judgment, decree, default judgment, directed verdict, dismissal, injunctive relief

judgment rates

Insurer Operations. Rates developed by an underwriter based on his or her experience and skills, rather than using actuarial analysis.

compare: manual rates; see: "A" rates, rate making, schedule rating

judicial bond

Surety. A general term applied to all bonds filed with a court.

see: appeal bond, bail bond, bond, court bond, defendant's bond to dissolve, fiduciary bond, financial guarantee bond, injunction bond, plaintiff's bond to secure, plaintiff's replevin bond, security for expenses

jumbo risk

Insurer Operations. An insurance policy with exceptionally high limits.

jumping juvenile life insurance

Life. A life insurance policy designed for children that has a low initial face value ($1,000 or $2,000), but significantly increases in face value automatically when the insured reaches a specified age (usually 21). The policy's annual premium remains the same throughout its term and no medical examinations are needed after it is issued.

compare: graded death benefit

jury duty reimbursement

Casualty. Business coverage which reimburses employers for a percentage (usually 80%) of wages paid to an employee who is called for jury duty.

juvenile insurance

Life. Insurance on children under sixteen years of age.

see: graded death benefit, jumping juvenile life insurance

191

K

Keene Doctrine

Casualty. Three theories concerning coverage for asbestos liability claims resulted from the decision handed down in *Keene Corp. v. Insurance Company of North America.* They are: 1) All insurers with policies in force between the time of initial exposure to asbestos and the manifestation of injury must respond on behalf of the policyholder; 2) Once coverage is triggered, all insurers are liable for their full policy limits in the event of a judgment – not their pro rata share with other policies; 3) Only one policy in force during the period of injury can apply to each injury, and the insured is allowed to select which policy is to respond.

   syn: **exposure in residence theory, triple trigger theory; see: exposure and manifestation theory**

Keeton-O'Connell Plan

Automobile. An automobile no-fault plan proposed by two law school professors – Robert Keeton and Jeffrey O'Connell – called "Basic Protection Insurance." The plan sought to eliminate most automobile tort liability lawsuits by having insureds paid by their own insurers (up to $10,000 per person). The plan would permit regular tort claims only for pain-and-suffering losses exceeding $5,000.

   see: **no-fault insurance**

Kenney Ratio

Insurer Operations. A property and casualty insurance company solvency rule-of-thumb, developed by the late Roger Kenney, an insurance journalist. It states that a property and casualty insurer should not have written premiums equal to more than twice the sum its capital and surplus.

Keogh Plan

Employee Benefits. A retirement plan for self-employed individuals, permitted under the Keogh Act (HR 10) passed by Congress in 1962. It allows an individual to make an annual tax deductible contribution to a retirement plan, up to a maximum limit of 25% of earned income (subject to a $30,000 maximum).

   syn: **HR-10 plan; compare: individual retirement account**

key employee insurance

Health/Life. A disability, life or health insurance program designed to financially protect an employer from the loss of an individual employee whose special skills or experience are vital to the firm. Proceeds from the plan would be used to cover lost income to the firm and/or to locate and hire a replacement for the key employee.

   syn: **key man insurance; see: cross purchase plan, overhead expense insurance, partnership insurance, sole proprietorship insurance**

key man insurance

Life.
   see: **key employee insurance**

kidnap insurance

Crime. Insurance that provides financial compensation when a person (usually an employee) is seized and used by criminals and/or terrorists to gain entry to a premises, to extract a ransom, or for the purpose of extortion. This coverage usually extends to the spouse and children of the covered individual.

   compare: **extortion insurance, kidnap-ransom-extortion insurance**

kidnap-ransom-extortion insurance

Crime. Originally an insurance policy for financial

kidnap-ransom-extortion insurance — continued
institutions, it has since been expanded for all corporate executives and individuals of wealth and fame.
The policy generally reimburses the insured for the
amount of a ransom payment, and provides the
assistance of professional negotiators to deal with the
kidnappers. Coverage is written on a worldwide basis.

   see: **extortion insurance, kidnap insurance,
ransom insurance.**

© 1991 NILS Publishing Company

labor and material bond

Surety. A form of payment bond that protects an owner contracting for work, against liens from subcontractors, suppliers or laborers who are not paid for their services and materials by the general contractor.

syn: **payment bond**

laches

General. Undue delay in asserting a right or privilege; specifically, undue delay in bringing a suit or complaint. Laches may be used as a defense if it can be proved by the defendant that he or she has suffered by the plaintiff's seeming acquiescence (i.e., delay in bringing suit).

see: **acquiescence, estoppel, reservation of rights, waiver**

lading

General.
see: **freight**

lagan

Ocean Marine. Cargo from a marine accident, lying at the bottom of the sea. Also, goods thrown into the sea with a buoy attached, so that they may be easily recovered later.

compare: **derelict**; see: **flotsam, jetsam**

land contract

Title. The sale of real property via a contract which conveys the title from one party to another upon full payment of the agreed purchase price. Under this form of sale, the title to the property remains with the seller until the buyer has paid the entire purchase price, with the buyer taking possession of the property immediately following payment of the purchase price.

landlords protective liability endorsement

Casualty. An endorsement (GL 99 02) available under the 1973 ISO liability rating program which allowed a significant rate credit for buildings leased to a single lessee. Under the 1986 ISO rating program, the need for this endorsement has been eliminated as rate credits previously allowed have been incorporated into new building and premises classifications.

lapse

Insurer Operations. Insurance policy termination caused by the failure of the policyholder to make premium payments.

see: **cancellation notice, reinstatement**

Life. A life insurance policy termination caused by the failure of the policyholder to make premium payments within the prescribed time period and where there is no nonforfeiture value.

see: **nonforfeiture benefit, reinstatement**

lapsed policy

Insurer Operations. An insurance policy which has been terminated because of the insured's failure to pay the premium.

lapse ratio

Insurer Operations/Life. A ratio used by life insurers to determine the effectiveness of their marketing efforts. It is the ratio of the number of life contracts that have lapsed within a specified period of time to the number in force at the beginning of the period.

compare: **persistency**; see: **termination rate**

larceny

Crime. The unlawful taking of another's personal property.

see: **theft**

large loss principle

Risk Management. A loss that would exceed a firm's

© 1991 NILS Publishing Company

large loss principle – continued
ability to absorb (finance) the loss. Generally, this type of loss is transferred through insurance.

see: **retention, risk transfer**

laser endorsement

Casualty. A series of endorsements developed in conjunction with the ISO "claims made" commercial liability policy in 1986. They exclude certain "claims made" accidents, products, work or locations by focusing on a very narrow subject, much the same as a laser.

last clear chance

General.
see: **doctrine of last clear chance**

last in, first out (LIFO)

Risk Management. An inventory accounting method by which sales are considered to be from among the latest merchandise or inventory purchased. This method of valuing inventory minimizes inventory profits and losses. An understanding of inventory valuation methods is important in estimating business interruption losses.

compare: **average cost; first in, first out**

latent defect

Casualty. A hidden, concealed or dormant defect which cannot be discovered by observation or a reasonably careful inspection.

see: **active malfunction, bench error, defective, hidden defect**

law of large numbers

Risk Management. A principle stating that the larger the number of exposures considered, the more closely the losses reported will equal the underlying probability of loss. This law forms the basis for statistical expectation of loss, upon which rates for insurance are calculated. *Example:* The more times a coin is flipped, the closer it will come to actually reaching the underlying probability of 50 percent "heads" and 50 percent "tails."

see: **degree of risk, homogeneity, odds, probability, reduction of risk, spread of risk**

layering

Casualty/Property. A method of structuring policies covering a risk, so that each policy provides a layer of coverage. This technique is used in both liability and property coverages. *Example:* A primary policy (Policy A) provides $100,000 in coverage limits. Policy B provides an additional $200,000 of coverage, in excess of Policy A's limits. Policy C provides an additional $300,000, in excess of Policy B, for a total of $600,000. The advantage to layering is the additional spread of

risk among insurers and the premium savings each company grants the insured.

see: **buffer layer, divided coverage, following form excess liability insurance, following form excess property insurance, nonconcurrency, quota share**

lay underwriter

Health/Life. A home office underwriter with extensive actuarial and medical knowledge.

lead fee

Agency/Insurer Operations. Payment of a fee to another party for the referral of a prospective insured or customer.

Leading Producers Round Table (LPRT)

Organizations. An award given annually by the National Association of Health Underwriters to producers who achieve certain levels of premium volume during the year.

see: **National Association of Health Underwriters**

lead insurance company

Insurer Operations. A large, recognized insurer that leads a group of other insurers and reinsurers in underwriting large risks. The lead insurer will usually assume a large percentage of the risk for its own account.

see: **lead underwriter**

lead underwriter

Insurer Operations. A Lloyd's term referring to the underwriter that leads on a Lloyd's slip. The lead underwriter is selected carefully, since the underwriter's prestige will determine the number and dollar amounts for which other underwriters will participate on the slip.

see: **slip**

leased employee

Casualty/Workers' Compensation. An employee that is sent by his or her employer to perform work or service for another organization and is under the exclusive control and direction of the management of the lessee organization. *Example:* A word processor sent by a temporary employment agency to work in the office of a bank.

see: **employee, employee leasing**

leasehold

General. A contract giving a party the right to use and occupy another party's property.

leasehold interest

Property.
see: **leasehold profit interest**

196

© 1991 NILS Publishing Company

leasehold interest insurance

Property. Coverage purchased by a lessee for a loss that would result from the premature cancellation of a lease, where the lessee's rent is lower than the rent being charged for similar property on new leases. The leasehold interest insurance covers the difference between the rent under the lease and the amount of rent that must be paid for similar property for the remainder of the original lease's term.

leasehold profit interest

Property. Coverage purchased by a lessee on leased space which is being sublet to another party for a higher rate than the lessee is paying. Under this coverage, the lessee can recover lost profit (the difference between the lease and sublease rates) in the event of the premature cancellation of the lease. Cancellation of the lease must have been triggered by an insured property loss.

syn: leasehold interest

lease payment insurance

Financial Guarantee Insurance. A form of credit insurance covering a lessor against non-payment of lease rental installments by the lessee in a capital equipment or real estate lease transaction.

see: credit insurance

ledger cost

Life. A life insurance policy's net cost, calculated by deducting the policy's cash value at a specific point in time from the premiums paid to that date, less the dividends paid on the policy.

legal department

Insurer Operations. The employees and operations of an insurance company that are responsible for defending the insurer in court; drafting and reviewing contracts; assisting in the drafting of insurance policy language; investigating and defending claims against policyholders; monitoring the changes in state insurance codes and regulations and pending legislation; and participating in industry lobbying activities.

legal expense insurance

Casualty. Insurance usually written on a group basis, covering legal advice and consultation, office work, various judicial and administrative proceedings and major legal expenses. Benefits are scheduled for each type of legal service, and maximum benefit limits apply.

see: business legal expense insurance

legal expense insurers

Insurer Operations. Insurers that write legal expense insurance. Regulators include under this category both commercial insurers and nonprofit organizations which operate legal expense service plans.

see: business legal expense insurance, legal expense insurance

legal expenses

Insurer Operations. Those legal expenses incurred in relation to the adjustment or settlement of a policyholder's claim.

see: claim expense, defense costs

legal liability

Casualty. An obligation imposed as a matter of law upon a party for its negligence, violation of law, or failure to fulfill contractual obligations. Liability insurance policies provide coverage for an insured's legal liability, excluding criminal acts, intentional torts or breach of contract.

see: casualty insurance, intentional tort, public policy, punitive damages; Fr: responsabilité légale; Gr: gesetzliche Haftpflicht; Sp: responsabilidad legal

legal liability indemnity association

Casualty. An association of attorneys who form an inter-indemnity trust to mutually insure themselves against claims which may arise out of their legal practice.

see: malpractice insurance

legal list

Insurer Operations/Regulation. A list of securities specified by regulations, in which pension funds and insurance companies are permitted to invest.

see: admitted assets

legal reserve

Life. Minimum reserves required by state law or regulation that life insurers must maintain to operate in that state.

legal reserve life insurance company

Life. A life insurance company which maintains reserves at least equal to the minimum prescribed by law or regulation in the state in which it does business. These reserves are based on actuarial formulas and are designed to allow the company to meet all of its financial obligations. An assessment life insurer, conversely, is permitted to assess its policyholders in the event of financial problems.

compare: assessment company; see: expense funds, old line company

legislated insurance coverage

Regulation. Coverages mandated by state or federal laws. *Examples:* Mandatory automobile liability insurance; earthquake insurance in California; crime insurance in New York; flood insurance to qualify for

© 1991 NILS Publishing Company

legislated insurance coverage – continued
federally insured loans; and COBRA extension/conversion rights.

see: **minimum coverage clauses, policy condition laws, standard provisions**

Health/Employee Benefits. Legislatively mandated health insurance coverages such as mammographies, in-vitro fertilization treatments, etc., that many employees and insurers point to as a significant contributor to the recent run-up in the cost of employee health plans.

lemon aid insurance

Automobile. Coverage indemnifying an auto dealer for a vehicle which has been returned by a purchaser under the provisions allowed by the Universal Commercial Code. The Code allows a vehicle to be returned if it suffers persistent mechanical problems over a specified period of time.

lender's bond

Surety. A bond guaranteeing the completion of construction of a building or an improvement to a property, required prior to a lender or mortgagee advancing monies to the owner or developer. After completion, the property replaces the bond as security for the loan.

syn: **completion bond; see: contract bond**

lender's holder in due course insurance

Casualty. Coverage usually provided in conjunction with a lender's single interest policy. The policy indemnifies the lender for any loss sustained under Federal Trade Commission (FTC) regulations. The coverage resulted from FTC regulations passed in 1976 which nullified a lending institution's defense as a holder in due course of loans purchased by the institution from dealers or vendors. Prior to the change, the institution was immune from any dispute between the purchaser of an item and the seller. The new regulation allows the purchaser to assert a claim against both the dealer or vendor and the holder in due course.

compare: **holder in due course insurance; see: holder in due course**

lending institutions

General. Use of this term is generally restricted to public institutions such as public banks, savings and loan associations and credit unions. Private organizations (such as investment bankers) are generally not included in this category.

lessee

General. A tenant who has signed a lease.
compare: **lessor**

lessees of safe deposit boxes coverage form

Crime. A crime coverage form providing burglary and robbery coverage for securities and property (other than money and securities) while located in a safe deposit box in a vault in a depository, leased or rented by the insured. The insurance covers insured property during the course of deposit or removal from the safe deposit box.

syn: **crime coverage form I; see: crime coverages, property other than money and securities, securities**

lessor

General. An owner of property who rents it to others under the terms of a lease.
compare: **lessee**

letter of credit (LOC)

General. A financial instrument issued by a bank guaranteeing payment of a customer's drafts up to a stated amount. The advantage of an LOC is that it confers the bank's credit upon the holder. LOCs can be either revolving (periodically renewing for a specified amount) or performance (guaranteeing performance depending upon the beneficiary's needs).

Reinsurance. A line of credit normally issued by a bank to a reinsurer, which can be drawn down to cover a liability. LOCs can cover the reserve for a loss or unearned premium in lieu of a cash deposit.

level commission

Agency/Insurer Operations. An agent's commission structure where first-year and renewal commissions for a particular type of policy are the same.

syn: **flat commission; compare: unlevel commission; see: agent's commission**

level death benefit option

Life. An option under universal life insurance allowing the beneficiary to choose either the face amount of the policy at the time of death, or a stipulated percentage of the accumulation value, whichever is greater.

see: **accumulation value, face amount**

level premium life insurance

Life. Whole life insurance where the premium remains the same for the policy's entire term. Under this plan, the premium is higher than necessary for the initial years of coverage, then is less than needed for the final years of coverage.

syn: **net level premium; see: net level premium reserve**

level term life insurance

Life. Term life insurance which has a constant face value from inception to expiration.

198

© 1991 NILS Publishing Company

liability

General. An accounting term signifying money owed or expected to be owed to another party. In law, a legal term signifying a legal obligation.

see: **assets, balance sheet, current liabilities, legal liability**

liability for guests' property – premises coverage form

Crime. A crime coverage form which provides coverage for the insured's legally imposed liability, arising out of damage to guests' property while on the insured's premises or in the insured's possession.

syn: **crime coverage form L; see: crime coverages, innkeepers legal liability**

liability for guests' property – safe deposit coverage form

Crime. A crime coverage form which covers the insured's legally imposed liability arising out of the loss or damage to guests' property while contained in a safe deposit box on the insured's premises. There is no limitation on the type of property that is covered.

syn: **crime coverage form K; see: crime coverages, hotel safe deposit box liability, innkeepers legal liability**

liability insurance

Casualty. Insurance that provides protection in the event the insured carelessly causes bodily injury or property damage to others and becomes legally obligated to pay damages.

see: **casualty insurance**

liability over suit

Workers' Compensation.
see: **third-party over suit**

Liability Risk Retention Act of 1986

Regulation. Federal legislation adopted in 1986 which expanded the provisions of the Product Liability Risk Retention Act of 1981. The primary changes in this bill were: expansion of risk retention groups (RRGs) and purchasing groups (PGs) to all types of liability insurance (except personal liability and workers' compensation); the expansion of authorized groups able to form RRGs and PGs from only product manufacturers to almost all businesses; and certain concessions to state regulators allowing them to regulate more RRG and PG activities.

syn: **Risk Retention Act; see: Product Liability Risk Retention Act of 1981, risk purchasing group, risk retention group**

libel

General. A defamatory or prejudiced written statement about another person or persons that harms their reputation, office, business, or livelihood.

compare: **slander; see: personal injury**

libel insurance

Casualty. Insurance providing coverage in the event that an insured without just cause intentionally publishes material or prints a picture that defames the reputation of another party.

compare: **slander; see: personal injury liability**

liberalization clause

Insurer Operations. A property insurance policy clause that extends broader legislated or regulated coverages to current policies if they do not affect premiums. A modifying endorsement is not required to add such coverage.

license

Regulation. Legal authority granted by the state. A state insurance department grants a license to an insurance company, an agent or a broker or to other entities transacting insurance-related business within its borders.

see: **admitted insurer, certificate of authority, certificate of convenience, licensee**

license bond

Surety. A bond guaranteeing that a person who has been issued a license will comply with the laws, regulations and ordinances associated with the issuance of the license.

see: **permit bond**

licensee

General. An individual or entity that is licensed, usually by a governmental regulatory agency.

see: **limited licenses**

Casualty. A person who enters or remains on the premises with the express or implied consent of the owner and for the licensee's own personal benefit, convenience or pleasure. The owner owes no duty of care with respect to correcting a condition of such premises.

compare: **invitee, trespasser; see: degree of care**

Agency/Insurer Operations. An individual or an organization that has been approved by a state department of insurance to act as an insurance company, agent, broker, solicitor, consultant or other entity conducting insurance-related business within that state.

see: **admitted insurer, prelicensing education requirement**

© 1991 NILS Publishing Company

lien

General. Legal action usually brought by a creditor or a service provider, upon real or personal property, in order to satisfy a debt.

see: encumbrance, mortgage, possessory lien, tax lien

lien plan

Life. A life insurance plan where policies are issued at a standard premium for substandard risks, but with a provision that less than the face benefit amount would be paid in the initial years of coverage. This type of plan is illegal in many states.

compare: graded death benefit

life annuity

Life.

see: annuity

life care contracts

Health. Contracts entered into by older adults where occasional, simple medical services are provided in addition to room and board, for the duration of the resident's life, or for a period in excess of one year. The consideration for such a service is an entry fee, with or without subsequent, periodic charges.

syn: life care providers; see: life care facilities

life care facilities

Health. Facilities providing board and lodging together with nursing services, medical services, or other health-related services, pursuant to an agreement effective for the life of the individual or for a period in excess of one year.

syn: continuing care facilities; see: life care contracts

life care providers

Health.

see: life care contracts

Life Communicators Association (LCA)

Organizations. Members: Specialists in the areas of life insurance advertising, sales promotion, public relations and corporate communications. *Objectives:* Conducts workshops for junior members. Distributes case histories describing activities of member companies. *Founded:* 1933. *Headquarters:* Des Moines, IA.

life expectancy

Life. The length of time an individual of a given age can be expected to live, based on mortality tables.

see: mortality rate, mortality table, normal life expectancy

life expectancy term insurance

Life. Term life insurance where the policy term is based on an individual's life expectancy, as opposed to a given period of time, such as five or ten years.

see: term life insurance

life income option

Life. A life insurance settlement option which a beneficiary may select, where the policy proceeds are converted to a life annuity for the beneficiary based upon his or her life expectancy, and are paid as long as the beneficiary lives.

compare: fixed amount option, fixed period option, interest option, life income with period certain option; see: optional life insurance settlement modes

life income with period certain option

Life. A life insurance settlement option which a beneficiary may select, where the policy proceeds are converted to a life annuity for the beneficiary with the benefit period based on the beneficiary's life expectancy and payments continuing for that period of time whether or not the beneficiary lives.

compare: fixed amount option, fixed period option, interest option, life income option; see: optional life insurance settlement modes

life insurance

Life. Insurance which will pay a specified sum of money if the individual insured by the policy dies during the policy term.

compare: annuity; see: adjustable life insurance, cash value, credit life insurance, decreasing term life insurance, deferred dividend policy, deferred life insurance, extended term life insurance, endowment policy, family income life insurance, family life policy, family maintenance life insurance, flexible premium life insurance, group life insurance, indexed life insurance, individual contract, industrial life insurance, interest-sensitive life insurance, joint life and survivor insurance, joint life insurance, jumping juvenile life insurance, level premium life insurance, level term life insurance, life expectancy term insurance, life insurance trust, limited payment life insurance, limited life insurance policy, monthly debit ordinary life insurance, multiple protection life insurance, National Service Life Insurance, ordinary life insurance, paid up at age life insurance, permanent life insurance, re-entry term life insurance, renewable term life insurance, savings bank life insurance, Servicemen's Group Life Insurance, single premium life insurance, split life insurance, survivorship life insurance, term life insurance, universal life

© 1991 NILS Publishing Company

insurance, universal variable life insurance, variable life insurance, variable premium life insurance, Veterans Group Life Insurance, whole life insurance

Life Insurance Agency Management Association (LIAMA)

Organizations. Members: Life insurance agency managers. *Objectives:* Seeks solutions to the problems of administering the agency force of a life insurer. *Founded:* 1945. *Headquarters:* Hartford, CT.

Life Insurance Association of America (LIAA)

Organizations. A former life insurance organization that served as the legislative relations arm for a large segment of the life insurance industry. It is now part of the American Council of Life Insurance.

see: American Council of Life Insurance

life insurance in force

Health/Life.

see: in-force business

Life Insurance Institute of Canada

Organizations. Members: Life insurers in Canada. *Objectives:* Encourages the development of a thorough knowledge of the business of life insurance. *Founded:* 1936. *Headquarters:* Toronto, Ontario.

Life Insurance Marketing and Research Association (LIMRA)

Organizations. Members: Life insurance companies. *Objectives:* Conducts market, consumer, economic, financial, manpower and human resources research. Provides executive and field management programs. *Founded:* 1916. *Headquarters:* Farmington, CT.

life insurance trust

Life. A life insurance policy whose benefits are used to establish a trust which distributes the policy proceeds based upon the trust agreement.

Life Insurers Conference (LIC)

Organizations. Members: Multiple line and combined life, accident and health insurance companies. *Objectives:* Promotes the exchange of ideas among its members. Supports the member's interests in legislative and regulatory activities. *Founded:* 1910. *Headquarters:* Atlanta, GA.

life maintenance contracts

Health/Life. Contracts providing life, health and disability income coverages on the condition that the subscriber maintain a healthy lifestyle. Health-promoting activities, such as exercise or stop-smoking programs, may be included.

Life Management Institute

Organizations. A unit of the Life Office Management Association (LOMA) which prepares and administers educational materials for the Fellow, Life Management Institute (FLMI) Program. Upon successful completion of its examinations, the student receives the FLMI designation.

see: Fellow of the Life Management Institute, Life Office Management Association

Life Office Management Association (LOMA)

Organizations. Members: U.S. and Canadian life and health insurers. Associate members include life insurers in 32 countries. Affiliate members include firms providing professional support to member companies. *Objectives:* Provides educational programs. Confers the Fellow, Life Management Institute (FLMI) designation upon individuals who pass a series of exams. *Founded:* 1924. *Headquarters:* Atlanta, GA

see: Fellow of the Life Management Institute, Life Management Institute

life risk factors

Insurer Operations/Life. Information needed to underwrite a life insurance policy such as an individual's age, sex, weight, height, tobacco use, heredity, and occupation. Statistically, these factors are related to an individual's life span. Some jurisdictions prohibit sex and heredity from being used as rating factors.

life salvage

Ocean Marine. A claim against the owner of a vessel, for a salvage award based upon the rescue of persons. Life salvage alone brings no salvage award, because reward is only out of the property saved. However, salvors of human life who take part in rescue actions on the occasion of the accident giving rise to the salvage of the property are entitled to a fair share of the remuneration awarded to the salvors of the vessel, its cargo and accessories.

see: salvage

lifetime disability benefit

Health. A disability benefit policy provision that provides periodic payments to replace lost income for as long as an insured is disabled, even if it is for a lifetime.

see: disability income insurance

lifetime policy

Health/Life. A life insurance or disability policy that is noncancellable or is guaranteed renewable, usually for as long as the insured lives. Some policies of this type will terminate when an insured reaches a specific age such as 65 years of age.

compare: optionally renewable contract; see: guaranteed insurability, guaranteed renewable, noncancellable policy

© 1991 NILS Publishing Company

life underwriter

Life. A life insurance agent.

Life Underwriter Political Action Committee (LUPAC)

Organizations. A life insurance lobbying organization created by the National Association of Life Underwriters (NALU).

see: **National Association of Life Underwriters**

Life Underwriters Association of Canada

Organizations. Members: Life insurance company underwriters in Canada. *Objectives:* Lobbies and educates those in the field of life insurance. Sponsors the Chartered Life Underwriter (CLU) designation in Canada. *Founded:* 1906. *Headquarters:* Don Mills, Ontario.

Life Underwriting Training Council (LUTC)

Organizations. Members: Students who are life underwriters taking sales training courses sponsored by local life underwriter associations. *Objectives:* Provide vocational sales training and life underwriter educational programs. *Founded:* 1947. *Headquarters:* Washington, D.C.

lighter

Ocean Marine.
see: **barge**

lighter aboard ship (LASH)

Ocean Marine. An ocean vessel which carries specially-designed barges.

lightning

Property. A large-scale natural electrical discharge in the atmosphere, from one cloud to another or from a cloud to the earth. Lightning is one of the insured perils in a standard fire insurance policy.

Fr: foudre; Gr: Blitzschlag; Sp: rayo

limitation of actions

Insurer Operations. Restrictions on the period of time during which an insured may bring actions under an insurance policy for certain claims or against which certain rights may be enforced.

see: **statute of limitations**

limitations

Insurer Operations. Exceptions and limitations on the coverages that are provided under an insurance policy.

see: **exclusion**

limited coverage for customers

Automobile. A garage policy provision which limits liability coverage for customers of auto dealerships to the financial responsibility law limits in the state where the vehicle being driven is principally garaged. This coverage does not apply if the customer has other insurance that would respond to an incident.

see: **dealer class plan, driveaway collision, garage coverage form**

limited damage waiver (LDW)

Automobile.
see: **collision damage waiver**

limited health service plan

Health. A health service plan providing services restricted to a medical specialty or a combination of related medical specialties, such as psychology and family counseling.

limited licenses

Regulation. Agents' licenses conferring limited or restricted powers, such as licenses limited to a single line of business or to transactions on out-of-state risks.

see: **certificate of convenience, license**

limited life and health insurers

Life. Stock or mutual health and life insurers providing nonassessable policies with limited benefits.

limited life insurance policy

Life. A life insurance policy that only pays its benefits when the insured dies from a specified peril, such as cancer or AIDS.

see: **cancer insurance, dread disease policy**

limited partnership

General. A partnership consisting of one or more limited partners (whose liability for partnership debts is limited to the amount originally invested) and one or more general partners (whose liability for partnership debts is unlimited). To create a limited partnership, a certificate must be filed with a state official. A limited partner may lose the shield of limited liability if he or she actively participates in the management of the business.

see: **partnership, partnership financial bond**

limited payment life insurance

Life. A life insurance policy that provides coverage for an individual's entire life, with premium payments made for a specified period of years, at which point they cease.

see: **paid up at age life insurance**

limited risk health insurance policy

Health. A health or Medicare supplement insurance policy often sold by newspapers or on television to their readers or viewers. Coverage is usually provided on restrictive forms with low limits.

see: **newspaper policy**

© 1991 NILS Publishing Company

limit of liability

Insurer Operations. The maximum amount an insured may collect, or for which an insured is protected, under the terms of a policy.

syn: amount of insurance, limits; see: aggregate benefits, aggregate limit, aggregate operations liability limit, aggregate products liability limit, aggregate protection liability limit, face amount, penalty, per cause maximum limit, per occurrence limit, per person limit

limit of liability rule

Property. A rule that allocates property insurance losses among insurers providing coverage on the same property.

see: contribution by limits, other insurance clause, pro rata liability clause

limits

Health/Life.
see: age limits

Insurer Operations.
see: limit of liability

line

General. A specific class of insurance. *Examples:* Property, casualty, workers' compensation and life are all "lines" of insurance.

syn: line of business; see: monoline policy, multiple line policy, package policy

Reinsurance. The amount or limit of insurance which a reinsurer has committed to a ceding company on a class of risks.

see: gross line, lines, net line

Insurer Operations. A term initially introduced at Lloyd's of London, it is the amount of liability assumed by an underwriter. A Lloyd's underwriter will indicate the amount of liability assumed and initial acceptance on one line of a slip.

see: Lloyd's of London, slip

line card

Property. A property underwriter's record of the limits of liability written on a specific policy.

line guide

Insurer Operations.
see: line sheet

line of business

Insurer Operations.
see: line

line of credit (LOC)

Risk Management. A prearranged borrowing limit established by an individual or organization with a financial institution.

syn: credit line; see: commitment fee

lines

Insurer Operations. The amount of risk a reinsurer assumes which is usually expressed in multiples of the net retention under a surplus treaty.

see: line

line sheet

Insurer Operations. The schedule an insurer maintains to guide its underwriters as to the maximum amounts of insurance that can be written on different classes of risks.

syn: line guide; see: rate card

line slip

Insurer Operations.
see: slip

Linton Yield Method

Life. A method developed by actuary M. Albert Linton to measure the cost of life insurance. A comparison is made between a whole life insurance policy, and a decreasing term policy combined with an investment fund. The yield or return on the investment fund is compared to the cash value of the whole life policy after a specified period of time, to determine which program should be selected.

see: interest adjusted cost

liquefied petroleum gas (LPG)

Loss Control. A compressed gas consisting of flammable light hydrocarbons (propane, butane, ethane or methane) and used as a fuel or as raw material for chemical synthesis.

liquidation

Regulation. A last-resort action taken by an insurance department after it has determined that a financially impaired insurer cannot be rehabilitated and is insolvent. When an insurer is liquidated, its affairs cease and any remaining assets are converted into cash to pay policyholder claims and creditors.

see: insolvency, rehabilitation, seizure order

liquidation charge

Life. A penalty fee charged by an annuity or mutual fund for an early withdrawal of funds that have accumulated. The charge is made to allow the insurer or fund administrator to recover expenses associated with marketing and administration which are higher in the initial years.

liquidation distribution

Regulation. The priorities of disbursements of the monetary assets of an insurance company that has been declared insolvent and for which a liquidation order has been issued by its domiciliary regulator. Generally, the order which an insurer's assets are distributed among its creditors could be, but are not necessarily in the following order: 1) The costs and

liquidation distribution — continued
expenses of the administration, insolvency, liquidation and rehabilitation, including claims handling expenses of any state guaranty funds; 2) Wages owed employees, other than officers of the insurer (often for a certain period preceding the action resulting in liquidation or a flat amount) and liens secured prior to regulatory proceedings; claims by policyholders, beneficiaries, insureds and liability claims against insureds covered by policies issued by the company, claims of any state guaranty fund, all other claims of general creditors not falling into any other priority, including unsecured governmental claims for taxes; claims of guarantee association certificate holders, guarantee capital shareholders and surplus note holders, shareholders, members and other owners.

liquidation period
Life. A period of time when an insurer is making annuity payments and, in effect, drawing down or liquidating the accumulated annuity benefits. Depending on whether the annuity is a pure or refund annuity, the liquidation period ends either when all payments have been made or when the annuitant dies.
see: **pure annuity, refund annuity**

liquidity
Risk Management. The ability of an organization to readily convert its assets into cash with little loss in the asset's value.

liquor bond
Surety.
see: **alcohol bond**

liquor control laws
Casualty.
see: **dram shop act**

liquor legal liability coverage
Casualty. Special liability coverage for insureds who are in the business of manufacturing, distributing, selling, serving or furnishing alcoholic beverages. For these insureds, liability can arise from such circumstances as contributing to the intoxication of an individual; the furnishing of alcoholic beverages to an individual that is under the legal drinking age or under the influence of alcohol; or violating any statute, ordinance or regulation relating to the sale, gift, distribution or use of alcoholic beverages.
see: **alcoholic beverage liability insurance, dram shop liability insurance, liquor liability laws**

liquor liability laws
Casualty. State or local statutes that establish the responsibilities of a business or individual that sells or serves alcoholic beverages to customers for injuries caused by customers to third parties.
see: **dram shop act, liquor legal liability coverage**

litigation
General. The process of carrying on a legal contest through the judicial process.
see: **adjudicate, defendant, plaintiff; compare: arbitration**

litigation bond
Surety.
see: **court bond**

livery use
Automobile. An archaic term denoting the use of a vehicle for hire to transport individuals. Use of a vehicle to carry persons or property for a fee is excluded by personal auto policies.

livestock auction market form
Inland Marine. A specialized livestock insurance form covering a livestock auction market owner for livestock consigned to the market, from the point of origin to when the livestock is unloaded.
see: **animal insurance, livestock floater**

livestock commercial feedlot reporting form
Inland Marine. Specialized livestock insurance written on a monthly reporting form basis, covering livestock of others while in the insured's commercial feedlot.

livestock floater
Inland Marine. Coverage on such livestock as cattle, sheep, swine, horses, mules or goats for death or destruction directly resulting from such named perils as fire, lightning, windstorm, earthquake, flood, crippling by wild animals, drowning or accidental shooting. Exclusions often include quarantine losses or confiscation by civil authority.
compare: **livestock mortality insurance; see: animal insurance**

livestock insurance
Inland Marine. A broad term which applies to insurance for losses involving domestic animals, such as cattle or horses raised for profit. Included within this term are animal mortality and named perils property insurance coverages.
see: **animal insurance, animal mortality insurance, livestock auction market form, livestock commercial feedlot reporting form, livestock floater, livestock mortality insurance, livestock transit insurance**

© 1991 NILS Publishing Company

livestock mortality insurance

Inland Marine. Specialized livestock insurance which provides the equivalent of life insurance coverage on such livestock as cattle, sheep, swine, horses, mules, goats or zoo animals. It provides coverage for death resulting from natural causes and "all-risks" coverage as respects physical perils, including acts of individuals other than the owner or employees of the owner.

compare: bloodstock insurance, livestock floater; see: animal insurance, breeder's policy, poultry insurance

livestock transit insurance

Inland Marine. Specialized livestock insurance covering the death or crippling of livestock while in transit by air, rail or truck.

see: animal insurance

living

Life. Possessing life; alive. Not having been pronounced dead by a medical doctor.

compare: death

living benefits

Life. An option offered by some life insurers in recent years, where a life insurance policy's proceeds (i.e., face amount, cash value and dividends, if any) are provided to a terminally-ill insured – suffering from Alzheimer's Disease, cancer, acquired immune deficiency syndrome, etc. – to assist the insured with their present living, medical and hospice expenses. The policy proceeds usually are discounted when this option is selected. Another approach to the problem has been the "purchase" of life insurance policies from terminally-ill individuals, by non-insurance financial organizations, in exchange for cash or annuity payments. (Actually, in these transactions, the insured names the financial organization as the policy's beneficiary.) Again, the terminally-ill receive the benefit of their life insurance when they most need it, but at a discount of the total amount.

syn: accelerated benefits; see: reverse-annuity mortgage

living trust

Financial Planning. A form of inter-vivos trust where the trust properties are distributed by the individuals establishing the trust while they are still living.

see: inter-vivos trust, trust

Lloyd's

Insurer Operations.
see: Lloyd's of London

Lloyd's association

Insurer Operations. A term used to refer to any association or joining together of a group of individuals to assume risks. It is patterned after the Lloyd's of London concept. Several Lloyd's associations exist in Texas and in other states.

see: Lloyd's of London

Lloyd's audit

Insurer Operations. An annual audit of the accounts of Lloyd's underwriters. Established in 1908 to assure the individual solvency of the underwriting accounts of all members of Lloyd's.

see: Lloyd's of London

Lloyd's broker

Insurer Operations. An individual – usually associated with a firm that is authorized to go onto the "floor" of Lloyd's of London – who negotiates contracts with a Lloyd's underwriter on behalf of clients seeking insurance coverage.

see: Lloyd's of London

Lloyd's member

Insurer Operations. An individual elected to membership of Lloyd's of London. Often referred to as "names." Individually, they are insurers; collectively, they are Lloyd's. Members must have substantial worth (about $200,000 for Americans). They pledge their entire personal assets to pay Lloyd's claims; usually, they join with other members and form a Lloyd's syndicate.

see: Lloyd's of London, Lloyd's syndicate

Lloyd's names

Insurer Operations.
see: Lloyd's member

Lloyd's of London

Insurer Operations. The centuries-old insurance exchange that traces its beginnings to Lloyd's Coffee House in London. It provides insurance and reinsurance coverages through underwriting syndicates. The syndicates, a form of insurance company, are funded by individual members or "names" who independently assume a proportionate part of the losses. The liability of the names is unlimited. The syndicates are managed by general managers who have underwriters on their staffs.

syn: Lloyd's; compare: insurance exchange; see: American Lloyd's, American Trust Fund, Committee of Lloyd's, line, Lloyd's association, Lloyd's audit, Lloyd's broker, Lloyd's member, Lloyd's Premium Trust Fund, Lloyd's property first loss scale, Lloyd's Register of Shipping, Lloyd's syndicate, Lloyd's underwriter, London Form B, London market, London rig slip, open slip, slip, tribunalization

Lloyd's Premium Trust Fund

Insurer Operations. A trust fund established by Lloyd's of London, in which Lloyd's underwriters must place premiums. These premiums are held until the

© 1991 NILS Publishing Company

Lloyd's Premium Trust Fund — continued
end of a specified period, and claims against the account are paid from this fund. After the specified period, has lapsed (usually three years) the underwriter is entitled to any profits that have been earned.

see: **American Trust Fund, guaranty funds, Lloyd's of London**

Lloyd's property first loss scale
Property. A scale frequently used by property underwriters in determining the allocation of premium between a primary and excess layer.

see: **layering**

Lloyd's Register of Shipping
Ocean Marine. A record of sea-going vessels maintained by Lloyd's in alphabetical order.

see: **American Bureau of Shipping Record, Lloyd's of London**

Lloyd's slip
Insurer Operations.
see: **slip**

Lloyd's syndicate
Insurer Operations. A group of individuals at Lloyd's of London who have entrusted their business to a team of underwriters, who underwrite on behalf of the group. The Lloyd's syndicates are the source of underwriting capacity for obtaining coverage on a risk.

see: **Lloyd's of London**

Lloyd's underwriter
Insurer Operations. An individual that sits or is located on the "floor" of Lloyd's of London and acts on behalf of a Lloyd's syndicate to accept or reject risks which are submitted by Lloyd's brokers.

see: **Lloyd's of London, Lloyd's syndicate, underwriter**

load fund
Financial Planning. A mutual fund that charges its participants a commission (load), and sells its shares through an outside sales organization.

compare: **low load fund, no load fund; see: mutual fund**

loading
General.
see: **expense loading**

loading or unloading
Automobile/Casualty. Liability coverage provided under a commercial automobile policy for bodily injury or property damage that may occur while merchandise or any other goods are on or in a vehicle. Loading or unloading of a vehicle begins when the

goods are removed from the site where they were accepted for shipment, including the period of time when the goods are being transported, and ends when the goods are delivered. Prior to loading and after unloading, liability coverage is provided by a commercial general liability policy or other form of premises liability policy.

see: **dual coverage**

loan receipt
Life. A written document signed by a policyholder which acknowledges that the funds from a life insurance policy loan have been received.

loan value
Life. The dollar amount that a life insurance policyowner can borrow against a life insurance policy which contains a cash value provision.

local
Automobile. A rating classification for commercial automobile insurance, applied to any vehicle customarily operated within a fifty-mile radius of the vehicle's garage location.

compare: **intermediate, long haul, radius of operation**

local agent
Agency/Insurer Operations. An agent that represents an insurance company in a specific geographic territory.

see: **agent**

lockbox plan
Insurer Operations. An arrangement between an insurer or agent and a bank, where premium payments are sent directly from the insured to the bank, which processes the checks and deposits them directly into the insurer's or agent's account. This procedure speeds up the collection process and increases investment income.

lock-out device
Loss Control. A locking device used during maintenance or repairs of equipment, to prevent someone from operating an electrical switch, valve, machine or equipment while it is being repaired or maintained. Each worker on the project holds a unique key to their own lock-out device, and the system under construction or repair can only be activated after all workers have removed their lock-outs.

lognormal distribution
Risk Management. An actuarial distribution curve that is skewed to the right. If the logarithms of individual severities are calculated, they will fall into a normal distribution.

see: **distribution curve**

© 1991 NILS Publishing Company

London Form B

Casualty. A property damage liability form developed in the London market that provides extremely broad property damage coverage.

London market

Insurer Operations. Lloyd's of London and English insurance companies with offices in London. Frequently, a Lloyd's broker's line slip will be completed using London market companies.

see: Lloyd's of London

London rig slip

Insurer Operations. An open slip on the London market, which offers coverage for the physical damage exposures of offshore drilling platforms during construction and operations. It is the largest market for rig insurance, affording close to $800 million in coverage for any one risk, anywhere in the world.

see: Lloyd's of London, open slip

long haul

Automobile. A rating classification for commercial automobile insurance, applied to any vehicle customarily operated at a distance of over 200 miles from where the vehicle is garaged.

compare: intermediate, local, radius of operation; see: zone rating

long hedge

Financial Planning.
see: buying hedge

Longshoremen's and Harbor Workers' Act Coverage endorsement

Workers' Compensation. An endorsement which extends coverage under a workers' compensation policy to include benefits to employees designated by the Longshoremen's and Harbor Workers' Compensation Act (33 USC Sections 901 *et seq*)

see: Longshoremen's and Harbor Workers' Compensation Act, workers' compensation insurance

Longshoremen's and Harbor Workers' Compensation Act

Workers' Compensation. A federal act (33 USC Sections 901 *et seq.*) passed in 1927 that specifies the liability of employers for maritime employees other than ships' officers and crew members. The law applies to longshoremen when loading and unloading cargo, and others "employed in maritime employment in whole or in part, upon the navigable waters of the United States." Amendments to the Act have extended this coverage to include shoreside areas.

see: Jones Act, Longshoremen's and Harbor Workers' Act Coverage endorsement

long-tail liability

Casualty. Liability incidents that take many years before they become known to the insured, and are reported as claims to an insurer. Examples are products liability and medical malpractice claims.

see: exposure and manifestation theory, Keene Doctrine, manifestation injury theory, occurrence trigger

long-term debt

Financial Planning. A debt that extends beyond twelve months and is considered a long-term liability.

compare: short-term debt; see: total debt

long term disability insurance (LTD)

Health. Coverage that provides an individual with monthly income payments during a period of disability in excess of 90 days due to a covered illness or accident. Most policies of this type terminate income payments at age 65.

see: disability income insurance

loss

General. A reduction, decrease or disappearance of value.

Fr: perte; Gr: Verlust; Sp: pérdida

Property. The amount of reduction in value of an insured property, caused by an insured peril.

Casualty. The payment of a claim on behalf of an insured.

Insurer Operations. The basis of a claim for indemnity or damages against an insurance policy.

see: notice of loss, proof of loss

loss adjustment expense

Insurer Operations. The expense involved in settling a loss, excluding the actual value of the loss.

see: claim expense

loss assessment coverage

Property. Property insurance coverage for a condominium unit owner, covering assessments charged by a condominium association for a loss to the property. The policy will pay the amount of the assessment, if the loss was caused by an insured peril. *ISO Form CP 04 19.*

see: condominium commercial unit owner's coverage

loss assumption

Reinsurance.
see: assume, assumption
Risk Management.
see: retention, risk management, self-insurance

loss avoidance
Risk Management.
see: avoidance

loss clause
Property.
see: automatic reinstatement clause

loss constant
Insurer Operations. A charge included in the premium calculation for smaller risks, to provide an adequate premium to cover the expense of writing low premium policies.
see: **minimum premium, minimum rate, rate making**

loss control
Loss Control. A term encompassing both loss prevention and loss reduction. It involves an insured taking action to reduce the frequency of loss occurrences and to minimize the financial impact of a loss.
see: **accident prevention, loss prevention, loss reduction; Fr: expertise; Gr: Schadenkontrolle; Sp: control de pérdida**

loss control policy statement
Risk Management. A formal, written document, usually prepared by a risk manager or loss control specialist and often approved by a company's officers and/or directors, designed to disseminate information about loss control objectives to management and throughout an organization.
see: **risk management policy statement**

loss control specialist
Loss Control. An individual charged with the responsibility of loss control, who is often referred to as a loss prevention engineer or a safety consultant. (The loss prevention engineer title is usually associated with property loss prevention. Safety consultants usually focus on safety for employees and the public.)
syn: **loss prevention engineer; see: Certified Safety Professional**

loss conversion factor (LCF)
Casualty/Workers' Compensation. A factor (e.g., 1.10, 1.15, 1.20) which is multiplied by incurred losses to cover claim adjusting expenses and the insurer's claim service. The resulting figure is "converted losses," which is often used in the calculation of retrospective rating and retention (dividend) plans.
compare: **loss development factor; see: converted losses, incurred losses, retrospective rating plan**

loss cost rating
Insurer Operations. A rating method adopted in many states by the Insurance Services Office (ISO) to replace advisory (manual) rates. Loss cost rates provide an insurer with that portion of a rate that does not include provisions for expenses (other than loss adjusting expenses) or profit and are based on historical aggregate losses and loss adjustment expenses projected through development to their ultimate value and through trending to a future point in time. The expense and profit components to develop final rates must be added by the individual insurers, based on their own costs for these items.
syn: **advisory loss cost rating; see: rate making**

loss development
Insurer Operations/Risk Management. The increase or decrease in the value of losses that occurs between two loss evaluation dates.
see: **loss development factor, trending**

loss development factor (LDF)
Insurer Operations/Risk Management. A factor (expressed as a percentage) designed to 1) correct for errors in estimating the reserves for known but unsettled losses, and 2) make an allowance for incurred but not reported losses.
compare: **loss conversion factor; see: incurred but not reported, rate making, trending**

losses
Insurer Operations.
see: **incurred but not reported, incurred losses, loss reserve, outstanding losses, paid losses**

losses paid
Insurer Operations.
see: **paid losses**

Loss Executives Association (LEA)
Organizations. Members: Loss executives for insurance companies. *Objectives:* Exchanges information between members and liaison with independent adjusters. *Founded:* 1921. *Headquarters:* Parsippany, NJ.

loss expectancy
Insurer Operations. An underwriter's estimate of the losses that a large risk will generate during the next policy period, based on prior loss experience and projected exposure bases (i.e., receipts, payroll, vehicles). Some consideration may be given to the potential for a reduction in losses from loss prevention activities or a change in the risk's operations.
syn: **loss pick**

loss experience
Insurer Operations. A summary of losses for a specific insured, agency, territory or class of business.
syn: **experience; see: accident experience, loss run**

208

© 1991 NILS Publishing Company

loss frequency

Insurer Operations/Risk Management. The number of losses that occur during a specified period of time (usually one year).

syn: claims frequency, loss rate; compare: accident frequency, accident severity, loss severity

loss frequency method

Risk Management. A method of projecting the number of future losses that occur within a specified time period. It is used by underwriters to develop a basic premium on large accounts to which insurance company loading for expenses, profits and contingencies are added.

see: loss expectancy

loss limitation

Casualty/Workers' Compensation. A factor or amount that limits the losses used to calculate the final premium in a retrospective rating plan or retention plan. This factor is designed to limit the adverse effect of a catastrophic loss on a plan's final premium calculation.

see: retrospective rating plan, stop loss

loss loading

Reinsurance. A method of calculating a reinsurance premium where pure losses are multiplied by a factor for inflation, expenses and other considerations.

loss of consortium

General. A legal term used to refer to the damages sought by a plaintiff, for the loss of the company, affection and service of their spouse.

loss of income benefit

Health. Benefit payments that replace a portion of an individual's lost wages because of a disabling injury or illness.

syn: loss of income insurance, loss of time insurance

loss of income insurance

Property.
see: business income coverage form
Health.
see: disability income insurance, loss of income benefit

loss of market

Inland Marine/Ocean Marine. The inability to sell a product to prospective buyers. This is usually considered a business risk and is not covered by most insurance policies. A limited form of loss of market coverage is provided in marine insurance policies, where loss of market due to spoilage of goods can be covered when caused by an insured peril. Product

recall and tampering insurance provide another limited form of this coverage.

see: business risk

loss of time insurance

Property.
see: business income coverage form
Health.
see: loss of income benefit

loss of use insurance

Property. Coverage for the loss of use of an insured's property, when it cannot be used for its intended purpose because of damage caused by an insured peril.

see: additional living expense insurance, business income coverage form, loss of use – value in improvements and betterments

loss of use – value in improvements and betterments

Property. Coverage for the loss of use of improvements made by a tenant in rented or leased property, which are destroyed and not replaced by the building owner.

see: improvements and betterments insurance

loss payable clause

Property. A property insurance policy provision that authorizes the insurer to make a loss payment to a party (loss payee) other than the insured to the extent that the loss payee has an insurable interest in the property.

compare: single interest policy; see: certificate of insurance, loss payee, mortgagee clause, underlying insurance policy

loss payee

Property. The party named in a loss payable clause, to whom insurance proceeds are to be paid in the event of damage to property in which the loss payee has an insurable interest. Loss payees include automobile lienholders and property mortgagees.

syn: mortgagee; see: incorporeal interest, insurable interest, loss payable clause

loss pick

Insurer Operations.
see: loss expectancy

loss portfolio transfer

Insurer Operations/Risk Management. An assumption of incurred losses by a third party. The assuming party hopes to profit by investing the sale price it has received over the length of time it requires to settle the claims it has assumed. Such transfers are also undertaken by insurers or self-insureds in order to

© 1991 NILS Publishing Company

loss portfolio transfer — continued
gain tax advantages, to clean up a financial statement or to exit from a line or class of insurance.

see: **portfolio runoff, portfolio transfer**

Reinsurance. An assumption of a ceding insurer's incurred losses by a reinsurer. This is done when an insurer desires to exit from a class or line of business they are writing or to bring their financial ratios into line with the industry.

compare: **portfolio return**

loss prevention

Loss Control. Measures designed to reduce the probability that a loss will occur.

syn: **accident prevention;** see: **loss reduction**

loss prevention engineer

Loss Control.
see: **loss control specialist**

loss prevention services

Loss Control. Survey, consultation or loss control management services provided to policyholders by an insurer to reduce the likelihood of accidents.

see: **inspection, insurance consultation services, loss prevention**

loss rate

Insurer Operations/Risk Management.
see: **loss frequency**

loss ratio

Insurer Operations. A formula used by insurance companies to relate income to loss expenses. *Formula:* Loss Ratio = (Incurred Losses + Loss Adjusting Expense)/Earned Premiums.

compare: **combined ratio, dividend ratio, expense ratio;** see: **accident year statistics, burning ratio, expected loss ratio, expected losses, insured loss ratio, underwriting margin**

loss ratio reserve method

Insurer Operations. A method of evaluating losses and loss adjusting expenses as a percentage of premium. Historic losses and loss adjusting expenses are evaluated to indicate the amount of reserves that must be maintained on future claims to adequately fund these expenses.

see: **reserve**

loss reduction

Loss Control. A loss control measure designed to reduce the severity of loss occurrences.

syn: **accident prevention;** see: **loss prevention, loss severity**

loss report

Insurer Operations.
see: **loss run**

loss reserve

Insurer Operations. An insurer's estimate of the amount an individual claim will ultimately cost. On an insurer's financial statement, it is the amount of estimated liabilities for known claims due but not paid, known claims not yet paid, and a provision for incurred but not reported claims.

syn: **claims reserve;** see: **incurred but not reported, incurred losses, reserve**

loss retention

Risk Management.
see: **retention**

loss run

Insurer Operations/Risk Management. A printed report summarizing the losses that have occurred over a specific period of time and are valued as of a specific date.

syn: **claims report, loss report;** see: **accident experience, loss experience**

loss severity

Risk Management. The value or dollar amount of a loss.

syn: **claims severity**

loss trends

Risk Management/Insurer Operations. Projections of future accidental losses based on analyses of historical loss patterns. Loss trends are used to determine the pure cost of protection and the resultant basic premium, contingency reserves, and whether or not the company should continue writing a specific policy, a specific line of business, or remain active in a particular geographical area.

see: **trending**

lost instrument bond

Surety. A bond which guarantees that the issuer of a stock certificate, bankbook or any other similar document will be indemnified should a lost or stolen document that has since been reissued be presented to them by another party at a later time.

see: **alteration bond, forgery bond**

lost or not lost clause

Ocean Marine. An obsolete ocean marine provision covering a vessel or cargo, whether or not the property existed when coverage began. Historically, this provision was needed because a vessel or cargo owner could not communicate with a foreign port or another vessel at sea before modern communication devices were available.

lost policy receipt

Insurer Operations. A form signed by a policyholder wishing to surrender a policy that has been lost. The signed receipt then becomes evidence that the policy

© 1991 NILS Publishing Company

is no longer in force and releases the insurer from all liability.

syn: lost policy release

lost policy release

Insurer Operations.

see: lost policy receipt

lower explosive level (LEL)

Loss Control.

see: flammable limits

low load fund

Financial Planning. A mutual fund that charges its participants a moderate sales commission (load).

compare: load fund, no load fund; see: mutual fund

low pressure steam

Loss Control. Steam reaching a pressure of no more than 15 pounds per square inch.

compare: high pressure steam

lump sum

Life. A life insurance provision calling for the benefit to be paid in a single payment rather than in installments.

see: cash refund annuity

lump sum refund annuity

Life.

see: cash refund annuity

211

© 1991 NILS Publishing Company

machine guard

Loss Control. Equipment or devices designed to prevent accidental contact with, or to enclose, moving or hazardous machine parts. Machine guards may be part of the original machine or installed (retrofitted) at some later date.

machinery

Property. Machines in general, or as a functional unit. For insurance purposes three property definitions exist: boiler and machinery, fixed machinery and mobile machinery.

compare: **equipment; see: boiler and machinery, fixed machinery, mobile machinery**

Ocean Marine. The term used to refer to apparatus for propelling a ship, including the ship's boilers, mechanical apparatus, refrigeration equipment and insulation, motors, generators and electrical equipment.

Fr: **machinerie;** Gr: **Maschinen;** Sp: **maquinaria**

machinery and equipment

Property. Coverage that can be included under either a building or personal property policy, for items or equipment that are permanently installed at an insured premises (e.g., heating and air conditioning equipment, engines or shafting).

see: **boiler & machinery insurance**

machinery breakdown insurance

Property.

see: **boiler & machinery insurance**

machine tool

Loss Control. A powered machine, generally metalworking, for making the parts of other machines. The two general classes of machine tools are: cutting tools (lathes, milling machines, grinders, drills, shapers) and forming tools (power press and breaks).

see: **barrier guard, inrunning nip point, point of operation**

MAERP Reinsurance Association

Casualty. Originally titled the Mutual Atomic Energy Reinsurance Pool and now officially known as the MAERP Reinsurance Association. Consists of over 120 mutual insurance company members and provides reinsurance for Mutual Atomic Energy Liability Underwriters (MEALU) and certain mutual fronting companies that write "all-risks" first-party property insurance for nuclear facilities.

syn: **Mutual Atomic Energy Reinsurance Pool;** see: **Mutual Atomic Energy Liability Underwriters**

mail coverage insurance

Inland Marine. Coverage on valuable mail shipments, purchased by financial institutions such as banks and stock brokerage firms. (*ISO Form CM 00 60*)

see: **parcel post insurance, registered mail insurance**

maintenance

Ocean Marine. A maritime term for room and board. It is one of a seaman's remedy while on a voyage.

see: **cure, Jones Act, seaman's remedies**

maintenance bond

Surety. A bond usually posted by a contractor, against defects in workmanship or materials for a stated period (usually two years) after the acceptance of completed work.

see: **faulty workmanship exclusion**

major hospitalization coverage

Health. Medical insurance that provides catastrophic

© 1991 NILS Publishing Company

major hospitalization coverage – continued
coverage for hospital expenses, subject to a large deductible. Full reimbursement is generally provided when the expenses paid by the insured reach the deductible level.

compare: comprehensive medical expense policy

major medical insurance

Health. Medical insurance providing catastrophic coverage for most types of medical expenses, subject to a large deductible. Full reimbursement is generally provided when the expenses paid by the insured reach the deductible level. Sublimits on services such as psychiatric care may be specified in the contract.

compare: basic medical expense, major hospitalization coverage; see: catastrophe policy, comprehensive medical expense policy, supplemental major medical coverage

makeup air

Loss Control. Clean exterior air supplied to a workspace to replace air removed by exhaust ventilation or other industrial processes.

malicious mischief

Property. A coverage included with vandalism insurance. It is the willful damage or destruction of another's property.

see: vandalism and malicious mischief coverage; Fr: dommage causé par acte de malveillance; Gr: Böswilligkeit; Sp: actos por personas mal intencionadas

malingering

Health/Workers' Compensation. Pretending to be ill or disabled, in order to avoid work and to collect insurance benefits or receive such benefits longer than necessary.

malpractice

General. An injurious act resulting from the dereliction of a professional duty or the failure of a professional skill or learning. Misconduct, negligence, or incompetence in the performance of a professional act.

see: malpractice insurance

malpractice arbitration panels

Casualty. A group of individuals selected to have original jurisdiction to hear and decide upon medical malpractice claims.

see: medical review panels

malpractice insurance

Casualty. Insurance for an individual or corporation in a professional field of endeavor. Coverage protects against claims filed with or without foundation, up to the limits of the policy.

see: ambulance service malpractice insurance, errors & omissions insurance, incidental medical malpractice liability, malpractice, malpractice arbitration panels, professional liability insurance

management expense

Reinsurance. A formula-based deduction from a reinsurer's income or profit, used to help defray the reinsurer's overhead expenses before calculation of a contingent commission.

see: ceding commission

managing general agent (MGA)

Insurer Operations. An agent authorized by an insurer to perform the insurance company's underwriting function in a specific geographical territory or for a specialized line of insurance, including the power to appoint and supervise other agents for the company.

compare: general agent; see: agent

managing physician

Health. Under an HMO or PPO plan, participants are either allowed to select a physician from a panel of physicians presented to them, or are assigned a physician who will manage their medical care needs within the HMO or PPO facilities.

see: health maintenance organization, preferred provider organization

mandatory retirement

Employee Benefits.

see: compulsory retirement

mandatory securities valuation reserve

Regulation. A method of valuing life insurance company investments in stocks and bonds, established by the National Association of Insurance Commissioners. This valuation method is designed to moderate the effect of large swings in stock and bond values on an insurer's mandatory reserves.

see: investment reserve, investment valuation reserve, securities valuation

manifest

Ocean Marine. A document prepared by a vessel's Master, listing all bills of lading by number and the type and quantity of all cargo carried by the vessel.

see: bill of lading

manifestation injury theory

Casualty. A theory in law that a claim or occurrence is charged against the policy(s) which were in force when the injury or death became known or manifested itself to the claimant or plaintiff.

see: Keene Doctrine, long-tail liability

© 1991 NILS Publishing Company

manometer

Health.
see: sphygmomanometer
Loss Control. A gauge that measures the pressure of gases and vapors.

manual

Insurer Operations.
see: rate manual

manual excess

Casualty. A table contained in a rate manual which provides rate factors to increase basic limits to higher limits of liability.
see: rate making, rate manual

manual rates

Insurer Operations. Rates contained in a manual published by an insurer or rating organization for a unit of insurance.
compare: "A" rates, judgment rates; see: rate making, rate manual, state exception pages, state rate pages, state territorial pages

manufacturers and contractors liability insurance (M&C)

Casualty. A policy form previously available under the 1973 ISO liability rating plan. The form was designed for less desirable manufacturing and contracting risks to provide limited coverage (i.e., not as broad as the comprehensive general liability form). The form excluded coverage for products and completed operations, independent contractors and structural alterations. The ISO 1986 liability rating plan does not include a similar form.
see: comprehensive general liability policy

manufacturers output policy (MOP)

Property. A commercial property policy covering the personal, off-premises property of a manufacturer, processor or assembler on an "all-risks" basis.

manufacturer's penalty insurance

Financial Guarantee Insurance. A commercial policy covering losses due to the unavailability of a product the insured has contracted to supply or manufacture. Coverage is purchased in amounts based on the contract between the insured and the buyer of the product. The objective is to protect the insured against responsibility for delays in completion due to non-delivery. Coverage is usually a percentage (i.e., 90%) of the penalty amount, but excludes coverage for delays due to a labor dispute.
compare: strike insurance; see: annual supply contract bond

manufacturer's selling price

Property. A method of valuing unsold finished goods: The actual cash value of finished stock manufactured by the insured equals that price (less all discounts and unincurred expenses) for which the stock would have been sold had not loss occurred.
see: actual cash value, selling price clause

manuscript policy

Insurer Operations/Risk Management. An insurance policy designed or tailored specifically for a large commercial insured, or a unique coverage written specifically at the request of a broker or a risk manager.
see: insurance contract, modification of contract; compare: contract of adhesion

map

Insurer Operations. A geographical chart or computerized representation used by an insurance underwriter to locate the area in which a risk is located. A detailed map, giving such details as elevation, soil conditions, terrain, proximity to other structures and to facilities such as airports or hospitals can be of great assistance in the underwriting process.
see: fire map; Sanborn Map Company, Inc.

map clerk

Property. A job position that no longer exists in most insurance companies. Prior to the 1950s, large fire maps (usually published by the Sanborn Map Company, Inc.) were maintained by insurers in their fire underwriting department. An individual from that department (the map clerk) was assigned to maintain these maps and record information concerning which risks were insured by that company and for what limit of liability. This function is now done by computer.
see: map; Sanborn Map Company, Inc.

marine definition

Ocean Marine/Inland Marine.
see: Nationwide Marine Insurance Definition

marine insurance

Inland Marine/Ocean Marine. A broad term including both ocean and inland marine insurance. The Nationwide Marine Insurance Definition, published by the National Association of Insurance Commissioners (NAIC), includes imports, exports, domestic shipments, means of communications, personal property floaters and commercial property floaters as marine insurance.
see: inland marine insurance, instrumentalities of transportation and communication, Nationwide Marine Insurance Definition, ocean marine insurance

marine insurance certificate

Ocean Marine. A certificate of insurance that is issued by the holder of an open cargo policy, which indicates a specific shipment is insured under the policy.

© 1991 NILS Publishing Company

marine insurance certificate — continued
Periodically, copies of the certificate and/or a bordereau is provided to the open cargo policy underwriter.
see: bordereau, declarations, open cargo policy

marine surveyor
Ocean Marine.
see: surveyor

Marine Syndicate B
Ocean Marine. An insurance syndicate created in 1920 by the Federal Maritime Commission. It is comprised of subscribing marine insurers who jointly underwrite certain American steamship vessel risks.
see: American Hull Insurance Syndicate, American Marine Insurance Clearinghouse

marital tax deduction
Financial Planning. A deduction under the federal tax code that allows an estate to be transferred to the surviving spouse without incurring any federal estate tax.
see: qualified terminable interest property trust

maritime
International/Ocean Marine. A term relating to navigation or commerce on the sea.
see: admiralty

market assistance plans (MAPS)
Regulation. Assistance given by the various states to insureds and producers in placing difficult lines of insurance such as medical malpractice, private dwellings, day-care centers and liquor liability coverage in a cooperative effort with insurers. Some states require or request that insurers participate in setting up these underwriting pools. *Examples:* Many states set up MAPs to assist day care facilities find coverage during the early to mid-1980s when such traditional market coverage disappeared.
see: assigned risk, Fair Access to Insurance Requirements, joint underwriting association

marketing department
Insurer Operations. The employees and operations of an insurance company that promote the company's insurance policies and services to potential buyers. Often this department participates in product research, personnel training and advertising.

marketing representative
Agency/Insurer Operations. An individual employed by an insurer to promote business from agents in a specific territory.
syn: field representative, special agent

market value
Property. The value of real or personal property based on the price a willing buyer would pay for the property.
compare: actual cash value, depreciated value, fair market value, functional replacement cost, replacement cost, reproduction cost, tax-appraised value; see: market value clause, valuation of potential property loss

market value clause
Property. Occasionally, property insurance policies are endorsed to allow a loss to be adjusted based on the price a willing buyer would have paid for the damaged or destroyed property, prior to the loss.
compare: actual cash value, replacement cost

masonry noncombustible construction
Loss Control. A structure built with exterior walls made of masonry materials, such as adobe, concrete, stone, tile, block or other materials. Other building components such as floors and the roof are often made with noncombustible materials.
see: construction

Mass Marketing Insurance Institute (MMII)
Organizations. Members: Independent brokers, insurers and other companies who sell their products through mass marketing techniques. *Objectives:* Disseminating mass marketing information and techniques. *Founded:* 1969. *Headquarters:* Kansas City, MO.

mass merchandising
Insurer Operations. An insurance marketing method which involves selling to an entire group of people, usually employees of a single company, members of a union or trade association, to insure as many members of the group with one insurer. Premiums are then deducted automatically from the payroll.
see: mass underwriting

mass underwriting
Insurer Operations. A method of underwriting that examines the demographic qualities of a group for its insurability, rather than the qualities of an individual.
see: mass merchandising, underwriting

master
Ocean Marine. Under admiralty law, the captain of a ship.

master air waybill
Aviation/Inland Marine. An air waybill issued by an originating airline when more than one airline is involved with a shipment, or when a freight forwarder issues a house waybill.
see: air waybill, house waybill, waybill

216

© 1991 NILS Publishing Company

master insurance policy

Property. The original complete policy contract issued to a property owner, to which underlying policies are issued to comply with the insurance requirements of mortgage holders.

Employee Benefits. The original complete policy issued to an employer, to which certificates of insurance are issued to its employees as evidence that they are included under an employee benefit insurance program.

Insurer Operations. An original, complete insurance policy contract that is issued by an insurer with the understanding that certificates of insurance or underlying policies will be issued to other parties.

syn: group contract; compare: **certificate of insurance, group certificate, underlying insurance policy**

master servant rule

Casualty. A rule requiring employers to be responsible for the acts committed by their employees while at work. Bodily injury, property damage and third-party liability damages fall under this rule.

see: **employee, respondeat superior**

material fact

General. A fact of such importance, that were it revealed, an underwriting decision or loss settlement would be altered.

see: **material misrepresentation**

material misrepresentation

General. The misrepresentation of a material fact to an insurer, which, were it discovered, a policy would likely be voided.

see: **concealment, contribute-to-the-loss statute, election to avoid a policy, material fact, representation**

maternity benefit

Health. Coverage provided under some health insurance policies for childbirth expenses. Many policies pay only a fixed amount, while others provide coverage based on actual expenses.

see: **childbirth, flat maternity benefit, swap maternity**

mature

Life. A life insurance policy is said to mature when the policy benefits are payable, such as upon the insured's death or a specified benefit payment date.

compare: **paid-up insurance; see: maturity date**

Employee Benefits. An employee group that has attained stability as to the distribution of age within the group. When it is mature, the group is close to having the same number of individuals of the same age year after year.

mature policies

Casualty. Claims-made insurance policies that have been continuously in force for at least five years with a retroactive date going back to the first claims-made policy. A mature claims-made policy is not eligible for rating credits assigned to immature policies.

compare: **immature policies; see: claims-made form**

maturity date

Life. The date a life insurance policy's benefits are payable because of the insured's death or because a specified benefit payment date has been reached.

see: **policy period**

maturity value

Life. The amount due an insured under an ordinary life insurance policy who has lived beyond a specified age; the amount due an insured at the end of an endorsement period.

maximum allowable concentration (MAC)

Loss Control. The concentration of an atmospheric contaminant during an eight-hour period below which it is unlikely that ill effects will be experienced by any except hypersensitive individuals.

maximum deductible contribution

Employee Benefits. The maximum contribution allowed by an employer to an employee under a salary reduction plan. The employer can set the amount to an amount less than the IRS maximum.

maximum disability income policy

Health. A noncancellable disability income insurance policy with a maximum limit of liability for any one claim, but no lifetime aggregate limit for multiple claims.

see: **disability income insurance**

maximum foreseeable loss

Loss Control/Property.

see: **maximum possible loss**

maximum line

Insurer Operations.

see: **gross line**

maximum period of indemnity

Property. An endorsement to the business income coverage form, which deletes the required coinsurance. The coinsurance requirement is replaced with coverage for the actual loss sustained during the initial 120 days after a loss up to the provided limit of liability.

compare: **monthly limit of indemnity; see: business income coverage form**

© 1991 NILS Publishing Company

maximum plan limits

Employee Benefits. Maximum benefits that would be paid to health plan participant(s). The maximum benefits limit will fall into one of the following definitions: 1) Defined maximum limit; 2) per cause (disability) maximum limit; or 3) all causes maximum limit.

see: **all causes maximum limit, per cause maximum limit**

maximum possible loss

Loss Control/Property. The worst possible loss that could occur under a policy. *Example:* It is assumed that in the event of a fire, the fire department did not respond, automatic sprinklers did not operate and fire divisions failed.

syn: **maximum foreseeable loss; compare: probable maximum loss**

maximum premium

Insurer Operations. The highest premium amount an insurance company can charge for a policy that is subject to an audit or a unique rating plan.

see: **maximum retrospective premium, premium**

maximum probable loss

Loss Control/Property.

see: **probable maximum loss**

maximum retrospective premium

Casualty/Workers' Compensation. The maximum premium that a policyholder would be required to pay under a retrospective rating plan, regardless of the amount of incurred losses. Usually the maximum is expressed as a percentage of premium (e.g., 110%, 125%, 150% of premium).

compare: **minimum retrospective premium;** see: **retrospective penalty insurance, retrospective rating plan**

maxi tail

Casualty. A provision contained in some claims-made policies that permits the insured an unlimited length of time to report a claim under the policy after its termination.

syn: **full tail, unlimited reporting period, unlimited tail;** see: **basic extended reporting period, claims-made form, extended reporting period, midi tail, mini tail, tail**

McCarran-Ferguson Act

Regulation. Federal legislation (15 USC Sections 1011 *et seq.*) enacted by Congress in 1945 to permit the states to continue the regulation of the insurance business after the Supreme Court, in the *U.S. v. South-*

Eastern Underwriters Association decision, had declared insurance to be interstate commerce and therefore eligible for federal regulation. Under the Act, insurance is exempt from some federal anti-trust statutes to the extent that it is regulated by the states. The exemption involves data gathering in concert for the purpose of ratemaking. Otherwise, the anti-trust laws prohibit insurers from boycotting, acting coercively or engaging in violations of the Sherman or Clayton Acts.

syn: **Public Law 15;** see: **anti-trust laws, Sherman Antitrust Act**

McClintock Table

Life. A life insurance mortality table developed by McClinton McClintock in 1896, based upon the experience of fifteen United States life insurers.

see: **mortality table**

mean

Risk Management. The expected average outcome after many exposures to chance. *Formula:* Mean = Sum of a Series of Numbers/The Number of Numbers in the Series.

syn: **arithmetic mean; compare: median, mode;** see: **central limit theorem**

mean reserve

Life. A life insurance reserve which is based on the average of the initial reserve and the terminal reserve for a life insurance policy.

compare: **initial reserve, terminal reserve**

mechanic's lien

Property.

see: **encumbrance**

median

Risk Management. A statistical term for the "middle most" or "most central" value of a set of numbers. It is the value halfway between two central observations.

compare: **mean, mode**

mediator

General.

see: **arbitrator**

Medicaid

Health. State medical benefit programs for individuals, regardless of age, whose income and resources are insufficient to pay for health care. As of January 1, 1966, federal matching funds were provided to the states for these programs under Title XIX of the Social Security Act.

syn: **Title XIX Benefits; compare: Medicare**

© 1991 NILS Publishing Company

medical deductible workers' compensation plan

Workers' Compensation. A form of deductible workers' compensation coverage where the policy deductible applies only to workers' compensation medical benefits.

compare: indemnity deductible workers' compensation plan; see: deductible workers' compensation plans

medical examination

General. A routine preventative examination or "check up" performed by a medical doctor on a patient to determine potential health or medical problems.

Employee Benefits. 1) A medical examination required and paid for by an employer on a prospective employee to determine his or her ability to perform a particular job.
2) A medical examination offered and paid for by an employer on a periodic basis to an employee as an employee benefit.

Health/Life. A medical examination required and paid for by a life or health insurance company on an applicant or claimant to determine acceptability for coverage or eligibility for benefits.

see: examined business, paramedical examination

medical examiner

Health/Life. A public officer who makes postmortem examinations of bodies to determine the cause of death.

medical expense insurance

Health. Health insurance covering medical, surgical and hospital costs.

see: hospital-surgical expense insurance

medical expense limit

Casualty. The highest amount recoverable under the ISO commercial general liability coverage form for medical payments to any one person – usually $1,000 or $5,000.

see: commercial general liability form, medical payments

medical expense reversionary trust

Casualty. A trust which a defendant as trustor establishes to make funds available for the actual medical needs of the plaintiff. Funds remaining in the trust after the death of the plaintiff revert, in whole or in part, back to the defendant. This is particularly useful in cases involving a potential for substantial future medical expenses, because it avoids a "windfall" to the plaintiff's estate.

see: structured settlement, trust

Medical Information Bureau (MIB)

Organizations/Health. *Members:* Health and life insurers. *Objectives:* Serves as a central computerized data base for storing the health histories of persons who have applied for insurance from subscribing companies. *Founded:* 1938. *Headquarters:* Westwood, MA.

see: Fire and Theft Index Bureau, Insurance Crime Prevention Institute, Insurance Services Office, interinsurer claim service organization, National Automobile Theft Bureau, Property Insurance Loss Register,

medical liability indemnity associations

Casualty. Any association, corporation or interindemnity trust formed by physicians, hospitals or other health care providers. Such associations mutually insure against claims arising from any aspect of professional practice, including public liability and medical malpractice claims.

medical licensing boards

Casualty. Composed of physicians and other specialists in a broad field of medical practice, these boards certify medical doctors as fit and able to practice medicine within their discipline. Also included are boards of medical osteopathic or podiatry examiners.

see: board certified

medical payments

Automobile. Medical and funeral expense coverage for individuals who sustain bodily injury from or while occupying an insured vehicle, regardless of the insured's negligence. Coverage is most commonly limited to $1,000 or $5,000. Coverage on personal automobile policies follows the insured, spouse and members of the household as passenger in other vehicles and as pedestrians if they are hit by an automobile.

syn: automobile medical payments

Casualty. Coverage for medical expenses to individuals who sustain bodily injury at an insured's premises or operations without regard to negligence. Medical expenses include first aid, surgery, x-rays, dental services, prosthetic devices, transportation by ambulance and funeral services. Coverage is included in the ISO commercial general liability form, as Coverage Part C and in homeowners' policies usually with a limit of $5,000.

see: commercial general liability form, medical expense limit

medical review panels

Casualty. Advisory panels usually established by the state which review and determine the validity of medical malpractice claims prior to the filing of such actions.

see: malpractice arbitration panels

219

medical service plan

Health. A plan by which medical services are rendered by participating physicians and other health personnel. The plan is funded from periodic payments made by the plan's members or subscribers.

see: health maintenance organization, preferred provider organization

Medicare

Health. A federally administered hospital insurance program and supplementary medical insurance for the aged (individuals over 65) created by 1965 amendments to the Social Security Act.

syn: Title XVIII of Social Security Act; compare: Medicaid

Medicare supplement policy

Health. A private insurance policy purchased by Medicare participants on a voluntary basis which covers medical and health services not covered by Medicare.

syn: medigap insurance

medigap insurance

Health.

see: Medicare supplement policy

membership termination

Employee Benefits. Discontinuance of membership in an organization or group. Such termination usually includes cessation of eligibility under a group policy (e.g., due to termination of employment or other changing circumstances) as well as voluntary withdrawal from an organization.

memorandum clause

Ocean Marine. An ocean marine cargo policy provision which acts like a deductible and does not hold an underwriter responsible for a cargo loss until the loss exceeds a specified percentage of the cargo's value.

mental anguish

General. An agonizing mental or emotional experience caused by a specific incident.

see: mental distress

mental disorder

Health. An emotional or organic mental impairment, other than retardation.

mental distress

Casualty. A painful mental or emotional experience caused by a specific incident (such as being involved in an automobile accident or seeing a family member killed). Often compensation for mental distress is included in court awards to claimants.

syn: emotional distress; see: mental anguish

mercantile open-stock burglary insurance

Crime. An obsolete crime form which covered a merchant's equipment and furniture from burglary and could be endorsed to include robbery and theft. This form has been replaced by the storekeepers burglary and robbery form.

syn: open-stock burglary policy; see: crime coverages, mercantile robbery insurance, mercantile safe burglary insurance, storekeepers burglary and robbery

mercantile robbery insurance

Crime. An obsolete crime form which covered loss by robbery committed on the premises of a merchant. This form has been replaced by the storekeepers burglary and robbery form.

see: burglary, crime coverages, mercantile open-stock burglary insurance, mercantile safe burglary insurance, messenger robbery insurance, robbery, storekeepers burglary and robbery

mercantile safe burglary insurance

Crime. An obsolete crime form which provided coverage if a merchant's safe was forcibly entered. This form has been replaced by the robbery and safe burglary form.

see: crime coverages, robbery and safe burglary form

merger

General. Any combination that forms one company from two or more previously existing companies.

see: articles of merger or consolidation, upstream merger, vertical merger

merger of plans

Employee Benefits. A merger or consolidation of two or more employee benefit plans. Such a merger can be accomplished if each participant receives benefits at least equal to those that would have been received prior to the merger or consolidation.

syn: consolidation of plans; see: plan sponsor

merit rating

Insurer Operations. A rating system used in several types of insurance that determines the insured's premium based on the insured's past loss record.

see: rate making

messenger robbery insurance

Crime. A variation of crime insurance covering money and other property against robbery away from the premises of the insured business (e.g., an employee is robbed while on the way to make a bank deposit).

see: robbery, securities, securities deposited with others coverage form

© 1991 NILS Publishing Company

Mexican automobile endorsement

Automobile. An endorsement that can be added to automobile policies, extending coverage across the U.S. border for 25 miles into Mexico. This coverage is not recognized by Mexican authorities as satisfying their financial responsibility requirements. When automobile coverage is also purchased from a Mexican insurance company, this endorsement's coverage is considered excess to the Mexican policy.

see: **Mexican automobile insurance**

Mexican automobile insurance

Automobile. United States citizens driving their autos into Mexico may be subject to detention by Mexican authorities following an accident, because insurance policies issued by U.S. insurers do not satisfy Mexican financial responsibility laws. Short-term automobile policies issued by Mexican insurance companies may be purchased at most border crossings at a reasonable cost, to protect U.S. citizens.

see: **international market categories, Mexican automobile endorsement**

midi tail

Casualty. A provision in some claims-made policies giving the insured an extended, but not unlimited, reporting period; generally longer than sixty days.

see: **claims-made form, extended reporting period, maxi tail, mini tail, tail**

military service exclusion

Health/Life. An exclusion in most life and health insurance policies excluding payment of benefits for death or injuries caused by military service during time of war.

see: **war clause, war risk accident insurance**

mill construction

Property. A type of building construction used in older factories and warehouses. A mill building is constructed of heavy timbers and masonry walls with no concealed wall spaces. It is considered a superior class of construction for fire insurance purposes.

see: **construction**

mill fever

Workers' Compensation.
see: **byssinosis**

Million Dollar Round Table (MDRT)

Organizations. Members: Life insurance agents who have sold $1 million or more in life insurance. *Objectives:* Recognizes life insurance agents who meet the organization's qualifications. *Founded:* 1927. *Headquarters:* Park Ridge, IL.

minimum amount policy

Life. A life insurance policy with a relatively high minimum face amount (i.e., $100,000, $300,000), allowing the rate for each thousand dollars of coverage to be lower than for policies with small face amounts. Theoretically, an insurance company's administrative expenses do not increase proportionately with the face amount of a policy.

see: **quantity discount**

minimum benefit

Employee Benefits. A minimum annuity amount that must be paid under some pension plans if the benefit formula produces a lesser amount. Usually, some minimum service period is required before the plan minimum benefit level applies.

minimum coverage clauses

Insurer Operations. Clauses stating that, notwithstanding any other terms and conditions of the policy, the coverage afforded shall be at least as extensive as the minimum coverage required by state statutes.

see: **legislated insurance coverage, policy condition laws**

minimum coverages

Casualty. Dollar amount minimum limits of coverage required in a liability insurance policy.

minimum funding

Employee Benefits. A minimum amount which an employer must contribute to a defined benefit, money purchase, or target benefit pension plan. A penalty in the form of an excise tax will be assessed against an employer who fails to contribute the minimum funding amount.

minimum funding standard

Employee Benefits. As respects an approved pension plan, the lesser of: 1) the excess of the total charges to the funding standard account for all plan years (beginning with the first plan year to which the funding provisions apply) over the total credits to such account for such years, or 2) the excess of the total charges to the alternative minimum funding standard account for such plan years over the total credits to such account for such years.

see: **accumulated funding deficiency, funding standard account, minimum funding**

minimum group

General/Regulation. The minimum number of individuals required to form a group insurance program under state law. Or, the minimum number of individuals required before an insurance company will issue a group insurance policy.

see: **discretionary groups, fictitious group, true group insurance**

minimum participation standards

Employee Benefits. Standards that apply to a qualified single employer pension plan that bases eligibility

© 1991 NILS Publishing Company

minimum participation standards – continued
for participation on age and service, which require that such a plan may not deny or delay participation beyond the time an employee achieves 25 years of age and has completed a year of credited service. In the event a plan provides full and immediate vesting of all accrued benefits, the denial of participation may be extended until the employee achieves 25 years and three years of credited service.

minimum premium

Insurer Operations. The lowest premium amount for which an insurance company will issue an insurance policy or will include a coverage within a policy.

see: loss constant, premium

minimum rate

Insurer Operations. The lowest rate which an insurer will charge for a specific coverage regardless of available protection or credits. Or, the rate that is applied to the lowest hazard risk.

see: loss constant, rate making

minimum retirement age

Employee Benefits.

see: normal retirement age

minimum retrospective premium

Casualty/Workers' Compensation. The minimum premium that a policyholder would be required to pay under a retrospective rating plan, even if there were no incurred losses. Usually, the minimum is expressed as a percentage of premium (e.g., 18 percent, 22 percent, or 30 percent of premium).

compare: maximum retrospective premium; see: retrospective rating plan

mini tail

Casualty. A provision in some claims-made policies granting the insured a very limited (i.e., 30 to 60 days) extended reporting period. The mini-tail provision will run concurrently with the midi-tail or maxi-tail.

see: claims-made form, extended reporting period, maxi tail, midi tail, tail

minor's compromise

General. A proposed settlement of a minor's claim which must be approved by a court.

see: settlement

miscellaneous hospital expenses

Health. Expenses involving hospital care other than room, board and doctors' fees, such as lab tests, drugs and radiology. Most hospital policies limit coverage for these expenses by scheduling the amounts covered or combining them for a specific maximum limit.

miscellaneous vehicles coverage

Automobile. Coverage that can be endorsed to a personal automobile policy to extend such coverage to other personal vehicles such as mopeds and motorcycles.

misdemeanor

Crime. A crime less serious than a felony; an offense in violation of law, punishable by fine and/or a relatively short term of imprisonment.

compare: felony

misrepresentation

General. A false oral or written statement with intent to defraud.

see: contribute-to-the-loss statute, election to avoid a policy, material misrepresentation, representation

misstatement of age

Life. An incorrect (usually lower) age given at the time a life insurance application is completed. When a misstatement of age is determined, the insurer will adjust the in-force policy to reflect the premium and coverages that would have applied if the correct age was known when the policy was issued.

see: age-adjustment clause

mobile equipment

Casualty. A term applied to any land vehicle (including attached machinery or apparatus) self-propelled or not which is not subject to motor vehicle registration. Also includes such vehicles or equipment when they are maintained for use exclusively on premises owned by or rented to the named insured, including the roadways immediately adjoining, or when they are designed for use principally off public roads, or vehicles or trailers whose sole purpose is to transport equipment attached to subject vehicles, such as power cranes, concrete mixers, air compressors and generators. Liability arising out of the operation of mobile equipment is usually covered by a general liability policy and is specifically excluded from automobile liability policies.

Property. Contractors' equipment, autos, aircraft, boats and ships, and other mobile machinery.

see: equipment floater, machinery

mobile home policy

Casualty/Property. A package policy, similar to a homeowner's policy, written on a permanently located mobile home.

see: homeowner's policy

mobile machinery

Property. Machinery that is readily movable and often covered by inland marine insurance.

© 1991 NILS Publishing Company

mode

General. A manner, method, approach or procedure used to accomplish a task.

Risk Management. The value with the highest probability; the outcome most likely to occur.

compare: mean, median

Model Insurers Supervision, Rehabilitation, and Liquidation Act of 1977

Regulation. A model act developed by the National Association of Insurance Commissioners, designed to provide state insurance regulators with the powers they need to deal with a financially troubled insurance company. The Act indicates the grounds for placing insurers in liquidation or in rehabilitation and sets standards to be followed when there are several insurance departments claimants from several jurisdictions involved in the liquidation of an insurer. Also sets forth order in which entities holding claims against an insolvent insurer will be paid.

see: liquidation, liquidation distribution, rehabilitation

mode of premium payment

Insurer Operations.

see: premium payment mode

modification of contract

Insurer Operations. An agreement whereby a standard insurance policy is changed to include special provisions for larger accounts or special programs. Such modifications may be instituted by the underwriter to attract more business or by an insurer or broker to handle unique exposures.

compare: contract of adhesion; see: insurance contract, manuscript policy

modification rating

Property. A property insurance rating method by which published manual rates are modified or adjusted by a classification factor and/or experience factor to determine a final policy rate.

see: experience rating plan, merit rating, rate making, retrospective rating plan, schedule rating

modified cash refund annuity

Employee Benefits/Life.

see: modified refund annuity

modified fire resistive construction

Loss Control. Buildings where the exterior walls, floors, and roof are constructed of masonry or fire resistant material, with a fire resistant rating of one hour or more, but less than two hours.

see: construction

modified life insurance

Life. An ordinary life insurance policy with premiums adjusted so that during the first three to five years, the premiums are lower than a standard policy, and in subsequent years are higher than a standard policy.

see: graded premium, ordinary life insurance

modified prior approval rating

Regulation. One of four generally recognized methods of rate approval used by state regulators. This method requires prior approval of rates, but allows new rates to go into effect immediately after filing without having to wait for official approval.

compare: prior approval rating; see: file-and-use rating, open competition rating, rate regulation

modified refund annuity

Employee Benefits. Form of annuity commonly used by contributory pension or employee benefit plans where, if an employee dies after retirement, their beneficiary or estate will receive an amount equal to the accumulated value of the employee's own plan contributions, with or without interest up to their retirement date, less the total retirement benefits they received prior to death.

syn: modified cash refund annuity; see: annuity

money

Crime. As defined in crime insurance forms, money is currency, coins and bank notes in current use with a face value; traveler's checks and registered checks; and money orders held for sale to the public. Older policy forms also included bullion in the definition of money.

see: Eurodollars, exchange rate

money and securities broad form insurance

Crime. A form of crime insurance covering loss by theft, disappearance or destruction of the insured's money and securities inside the insured's premises as well as outside the insured's premises while in the custody of a messenger.

syn: disappearance and destruction coverage form; see: crime coverages, theft

money damages

General. Court awards in a liability suit which are broken down between compensatory and punitive damages.

syn: pecuniary damages; see: damages

money orders and counterfeit paper insurance

Crime. A form of crime insurance covering loss due to an acceptance in good faith of any money order which has been issued or is purported to have been issued by

money orders and counterfeit paper insurance —
continued
> a post office or express company. Also covered is
> acceptance of counterfeit paper currency of the Unit-
> ed States or Canada.
>> see: alteration bond, forgery bond

money purchase plan
Employee Benefits. A pension plan where the employer's contributions are assigned to a specific employee's account and his or her final benefits are based
on the final funds in each individual's account.
> compare: target benefit plan; see: benefit plan,
> civil damages

monoline policy
Insurer Operations. An insurance policy that provides coverage for a single line of insurance.
> compare: multiple line policy, package policy

monopolistic markets
International.
> see: international market categories

monopolistic state fund
Workers' Compensation. A state-operated insurance
fund in those states having laws that require all
businesses to buy workers' compensation insurance
from the state. Private insurers cannot operate in
these monopolistic fund states: Nevada, North Dakota, Ohio, Puerto Rico, Washington, West Virginia
and Wyoming.
> compare: competitive state funds

monthly debit ordinary life insurance
(MDO)
Life. Debit life insurance where premiums are collected (usually at the home of the policyholder) on a
monthly basis.
> see: industrial life insurance

monthly limit of indemnity
Property. An endorsement to the business income
coverage form, which deletes the coinsurance requirement and replaces it with a provision that recovery is
limited during each 30-day period to a preselected
percentage of the business income limits. This coverage form is designed for insureds having material
monthly income fluctuations.
> compare: maximum period of indemnity; see:
> business income coverage form

mooring
Aviation. A term found in aircraft policies for water-
alighting aircraft, when they are on water and are
anchored or moored, or during launching onto or
hauling up from the water, except under its own
power or momentum.

Ocean Marine. 1) A pier, wharf, or weighted buoy or
other such device or structure to which a vessel is
secured.
2) The act of securing a vessel to a mooring buoy,
wharf, pier or dock by chains or ropes.

moral hazard
Property. Circumstances of morals or habits which
increase the probability of a loss from an insured peril.
Example: An insured previously convicted of arson.
> see: hazard

morale hazard
Property. An increase in the hazards presented by a
risk, arising from the insured's indifference to loss
because of the existence of insurance. *Example:* An
insured fails to repair faulty wiring, believing it is less
expensive to pay insurance premiums than to pay an
electrician.
> see: hazard

morbidity
Life. The frequency of the incidence of disease, illness
or sickness.
> compare: mortality; see: morbidity table

morbidity assumption
Health/Life. A statistical projection of future illness,
sickness, and disease.
> compare: morbidity rate

morbidity rate
Health/Life. A rate of incidence of sickness to the
number of well people in a given group of people
(usually 100,000) over a specified period of time.
> compare: morbidity assumption; see: expected
> morbidity

morbidity table
Health/Life. A table showing the number of individuals exposed to the risk of illness, sickness, and disease
at each age, and the actual number of individuals who
incurred an illness, sickness, and disease at each age.
> compare: morbidity assumption, morbidity
> rate; see: natural premium

mortality
Life. The ratio of deaths to a specific population. The
number of deaths resulting from specific types of
illness or disease.
> syn: death rate; see: life expectancy, mortality
> table, normal life expectancy; compare:
> morbidity

mortality assumption
Life. An actuarial assumption of the probability of
death at given ages.
> syn: death rate; compare: mortality rate

© 1991 NILS Publishing Company

mortality rate

Life. The relationship of the frequency of deaths of individual members of a group to the entire group membership over a particular time period.

compare: mortality assumption; see: expected mortality, life expectancy

mortality savings

Life. The number which results when actual experienced mortality is subtracted from expected mortality. *Formula:* Mortality Savings = Expected Mortality – Actual Mortality.

mortality table

Life. A table which indicates the number of individuals within a specified group of individuals (males, females, airline pilots, etc.), starting at a certain age, who are expected to be alive at a succeeding age. It will indicate the "natural premium" for an individual applying for life insurance.

compare: morbidity table; see: American Annuitants Mortality Table, American Experience Table of Mortality, American Men Table, annuity table, Annuity Table for 1949, Commissioners Standard Ordinary Table, graduated life table, increased limits table, McClintock Table, National Fraternal Congress Mortality Rate Table, natural premium, select mortality table, smoker and nonsmoker mortality table, special mortality table, ultimate mortality table, z table

mortgage

Mortgage Insurance. A formal written instrument executed by a borrower (mortgagor) on behalf of a lender (mortgagee) that establishes a lien on the property allowing the lender to receive title to it in the event that the borrower is unable to repay the lender.

see: encumbrance, lien, mortgagee, mortgagor, second mortgage

mortgage banker

Mortgage Insurance. An organization that originates mortgage loans and then sells the loans to investors. Frequently the mortgage banker will service the loans sold and receive both origination and service fees.

mortgage bonds

Financial Planning. Debt instruments, used by a business entity to raise cash, which are secured by a pledge of properties and real estate assets.

mortgage correspondent

Mortgage Insurance. A lending institution agent who is authorized to process and service mortgage loans.

mortgagee

Mortgage Insurance. The person to whom property is mortgaged; that is, the person who extends credit to another, based on the other party's possession of collateral property.

compare: mortgagor; see: loss payee

mortgagee clause

Property. An endorsement attached to a fire or other direct damage policy that covers mortgaged property, specifying that 1) the loss reimbursement shall be paid to the mortgagee as the mortgagee's interest may appear, 2) that the mortgagee's rights of recovery shall not be defeated by any act or neglect of the insured, and giving the mortgagee other rights, privileges, and duties.

see: certificate of insurance, loss payable clause, noncontribution mortgage clause, underlying insurance policy

mortgage guarantee insurance

Mortgage Insurance. Insurance that indemnifies a lender from loss if a borrower fails to meet required mortgage payments. Typically, the mortgagee must report to the insurer when the mortgagor is two months in default. Should foreclosure be required, the mortgagee usually must acquire title to the property before the claim is paid.

mortgage insurance

Mortgage Insurance. A reducing term life or life and disability policy whose benefits are designed to 1) pay the balance due on a mortgage upon the death or injury of the insured; or 2) meet monthly payments on a mortgage upon death or disability of the insured.

syn: mortgage redemption insurance; see: collateral assignment, credit health insurance, credit life insurance

Mortgage Insurance Companies of America (MICA)

Organizations. Members: Mortgage insurance companies. *Objectives:* Promotes interests of its members before state and federal regulatory agencies. *Founded:* 1973. *Headquarters:* Washington, D.C.

mortgage redemption insurance

Health/Life.

see: mortgage insurance

mortgagor

Mortgage Insurance. A person who mortgages property; that is, the person who receives credit from another and pledges property as collateral.

compare: mortgagee

motor truck cargo insurance

Inland Marine. A form of inland marine insurance covering cargo while being transported in a truck. There are two basic forms – the Carrier's Form and the Owner's Form. The Carrier's Form covers a common carrier's legal liability for damage to or destruction of a

225

© 1991 NILS Publishing Company

motor truck cargo insurance — continued
customer's property, when that property is being transported as prescribed by the Federal Motor Carrier Act of 1935 and 1980. It does not insure against any loss for which the trucker is not legally liable. Statutory law requires a truckman to carry a minimum amount of coverage. The Owner's Form covers truck owners against loss or damage to their own property while being transported. It pays for the loss or damage of cargo for the perils insured against, regardless of the legal liability.

syn: carrier's form, owner's form; see: cargo insurance, Federal Motor Carrier Act

motor truck cargo radioactive contamination insurance
Inland Marine. A form of inland marine insurance covering a common carrier for damage or destruction due to radioactive contamination from commercial radioisotopes to property being transported.

motor vehicle record (MVR)
Automobile. Records maintained by a state motor vehicle department of a driver's accidents and traffic violations.

movable barrier guard
Loss Control. A barrier guard designed to enclose the point of operation of machinery or equipment completely, before the clutch can be engaged.

syn: gate guard; see: barrier guard

movie completion bond
Financial Guarantee Insurance. A form of financial guarantee insurance, which provides assurance to the financial backers of a motion picture that it will be completed on time.

moving average rating method
Risk Management. A rate development method which smooths out irregularities in data, such as nonhomogeneous exposure units, unrepresentative historical losses, adverse selection of data, social inflation and distortions resulting from misleading averages.

see: adverse selection, homogeneous exposure units

multiemployer plan
Employee Benefits. A plan maintained pursuant to a collective bargaining agreement to which two or more employers contribute. Plan contributions by an employer must be detailed in a labor agreement. Within one year of enactment of a plan, it may irrevocably elect not to be treated as a multiemployer plan if it was categorized as a single employer plan for each of the last three years.

see: multiemployer welfare association

multiemployer welfare association (MEWA)
Employee Benefits. Formerly known as a multiemployer trust (MET), MEWAs are formal trusts for self-funding a corporate group benefit plan that covers medical and dental insurance and pensions. Generally a MEWA is geared toward small employers and is regulated by the Department of Labor under ERISA, not state insurance regulators.

compare: multiemployer plan

multinational absolute liability
International. The emerging theory that extends the doctrine of strict or absolute liability, as it is known in the U.S., to subsidiaries or affiliated companies of American corporations.

see: multinational corporation

multinational corporation (MNC)
International. A corporation that has significant operations, investments, or revenues from countries other than its country of origin. A multinational corporation will encourage local participation in their operation as compared to corporations that operate in, or export to foreign countries, but do not have an international business philosophy.

see: multinational absolute liability

multi-peril crop insurance (MPCI)
Property. An archaic term covering what is now open perils crop insurance.

see: crop-hail insurance, crop insurance, open perils crop insurance

multi-peril policies
Insurer Operations. Policies that provide coverage for more than one peril in a single contract.

multiple indemnity
Life. A life insurance policy provision under which certain benefits are increased by a stated multiple (double, triple) when death results from an accident. Some policies require a more specific circumstance such as an accident involving a public conveyance.

syn: accidental death benefit, double indemnity; compare: double protection life insurance

multiple line law
Regulation. Legislation adopted in all states which allows an insurer to underwrite both property and casualty insurance. Prior to this legislation most states only allowed an insurer to be licensed for either property insurance or casualty insurances, but not both.

see: line

multiple line policy
Insurer Operations. A policy which insures more than one line of insurance, such as property and

226

© 1991 NILS Publishing Company

casualty. A package policy or the ISO commercial lines policies are examples of multiple lines policies.

compare: monoline policy; see: line, package policy

multiple location policy

Property. A policy which provides coverage on more than one location of the insured.

multiple location rating plan

Property. A rating method used to rate property insurance policies which provides coverage on five or more individual, dispersed locations. It allows a credit for the reduced hazard because of the dispersed locations, and lower insurer expenses in writing a large amount of premium under a single policy.

syn: premium and dispersion credit plan; see: premium discount, rate making

multiple protection life insurance

Life. A life insurance policy which 1) combines both term and whole life insurance; 2) pays a multiple of the face amount during the term policy period; and 3) converts to a whole life policy after a specified period of time. During the initial years – when both the term and whole life policies are in force – the multiple protection period is in effect.

multiple retirement ages

Employee Benefits. Ages at which, under some pension plans, an employee can retire and receive full benefits without reduction or penalty.

see: deferred retirement, early retirement, normal retirement age

multiple table extra premium

Health. A method of providing health insurance for insureds who are substandard risks. The rate used is developed by increasing the premium by a multiple of a standard premium. Under this method the insurance policy is issued without excluding particular risks from coverage.

municipal bond insurance

Financial Guarantee Insurance. Coverage that guarantees bondholders against default by a municipality. This form of financial guarantee was introduced in the early 1970s. Municipalities embraced it because their offerings took on the credit rating of the company that wrote the insurance, rather than their own ratings. It meant that most municipal bond offerings were elevated to Triple-A, and municipalities could raise money at a lower rate of interest. For investors, it made municipal bonds less risky.

see: municipal bonds

municipal bonds

Financial Planning. Bonds issued by counties, municipalities, water districts, school districts or other public authorities below the state level. They are long-term promissory notes with their interest payments exempt from federal income taxes. State and local income taxes are exempt within the state of issue.

see: municipal bond insurance

municipal insurance

Insurer Operations. Insurance coverage for cities or municipalities.

see: public entity insurance

musical instrument dealers coverage

Inland Marine.

see: camera and musical instrument dealers coverage

mutual assent

General.

see: acceptance

Mutual Atomic Energy Liability Underwriters (MAELU)

Organizations. Members: Casualty insurance companies who write nuclear energy liability coverage. *Objectives:* Providing atomic energy liability insurance. *Founded:* 1956. *Headquarters:* Chicago, IL.

see: MAERP Reinsurance Association

Mutual Atomic Energy Reinsurance Pool

Casualty.

see: MAERP Reinsurance Association

mutual benefit association

Insurer Operations. An association organized to provide benefits to its members under a plan which does not prefund the benefit (life insurance), but rather levies an assessment on members after a specific loss occurs.

mutual fund

Financial Planning. An investment company or trust which combines many investor's contributions, to invest in any one or a combination of stocks, bonds, commodities, options, money market funds, precious metals or securities in foreign corporations. The funds are managed by professional money managers whose services would generally not be available to smaller investors.

syn: crime coverage form C, investment company, mutual investment trust; see: closed-end mutual fund, liquidation charge, load fund, low load fund, no load fund, open-end mutual fund

mutual fund insurance

Financial Guarantee Insurance. A form of financial guarantee insurance that guarantees the repayment of the principal invested in the fund.

© 1991 NILS Publishing Company

mutual insurance company

Insurer Operations. An insurance company that has no capital stock, but rather is owned by its policyholders who elect a board of directors or trustees through whom business is conducted. Any earnings belong to the policyholders and may be distributed to them as policy dividends or reduced premiums.

compare: **reciprocal insurance exchange, stock insurance company**; see: **assessment mutual, demutualization, farmers mutual insurers, mutualization**

mutual investment trust

General.

see: **mutual fund**

mutualization

Insurer Operations. The converting of an insurance company's ownership structure from a stock insurance company to a mutual insurance company, by having the stock company buy up all the shares of the stock and retiring them.

compare: **demutualization**

mutual mortgage insurance fund

Mortgage Insurance. A fund – managed by the Federal Housing Administration – which insures mortgages on homes, property improvement loans and disaster relief loans.

mysterious disappearance

Crime/Inland Marine. A disappearance of property without knowledge as to the location, time or how the property was lost. Mysterious disappearances (or losses that cannot be identified as to time and place) are excluded from most "all-risk" property and inland marine policies.

see: **disappearance**

228

© 1991 NILS Publishing Company

named driver exclusion

Automobile. An endorsement added to an automobile policy which specifically excludes from all coverage losses involving a named individual. Usually attached when the underwriter is aware of a problem driver who might be allowed to use an insured automobile (e.g., the son of the named insured) in the absence of this endorsement.

named insured

Aviation. Under an aircraft policy, the named insured is usually extended to include any person while using or riding in the aircraft and any person or organization legally responsible for its use, provided the actual use is with the express permission of the named insured.

Automobile/Casualty/Property. An individual, business or organization that is specified in its declarations by name as the insured(s) under a policy. Other insureds may be covered in the context of the policy without necessarily being named in the policy declarations; these individuals and organizations may be included for coverage as "insureds" or "additional insureds" by other provisions (e.g., definitions) of the policy. The named insured is responsible for premium payments, receipt of notices, and adjustment of losses. Under general liability policies, the named insured is required to maintain records of such information as is necessary for premium computation, and the insurer is permitted to inspect the named insured's property and operations at any time. Only a named insured may make agreements and representations as to statements in the policy declarations.

   see: **additional insured, broad named insured definition endorsement, insured**

named nonowner endorsement

Automobile. An endorsement that can be added to an automobile policy that covers the individual operating any non-owned automobile or trailer. This type of coverage is needed by individuals driving employer-furnished autos who do not own vehicles themselves.

   see: **broad form drive other car coverage**

named perils

Property. A term used to describe the breadth of coverage provided under a property insurance policy which lists specific covered perils. No coverage is provided for unlisted perils.

   syn: **specified perils;** compare: **"all-risks" insurance;** see: **broad form, open perils;** Fr: énumeration des risques; Gr: benannte Gefahren; Sp: riesgos especificados

name position bond

Crime. A fidelity bond which provides coverage in a specified amount for each employee holding a specific position listed in the bond schedule. *Example:* A $25,000 per position bond covering cashiers would cover a $100,000 loss caused by four cashiers; however, if four clerks were responsible for the same loss, there would be no coverage as only cashiers were specifically covered. If three cashiers and a clerk were responsible for a $100,000 loss, only the $25,000 per covered position limit ($75,000) would be covered.

   compare: **blanket fidelity bond, blanket position bond, name schedule bond**

name schedule bond

Crime. A fidelity bond which provides coverage for an act by one or more employees specifically named in a schedule. Specific limits applying to each employee are listed in the schedule, as well.

   compare: **blanket fidelity bond, blanket position bond, name position bond**

229

© 1991 NILS Publishing Company

National Association of Bar-Related Title Insurers (NABRTI)

Organizations. Members: Title insurance companies known as "bar-related," which is a registered trademark of the association. *Objectives:* Promotes interests of its members. *Founded:* 1953. *Headquarters:* Chicago, IL. Until 1979, known as the National Conference of Bar-Related Title Insurers.

National Association of Casualty and Surety Agents (NACSA)

Organizations. Members: Agents handling fire, casualty and surety insurance. *Objectives:* To safeguard the public's insurance interests, to preserve a stable, competitive insurance market, to foster self-regulation and good public relations and to lobby state and federal governments. *Founded:* 1913. *Headquarters:* Bethesda, MD.

National Association of Casualty and Surety Executives (NACSE)

Organizations. Members: Casualty and surety insurance company executives. *Objectives:* Promotes discussion of industry issues among insurance agents. *Founded:* 1911. *Headquarters:* Washington, D.C.

National Association of Catastrophe Adjusters (NACA)

Organizations. Members: Catastrophe claims adjusters. *Objectives:* Promote the interests of the membership. *Founded:* 1976. *Headquarters:* Hilltop Lakes, TX.

National Association of Crop Insurance Agents (NACIA)

Organizations. Members: Service agents and insurance agencies selling federal All-Risk Crop Insurance to farmers. *Objectives:* Disseminates information to its membership about crop insurance. *Founded:* 1981. *Headquarters:* Anoka, MN.

National Association of Fire Investigators (NAFI)

Organizations. Members: Fire investigators, insurance adjusters, firefighters, attorneys and related professions. *Objectives:* Improve the skills of those involved in investigating fires, explosions, arson, subrogation and fire prevention. *Founded:* 1961. *Headquarters:* Chicago, IL.

National Association of Fraternal Insurance Counselors (NAFIC)

Life/Organizations. Members: Sales personnel for fraternal benefit life insurance societies. *Objectives:* Promoting and educating the membership's sales force. *Founded:* 1950. *Headquarters:* Sheboygan, WI.

National Association of Health Underwriters (NAHU)

Organizations. Members: Insurance agencies and individuals engaged in the promotion, sale and administration of disability income and health insurance. *Objectives:* Sponsors educational seminars. Represents its members before federal and state legislators. *Founded:* 1930. *Headquarters:* Washington, D.C.

see: **Disability Insurance Training Council, Leading Producers Round Table**

National Association of Independent Insurance Adjusters (NAIIA)

Organizations. Members: Claims adjusters and firms operating independently on a fee basis for all insurance companies. *Objectives:* Provides educational courses for adjusters. *Founded:* 1937. *Headquarters:* Chicago, IL.

National Association of Independent Insurers (NAII)

Organizations. Members: Independent property and liability insurance companies. *Objectives:* Operates as an independent statistical service which collects, compiles and files statistics. Develops simplified statistical plans. *Founded:* 1945. *Headquarters:* Des Plaines, IL.

National Association of Independent Life Brokerage Agencies (NAILBA)

Organizations. Members: Licensed independent life brokerage agencies which represent at least three insurers, but are not owned or controlled by an insurance company. *Objectives:* Promotes the interests of its member agencies. *Founded:* 1982. *Headquarters:* Washington, D.C.

National Association of Insurance Agents, Inc. (NAIA)

Organizations. The former name of the Independent Insurance Agents of America.

see: **Independent Insurance Agents of America**

National Association of Insurance Brokers, Inc. (NAIB)

Organizations. Members: Insurance brokers, primarily in the areas of commercial, industrial and institutional risks and related insurance. *Objectives:* Promotes the interests of the insurance brokerage industry. *Founded:* 1934. *Headquarters:* Washington, D.C.

National Association of Insurance Commissioners (NAIC)

Organizations. Members: State insurance regulators. *Objectives:* Promotes uniformity in regulation by drafting model laws and regulations for adoption by the states. Also provides support services to insurance

© 1991 NILS Publishing Company

departments such as examinations and statistical information. The organization holds four meetings each year to work on model laws and regulations and discuss other pertinent issues. *Founded:* 1871. *Headquarters:* Kansas City, MO.

see: **Commissioners Standard Ordinary Table; McCarran-Ferguson Act; Model Insurers Supervision, Rehabilitation and Liquidation Act of 1977; Schedule P; Statutory Accounting Principles; statutory earnings or losses**

National Association of Insurance Women (NAIW)

Organizations. Members: Women in the insurance business. *Objectives:* Sponsors educational programs. Awards the Certified Professional Insurance Woman designation to qualified members who pass examinations. *Founded:* 1940. *Headquarters:* Tulsa. OK.

National Association of Life Companies (NALC)

Organizations. Members: Life and health insurance companies. *Objectives:* Promotes the interests of its members. *Founded:* 1955. *Headquarters:* Washington, D.C.

National Association of Life Underwriters (NALU)

Organizations. Members: Life insurance agents, general agents and managers. *Objectives:* Supports the principles of legal reserve life and health insurance. *Founded:* 1890. *Headquarters:* Washington, D.C.

see: **Life Underwriter Political Action Committee**

National Association of Mutual Insurance Companies (NAMIC)

Organizations. Members: Mutual fire and casualty insurance companies. *Objectives:* Gathering, compiling and analyzing information relating to insurance and reducing or preventing losses. *Founded:* 1895. *Headquarters:* Indianapolis, IN.

National Association of Professional Surplus Lines Offices (NAPSLO)

Organizations. Members: Brokerage firms and companies providing excess and surplus lines of insurance. *Objectives:* Provides services for its members, including conventions and educational seminars. Lobbies at the federal and state levels for its members' interests. *Founded:* 1975. *Headquarters:* Kansas City, MO.

National Association of Public Insurance Adjusters (NAPIA)

Organizations. Members: A professional society of public insurance adjusters. *Objectives:* Sponsors educational programs, and presents certificates and awards. *Founded:* 1951. *Headquarters:* Washington, D.C.

National Association of Securities Dealers (NASD)

Organizations. Members: Brokers and securities dealers. *Objectives:* Produces rates, rating plans and language for stocks. *Founded:* 1938. *Headquarters:* Rockville, MD.

see: **registered representative**

National Association of Surety Bond Producers (NASBP)

Organizations. Members: Insurance agents and brokers who write surety bonds. *Objectives:* Considers matters pertaining to contract bonds. *Founded:* 1942. *Headquarters:* Bethesda, MD.

National Automobile Theft Bureau (NATB)

Organizations. Members: Insurance companies who write physical damage coverage on motor vehicles. *Objectives:* Preventing and reducing fraudulent automobile fire and theft claims. Compiling and issuing reports on stolen vehicles. Offering assistance in finding and recovering vehicles. *Founded:* 1912. *Headquarters:* Palos Hills, IL.

see: **Fire and Theft Index Bureau, Insurance Crime Prevention Institute, Insurance Services Office, interinsurer claim service organization, Medical Information Bureau, Property Insurance Loss Register**

National Board of Fire Underwriters (NBFU)

Organizations. A now-defunct organization founded by fire insurance underwriters in 1866. The Board's main objectives were to promote fire prevention and property loss control. The NBFU was instrumental in developing the standard fire insurance policy. In the mid-1960s, the NBFU merged into the American Insurance Association; in the early 1970s, thirty rating bureaus formed the Insurance Services Office (ISO).

see: **American Insurance Association, Insurance Services Office**

National Building Code

Loss Control. A set of standard safety guidelines developed by the American Insurance Association. It is designed to be adopted by local governments, to provide uniformity in building construction.

National Bureau of Standards

Regulation. A division within the U.S. Department of Commerce, that establishes minimum standards for certain industries or products, which must be met by manufacturers of those products.

© 1991 NILS Publishing Company

National Commission on State Workers' Compensation Laws

Workers' Compensation/Regulation. A group appointed by President Richard M. Nixon in 1971, to study the state workers' compensation system. The Commission made recommendations to upgrade state workers' compensation laws (higher benefits, mandatory coverage, and unlimited medical care and rehabilitation benefits). After most states adopted the recommendations, an increase in premiums for the new benefits resulted.

National Committee on Property Insurance (NCPI)

Organizations. Members: Property and casualty insurance companies. *Objectives:* Assists insurers who write property coverage in distressed or residual insurance markets. Operates the Property Insurance Plans Service Office, which assists state property and casualty insurance plans in their administration, operation and functions. *Founded:* 1977. *Headquarters:* Boston, MA.

see: **Property Insurance Plans Service Office**

National Conference of Insurance Legislators (NCOIL)

Organizations. Members: Chairpersons or members of insurance or insurance-related committees in state legislatures. *Objectives:* Support legislators by providing information, to assist them in drafting laws regulating the insurance industry. *Founded:* 1969. *Headquarters:* Brookfield, WI.

National Convention of Insurance Commissioners

Organizations. The former name for the National Association of Insurance Commissioners (NAIC).

See: **National Association of Insurance Commissioners**

National Coordinating Committee for Multiemployer Plans (NCCMP)

Organizations. Members: Trade unions, multiemployer pension and welfare funds and jointly administered employee benefit trusts. *Objectives:* Promotes and lobbies for improved retirement security. *Founded:* 1975. *Headquarters:* Washington, D.C.

National Council of Self-Insurers (NCSI)

Organizations. Members: Associations, companies and others involved in or concerned with self-insurance and workers' compensation. *Objectives:* Promotes the interests of self-insurers or legally noninsured employers. *Founded:* 1945. *Headquarters:* Chicago, IL.

National Council on Compensation Insurance (NCCI)

Organizations. Members: Insurance companies that write workers' compensation insurance. *Objectives:* Collects statistics on the frequency and severity of job-related injuries (to establish a rate structure for member companies); files rate plans with insurance commissioners for member companies and generates forms and policies for member companies. *Founded:* 1923. *Headquarters:* New York, NY.

National Credit Union Administration (NCUA)

Organizations. An organization similar to the Federal Deposit Insurance Corporation (FDIC), that provides protection for credit union depositors.

see: **Federal Deposit Insurance Corporation**

National Crop Insurance Association (NCIA)

Organizations. An association that merged with the Crop Hail Insurance Actuarial Association in 1989 to form National Crop Insurance Services.

see: **National Crop Insurance Services**

National Crop Insurance Services (NCIS)

Organizations. Members: Insurers covering agricultural crops against hail, fire and other weather perils. *Objectives:* Serves as a statistical and rating organization. *Founded:* 1989. *Headquarters:* Overland Park, KS. Formed by a merger of the Crop-Hail Insurance Actuarial Association and the National Crop Insurance Association.

see: **crop insurance, crop-hail insurance**

National Employee Benefits Institute (NEBI)

Organizations. Members: Fortune 1000 corporations. *Objectives:* To reduce government regulation of employee benefits and to promote legislation and regulation favorable to their member's interests. *Founded:* 1977. *Headquarters:* Washington, D.C.

National Federation of Grange Mutual Insurance Companies (NFGMIC)

Organizations. Members: Grange insurance companies. *Objectives:* Provides reinsurance and promotes Grange mutual insurance. *Founded:* 1934. *Headquarters:* Glastonbury, CT.

national fire code

Property.

see: **National Fire Protection Association**

National Fire Protection Association (NFPA)

Organizations. Members: Business, industry, fire service, healthcare, educational groups and other institutions and people in the fields of insurance, government, architecture and engineering. *Objectives:* Sets fire safety standards, and serves as a clearing house of information concerning fire loss control. Publishes a

© 1991 NILS Publishing Company

national fire code. *Founded:* 1896. *Headquarters:* Quincy, MA.

National Flood Insurance Program (NFIP)

Property. A federal program, administered by the Federal Insurance Administration, providing flood insurance under the National Flood Insurance Act passed in 1968. Under a "dual" program, coverage may be written directly by the NFIP or by private carriers whose losses are reimbursed by the NFIP.

see: **Emergency National Flood Insurance Program, Federal Insurance Administration, Flood Disaster Protection Act of 1973, Flood Hazard Boundary Map, flood insurance, Flood Insurance Manual, flood insurance rate map, Regular National Flood Insurance Program**

National Fraternal Congress Mortality Rate Table

Life. A mortality table prepared for fraternal insurers in 1898.

National Fraternal Congress of America (NFCA)

Organizations. Members: Fraternal benefit societies writing life, accident and health insurance. *Objectives:* To promote the general welfare of the fraternal benefit system by uniting fraternal benefit societies in all matters of mutual concern. *Founded:* 1913. *Headquarters:* Naperville, IL.

National Health Care Anti-Fraud Association (NHAFA)

Organizations. Members: Public and private agencies involved in health care and insurance. *Objectives:* Seeks to reduce health care fraud and costs. *Founded:* 1985. *Headquarters:* Washington, D.C.

national health insurance

Health/International. A form of health insurance found in some countries such as Great Britain and Canada, where all of the country's citizens are covered by a national health insurance program. These programs are administered by the national government and financed through taxes.

syn: **socialized health insurance**

National Health Planning and Resource Development Act of 1974 (Public Law 93-641)

Health.

see: **annual implementation plan**

National Institute for Occupational Safety and Health (NIOSH)

Regulation. A division of the U.S. Department of Health, Education and Welfare, which is responsible for researching injury and illness arising from workplace hazards. As a result of its research, recommendations are made covering standards for employees' maximum exposures to hazardous substances.

see: **Occupational Safety and Health Act**

National Institute of Pension Administrators (NIPA)

Organizations. Members: Individuals with a minimum of one year's experience in pension administration. *Objectives:* Provides educational programs for the accreditation of pension administrators. *Founded:* 1983. *Headquarters:* Tustin, CA.

National Insurance Association (NIA)

Organizations. Members: U.S. insurance companies. *Objectives:* Exchanges information and ideas on common problems that especially affect the black community. *Founded:* 1921. *Headquarters:* Chicago, IL.

National Insurance Consumer Organization (NICO)

Organizations. Members: Consumer advocates. *Objectives:* Supports reform of unfair industry practices and marketplace abuses. Educates consumers about insurance. *Founded:* 1980. *Headquarters:* Alexandria, VA.

National Insurance Development Corporation (NIDC)

Reinsurance. A government corporation that provides reinsurance for private insurers that write riot and civil commotion insurance. Riot losses in major cities in the 1960s caused insurers to stop writing this coverage in certain urban areas, whereupon Congress created federal crime insurance and the National Insurance Development Corporation.

see: **federal crime insurance program**

National Insurance Producers Conference

Organizations. An organization of insurance broker and agent associations (e.g., the Independent Insurance Agents of America, National Association of Professional Insurance Agents, National Association of Insurance Brokers, etc.).

National Safety Council (NSC)

Organizations. Members: Representatives from all kinds of industries. *Objectives:* Publishes and disseminates safety education material and statistics on accidents and workplace injuries. *Founded:* 1913. *Headquarters:* Chicago, IL.

National Service Life Insurance (NSLI)

Life. Life insurance underwritten by the federal government, for those who served in the United States armed forces from 1940 to 1951.

syn: **United States Government Life Insurance**

© 1991 NILS Publishing Company

National Society of Insurance Premium Auditors (NSIPA)

Organizations. Members: Employees of insurance companies who are involved in field, administrative or support service policy auditing to determine insurance premiums. *Objectives:* Establishes uniform standards for auditing, promoting the interests of the members, and conducting research. Develops professional courses of study and proficiency test procedures. *Founded:* 1975. *Headquarters:* Boys Town, NE.

Nationwide Definition and Interpretation of the Powers of Marine and Transportation Underwriters

Inland Marine. The full title for the Nationwide Marine Insurance Definition.

see: Nationwide Marine Insurance Definition

Nationwide Inter-company Arbitration Agreement

Insurer Operations. An agreement that covers controversies between insurance companies, including those involving policy coverage and interpretations, or subrogation. Participating companies agree that certain controversies must be submitted to arbitration.

see: arbitration, dual coverage, other insurance clause, subrogation

Nationwide Marine Insurance Definition

Ocean Marine/Inland Marine. A statement about the types of coverage that may properly be written on inland marine and ocean marine insurance forms. The National Association of Insurance Commissioners (NAIC) adopted a Nationwide Marine Insurance Definition in 1953, and revised it in 1976. This definition is used principally for classification purposes, rather than as a definition of underwriting powers. The majority of states have adopted the 1976 version, but the 1953 version is still in effect in some states.

syn: marine definition, Nationwide Definition and Interpretation of the Powers of Marine and Transportation Underwriters; see: inland marine insurance, instrumentalities of transportation and communication, ocean marine insurance, transportation insurance

natural expiry

Insurer Operations. The normal termination date of an insurance policy.

see: expiration date, policy period

natural perils

Property. One of three categories of perils, the others being "human perils" and "economic perils." Natural perils include property damage caused by such natural elements as rain, ice, wind, earthquake, flood, rot and rust, etc.

see: economic perils, human perils, peril

natural premium

Life. A life insurance premium, developed from a mortality table, which is the amount of money that must be collected from each member of a group composed of the same age and sex, in order to pay $1,000 for each death that will occur in the group each year.

see: morbidity table, mortality table, pure mortality cost

negative cash flow

Risk Management. A financial situation where a business' cash needs exceed its cash intake. Short periods of negative cash flow create no problem for most businesses; however, longer periods of negative cash flow may require additional capital investment if the business is to avoid insolvency.

see: cash flow, insolvency

neglect

Property. To give little attention, leave undone or unattended through carelessness. Most property insurance policies contain exclusions for losses caused by neglect.

negligence

Casualty. The failure to use the care that a reasonable, prudent person would have taken under similar circumstances.

see: comparative negligence, contributory negligence, degree of care, degree of negligence, doctrine of last clear chance, gross negligence, reasonable care, res ipsa loquitur

negotiated contribution plan

Employee Benefits. A form of defined contribution plan, where a collective bargaining agreement establishes the amount of employer contributions. Frequently, these plans involve several employers and are administered jointly by the employer(s) and a union representing the employees.

see: collectively bargained contribution plan

net amount at risk

Life. The difference between a life insurance policy's face amount and its reserve or cash value.

net cash value

Life. The net amount of cash that the policyholder will receive from the insurance company upon surrendering a life insurance policy for its cash value. It is arrived at by taking the cash value, subtracting any policy loans, and adding accumulated dividends.

see: cash value, life insurance

© 1991 NILS Publishing Company

net change

Financial Planning. The amount of increase or decrease in a stock's price from a specified day's closing price and the closing price of that stock on the next trading day.

net current assets

Financial Planning.
see: **working capital**

net income

Financial Planning/Risk Management. The balance of funds remaining after all of an organization's expenses are subtracted from gross sales. Net income is the amount that can be distributed to an organization's owners or retained within the organization as retained earnings.
see: **financial statement, financial underwriting, retained earnings**

net increase

Insurer Operations. The increase in an insurance company's total business as measured by premium volume during a specified period of time. The increase is calculated by adding the new and renewal policy premiums and subtracting the premium from lapsed and cancelled policies.

net interest earned

Insurer Operations. The average interest an insurance company earns during a specified period of time. The amount is calculated prior to tax considerations, by taking the interest earned on investments and subtracting investment expenses.
see: **interest, investment income**

net level premium

Life.
see: **level premium life insurance**

net level premium reserve

Life. A premium reserve established for level premium ordinary life insurance policies in their initial years of coverage, to offset inadequate premiums charged in later years. The reserve is based on the amount of excess premium charged in the initial years, plus the interest earned on the accumulated excess premium. As long as such a reserve exists for a policy, it comprises part of that policy's death benefit.
see: **level premium life insurance**

net line

Reinsurance. The amount of coverage retained by a ceding company on an individual risk (before a loss) or occurrence (after a loss).
syn: **net retained line; see: gross line, line, net retained lines clause, net retention**
Insurer Operations. The maximum amount of loss to

which an insurer will expose itself on a particular risk without reinsurance.
syn: **retention; compare: remainder; see: line, gross line**

net loss

Insurer Operations. An amount of loss sustained by an insurer after deducting any recoveries, salvage and reinsurance.
see: **net underwriting loss, ultimate net loss**

net net income

Financial Planning. A term used in real estate investments, where the word net is repeated to indicate actual profits after *all* expenses are paid, (including mortgage reduction payments, principal and interest). It indicates whether or not the investment will generate a positive cash flow.
see: **cash flow**

net premium

Life. An initial participating life insurance policy premium minus policy dividends when the insured applies such dividends to pay part of the policy premium.
see: **initial premium, participating policy, policy dividend**
Insurer Operations. Gross policy premium, less agent's or broker's commissions. Premium available to pay anticipated losses, prior to any loading for other expenses.
syn: **net single premium; compare: gross premium, pure premium; see: premium**

net premiums written

Insurer Operations. An insurer's retained premium income – direct or through reinsurance – less payments made for reinsurance ceded.
see: **premium, reinsurance premium**

net present value method (NPV)

Financial Planning. A method of ranking investment proposals. The net present value is equal to the present value of future returns, discounted at the marginal cost of capital, minus the present value of the cost of the investment.
see: **present value**

net quick assets

Surety. Net current assets minus inventory. It is of interest to surety underwriters, because it indicates a business' ability to respond to financial obligations.
see: **working capital**

net retained liability

Reinsurance.
see: **net retention**

© 1991 NILS Publishing Company

net retained line
Insurer Operations.
see: net line

net retained lines clause
Reinsurance. A clause in an excess of loss reinsurance contract stating that the contract covers liability on net retentions only.
see: excess of loss reinsurance, line, net line

net retention
Insurer Operations. The amount of liability that an insurer keeps for its own account and does not reinsure in any way.
syn: first loss retention, net line, net retained liability; compare: remainder; see: net retention clause

net retention clause
Reinsurance. A provision in a reinsurance contract which indicates the amount that the ceding company will retain and that the reinsurance will apply only to the business assumed by the ceding company.
syn: retainer clause; see: net line, net retained liability, net retention

net single premium
Insurer Operations.
see: net premium

net underwriting loss
Insurer Operations. A negative amount which may result when policyholder dividends are subtracted from statutory profit or loss.
compare: net underwriting profit; see: net loss

net underwriting profit
Insurer Operations. A positive amount which may result when policyholder dividends are subtracted from statutory profit.
compare: net underwriting loss; see: underwriting profit or loss

net worth
Financial Planning/Surety. Total value of all assets minus liabilities. In a stock corporation, the amount of equity available to stockholders is the total common stock, capital surplus, earned surplus and accumulated retained earnings. Net worth is of interest to surety underwriters, since it indicates the ability of a business to respond to financial obligations.

net worth ratio
Risk Management. A financial analysis ratio which is a test of an organization's earning power based on its capitalization. It is a measure of what the stockholders earned from all sources as a percentage of the stockholders' investment. *Formula:* Net Worth Ratio

= Net Income/Owner's Equity. The higher the ratio, the more willing investors would be to invest in the company.
see: financial ratios, financial underwriting

new for old
Ocean Marine. A provision contained in older marine policies which meant that when repairs are made and new parts or equipment are supplied in place of old parts that have been lost or damaged, there shall be an agreed discount to represent the depreciation of the old items.
syn: no thirds off; see: repair or replace

newly acquired
Automobile. A provision in a business auto policy that will automatically cover an auto if it was acquired since the policy was issued and if the auto either replaced a scheduled auto or was an addition to a fully scheduled fleet. Such automatic coverage usually expires in 30 or 90 days, after which the insured must report the new vehicle to the insurer and formally add the vehicle to the policy.
see: fleet automatic, nonfleet automatic

newspaper policy
Health/Life. A limited health insurance policy, often sold by newspapers to increase circulation.
see: limited risk health insurance policy

New York Insurance Exchange
Insurer Operations. An insurance exchange that began operation in New York City in March 31, 1980 and ceased operation in 1987.
see: insurance exchange

New York standard fire policy
Property. A fire insurance policy form, initially drafted in 1918 and amended in 1943, which was used by most states until it was replaced by the ISO simplified language policies in the 1980's. The policy included coverage for not only fire, but also lightning and the removal of property after a fire to protect it from further damage.
syn: standard fire policy

nimble dividend
Insurer Operations. Dividends paid out of current earnings at a time when there is a deficit in earned surplus (or other financial account from which dividends might otherwise be paid). Some state statutes do not permit nimble dividends; these statutes require current earnings to be applied against prior deficits, rather than being used to pay a current dividend. Some insurers occasionally pay nimble dividends to maintain a consistent dividend record.
see: dividend

© 1991 NILS Publishing Company

nip point

Loss Control.
see: inrunning nip point

no-fault insurance

Automobile. A form of automobile insurance enacted by law in many states, where compensation for auto accident victims is made by their own insurance companies. Legal liability or fault is not usually determined, unless certain damages exceed a specified amount and an insured takes legal action.
see: add-on no-fault benefits, Keeton-O'Connell Plan

noise level

Loss Control. The amount of sound reaching a person's ear, measured in decibels (dB). Current United States requirements assign a sound level of 90 dB (A-scale) as a safe level during an eight-hour work day. Higher noise levels are permitted for shorter periods of time, ranging up to 115 dB (A-scale) for 15 minutes.
see: decibel, hearing level

no load fund

Financial Planning. A mutual fund that does not charge its participants commissions (load). Shares are sold directly to the participant by the fund, and no outside sales organization is involved.
compare: load fund, low load fund; see: mutual fund

nominal damages

General. The money awarded by a court to a plaintiff when no real damage has occurred from another's wrongful act.
compare: punitive damages; see: damages

nonadmissible assets

Insurer Operations.
see: excluded assets, nonadmitted assets

nonadmitted assets

Insurer Operations. Assets of an insurer that are not permitted by the state insurance department or other regulatory authority to be taken into account in determining an insurer's financial condition. Nonadmitted assets often include furniture, fixtures, agents' debit balances, and receivables over 90 days old.
syn: excluded assets, nonadmissible assets; compare: admitted assets; see: annual statement, assets, Statutory Accounting Principles

nonadmitted insurer

Insurer Operations. An insurance company not licensed to do business within a certain state.
compare: admitted insurer

nonadmitted market

Insurer Operations. Insurers doing business in a state as nonadmitted insurers, that is, where such insurers are not licensed to sell and service their policies. Usually, such insurers can sell insurance in a state where they are not licensed only through excess and surplus lines brokers.
compare: admitted market; see: excess and surplus lines broker

nonadmitted reinsurance

Insurer Operations. Reinsurance that is ceded to a reinsurer not admitted to operate in the state of the primary insurer, and for which an annual statement credit will not be given by state insurance regulators.
compare: admitted reinsurance; see: reinsurance credit

nonassessable mutual

Insurer Operations. A mutual insurance company with sufficient policyholder surplus to cover projected losses and whose corporate charter and bylaws prohibit it from assessing its policyholders any funds in excess of initial premiums.
compare: assessment mutual; see: mutual insurance company

nonassessable policy

Insurer Operations. An insurance policy which prohibits an insurer from assessing the policyholder for any adverse loss or expense experience. The term is usually applied to policies issued by a nonassessable mutual insurer.
compare: assessable policies; see: assessment mutual, nonassessable mutual

nonassignable

Insurer Operations. An insurance policy that does not allow the policyholder to assign or transfer the policy to a third party. Most policies cannot be assigned without prior approval by the insurer.
see: assignment

noncancellable policy

Health. A health insurance policy which must be maintained in force by the insurance company for an extended period of time as long as its premiums are paid. Many states have adopted standards suggested by the National Association of Insurance Commissioners which require that noncancellable health policies must continue in force until age 50, or for at least five years when issued after age 44.
compare: guaranteed insurability, guaranteed renewable, optionally renewable contract; see: lifetime policy

© 1991 NILS Publishing Company

noncomplying policies

Insurer Operations. Insurance policies which do not state requirements as respects their rates or forms.

see: insurance contract

nonconcurrency

Casualty. A situation where liability policies in a layered program (i.e., primary, umbrella and excess policies) do not agree with respect to policy effective dates or other policy provisions, creating the potential for coverage gaps (e.g., the application of annual aggregate limits) in the event of a large loss.

compare: following form excess liability insurance; see: Cromie rule, layering, nonconcurrent apportionment rules

Property. A situation where two or more insurance policies are issued to cover an insured's property, but they do not provide the same coverage when this situation exists. It is possible that an insured will not recover the full amount of a loss.

compare: following form excess property insurance; see: Cromie rule, nonconcurrent apportionment rules

nonconcurrent apportionment rules

Insurer Operations. Rules developed in 1963 by property and casualty insurance companies, which provide a basis to determine how multiple policies providing overlapping coverage should respond to a specific claim.

see: Cromie rule, nonconcurrency

nonconfining sickness

Health. A sickness or illness that prevents an individual from working, but does not confine them indoors.

compare: house confinement

noncontribution mortgage clause

Property. An endorsement that can be added to a commercial property policy if more than one policy is in force on a mortgaged property. The endorsement allows a mortgagee to require that in the event of a loss involving the property, the mortgagee's claim will not be apportioned with other policies and the lender's interest will be paid up to the limit of the policy to which this endorsement has been attached.

see: apportionment, loss payable clause, mortgagee clause

noncontributory group insurance

Employee Benefits. A term used to describe an employee benefit plan where the employer pays the entire premium and the employee contributes no part of the premium.

compare: contributory group insurance

nondisabling injury

Health/Workers' Compensation. An injury that is not serious in nature and where little or no disability is noticeable. Such an injury does not qualify an individual for disability or workers' compensation benefits, except that some disability policies provide 25% to 50% of one month's disability payment.

see: disability

nondiscriminatory

Regulation. A requirement of most state insurance department regulations, which stipulates that the rates an insurer charges can not unfairly discriminate against any segment of the population.

see: adequate, discrimination, equity, excessive, rate making

nonduplication of benefits

Health. A clause contained in some health insurance policies which provides that the insurer will not pay for benefits which are reimbursed by other insurance.

see: coordination of benefits

noneconomic loss

Casualty. Pain, suffering, inconvenience and other non-money damages associated with liability insurance claims.

compare: economic loss

nonfleet automatic

Automobile. Business or commercial auto coverage that requires the reporting of newly acquired vehicles to the insurance company within a certain number of days for coverage to remain in effect on those vehicles. (Such policies provide basic coverage for newly acquired vehicles – but usually for a limited number of days.)

compare: fleet automatic see: newly acquired

nonforfeiture benefit

Life. A life insurance policy clause which provides that an insured's equity in the policy cannot be forfeited. To recover policy equity, the insured can either: accept the cash surrender value; direct the insurer to use any equity to obtain extended term insurance; take any equity in the form of a loan, or direct the insurer to purchase reduced paid-up insurance. In the event one of these options is not elected, a policy specifies which of the above options is automatically effective.

see: nonforfeiture cash surrender value benefit, nonforfeiture extended term benefit, nonforfeiture loan value benefit, nonforfeiture reduced paid-up benefit

nonforfeiture cash surrender value benefit

Life. A life insurance policy nonforfeiture benefit option where, upon surrender of the policy, the policyholder receives the policy cash value as specified in a table attached to the policy, minus any outstanding loans and accrued interest. Some policies have a

© 1991 NILS Publishing Company

waiting period of up to six months before they make the cash payment.

see: cash surrender value, nonforfeiture benefit

nonforfeiture extended term benefit

Life. A life insurance policy nonforfeiture benefit option where the cash surrender value of the policy is used to pay the policy premium for a specific period of time after which coverage terminates.

see: extended term life insurance, nonforfeiture benefit

nonforfeiture loan value benefit

Life. A life insurance policy nonforfeiture benefit option where the cash surrender value of the policy is used as collateral for a loan to the policyholder.

see: nonforfeiture benefit, policy loan

nonforfeiture reduced paid-up benefit

Life. A life insurance policy nonforfeiture benefit option where the cash surrender value of the policy is used to purchase a fully paid up life insurance policy for a lesser limit. The new policy limit will be based on the insured's age and the policy cash surrender value.

syn: reduced paid-up insurance; see: nonforfeiture benefit

noninsurable risk

General.

see: uninsurable risk

noninsurance

Risk Management. The *intentional* election not to purchase insurance for a known exposure. Losses arising from such an exposure are not prefunded (self-insured), but rather will be absorbed as a direct business expense when they occur.

compare: avoidance, insurance, passive retention, risk transfer, self-insurance, small loss principle, underinsurance

noninsurance transfer

Risk Management. A risk management technique for shifting an organization's potential losses to others. Many alternatives are available that may be less costly than insurance, such as subcontracting part of a project or inserting a hold-harmless agreement in a contract.

see: risk transfer

nonledger assets

Risk Management. Assets which have not been received and have not been entered on the balance sheet, but are due and payable in the current year nonetheless.

see: assets

nonlegal reserve life insurance company

Life.

see: legal reserve life insurance company

nonmedical insurance

Health/Life. A life or health insurance policy which is issued based solely on the insured's application; that is, the underwriter does not require the applicant to take a medical examination.

compare: examined business

nonoccupational disability

Health/Workers' Compensation. A disability which did not occur as a result of an individual's employment, but is still covered by workers' compensation in some states.

compare: occupational accident, occupational disease

nonoccupational policy

Health. A provision in most health insurance policies, excluding coverage for injuries covered by workers' compensation or work-related injuries. This provision makes most health insurance policies so-called "nonoccupational policies."

compare: workers' compensation insurance

nonowned aircraft liability insurance

Aviation. Liability coverage for an employer when employees or agents use their aircraft on behalf of the employer. The coverage can be provided by an aviation policy, or by an endorsement to the commercial general liability policy. This is also a coverage included in many umbrella liability policies.

syn: aircraft nonowned coverage

nonowned automobile

Automobile. An auto used for business purposes but which is not owned, leased, hired or borrowed by the insured. *Example:* An employee's owned automobile, when used in making sales calls or deliveries for a commercial insured.

compare: hired automobile; see: nonowned automobile liability

nonowned automobile liability

Automobile. Liability coverage for an employer when employees or agents use their own autos on behalf of the employer. The coverage can be provided by a commercial auto policy or endorsed to a commercial general liability policy.

syn: automobile nonowned coverage, employers nonownership liability

nonowned watercraft liability

Casualty. Liability coverage for an employer when employees or agents use their watercraft on behalf of the employer. This coverage is usually endorsed to a

© 1991 NILS Publishing Company

nonowned watercraft liability – continued
commercial liability policy, but may also be provided by a separate policy.

syn: **watercraft nonowned coverage**

nonparticipating policy

Casualty/Workers' Compensation. An insurance policy which does not pay policy dividends.

compare: **participating policy**

nonprofit insurers

Insurer Operations. Insurers such as the Blue Cross and Blue Shield Plans that provide medical expense reimbursement insurance without a profit motive. They are organized according to certain state laws and usually exempted from certain standard insurer taxes.

see: **Blue Cross and Blue Shield Association**

nonprofit organization

General. An organization not intended to show a profit or to operate on a for-profit basis. The largest difference between a for-profit and nonprofit organization is in the tax treatment of each organization. Nonprofit organizations include religious, charitable, recreational, educational and civic organizations.

see: **favored institution**

nonproportional automatic reinsurance

Reinsurance. A reinsurance contract under which the reinsurer is obligated to automatically assume all or a large share of all losses up to a specified limit when these losses exceed the reinsured (ceding) company's retention limit.

see: **aggregate excess of loss reinsurance, nonproportional reinsurance;** compare: **excess of loss reinsurance**

nonproportional facultative reinsurance

Reinsurance. A reinsurance contract that is issued to cover a specific policy or group of policies. The reinsurer is obligated to assume all or a large share of all losses for those policies, up to a specified limit, when losses exceed the reinsured (ceding) company's retention level.

see: **facultative reinsurance, nonproportional reinsurance**

nonproportional reinsurance

Reinsurance. A reinsurance contract where the reinsurer is not involved in the direct sharing of risks. The reinsurer is obligated only after the ceding insurer's loss payments exceed some predetermined amount, after which time the reinsurer's share of subsequent losses is substantial or even total. The term "nonproportional" is used because the reinsurer's share of loss is not proportional to the share of original premiums.

compare: **aggregate excess of loss reinsurance;** see: **nonproportional automatic reinsurance, nonproportional facultative reinsurance**

nonqualified plan

Employee Benefits. An employee benefit plan which is not qualified under IRS rules to receive federal tax deductions for employer contributions paid to fund the plan. Employers use this type of plan, because it will allow discriminatory coverage for certain employees and reward specific employees with special benefits – practices which are not allowed under "qualified plans." A nonqualified plan may be constructed so that it is less expensive for an employer, since less employees can be included for coverage.

compare: **qualified plan;** see: **top-heavy plan**

nonresident agent (broker)

Agency. An agent domiciled in one state who becomes licensed to write insurance in another state. Agents who do business in more than one state require such additional licenses to legalize their representation, and to earn commissions in the states in which they do not have their principal offices.

compare: **resident agent;** see: **agent, countersignature**

nonsmoker discount

Life. A premium credit offered by some life insurers to their insureds, in recognition of their not using tobacco. This discounting is based on the actuarially supported belief that the hazard of smoking increases the perils of cancer and heart disease, which adversely affect longevity.

see: **smoker and nonsmoker mortality table**

nontrading partnership

General. A partnership in the business of selling only services.

see: **partnership**

nonvalued policy

Property. A policy that does not specify the amount of compensation for a loss. Loss reimbursements are calculated on an actual cash value basis.

compare: **limit of liability, valued policy;** see: **insurance contract**

nonvoting common stock

Insurer Operations. Shares of stock that do not grant their holder a right to vote. Such shares may be created in most states; in certain states, however, nonvoting shares may be entitled to vote as a class on certain proposed changes that would adversely affect that class.

see: **share of stock**

nonwaiver agreement

Insurer Operations. A document signed by an insured shortly after a claim has been filed, stating that

© 1991 NILS Publishing Company

the participation of a claims adjuster in a loss adjustment does not waive the insurer's continued ability to deny coverage under the policy.
see: estoppel, reservation of rights

noon clause
Property. An insurance policy provision starting coverage at noon, standard time, at the insured's property. However, most property policies now specify 12:01 a.m. as the effective time.
see: policy period

no par stock
Insurer Operations. Shares of stock which are stated to have no par value. Such shares are issued for the consideration designated by the board of directors; such consideration is allocated to the capital stock account, unless the directors or shareholders determine to allocate a portion to capital surplus. As a result, in many respects no par shares do not differ significantly from par value shares.
see: par value, share of stock

normal annuity form
Employee Benefits. A method for computing a pension plan's cost, assuming that retirement and plan benefits both begin on the first day of the month nearest the plan participant's retirement-year birthday, which is generally 65.
compare: optional annuity form

normal life expectancy
Life. The number of years that a person is expected to live, statistically determined by sex and chronological age.
see: life expectancy, mortality

normal probability distribution
Risk Management. A statistical curve that is symmetrical and bell-shaped. It is often used to plot probable losses.
syn: bell curve; see: probability

normal retirement age
Employee Benefits. The age specified by a pension plan as the earliest date at which an employee can retire without being penalized by a reduction in pension benefits. To receive maximum benefits, the employee must have reached his or her minimum retirement age and worked a minimum number of years for the employer. Historically, the minimum retirement age has ben 65 years, but some plans provide earlier or later normal retirement ages.
syn: minimum retirement age; see: deferred retirement, early retirement, normal annuity form, normal retirement date, retirement age

normal retirement benefit
Employee Benefits. Under a pension plan, the greater of 1) early retirement benefits, or 2) benefits that would be paid upon reaching the normal retirement age.
see: early retirement, normal retirement age

normal retirement date
Employee Benefits. Under a pension plan, the earliest date at which a plan participant qualifies for normal retirement; usually the later of the date on which the employee reaches minimum retirement age, or the date on which the employee has worked the minimum number of years for the employer as established under the plan.
see: normal retirement age

note
Financial Planning. A written promise to pay a debt.
see: debt securities

no thirds off
Ocean Marine.
see: new for old

notice of cancellation
Insurer Operations.
see: cancellation notice

notice of loss
Insurer Operations. A form or statement from an insured to an insurer, informing the insurer that events leading to a possible claim have occurred. The notice will include information as to how, when and where the loss took place. For a loss to be covered by a policy, notice of loss usually must be submitted to the insurer within a specified period of time.
syn: notice to company; see: accident report, claim, incident report, nonwaiver agreement, proof of loss, reportable event

notice of occurrence
Casualty. A provision in a casualty insurance policy, requiring the insured to inform the insurer of an occurrence (i.e., an event that might lead to liability claims), including the time, place and circumstances. Other pertinent information must be given to the insurer or an authorized agent as soon as possible.
see: accident, cause of action, cause of loss, fortuitous event, occurrence

notice to company
Insurer Operations.
see: notice of loss

not in motion
Aviation.
see: in motion

© 1991 NILS Publishing Company

not otherwise classified (NOC)

Insurer Operations. A classification used in underwriting various lines of insurance, when no specific classification applies. Most often used in liability or workers' compensation rating and classification.

not taken

Insurer Operations. A policy that is applied for and issued, but rejected by the applicant.

compare: delivered business, examined business, issued business, paid business, placed business, written business

novation

General. A principle in contract law, by which a third person takes over the rights and duties of a party to a contract, such party thereby being released from obligations under the contract. In the law of corporations, the concept may be applied to the release of a promoter who is personally liable on a preincorporation contract when the corporation is formed and adopts the contract. A novation requires the consent of the other party to the contract, but that consent may be implied from the circumstances.

see: assignment, assignment and assumption, assume, contract

nuclear energy liability insurance

Casualty. A liability insurance policy which will respond to claims alleging bodily injury and property damage caused by nuclear energy material located on the company's premises or while in transit. Most liability policies exclude nuclear energy liability, so this coverage must be purchased separately.

see: American Nuclear Insurers, Price-Anderson Act

nuclear hazard exclusion

Property. A property policy exclusion that specifically eliminates coverage for a loss caused by any weapon using atomic fission or fusion, or by any nuclear reaction, radiation or radioactive contamination, regardless of cause. However, an exception is ensuing fire loss which is covered.

syn: nuclear reaction exclusion; see: radioactive contamination insurance

nuclear pool

Casualty.

see: American Nuclear Insurers, MAERP Reinsurance Association

nuclear reaction exclusion

Property.

see: nuclear hazard exclusion

Nuclear Regulatory Commission (NRC)

Regulation. A federal agency that regulates the nuclear power industry. The NRC also offers supplemental insurance for nuclear facilities, in addition to private insurance pools.

nuisance value

Insurer Operations. An amount that an insurer will pay to settle a claim that may not be valid. Such values are sometimes set by insurers beforehand, and claim representatives are authorized to settle any claims within that amount unless a claim is clearly fraudulent.

see: ex gratia payment

numerical rating system

Life. An underwriting system that categorizes life insurance applicants by applying numerical values to certain demographic factors, such as physical condition, habits, morals and family history. The values for all factors are totalled, and applicants are then classified as either preferred, standard, substandard or uninsurable, according to the final score.

see: preferred risk, rate making, standard risk, substandard risk, uninsurable risk

nurse fees

Life. A medical expense reimbursement policy provision that reimburses the insured for fees for nurses who are not hospital employees.

nursing expense benefit

Health. A health insurance policy provision which pays for in-hospital nursing care that is required in conjunction with the treatment of a covered injury or sickness. The coverage is usually written to provide only for care by a private duty registered nurse.

© 1991 NILS Publishing Company

object

Property. A term used in boiler and machinery policies which refers to apparatus.

see: **covered boiler & machinery property; Fr: objet; Gr: Gegenstand, Objekt; Sp: objeto**

objective probability distribution

Risk Management. An actuarially-based probability distribution which emphasizes or expresses reality, compared to personal reflections or feelings.

see: **probability**

obligatory reinsurance treaty

Reinsurance. A reinsurance contract under which the business must be ceded by the ceding company in accordance with contract terms and accepted by the reinsurer.

compare: **facultative obligatory reinsurance treaty, facultative semi-obligatory reinsurance treaty**

obligee

Surety. The individual, business or organization named in a surety bond in whose favor the obligor promises performance. The person, firm or corporation protected by the bond.

compare: **obligor, principal, surety; see: bond; Fr: obligataire; Gr: Gläubiger; Sp: el que se beneficia**

obligor

Surety. In a surety bond, the principal or party bound by the obligation. Under a surety bond, both the principal and the surety are obligors, as the surety must respond should the principal default.

compare: **obligee; see: bond, principal, surety**

occupancy

Property. In fire insurance underwriting, "occupancy" is used to refer to the type or character of the property and how it is used. It is an important consideration in computing rates and determining the amount of insurance a company is willing to write on that property.

compare: **construction, exposure, protection**

occupancy permit

Property. An endorsement to a property policy allowing an occupancy which might otherwise suspend the policy or invalidate it.

see: **change in occupancy or use, increased hazard, vacancy or unoccupancy permit**

occupational accident

Health/Life/Workers' Compensation. An accident which results during, and is related to, the individual's employment.

compare: **nonoccupational disability; see: arising out of and in the course of employment, workers' compensation insurance; Fr: accidents du travail; Gr: Arbeitsunfall; Sp: accidentes de trabajo**

occupational disease (OD)

Health/Workers' Compensation. An impairment of health, or even death, caused by exposure to adverse conditions inherent in an individual's occupation, frequently over a period of time. Workers' compensation provides coverage for occupational diseases such as black lung disease.

see: **arising out of and in the course of employment, black lung disease, brown lung disease, byssinosis, silicosis, workers' compensation insurance**

243

© 1991 NILS Publishing Company

occupational hazard

Health/Life/Workers' Compensation. A risk that is inherent in certain occupations that increases the risk for an accident or disease.

see: hobbies or avocations, impaired risk, occupational disease, uniform premium

Occupational Safety and Health Act (OSHA)

Regulation. Federal legislation passed in 1970 which created safety and health standards on a national level. U.S. Department of Labor safety inspectors enforce the law. The act also requires employers to keep records of job-related injuries and illnesses.

see: National Institute for Occupational Safety and Health, occupational accident, occupational disease

occupying

Automobile. Under an automobile policy, an individual is said to be occupying an auto while in, upon, getting in, on, off, or out of the vehicle.

occurrence

General. An accident, sickness or other event that results in an insured loss.

Casualty. An accident, including continuous or repeated exposure to conditions, resulting in injury to persons or damage to property. An act or related series of acts which inflict injury to persons or damage to property.

compare: accident; see: cause of action, cause of loss, fortuitous event, notice of occurrence, occurrence coverage

occurrence coverage

Casualty. A liability policy covering all claims arising out of incidents occurring during the policy period, regardless of whether or not the policy is still in effect at the time that the claim is made.

compare: claims-made form; see: occurrence trigger

occurrence limit

Casualty/Property. The maximum limit of insurance coverage for the payment of all claims arising from any one incident.

compare: aggregate limit, per person limit

occurrence trigger

Casualty. Under an occurrence policy, coverage is activated ("triggered") when a covered event occurs during the policy period. Coverage for the insured is found under the policy in force at the time the event triggering coverage occurred.

compare: claims-made trigger, Keene Doctrine; see: occurrence coverage

ocean cargo insurance

Ocean Marine. A form of marine insurance covering goods lost or damaged during transport by water.

ocean marine insurance

Ocean Marine. Coverage for these types of ocean transportation exposures: 1) ships or hulls; 2) goods or cargos; 3) earnings (such as freight, passage money, commissions, or profit); and, 4) liability (known as protection & indemnity). This insurance may be purchased by the vessel owner, or any party interested in or responsible for insurable property by reason of maritime perils.

see: marine insurance, river marine insurance, wet marine insurance; Fr: assurance maritime; Gr: Seetransport Versicherung; Sp: seguro marítimo

odds

General. The probability that one event will occur rather than another event. A ratio expressing the probability of an event or outcome.

see: degree of risk, law of large numbers, probability

offer

General. One of the elements needed to form a legal contract. An offer is a promise made by one party in exchange for another party's act, forbearance, or return promise.

see: contract, offeree, offeror

offered price

Financial Planning.
see: asking price

offeree

General. The party to whom an offer is made.
compare: offeror; see: offer

offering price

Financial Planning.
see: asking price

offeror

General. The party that makes an offer.
compare: offeree; see: offer

office burglary and robbery insurance

Crime. A crime plan designed for business and professional offices which covers money, securities and other property against burglary and robbery inside the premises, and robbery of messengers outside the premises.

syn: crime plan 5; see: crime coverages, premises burglary coverage form

© 1991 NILS Publishing Company

office personal property form

Crime. A commercial property insurance endorsement which provides coverage for all office equipment (whether or not owned), improvements made by the insured in leased office space, and valuable papers and documents.

officers & directors liability insurance

Casualty.

see: directors & officers liability insurance

officers protective policy

Ocean Marine. A policy providing all-risks coverage for the personal property of a ship's crew and passengers. This property is not covered by marine cargo insurance.

see: cargo insurance

off-premises coverage

Property. A provision in some property insurance policies, which (subject to limitations) extends protection to personal property located away from the premises described in the policy for a lesser amount than the policy limit. Usually, coverage is provided for a specified amount – between $10,000 to $50,000 – or a percentage of the policy limit, subject to a maximum limitation.

see: coverage extension

offset

Regulation. A broad legal and business concept that allows two parties transacting business to cancel debts owed to each other. As regards insurance, offsets owed reinsurers by insurers in liquidation proceedings would allow reinsurers access to insurer assets ahead of policyholders. Under order of liquidation distribution, policyholders normally hold priority over reinsurers. Regulators (acting as liquidators) feel offsets unfairly move reinsurers ahead of policyholders in access to assets.

offset approach

Employee Benefits.

see: Integration with Social Security

off-shore insurers

Insurer Operations/Risk Management.

see: captive insurance company

ohm meter

Loss Control. A meter used to measure the resistance of a material to an electric current.

oil and gas deficiency insurance

Financial Guarantee Insurance. A form of guaranteed performance insurance that indemnifies the insured against loss if an oil or gas field's actual output falls short of engineering report projections. Coverage is generally limited to fields with proven reserves, that

are currently yielding through at least three producing wells.

oil landmen and lease brokers errors & omissions insurance

Casualty. Errors & omissions coverage for oil landmen, who search for titles and purchase oil leases for clients.

oil well liability

Casualty. Coverage for contractors against bodily injury and property damage arising out of their ownership, operation or use of oil wells.

see: blowout and cratering, platform insurance, saline contamination exclusion

Old Age, Survivors, Disability, and Health Insurance (OASDHI)

Health.

see: Social Security

old line company

Life. A nonfraternal life insurance company which operates on a legal reserve basis. It is believed that the term grew from the early competition between the "new" fraternal insurance companies and the commercial insurance companies who referred to themselves as old line legal reserve companies. Most fraternal companies now operate on a legal reserve basis.

syn: old line legal reserve company; see: insurance company, legal reserve

old line legal reserve company

Life.

see: old line company

omission

Casualty. A peril insured under some liability policies, which is defined as a failure to act or inactivity.

see: errors & omissions insurance

omissions clause

Reinsurance. A treaty reinsurance contract provision stating that should a ceding company fail to report a risk that would normally be covered, the reinsurer would still be liable for the risk, provided the omission was unintentional.

see: treaty reinsurance

omnibus clause

Automobile. A standard automobile liability policy provision that extends coverage to others who may use an insured automobile, without specifically naming them in the policy.

on board bill of lading

Ocean Marine. A bill of lading issued by a steamship

© 1991 NILS Publishing Company

on board bill of lading — continued
company, that confirms the receipt of merchandise
and its loading on board a vessel.
see: bill of lading

on-consignment policy
Inland Marine.
see: in-trust policy

on-deck cargo
Ocean Marine.
see: deck cargo

open cargo policy
Inland Marine/Ocean Marine. A marine insurance
policy primarily used to insure goods in transit. Once
the policy is issued, it remains in force until cancelled
by either party. The policy usually indicates the types
of goods to be insured, sets geographical limits,
establishes a maximum limit of liability for any one
shipment, and enumerates the perils insured against.
Provisions also allow certificates of insurance to be
issued by the insured, based upon the master policy. A
monthly report of shipments is provided to the
insurer, and it forms the basis for determining the
premium.
see: cargo insurance, certificate of insurance,
master insurance policy, warehouse-to-warehouse coverage

open competition rating
Regulation. A method of insurance rate regulation
allowing insurers to compete openly by developing
their own rates, subject to their being adequate and
nondiscriminatory.
syn: open rating; see: adequate, excessive, file-
and-use rating, modified prior approval rating,
nondiscriminatory, prior approval rating, rate
making, rate regulation

open cover
Reinsurance. A term used to refer to any reinsurance
treaty under which a cedent may declare and reinsure
risks of a certain category (e.g., a facultative obligatory
reinsurance treaty).

open debit
Agency. A geographical territory of life and health
insurers that is not serviced by an agent.
see: debit system

open-end mutual fund
Financial Planning. A mutual fund that issues its own
shares to investors continuously, and then redeems
shares as required. Shares are not listed on any
exchange, and participants buy and sell at a unit price
based on the appraised value of the fund's total assets.
compare: closed-end mutual fund; see: mutual
fund

open end policy
Insurer Operations. A policy having no stated expiration
date; it continues in effect until cancelled. Many
ocean cargo policies are written on this basis.
see: policy period; compare: perpetual
insurance

open group actuarial cost method
Employee Benefits/Risk Management. A method
for determining the cost of employee benefit plans,
where the actuarial present values associated with
expected future entrants are considered.
see: actuarial cost method

open perils
Property. A property insurance form that insures
against any "risks of loss" that are not specifically
excluded. This term is replacing the use of the term
"all-risks."
compare: "all-risks" insurance

open perils crop insurance
Property. Crop insurance coverage that is written
under the jurisdiction of the National Crop Insurance
Services. Under a crop insurance policy, the perils
insured can include fire, hail, wind, flood, insects, and
plant disease.
see: crop insurance, crop-hail insurance, multi-
peril crop insurance

open rating
Regulation.
see: open competition rating

open reporting form
Property. A broad term used for several forms of
commercial property insurance which cover all types
and locations of an insured's property within a single
policy.
see: blanket insurance, manufacturers output
policy, stock throughput policy

open slip
Insurer Operations. A Lloyd's of London slip obtained
by a broker that indicates an underwriter's
preapproval for any account which falls within specified
requirements.
see: London rig slip, slip

open-stock burglary policy
Crime.
see: mercantile open-stock burglary insurance

operating income/profit
Insurer Operations. The sum of the net investment
income and net underwriting income in a reporting
period.
see: financial statement, investment income

© 1991 NILS Publishing Company

operating margin

Financial Planning. Operating earnings (before deduction for depreciation, depletion, amortization, interest, and income tax) as a percentage of sales or revenues.

operating ratio

Financial Planning. A financial/management ratio which indicates the efficiency of management. *Formula:* Operating Ratio = Operating Expenses/Net Sales. The smaller the ratio, the greater the organization's ability to generate profit if revenues decrease.

see: **financial ratios, financial underwriting**

operating rights

Automobile. A term that refers to the area in which a truck or trucking company is licensed to operate.

see: **radius of operation**

operations liability

Casualty. Under a commercial general liability policy, that liability which arises from the activities of the insured and his or her employees in the conduct of a business. It does not include completed operations liability. More commonly called premises liability or premises-operations liability.

see: **premises-operations liability**

opportunity cost

Risk Management. The rate of return on the best available investment alternative. The opportunity cost is the greatest return that *will not* be earned if the funds are invested in a specific investment, and not in another.

see: **return on investment**

option

Life. The right of an insured to choose the form in which payments are received from a life insurance policy.

see: **optional life insurance settlement modes, paid-up additions**

Financial Planning. The right to purchase a stock during a specified period of time at a specified price.

see: **call option, put option, warrant**

optional annuity form

Employee Benefits. A provision in a pension plan which allows a participant to elect early retirement, or to continue working past the normal retirement age. Employees that elect early retirement receive reduced benefits, and employees that continue working usually receive enhanced benefits.

compare: **normal annuity form; see: annuity, early retirement, normal retirement age**

optional benefits

Health.

see: **elective benefits**

optional life insurance settlement modes

Life. A beneficiary of the proceeds of a life insurance policy may choose one of five settlement options: interest option, fixed amount option, fixed period option, life income option, or life income with period certain option.

see: **dividend addition, dividend option, fixed amount option, fixed period option, interest option, life income option, life income with period certain option**

optionally renewable contract

Health. A group contract of health insurance allowing the insurer to terminate coverage (i.e., refuse to continue the policy) only at an anniversary or a premium-due date.

compare: **guaranteed renewable, guaranteed insurability, lifetime policy, noncancellable policy**

oral contract

General.

see: **quasi-contract**

order bill of lading

Inland Marine. A bill of lading which is a negotiable document, with interest transferred from one party to another by endorsement. The shipper or buyer is the consignee.

see: **bill of lading, certificate of insurance**

ordinance

General. A law enacted by a governmental authority, especially a municipal political subdivision.

see: **statute**

ordinance or law coverage endorsement

Property. An endorsement that can be added to a property policy written on a replacement cost basis. It covers a building in the event that the enforcement of any building, zoning, or land use law results in 1) loss or damage, 2) any increased cost of repairs or reconstruction, 3) demolition and removal costs. This endorsement incorporates the coverages that were provided by the contingent liability from operation of building laws endorsement, the demolition cost endorsement, and the increased cost of construction endorsement.

syn: **building ordinance or law coverage; see: contingent liability from operation of building laws endorsement, demolition cost endorsement, increased cost of construction endorsement, ordinance or law exclusion**

© 1991 NILS Publishing Company

ordinance or law exclusion

Property. An exclusion in most property insurance policies for loss, or an increase in loss, caused by enforcing any ordinance or law regulating the construction, use or repair of any property, or requires the tearing down of any property, including the cost of removing debris.

see: **civil authority clause, ordinance or law coverage endorsement**

ordinary agent

Agency/Life. An insurance agent who specializes in selling and servicing ordinary life insurance and who may sell other types of life insurance.

see: **agent**

ordinary construction

Loss Control. A term no longer in frequent use, which referred to a building with wood floors on wood joists, with concealed interior wall space, and limited stairwell protection. A fire would spread rapidly through this type of construction.

see: **construction**

ordinary income

Financial Planning. Income from the normal operations of a firm, specifically excluding income from unusual events (e.g, the sale of capital assets).

ordinary life insurance

Life. A form of whole life insurance which is issued in multiples of $1,000, with premiums payable on a monthly, quarterly, semiannual or annual basis until the insured dies.

syn: **straight life policy**; see: **limited payment life insurance, modified life insurance, permanent life insurance, term life insurance, whole life insurance**

ordinary payroll

Property. The payroll of an insured's employees (excluding officers, department managers, executives, contract employees and others). Ordinary payroll is a coverage provided by business interruption policies, depending or whether the ordinary payroll coverage endorsement or the ordinary payroll exclusion endorsement has been attached.

see: **ordinary payroll coverage endorsement, ordinary payroll exclusion endorsement**

ordinary payroll coverage endorsement

Loss Control. An endorsement that can be added to certain business interruption policies which provides coverage for the payroll of employees other than officers, executives, department managers, employees under contract and other important employees, who are automatically included.

compare: **ordinary payroll exclusion endorsement**

ordinary payroll exclusion endorsement

Property. An endorsement that can be added to certain business interruption policies, which excludes coverage for the payroll of all employees except officers, executives, department managers, employees under contract and other important employees. In other words, ordinary workers would not be paid.

compare: **ordinary payroll coverage endorsement**

organizational expenses

General. The costs of organizing a corporation, including filing fees, attorneys' fees, and related expenses. Organizational expenses may also include the cost of raising the initial capital through the distribution of securities.

see: **capital requirement**

Organized Flying Adjusters (OFA)

Organizations. Members: Aircraft insurance adjusters, rated pilots and/or pilots with equivalent aircraft experience. Associate members include company claims personnel, manufacturers and general insurance members. *Objectives:* Promotes high standards in the processing of aviation insurance claims. *Founded:* 1958. *Headquarters:* Corpus Christi, TX.

original age

Life. The age of an insured on the inception date of a term life insurance policy.

see: **attained age**

original age option

Life.

see: **retroactive conversion**

original cost

Property. The actual price paid for a property when it was purchased. "Property" in this context includes buildings, land, equipment and other items.

see: **actual cash value, replacement cost**

original cost new

Automobile. The retail cost paid by the original purchaser for an auto and its equipment.

see: **actual cash value**

other insurance

Insurer Operations. Insurance policies covering the same conditions and perils as an existing contract.

see: **concurrent insurance, other insurance clause**

other insurance clause

Insurer Operations. A clause in property, casualty and health insurance policies, outlining how a policy's benefits will be paid if more than one contract covers the same risk.

syn: **contribution clause**; see: **apportionment,**

© 1991 NILS Publishing Company

coordination of benefits, joint loss agreement, nonduplication of benefits, proration of benefits

other-than-collision coverage (OTC)
Automobile.
see: comprehensive coverage

outage insurance
Property. Coverage that insures against a loss of earnings caused by an insured peril that damages property and prevents machinery from operating.
see: business income coverage form

out-of-court settlement
General.
see: settlement

out of trust
Agency. A term used when an agent's trust is inadequate to meet the payment of agent's balances. This can occur when an agent has made inadequate payments to the trust or illegally withdrawn funds from the trust.
see: bucking arrears

out-patient
Health. An individual who does not need to stay overnight in a hospital, but who receives care, diagnosis or treatment in a clinic, emergency room or health care facility.
compare: in-patient

out-patient facility
Health.
see: ambulatory care facility

outside directors
Casualty. Directors of publicly-held corporations who do not hold executive positions within the corporation. Outside directors may include investment bankers, attorneys, or others who provide advice or services to incumbent management and thus have financial ties with management. The number of inside and outside directors in a corporation is of interest to a D&O liability underwriter.
compare: inside directors; see: directors & officers liability insurance

outstanding claims account
Reinsurance.
see: funding of reserves

outstanding losses
Insurer Operations. Losses that have occurred which are known to an insurer, but which have not yet been settled.
compare: incurred but not reported; see: loss

outstanding premiums
Insurer Operations. Premiums due on issued policies or business, which have not yet been received by an insurer.
see: premium

over-age insurance
Health. Health insurance coverage written for a person who is above the standard limit, which is usually 65 years old.
syn: extended health insurance

overhead expense insurance
Health. Insurance that provides coverage for rent, utilities, and employee salaries when a business owner becomes disabled. The insurance benefit is generally not a fixed amount, but pays the amount of expenses actually incurred.
see: key employee insurance

overinsurance
General. A term used to describe the situation that is created when a risk is insured for an amount exceeding its actual cash value or replacement cost, or when excessive limits of coverage are purchased on liability risks or in life insurance programs.
compare: underinsurance; see: pyramiding of limits, stacking of limits, valued policy law

overlapping insurance
General. Duplicate coverage, involving at least two policies covering the same risk.
see: concurrent insurance, other insurance

overline
Reinsurance. 1) A term used to describe a risk which exceeds an insurance company's normal capacity (including automatic reinsurance treaties on a specific policy). 2) An insurer's agreement to provide insurance or a reinsurer's agreement to assume reinsurance in excess of normal capacity.
see: line

overriding commission
Agency/Insurer Operations. A commission paid to agents who have exclusive territorial or class-of-business agreements with an insurance company, for all policies written in their territory or for that class of business, even if the business is written by other agents.
see: agent's commission, compensation agreement

Overseas Private Investment Corporation (OPIC)
Insurer Operations. A federal program to provide political risk insurance on U.S. investments in developing countries. Protects those businesses/investments it insures against confiscation, expropriation,

© 1991 NILS Publishing Company

OPIC — continued

devaluation of currencies, war exposures and other perils for an agreed limit of liability and time period.

see: **expropriation insurance, political risk insurance**

owned automobile

Automobile. For automobile liability purposes, any automobile owned by the insured including unowned trailers while attached to an owned auto.

owners and contractors protective liability (OCP)

Casualty. An endorsement that can be added to liability policies which provides coverage for claims caused by the negligence of a contractor or subcontractor hired by the insured.

syn: **independent contractors insurance**

owner's equity

Risk Management. An interest in property which is in excess of any claims or liens against it. As a balance sheet item, "owner's equity" is established by capital contributions to an organization by its owners for formation or expansion. Also included in "owner's equity" are profits retained in the company (retained earnings).

see: **balance sheet, capital, financial statement, retained earnings**

owner's form

Inland Marine.

see: **motor truck cargo insurance**

ownership of expirations

Agency/Insurer Operations. Property and casualty insurance policy expirations are considered the exclusive property of the independent agent producing the business, and an insurer cannot reveal this information to anyone other than the originating agent. Expirations of direct writing and exclusive agency companies usually belong to the insurance company.

see: **agency agreement**

ownership provision

Life. A provision that allows policy ownership by a person other than the insured.

owners, landlords, and tenants liability insurance (OL&T)

Casualty. A policy form available under the 1973 ISO liability rating plan still used by some insurers. The form was designed for the less desirable owner, landlord or tenant risks to provide limited coverage (i.e., not as broad as the comprehensive general liability form). As it was limited to this premises liability coverage, the form did not include protection for other-than-designated premises, products and completed operations, independent contractors and

structural alterations. The 1986 ISO liability rating plan does not include a similar form.

oxidation

Inland Marine/Loss Control/Ocean Marine. A physical or chemical change in metal (such as rusting) or a possible cause of spontaneous combustion in flammable materials.

© 1991 NILS Publishing Company

package policy

Insurer Operations. An insurance policy that includes two or more lines or types of coverage in a single contract. *Examples:* Homeowner's (including property and personal liability) and special multi-peril policies (including commercial property and liability).

see: **multiple line policy**

paid business

Life. A policy for which an application for coverage has been signed by the prospective insured, the medical examination has been completed, the initial premium payment has been tendered and accepted by the insurer, but the policy has not yet been delivered.

compare: **delivered business, examined business, issued business, not taken, placed business, written business**

paid claim count

Insurer Operations. The total number of claims for which indemnity payments have been made and for which the claims files have been closed.

see: **claim expense**

paid expense

Insurer Operations. An amount paid for the costs associated with a claim, but not including insurance company claim handling expenses. It includes defense costs (such as attorneys' fees, filing fees, and expert witness fees).

syn: **allocated claim expense;** see: **claim expense**

paid-in capital

General. Money invested in a corporation by its owners, for which shares of stock are received. On a corporation's balance sheet, paid-in capital amounts are reflected in owner's or stockholder's equity.

see: **capital**

paid-in surplus

Insurer Operations. Surplus paid in by stockholders in excess of paid-in capital, to meet minimum policyholders surplus requirements established by applicable state insurance codes. No stock is issued for paid-in surplus, rather it is usually in the form of a stockholder's loan.

see: **policyholder surplus, surplus**

paid losses

Insurer Operations. The actual dollar total that has been paid on incurred losses by issuing checks or drafts to claimants. Paid losses for a specified accounting period are the aggregate of such payments recorded on the books of the insurer within that period.

compare: **incurred losses;** see: **loss**

paid loss retrospective rating plan

Casualty. A conventional retrospective rating plan with an amended premium payment provision. The advance premium remains unchanged, but the insurer agrees to accept a substantially lesser amount in cash and, typically, a promissory note secured by an irrevocable letter of credit or surety bond for the balance. As claims are paid, the insured makes further payments to the insurer, usually on a monthly basis.

see: **cash flow program, retrospective rating plan**

paid-up additions

Life. Some participating life insurance policies allow the policyholder the option to use policy dividends to purchase increments of permanent life insurance which are fully paid-up.

see: **option, policy dividend**

251

© 1991 NILS Publishing Company

paid up at age life insurance
Life. A form of life insurance that provides protection for an entire lifetime, but the premium payments cease at a specific age. Usually stated as "Life paid up at age 45," etc.
see: **limited payment life insurance**

paid-up insurance
Life. A life insurance policy that has all of its premiums paid, but which has not matured by either death or endowment.
compare: **mature**

pair and set clause
Inland Marine/Property. A clause in many property and inland marine policies which provides that the insurer is not obligated to pay for the total value of a set of items if only one item has been lost, damaged or destroyed. The loss settlement would be based on the reasonable and fair proportion that the lost or damaged part bears to the total value of the set.

pallet
Inland Marine/Ocean Marine. A portable, shallow wooden or metal platform – usually about four feet square – for holding and moving material in storage or during transport.

panel wall
Loss Control/Property. An exterior non-bearing wall in multi-story buildings. The panel itself is one story in height, and is supported at each floor level.
see: **construction, curtain wall**

paper losses
Ocean Marine. A form of cargo loss which does not involve a physical loss, but rather a loss due to the incorrect measurement of a cargo upon loading or unloading, because of erroneous mathematical calculations or other mistakes in documentation or measurement of the cargo.

paper title
Title. Title of a property that is evidenced only by deeds or matters appearing on record.
see: **certificate of title, title**

paramedic
Health. An individual who has received formal professional training in routine and emergency medical care. Licensing of paramedics is required by law in most states.
see: **paramedical examination, paramedics professional liability**

paramedical examination
Health/Life. A medical examination performed by a paramedic, on a person applying for life or health insurance.
see: **medical examination**

paramedics professional liability
Casualty. Insurance for licensed paramedics, covering liabilities arising from their professional activities. The policy form is similar to a doctor's or nurse's malpractice liability policy.
compare: **ambulance service malpractice insurance**

parapet
Loss Control. That portion of a solid masonry division or fire wall that extends through the roof by at least three feet.
see: **fire division, fire wall**

parasol policy
Property. A British term for a policy similar to a difference in conditions policy.
compare: **bumbershoot, umbrella liability insurance;** see: **difference in conditions insurance**

parcel post insurance
Inland Marine. Insurance to cover the interest of a shipper for loss against damage to or loss of property being transported by the United States Postal Service via parcel post, first class registered mail, registered air mail, certified mail or ordinary first class mail. Coverage can be provided either by the U.S. Postal Service or through private insurers.
compare: **trip transit insurance;** see: **mail coverage insurance, registered mail insurance**

parent company
Insurer Operations. A term used to refer to a larger company or holding company which owns other smaller companies.
compare: **pup company;** see: **affiliated companies, fleet of companies, holding company, subsidiary company**

parent liability
General. Liability that parents incur through a tort committed by their minor child.

parol evidence rule
General. A rule of law that prohibits modification of a written contract, such as an insurance policy, by a prior oral agreement.
see: **evidence**

partial disability
Employee Benefits. A disability which prevents individuals from performing one or more functions of

© 1991 NILS Publishing Company

their occupation, but does not impair their capability of performing less demanding employment.

compare: **permanent partial disability, permanent total disability, total disability; see: disability, temporary partial disability**

partial disability insurance

Health. A disability income policy provision that provides for partial benefit payments (usually 50% of the total disability limit) for a limited time period (usually six months) when the insured is partially disabled.

see: **disability income insurance, partial disability**

partial loss

Property. A loss to an insured property that does not completely destroy the property.

compare: **total loss**

partial pension plan termination

Employee Benefits. A method developed to allow employers to recapture excess pension plan assets by dividing a qualified plan into two parts, and then terminating one part. Generally, the employer will buy annuities to pay retirees their benefits under the plan and then reclaim the excess assets.

participant

Employee Benefits. An individual who is eligible for or covered under an employee benefit plan, a group insurance plan or a pension plan.

participate

Insurer Operations. To share in the writing of a risk with another insurer.

see: **pro rata, quota share**

participating policy

Insurer Operations. A term used to refer to any insurance policy that distributes its dividends by cash payments, reduced premiums, units of paid-up life insurance, a savings program, or by the purchase of term insurance.

compare: **nonparticipating policy; see: initial premium, net premium, policy dividend**

participating preferred shares

Insurer Operations.
see: **preferred stock**

participating reinsurance

Reinsurance.
see: **pro rata reinsurance**

particular average

Ocean Marine. A concept providing that where a portion of cargo, hull or freight is jettisoned to save the entire venture from peril at sea, the resulting loss

is borne entirely by the individual owning the property which is damaged or sacrificed. The loss must be less than a total loss and not subject to the provisions of general average. Some ocean marine policy forms will provide limited coverage for a particular average loss.

compare: **free of particular average, general average**

partnership

General. An association of two or more persons operating as co-owners of a business for profit.

syn: **general partnership; see: apparent partner, common name statutes, limited partnership, nontrading partnership, partnership insurance, Subchapter S, trading partnership**

partnership financial bond

Surety. A bond used for guaranteeing that an individual investing in a private limited partnership will meet future financial obligations to the partnership.

see: **limited partnership**

partnership insurance

Health/Life. Life or health insurance coverage for a partnership, to guarantee business continuity should one of the partners die or become disabled.

see: **cross purchase plan, key employee insurance, partnership**

party

General. An entity or individual taking part in a legal proceeding or transaction, such as a contract or lawsuit.

party wall

Loss Control. A wall shared by buildings constructed on either side of it.

syn: **common wall; see: adjoining building**

par value

Financial Planning. The nominal (or face value) of a stock or bond.

compare: **no par stock; see: share of stock**

passenger

Aviation. Any person who is in, on, boarding or disembarking an aircraft for the purpose of riding or flying on a flight or attempted flight. In its broadest interpretation, "passenger" includes pilots or crew members.

Fr: **passager**; Gr: **Passagier**; Sp: **pasajero**

passenger bodily injury

Aviation. The basic aircraft liability policy specifically excludes coverage for claims arising out of injury to passengers; this must be added to the policy by a separate insuring agreement.

253

© 1991 NILS Publishing Company

passenger hazard exclusion

Automobile. An endorsement frequently added to motorcycle policies, which excludes coverage for claims against the insured for bodily injury to a passenger.

see: **guest law**

passenger yield

Aviation. The average revenue per mile paid by each passenger of an airline. *Formula*: Passenger Yield = Total Passenger Revenues/Revenue Passenger Miles.

see: **revenue passenger miles**

passive restraint systems

Automobile. Systems within an automobile which restrain passengers from injury during collisions. These include air bags, automatic seat belts and other devices. Insurers encourage their use and installation in automobiles, since they have been shown to reduce the severity of injuries to drivers and passengers. Some insurers offer discounts on automobiles equipped with such devices.

passive retention

Risk Management. A "method" of loss assumption, where an entity does not establish or maintain a fund to pay expected losses arising from an exposure, or purchase insurance for the exposure, because they are 1) unaware of the exposure, 2) the cost of funding the exposure is prohibitive, or 3) any loss, if it occurred, would be insignificant.

compare: **avoidance, insurance, risk transfer, self-insurance**; see: **noninsurance, retention**

past consideration

General. A contract law term referring to an event performed in the past which, therefore, cannot be considered for a promise made in the present.

see: **consideration, contract**

past service benefit

Employee Benefits. A credit allowed to a pension plan participant for their years of service prior to the plan's commencement.

syn: **prior service benefit**; see: **past service liability**

past service liability

Employee Benefits. An employer's obligation to fund pension benefits on newly created plans for employees who are qualified to participate prior to the plan's inception date.

see: **past service benefit**

patent

General. A governmental grant to an inventor of an exclusive right to make and sell his or her invention for a single, nonrenewable period of 17 years.

see: **patent insurance**

patent insurance

Casualty. A term used to refer to either insurance that protects a patent holder, or insurance that protects a party who may infringe on the rights of a patent holder. Patent holders are protected against loss due to infringement of their patent, and non-patent holders are protected from claims due to infringing other parties' patents.

see: **advertising injury coverage**

pattern and die floater

Inland Marine. Patterns and dies can represent a major investment for manufacturing concerns, and a loss can severely impact their business income. Often the patterns and dies are sent out to various subcontractors, which use them to manufacture parts for the insured. The pattern and die floater ordinarily provides "named perils" coverage at subcontractors' locations, and "all risks" coverage for patterns and dies in transit.

see: **die, dies insurance**

Paul v. Virginia

Regulation. An 1869 U.S. Supreme Court ruling which found that an insurance policy did not constitute interstate commerce and therefore was not subject to federal regulation. *Paul* gave the states the power to regulate insurance for over 60 years. This ruling was later modified when the U.S. Supreme Court revised the definition of "commerce" in its *United States v. South-Eastern Underwriters Association* decision. As a result of this decision, the McCarran-Ferguson Act was passed by Congress to maintain state regulation.

see: **McCarran-Ferguson Act, South-Eastern Underwriters Association**

payback period

General. The length of time required for the net revenue from an investment to return the cost of the investment.

syn: **amortization period**

Reinsurance.

see: **amortization period**

paymaster robbery insurance

Crime. Coverage against loss by robbery of payroll monies, while in the care of a custodian or carrier.

payment bond

Surety. A bond guaranteeing a construction project owner that a project contractor will pay for the labor and material it will supply.

syn: **labor and material bond**

payment certain

Life.

see: **annuity certain**

254

© 1991 NILS Publishing Company

pay on behalf of

Casualty. Most liability insurance policies provide that the insurer will pay directly to the appropriate parties those sums that the insured becomes legally obligated to pay as damages. This term signifies that the insured need not first make payment and subsequently obtain reimbursement from the insurer.

compare: indemnification

payor benefit

Life.

see: payor disability

payor disability

Life. A rider attached to a life insurance policy, that pays the premium for the insured if the payor dies or is disabled. When this rider is used, the payor of the policy is usually someone other than the insured person. It is often used on juvenile policies, where the payor is a parent.

syn: death waiver, payor benefit; see: disability income insurance

payout illustration

Employee Benefits. A computer-generated employee benefit schedule which indicates future periodic payments and cumulative payout figures.

payroll audit

Casualty/Workers' Compensation. An examination and verification of an insured's records of employee compensation, which is used in determining the final premium for certain lines of insurance such as workers' compensation.

see: audit, initial premium, remuneration

payroll deduction insurance

Employee Benefits. Insurance coverage provided through an employer, where an employee authorizes all of the premium to be deducted from his or her salary. Initially, this plan was only used for term life insurance policies, but now it has now been expanded to disability, homeowner's, automobile and legal expense insurance.

syn: salary savings insurance; see: group insurance

peak season endorsement

Property. An endorsement providing additional coverage for seasonal risks (resorts, agricultural) where greater inventories or a large percentage of a year's business is at risk during peak seasons. The peak season limit begins and ends on the dates stated in the endorsement.

see: reporting form, seasonal risk

pecuniary damages

General.

see: money damages

penalty

Surety. Maximum amount for which an insurance company, acting as a surety, is held liable under a bond.

see: bond, limit of liability, surety

pension benefit formula

Employee Benefits.

see: benefit formula

Pension Benefit Guaranty Corporation (PBGC)

Regulation. A federal agency, administered by the U.S. Department of Labor, which was authorized by the Employee Retirement Income Security Act of 1974 (ERISA). It insures qualified and defined pension plans and protects vested pension benefits in those cases where the employer or pension trust is insolvent or otherwise unable to meet its commitments. Premiums are paid to the PBGC by employers, based on the number of employees in their plan.

see: Employee Retirement Income Security Act of 1974, restoration of plan

pension liability

Employee Benefits. The total of all unfunded vested pension benefits that have accrued.

per capita

Financial Planning. The distribution of an estate among the deceased's beneficiaries on an equal basis.

compare: per stirpes

per cause maximum limit

Health. Maximum benefits under a health insurance plan that apply separately to each accident or illness incurred by a covered participant. Policies with a per cause maximum limit do not have a maximum policy benefit limit.

see: inside limits, limit of liability, maximum plan limits

percentage of loss deductible

Insurer Operations. A preset percentage deducted from the amount of a loss, usually subject to minimum and maximum amounts. *Example:* A five percent deductible applied to a $12,000 loss leaves the insured responsible for $600 of the loss.

see: deductible, franchise deductible

percentage of value deductible

Property. A deductible whose amount is based on a percentage of the value of the property insured at the time of loss. Most earthquake and some flood insurance policies are written with this type of deductible. *Example:* A building valued at $120,000 with a five percent deductible at the time of loss would result in

© 1991 NILS Publishing Company

percentage of value deductible — continued
the insured being responsible for the first $6,000 of loss.

compare: flat deductible; see: deductible, earthquake insurance, first loss earthquake insurance, franchise deductible

percentage participation

Health. A condition in many health insurance policies, requiring that the insured pay a percentage of covered medical expenses. *Example:* A 10 percent participation would require the insured to pay 10 percent of a claim and the insurer to pay 90 percent.

compare: co-payment; see: coinsurance

per curiam opinion

General. An opinion written "by the court" rather than by a named judge, when all the judges of a court agree on a matter, and it is not deemed to merit any discussion.

per diem

General. The payment of funds on a daily basis.

per diem business interruption coverage

Property. A business interruption coverage where the insured receives a specified amount of money for each day that the business is interrupted as the result of an insured peril. If the interruption is partial (i.e., some business can be transacted), the percentage of interruption is calculated and this percentage of the per diem amount is paid.

see: business income coverage form

performance bond

Surety. A bond guaranteeing that one party (usually a contractor) will faithfully perform contractual obligations to another party.

see: bid bond, contract bond

peril

Insurer Operations. The potential cause of a loss. Perils include such things as fire, wind, legal liability, errors and omissions, bodily injury and collision.

syn: cause of loss; compare: exposure, hazard, insured peril, risk; see: economic perils, human perils, natural perils; Fr: risque assuré; Gr: versicherte Gefahren; Sp: riesgo asegurado

perils of the sea

Ocean Marine. A term found in ocean marine contracts that means the peril must be something peculiar to transportation by water, such as heavy weather, strandings, striking on rocks or on the ocean floor, collisions with other vessels, or contacts with floating objects such as logs or icebergs.

periodic payment

Insurer Operations.
see: structured settlement

period of restoration

Property. Under business income coverage, this is the period of time during which the insured will receive compensation for lost income. It is not the actual period of the restoration, but rather the time it would normally take to restore the damaged property.

see: business income coverage form

permanent life insurance

Life. A general term used to refer to ordinary life and whole life insurance policies that remain in effect so long as their premiums are paid.

compare: term life insurance; see: ordinary life insurance, whole life insurance

permanent partial disability

Employee Benefits. A disability which prevents individuals for the remainder of their lives from performing one or more functions of their occupation, but does not impair their capability of performing less demanding employment.

compare: partial disability, permanent total disability, total disability; see: disability

permanent total disability

Employee Benefits. A disability which prevents individuals for the remainder of their lives from performing any duty pertaining to their occupation and does not allow them to perform any other employment.

compare: partial disability, permanent partial disability, total disability; see: disability, presumptive disability

permit bond

Surety. A bond guaranteeing that the recipient of a permit will comply with the laws, regulations and ordinances associated with the use of the permit.

see: license bond

per occurrence limit

Casualty. A sub-limit contained in some liability policies, which places a cap on payment for all claims which arise out of a single incident. Under the ISO Commercial General Liability Policy, a per occurrence limit applies to Coverage A (bodily injury and property damage liability) and Coverage C (medical payments).

see: commercial general liability form, limit of liability

per person limit

Casualty. A sub-limit contained in some liability policies which places a cap on the payment of a claim to any one person. Under the ISO Commercial General Liability Policy, a per person limit applies to

© 1991 NILS Publishing Company

Coverage B (personal and advertising injury liability) and Coverage C (medical payments).

compare: aggregate limit, occurrence limit;
see: commercial general liability form, limit of liability

perpetual insurance

Property. A unique form of insurance policy written on buildings. For a flat initial premium of sufficient amount, the insurer agrees to cover the building named in the policy without an expiration date. A few of these policies are still in force from the 1700s!

compare: open end policy

perpetual succession

General. A term used to describe the life of a corporation, which continues despite the death of any stockholder or any stockholder's transfer of stock.

see: corporation

persistency

Insurer Operations. A term used to describe the percentage of insurance policies remaining in force or which have not been cancelled for non-payment of premium during their term.

compare: lapse ratio, termination rate

person

General. A legal term that includes both "natural persons" (living people) and artificial persons (such as corporations) created by an act of government.

see: corporation

personal and advertising injury liability

Casualty. Coverage Part B of the ISO Commercial General Liability form, which combines both personal injury and advertising injury into a single insuring agreement and limit of liability.

see: advertising injury coverage, commercial general liability form, per person limit, personal injury, personal injury liability

personal articles floater

Inland Marine. Insurance coverage for specific personal articles (such as jewelry, cameras, fine arts and musical instruments) where each item to be covered is specifically listed (along with its value) in the policy. Coverage is provided on an "all-risks" basis, usually with no deductible.

syn: personal effects floater; see: floater policy

personal automobile policy (PAP)

Automobile. A common automobile insurance policy providing individual or family coverage. This policy replaced the family automobile policy.

compare: basic standard auto policy, family automobile policy

personal contract

Insurer Operations. An insurance policy is a personal contract between an insurer and the insured. Each party relies implicitly on the other for disclosing critical information, and the insurer promises to indemnify the insured against certain events in return for the payment of premiums.

see: contract

personal defense

General. A legal defense involving negotiable instruments, by which a party to such an instrument can avoid liability under the instrument because of their participation in or knowledge of certain transactions or facts. Such a defense is not valid against a holder in due course of the instrument.

see: holder in due course

personal effects floater

Inland Marine.

see: personal articles floater

personal income insurance

Health.

see: disability income insurance

personal injury

Casualty. Libel, slander, false arrest and invasion of privacy. In its broadest sense, it is defined as any physical or mental harm, although in liability insurance personal injuries (the less physical of these injuries) and bodily injuries (the more physical) are dealt with separately.

see: defamation of character, disparagement of goods, libel, personal injury liability, slander

personal injury liability (PI)

Casualty. Coverage automatically included in the ISO Commercial General Liability form under Coverage Part B. This coverage acts to extend bodily injury coverage to include coverage for personal injury.

see: personal and advertising injury liability, personal injury

personal injury protection (PIP)

Automobile. An automobile insurance coverage required by law in some states, which provides coverage for basic medical expenses to victims, regardless of legal liability or fault.

see: no-fault insurance

personal lines

Insurer Operations. A general term used to describe insurance for individuals or families, as opposed to "commercial lines" which refers to insurance for businesses.

compare: commercial lines

© 1991 NILS Publishing Company

personal property

Property. Property that is movable or separable from the realty; any property other than real property.

syn: **business personal property**; compare: **improvements and betterments, real estate;** see: **equipment floater, intangible personal property, machinery, machinery and equipment, personal articles floater**

personal property floater (PPF)

Inland Marine. Worldwide coverage on an "all-risks" basis for personal property owned, used or worn by the insured. Coverage extends to personal property of family members residing in the same household. Coverage is divided between blanket property and scheduled property sections.

see: **floater policy**

personal property of others

General. Personal property which is not owned by the insured.

see: **bailment**

Property. That personal property lost or damaged while in the possession of or otherwise in the care, custody, or control of an insured. Many property forms provide limited coverage for personal property of others, and allow additional coverage to be purchased.

Casualty. Personal property of another damaged or lost while in the care, custody or control of another. Liability forms generally exclude coverage for liability arising out of damage to the personal property of others in an insured's care, custody or control. This coverage can be purchased for an additional premium.

personal protective equipment

Loss Control. Clothing or devices worn or used to protect various parts of the body. *Examples:* Hard hats, protective eyewear, gloves, etc.

personal surety

Surety. An individual – instead of an insurance company – acting as a surety, guaranteeing the acts of another.

see: **surety**

personal theft insurance

Crime.
see: **broad form personal theft insurance**

personal trust

Financial Planning. A form of inter-vivos trust, where the owner of a property gives it to another person to safeguard, hold, and use for a third party's benefit.

see: **inter-vivos trust, trust**

personal umbrella

Casualty. A liability policy which provides increased limits and expanded coverage over underlying casualty coverages in homeowner's and personal automobile policies.

see: **umbrella liability insurance**

per stirpes

Financial Planning. From the Latin term for "by branches," the distribution of a deceased beneficiary's share of an estate among heirs related to the beneficiary in a descending order, according to the proximity of each heir's relationship to the deceased.

compare: **per capita**

pet insurance

Casualty. Coverage provided on specified household pets, for veterinarian fees on a per accident or per illness basis, usually subject to a deductible. Broader coverages (including death benefits, theft and loss in value of the pet) are also available.

see: **animal insurance**

petition

General. A formal request to a court, asking for judicial action on a matter; also referred to as a "motion" or an "application."

see: **answer, complaint, pleadings, summons**

pet salon liability coverage

Casualty. Coverage designed for pet salons and grooming establishments that clip nails or hair, or dock tails of cats and dogs. It provides malpractice coverage similar to that provided for beauticians and barbers.

phantom stock plan

Employee Benefits. An employee benefit plan where the plan benefits are tied to the employing corporation's common shares. Actual shares are not utilized in funding the plan, rather "phantom shares" are assigned to each plan participant and the value of their increase (decrease), dividends and splits are accrued for their benefit. This plan allows the employees to participate in the corporation's results.

see: **share of stock**

pharmacists professional liability

Casualty. Coverage for employed pharmacists, against claims for personal injury arising from alleged malpractice, error or omission in rendering professional services.

compare: **druggists liability coverage**

physical damage

Automobile. A broad term that refers to any automobile insurance coverage that insures against damage to the vehicle. Perils such as collision, vandalism, fire and theft would be included under this term.

see: **collision coverage, comprehensive coverage; Fr: dommages éprouves par les (voitures**

© 1991 NILS Publishing Company

or automobiles); Gr: Kasko (Auto); Sp: daño físico (automóvil)

physical depreciation
General.
see: depreciation

physical hazard
Loss Control. A hazard which results from material or structural features of a risk, as opposed to human or management factors.
see: hazard

physicians and surgeons floater
Inland Marine. Coverage on an "all-risks" basis, designed specifically for physicians and surgeons to cover medical, surgical and dental equipment and instruments (including tools, materials, supplies and scientific books) used in their profession. The policy may be extended to cover furniture, fixtures and tenants' improvements and betterments. *(ISO Form CM 00 26)*
see: floater policy

physicians professional liability insurance
Casualty. Coverage for physicians, against claims for bodily injury arising from alleged malpractice, error or omission in rendering professional services. This coverage is usually written on a claims-made form.
see: physicians, surgeons, and dentists professional liability insurance, professional liability insurance

physicians, surgeons, and dentists professional liability insurance
Casualty. An ISO liability program which includes policy forms and general rules for writing physicians, surgeons and dentists professional liability coverage. Coverage is written in programs developed for each specialty.
see: dentists professional liability insurance, physicians professional liability insurance

picketing
General. The presence outside an employer's business of one or more employees and/or other persons, to publicize a labor dispute, influence employees or customers to withhold their work or business (respectively), or show a union's desire to represent the employees.
see: strike, strike insurance

pickling
Loss Control. The process of removing a coating of scale, oxide, or tarnish from metals by immersion in an acid bath to obtain a chemically clean surface.

pilferage
Crime. Petty theft; sneak thievery; stealing small amounts of property.
see: theft; Fr: petit vol, larcin; Gr: Plünderung; Sp: ratería

pilot and crew occupational disability insurance
Aviation/Health. Disability coverage for professional pilots and crew members, when they are unable to perform their normal flight duties.
see: disability income insurance

pilot light
Loss Control. 1) A colored light on or near electrical equipment, indicating the equipment power is on or that it is in use. 2) A low flame in a gas-fired vessel or heater, which ignites the main heating elements when they are supplied with gas.

pilot warranty
Aviation. A warranty to aircraft policies requiring that a covered aircraft be piloted by a specifically named pilot or by a pilot meeting specified (required) qualifications. The pilot qualifications can be stated as a minimum number of total flight hours, minimum number of hours in a specific type of aircraft, by a specific Federal Aviation Administration (FAA) flight rating, or a combination of these. An additional requirement is that a pilot must have a valid FAA license and medical certificates, and operate the aircraft within the limits of the pilot's FAA rating.

pipeline insurance
Inland Marine. Coverage, generally on an "all-risks" basis, for pipeline systems (including buildings, pipelines, meters and machinery, pumping stations and tanks).
see: platform insurance

piracy
Ocean Marine. An act committed by unauthorized persons who seize or plunder property, solely for their own purposes, on the high seas. "Piracy" can include seizure of a ship's cargo by a mob from on shore or seizure of a ship by her passengers.
see: assailing thieves, barratry

placed business
Life. An application for coverage which has been signed by the prospective insured, the medical examination has been completed, the initial premium payment has been tendered, and the policy has been delivered.
compare: delivered business, examined business, issued business, not taken, paid business, written business

259

© 1991 NILS Publishing Company

placement

Agency. The process of binding or underwriting an insurance policy once an agent or broker has found a company to accept the risk.

plain language laws

Regulation. Laws that have been instituted by many states, which require insurance policies to be written in easily understandable ("everyday") language.

see: easy read, Flesch Test

plaintiff

General. A party filing a lawsuit against another party, who is the defendant.

compare: defendant; see: claimant

plaintiff's bond to secure

Surety. One of two forms of injunction bonds. As the result of a judicial process, an order granting an injunction may be conditioned upon the plaintiff furnishing a bond to indemnify the defendant against loss in the event it is finally decided that the injunction should not have been granted.

compare: defendant's bond to dissolve; see: bond, injunction bond

plaintiff's replevin bond

Surety. A bond that guarantees that a plaintiff will pay damages or return property if the replevin action is defeated.

see: bond, court bond, replevin

plan's benefit formula

Employee Benefits.

see: benefit formula

plan sponsor

Employee Benefits. The entity or organization that sponsors an employee benefit plan; it may be a single employer, a group of employers (multi-employer trust), an employee organization (union), an association, committee or joint board of trustees.

see: merger of plans

plant age

Risk Management. An estimate of the average age of capital assets used in a business, derived by dividing accumulated depreciation at the most recent year end by the depreciation allowance in the most recent year.

plate glass insurance

Property.

see: glass coverage form

platform insurance

Ocean Marine. Property and liability coverages written on an ocean marine form, for oil and gas drilling barges and platforms located offshore in an ocean or a lake.

see: oil well liability, pipeline insurance, saline contamination exclusion

pleadings

General. The papers filed by the parties involved in a legal action, setting forth the facts and framing the issues to be tried.

see: answer, complaint, demurrer, petition, summons

pleasure and business

Aviation.

see: business and pleasure

pleasure use

Automobile. An automobile rating classification used when a vehicle is not used for business purposes. Pleasure use includes driving to and from work.

compare: business use, drive to or from work, farm use

pluralistic markets

International.

see: international market categories

pluvious insurance

Property.

see: rain insurance

point of operation

Loss Control. The point of contact between the principal functional part of a machine or tool and the material or substance being worked on by the machine or tool.

see: barrier guard, inrunning nip point, machine tool, two-hand controls

Poisson distribution

Risk Management. An actuarial distribution curve which is applied to independent, random events where the frequency is small compared to the number of exposure units.

see: distribution curve, probability

policy

Insurer Operations. The written forms, endorsements, riders and attachments that make up an insurance contract between an insured and insurer. A policy includes the terms and conditions of the coverage, the perils insured or excluded, the limits of insurance provided, the interests insured, the effective dates of the coverage, etc.

see: insurance contract, policy condition laws, policy conditions, policy declarations; Fr: police; Gr: Police; Sp: poliza

© 1991 NILS Publishing Company

policy anniversary

Insurer Operations. A date twelve months after the date when a policy is issued, or as specified in the declarations.

see: **anniversary date, policy period**

policy condition laws

Regulation. Specific state regulations that require insurance policies issued in that state to include "statutory conditions." If a policy is issued which is inconsistent with the statutory conditions, the statutory conditions will apply, as they are held to be of greater effect because of their statutory origins. Occasionally, statutory conditions may be waived or modified by noting such a change in clear type with a different colored ink; the courts sometimes must decide (after a loss) whether such waivers or modifications were reasonable.

see: **legislated insurance coverage, minimum coverage clauses**

policy conditions

Insurer Operations. The section of a policy or provisions scattered throughout an insurance policy, indicating the general rules or procedures that the insurance company and insured agree to follow under the contract.

syn: **condition**; see: **exclusion, face, insurance contract, policy declarations**

policy declarations

Insurer Operations. The section of an insurance policy containing basic underwriting information, such as the insured's name, address, a description of insured locations or receipts. Also, a statement that an applicant for insurance makes to obtain an insurance policy.

syn: **declarations**; see: **exclusion, face, insurance contract, insuring agreement, policy conditions**

policy dividend

Insurer Operations. An amount of money paid to policyholders by a mutual insurer because of their ownership interest in the company. A stock insurer may also pay a policy dividend if it writes participating insurance. The amount of dividend payable is based on certain savings in losses or expenses realized by the insurer on that participating class of business.

see: **initial premium, paid-up additions, participating policy**

policy fee

Insurer Operations. An amount sometimes charged in addition to the initial policy premium, for issuing the policy. In many states such a fee is illegal.

see: **premium, service fee**

policyholder

Insurer Operations. The party in whose name an insurance policy is issued; the first named insured.

compare: **insured, named insured, policyowner**

policyholder surplus

Insurer Operations. The amount by which an insurance company's assets exceed its liabilities, as reported in its annual statement. For a stock insurer the policyholder surplus would be the sum of its capital and surplus; for a mutual insurer, the policyholder surplus equals the company's surplus.

syn: **surplus to policyholders**; see: **surplus**

policy jacket

Insurer Operations.

see: **jacket**

policy loan

Life. A loan made by a life insurer to the owner of a life policy having a cash value equal to all or part of the cash surrender value. Such a loan is one of the usual nonforfeiture values of a life policy.

see: **delay clause, nonforfeiture loan value benefit**

policyowner

Insurer Operations. An individual that has an ownership interest in an insurance policy.

compare: **insured, named insured, policyholder**

policy period

Insurer Operations. The period during which an insurance policy provides coverage.

syn: **policy term**; see: **anniversary date, annual policy, duration of risk, effective date, expiration date, maturity date, natural expiry, noon clause, open end policy, policy anniversary, term**; Fr: **durée de la police**; Gr: **Vertragsdauer**; Sp: **vigencia de la póliza**

policy reserve

Life/Health. An amount set aside by an insurer specifically to fulfill the obligations of a policy. While such reserves may be calculated as an aggregate amount, covering many policies, it is assumed that each policy has a pro rata share of the total reserve. This reserve is for the increased claim rate encountered as the policyholder population ages.

syn: **active life reserve**

policy term

Insurer Operations.

see: **policy period**

© 1991 NILS Publishing Company

policywriting agent

Insurer Operations. An agent who is authorized to issue an insurer's policies.

see: agent, general agent, recording agent

policy year

Insurer Operations. The 12-month period commencing with a policy's effective date or renewal date, as distinguished from the calendar year, which always starts on January 1.

compare: calendar year, fiscal year; see: policy period

policy year experience

Insurer Operations. The losses incurred by a specific policy or line of business that was in force for a defined twelve-month period. In long-tail liability coverages, the incurred losses produced from a policy or line of business may not become known until several years after expiration of the defined policy period.

see: long-tail liability

political action committee liability

Casualty. Coverage for political action committees (PACs), which are formed to raise funds for political candidates. It provides liability protection for committee members from lawsuits, including protection for the exposures set forth under the Federal Election Campaign Act of 1971, as well as Chapters 95 and 96 of the Internal Revenue Code.

political risk insurance

International. Coverage for United States firms operating outside the United States in the event of confiscation or expropriation of property by a foreign government. Coverage can also be provided for loss due to the devaluation of currencies. Political risk insurance is available from private insurers and governmental bodies.

see: expropriation insurance, Overseas Private Investment Corporation

pollutant

Casualty. As used in most liability policies written after the mid-1980s, this term is used to refer to any solid, liquid, gaseous or thermal irritant or contaminant, including smog, vapor, soot, fumes, acids, alkalines, chemicals and waste. Waste is further defined as materials to be recycled, reconditioned or reclaimed.

see: hazardous waste, pollution exclusion, pollution insurance

pollution exclusion

Casualty. An exclusion contained in the ISO Commercial General Liability form which denies coverage for bodily injury or property damage arising out of the actual, alleged or threatened discharge, dispersal,

release or escape of pollutants. Occasionally, portions of this exclusion can be eliminated for an additional premium, or pollution coverage can be purchased in a separate policy. Prior to the 1986 CGL form, coverage was provided for pollution arising out of a sudden and accidental event.

see: commercial general liability form, environmental impairment liability, pollutant, pollution insurance, pollution liability extension endorsement

pollution insurance

Casualty. Coverage against third-party claims for contamination of air, water, or land, from sudden and accidental release of chemicals or pollutants.

see: environmental impairment liability, pollutant, pollution liability extension endorsement, pollution liability – limited form

pollution legal liability

Casualty.

see: environmental impairment liability

pollution liability extension endorsement

Casualty. An endorsement to the ISO Commercial General Liability (CGL) policy, which deletes part of the pollution exclusion, thereby providing coverage for sudden and accidental pollution.

see: commercial general liability form

Pollution Liability Insurance Association (PLIA)

Organizations. Members: Primary and reinsurance companies. *Objectives:* Promotes the availability of pollution and hazardous waste insurance. Policies are issued by member companies and reinsured through the association. *Founded:* 1982. *Headquarters:* Downers Grove, IL.

pollution liability – limited form

Casualty. An ISO form providing pollution liability coverage on a "claims-made" basis; coverage for clean-up costs is excluded *(ISO Form CG 00 40)*.

pool

Insurer Operations. A group of self-insurers, insurers or reinsurers which underwrites certain risks, with premiums, losses and expenses shared among members of the pool in predetermined ratios.

syn: syndicate

portfolio

General. A collection of items belonging to a single owner.

see: loss portfolio transfer, portfolio return, portfolio runoff, portfolio transfer, premium portfolio

Financial Planning. A collection of financial assets (securities, bank deposits, notes, etc.) belonging to a

© 1991 NILS Publishing Company

single owner. In the securities industry, a portfolio consists of common stocks, preferred stocks, bonds, cash, etc. belonging to a single owner.

portfolio return

Reinsurance. The reassumption of a specific book of reinsured business by an insurer, from the reinsurer that had assumed the business.

compare: loss portfolio transfer, portfolio transfer

portfolio runoff

Reinsurance. The continuing obligation of a reinsurer under a cancelled reinsurance contract until all ceded premiums from that contract are earned and all losses paid.

portfolio transfer

Reinsurance. The transfer of an entire portfolio of policies by a cession from a primary carrier to a reinsurer; the reinsurance of an entire book of business that a primary insurer no longer desires to write.

compare: portfolio return; see: loss portfolio transfer

port risk insurance

Ocean Marine. Coverage for a ship that remains in a port for a protracted period of time. The ship may move within the port limits, and even prepare for a voyage and load cargo, but once leaving port, coverage ceases.

syn: port risk only clause

port risk only clause

Ocean Marine.

see: port risk insurance

position schedule bond

Surety. A fidelity bond that provides coverage only for individuals filling specific positions for the insured, and which are described in a schedule attached to the bond.

see: blanket position bond, fidelity bond, name position bond

possession

General. A term used to describe an exclusive domain over and control of property, either as an owner or as the proprietor of a qualified right to a property.

see: adverse possession

possessory lien

General. A lien allowing a party the right to retain possession of another's property as security for a debt or obligation owed. The lien continues only as long as the possession is retained.

see: encumbrance, lien

postdate

General. To insert or place a later date on a document than the actual date on which it was executed.

compare: antedate

postdated check plan

Insurer Operations. A program no longer in common use, where a policyowner provides the insurer with a series of postdated checks, which are used to make premium payments due throughout the year. This concept has been replaced by the preauthorized check plan.

compare: preauthorized check plan

post-FIRM rates

Property. A category of rates published in the National Flood Insurance Program Manual, applying to buildings located in a community qualifying for the regular flood program. Post-FIRM rates are used on building construction that started after December 31, 1974, or after the community's initial Flood Insurance Rate Map was published, whichever is later. These rates are lower than pre-FIRM rates.

compare: pre-FIRM rates; see: flood insurance rate map, National Flood Insurance Program

post-judgment interest

General. Interest payable on court-awarded damages, from the date of judgment until the date the damages are paid to the plaintiff.

compare: prejudgment interest; see: damages

post-mortem dividend

Life. A dividend paid under a participating life insurance policy, which includes dividends earned from the last dividend date to the date of death.

see: participating policy

post-retirement funding

Employee Benefits. A pension plan funding concept which is no longer allowed by ERISA where an employer would purchase an annuity or fund pension benefits only upon retirement of a participant. ERISA now requires all pension benefits to be funded on a current basis.

see: Employee Retirement Income Security Act of 1974

poultry insurance

Inland Marine. Coverage on poultry which insures against death directly and immediately resulting from fire only, or from such "named perils" as fire and lightning, extended coverages, flood, and collision or overturn of a vehicle within which the poultry is being transported. The requirement for this coverage to

© 1991 NILS Publishing Company

poultry insurance — continued
apply is that death must result directly and immediately from an insured peril.

see: **animal insurance, livestock mortality insurance**

power interruption insurance
Property. Coverage that indemnifies the insured for loss of earnings if power supplied by a public utility is interrupted by an insured peril.

see: **contingent business income coverage**

power of attorney
General. A written authorization given by one person or entity to a second party, to authorize the second party to act for and obligate the first to the extent set forth in the authorization.

see: **attorney-in-fact**

power plant insurance
Property. A form of boiler and machinery insurance that insures electrical generating stations against loss.

preaction automatic sprinkler system
Loss Control. An automatic sprinkler system that is similar to a dry-pipe system; however, air pressure may or may not be used. The main sprinkler system control valve is opened by an actuating device, which permits water to flow to the individual sprinkler heads and the system then functions as a wet-pipe system. It is generally used in areas where piping systems are subject to mechanical damage and where it is important to prevent accidental discharge of water.

see: **automatic sprinkler system, dry pipe automatic sprinkler system, wet pipe sprinkler system**

preauthorized check plan
Insurer Operations. A system that allows a policyowner to authorize the insurer to withdraw funds on a periodic basis directly from the insured's bank account for premium payments.

syn: **electronic funds transfer plan;** compare: **postdated check plan**

preexisting condition
Health/Life. An illness or disability that existed before the effective date of a health or life insurance policy. Such a preexisting condition can result in cancellation of a policy or exclusion from coverage.

see: **impairment exclusion rider, injury independent of all other means**

preferred creditor
General. A creditor given a statutory right to first payment or payment before other creditors.

preferred provider organization (PPO)
Health. The joining together of hospitals, physicians, dentists and other health care providers to provide comprehensive medical services on a contractual, predetermined-fee basis to individuals, employers, insurers or third-party administrators.

see: **direct health care corporation, health indemnity plan, health maintenance organization, managing physician, prepaid group practice program**

preferred risk
Insurer Operations. An insurable risk with underwriting characteristics that are superior to the standard risk.

see: **standard risk**

preferred shareholder
General. A term used to refer to a beneficial holder of preferred shares of corporate stock.

see: **preferred stock**

preferred stock
General. Shares that have preferential rights (ahead of common shareholders) to dividends, to amounts distributable on liquidation, or to both, ahead of common shareholders. Preferred shares are usually entitled only to receive specified, limited amounts as dividends or on liquidation. If preferred shares are entitled to share in excess distributions with common shareholders on some defined basis, they are called "participating preferred shares." Participating preferred shares may also be called "class A common," or some similar designation to reflect their open-ended rights.

syn: **participating preferred shares;** see: **preferred shareholder, share of stock**

pre-FIRM rates
Property. A category of rates published in the National Flood Insurance Program Manual. They apply to buildings located in a community that has qualified for the regular flood program. Pre-FIRM rates are used on building constructions that started on or before December 31, 1974, or before the community's initial Flood Insurance Rate Map was published, whichever is later. These rates are higher than post-FIRM rates.

compare: **post-FIRM rates;** see: **flood insurance rate map, National Flood Insurance Program**

prejudgment interest
Casualty. Interest that accrues on any money awarded by a court during that time prior to the entry of a trial judgment. Most liability policies will pay the cost of interest on a judgment only from the time of a court decree until the date of payment.

compare: **post-judgment interest;** see: **damages**

© 1991 NILS Publishing Company

prelicensing education requirement

Agency/Regulation. An educational program specified by state law which agent or broker applicants must complete before receiving a license.

see: licensee

preliminary term

Life/Insurer Operations. An accounting method for life insurers which does not require any terminal reserve to be established during the first year of a policy, thereby making the policy more attractive to prospective buyers.

see: terminal reserve

premises

Aviation. As used in aircraft policies, a term describing areas at an airport used for parking or storing aircraft.

Insurer Operations. A specified property, location or portion of a property that is designated for coverage in an insurance policy.

Fr: lieux, locaux; Gr: Grundstück; Sp: predios

premises burglary coverage form

Crime. A crime coverage form providing coverage against actual or attempted robbery of a watchperson and actual burglary of property from an insured premises.

syn: crime coverage form E; see: burglary, crime coverages

premises liability insurance

Casualty. Legal liability insurance coverage for damages caused by accidents or occurrences arising from the condition, maintenance or upkeep of the insured's premises.

see: owners, landlords, and tenants liability insurance

premises-operations liability

Casualty. Legal liability coverage for damages caused by accidents or occurrences arising from the condition, maintenance or upkeep of the insured's premises and from the insured's business operations. Most basic business liability policies provide this coverage.

compare: products-completed operations insurance; see: commercial general liability form

premises theft and outside robbery coverage form

Crime. A crime coverage form providing coverage against actual or attempted theft within or outside an insured premises. It also covers damage to the premises or its exterior resulting directly from an actual or attempted theft.

syn: crime coverage form H; see: crime coverages, theft

premium

Insurer Operations. A sum of money paid for an insurance policy; the amount of money an insurer charges to provide coverage.

see: additional premium, adjustable premium, basic premium, deferred premium, deferred premium payment plan, deposit premium, direct bill, direct written premium, discounted premium, dividend, earned premium, earned reinsurance premium, estimated annual premium, excess loss premium factor, financed premium, fully earned premium, graded premium, gross premium, guideline premium, initial premium, itemized premium charges, Lloyd's Premium Trust Fund, maximum premium, maximum retrospective premium, minimum premium, minimum retrospective premium, multiple table extra premium, natural premium, net premium, net premiums written, outstanding premiums, policy fee, premium adjustment provision, premium deficiency, premium discount, premium financing, premium income per share, premium in force, premium load, premium payment mode, premium payment notice, premium portfolio, premium receipt, premium tax, premium written per share, premium written to surplus, provisional premium, pure premium, reinsurance premium, reserve premium, restoration premium, retrospective premium, return of premium, return premium, risk premium, standard premium, step-rate premium, subject premium, unearned premium, unearned premium reserve, unearned reinsurance premium, uniform premium, unscheduled premium payments, valuation premium, vanishing premium, waiver of premium, waiver of restoration premium, whole dollar premium, written premiums; Fr: prime; Gr: Beitrag, Prämie; Sp: prima

premium adjustment provision

Insurer Operations. A provision contained in or endorsed to some insurance policies stating that an initial or deposit premium will be charged, but that the final premium will be subject to adjustment during the period of coverage or at the end of coverage, based on loss experience or change in the rating base.

see: audit provision, deposit premium, initial premium, retrospective rating plan

premium and dispersion credit plan

Property.

see: multiple location rating plan

265

© 1991 NILS Publishing Company

premium audit
Insurer Operations.
see: audit

premium base
Insurer Operations/Reinsurance.
see: subject premium

premium deficiency
Insurer Operations. An amount by which anticipated losses, loss adjustment expenses, policyholder dividends, unamortized deferred acquisition costs and other underwriting expenses exceed the related unearned premiums and related future investment income.

premium deficiency reserve
Life/Regulation. A reserve sometimes required by state regulators of life insurers, when the gross premium is less than the valuation premium, because their experience reflects different loss statistics than current mortality tables.
see: Statutory Accounting Principles, statutory reserve

premium discount
General. A percentage reduction based upon the size of the premium. The justification for such a discount is that the proportionate cost of issuing and servicing a policy is generally less as the premium increases.
see: multiple location rating plan

premium finance company errors & omissions insurance
Casualty. Errors and omissions coverage for insurance premium finance companies to pay damages in the event they allow an insurance policy to be incorrectly cancelled or let a policy lapse.
see: premium financing

premium financing
Insurer Operations. A method of paying for insurance coverage, whereby a premium finance company (which may or may not be affiliated with an insurance company) pays a policy's premium, and then bills the policyowner in installments, for a portion of the premium plus a finance charge or interest. If the policyowner fails to make a scheduled payment, the premium finance company may request pro rata or short-rate cancellation of the policy and receive any return premium.
see: deferred premium payment plan, financed premium, pro rata cancellation, short-rate cancellation

premium income per share
Insurer Operations. A financial measure of insurer strength, calculated by dividing premium income received by an insurer by the number of common shares outstanding at year-end.
compare: premium written per share

premium in force
Insurer Operations. The total of initial premium on all policies which have not expired or been cancelled.

premium load
Life. The percentage of premium deducted from premium payments for universal life insurance policies, to cover policy expenses. Some policies are issued on a "no load" basis.
syn: front-end load

premium offset
Life.
see: vanishing premium

premium payment mode
Insurer Operations. The method by and frequency with which the policy premium is to be paid to the insurer. *Examples:* Annually, or in quarterly or monthly installments; 10 percent deposit and 11 monthly installments; or a 20 percent deposit with monthly reports.

premium payment notice
Insurer Operations. An invoice from an agent or insurer to the insured, indicating that a premium will be due by a specified date.

premium portfolio
Insurer Operations. A specified group of insurance policies issued by an insurer and in force.
see: portfolio

premium receipt
Insurer Operations. A receipt issued by an agent or insurer indicating that a premium payment has been received from the insured.

premium tax
Insurer Operations. A tax applied by states against the gross premium written by an insurer on risks in that state. It is usually indicated as a percentage of premium, and can range from 1.5% to 6%.

premium written per share
Insurer Operations. A financial measure of insurer strength, calculated by dividing the total premiums written by a property and casualty insurer during the year, by the number of common shares outstanding.
compare: premium income per share

premium written to surplus
Insurer Operations. The total premiums received from property and casualty policies sold during the year, divided by statutory "net worth."

© 1991 NILS Publishing Company

prepaid expense

General. A payment made for various goods or services which have not yet been received, and whose benefit will only be enjoyed in the future.

see: current assets

prepaid freight

Inland Marine/Ocean Marine. Freight for which the full bill-of-lading has been paid in advance. The freight is payable whether the goods are delivered or not, provided that the failure to deliver the goods resulted from causes beyond the carriers's control.

compare: collect freight; see: freight

prepaid group practice program

Health. An early form of preferred provider organization, where a group of physicians and dentists joined together to provide medical services to individuals for a predetermined fee.

see: preferred provider organization

present value

Risk Management. The amount that, if invested today at a reasonably likely rate of return, would equal some future payment. The present value concept takes into consideration the investment value of money. *Example:* If money is worth 20 percent, the present value of a $10,000 premium payment due twelve months from now would be $8,333.

syn: actuarial liability; see: discount factor, discounted cash flow techniques, time value of money

present value of sprinkler reduction

Reinsurance/Loss Control. A method used in risk management to evaluate the value of installing an automatic fire sprinkler system. The method compares the cost of installing the system today with the reduction in fire insurance premiums in the future. A formula is calculated to make the comparison on a present value of money basis, or on an organization's required rate of return basis.

see: automatic sprinkler system

pressure vessel

Property. A container made to hold materials under pressure. Boiler and machinery policies divide such vessels into two categories: fired pressure vessels (such as boilers or gas water heaters) and unfired pressure vessels (such as air tanks, electric water heaters, steam cookers, and hydropneumatic tanks).

see: object

presumed negligence

General.

see: res ipsa loquitur

presumption of death

Life. The rebuttable presumption that a person has died when they have been continuously absent and not heard from for a period of seven years.

presumptive disability

Health/Life. An insurer's assumption of an insured's total disability when the insured loses sight, hearing, speech or a limb. If such a disability occurs, the insurer generally assumes that the disability will continue for the insured's life.

see: permanent total disability

pretax margin

General. Profits before federal, state, and foreign income taxes, expressed as a percentage of sales or revenues.

pretrial conference

General. A conference held before a trial, where the judge and the attorneys seek to simplify the issues in the controversy and eliminate matters not in dispute.

Price-Anderson Act

Regulation. A federal statute enacted in 1957, which requires owners or operators of nuclear facilities to provide proof of financial responsibility before they are licensed. The act limits a facility's liability to $700 million per nuclear accident.

see: nuclear energy liability insurance

Priestly v. Fowler

Workers' Compensation. A landmark case in the development of workers' compensation. The 1837 British decision established that an employer was not responsible for injury to an employee if that injury was caused by a fellow employee. *Priestly* also laid the groundwork for the "assumption of risk" defense. Prior to *Priestly*, English common law dictated that employers were responsible for any injury to their employees.

see: assumption of risk, common law defense, fellow servant rule

prima facie evidence

General. A legal term referring to evidence that by itself would establish the claim or defense of the party if the evidence is not rebutted or contradicted.

see: evidence

primary beneficiary

Life. The person designated as the first individual to receive the proceeds of a life insurance policy, as distinguished from a contingent beneficiary who will receive the proceeds only if the primary beneficiary dies before the insured.

see: contingent beneficiary, second beneficiary

primary insurance

Insurer Operations. Insurance covering losses on a first-dollar basis, sometimes subject to a deductible. A

© 1991 NILS Publishing Company

primary insurance – continued
low-limits insurance policy, over which excess or umbrella policies are issued. The insurance contract issued to the insured, as opposed to the liability ceded to a reinsurer by the primary (ceding) insurer.

syn: **underlying insurance;** see: **layering, primary insurance company, reinsurance**

primary insurance amount (PIA)
Employee Benefits. Social Security benefits are considered as primary insurance, over which private pension or medical plans build their benefits. The amount of Social Security primary insurance is determined by taking the average monthly wage and referring to the Social Security Wage Index, which translates it into a monthly benefit.

see: **average monthly wage, Social Security Wage Index**

primary insurance company
Insurer Operations. An insurer that sells insurance directly to consumers or businesses and may cede reinsurance to a reinsurer.

syn: **ceding company, reinsured**

primary insured
Insurer Operations. The first insured named in an insurance policy.

see: **first named insured**

primary policy
General. The initial policy issued by the primary insurance company to the primary insured; the policy covering losses on a first-dollar basis; the underlying insurance policy; the insurance policy covering the first (bottom) layer in a layered program.

see: **layering, primary insurance, primary insurance company**

Insurer Operations. To avoid multiple compensation for a loss covered by more than one policy, the covering policies accept responsibility for insurance in an established order. The order varies by the type of loss and the coverages provided by the various policies in force. The first policy in order is sometimes called the primary policy.

see: **apportionment, coordination of benefits, other insurance clause**

prime rate
General. The lowest rate of interest that a commercial bank will charge its best customers – usually large, financially sound corporations.

see: **interest**

principal
General. A person who has authorized an agent to act on his or her behalf.

Fr: **principal;** Gr: **Prinzipal;** Sp: **principal**

Surety. The debtor in a suretyship arrangement, the person or entity who purchases a bond.

compare: **obligee, surety;** see: **obligor**

principal sum
General. The capital sum of a money debt.

see: **interest**

Health/Life. The amount specified in a disability income policy to be paid in the event of accidental death, dismemberment or loss of sight.

see: **capital sum**

principle of indemnity
General.
see: **indemnification**

prior acts coverage
Casualty. Coverage that may be necessary for an insured who has been uninsured or who has cancelled a claims-made liability policy that does not provide an adequate claims discovery period. Insurance may be available from the new insurer providing coverage, or occasionally from a separate insurer who provides a policy only for claims arising from acts that occurred before the beginning of the policy period.

see: **claims-made form**

prior approval rating
Regulation. A method of rate insurance regulation under which rates and policy forms must be approved by regulators before they can be used in that state.

compare: **file-and-use rating, modified prior approval rating, open competition rating;** see: **rate making**

prior service benefit
Employee Benefits.
see: **past service benefit**

prison guard captivity coverage
Casualty. Coverage for prison guards, that responds when they are taken and held as hostages or injured in a prison riot. Provides compensation to a guard and/or their family in case of injury or death.

private carrier
Automobile. A fleet of trucks owned by the shipper and used for carrying its own cargo (i.e., a firm's own fleet of trucks).

compare: **common carrier, contract carrier;** see: **carrier**

private passenger automobile
Automobile. A four-wheeled vehicle designed for roads, that must be registered. An automobile used for personal purposes; to be covered by a personal auto policy (as opposed to a business policy), the auto must be owned by an individual and not used for public or livery use.

© 1991 NILS Publishing Company

privileged communication

General. A legal term referring to statements that a witness may refuse to testify to in court because of the relationship with the party being tried. *Example:* Husband/wife and attorney/client communications are considered privileged.

privity of contract

General. A legal term referring to the rights or duties that two parties to a contract have, as a result of their creation of the contract.

   see: contract

prize indemnification insurance

Inland Marine. A specialized inland marine coverage, which pays for prizes offered at fund raisers or sporting events. Frequently the winners of large prizes are paid by underwriters in the form of an annuity over several years. The premium charged for this insurance is based on the odds faced by the insurer.

   see: hole-in-one coverage, record fish coverage, tagged fish coverage

probability

Risk Management. A mathematical forecast that, for an exhaustive set of outcomes, is the ratio of the outcomes that would produce a given event to the total number of possible outcomes. The outcome of the forecast (or relative frequency of an event occurring) is expressed as a number between zero (certain not to occur) and one (certain to occur).

   see: degree of risk, law of large numbers, odds

probable maximum loss (PML)

Loss Control/Property. A maximum loss estimate developed for property insurance underwriters, which assumes normal conditions exist at the time of loss. A PML estimate may be exceeded if other-than-normal conditions exist, such as a delayed fire alarm, insufficient water supply or delayed fire department responses.

   compare: maximum possible loss; see: above-normal loss, amount subject, segregation of exposure units

probate

General. The procedure for formally establishing or providing that a given writing is the last will and testament of the person purporting to have signed the document.

   see: probate bond, probate court

probate bond

Surety. A fiduciary bond required by a probate court, to protect the administration of a will, estate or guardianship.

   see: fiduciary bond, probate

probate court

General. A court having jurisdiction over the proof of wills, the settlement of estates and guardianships.

   see: probate

probationary period

Health. The period of time in a health insurance policy between the effective date and the first day of coverage for certain disabilities, illnesses or accidents.

   syn: excluded period

proceedings

General.

   see: actions and proceedings

proceeds

Life. A life insurance policy's face value, including any additional benefits which may be payable at its maturity or upon the death of the insured.

   see: face amount

processing endorsement

Ocean Marine. An endorsement to a cargo policy written on a warehouse-to-warehouse basis, that extends coverage while the merchandise is being processed at its destination.

   see: warehouse-to-warehouse coverage

processor

Loss Control/Inland Marine. A business that is involved in the physical modification of a product, but which does not modify the fundamental nature of the product.

   see: processor's policy

processor's policy

Inland Marine. An inland marine policy that provides coverage on raw materials or goods in process which have been sent to another firm for processing. Coverage extends while in transit to and from the off-site location and while on the premises of the processing firm.

   see: processor

producer

Agency. An agent, solicitor, broker or any other person directly involved in the sale of insurance.

   see: agent, broker, solicitor

Product Liability Risk Retention Act of 1981

Regulation. Federal legislation adopted in 1981 to facilitate the ability of product manufacturers to establish group self-insurance programs or group captives for their products liability exposures (risk retention groups) and to purchase products liability insurance on a group basis (risk purchasing groups). The 1981 Act contained provisions that limit the states' control over insurance as respects products

© 1991 NILS Publishing Company

*Product Liability Risk Retention Act of 1981 —
continued*
liability. The 1981 bill also provided that a risk
retention or purchasing group could be domiciled in
one state (where it would be regulated), but would be
authorized to operate in all other states, exempt from
most state insurance regulation and state guaranty
funds. The initial objectives of the 1981 Act were
expanded by the Liability Risk Retention Act of 1986.

see: **Liability Risk Retention Act of 1986, risk
purchasing group, risk retention group**

products-completed operations aggregate limit

Casualty. The total amount an insured can recover
under the ISO commercial general liability coverage
form, for all claims arising under Coverage Part A of
the products-completed operations hazard during a
single policy year.

see: **aggregate limit, broad form products liability, commercial general liability form, general aggregate limit**

products-completed operations insurance

Casualty. Coverage against loss arising out of the legal
liability incurred by a manufacturer, merchant or
distributor, due to injury or damage resulting from the
use of a covered product. Coverage also includes
liability incurred by a contractor as the result of
improperly performed work (construction or installation) after a job has been completed. This coverage
can be included in the ISO commercial general
liability form under Coverage Part A.

see: **commercial general liability form, completed operations coverage, defective, defective product, products-completed operations
aggregate limit, your product, your work**

products extortion insurance

Casualty. Coverage that indemnifies an insured for a
percentage of the loss incurred from the insured's
payment of extortion, or for recalling a threatened or
contaminated product, or destroying a contaminated
product.

see: **products recall expense insurance**

products liability insurance

Casualty.
see: **products-completed operations insurance**

products recall exclusion

Casualty. A provision contained in commercial general liability policy forms (since 1966) which specifically
excludes from coverage the cost or expense incurred
by an insured for the withdrawal, recall, inspection,
repair, replacement, adjustment, removal or disposal
of an insured's product. It is sometimes referred to as
the "sistership" exclusion, because defective products
which have already generated liability claims have

sister products of the same production run or lot still
in the hands of consumers.

syn: **sistership exclusion;** see: **products recall
expense insurance**

products recall expense insurance

Casualty. Extra expense coverage that indemnifies
the insured for the cost of recalling a product that is
suspected of being defective and causing bodily harm
to consumers. Coverage usually includes such expenses as communications, shipping charges, radio and
television announcements, newspaper advertise-
ments, hiring additional personnel, and destroying
the product if necessary.

see: **products extortion insurance, products
tampering insurance**

products tampering insurance

Casualty. Coverage that protects a manufacturer
whose product has been tampered with, which pays
the cost of necessary inventory destruction, lost profits, business interruption and product rehabilitation.
Coverage does not apply to third-party liability or
extortion payments.

see: **products-completed operations insurance,
products extortion insurance, products recall
expense insurance**

products warranty inefficacy insurance

Casualty. A form of product warranty insurance which
guarantees systems performance on newly constructed facilities. It guarantees that the system will perform
up to its engineer-designed level.

see: **efficacy coverage**

Professional Insurance Agents (PIA)

Organizations. Members: Independent property and
casualty agents. *Objectives:* Provide educational programs and support services. *Founded:* 1931. *Headquarters:* Alexandria, VA.

Professional Insurance Communicators of America (PICA)

Organizations. Members: Publication editors from
mutual insurance organizations. *Objectives:* Reviewing and evaluating in-house publications; sponsoring
educational programs and giving awards. *Founded:
1955. Headquarters:* Indianapolis, IN.

Professional Insurance Mass-Marketing Association (PIMA)

Organizations. Members: Insurance companies,
agencies and others servicing the insurance industry.
Objectives: Promotes the marketing of insurance.
Founded: 1975. *Headquarters:* Bethesda, MD.

professional liability insurance

Casualty. A term that has replaced the use of the

© 1991 NILS Publishing Company

terms "malpractice insurance" and "errors & omissions insurance" to describe the coverage of specialists in various professional fields.

see: architects professional liability insurance, broadcasters liability insurance, educators professional liability insurance, engineers professional liability insurance, errors & omissions insurance, hospital professional liability insurance, malpractice insurance

professional reinsurer

Reinsurance. An organization whose business is mainly reinsurance and related services – as contrasted with other insurance organizations that may assume reinsurance in addition to their basic primary insurance business.

see: reinsurance

Professional Standards Review Organization (PSRO)

Organizations. Members: Physicians and healthcare institutions. *Objectives:* Monitors government health insurance programs. *Founded:* 1973. *Headquarters:* Washington, D.C.

profit

General. The compensation accruing to an enterprise for the assumption of a business risk. The excess of the selling price of a good over its cost.

compare: deficit

profit and loss statement

Risk Management.
see: income statement

profit center

General. A unit of a large, decentralized firm that has its own investments and for which a rate of return on investment can be calculated.

see: return on investment

profits and commissions insurance

Property. Coverage which protects an individual or firm that has sold a product from lost profit or commission because of damage to that product prior to its delivery to the buyer.

profit sharing plan

Employee Benefits. A plan established by an employer to share the profits of the business with employees.

pro forma

General. A financial or business projection. *Example:* A pro forma financial statement simulates an actual statement with certain assumptions.

prohibited list

Insurer Operations. An insurance company's listing of the types or classes of risk they will not insure.

syn: do not solicit list, undesirable list; compare: target risk; see: redlining

promissory note

General. An unconditional promise in writing, made by one person to another and signed by the maker, guaranteeing to pay on demand (or at a definite time) a certain sum of money.

promissory warranty

Insurer Operations. A representation made by an applicant for insurance to an insurer, as to a future event which the applicant guarantees will occur.

promoters

General. Persons who develop or take the initiative in founding or organizing a business venture. If more than one promoter is involved in a venture, they are usually described as co-promoters.

promulgate

Insurer Operations. To develop or establish, publish and place in effect insurance forms or rates. Rates and forms may be promulgated by insurers, rating bureaus, insurer organizations or state agencies (insurance departments or state rating bureaus).

see: rate making

Regulation. To develop or establish, publish and place in effect regulations and administrative rulings.

compare: enact

proof of loss

Insurer Operations. A sworn statement which usually must be furnished by the insured to an insurer before any loss under a policy can be paid. This form is usually used in the settlement of first-party losses, and includes the date and description of the occurrence and the amount of indemnity claimed.

syn: statement of loss; see: affidavit of claim, notice of loss

property

General. A term used to describe the ownership rights and interests that a party has in relation to land and attachments (real property) and movable objects not attached to land (personal property). Also used to refer to the subjects of those rights and interests (e.g., the real estate, buildings, personal articles, etc).

see: machinery, personal property, real estate

property damage liability coverage

Casualty. Coverage for sums that the insured becomes legally obligated to pay to third parties as damages because of the physical injury to tangible property, including the loss or use of that property. This coverage is included in most personal and

© 1991 NILS Publishing Company

property first loss scale

property damage liability coverage — continued
commercial liability policies along with bodily and
personal injury coverages.

see: **bodily injury and property damage
liability**

property first loss scale
Property.
see: **Lloyd's property first loss scale**

property insurance
Property. First-party insurance providing financial
protection against loss to real and personal property,
marine and aviation properties. The terms "property
insurance," "liability insurance" and "life and health
insurance" take in almost the entire spectrum of
insurance coverages.

see: **excess property insurance, taxation of
property insurance claims payments**

Property Insurance Loss Register (PILR)
Property. A listing maintained by the American Insurance Association of all fire losses over $500. The listing
is maintained on a database which insurance companies can access to determine undisclosed duplicate
insurance coverage.

see: **American Insurance Association, Fire and
Theft Index Bureau, Insurance Crime Prevention Institute, Insurance Services Office, interinsurer claim service organization, Medical Information Bureau, National Automobile Theft
Bureau**

Property Insurance Plans Service Office
Organizations. An organization that provides technical and administrative services to state property insurance plans. A division of the National Committee on
Property Insurance.

see: **National Committee on Property
Insurance**

Property Loss Research Bureau (PLRB)
Organizations. Members: Mutual and stock insurance
companies. *Objectives:* Sponsors property loss research. *Founded:* 1947. *Headquarters:* Schaumburg,
IL.

property other than money and securities
Crime. A term used in crime coverages forms to
extend coverage to tangible property other than
money and securities that has monetary value. The
individual crime coverage forms will contain exclusions for many forms of property that would be
included under this broad definition.

see: **crime coverages, money, securities**

proportional reinsurance
Reinsurance.
see: **pro rata reinsurance**

proposal
Agency. The written presentation of insurance terms,
conditions and pricing presented by an agent to a
client.

International. The term used in the London Market
for an insurance application.

Proposition 103
Regulation. A ballot initiative approved by California
voters in 1988, as a revolt against what consumers
perceived as excessive private passenger automobile
rates. Provisions included a 20 percent rate rollback
for auto insurance, homeowner's and commercial or
municipal liability insurance; good driver discounts;
an elected insurance commissioner; elimination of
territorial (zip code-based) rating; elimination of the
insurance industry's anti-trust exemptions; allowing
banks to sell insurance; allowing insurance agents to
rebate their commissions to insureds; legalizing group
property and casualty insurance plans; and restricting
policy cancellations by insurers to nonpayment of
premiums, fraud or a substantial increase in the
insured hazard. Some of Proposition 103's provisions
have been implemented; other provisions have met
insurer opposition in the form of lawsuits. The importance of the proposition is that it triggered similar
legislation in other states.

see: **anti-rebate law, reasonable rate of return**

pro rata
General. A term used to describe any proportionate
division or sharing, usually according to a rate or
standard.

see: **participate, quota share, pro rata cancellation, pro rata distribution clause, pro rata liability clause, pro rata reinsurance**

pro rata cancellation
Insurer Operations. Termination of an insurance
contract before the expiration date by the insurer.
Premiums returned to the insured are in direct
proportion to the days remaining in the policy period,
with no penalty, because the insurer initiated the
action.

compare: **short-rate cancellation;** see: **cancellation, earned premium, pro rata, return
premium**

pro rata distribution clause
Property. A penalty clause found in older property
insurance policies, which provides for the automatic
distribution of insurance coverage on insured properties at various locations in the same proportion as
their values bear to the total of values on all properties
insured, if the insured is carrying inadequate insurance coverage at the time of a loss.

syn: **distribution clause;** see: **average clause,
pro rata**

© 1991 NILS Publishing Company

pro rata liability clause

Property. A clause in most property insurance policies which provides for the automatic distribution of a claim payment among two or more insurance policies that are providing coverage on the same claim. Each policy would pay a share of the claim, in the same proportion as the limit of liability provided by that policy bears to the total of all insurance on the property.

see: apportionment, assignment quota, other insurance clause, pro rata

pro rata reinsurance

Reinsurance. A form of reinsurance where the reinsurer shares a proportional part (a stated percentage) of the original losses and premiums of the ceding company.

syn: participating reinsurance, proportional reinsurance; see: pro rata, reinsurance

proration of benefits

Health. The proportionate division or adjustment of benefits between two or more insurance policies which provide coverage for the same accident or disability.

see: coordination of benefits, other insurance clause, pro rata distribution clause, pro rata liability clause

prospect

Agency. A potential purchaser of insurance.

prospective rating plan

Insurer Operations. The most frequently used method of establishing an insurance rate. A rate is developed in advance to be used on future policies. This rate is based on historical loss experience for similar exposures.

compare: retrospective rating plan

prospective reserve

Health/Life. A reserve amount designated as a liability for life or health insurers, to pay the difference between projected benefits and projected premiums, including investment income.

protected risk

Loss Control/Property. A property risk which is located within a fire protection district or area serviced by a recognized fire department.

see: grading schedule, highly protected risk, protection

protection

Property. The existence, location and proximity to an insured risk of facilities for fighting fires. This can include the location of hydrants; adequacy and reliability of water supplies; firefighting personnel training and performance; and adequacy and effectiveness of firefighting equipment, etc.

syn: fire protection; compare: construction, exposure, occupancy; see: grading schedule, protection class

protection & indemnity insurance (P&I)

Ocean Marine. A broad form of marine legal liability insurance that covers the operator of a ship for such things as liability to crew members and other individuals on board the vessel, and for damage to fixed objects, such as docks, resulting from the insured's negligence.

protection class

Loss Control/Property. A grade assigned to a fire protection district, usually expressed in a number between 1 (best) and 10 (worst).

syn: class; see: grading schedule, protection

protective safeguards clause

Property. A policy provision which voids coverage if the insured fails to exercise due diligence in maintaining protective safeguards such as automatic sprinklers or burglar alarms.

see: automatic sprinkler clause

provisional premium

Insurer Operations. A premium based on a rough estimate of exposures and/or using a provisional rate, used to issue a policy. The premium is subject to subsequent adjustment, when additional information is available.

syn: tentative premium; see: deposit premium, premium

provisional rate

General. A tentative rate used to issue a policy, subject to subsequent adjustment when sufficient information to develop a final rate is obtained.

syn: tentative rate; see: provisional premium

provisions

Insurer Operations. A broad term used to refer to the sections or clauses of an insurance policy that communicate the policy's benefits, conditions, exclusions, etc.

see: insurance contract

proximate cause

General. An act or event which is the natural and reasonably foreseeable cause of the harm or event which occurs and injures a plaintiff or damages his or her property.

compare: concurrent causation, direct cause

Property. Most property insurance policies require that an insured peril be the proximate cause of a loss

© 1991 NILS Publishing Company

proximate cause — continued
for coverage to apply; that is, the loss must be a direct result of an insured peril.
see: concurrent causation

proxy
General. A shareholder's written authorization to vote the stock owned by the shareholder; the person holding or exercising such a written authorization.
compare: voting trust; see: share of stock

proxy solicitation machinery
Insurer Operations. A phrase commonly used to describe the phenomenon whereby the incumbent management of a publicly held corporation may usually produce large majorities of shareholder votes on any issue it desires. This power is based in part on the ability of incumbent management to use corporate funds to communicate at will with the shareholders, and partially on the ability to represent their views as the views of "management."

public adjuster
General. An organization or individual (other than a lawyer) who represents the insured in loss adjustments, charging a fee for settling claims with insurers.
compare: independent adjuster; see: claims adjuster

Public Agency Risk Managers Association (PARMA)
Organizations. Members: Risk and insurance managers from public agencies, private agencies and professionals. *Objectives:* Promotes the interests of those involved in risk management. *Founded:* 1974. *Headquarters:* San Jose, CA.

public and institutional property
Property. An obsolete property insurance rating program that was developed specifically for educational, religious, charitable, government and non-profit organizations. The program provided reduced rates for these properties and extremely broad coverage forms.

public domain
General. Public or government-owned property.
see: eminent domain

public easement
General. A right-of-way for use by members of the public at large.
see: dedicate, easement, inverse condemnation, public domain

public entity insurance
Insurer Operations. Insurance on public entities such as municipalities, counties, state and federal governments and their agencies. Such entities have significant property and casualty exposures. Many of their exposures (such as police and fire department liability, road design and maintenance, public beaches and playgrounds) are unique and difficult to insure.
compare: government insurance; see: county clerks and recorders errors & omissions insurance, municipal bond insurance

public exchange offer
Insurer Operations. A technique by which an aggressor corporation seeks to obtain control over a target corporation, by offering to exchange a package of its securities for the target corporation's voting shares. Usually a specified number of target corporation shares must be presented for exchange before it will take place.

Public Law 15
Regulation.
see: McCarran-Ferguson Act

Public Law 91-508
Agency/Insurer Operations.
see: Fair Credit Reporting Act

public offering
Financial Planning. The sale of securities by an issuer (or a person controlling the issuer) to members of the public. Generally, any offering that is not exempt under the private offering exemption of the Securities Act of 1933 and/or similar exemptions under state "blue sky" laws is considered a "public offering." Normally, registration of a public offering is required, though in some instances, exemption from registration may be available.
see: blue sky laws

public official bond
Surety. A bond in which the surety company guarantees that a public official will faithfully perform his or her official duties and honestly administer all funds entrusted to them. These bonds are issued so as to comply with a statute requiring them, and cover whatever liability the statute imposes.
syn: federal official bond; see: bond, state bonding funds

public policy
General. Objectives relating to the health, morals and integrity of society that the law seeks to advance or maintain, by declaring invalid any contract which conflicts with those objectives, even though there is no statute expressly declaring such a contract illegal. Insurance against liability imposed or fines assessed for certain anti-social acts is usually considered against public policy and therefore without effect.
see: intentional tort, punitive damages

274

© 1991 NILS Publishing Company

Public Risk Management Association (PRIMA)

Organizations. Members: Risk, insurance and/or safety managers for cities, counties, villages, towns, school boards, water districts, utility districts and highway authorities. *Objectives:* Provides information on risk and safety management. Represents the members' interests before state and federal legislative bodies. *Founded:* 1978. *Headquarters:* Arlington, VA. Known as the Public Risk and Insurance Management Association until 1989.

punitive damages

Casualty. Damages awarded in excess of those required to compensate the plaintiff for the wrong committed. Generally imposed to punish the defendant for the wanton or willful action that resulted in the injury or other tort, or to serve as an example and deterrent to others who would contemplate similar torts. Some states prohibit the insuring of punitive damages. Some policies specifically exclude coverage for punitive damages, while others rely on state public policy.

syn: exemplary damages; compare: actual damages; see: damages

pup company

Insurer Operations. A smaller subsidiary insurance company owned by a larger company.

compare: parent company; see: affiliated companies, fleet of companies, subsidiary company

purchase date

Life. A specific date set for buying an annuity, used in calculating an annuity's cost.

purchase payment fund

Life.

see: active life fund

purchasing group

Regulation.

syn: purchasing group

pure annuity

Life. An annuity contract which pays a periodic income benefit for the life of the individual annuitant. All payments end when the annuitant dies.

see: annuity

pure captive

Risk Management. A captive insurance company that insures only its parent's business.

see: captive insurance company

pure loss cost

Reinsurance. The ratio of reinsured losses incurred under a reinsurance agreement to the ceding company's subject earned premium for that agreement, before any loading factors are added.

syn: burning cost

pure mortality cost

Life. The face amount of a life insurance policy, multiplied by a factor indicated on a mortality table. The result – the pure mortality cost – is the first element considered in developing a life insurance policy premium.

see: mortality table, natural premium

pure premium

Risk Management. That portion of the premium which covers losses and related loss expenses (i.e., includes no loading for commissions, taxes or other expenses).

see: expense loading, field expenses, general and insurance expenses, premium

pure risk

Risk Management. A risk involving the probability or possibility of loss with no chance for gain. A pure risk is generally insurable.

compare: speculative risk; see: indemnification

purging

Loss Control. The filling of a tank with water or inert gases, to remove toxic or flammable vapor or gases.

put option

Financial Planning. A contract granting the holder of stock to sell a given number of those shares at a specified price on or before a certain date. For this hedge against the stock dropping in price, the holder pays an "option premium."

compare: call option; see: option

pyramiding of limits

Life. A situation where credit life insurance policies are issued to a consumer without the cancelling of existing policies which duplicate coverage.

see: overinsurance

Casualty. A term applied to the judicial interpretation that when several liability policies (usually involving products liability or pollution liability) are in force covering the same risk of loss, higher limits of coverage than originally intended (i.e., as much as the total of all limits insured) thereby result.

see: dual coverage, overinsurance, stacking of limits

275

© 1991 NILS Publishing Company

Q Schedule
Regulation.
  see: Schedule Q

qualified assignment
Insurer Operations. A transfer of rights of a defendant/insurer's obligation to an assignee, pursuant to Internal Revenue Code Section 130. Often the plaintiff releases the original obligor.

qualified funding asset
General. The resolution of a claim involving a structured settlement which must be funded by annuities or U.S. government obligations.
  see: **structured settlement**

qualified impairment insurance
Health. An endorsement attached to a health insurance policy which waives exclusion of an impairment for a policy applicant who would not otherwise qualify for coverage.
  see: **impaired risk, impairment exclusion rider, preexisting condition, substandard risk**

qualified plan
Employee Benefits. An employee benefit plan approved by the Internal Revenue Service, meeting requirements set forth in IRS Code Section 401(a). Employer contributions to such plans are subject to favorable tax treatment.
  compare: **nonqualified plan**

qualified terminable interest property trust (Q TIP Trust)
Life. A trust under which a surviving spouse receives all income from trust assets. Such income must be paid to the spouse annually. This acts to reduce any estate tax and provide for the surviving spouse. Often, this type of trust contains a provision which prohibits transfer of any assets to another person, but allows the surviving spouse to will the remaining assets to one or more persons specifically designated by the surviving spouse upon his or her death. This allows the estate to escape taxation on any assets remaining at the death of the surviving spouse.

quality control (QC)
Loss Control. Procedures established to prevent or reduce the chance that products or services and negligently manufactured or performed.

quantity discount
Life. Life insurance policy premium discount allowed on policies that are written with a large face amount.
  see: **minimum amount policy**

quarantine benefit
Health. Health insurance coverage extension which indemnifies individuals for lost wages while they are quarantined by health authorities.
  syn: **quarantine indemnity**; see: **disability income insurance**

quarantine exclusion
Ocean Marine. Extra expenses resulting from a ship being ordered into detention or isolation by port authorities when it is suspected of carrying an infectious disease. These expenses are excluded from most marine insurance policies.

quarantine indemnity
Health.
  see: **quarantine benefit**

quasi-contract
General. A contract implied in law where no specifically drawn contract exists. The courts will find such a

© 1991 NILS Publishing Company

quasi-contract — continued
contract exists to prevent an unjust enrichment or an injustice.

syn: oral contract; see: contract

quasi-insurance institutions

General. Government institutions (such as the Federal Insurance Administration and the Department of Health, Education, and Welfare) which have programs with some characteristics of private insurance.

quick assets

Surety. Assets that can be quickly converted into cash, such as trade receivables and marketable securities.

see: current assets, quick ratio

quick ratio

Risk Management. A measure of an organization's ability to expediently pay all of its current liabilities. *Formula:* Quick Assets(cash, trade receivables, marketable securities)/Current Liabilities. The higher the ratio, the greater the immediate debt paying ability.

syn: acid-test ratio; see: current liabilities, financial ratios, financial underwriting, quick assets

quid pro quo

General. A Latin term meaning something given or received in return for something else given in return, usually at a later date. For example, an insured pays a premium to an insurer, who promises to compensate the insured for a loss.

see: consideration

quit claim deed

Title. A deed against which any claim has been released or relinquished in the process of the conveyance of real estate to another party.

see: deed

quota share

Property. Property insurance program where several policies share the exposure of a risk on a percentage, or quota basis. *Example:* $1,000,000 in fire insurance is split on a quota share basis, with Company A assuming 50 percent ($500,000), Company B assuming 30 percent ($300,000), and Company C assuming 20 percent ($200,000). The companies will usually share the premium in the same proportion as they share the risk.

syn: assignment quota; see: participate

quota share reinsurance

Reinsurance. A proportional or pro rata reinsurance treaty where the same proportion is ceded on all cessions. The reinsurer assumes a set percentage of risk for the same percentage of the premium less an allowance for the ceding company's expenses.

see: treaty reinsurance

quote

General.

see: bid

© 1991 NILS Publishing Company

R

racial discrimination
Casualty.
see: discrimination

radiation
Loss Control. The emission and propagation of energy in the form of waves through space or through a material medium. It usually refers to electromagnetic radiation such as gamma rays and ultraviolet rays, but may also apply to alpha and beta particles or heat waves.
compare: radioactivity

radioactive contamination insurance
Property. Property insurance coverage which indemnifies an insured for contamination to property from radioactive materials stored or used on the premises. Coverage is specifically excluded for radiation from nuclear reactors and nuclear fuel.
see: nuclear hazard exclusion, shippers radioactive contamination insurance

radioactivity
Loss Control. Spontaneous atomic disintegration accompanied by the emission of one or more types of radiation, such as alpha particles or gamma rays.
compare: radiation

radius of operation
Automobile. A factor used in the rating of commercial trucks based on the distances travelled from its place of principal garaging. This factor was developed with the belief that the exposure to risk is greater for trucks traveling long distances (usually more than 50 miles) and are more hazardous (because of driver fatigue,

higher speeds, etc.), than those confined to a smaller territory.
see: intermediate, local, long haul, operating rights

railroad protective liability
Casualty. Insurance obtained by a contractor or a railroad on behalf of a contractor, naming the contractor and the railroad as named insureds, and covering the railroad against bodily injury and property damage losses sustained by the public, employees of the railroad, the general contractor or subcontractors. Coverage is also provided for physical damage to rolling stock, and its contents and equipment.

Railroad Retirement Act
Employee Benefits. The Railroad Retirement Act passed by Congress in 1937 specifies death, retirement, disability and unemployment coverages for railroad employees. Retirement benefits provided under the Act are tied to the Social Security cost-of-living increases.
syn: railroad retirement system

railroad retirement system
Employee Benefits.
see: Railroad Retirement Act

railroad rolling stock coverage
Casualty/Inland Marine. A package policy for a railroad which incorporates both "all-risk" coverage on the rail cars and equipment with property damage liability to the rail cars or equipment of others along the railway and to property of others in the railroad's care, custody and control.

railroad sidetrack agreement
Casualty.
see: sidetrack agreement

© 1991 NILS Publishing Company

railroad subrogation waiver clause
Casualty.
see: sidetrack agreement

railroad travel policy
Health. A travel accident policy for a specific train trip sold in railroad stations through ticket agents or vending machines.
see: travel accident insurance

rain insurance
Property. Insurance which indemnifies an insured for financial loss caused by rain. Coverage is written for a specific period of time to cover a specific outdoor event, where financial success depends largely on the weather. The definition of rain includes snow, sleet and hail.
syn: pluvious insurance; see: weather insurance

raise
Loss Control. An exploratory mining tunnel, excavated upward, to reach an ore load.
see: adit, cross-cut

ranchowners personal liability form
Casualty. A personal liability endorsement covering a rancher's liability arising out of a collision between covered animals and a motor vehicle not owned or operated by the insured or an employee of the insured. The collision must have occurred on a public highway and not while the animal was being transported in a vehicle.
see: animal insurance, farmowners personal liability form

ransom insurance
Crime. Indemnification of an insured for payments made to kidnappers for the release of an insured or the employees of the insured.
see: kidnap insurance

rate
Insurer Operations. The actuarially concluded unit of cost that is applied against the rating basis (i.e., payroll, receipts, values) from which a policy premium is developed.
see: rate making, specific rate, tariff rate; Fr: taux; Gr: Prämiensatz; Sp: cuota, tipo;
Reinsurance. The unit or cost which is applied against the subject premium of the ceding company to develop a reinsurance premium.
see: reinsurance premium

rate card
Insurer Operations. A pocket-sized card issued by an insurer to agents, listing rates for various coverages.
see: line sheet, rate manual

rate discrimination
Regulation. An illegal practice of applying different premium rates to consumers or risks that are in the same insurance class or that have the same general characteristics.
see: discrimination, unfair discrimination

rated policy
Life. A life insurance policy that is issued at a higher than standard rate to cover an individual classified as a substandard risk. The policy may also contain special limitations and exclusions.
syn: rated up; see: substandard life expectancy, substandard risk

rated risk
Life.
see: rated policy

rated up
Life.
see: rated policy

rate making
Insurer Operations. A process for determining rates and premiums by combining losses, expenses, and provisions for profit factors.
see: absorption rate, adequate, aftercharge, American Association of Insurance Services, annuity conversion rate, "A" rates, average blanket rate, Aviation Insurance Rating Bureau, base rate, building rate, bureau rate, class rate, contents rate, deviated rate, discretionary groups, discrimination, driver training credit, empirical rate calculation, equity, excessive, expense constant, expense loading, experience rating plan, file-and-use rating, filing requirements, flat rate, flood insurance rate map, gender rating, governing classification, group I rates, group II rates, increased limits table, independent filing, individual risk premium modification rating plan, inflation factor, Insurance Services Office, judgment rates, loss constant, loss cost rating, loss trends, manual excess, manual rates, merit rating, minimum rate, modification rating, modified prior approval rating, moving average rating method, multiple location rating plan, National Council on Compensation Insurance, National Crop Insurance Services, nondiscriminatory, numerical rating system, open competition rating, paid loss retrospective rating plan, post-FIRM rates, pre-FIRM rates, prior approval rating, promulgate, prospective rating plan, provisional rate, rate, rate discrimination, rate manual, rate regulation, rating, rating bureau, rating class, reasonable rate of

© 1991 NILS Publishing Company

return, retrospective rating plan, schedule rating, short-rate table, specific rate, state rate pages, statistical agent, step-rate premium, tariff rate, territorial rating, universal mercantile system, zone rating

rate manual

Insurer Operations. A loose leaf manual that can be periodically updated or revised which contains rules, rates and other information prepared by an insurance company or rating bureau to develop premiums for insurance policies.

see: rate card, state exception pages, state rate pages, state territorial pages

rate of loss

Property.
see: time-loss unit

rate of natural increase or decrease

General. A census figure that is determined by subtracting the death rate from the birth rate. The rate of natural increase or decrease excludes changes in population due to migration.

rate of return

Risk Management. The interest rate at which the present value of the payment in the future equals the cost of that payment.

see: internal rate of return, present value, required rate of return, return on investment

Life. A method developed by the Federal Trade Commission to compare the cost of various life insurance policies.

Formula: Step 1 – Savings Element = Gross Policy Premium – Pure Cost of Protection (Mortality Expectation) + Policy Dividends (if any).

Step 2 – Calculate the rate of return needed to match the savings element that must be accumulated in order to equal the cash value of the policy at some specified future date.

rate regulation

Regulation. Insurance rates are controlled through legislation established by each state. State insurance laws usually provide that insurance rates be adequate, equitable and not excessive. Most states assign the responsibility of approving and monitoring insurance rates to its department of insurance. Generally, the development of rates and forms follows one or a combination of the following methods: open competition rating, prior approval rating, modified prior approval rating or file and use rating.

see: adequate, equity, excessive, file-and-use rating, modified prior approval rating, open competition rating, prior approval rating, rate making, ratification

ratification

Regulation. A formal approval by a state insurance department of rates or policy forms filed by insurers.
see: rate regulation

rating

Insurer Operations. The process of developing rates and premiums for a policy to cover a specific risk which will be covered by the policy.

see: adverse selection, homogeneous exposure units, inflation, loss cost rating, loss expectancy, loss frequency, moving average rating method, premium, probability

rating bureau

Organizations. An organization (usually formed by, or on behalf of, a group of insurers) to develop rates for those insurers. This may include not only rate promulgation, but the bureau may also act as a collection point for actuarial data and to survey individual risks.

syn: inspection bureau; see: advisory organization, American Association of Insurance Services, bureau insurer, bureau rate, Insurance Services Office, National Council on Compensation Insurance

rating class

Insurer Operations. A group of risks which have the same general characteristics and which are placed into the same "class" for rating purposes. The same rate then applies to all risks in this class.

see: classification, homogeneous exposure units

readjustment income

Life. An estimate of the financial requirements of a family for a six-month period after the death or disability of its principal financial provider. This estimate is used as a benchmark in financial planning and recognizes that more funds than usual will be required during this period.

see: adjustment income, emergency fund

real chattel

General. Any item of property which is annexed with or connected with, or concerned with real estate.
see: chattel, chattel mortgage, real estate

real estate

General. Land and immovable structures attached to the land.

syn: improvements and betterments, real property, realty

real estate agents errors & omissions insurance

Casualty. Coverage for a real estate agent against third-party claims for damages alleging negligence in

© 1991 NILS Publishing Company

real estate agents errors & omissions insurance –
continued

the conduct of negotiations and business performance for others.

real estate investment trust (REIT)

Financial Planning. A financial intermediary that invests its equity capital and debt in income-producing real estate and mortgages. Under legislation passed in 1961, REITs were granted conduit tax treatment (the same as that permitted mutual funds), under which the part of earnings that is flowed through to shareholders in the form of dividends is exempt from federal income taxes at the trust (or corporate) level, provided several conditions are met. Some of the conditions for qualification as a REIT under the Internal Revenue Code are that at least at least 95 percent of otherwise taxable income must be distributed to shareholders, and that specified percentages of both investments and gross income must be related to real estate. Many trusts that started out as REITs and are still reviewed as part of the REIT industry, in fact, no longer qualify for the special tax treatment.

real estate values

Financial Planning. The fair market value of real estate, usually determined by one of the following three methods: 1) cost method, 2) market method, or 3) income method.

see: **fair market value**

real property

Property.

see: **real estate**

realty

General.

see: **real estate**

reasonable and customary charge

Health. The usual fee charged in a geographical area by a medical provider for a specific medical procedure or service. The fee is based upon a consensus of what most other local hospitals, physicians or laboratories are charging for a similar procedure or service.

see: **approved charges, diagnostic related group, schedule**

reasonable care

General. The degree of care or concern that a reasonable person would have taken under all known circumstances.

see: **degree of care, negligence**

reasonable rate of return

Insurer Operations. A concept that emerged from the passage in 1988 of California's Proposition 103. In its interpretation of the proposition, the California

Supreme Court stated that automobile insurers must be allowed a "reasonable rate of return" on their operations.

see: **Proposition 103**

reassured

Reinsurance.

see: **ceding company**

rebate

Regulation. The return of a portion of an insurance agent's commission (or the giving of something else of value) to induce someone to purchase insurance. Anti-rebate laws – which make it illegal to give such rebates on commissions – exist in most states.

see: **anti-rebate law, Proposition 103**

recapture

Reinsurance. A ceding company taking back previously ceded insurance from a reinsurer.

compare: **return portfolio;** see: **reinsurance**

recapture of plan assets

Employee Benefits. The return of all or a portion of an employer's contributions to a pension plan because of an IRS determination that the plan does not qualify or that portions of the plan do not qualify for tax considerations under provisions of the Internal Revenue Code.

receivables

General. The value of goods and services that are sold, shipped or provided to customers, but for which the company has yet to be paid.

see: **accounts receivable**

Insurer Operations. In insurer operations, "receivables" is often used to refer to earned premiums not yet received.

received for shipment bill of lading

Inland Marine/Ocean Marine.

see: **dock receipt**

recipient property

Property. A principal customer. A contingent business income term referring to a location where most of the insured merchandise or manufactured goods flow.

see: **contingent business income coverage, dependent property**

reciprocal insurance company

Insurer Operations.

see: **reciprocal insurance exchange**

reciprocal insurance exchange

Insurer Operations. Insurance resulting from an interchange of reciprocal agreements of indemnity among persons known as subscribers, collectively

© 1991 NILS Publishing Company

known as a reciprocal insurance exchange. The interchange is effected through an attorney-in-fact common to all persons. Subscribers agree to become liable for their share of losses and expenses incurred among all subscribers, and authorize the attorney-in-fact to exchange insurance with the other subscribers, pay losses, invest premiums, recruit new members, underwrite new business, receive premiums and effect contracts of reinsurance.

syn: exchange, reciprocal insurance company; see: assessment company, attorney-in-fact, insurance company

reciprocal legislation

Insurer Operations/Regulation. State legislation which allows insurers domiciled in another state favorable tax treatment if the insurer's domiciliary state does the same for insurance companies domiciled in the first state. Reciprocal arrangements also exist with respect to offsets of payments due ceding insurers and reinsurers in cases of liquidations.

compare: retaliatory legislation, retaliatory tax

Agency. State legislation enacted by any two states, providing for mutual regulatory considerations. Most common reciprocal laws address premium taxes, countersignature requirements and agent licensing requirements.

compare: retaliatory legislation

reciprocity

Reinsurance. The mutual exchange of reinsurance, whereby one reinsurer accepts (assumes) risk in exchange for the other company's acceptance of its ceded business.

record

General. The official collection of all pleadings, exhibits, orders, and verbatim testimony that took place during a hearing or trial.

record fish coverage

Inland Marine. A form of prize indemnification insurance which indemnifies the insured (usually the tournament sponsor) if a record-size fish is caught by a participating fisherman during a specified fishing tournament.

see: prize indemnification insurance, tagged fish coverage

recording agent

Property. A policywriting agent for property insurance coverage.

see: agent, general agent, policywriting agent

record owner

Financial Planning. A person in whose name shares of stock are registered on the records of the corporation. A record owner is treated as the owner of the

shares by the corporation, whether or not he or she is the beneficial owner of the shares.

see: share of stock

recoverables

Insurer Operations. Money or any other item of value which an insurance company recoups through reinsurance, salvage, or by subrogation against a third party at fault.

see: reinsurance, salvage, subrogation

recurrent disability

Life/Health. A disability which returns from time to time and has the same or related causes.

recurring clause

Health. A clause found in health insurance policies which specifies the period of time that must elapse between two illnesses in order for a new set of benefits to be available for the second illness.

redemption

Insurer Operations. The reacquisition of a security by the issuer, pursuant to a provision in the security that specifies the terms on which the reacquisition may take place. A security is "called for redemption" when the issuer notifies the holder that the redemption privilege has been exercised. Typically, a holder of a security that has been called for redemption will have a limited period thereafter to decide whether or not to exercise a conversion right, if one exists.

redlining

Regulation. An underwriting practice whereby a risk is rejected based upon its geographical location. Most states prohibit this practice ruling that it tends to be discriminatory against minorities.

see: discrimination, prohibited list, unfair discrimination

reduced earnings

Casualty. The amount an individual who is partially disabled is able to earn. This amount, when subtracted from the amount the employee was able to earn before the accident, determines the amount of disability benefits payable.

compare: wage loss; see: able to earn, partial disability

reduced paid-up insurance

Life.

see: nonforfeiture reduced paid-up benefit

reduction

Insurer Operations. The decrease in insurance policy benefits or limits imposed because a known specific

© 1991 NILS Publishing Company

reduction — continued
condition exists. A property policy may place a sublimit on a specific location because of hazardous activities, or an accident policy may reduce benefits for a hazardous activity such as auto racing.

reduction of risk

Risk Management. A method of handling risk by the scope or volume of a firm's operations, or through the purchase of insurance. *Example:* The risk of loss to billboards is reduced by a large outdoor advertising company simply by virtue of the fact that they have a large number of geographically dispersed exposure units. The scale of operations makes the loss relatively predictable, so there is little uncertainty. Insurance also reduces risk (e.g., for a small billboard company), by combining a number of smaller companies' risks into a more predictable group.

see: **homogeneity, law of large numbers, spread of risk**

re-entry term life insurance

Life. A rider to an annual renewable term life insurance policy allowing the policyholder to periodically (every three or five years) re-apply for increased coverage at a reduced premium.

see: **term life insurance, yearly renewable term**

referee

General. An impartial person selected by involved parties or appointed by a court to determine facts or decide matters in dispute.

compare: **arbitrator**

refund annuity

Life. An annuity where, if the annuitant dies during the accumulation period, all premiums (plus interest) are returned to the beneficiary.

see: **annuity**

regionalism

International. The duplication of special permissive rules related to insurers domiciled in different countries within a given region. Regionalism is related to the integration of insurance operations in common markets as well as establishing regional insurers and reinsurers.

regional office

Insurer Operations. An insurance company office which has greater authority than a branch office and is generally staffed to underwrite all lines of business in a specific geographical area.

compare: **branch office, home office**

register

Life. A listing or accounting of debit or industrial insurance policies.

see: **industrial life insurance**

registered bond

Financial Planning. A bond with the owner's name registered on the books of the issuing corporation as with a stock share. For the bond to be negotiable, it must be endorsed by the registered owner.

see: **bonds**

registered mail insurance

Inland Marine. Coverage on an "all-risks" basis for loss of highly valued property (such as jewelry or watches) sent through the postal service.

see: **mail coverage insurance, parcel post insurance**

registered mutual fund representative errors & omissions insurance

Casualty. Coverage for registered representatives of broker-dealers against third-party legal liability caused by alleged negligent acts, errors or omissions when operating in their professional capacities in the sale of mutual funds or variable annuities.

registered representative

General. An individual who is licensed by the National Association of Securities Dealers to sell securities to the public.

see: **National Association of Securities Dealers**

registered retirement saving plan (RRSP)

Employee Benefits. A program which allows citizens of Canada to accumulate retirement funds on a tax deductible basis. It is similar to the U.S. Individual Retirement Account.

see: **individual retirement account**

registered tonnage

Ocean Marine. The tonnage on which an ocean marine policy's limit of liability is calculated in England. For sailing, it is the net register tonnage, and for steamers it is the gross registered tonnage without deduction for engine room space.

regression analysis

Risk Management. A statistical procedure for predicting the value of one variable (the dependent variable) on the basis of knowledge about one or more other variables (independent variables).

Regular National Flood Insurance Program

Loss Control. One of two National Flood Insurance Programs available to a community. This program requires the completion of a flood study of the community by the Federal Insurance Administration, and publication of a Flood Insurance Rate Map. Once a community is approved, individuals within it can purchase flood coverage in excess of the Emergency National Flood Insurance Program. The amounts of additional coverage available in excess of the emergency program are — 1) single family dwelling:

© 1991 NILS Publishing Company

$150,000 on the structure and $50,000 on contents; 2) small business: $150,000 on the structure and $200,000 on the contents.

compare: Emergency National Flood Insurance Program; see: National Flood Insurance Program

regulation

Regulation. Supervision of business and financial practices by a governmental entity.

see: insurance commissioner, insurance department

rehabilitation

Workers' Compensation. Efforts taken to restore an injured employee, through education or physical therapy, to a point where gainful employment is possible.

Regulation. An initial action taken by an insurance department to salvage a financially impaired insurance company. Under rehabilitation, the affairs of the troubled insurer are supervised by the insurance department until such time as it returns to financial stability, or the decision is made to liquidate the company.

see: guaranty funds, insolvency, liquidation

rehabilitation clause

Health. A clause contained in many health and disability insurance policies which provides vocational rehabilitation for disabled policyholders.

reimbursement

Insurer Operations. Payment of an amount of money by an insurance policy in the event of a covered loss.

compare: pay on behalf of; see: indemnify

reinstatement

Reinsurance. Restoration of a reinsurance contract's limit to its full amount by a reinsurer after the payment of a large loss. Often, this will involve the payment of additional premium.

Casualty/Property. Restoration of a policy that has lapsed or been cancelled for nonpayment of premium.

see: lapse

Life. Restoration of a policy that has lapsed due to nonpayment of premiums and whose grace period has expired.

see: lapse

reinsurance

Reinsurance. A form of insurance whereby one insurance company (the reinsurer) in consideration of a premium paid to it, agrees to indemnify another insurance company (the ceding company) for part or all of its liabilities from insurance policies it has issued. The basis of all insurance; i.e., spreading the risk.

Reinsurers often reinsure risks with other reinsurers, a process known as a retrocession.

compare: retrocession; see: admitted reinsurance, agency reinsurance, aggregate excess of loss reinsurance, aggregate working excess reinsurance, American Cargo War Risk Reinsurance Exchange, arbitration clause, assume, assuming reinsurer, assumption, authorized reinsurance, automatic reinsurance, automobile reinsurance facility, Cargo Reinsurance Association, Carpenter Plan, catastrophe reinsurance, cede, ceded reinsurance, ceding company, certificate of reinsurance, cession, earned reinsurance premium, excess loss-ratio reinsurance, excess of loss reinsurance, facultative obligatory reinsurance treaty, facultative reinsurance, facultative semi-obligatory reinsurance treaty, fiduciary, first surplus reinsurance treaty, flat rate, follow the fortunes, intermediary, letter of credit, MAERP Reinsurance Association, nonadmitted reinsurance, nonproportional automatic reinsurance, nonproportional facultative reinsurance, nonproportional reinsurance, obligatory reinsurance treaty, professional reinsurer, pro rata reinsurance, quota share reinsurance, recapture, reciprocity, recoverables, Reinsurance Association of America, reinsurance assumed, reinsurance capacity, reinsurance clause, reinsurance credit, reinsurance exchange, reinsurance premium, retrocedent, retrocessionaire, surplus reinsurance treaty, surplus relief reinsurance, ticket reinsurance, treaty reinsurance, uberrimae fidei, unauthorized reinsurance, unearned reinsurance premium, utmost good faith

Reinsurance Association of America (RAA)

Organizations. Members: Property and casualty reinsurance companies. *Objectives:* Promotes the industry's interests by representing it before Congress and federal and state regulators. *Founded:* 1968. *Headquarters:* Washington, D.C.

reinsurance assumed

Reinsurance. The portion of risk that the reinsurer accepts from the original insurer or ceding company.

syn: assumed reinsurance; see: assumption, cession

reinsurance broker

Reinsurance.

see: intermediary

reinsurance capacity

Reinsurance. 1) The capacity for a particular reinsurer is the largest line it will commit to a risk; this may vary for casualty lines and property lines.

2) The capacity for a class of insurance (e.g., earthquake, off-shore platforms) that is available in the

© 1991 NILS Publishing Company

reinsurance capacity — *continued*
world insurance markets, including reinsurance markets.
3) A reinsurer's ability to accept premium, which may be limited by its policyholder's surplus.

reinsurance ceded
Reinsurance.
see: cession

reinsurance clause
Reinsurance. A provision in a reinsurance contract that describes the business to be insured.

reinsurance commission
Reinsurance.
see: ceding commission

reinsurance credit
Regulation/Reinsurance. Credit allowed for ceded reinsurance premiums and losses recoverable on the ceding insurer's annual statement.
see: admitted reinsurance, annual statement, recoverables

reinsurance exchange
Reinsurance. An organized facility or market established by reinsurers having rules for the assumption or ceding of reinsurance between its participants.
compare: insurance exchange

reinsurance intermediary
Reinsurance.
see: intermediary

reinsurance premium
Insurer Operations/Reinsurance. An amount paid by the ceding insurer to the reinsurer in consideration for the liability assumed by the reinsurer.
see: net premiums written, premium, rate

reinsured
Reinsurance.
see: ceding company

reinsurer
Reinsurance. An insurer assuming the liability of another insurer through reinsurance.
compare: ceding company, retrocessionaire; see: assume, assuming reinsurer

rejection
Insurer Operations. The declination of a risk by an underwriter.
compare: acceptance; see: submitted business

release
General. A document by which a legal right is discharged.
see: forthwith payment
Insurer Operations. A document used by insurance adjusters to obtain a formal discharge by a claimant of any additional rights to recovery after a claims settlement agreement.

released bill of lading
Inland Marine. A bill of lading on which no stated value has been indicated, thereby limiting the carrier's liability to statutory amounts or to the specified rate per pound of merchandise shipped.
see: bill of lading

religious discrimination
Casualty.
see: discrimination

remainder
Reinsurance. The amount a reinsurer assumes from a ceding company on an individual risk. The amount remaining after subtracting the ceding company's retention from the total limit insured.
compare: net line, net retention

removal
Property. A covered peril of a property insurance policy providing for the removal of insured items from insured property for safekeeping purposes.

remuneration
Casualty/Workers' Compensation. Often used as a rating base, the salary or other earnings of employees, which make up the payroll of an organization. It includes regular earnings, piece goods payments and overtime.
see: exposure unit, payroll audit; Fr: rémuneration; Gr: Vergütung; Sp: remuneración

renewable term life insurance
Life. Term life insurance which may be continued beyond its original term by acceptance of a premium for a new policy term without evidence of insurability.
see: term life insurance, yearly renewable term

renewal
Insurer Operations. The act or process of maintaining insurance in force by issuing a new policy to replace an expiring policy or the issuance of certificates or endorsements extending the term of an expiring policy.
see: anniversary date, annual renewal agreement, renewal certificate

renewal certificate
Insurer Operations. A form notifying the insured that

© 1991 NILS Publishing Company

an insurance policy is renewed on the same terms as the expiring policy.

see: renewal

renewal commission

Agency/Insurer Operations. A commission paid to an agent or broker for premiums on policies that have been renewed.

compare: first-year commission; see: agent's commission, graded commission, unlevel commission

rental income insurance

Property. A form of property insurance that pays the owner of a building for the amount of rent lost due to damage from an insured peril. The form will also cover the tenant of a building for rent that must continue to be paid, even if the premises cannot be occupied.

compare: rental value insurance

rental reimbursement coverage

Automobile. Coverage that can be endorsed to an automobile policy, which pays for the cost of renting a substitute vehicle if a policyholder's auto is disabled by a covered physical damage loss.

see: physical damage, temporary substitute automobile, transportation expense coverage

rental value insurance

Property. A form of property insurance that covers the use interest of owners occupying their own building or tenants in a building. For a building owner, coverage will pay to secure other facilities similar to the damaged building or will pay the amount the owner would have received if the building were leased to others. For a tenant, coverage pays the amount that the tenant must pay to secure comparable facilities.

syn: rent insurance; compare: rental income insurance

renter's insurance

Casualty/Property. A personal property/liability package policy designed to protect a renter (individual or family). It combines broad coverage on personal property with broad personal liability coverage. The policy is similar to a homeowner's policy, except there is no property coverage for the structure itself. The coverage is similar to that provided by the homeowner's policy form 2.

syn: homeowner's policy form 4; compare: rental income insurance, rental value insurance; see: homeowner's policy form 2

rent insurance

Property.

see: rental value insurance

reorganization

General. The restructuring of a financially troubled organization. A firm's assets are restated to reflect their current market value, and its financial structure is restated to reflect any changes on the asset side of the statement. The organization continues in existence – in contrast to bankruptcy – where the organization is liquidated and ceases to exist.

compare: rehabilitation

repair or replace

Inland Marine. A condition commonly found in inland marine policies which refers to the insurer's right to settle a loss by repairing or replacing damaged property with property of like kind and quality.

see: new for old

replacement cost

Property. A property valuation method; the cost to replace damaged property with property of like kind and quality; the cost to replace property at its current price, without a deduction for depreciation.

compare: actual cash value, depreciated value, depreciation insurance, economic value, fair market value, functional replacement cost, market value, reproduction cost, tax-appraised value; see: functional obsolescence, replacement cost insurance, valuation of potential property loss; Fr: valeur à neuf; Gr: Neuwert, Ersatzwert; Sp: costo de reposición

replacement cost insurance

Property. Insurance that compensates property owners for losses on a replacement cost basis.

see: depreciation insurance, replacement cost

replacement policy

Insurer Operations. A policy which has been issued to replace one currently in force.

replacement ratio

Agency/Life. A ratio used by life insurers and their agents to determine the amount of new insurance premium which must be developed to replace lost premium. The ratio can be developed based on the number of new to lost policies, or based on policy face amounts lost to the face amounts of new policies.

replevin

General. The recovery by a plaintiff of goods or chattels claimed to be wrongfully taken or detained upon the plaintiff's giving security until the matter can be tried in court. The plaintiff is bound to return the goods if defeated in the court action.

see: plaintiff's replevin bond

replevin bond

Surety.

see: plaintiff's replevin bond

© 1991 NILS Publishing Company

reportable event

Insurer Operations. A loss from any insured peril. An insured is obligated to report such losses to the insurer or its representative as soon as possible.

see: **accident report, incident report, notice of loss**

reported claims count

Risk Management. The total number of claims reported by an insured to an insurance company.

reporting arrangement

Automobile. A reporting form method of arranging automobile physical damage under a garage policy. This method of coverage provides a maximum limit of liability for all vehicles, basing the premium on a rate applied against reports of monthly or quarterly values at risk.

see: **garagekeepers insurance**

reporting form

Workers' Compensation. A form which must be completed by a policyholder on a periodic basis (e.g., monthly or quarterly), to report the workers' compensation payroll for that period. These figures are then used to determine the premium to be charged for that period.

Casualty. A form which must be completed by a policyholder on a periodic basis (monthly, quarterly) to report that period's exposure basis (receipts, payroll, units produced) which is used to determine the premium to be charged for that period.

Property. A form which must be completed by a policyholder on a periodic basis (e.g., monthly or quarterly) to meet insurance policy requirements. A reporting form policy requires the insured to report property values that frequently vary (up or down) during the policy period. This method of coverage usually will result in a premium savings to the policyholder, since coverage does not have to be purchased for the maximum exposure during the year, but instead the insured pays a premium based on the actual or average exposure. Often policies written on this basis have a penalty provision for late reporting.

syn: **value reporting form**; see: **full reporting clause, peak season endorsement, seasonal risk**

reporting policy

Property.

see: **adjustable policy**

representation

General. A written response to questions or statements made on an application for insurance which the applicant indicates are fact and the underwriter relies upon to issue a policy.

see: **affirmative warranty, application, material misrepresentation, misrepresentation, warranties of insured**

representative

Agency/Insurer Operations. An agent of a direct writing insurance company.

see: **direct writer**

reproduction cost

Property. Occasionally, a property insurance policy will provide for loss adjustment on the basis of reproduction cost, which is the cost to replace an identical property at the same location. When insuring on this basis, the insurer's responsibility is to replace the building using existing plans and specifications, with the expense for these items deducted from the insurable value.

compare: **actual cash value, depreciated value, fair market value, functional obsolescence, functional replacement cost, market value, replacement cost, tax-appraised value**; see: **valuation of potential property loss**

request for proposal (RFP)

Surety.

see: **advertisement to bid**

required rate of return

General. The rate of return that stockholders expect to receive on common stock investments.

see: **rate of return**

rescind

Insurer Operations. To void or cancel an insurance policy back to its inception as if the policy had never been issued.

see: **flat cancellation, rescission**

rescission

General. The cancellation of a contract – back to its inception date – as though the contract had never existed. Usually, rescission is allowed by courts when fraud, misrepresentation or duress by one of the parties to the contract is present.

see: **duress, fraud, misrepresentation, rescind**

reservation of rights

Insurer Operations. A written notification to an insured from an insurer stating its right to affirm or deny its liability when coverage for a claim appears questionable. However, the insurer agrees to defend the insured.

see: **acquiescence, estoppel, laches, nonwaiver agreement, waiver**

reserve

General. Funds set aside by an organization to assure the fulfillment of commitments for future liabilities; or the total unpaid amount of self-insured or employee

© 1991 NILS Publishing Company

benefit plan claims which have been reported at the accounting date.

see: pension liability, self-insurance reserve

Insurer Operations. Funds set aside by an insurance company to assure that it can cover future liabilities; or the total unpaid amount of claims which have been reported at a specific accounting date.

see: balance sheet reserves, deficiency reserve, expense reserve, funding of reserves, initial reserve, investment reserve, investment valuation reserve, legal reserve, loss ratio reserve method, loss reserve, mandatory securities valuation reserve, mean reserve, net level premium reserve, policy reserve, premium deficiency reserve, prospective reserve, reserve premium, self-insurance reserve, statutory reserve, tabular-value reserve method, technical reserves, terminal reserve, unearned premium reserve, valuation reserve, voluntary reserve

reserve premium

Insurer Operations. A premium that is collected in addition to the policy premium, to offset unexpected claims. It is calculated as a proportion of the policy premium and maintained in a separate reserve account. To the extent it is not used to pay losses, it is returnable to policyholders along with a specified interest rate. No insurance company expenses are charged against the premium, with the exception of unexpected losses and state premium taxes.

see: premium

residence employee

Workers' Compensation. A person hired by the owner of a private residence, who does domestic work at that residence on a full or part-time basis. In some states, workers' compensation coverage for such an employee must be included in a homeowner's or renter's policy.

see: domestic

resident agent

Agency. An agent who is domiciled in the state where he or she does business.

compare: nonresident agent (broker); see: agent, countersignature

residual disability income policy

Health. A policy providing benefits for loss of income following disability, rather than the inability to perform the duties of an occupation. An important coverage for a professional, whose disability causes a business interruption resulting in a loss of clients, even though recovery from the disability is complete.

residual markets

Insurer Operations. Specialty insurance markets or facilities designed to assume risks which are generally unacceptable to the normal insurance market. Such markets include assigned risk plans, government insurance programs, and aviation or nuclear pools.

see: assigned risk, Fair Access to Insurance Requirements

residual value

General. The value of leased property at the end of the lease term.

see: residual value insurance

residual value insurance

Financial Guarantee Insurance. A form of financial guarantee insurance that protects a lessor against unexpected declines in the market value of leased equipment (automobiles, aircraft, heavy machinery) upon termination of the lease agreement.

see: equipment value insurance, residual value

res ipsa loquitur

General. A Latin phrase which means "the facts speak for themselves." This is a legal term for the permissible inference that a defendant was negligent, because the facts are clear and the circumstances are such that, ordinarily, the plaintiff could not have been injured if the defendant had not been at fault.

syn: presumed negligence

Resource Conservation and Recovery Act of 1976 (RCRA)

Regulation. A federal act which established the financial responsibility requirements for the hazardous waste industry.

see: closure and post-closure insurance, environmental impairment liability, pollution insurance

respondeat superior

General. A Latin phrase which means "let the superior reply." It is a legal doctrine holding that the principal or employer is vicariously liable in certain situations for unauthorized torts committed by its agents or employees while acting in the scope of the agency or during employment.

see: agency, master servant rule

rest cure

Health. Custodial care at a sanitarium or nursing home.

restoration of plan

Employee Benefits. The act of restoring a pension plan that has been terminated to its previous status by funding all or a portion of the plan's previous assets. Such a restoration must be approved by the Pension Benefit Guaranty Corporation.

compare: recapture of plan assets; see: Pension Benefit Guaranty Corporation

© 1991 NILS Publishing Company

restoration of vested benefits

Employee Benefits. An Employee Retirement Income Security Act (ERISA) provision allowing employees of a pension plan who are less than 50 percent vested to buy back retirement benefits lost because contributions are withdrawn.

see: Employee Retirement Income Security Act of 1974

restoration premium

Insurer Operations. A premium that must be paid by the policyholder to restore a policy's benefit limits following their exhaustion by the payment of claims. Most policies do not reduce their limits because of claims payments, but some London market policies and bonds do contain such a provision.

compare: automatic reinstatement clause; see: aggregate limit, first loss insurance, premium

retail credit report

Insurer Operations. A report used by insurers as an underwriting tool, to determine an applicant's financial condition. These reports are developed and supplied by credit reporting agencies that collect the data from various sources.

see: Fair Credit Reporting Act

retained earnings

General. The sum of a company's net profit during its existence, minus all dividends (common and preferred) ever paid.

syn: earnings retained; see: balance sheet, capital, common equity, financial statement, owner's equity

retainer

General. An initial fee paid to ensure an attorney's services, should such a need arise.

see: contingent fee agreement, defense costs

retainer clause

Reinsurance. A nonproportional, reinsurance contract provision which specifically limits coverage under the contract to business that the ceding insurer retains for its own account.

syn: net retention clause

retaliatory legislation

Insurer Operations/Regulation. State legislation which provides that insurance companies domiciled in another state must pay the same tax rate that insurance companies domiciled in that state pay, but only if the tax rate is higher.

compare: reciprocal legislation; see: retaliatory tax

Agency/Regulation. State legislation which imposes the same licensing requirements on out-of-state agents or brokers as their home state requires of out-of-state agents or brokers.

retaliatory tax

Insurer Operations/Regulation. The tax imposed by retaliatory legislation.

compare: reciprocal legislation; see: retaliatory legislation

retention

Reinsurance. A term which refers to the amount of liability which an insurer does not reinsure, but instead retains for its own account.

Risk Management. The planned assumption of risk by an insured through the use of deductibles, insurance policy retentions, or self-insurance. Retention usually results from three basic desires of the insured: 1) to reduce expenses and improve cash flow; 2) to increase control of claims reserving and claims settlements; and 3) to fund for losses that cannot be insured.

syn: loss assumption, loss retention, net line, risk assumption, risk retention; compare: non-insurance, passive retention; see: avoidance, diversification, insurance, large loss principle, transfer of risk

retention and limits clause

Reinsurance. A clause found in excess of loss reinsurance contracts which provides that the reinsurer will pay all claims in excess of the ceding company's retained limit (retention) up to the reinsurer's limit of liability.

see: excess of loss reinsurance, retention

retention limit

Casualty. The amount an insured must pay before a liability policy with a self-insured retention will respond to a loss. In regard to an umbrella policy, it is the amount an insured must pay for a loss not covered by an underlying policy, before the umbrella policy will respond.

see: deductible, retention, self-insured retention

retired life fund

Life.

see: annuity purchase fund

retirement age

Employee Benefits. The age at which a participant in a pension plan terminates his or her employment and thereby becomes qualified to receive the retirement benefits.

see: deferred retirement, delayed retirement credit, early retirement, normal retirement age

retirement annuity

Life. An insurance contract which does not contain an element of pure insurance. The death benefit of the

© 1991 NILS Publishing Company

contract is based on the remaining reserve or the premium paid, without interest, whichever is larger.

see: annuity

retirement income policy

Life. A deferred annuity policy which does not provide any life insurance coverage and begins paying benefits at a specified age. The premium, less the insurer loading, is accumulated with interest to fund the periodic annuity payments.

see: annuity

retiring from a line

Insurer Operations. The withdrawal of an insurance company from an insurance line of business by cancelling or non-renewing policies.

retroactive conversion

Life. Converting a term life insurance policy to a cash value policy, using the term policy's original inception date rather than the date of conversion.

syn: original age option

retroactive date

Casualty. A date stipulated in the claims-made liability form declarations section as the first date on which an incident may occur and be covered by the policy. The retroactive date is designed to provide coverage for claims resulting from incidents that take place prior to the current policy term

see: claims-made form, claims-made trigger

retroactive extension

Casualty. An extension of the terms of a current insurance policy back into a prior period of time.

retrocedent

Reinsurance. A reinsurer who cedes a portion of the business it assumes to another reinsurer.

compare: ceding company, retrocessionaire

retrocession

Reinsurance. The purchasing of reinsurance by a reinsurer. The further spreading of a large risk assumed by a reinsurer among a number of other reinsurance companies.

retrocessionaire

Reinsurance. A reinsurer who assumes reinsurance from another reinsurer.

compare: ceding company, reinsurer, retrocedent

retrofit

Loss Control. To go back and fix or adjust something that has already been constructed or manufactured in order to bring it up to current standards. *Example:* Bringing an existing building up to current earthquake standards.

retrospective penalty insurance

Casualty/Workers' Compensation. A separate insurance policy, written in conjunction with a retrospective rating plan policy, that protects the policyholder against having to pay a penalty or extra premium in excess of the standard retrospective premium in the event of an adverse loss ratio.

see: maximum retrospective premium, retrospective rating plan

retrospective premium

Insurer Operations. The final premium developed under a retrospective rating plan.

see: retrospective rating plan

retrospective rating plan

Insurer Operations. A method of establishing a premium on large commercial accounts. The final premium is based on the insured's actual loss experience during the policy term, subject to a minimum and maximum premium, with the final premium determined by a formula. Under this plan, the current year's premium is based on the current year's losses, although the premium adjustments may take months or years beyond the current year's expiration date. The rating formula is guaranteed in the insurance contract. *Formula:* Retrospective Premium = Converted Loss + Basic Premium x Tax Multiplier. Numerous variations of this formula have been developed and are in use.

compare: experience rating plan, maximum retrospective premium, paid loss retrospective rating plan, prospective rating plan; see: basic premium, converted losses, excess loss premium factor, retrospective penalty insurance, tax multiplier

Reinsurance. A reinsurance contract rating formula where the final premium is based on the primary carrier's loss experience over a specified period of time.

return commission

Agency. The portion of a commission that has been received by an agent that must be returned to an insured as the result of cancellation, rate adjustment, deletion or reduction in coverage, or an error in calculation of the initial premium.

compare: flat cancellation, pro rata cancellation, short-rate cancellation

return of cash value

Life. A life insurance policy provision stating that if death occurs during a certain period of time, the policy will pay its cash value, in addition to the face amount.

compare: return of premium

© 1991 NILS Publishing Company

return of premium
General.
see: return premium

Health. A provision in a health insurance policy providing for the payment of a benefit equal to the sum or a stated percentage of all the premiums paid, less claims paid, if the claims paid over a stated period of time do not exceed a fixed percentage of the premiums paid.

Life. A life insurance policy provision that the death benefit paid will be the face amount, plus the sum of all the premiums paid, should death occur within a specified period of time after inception of the policy.

compare: return of cash value

return on investment (ROI)
Insurer Operations. A frequently used financial analysis ratio which indicates both an investor's return on his or her investment and whether or not the volume of income generated is adequate relative to the amount of capital invested in the organization. *Formula:* Return On Investment = Net Income/Total Assets. The higher the ratio, the greater the profitability.

see: financial ratios, financial underwriting, internal rate of return, opportunity cost

return portfolio
Reinsurance. The reassumption by a ceding company of a portfolio of risks that were previously assumed by a reinsurer.

see: recapture

return premium (RP)
Insurer Operations. The portion of the premium returned to an insured as the result of cancellation, rate adjustment, deletion or reduction in coverage or an error in calculation of the initial premium.

syn: return of premium; compare: additional premium, initial premium; see: flat cancellation, pro rata cancellation, short-rate cancellation; Fr: ristourne de prime; Gr: Rückvergütete Prämie; Sp: prima de devolución

revenue passenger miles
Aviation. A measure of airline traffic. Each revenue passenger mile represents one revenue-paying passenger flown one mile.

see: available seat miles, passenger yield

reverse-annuity mortgage (RAM)
Financial Planning. A quasi-annuity, whereby a homeowner receives lifetime monthly payments from a lender, based on the value of the house and the homeowner's life expectancy. Upon the death of the homeowner, title to the house automatically transfers to the lender. An especially useful technique for elderly persons, who usually own their homes free and clear, since it allows them to benefit from the equity tied up in their homes yet it guarantees them a place to live.

see: annuity, living benefits

reverse flow business
International. A term referring to the insuring of businesses or properties in the United States, owned by foreign investors. Many insurance companies have established special departments to concentrate on this business, because of the tremendous increase of foreign investments in the United States.

see: foreign/home insurance

reversionary annuity
Life.
see: joint and survivor annuity

revival
Insurer Operations.
see: reinstatement

revocable beneficiary
Life. A life insurance policy in which the owner reserves the right to revoke or change the beneficiary.

compare: irrevocable beneficiary;
see: beneficiary

Richter scale
Loss Control.
see: seismograph

rider
Insurer Operations. A term usually applied to an attachment which modifies life insurance policies or a contract of insurance or a bond, often by adding or excluding various coverage.

syn: attachment, waiver; compare: endorsement

right of exoneration
Surety. After a principal defaults on its obligation to the obligee, and the surety performs under the terms of the bond, most bonds provide the surety recourse to recover from the principal the amounts which the surety was required to pay. This right to recourse is called, within the field of surety, the surety's right of exoneration.

riot
Property. Public uproar or disturbance involving three or more people. Damage caused by riot is covered by most property insurance policies.

Fr: émeute; Gr: Aufruhr; Sp: alboroto popular

risk
General. The possibility of loss.

syn: uncertainty; compare: exposure, hazard,

© 1991 NILS Publishing Company

peril; see: business risk, degree of risk, financial risk

Risk Management. The term "risk," as used in risk management and insurance, has several definitions – the possibility of loss or injury; the chance of loss; the perils to which the subject matter of an insurance contract is exposed; a specified hazard to an insurance company; the property or person exposed to damage or injury; and, the uncertainty concerning loss.

risk-adjusted discount rate

Financial Planning. The discount rate applicable to a particularly risky (uncertain) stream of income; the risk-free rate of interest, plus a risk premium appropriate to the level of risk attached to the particular income stream.

see: discount factor, discounting, risk premium

Risk and Insurance Management Society, Inc. (RIMS)

Organizations. Members: Corporate risk, insurance and employee benefits managers. *Objectives:* Sponsors educational programs. Promotes risk management concepts. *Founded:* 1950. *Headquarters:* New York, NY. Originally known as National Insurance Buyers Association until 1954, when the name was changed to the American Society of Insurance Management. The association took its current name in 1975.

risk appraiser

Life. A life insurance company employee responsible for deciding whether an application for life insurance coverage will be approved or rejected, or if alternative coverage will be offered.

see: risk classification, underwriter

risk assumption

Risk Management.
see: retention

risk classification

Life. The process by which a life insurer determines the premium that should be charged for a policy according to such factors as an applicant's age, occupation, sex and health.

see: classification, risk appraiser, underwriting

Workers' Compensation. The placing of employees into various job classifications to determine the rate that should be used to develop a workers' compensation policy premium.

see: classification, governing classification, underwriting

Casualty. The placing of an insurance applicant's operations, properties, products, etc., into specific rating classifications to determine the rate that should be used to develop a policy premium.

see: classification, underwriting

risk control

Risk Management. Techniques or programs used to reduce the total amount of physical damage, injury or loss should an event occur that results in a fortuitous loss.

see: loss control, loss prevention, risk management process

risk financing

Risk Management. Techniques or methods used to provide funds to pay for losses due to fortuitous events.

compare: noninsurance; see: captive insurance company, insurance, retention, self-insurance

risk identification

Risk Management. The risk management process of determining the potential sources of loss faced by individuals and organizations.

see: risk management process

risk management

Risk Management. The procedures used to identify, analyze, assess and minimize loss exposures; management of the pure risks to which an organization might be subject; a process that uses physical and human resources to accomplish certain objectives (risk reduction, insurance, etc.) concerning identified loss exposures.

compare: insurance management; see: risk management process

risk management audit

Risk Management. A systematic evaluation of an organization's exposure to risks, insurance coverages or retentions as they relate to those risks, and how the organization is coordinating its risk management program, including any necessary recommendations for improvements.

see: risk identification, risk management process

risk management consultant

Risk Management. An individual or firm that provides risk management and insurance consulting – e.g., risk management audits, policy analysis, feasibility studies, etc. – on a fee basis. As a rule, the risk management consultant does not sell insurance, and so maintains its independence and objectivity. Usually such an individual will have a CPCU (Chartered Property and Casualty Underwriter) or ARM (Associate in Risk Management) designation.

see: Associate in Risk Management, Chartered Property and Casualty Underwriter

© 1991 NILS Publishing Company

risk management manual

Risk Management. A manual developed for an organization – usually by its risk manager, risk management consultant, or broker – which includes a risk management policy statement, a description of all insurance contracts purchased by the organization, and procedures to report changes in exposures, and claims.

compare: **risk management policy statement**

risk management policy statement

Risk Management. A statement developed and approved at a high management level within an organization for the following purposes: 1) To commit top managers to the risk management function; 2) To disseminate the risk management function throughout the organization in; and 3) To set a standard against which the firm's risk management performance can be judged.

see: **loss control policy statement**

risk management process

Risk Management. The risk management process is a series of steps: 1) Identifying and analyzing loss exposures; 2) Measuring loss exposures; 3) Selecting the technique or combination of techniques to be used to handle each exposure; 4) Implementing the techniques chosen; and 5) Monitoring the decisions made and implementing appropriate changes.

see: **feasibility study, insurance, risk control, risk financing, risk identification, risk management, risk management audit, risk transfer**

risk premium

Financial Planning. The difference between the rate of return on a particularly risky asset, and the rate of return on an asset without risk, with the same expected life.

see: **rate of return, return on investment, risk-adjusted discount rate**

risk premium insurance

Life.

see: **yearly renewable term**

risk purchasing group (RPG)

Regulation. An entity which offers insurance to groups of similar businesses with similar exposures to risk. (Personal lines and workers' compensation policies cannot be written by risk purchasing groups.) The policy is based on the insured's loss and expense experience and is not afforded to other policyholders with respect to rates, policy forms or coverages. Such programs and the groups that offer them are exempt from most state laws, rules or regulations, except for the state in which the group is domiciled. RPGs were originally created, along with risk retention groups

(RRGs) by the Product Liability Risk Retention Act of 1981.

compare: **risk retention group**; see: **Liability Risk Retention Act of 1986, Product Liability Risk Retention Act of 1981**

risk quantification

Risk Management. The measurement criteria used to evaluate loss frequency and loss severity.

see: **loss frequency, loss severity**

risk retention

Risk Management.

see: **retention**

Risk Retention Act

Regulation.

see: **Liability Risk Retention Act of 1986**

risk retention group (RRG)

Regulation. A group self-insurance program or group captive insurance company formed under provisions of the Liability Risk Retention Act of 1986, by or on behalf of businesses joined to insure their liability exposures. Such a group is exempt from most state laws, rules or regulations except, in most cases, for the state in which it is domiciled.

see: **association captive insurance company, group captive insurance company, Liability Risk Retention Act of 1986**

risk transfer

Risk Management. The contractual shifting of a pure risk from one party to another. The purchase of an insurance policy, where the risk is passed from the policyholder to the insurer is risk transfer. Other examples would be the hold harmless agreements contained in many contracts, or a contractual requirement to provide insurance coverage for another party's benefit.

compare: **avoidance, noninsurance, passive retention, retention, self-insurance**; see: **hold harmless agreement, insurance, noninsurance transfer, risk management process**

river marine insurance

Ocean Marine. Ocean marine insurance coverage for vessels operating on inland waterways.

see: **ocean marine insurance**

robbery

Crime. The taking of property from a person or the possession of another by using violence or threats.

see: **holdup; Fr: vol; Gr: Raub; Sp: robo con violencia**

robbery and safe burglary form

Crime. A crime coverage form providing "robbery and burglary from a safe" coverage inside a premises, as

© 1991 NILS Publishing Company

well as "robbery of messengers" coverage outside of the premises.

syn: **crime coverage form D; see: crime coverages**

rollover individual retirement account

Employee Benefits. An individual retirement account (IRA) created specifically for the purpose of receiving funds distributed from a qualified pension plan, usually without incurring any tax liabilities. Some restrictions exist for the amount, frequency and timing of these rollovers with respects to their tax exempt status.

see: **individual retirement account, tax free rollover**

rule of strict construction

General.

see: **strict construction**

running down clause

Ocean Marine. Liability coverage that can be added to an ocean marine hull policy for damage caused by a collision with another vessel.

syn: **both to blame collision clause, collision clause**

run-off cancellation

Reinsurance. A reinsurance contract termination provision requiring the reinsurer to remain liable for a losses under reinsured policies in force at the date of termination, as a result of an occurrence after the date of termination.

compare: **cut-off cancellation; see: cancellation**

295

© 1991 NILS Publishing Company

safe

Crime. A container, usually made of metal, designed to be opened only by an authorized person, that can be used for storing valuables.

see: iron safe clause, vault

safe burglary insurance

Crime. Coverage against the taking of covered property from within a locked safe or vault inside a premises, or the actual taking of the safe or vault from the premises. Some older forms of the coverage required that there be visible signs of forcible entry.

safe deposit box coverage

Crime. Coverage for a bank or savings and loan from liability for loss to property in a safe deposit box against burglary from the box or against robbery from within the vault containing the box or the customers' section of the safe deposit department. Money is excluded from coverage, but may be added by an endorsement.

compare: safe depository direct loss coverage form; see: hotel safe deposit box liability, safe depository liability coverage form

safe depository direct loss coverage form

Crime. A crime coverage form which provides direct damage coverage for customers' securities and property (other than money and securities) that have been entrusted with an insured safe depository facility that is not a financial institution (e.g., a hotel). Money may be included for coverage by endorsement.

syn: crime coverage form N; compare: safe deposit box coverage; see: crime coverages, hotel safe deposit box liability, money, property other than money and securities, securities

safe depository liability coverage form

Crime. A crime coverage form which provides legal liability coverage for loss of a customer's securities and property other than money and securities while in an insured safe depository facility.

syn: crime coverage form M; see: safe deposit box coverage

safe driver plan

Automobile. A rating system for automobile insurance. Good drivers are charged lower rates, while bad drivers must pay higher rates. Good and bad drivers are designated by use of a point system, with points assigned for traffic violations and certain accidents. Each assigned point brings with it a surcharge to a drivers' rate base.

see: chargeable offense, good driver discount, merit rating

safety

Loss Control. A means of preventing or reducing accidents and injuries.

safety audit

Loss Control. A systematic study and inspection of an organization's operations to discover existing and potential hazards and those actions that are necessary to reduce or eliminate such hazards.

safety can

Loss Control. An container approved by an accredited safety organization for the handling of flammable liquids not exceeding five gallons in capacity. It is fitted with a spring-closing lid and spout cover which will remain closed when not in use, but will relieve internal pressure due to extreme heat.

salamander

Loss Control. A portable oil-fired heater used at construction sites or in large warehouses.

© 1991 NILS Publishing Company

salary continuation plan

Employee Benefits. A plan to continue an employee's salary to a spouse or other beneficiary for a specific period of time after an employee's disability or death. This type of plan is usually funded by disability and/or life insurance.

salary savings insurance

Life.
see: payroll deduction insurance

sale

General. The transfer of title from seller to purchaser for some form of consideration.

sales

General. Gross revenue less returns, discounts, and allowances.
Fr: ventes; Gr: Umsatz; Sp: ventas
Casualty. An exposure unit used to rate many casualty insurance coverages.
see: exposure unit

salesmen's samples floater

Inland Marine. Inland marine coverage for business firms insuring against loss or damage to their salesmen's samples on an "all-risks" basis.
see: floater policy

sales representative

Agency/Insurer Operations.
see: special agent

saline contamination exclusion

Casualty. An endorsement attached to commercial general liability policies insuring oil drilling risks which excludes coverage for damage to underground resources resulting from contamination caused by pumping saline water into wells to increase recovery of oil.
see: oil well liability, platform insurance

salvage

Ocean Marine. The amount of money realized from the sale of damaged merchandise; services rendered by the rescuers of a ship or cargo.
see: life salvage, recoverables, salvage charges, salvor
Insurer Operations. The title of property recovered from an insured loss that is transferred to the insurer paying the loss. The insurer then sells the property to reduce the loss.
Fr: sauvetage; Gr: Bergung; Sp: salvamento

salvage charges

Ocean Marine/Property. Payment by the property owner to a salvor following the salvage or recovery of property. Frequently, the amount will be determined by a court and will be based on the value of the salvaged material and the salvor's expenses.
see: salvage, salvor

salvage loss

Ocean Marine. The amount of a loss that is the difference between the amount of funds raised by the sale of merchandise at a salvage sale and the insured value. This amount is important when an insured and an insurer cannot agree on the value of damaged goods, because it is used to determine the actual value of the salvage.
see: salvage sale

salvage sale

Ocean Marine. The public sale of damaged property recovered by salvage.
see: salvage loss

salvor

Ocean Marine. The person(s) who save property from loss or damage; those involved with the salvaging of property.

Sanborn Map Company, Inc.

Property. The Sanborn Map Company was formed in 1866 to provide fire maps for the insurance industry. These maps were used for basic underwriting of property insurance and by individual insurers to monitor their accumulations of liability within specific geographical areas. By the mid-1950s, Sanborn maps covered most communities in the United States with populations in excess of 2,500. The high cost involved in maintaining the maps and the use of computers in the underwriting process has eliminated the use of these maps by most insurers.
see: fire map

satellite and space vehicle insurance

Aviation. Coverage that insures against the loss of capital expended to launch a satellite. There are four types of satellite insurance: 1) *Preignition insurance.* Provides coverage up to the time of the intended ignition of the launch vehicle; 2) *Launch insurance.* Protects the insured against physical loss or damage to the spacecraft in the launch sequence, failure of the spacecraft to arrive at its designated orbit, or failure of the satellite to perform as specified once it arrives in orbit; 3) *In-orbit insurance.* Protects the insured against failure of the spacecraft to continue to operate successfully in its required orbit; and 4) *Ground-support insurance.* Protects the insured against third party liability claims from an occurrence associated with the satellite launch mission.

satisfaction of judgment

General. The act of the losing party in complying with

© 1991 NILS Publishing Company

the requirements of the judgment (e.g., paying a specific sum to the prevailing party).

see: post-judgment interest, prejudgment interest

savings bank life insurance (SBLI)

Life. Life insurance which is permitted to be sold by mutual savings banks in certain states such as New York, Connecticut, and Massachusetts.

savings element

Life. The cash value accumulation within a life insurance policy which is considered the policy's savings element. The policyholder can borrow against this accumulation in some policies; it is returned to the policyowner if the policy is cancelled or has reached maturity.

see: cash surrender value, cash value, mature

schedule

Health. A listing of medical and surgical procedures and ancillary expenses with corresponding maximum fees or benefits payable for hospital and medical reimbursement policies. Usually published by health insurers.

syn: fee schedule, table of allowances; compare: unallocated benefit; see: approved charges; diagnostic related group; reasonable and customary charge; usual, customary and reasonable fees

Property. A listing of buildings, structures and contents that is covered by a multiple location property policy.

Inland Marine. A listing of the items (such as jewelry, furs, silverware or cameras) covered by an inland marine floater policy. For each item listed there is a description and a value indicated.

schedule bond

Crime. A bond listing the various covered principals, by name or position.

see: name position bond, name schedule bond

scheduled coverage

Inland Marine/Property. Coverage that insures items of property that are specifically listed. The schedule indicates amount of insurance applicable to each item.

compare: blanket insurance; see: schedule, scheduled item

scheduled item

Inland Marine/Property. An insured item which is specifically listed in the policy and for which a amount of insurance is indicated.

see: scheduled coverage

scheduled personal property endorsement

Inland Marine. A homeowner's policy endorsement

that provides coverage on specifically scheduled articles on an "all-risks" basis. Each insured article is listed on the schedule, along with its stated value. Articles that can be covered under this endorsement include jewelry, furs, cameras, silverware, appliances, and musical instruments.

compare: personal articles floater

Schedule P

Regulation. Considered to be the most important loss reserve development schedule in the National Association of Insurance Commissioner's annual statement for a property and casualty insurance company. This schedule includes reserve development for auto liability, other liability, workers' compensation, package policies, ocean marine, aircraft and boiler and machinery and consists of three parts: 1) cumulative loss experience by accident year – the basis used to determine the minimum statutory reserve, 2) the historical development of incurred losses, and 3) comparison of the claims settling experience of the last seven accident years.

Schedule Q

Regulation. A schedule that life insurers doing business in New York must file with the insurance department. The schedule includes a listing of all life insurance selling expenses and places a maximum limitation on commissions paid to agents.

syn: Q Schedule

schedule rating

Automobile/Casualty/Property. A method of developing property and liability insurance premiums by applying debits and/or credits within established ranges for various characteristics of the risk, which are either above or below a schedule of standards.

see: "A" rates, account premium modification plan, judgment rates

scrub tower

Loss Control. An item of equipment that removes airborne impurities by passing (scrubbing) exhaust gases or dust through a system of fine water spray or through a system of wet slats which collects the impurities.

scuppers

Loss Control. Floor level openings in a building wall covered by hinged metal flaps which allow water from sprinkler systems to flow through, reducing the weight and possible collapse of the floors.

see: automatic sprinkler system, sprinkler leakage coverage

seal

General. A symbol attached to a document, attesting that it is a legal or official document.

© 1991 NILS Publishing Company

seaman's remedies

Ocean Marine. General maritime law provides a seaman with a right to wages until the end of the voyage or period of hire, and to board and care during that period of time or while on the voyage.

see: cure; Jones Act; wages, maintenance and cure

seasonal risk

Insurer Operations. A business that operates on a seasonal basis, such as a farm or resort hotel, where there is little or no exposure for part of the year. Or, a risk having a seasonal fluctuation in insured exposures (changes in inventory or sales, increased or decreased use of facilities, etc.). Underwriters allow for such seasonality, because of the reduced exposures during part of the policy period.

see: peak season endorsement, reporting form

seat belt

Automobile.

see: passive restraint systems

SEC liability insurance

Casualty. Insurance which provides coverage for securities underwriters or issuers of stocks sold in secondary offerings. These policies protect against third party claims arising out of liability imposed under the Securities Act of 1933, the Securities Exchange Act of 1934, or any similar common or statutory law of any state.

see: Securities Act of 1933

second beneficiary

Life. The individual named to receive a life insurance policy's death benefits in the event that the primary or first-named beneficiary dies and is unable to collect all or part of the benefits.

syn: contingent beneficiary, secondary beneficiary; see: primary beneficiary

secondary beneficiary

Life.

see: second beneficiary

second death insurance

Life. Coverage on two individuals that pays its benefit after the second of the two insureds dies.

compare: joint life insurance; see: joint life and survivor insurance, survivorship life insurance

second injury fund

Workers' Compensation. To encourage the hiring of the handicapped, many states have established workers' compensation second injury funds. The employer of an injured, handicapped worker is responsible only for the worker's compensation benefit for the most recent injury; the second injury fund would cover the cost of any additional benefits for aggravation of a prior condition or injury.

second mortgage

Financial Planning. A mortgage that is second to, junior to, or subordinate to the first mortgage.

see: mortgage

second surplus treaty

Reinsurance. A reinsurance treaty used in writing large industrial risks where the limits of liability are too large to be covered by a first surplus treaty.

see: first surplus reinsurance treaty

secured creditor

General. A creditor with an interest in the specific assets of a debtor which is supported by written documents.

securities

General. Documents which show a debt or ownership such as stocks, bonds, and checks.

see: bonds, securities valuation, stock

Crime. As defined in crime insurance forms, securities are both negotiable or non-negotiable instruments or contracts, representing either money or other property such as tokens, tickets, revenue and other stamps (actual stamps and unused value in a stamp meter), and evidence of debt issued in connection with credit or charge cards not issued by the insured.

see: crime coverages

Securities Act of 1933

Regulation/Life. Legislation adopted by Congress in 1933 which authorizes the Securities and Exchange Commission to require registration of securities issued and full disclosure of material information concerning the financial condition of the organization issuing the securities. The definition of securities includes variable annuity and variable life insurance policies.

syn: Full Disclosures Act

securities analyst

Financial Planning. An individual skilled in investigating the facts concerning a security or the securities industry. An individual who provides investment advice concerning securities.

syn: analyst

Securities and Exchange Commission (SEC)

Regulation. A federal agency created by Congress as part of the Securities Exchange Act of 1934. The SEC establishes rules for and regulates issuers of securities, securities firms, investment firms and investment advisors.

© 1991 NILS Publishing Company

securities deposited with others coverage form

Crime. A crime coverage form providing theft, disappearance or destruction of securities deposited with others, such as banks, trust companies, public officials or stockbrokers while the securities are inside the custodian's premises or being conveyed outside by employees of the custodian.

syn: crime coverage form J; see: crime coverages, securities, theft

Securities Investor Protection Corporation (SIPC)

Regulation. A non-profit corporation created by Congress in 1970 under the Securities Investor Protection Act that provides insurance to protect the assets of client accounts held by registered securities broker-dealers. The maximum coverage for cash and securities in a client account is $500,000 with a sublimit of $100,000 on the amount of cash.

see: Federal Deposit Insurance Corporation, Federal Savings and Loan Insurance Corporation

securities valuation

Insurer Operations/Regulation. A method used by state insurance regulators to value securities on the books of insurance companies. Bonds meeting certain credit requirements are carried at face value, plus or minus any purchase discount or premium. Preferred stock is valued at cost and common stock at market price. The National Association of Insurance Commissioners (NAIC) values impaired securities such as bonds in default.

see: investment reserve, investment valuation reserve, mandatory securities valuation reserve

security for expenses

Surety. A term used to describe state statutes that require certain plaintiffs in a derivative suit to post a bond with sureties, from which corporate or other defendants may be reimbursed for their expenses if they prevail. Designed as a protection against strike suits, they have been widely criticized as illogical and unnecessary.

see: judicial bond

security interest

General. An interest by a creditor in personal property or fixtures which secures payment or performance of an obligation.

seedmens errors & omissions insurance

Casualty. Coverage that protects seed growers, seed dealers, wholesalers, seed packagers, seed brokers and any other individual or firm that handles seeds, against claims arising from errors or omissions in germination tests, failure to germinate, mislabeling of seeds and similar claims.

segregation of exposure units

Risk Management. A risk management concept used to reduce the maximum potential loss of an organization by physically separating assets or operations. This is commonly accomplished by constructing separate fire divisions at a single plant site, or by using multiple plant sites.

see: fire division, probable maximum loss

seismograph

Loss Control. An instrument to measure and record vibrations and tremors within the earth, using the Richter scale. The Richter scale is logarithmic, meaning that each whole number increase on the scale indicates an earthquake ten times more powerful than one recorded at the preceding whole number reading. An earthquake reading 1.5 is the smallest tremor that can be felt; a 4.5 earthquake causes slight damage; and an earthquake of 8.5 causes widespread devastation.

see: earthquake

seizure order

Regulation. A court order directing an insurance commissioner to take possession and control of the property, accounts, records and other items of an insurer.

see: liquidation

selection of risk

Insurer Operations. Practice of an insurer to select, through underwriting, better risks over poorer risks.

see: underwriter

select mortality table

Life. A mortality table based only on individuals that have recently purchased life insurance policies; such individuals historically produce lower mortality rates because they are younger and have experienced better medical care than older policyholders.

see: mortality table

self-administered plan

Employee Benefits/Health. A qualified employee benefit plan funded and administered by an employer rather than an insurer. The most important distinction of such plans is that they are not subject to regulation by state insurance departments and need not submit to state-mandated laws such as required coverages in health insurance plans. Instead, these plans are regulated by the federal government through the Employee's Retirement Income Security Act (ERISA) of 1974.

see: Employee Retirement Income Security Act of 1974

© 1991 NILS Publishing Company

self-inflicted injury

Life/Health/Workers' Compensation. An intentional injury a person causes to one's self. Generally, this type of injury is not covered by a health plan or a workers' compensation policy, since it is not an accident, but self-inflicted injuries that result in death (i.e., suicide) are often covered by a life insurance policy after a specified time period.

self-insurance

Risk Management. An alternative to the purchase of insurance where an organization develops a formal program for identifying, evaluating and funding its losses. It is frequently used for workers' compensation where losses are fairly predictable and states have established regulations for self-insurance. Smaller losses which occur frequently are a better subject for self-insurance as opposed to large infrequent losses. Self-insurance programs are frequently structured to retain losses up to a specific limit and insurance is purchased above that level.

> compare: noninsurance, passive retention, risk transfer; see: captive insurance company, excess insurance, self-insured retention

Self-Insurance Institute of America (SIIA)

Organizations. Members: Actuaries, attorneys, adjusters, insurance consultants, corporations, employers, insurers, risk managers, third party administrators and others interested in self-insurance. *Objectives:* Promotes self-insurance concepts, plans and interests. Supports educational programs. *Founded:* 1981. *Headquarters:* Santa Ana, CA.

self-insurance reserve

Risk Management. Funds set aside by an organization to cover liability for future claims under its self-insurance program.

> see: reserve

self-insured retention (SIR)

Casualty/Risk Management. The portion of a risk or potential loss assumed by an organization. The SIR differs from a deductible because the insured performs all the functions normally undertaken by an insurance company for losses within the SIR, including claims adjusting and audits, funding and paying claims, and complying with applicable state and federal laws and regulations.

> see: retention, umbrella liability insurance

selling price clause

Property. A property policy provision that pays at selling price (established market value) those losses to finished stock which is sold, but not delivered. This includes the insured's profit. Normally, such stock would be valued at its production or replacement cost, whichever is lower.

> see: manufacturer's selling price

separation of insureds

Casualty. A condition in liability policies obligating an insurance company to provide a separate defense for each insured, and to settle each claim or suit against each insured independently.

> see: duty to defend

sequential approach

Loss Control. A method of examining potential business income losses by following the activities or operations of a business from where they begin (raw materials, or telephone order) to where they end (delivery of a finished product or completion of a service).

> see: business income coverage form

servant

Casualty/Workers' Compensation. An agent whose physical conduct is under the control of a master (principal).

> see: agency, employee, master servant rule

service

General. Labor rendered by one person for another.
Employee Benefits. A term which refers to employment by an employer of an employee.

> see: years of service

service adjustment

Employee Benefits. An increase or decrease in years of service credited to an employee when pension benefits are calculated.

service charges

General. Handling fees charged in addition to the base costs of a transaction.

> see: interest

service fee

Agency. A fee paid directly to an insurance broker for services rendered. In many states, fees to brokers are illegal, or are illegal if they are combined with commission.

> compare: agent's commission; see: policy fee

service insurance corporation

Insurer Operations. A general term used to refer to corporations providing insurance or prepayment plans which pay benefits in services rather than dollars, with or without additional provision for the incidental payment of indemnity under certain circumstances.

> see: Blue Cross Plan, Blue Shield Plan, health maintenance organizations, legal expense insurers

Servicemen's Group Life Insurance (SGLI)

Life. Life insurance underwritten by private insurance companies for members of the United States Armed

© 1991 NILS Publishing Company

Forces on active duty. Policies are issued based on standard mortality tables, with the federal government providing reimbursement for any increased risk from the individual's military duty. Upon leaving active duty, the SGLI policy can be converted to either a Veterans Group Life Insurance Policy or to a standard policy based on the veteran's current age.

see: **Veterans Group Life Insurance**

service plans

Health. An insurance plan that provides actual service rather than benefits.

see: **Blue Cross Plan, Blue Shield Plan**

service provider

Insurer Operations. A person or organization whose profession or business function is to provide insurance services to covered individuals, e.g., an HMO (health maintenance organization).

servicing facility

Insurer Operations. Offices designated to process claims on the behalf of a joint underwriting association (JUA) or a guaranty association.

see: **joint underwriting association**

servicing insurer

Insurer Operations. An insurer designated to process claims for a joint underwriting association (JUA) or a guaranty association.

see: **joint underwriting association**

setoff clause

Insurer Operations. An insurance policy provision which reduces the amount of an insured's recovery for a loss by amounts that are recovered from other sources stipulated in the policy.

compare: **salvage, subrogation;** see: **other insurance clause**

settlement

Insurer Operations. An agreement between a claimant or beneficiary to an insurance policy and the insurance company as to the amount and method of a claim or benefit payment.

syn: **out-of-court settlement;** see: **minor's compromise**

several liability

Casualty. Liability arising from a contract in which several parties have each individually promised the performance indicated in the contract.

compare: **joint liability;** see: **joint and several liability**

sex

Automobile/Health/Life.

see: **gender rating, sex discrimination**

sex discrimination

Health/Life. The risk classification factors – male or female – used by life and health insurance underwriters to establish rates, have been found to be discriminatory in some states and are prohibited.

see: **risk classification**

Casualty. The illegal refusal by an employer to hire or promote an individual because of gender.

see: **sexual harassment, unfair discrimination, unisex legislation**

sexual harassment

Casualty. A term used to describe an employment setting wherein unwelcome sexual advances from an employer or fellow employee, requests for sexual favors, and other verbal or physical conduct of a sexual nature are allowed to occur. The offending employer usually makes submission to or agreement with such conduct explicitly or implicitly a term or condition of an individual's employment, or the employee's response to such conduct is used as the basis for employment decisions. In any event, sexual harassment is usually determined to have occurred when such conduct has the effect of interfering with an employee's performance or creating an intimidating, hostile, or offensive working environment. Sexual harassment is a violation of Title VII of the U.S. Civil Rights Act, and can be the basis for employment discrimination suits by employees against employers who engage in such practices, or who allow conditions of sexual harassment to exist in their workplace.

see: **discrimination, sexual harassment defense coverage, unfair discrimination, unfair labor practices**

sexual harassment defense coverage

Casualty. Coverage on a claims-made basis that protects an employer against sexual harassment lawsuits and/or administrative proceedings.

see: **sexual harassment**

shareholder

General.

see: **stockholder**

share of stock

General. A unit of ownership in a corporation.

see: **capital stock, combined stock and mutual insurer, common stock to surplus, common stock to total investment, cumulative dividend, cumulative voting, employee stock ownership plan, issued stock, no par stock, nonvoting common stock, par value, phantom stock plan, preferred stock, proxy, record owner, stock, stock dividend, stockholder, stock split, watered stock**

© 1991 NILS Publishing Company

Sherman Antitrust Act

Regulation. Federal Legislation passed by Congress in 1890 which included a provision prohibiting monopolies and restraint of trade in interstate commerce. This legislation did not apply to the insurance industry because the U.S. Supreme Court found in *Paul v. Virginia* that insurance was not commerce and thus not subject to federal regulation.

see: anti-trust laws, Clayton Act, McCarran-Ferguson Act

shipper

Inland Marine/Ocean Marine.

see: consignor

shippers radioactive contamination insurance

Inland Marine. Inland marine coverage available to shippers of radioactive materials (except those who ship radioactive waste and nuclear reactor fuel), insuring against direct loss or damage caused by radioactive contamination.

compare: motor truck cargo radioactive contamination insurance; see: radioactive contamination insurance

shop right

Casualty. An employers' free, nonexclusive, irrevocable, nonassignable license to use an invention or discovery made by an employee who has used employment time or the employer's facilities in connection with such invention or discovery.

shore risk clause

Ocean Marine. An extension of an ocean marine cargo policy to provide coverage for onshore perils such as fire, sprinkler leakage, collapse of docks, flooding and damage from accidents during ground transportation.

short form bill of lading

Inland Marine/Ocean Marine. A bill of lading in summary form that does not spell out all obligations and responsibilities of the parties to the bill. Not generally used, unless the shipper is familiar with a carrier's tariff.

see: bill of lading

short-rate cancellation

Insurer Operations. The termination of a policy contract before the expiration date at the request of the insured. Premiums returned to the insured are not in direct proportion to the days remaining in the policy period, because of fixed expenses incurred by the company.

compare: pro rata cancellation; see: cancellation, return premium

short-rate table

Insurer Operations. A table used to calculate the refund due on a policy cancelled by the insured prior to its full term. The table displays a percentage of earned premiums which include a component for policy administration and other services, and a pro rata component based on the number of days the policy has been in force.

see: short-rate cancellation

short tail

Casualty. As respects liability insurance, short tail liability is that where claims become known within a relatively short period of time (i.e., during the policy period or within 12 months of expiration).

compare: long tail

short-term debt

Financial Planning. Debt that is due within twelve months and therefore is considered a current liability.

compare: long-term debt; see: total debt

short-term disability

Health. A disability which impairs an injured party's earning capacity for a short period of time, usually less than 90 days.

see: disability

short-term disability insurance (STD)

Health. Disability coverage for a period of two weeks to two years. Coverage in excess of two years is considered long-term disability insurance.

compare: long term disability insurance; see: disability income insurance

short-term reversionary trust

Employee Benefits. A form of trust frequently used prior to the Tax Reform Act of 1969 to defer taxes. An irrevocable trust was established for a minimum of ten years, and upon termination the principal was returned to the grantor. This usually allowed the earnings on the principal to be taxed at the beneficiary's tax rate, instead of the higher tax rate of the grantor. This tax deferral arrangement is no longer allowed.

see: irrevocable trust, tax bracket shifting, trust

sickness insurance

Health.

see: health insurance

sidetrack agreement

Casualty. A contractual hold-harmless agreement between a railroad and a property owner pertaining to the use of a sidetrack leading to the property owner's premises. The railroad will require that the property owner assume certain liabilities in exchange for constructing the sidetrack, such as transferring liability for damaged goods or bodily injury resulting from use of

© 1991 NILS Publishing Company

the sidetrack. The contractual liability resulting from a sidetrack agreement is provided automatically under the ISO Commercial General Liability insurance coverage forms.

sign coverage

Inland Marine. An "open perils" coverage form that can be endorsed to commercial property policies to provide coverage for neon, fluorescent, automatic, or mechanical electric signs and lights.

compare: sign floater

signed

General. A signature or any symbol executed or adopted by an individual with the present intention to authenticate a signature.

sign floater

Inland Marine. An inland marine policy that provides broad coverage on neon signs during their installation or repair, as well as providing coverage after they are installed.

compare: sign coverage

silent alarm

Loss Control.
see: burglar alarm

silicosis

Health/Workers' Compensation. A chronic disease of the lungs caused by the continued inhalation of silica dust. Silicosis is a frequently encountered condition among coal miners.

see: black lung disease, brown lung disease, occupational disease

simple interest

Financial Planning. Interest that is earned on the initial principal, without compounding.

compare: compound interest; see: interest

simplified earnings form

Property. An older, rarely used form for loss of earnings coverage for small businesses, that provides reimbursement when a property is destroyed and a business is unable to continue. The inability of the business to continue must be as a result of a direct loss. Coverage under such a policy protects income and is subject to a monthly limitation.

see: earnings insurance form

simplified employee pension (SEP)

Employee Benefits. An Individual Retirement Account (IRA) funded by an employer or jointly funded by the employer and the employee. These plans are used by smaller employers and under the Tax Reform Act of 1986, such plans may be used as an alternative to Section 401(k) Plans when 25 or less employees are

involved. Any employer contributions to such plans must be included as income to the employee, but an offsetting deduction to the IRA, subject to the maximum contribution limitation, is allowed on the employee's tax return. The employer's contribution is regulated by the limitations contained in an HR 10 plan. Employees benefit from these plans as employer contributions are vested immediately and investment decisions rest completely with the employee.

compare: Internal Revenue Code: Section 401(k); see: Keogh Plan

simulation

Risk Management. A technique whereby probable future events are constructed by a computer model and from which certain assumptions concerning risk can be made.

simultaneous death

Life/Regulation.
see: uniform simultaneous death act

sine qua non rule

General. A Latin legal term which translates to "without which not." It is applied to tort law where the plaintiff must prove that an injury was a direct result of a negligent act caused by the defendant, and that the injury would not have occurred without the negligent act.

see: comparative negligence, contributory negligence

single annuitant

Life. An annuity that pays benefits until the annuitant dies.

syn: single life annuity; see: annuity

single interest policy

Property. An insurance policy that protects only the insurable interests of one party, usually the named insured. *Example:* An automobile physical damage policy purchased to cover the insurable interest of the lending institution, and not that of the owner/driver.

compare: loss payable clause, underlying insurance policy

single life annuity

Life.
see: single annuitant

single limit

Automobile/Casualty.
see: combined single limit

single premium life insurance

Life. A life insurance policy where the entire premium is paid in one lump sum at the policy's inception.

© 1991 NILS Publishing Company

single risk cargo insurance

Ocean Marine. A cargo policy issued on a single shipment of goods.

syn: **special risk insurance, trip transit insurance; compare: open cargo policy**

sinkhole coverage

Property. Property insurance policies which provide coverage for the unexpected sinking or collapse of land into a hollow place or depression underground.

sinking fund

Risk Management. A fund established by a self-insurer to accumulate a specified amount of money for the payment of large losses when they occur. As losses are paid from this fund, it is replenished so as to maintain a specified amount.

see: **imprest account**

Financial Planning. A fund established and accumulated by using regular deposits for paying off the principal of a debt, redeeming debt securities or preferred stock issues.

sistership exclusion

Casualty.

see: **products recall exclusion**

skewed curve

Risk Management. An actuarial term which refers to the shape of a distribution curve that is not symmetrical. Most curves involving loss projections are skewed to the right because of the small chance for large losses.

syn: **asymmetrical curve; compare: symmetrical curve; see: distribution curve**

slander

General. A defamatory or prejudiced spoken statement or gesture made against another person or persons that harms their reputation, office, business, or means of livelihood.

compare: **libel; see: personal injury**

sliding scale commission

Reinsurance. A reinsurance contract commission formula which is designed to reward a ceding insurer for a profitable loss ratio. The formula provides that the reinsurer will pay a ceding insurer a commission which varies inversely with the loss ratio, subject to a minimum and maximum commission rate.

see: **ceding commission**

slip

Insurer Operations. An application submitted by a broker to the underwriters at Lloyd's of London which, when accepted by underwriters of syndicates, becomes a binder of insurance.

syn: **line slip; see: line, Lloyd's of London, open slip**

small loss principle

Risk Management. A risk management principle stating that small losses can be absorbed more efficiently as normal business expenses through deductibles or self-insured retentions than they can through insurance, since insurers add expense loadings (for its own profit, administrative and selling expense, etc.) to the basic premium.

see: **noninsurance**

smoke damage

Property. Damage caused by the smoke created by combustion, as distinguished from the damage caused by the combustion itself.

smoker and nonsmoker mortality table

Life. A mortality table that indicates separate mortality rates for smokers and nonsmokers.

see: **mortality table, nonsmoker discount**

snowmobile coverage

Automobile/Property. Coverage that can be endorsed to a homeowner's or personal automobile policy, that covers physical damage to snowmobiles on a named perils or "all-risks" basis.

social engineering

General. Effecting social change through the enactment of laws designed to accomplish specific societal goals. For example prior to 1935, few Americans elected to or were able to put aside money specifically for retirement. Through the passage of the Social Security Act, individuals were forced to set aside money for their retirement.

see: **public policy, social insurance, Social Security**

social insurance

General. Compulsory insurance which has been legislated into existence to provide economic security for a large percentage of the population, many of whom could not otherwise afford its cost. Workers' compensation and compulsory auto liability insurance sometimes have been characterized as social insurance.

see: **Social Security**

socialized health insurance

Health.

see: **national health insurance**

Social Security

Employee Benefits. Federal legislation enacted as the United States Social Security Act of 1935, and its amendments. This legislation is now called Old Age, Survivors, and Disability Insurance and is funded by both employer and employee contributions, as taxes, under the Federal Insurance Contributions Act. The program pays the loss of income benefits on retirement at age 65, or earlier at age 62, at a reduced

© 1991 NILS Publishing Company

benefit if early retirement is chosen by the employee; survivor benefits on death of the employee and financial benefits to employees under 65 who are physically disabled.

syn: Old Age, Survivors, Disability, and Health Insurance; see: currently insured status, Federal Insurance Contributions Act, fully insured status, Integration with Social Security

Social Security Integration

Employee Benefits.

see: Integration with Social Security

Social Security offset

Employee Benefits.

see: Integration with Social Security

Social Security Wage Index

Employee Benefits. A Social Security Administration table indicating the amount of Social Security benefits due to a participant or the primary insurance amount that will be paid monthly based on the average monthly wage.

syn: wage index; see: average monthly wage, primary insurance amount

Society for Risk Analysis (SRA)

Organizations. Members: Risk assessment professionals. *Objectives:* Studies risks posed by technological development on a scientific basis. Gathers and disseminates pertinent information. *Founded:* 1982. *Headquarters:* McLean, VA.

Society of Actuaries (SOA)

Organizations. Members: Professional society of those trained in the application of mathematical probabilities to the design of insurance, pension and employee benefit programs. *Objectives:* Sponsors a series of examinations leading to the designation of Fellow or Associate within the Society. *Founded:* 1949. *Headquarters:* Schaumburg, IL.

see: Associate in Society of Actuaries, Fellow of the Society of Actuaries

Society of Certified Insurance Counselors (SCIC)

Organizations. Members: Licensed agents, brokers, solicitors, corporate risk managers and insurance faculty of accredited colleges or universities. *Objectives:* Organizes examinations and certifications. *Founded:* 1969. *Headquarters:* Austin, TX.

Society of Chartered Property and Casualty Underwriters (SCPCU)

Organizations. Members: Insurance underwriters. *Objectives:* Promotes professionalism, social responsibility, education and research in the insurance industry. Awards the CPCU designation to those successfully completing examinations offered by the American

Institute for Property and Liability Underwriters. *Founded:* 1944. *Headquarters:* Malvern, PA.

see: American Institute for Property and Liability Underwriters, Chartered Property and Casualty Underwriter

Society of Insurance Accountants (SIA)

Organizations. Members: Insurance accountants, statisticians, actuaries and others interested in insurance accounting procedures and use of data processing equipment. *Objectives:* To provide a forum for discussion of accounting statistical and related problems, an interchange of ideas and for the dissemination of information to its membership. *Founded:* 1960. *Headquarters:* Hollowville, NY.

Society of Insurance Research (SIR)

Organizations. Members: Industry personnel actively involved in insurance research. *Objectives:* Promoting insurance research concepts and methodology. *Founded:* 1970. *Headquarters:* Appleton, WI.

Society of Insurance Trainers and Educators (SITE)

Organizations. Members: Individuals, teachers and others engaged in educating and training those in the insurance industry. *Objectives:* Furthering the education and training of insurance within the industry. *Founded:* 1953. *Headquarters:* Cary, IL. Formerly known as the Insurance Company Education Directors Society.

Society of Professional Benefit Administrators (SPBA)

Organizations. Members: Independent third-party contract employee benefit plan administration firms. *Objectives:* Promotes public understanding and acceptance of contract administration. *Founded:* 1975. *Headquarters:* Chevy Chase, MD.

Society of Risk Management Consultants (SRMC)

Organizations. Members: Independent risk management and insurance consultants. *Objectives:* Promotes professional standards for risk managers and insurance consultants. *Founded:* 1984. *Headquarters:* Orinda, CA. Formed in 1984 by the merger of the Insurance Consultants Society and the Institute of Risk Management Consultants.

soft market

Insurer Operations. A period of time during the insurance underwriting cycle when insurance coverage is readily available and underwriters are actively competing for business. Generally, during this period there are significant rate reductions, and higher limits of liability and new coverages are available.

compare: hard market, tight market; see: buyer's market, underwriting cycle

© 1991 NILS Publishing Company

sole proprietorship insurance

Health/Life. Life and disability insurance designed for an owner of a small business. Provides benefits to family members adequate to continue operations of the business or arrange for its sale.

see: **key employee insurance**

solicitor

Agency. An individual employed or contracted by an agent to solicit, but not to conclude, contracts of insurance on behalf of the agent.

see: **agent, broker, producer**

sonic boom

Property. Noise, pressure, and shock waves resulting from an aircraft or missile exceeding the speed of sound. Most property policies cover damage from this peril.

South-Eastern Underwriters Association (SEUA)

Regulation. A property insurance rating organization which pressed a lawsuit leading to the 1944 United States Supreme Court decision which declared insurance to be interstate commerce and thus subject to federal regulation. As a result of this decision, Congress passed the McCarran-Ferguson Act returning the business of insurance to state regulators.

see: **McCarran-Ferguson Act, Paul v. Virginia**

sovereign immunity

Casualty. A right reserved by a government to preclude action against itself by virtue of its political prerogative and the necessity of making judgments in the interest of the state which may, in fact, deprive some individuals or businesses of certain rights.

spacecraft insurance

Aviation. Insurance on rockets and satellites designed for voyages in outer space.

see: **satellite and space vehicle insurance**

special acceptance

Reinsurance. An agreement by a reinsurer to make an exception to a reinsurance contract, allowing a specific risk (which ordinarily would not qualify for coverage under the contract) to be included in coverage.

special agent

Agency/Insurer Operations.

see: **marketing representative**

Life. An individual who has an exclusive agreement with an insurer to sell and service life insurance in a specific territory.

syn: **sales representative**

special cargo policy

Ocean Marine. A policy used in the shipping of merchandise that is similar to a certificate of insurance, except that it is an entire insurance policy and not subject to the underlying terms of an open policy when title has been transferred to a third party.

see: **cargo insurance**

special damage

Property.

see: **consequential damage**

special damages

General. Those damages that are a natural – but not necessary – result of an act of negligence or intentional tort.

see: **damages**

special form

Property. A property form which insures against *all risks* of direct physical loss that are not specifically stated in the exclusions and limitations sections of the form. Any accidental loss is presumed covered, unless the insurer can show that the loss was caused by an excluded peril.

special homeowner's policy

Property.

see: **homeowner's policy form 3**

special mortality table

Life. A mortality table developed specifically for purchasers of annuities which shows that individuals purchasing annuities often have a longer life expectancy than the population as a whole.

see: **mortality table**

special multi-peril program (SMP)

Property. A combination/package policy developed for commercial risks, which has largely been replaced by new commercial forms. The program required the inclusion of property and liability coverages as minimum coverages, with crime and boiler and machinery as optional coverages. Prior to 1977, only seven carefully defined classes of business firms were eligible for the SMP program. However, in 1977 the program was broadened to include almost any type of business.

see: **commercial package policy, industrial property policy program, special personal property form**

special package automobile policy

Automobile. An obsolete automobile policy form created in the 1960s which provided a single limit of liability for bodily injury and property damage and a corresponding limit for medical payments. Physical damage coverage could be included as a separate item.

© 1991 NILS Publishing Company

special personal property coverage endorsement

Property. An ISO Homeowner's Form (HO-15) which, when attached to Homeowner's Form HO-3, provides "all risks" coverage on personal property.

special personal property form

Property. A form used in the special multi-peril program that provided "all-risks" coverage on business personal property. It has largely been replaced by the building and personal property coverage form. It was once the broadest coverage available for the personal property of a business.

see: special multi-peril program

special risk insurance

Ocean Marine.

see: single risk cargo insurance

special risks

Insurer Operations. A risk which, due to its unusual nature, high hazard of loss, or other special circumstance, may be exempted from applicable rate filing requirements.

see: insurable risk, specialty insurer, uninsurable risk

specialty insurer

Insurer Operations. An insurance company that writes a narrow spectrum of risks which often involves unusual, nonstandard or difficult-to-place risks.

see: special risks

specific excess workers' compensation insurance

Workers' Compensation. Insurance coverage for organizations that self-insure their workers' compensation benefits. It indemnifies the insured for claims on a per-occurrence basis in excess of a specific retention ($50,000, $100,000, $250,000), subject to a maximum limit which can range from $1 million to statutory benefits. Coverage is based on the coverages provided by a standard worker's compensation policy.

compare: aggregate excess workers' compensation insurance

specific insurance

Property. An insurance policy that covers a specific kind or unit of property, in contrast to a policy that covers on a blanket basis all property at one or more locations. Generally, a specific policy is considered as primary coverage in the event of overlapping coverage between multiple policies.

compare: blanket insurance

specific rate

Property. A published rate (as opposed to a tariff rate) applying specifically to an individual location or building.

compare: average blanket rate, tariff rate;
see: rate

specific reinsurance

Reinsurance.

see: facultative reinsurance

specified perils

General.

see: named perils

specimen policy

Insurer Operations. A sample policy used to discuss protection features with a prospective insured.

speculative risk

Risk Management. A risk for which it is uncertain as to whether the final outcome will be a gain or loss. Gambling is a speculative risk. Generally, speculative risks cannot be insured.

compare: pure risk

spendthrift trust clause

Life. A life insurance policy provision that prevents creditors of beneficiaries from making a claim against the policy benefits before the beneficiaries are paid.

sphygmograph

Health. An apparatus used to measure an individual's pulse.

sphygmomanometer

Health. An apparatus used to measure an individual's blood pressure, especially arterial blood pressure.

syn: manometer; see: blood pressure

split deductible

Insurer Operations. A combination of two or more deductibles within a policy, with each applying to a different form of coverage. *Example:* A property policy with a $5,000 deductible on fire losses, $100,000 deductible on flood losses and $250,000 deductible on earthquake losses.

see: deductible

split dollar insurance

Life. Life insurance jointly paid for by an employer and employee or a parent and a child. The ownership right and death proceeds of the policy may also be divided between the parties paying the premium.

see: contributory group insurance

Health. Disability income insurance jointly paid for by an employer and an employee. The employer pays for the basic or primary level of coverage and the employee pays for an extended period of coverage.

309

© 1991 NILS Publishing Company

split life insurance

Life. A combination of annuity and term insurance, where the term insurance is based on a factor of the installment annuity premium paid.

compare: double protection life insurance

split limits

Automobile/Casualty. Separately stated limits of liability for different coverages. The limits may be stated on a per person, per occurrence, per policy period basis, or can be split between bodily injury and property damage, or expressed in other ways. *Example:* An auto liability policy with limits of $200,000/ $500,000/$100,000 would have a maximum of $200,000 bodily injury coverage for each person; coverage of $500,000 for bodily injury per accident; and total coverage of $100,000 for property damage liability per accident.

compare: combined single limit

spoliation

Insurer Operations. Alterations made to an insurance policy by a stranger to the contract. Such alterations do not affect the contract if the original words can be ascertained with certainty.

see: alteration

spontaneous combustion

Loss Control. The self-ignition of combustible material through chemical action (e.g., oxidation) of its constituents.

spouse's benefit

Employee Benefits. Benefits payable to the spouse of a worker after retirement or death, such as benefits under the Federal Retirement Equity Act, the Social Security Act, or through a special provision by an employer.

see: dependent

spread loss plan

Risk Management. A form of banking plan involving a long-term contract of insurance (three to ten years), under which an annual premium is paid based on projected losses and the insurer's expense loading. The final premium paid to the plan is based on a retrospective rating formula, which, if the premium and investment income exceeds the losses and loading over the life of the plan, is returned to the policyholder. In the event losses exceed funds accumulated in this plan, the insurer loans the insured funds to pay losses up to the policy limit and increases the annual premium over the remainder of the plan to repay the funds loaned.

syn: funded spread loss plan; see: banking plan, chronological stabilization plan

spread loss reinsurance

Reinsurance.

see: Carpenter Plan

spread of risk

Risk Management. A principle of insurance which states that insurers need to accept homogeneous exposure units spread over a wide geographical area, with the certain knowledge that only a given number of risks will result in claims or losses. This dispersion of exposure units allows insurers to project expected losses from the entire body of insureds, lessens the potential for catastrophic losses that could occur to exposure units in close proximity to one another, and allows for the development of rates.

see: homogeneity, law of large numbers, reduction of risk

spreadsheet

Risk Management. A graphic display of information, usually columnar in format, that is in most cases, computer generated. Generally used by management to monitor and/or display business information, risk managers use spreadsheets to track exposure and claim information in a form that can be easily modified and updated.

sprinkler leakage coverage

Property. A peril that can be insured under a property insurance form. This coverage protects an insured in case of direct damage to buildings or contents caused by the leakage or discharge of water or other substances from any automatic sprinkler system, or caused by the fall or collapse of tanks that are part of the system. Coverage for loss from this peril is included under the ISO commercial property basic, broad, and special coverage forms.

compare: water damage clause; see: automatic sprinkler system, scuppers

sprinkler leakage legal liability insurance

Casualty. A liability coverage which protects the insured should a sprinkler leakage loss occur on rented premises or on premises loaned to the insured. Coverage applies when an automatic sprinkler system discharges or leaks water or other substances as the result of the insured's negligence.

compare: water damage legal liability; see: automatic sprinkler system

stacking of limits

Casualty. The application of two or more policies to the same loss or occurrence, allowing for significantly higher limits of liability to pay claims. This is frequently seen with pollution and products liability claims where damage has occurred over many years and it is

© 1991 NILS Publishing Company

impossible to determine which policy applies to a specific claim.

see: **dual coverage, overinsurance, pyramiding of limits**

staff adjuster
Insurer Operations. An individual employed by an insurance company to settle claims with or for policyholders of the company.

see: **claims adjuster**

stamp and coin dealers insurance
Inland Marine. A special inland marine coverage designed for stamp and coin dealers, written on an "all-risks" basis. Coverage includes the time that the insured items are in transit.

stamping office
Insurer Operations.

see: **audit bureau**

standard deviation
Risk Management. An arithmetic mean of the differences between each outcome and the average of all outcomes within a set. It is utilized by actuaries to indicate the degree of dispersion that exists between a set of outcomes. *Formula:* Standard Deviation Square Root of the Arithmetic Mean of the Squares of the Deviation subtracted from the Arithmetic Mean of a Frequency Distribution.

syn: **standard variation**; see: **frequency distribution**

standard fire policy
Property.

see: **New York standard fire policy**

standard homeowner's policy
Property.

see: **homeowner's policy form 1**

standard limit
General.

see: **basic limits**

standard policy
Insurer Operations. An insurance contract or policy used by insurers, adopted by a group of insurers, and/or approved by insurance regulators or prescribed by law.

standard premium
Casualty. A factor used in a retrospectively rated casualty program. It is the premium developed for the risk at standard rates (i.e., the premium that would apply if no retrospective plan were to be used).

see: **basic premium, retrospective rating plan**

Workers' Compensation. A factor used in a retrospectively rated workers' compensation program. The standard premium is generally derived by multiplying the workers' compensation rates by the applicable payroll amounts, to which the insured's experience modification factor is then applied.

see: **basic premium, retrospective rating plan**

standard provisions
Insurer Operations/Regulation. Those provisions of an insurance policy that are in common use by most insurers or required by legislation.

see: **minimum coverage clauses, policy condition laws, standard policy**

standard risk
Insurer Operations. A risk that is considered by the underwriter as a basis by which to judge other risks. Material deviations from the standard risk will result in higher or lower rates based on the degree of deviation, and a risk that deviates too far may be rejected.

syn: **average risk**; see: **benchmark, preferred risk, substandard risk**

standard variation
Risk Management.

see: **standard deviation**

standing timber insurance
Property. Coverage on living trees that show no signs of decay and have a minimum diameter and are therefore saleable, or on all living trees in an area of reforestation. The insured value is determined by the current price for standing timber. Coverage is limited to the perils of fire and lightning. Since most fires occur in spring and summer months, policy premium is considered fully earned if coverage is provided at any time during those seasons. Used by investors and timber owners seeking financing to secure their interests and the interests of lenders.

stare decisis
General. A Latin phrase meaning "to stand by the decisions." A principle of law whereby courts will follow a case precedent if it is still applicable.

state agent
Agency/Insurer Operations. An obsolete term, used to refer to 1) an agent that has an exclusive agreement for representing an insurer in a specific state, and 2) a special agent.

see: **agent, special agent**

state bonding funds
Surety. Funds maintained by a state for the bonding of public employees.

see: **public official bond**

stated amount
Property. An amount of insurance scheduled in a

stated amount — continued
property policy which is not subject to any coinsurance requirement in the event of a loss. The amount scheduled is the maximum amount of insurance available in the event of loss.

> see: agreed amount

Automobile. A method of writing automobile physical damage coverage where the limits that can be recovered in the event of a total loss cannot exceed the amount of insurance specified for the vehicle. Used for older cars or vehicles whose value after a loss might prove difficult to establish.

> compare: actual cash value; see: valued clause, valued policy

state exception pages

Insurer Operations. Rating manual pages that contain special rating provisions or exceptions to the general rules for policies issued in a particular state or territory.

> see: manual rates, rate manual

state fund

Insurer Operations/Workers' Compensation. A state government-operated insurance facility used to insure workers' compensation benefits. Some states have monopolistic funds that require employers to purchase coverage from them, while other state funds compete with private insurers.

> see: competitive state funds, monopolistic state fund

statement blank

Regulation.
> see: annual statement

statement of changes in financial position

General. A section of the financial statement which summarizes the cash flow or working capital of an organization which brings about changes in the assets, liabilities, and equity of the owners in the period between two consecutive balance sheets. This statement will reveal certain aspects of an organization's financing and investment activities, whether or not these affected the balance sheet or other working capital.

> see: financial statement

statement of loss

Insurer Operations.
> see: proof of loss

statement of opinion

General. A statement made by a certified public accountant (CPA) which gives an opinion as to the true financial condition of an organization as expressed by its financial statements. The opinion will be in one of three forms: 1) unqualified (or "clean"), which means

no exceptions were found; 2) qualified, which means that the financial statements fairly represent the organization's condition except there are some important uncertainties which cannot be determined at this time; and 3) adverse, which means the financials are unacceptable to the accountant.

> see: financial statement, Statutory Accounting Principles

statement of policy information

Life. An annual statement or document issued for universal life insurance policies which indicates all transactions (premiums, death benefits, interest credited, etc.) that occurred during the year.

> see: universal life insurance

statement of values

Property. A property insurance form used when coverage is written on a blanket basis, listing all insured locations and the buildings that are insured, contents and loss of earnings values. The form is used to develop a blanket rate and usually must be signed by the insured if an agreed amount endorsement is attached to the policy.

> see: agreed amount clause

state rate pages

Insurer Operations. Rating manual pages containing base rates for the coverages available in a particular state or territory.

> see: manual rates, rate manual

state territorial pages

Insurer Operations. Rating manual pages that indicate codes for each rating territory (city, county, zip code) in a state. These pages are used to locate base rates.

> see: manual rates, rate manual

statewide average weekly wage (SAWW)

Workers' Compensation. A periodically prepared report, indicating the average state-wide weekly wages paid over a specific period of time. This report is used to determine the adequacy of workers' compensation benefit levels.

static electricity

Loss Control. An electrical charge generated by the friction of two dissimilar bodies, either solids or liquids. A static electrical spark can ignite an atmosphere laden with combustible dusts or vapors resulting in an explosion.

statistical agent

Organizations. An organization which prepares statistical studies used in formulating rates.

> see: rating bureau

© 1991 NILS Publishing Company

statistics

Risk Management. A branch of mathematics dealing with the collection, analysis, interpretation and presentation of masses of numerical data; a collection of quantitative data. A leading branch of statistics – actuarial science – deals with insurance.

see: actuarial science

statute

General. A specific law enacted by the legislative branch of a municipal, county, state or federal governmental entity.

see: ordinance, statutory law

statute law

General.

see: statutory law

statute of frauds

General. A law which requires that certain types of contracts must be written in order to be enforced. Most contracts involving real estate fall into this category of contracts.

see: contract

statute of limitations

General. A statute limiting the time in which a claim may be asserted in a court; expiration bars enforcement of a claim.

see: limitation of actions

Statutory Accounting Principles (SAP)

General. Statutory requirements based on criteria established by the National Association of Insurance Commissioners in regards to the preparation of financial statements by an insurance company to be filed with a state insurance department. The required principles differ considerably from generally accepted accounting principles requirements. SAP, being more regulatory by nature, generally give a more conservative depiction of an insurer's financial condition.

compare: Generally Accepted Accounting Principles; see: accounting, Financial Accounting Standards Board, financial statement

statutory conditions

Regulation.

see: policy condition laws

statutory disability income

Health. Compulsory nonoccupational disability income coverage which must be provided by employers in California, Hawaii, New Jersey, New York, Rhode Island and the territory of Puerto Rico.

see: disability income insurance, unemployment compensation disability insurance

statutory earnings or losses

Regulation. An insurer's earnings or losses as indicated on the National Association of Insurance Commissioners convention blank.

see: annual statement

statutory law

General. The body of principles and rules of law enacted by legislation, bills or ordinances, or other statutory instruments which are passed by the legislative branch of government and signed into law by the executive branch. Statutory law is distinct from common, or case law.

syn: statute law; compare: common law

statutory reserve

Regulation. A reserve maintained by an insurer in order to comply with requirements for such reserves mandated by state law. These reserves are required to ensure that an insurer can pay policyholder claims.

statutory underwriting profit or loss

Insurer Operations. Premiums earned less losses and expenses.

statutory violation

General. The breaking of an enacted law. Such a violation is evidence of negligence, but is not necessarily proof of negligence. Therefore, a statutory violation, when followed by a third-party injury does not always result in the violator being found to be negligent.

see: statutory law

step-rate premium

Health/Life. A life or health insurance policy that has built-in rate increases which are based on reaching certain ages or numbers of years in force.

stevedore

Ocean Marine/Workers' Compensation. An individual or firm who works at or is responsible for unloading a ship in port.

stevedores legal liability insurance

Casualty. Liability coverage that protects a stevedore against loss or damage to vessels or cargo arising out of loading or unloading operations.

stipulation

General. A voluntary agreement to any point or issue raised by parties to an agreement or contract. A requirement or insistence as an essential condition to an agreement or contract, or an express demand for an essential condition.

stock

General. A certificate of ownership in a corporation. A contract between the issuing corporation and the stockholder that gives the stockholder an interest in

© 1991 NILS Publishing Company

stock — continued
the management of the corporation, the right to participate in profits, and, if the corporation is dissolved, a claim upon the corporation's assets.

see: dividend, share of stock, stock dividend, stock split; Fr: marchandise; Gr: Vorräte, Lager; Sp: existencias

Property. Merchandise or property that is, or will become, the sales inventory of a commercial enterprise. Certain other property of an organization falls in this category, including materials and supplies used in packing and shipping.

stock dividend

Financial Planning. The issuance of additional common shares of stock on a pro rata basis to common stockholders, with no change in total common equity.

see: stock split

stockholder

General. An individual or entity owning one or more shares of stock in a corporation. Stockholder dividends are paid to this party.

see: stock

stock insurance company

Insurer Operations. An insurance company, formed as a corporation, that is owned and controlled by its stockholders, usually for the purpose of making a profit. Initial capital is contributed by its stockholders, to whom any profits are distributed as stock dividends. Policies are issued at a fixed cost and should losses exceed premiums received, the stockholders investment and equity must make up the difference.

syn: capital stock insurance company; compare: mutual insurance company

stock split

Financial Planning. A proportional increase in the number of a corporation's outstanding stock shares. Generally, a corporation will elect to increase the number of shares to reduce each share's market value and increase trading in the shares.

see: share of stock, stock dividend

stock throughput policy

Inland Marine/Ocean Marine. A personal property insurance form developed in the London market covering the personal property of manufacturers, processors, importers/exporters or assemblers anywhere in the world on an "all-risks" basis. Coverage can include machinery, electronic data processing, equipment, furniture and fixtures, and raw materials. The policy itself is a combination of ocean cargo/inland marine/personal property coverages. The premium is usually based on a rate applied to the insured's annual sales.

stop loss

Insurer Operations. Any provision in a policy limiting the maximum claim amount payable. It may take the form of a maximum aggregate limit payable or a maximum limit payable for any one event.

see: limit of liability, loss limitation

stop loss reinsurance

Reinsurance.

see: aggregate excess of loss reinsurance

storekeepers broad form

Crime. A crime coverage plan developed under the 1986 ISO crime program which is designed for small storekeepers, providing "all-risk" protection on money and securities, depositor's forgery, limited employee dishonesty coverage, plus nine specific crime coverages on the same basis as a storekeeper's burglary and robbery policy.

syn: crime plan 3; see: crime coverages, storekeepers burglary and robbery

storekeepers burglary and robbery

Crime. A crime coverage plan developed under the 1986 ISO crime program which combines seven different burglary and robbery coverages for storekeepers into a single form. The selected limit of liability applies separately to each one of the coverages, which include: safe burglary, damage caused by robbery and burglary, robbery of a guard, burglary of merchandise, robbery inside and outside the insured premiums, kidnapping to force the opening of a premises, and theft of money and securities from a messenger.

syn: crime plan 4; see: crime coverages, storekeepers broad form

straight life policy

Life.

see: ordinary life insurance

straight line depreciation

Risk Management. A method of depreciating a fixed asset where the asset's cost (less salvage value and depreciation) is divided by the asset's useful life. The result is the annual depreciation expense which is then subtracted from pretax income.

see: accelerated depreciation, depreciation

stranded

Ocean Marine. A term which refers to a ship that has run aground, in some unusual place or manner.

strict construction

General. A legal rule of contract law that applies to insurance policies, which states that unclear language found in an insurance policy shall be interpreted against the party who wrote it (the insurer).

see: contract of adhesion

© 1991 NILS Publishing Company

strict liability

General.

see: absolute liability

strike

General. An organized work stoppage by a group of employees for the purpose of coercing their employer to accede to some demand.

see: picketing, strike insurance; Fr: grève; Gr: Streiks; Sp: huelga

strike insurance

Casualty. A form of financial guarantee insurance designed to protect employers from lost income caused by labor disruptions.

compare: manufacturer's penalty insurance; see: strikes, riots and civil commotions exclusion

strikes, riots and civil commotions exclusion (SR&CC)

Ocean Marine. A marine policy clause which excludes coverage for losses caused by acts of strikers, locked-out workers or persons taking part in labor disputes, riots or civil commotions, or for losses which are directly caused by persons acting maliciously. This exclusion may be deleted for an additional premium.

structured settlement

Insurer Operations. A claim settlement involving periodic payments to the claimant for a specific number of years, or for life in cases where special medical care must be provided. Often such payments are funded by an annuity policy, and because the time value of money is contemplated in the settlement, a structured settlement is usually less costly to an insurer or self-insurer than a lump sum settlement.

syn: periodic payment; see: constructive receipt, medical expense reversionary trust, qualified funding asset, Internal Revenue Code: Section 461(h)

sub-agent

Agency. An individual acting as an agent who reports to another agent or to a general agent or managing general agent (MGA), and not directly to an insurer.

see: solicitor

sub-broker

Reinsurance. A reinsurance broker from whom another reinsurance broker is able to obtain reinsurance business.

Subchapter S

Financial Planning. A tax option under the Internal Revenue Code of 1954, which permits certain closely held corporations to be taxed in a manner similar to that applicable to partnerships. Under Subchapter S, corporate income is taxable directly to shareholders whether or not it is actually distributed to them. Subchapter S was designed to eliminate the double taxation problem; however, the provisions of Subchapter S are complex and create a number of unique problems that are not present in the tax treatment of partnerships.

see: partnership

sub-contractor

General. An independent contractor who does not work directly for the property owner, but instead works for or through a general contractor. Typically, a general contractor will use several specialty sub-contractors on a project.

compare: general contractor; see: independent contractor

subject premium

Reinsurance. The premium of a ceding company to which a rate is applied, to develop the premium due to a reinsurer for reinsurance coverage.

syn: base premium, premium base, underlying premium; see: premium

sublease

General. A lease by a tenant or lessee of part or all of a leased premises. The tenant or lessee retains some rights or interests under such an arrangement.

sublimits

Health.

see: inside limits

submitted business

Insurer Operations. An insurance application possessed by an insurer and which is in the approval/disapproval process.

see: acceptance, rejection

subrogation

Insurer Operations. The right of a party to proceed against another for recovery. The acquisition by an insurer of an insured's rights against third parties for indemnification of loss or other payment, to the extent that the insurer pays the loss.

see: recoverables; Fr: subrogation; Gr: Regress; Sp: subrogación

Surety. The right of a surety to seek indemnification for a bond loss from the principal or any other party liable for the loss. This term is also referred to as right of exoneration.

see: right of exoneration

subrogation release

Insurer Operations. A document executed by an insured upon receiving a property loss claims payment, which assigns the right of recovery that the insured possesses against any responsible party for the loss to the insurer.

© 1991 NILS Publishing Company

subrogation waiver

Property. The intentional relinquishing by a named insured of any right to recover damages from another party who may be responsible in some way for those damages. Commercial property insurance policies recognize a written subrogation waiver issued prior to the policy's effective date. A waiver issued during the policy period must be approved by the insurer.

subscribers agreement

Regulation. Basic documents organizing reciprocal, and occasionally, assessment mutual insurers.

subscription policy

Insurer Operations. Insurance on a risk using a single policy form to which two or more insurers subscribe for a share of the coverage. Their participation can be expressed either as a percentage of the coverage provided or a dollar amount which is indicated as being part of the entire liability limit.

see: participate

subsidence

Property. Sinking or settling of land caused by heavy rains or man-made caverns. Subsidence does not include earth movement caused by an earthquake.

see: earthquake, sinkhole coverage; Fr: glissement de terrain; Gr: Senkung; Sp: desmoronamiento, hundimiento

Casualty. An excluded coverage in most liability policies.

see: subsidence coverage

subsidence coverage

Casualty. Coverage that can be endorsed to the general liability policy or purchased as a separate policy by a developer or contractor. It provides coverage for the unexpected subsidence of land causing damage to the homes or buildings on it.

compare: sinkhole coverage

subsidiary company

Insurer Operations. A term used to refer to a company wholly owned by a larger company or holding company.

see: affiliated companies, parent company, pup company

substance abuse

Health. The over-use of bodily-ingested chemicals such as alcohol, cocaine or prescription drugs to the extent that medical attention is, or should be, sought.

substandard life expectancy

Life. Life expectancy of an individual that is materially less than indicated on a standard mortality table.

syn: age "rate up;" see: rated policy

substandard risk

Health/Insurer Operations/Life. A risk that is considered by the underwriter as not measuring up to minimum underwriting standards. Such a risk may be written at surcharged rates or be rejected.

compare: standard risk; see: classified insurance, impaired risk, qualified impairment insurance, rated policy, substandard life expectancy, uninsurable risk

sue and labor clause

Ocean Marine. An ocean marine policy provision which provides coverage for expenses reasonably insured by the policyholder or its agents to protect insured property from further harm and to assist in recovering the damaged property to minimize the loss.

suicide

Life.

see: self-inflicted injury

summons

General. A writ or process served on the defendant by the plaintiff in a civil suit notifying the defendant of the complaint and summoning the defendant to appear and answer.

see: answer, summons and complaint, writ

summons and complaint

General. A legal document served on a defendant by a plaintiff to commence a lawsuit. This particular form combines both a summons requiring the response of the plaintiff and the complaint which must be answered.

see: answer, complaint, summons

superaddition

General. A legal term denoting the inclusion of an amount over and above, or a superfluous amount.

compare: additur

Superfund

Regulation.

see: Comprehensive Environmental Response, Compensation and Liability Act

superintendent of insurance

Regulation.

see: insurance commissioner

superseded suretyship rider

Surety. An endorsement or a provision in a new fidelity bond superseding a bond that has been cancelled, providing that the new bond will cover a loss that occurred while the old bond was in force and that would have been covered under that bond had it

© 1991 NILS Publishing Company

been discovered within the discovery period. Coverage is limited to the amount provided by the previous bond.

see: bond

supplemental extended reporting period

Casualty. A provision found in many claims-made liability policy forms allowing an insured to purchase an optional time period (12 months to unlimited) during which claims occurring may be reported. The ISO commercial liability claims-made form provides an unlimited time in which to report claims.

see: basic extended reporting period, claims-made form

supplemental major medical coverage

Health. Medical insurance providing coverage for expenses not covered by a basic medical plan. It usually will reimburse the insured for uncovered expenses with no deductible or copayment.

see: major medical insurance

supplementary payment

Casualty. A payment included as benefits in a liability policy which is made in addition to any payments for other coverages provided by the policy. The cost of bail bonds or prejudgment interest are examples of supplementary payments.

see: commercial general liability form

surety

Surety. The individual or entity that guarantees the legal liability for the debt, default, or failure to perform a duty (such as an appearance in court) of a principal.

compare: obligee, principal; see: bond, guarantor, obligor

Surety Association of America (SAA)

Organizations. Members: Insurers writing fidelity, surety and forgery bonds. *Objectives:* Classifying risks, rates, minimum premiums and rating plans. Preparing forms, provisions, terms and riders. Making filings with regulatory authorities. *Founded:* 1908. *Headquarters:* Iselin, NJ.

surety bond

Surety. A promise by a professional surety insurer to pay should the principal default or commit a wrongful act. A written guarantee that a party will perform an expressed obligation.

see: bond

Surety Bond Guarantee Program

Surety. A program developed by the Small Business Administration (SBA), by which the SBA acts as a guarantor of bonds issued by a surety company to minority contractors.

suretyship

Surety. The function of being a surety. It is the obligation of a surety to pay the debts of or answer for the default of another. A three-party contract is the basis for a suretyship, insuring that one party (surety) undertakes to answer to a second party (obligee) for the debt or default of a third party (principal) resulting from the third party's failure to pay or perform as required by an underlying contract.

surgical expense insurance

Health. A health insurance policy that covers surgery.

surgical schedule

Health.

see: schedule

surplus

General. On a financial statement, the amount by which assets are higher than liabilities.

see: policyholder surplus

Reinsurance. The portion of a reinsurer's risk which remains after deducting the ceding company's retention.

see: surplus reinsurance treaty

surplus deposit

Insurer Operations. A deposit maintained by reciprocal subscribers in lieu of an assessment liability.

surplus lines

Insurer Operations. Insurance coverage for which there is no readily available admitted market. Such coverages are marketed through nonadmitted insurers on an unregulated basis under each state's surplus lines laws.

compare: unauthorized insurance; see: excess lines

surplus lines broker

Agency. A broker licensed and authorized by a state to conduct business within the state on behalf of nonadmitted insurers.

see: excess and surplus lines broker, excess lines, nonadmitted insurer, surplus lines

surplus reinsurance treaty

Reinsurance. A reinsurance treaty where the reinsurer automatically assumes a layer of each risk written in excess of the ceding company's retention. Generally, the layer assumed by the reinsurer is a multiple of the ceding company's retention.

see: first surplus reinsurance treaty, second surplus treaty

surplus relief reinsurance

Reinsurance. A reinsurance contract where an admitted reinsurer assumes a portfolio of a ceding company's business to relieve stress on the company's

© 1991 NILS Publishing Company

surplus relief reinsurance — continued

policyholder surplus. The portfolio transfer allows the ceding company to recapture the equity found in unearned premium reserves on the business ceded.

compare: **loss portfolio transfer, portfolio transfer**

surplus share

Reinsurance.

see: **surplus relief reinsurance**

surplus to policyholders

Insurer Operations.

see: **policyholder surplus**

surrender

Life. The relinquishing of a cash value life insurance policy by the owner for its cash surrender value.

see: **cash surrender value**

surrender value

Life.

see: **cash surrender value**

survey

Inland Marine/Ocean Marine. 1) The examination of damaged cargo after a marine loss, to determine the cause and extent of damage.
2) The inspection of a ship's hull to determine its insurability.
3) After a loss, the inspection of a ship's hull to determine the cause and extent of damage.

see: **surveyor**

surveyor

Ocean Marine. An individual that performs inspections of marine cargos and hulls, generally for insurance purposes.

syn: **marine surveyor**; see: **survey**

surviving companies

General. Corporate entities that remain after consolidations or mergers.

survivorship annuity

Life.

see: **joint and survivor annuity**

survivorship benefits

Employee Benefits. Benefits paid to a survivor of a retired individual who was receiving pension benefits. Survivor benefits are based on a formula contained in the plan.

syn: **benefits of survivorship**

Life. A retirement income benefit for an insured's survivor that is set according to a predetermined formula.

syn: **benefits of survivorship**

survivorship life insurance

Life. A life insurance policy which is written to cover two or more individuals with the policy benefits payable only after all of the covered individuals die. It is used as a vehicle to fund estate taxes upon the deaths of both the husband and wife, or to fund the continuation of a business in the event its principals die.

see: **joint and survivor option, tontine**

swap maternity

Health. Maternity coverage that is provided at the beginning of a group health insurance plan, but terminates on pregnancies in progress upon the plan's termination. This is the reverse of the way coverage is usually provided, and therefore explains the term "swap" maternity.

see: **maternity benefit**

symmetrical curve

Risk Management. An actuarial term for a distribution curve where the mean, median and mode have the same numerical value. A bell-shaped curve.

syn: **bell-shaped curve**; compare: **skewed curve**; see: **distribution curve**

syndicate

Insurer Operations. Insurers or reinsurers that have joined or become associated to underwrite a risk or risks. They will usually take agreed-upon shares of premiums, expenses, profits and losses. A syndicate is often formed to underwrite large risks that are beyond the ability of a single member to insure.

syn: **pool**; see: **Lloyd's syndicate**

© 1991 NILS Publishing Company

T

table of allowances
Health.
see: fee schedule, schedule

tabular mortality
Life. Expected mortality as indicated on mortality tables.
see: mortality table

tabular plan
Casualty/Workers' Compensation. A retrospective rating plan in which the factors (i.e. basic, minimum, maximum) used in the rating formula are indicated in a table. The factors vary, depending on the risk's premium size and prior loss experience.

tabular value reserve method
Life. A life insurance reserving method which uses a mortality table to indicate the reserve that applies to the rating of specific insureds.

Taft-Hartley Act
Employee Benefits. Federal legislation which amended the National Labor Relations Act of 1935. Among other things, it defined unfair labor practices; granted individual employees the right to prosecute union or company officials for unfair labor practices; restricted closed shops and prohibited secondary boycotts. It also prohibits employers from making direct contributions to unions for employee benefits, but allows employee contributions to be paid to a separate benefit trust fund managed by the union.
see: unfair labor practices

tagged fish coverage
Inland Marine. A form of prize indemnification insurance which indemnifies the insured (usually the tournament sponsor) should a tagged fish be caught by a participating fisherman during a specified fishing tournament.
see: prize indemnification insurance, record fish coverage

tail
Casualty. 1) Liability that exists after the expiration of a policy.
2) Outstanding liability claims that are not yet known to an insured or insurer.
see: claims-made form, incurred but not reported, tail coverage

tail coverage
Casualty. Coverage that can be purchased after the expiration of a claims-made liability policy which extends for a period of time, with or without limit, the right to report events that occurred before the policy was terminated.
see: claims-made form, extended reporting period

takeover attempt insurance
Casualty.
see: tender offer defense expense insurance

tangible assets
General. Physical property, such as land, buildings, machinery and equipment, timber and other growing crops, mineral resources and merchandise.

target benefit plan
Employee Benefits. A defined contribution plan that is structured so that benefits may change according to the investment performance of the pension plan assets. Plan contributions are set at a level to fund a target benefit, such as 30 percent of compensation,

© 1991 NILS Publishing Company

target benefit plan — continued
using acceptable mortality and interest rate assumptions.

compare: **money purchase plan**; see: **benefit plan, defined contribution plan**

target risk

General. A risk which is large, hazardous, or generates sizable premiums.

Reinsurance. A risk that involves the concentration of values – such as a bridge, tunnel, or art collection – which could produce an exceptionally large loss. Such risks will frequently be excluded from treaty reinsurance and must be reinsured on a facultative basis instead.

Insurer Operations/Agency. 1) A large account that is considered a target for competing brokers or insurance companies.
2) Prospective buyers of insurance classified according to various demographics such as age, sex, and type of insurance.

compare: **prohibited list, uninsurable risk**

tariff rate

Insurer Operations. A rate developed by rating organizations for a general category of property or liability insurance.

compare: **specific rate**

taxable income

Financial Planning. Earned and unearned income on which current taxes must be paid.

tax-appraised value

Financial Planning. The value of real or personal property based on the valuation established by a government tax assessor.

compare: **actual cash value, depreciated value, fair market value, functional replacement cost, market value, replacement cost, reproduction cost**; see: **valuation of potential property loss.**

taxation of business income loss payments

Risk Management. Claims payments from business income insurance, by nature, pay for profits which were not realized, plus continuing expenses; therefore, like profits, these claims payments are subject to taxation.

compare: **taxation of uninsured business interruption insurance losses**; see: **business income coverage form**

taxation of interest on life insurance dividends

Life. Interest earned on participating life insurance

policy dividends, left on deposit with the insurance company that is subject to taxation.

see: **dividend accumulation**

taxation of property insurance claims payments

Risk Management/Property. Claims payments for business property insurance losses are generally taxed as ordinary income to the extent that they exceed the book value of the damaged property. It is sometimes possible to defer taxation if the property is replaced with similar property.

compare: **taxation of uninsured property losses**

taxation of uninsured business interruption insurance losses

Risk Management/Property. Uninsured business interruption losses are not directly tax deductible; however, since such a loss would result in lower income, it would result in lower taxes.

compare: **taxation of business income loss payments**

taxation of uninsured property losses

Risk Management/Property. Uninsured business property losses are generally tax deductible, but only up to the amount of book value at the time of loss. When the book value is zero, no deduction is allowed.

compare: **taxation of property insurance claims payments**

tax audit insurance

Casualty. A specialized form of insurance that reimburses taxpayers for additional expenses involved if their tax attorney or CPA-prepared tax returns (with deductions claimed within the Internal Revenue Service laws and regulations) are audited by the IRS.

tax avoidance

General. The utilization of certain provisions of the tax laws to reduce or avoid income tax by legally permitted methods. Also, the non-payment of taxes attached to the purchase of taxable goods and services by not purchasing such goods and services.

compare: **tax deferral, tax evasion**

tax benefits of life insurance

Financial Planning/Life. Two principal tax advantages of purchasing life insurance: 1) Tax deferral of the buildup of earnings in whole life policies and annuities, which go untaxed, and 2) tax-free death benefits of a life insurance policy.

see: **Tax Equity and Financial Responsibility Acts of 1982 and 1983**

tax bracket shifting

Financial Planning. A method of reducing taxes for a family, by shifting income from one family member in

© 1991 NILS Publishing Company

a high tax bracket to another one in a lower tax bracket. This is possible when the family members file separate tax returns.

see: **irrevocable trust, short-term reversionary trust**

tax deferral

Financial Planning. Postponing taxes to a future tax year because of an anticipated lower tax bracket, or for current use of the funds. This differs from the illegal practice of tax evasion.

compare: **tax avoidance, tax evasion**

tax deferred annuity (TDA)

Life. A retirement program specifically for employees of a public school system or a qualified charitable organization, permitted under Section 403 (b) of the Internal Revenue Code.

see: **Internal Revenue Code: Section 403(b)**

tax depreciation

General.

see: **depreciation**

Tax Equity and Financial Responsibility Acts of 1982 and 1983 (TEFRA)

Employee Benefits/Life. Federal legislation which altered the traditional taxation of life insurance and life insurance companies. It increased the corporate tax rate on life insurance companies; redefined flexible premium life insurance so that it no longer provides favorable tax benefits; and reduced the estate tax exclusion for a retirement plan death plan benefits to a maximum of $100,000. It also lowered pension plan contributions and benefits; specified that certain loans from plans are to be treated as distributions and repealed special Keogh Plan and Subchapter S restrictions.

see: **tax benefits of life insurance, Tax Reform Act of 1984**

tax evasion

General. The nonpayment of taxes through illegal means, such as under-reporting income or reporting invalid deductions.

compare: **tax avoidance, tax deferral**

tax factor

Casualty/Workers' Compensation.

see: **tax multiplier**

tax free rollover

Employee Benefits. ERISA and IRS provisions allowing an individual to transfer funds within a 60-day period from a qualified pension plan to an IRA or from an IRA to a qualified pension fund or from one IRA to another one. Under these provisions an individual is not required to pay a tax for withdrawing funds if they are transferred within 60 days.

see: **rollover individual retirement account**

tax interruption policy

Property. A form of contingent business income coverage purchased by a public entity that insures against a large fire, windstorm or other disaster that destroys a leading industry, convention or entertainment center in the community that contributed a sizable portion of the community's tax income.

see: **contingent business income coverage**

tax lien

Financial Planning. A claim upon real or personal property for the satisfaction of taxes.

see: **lien**

tax multiplier

Casualty/Workers' Compensation. A factor applied in retrospective rating plans to cover the insurer's costs for licenses, fees, assessments and taxes that the insurer must pay on collected premiums. The factor varies by state, and sometimes is a composite of several state factors.

syn: **tax factor;** see: **retrospective rating plan**

tax penalty

General. Monies assessed for deficiencies in tax returns, due to late filings or computation errors. They differ from fines assessed for illegal acts, such as tax evasion.

see: **tax evasion**

tax planning

Financial Planning. The systematic structuring of discretionary income, expenses, and investments to enhance after-tax wealth. Frequently, life insurance annuities and employee benefit plans can be used to increase after-tax income through their tax-deferral features.

see: **exemption, marital tax deduction, qualified terminable interest property trust, tax avoidance, tax deferral**

tax preparers errors & omissions insurance

Casualty. A policy insuring against claims alleging errors or omissions of tax preparers, including incorrect or incomplete preparation of forms, errors in calculations, and erroneous professional advice.

Tax Reform Act of 1976

Employee Benefits. Federal legislation that extended tax credit provisions for ESOPs contained in the Tax Reduction Act of 1975. These were used as temporary

© 1991 NILS Publishing Company

Tax Reform Act of 1976 — continued
rules and regulations for implementation of the Employee Retirement Income Security Act of 1974 (ERISA).

see: **Employee Retirement Income Security Act of 1974**

Tax Reform Act of 1984

Life/Insurer Operations. Federal legislation that included provisions to tighten the life insurance tax provisions of the Tax Equity and Financial Responsibility Acts of 1982 and 1983. This act further raised the corporate tax on life insurance companies and broadened the definition of life insurance to include all life insurance contracts, not just those with flexible premiums. The act also addressed redistribution of the tax burden between mutual and stock life insurance companies.

see: **Tax Equity and Financial Responsibility Acts of 1982 and 1983**

Tax Reform Act of 1986

Employee Benefits. Federal legislation that included provisions to eliminate many tax shelters and deductions previously allowed. It also reduced individual and corporate tax rates. The Act further restricted personal tax deductions for Individual Retirement Accounts (IRAs), restricted use of corporate sponsored 401(k) payroll deduction plans, and increased corporate expenses to start and maintain pension plans. An alternative minimum tax for corporations originated with this Act and has had a material effect on insurance company tax payments.

tax shelter

Financial Planning. An investment or employee benefit structured to provide a tax savings by reducing taxable income or creating losses to offset taxable income.

see: **Tax Reform Act of 1986**

tax shelter legal expense insurance

Casualty. Coverage designed for partnerships, syndicates and joint ventures providing tax shelter benefits to investors. The insurance benefit reimburses these ventures for their legal expenses in contesting disallowances by the Internal Revenue Service.

technical reserves

Insurer Operations/Reinsurance. Reserves made for future underwriting liabilities on an insurance or reinsurance account.

television closed circuit breakdown insurance

Property. Coverage that indemnifies a sponsor of a closed circuit telecast (a seminar, sporting event, etc.) for loss of revenues because of interruption of service

for technical reasons that necessitates the refund of admissions.

see: **entertainment insurance**

temperature extremes exclusion

Property/Inland Marine. A provision in "all-risks" property and inland marine policies, excluding coverage for loss from extremes of temperature to such things as fruits, vegetables, and living plants.

temporary disability benefits (TDB)

Health. Benefits in the form of income payments made to a sick or disabled worker who is not receiving workers' compensation benefits. Often these benefits are prescribed by state legislation.

see: **disability income insurance**

temporary life annuity

Life. An annuity that makes benefit payments for a limited period of time (i.e. five years) while the annuitant is alive. Payments cease after the end of the stipulated period or upon the death of the annuitant.

see: **annuity**

temporary life annuity due

Life. An annuity with a limited number of payments, the first of which is paid immediately; thereafter payments continue until the limit set for such payments is reached or until the death of the annuitant.

temporary nonoccupational disability plan

Health. A social insurance program established in California, Hawaii, New Jersey, New York and Rhode Island to provide benefits to temporarily disabled workers.

temporary partial disability

Health/Workers' Compensation. An injury to an individual that impairs his or her capacity to work for a limited period of time. The impairment is such that the individual is able to continue to work at reduced efficiency, and is expected to fully recover.

syn: **intermediate disability**; see: **partial disability**

temporary substitute automobile

Automobile. A rented or borrowed auto operated by an insured provided for under an automobile insurance policy when the insured's damaged vehicle is being repaired.

see: **rental reimbursement coverage, transportation expense coverage**

temporary total disability

Health/Workers' Compensation. An injury to a worker rendering him or her unable to work at all during the recovery period. After the recovery period, a full return to previous work is anticipated.

see: **total disability**

© 1991 NILS Publishing Company

tenancy

General. The possession or occupancy of land or real property by means of a lease or payment of rent.

see: joint tenancy, tenancy by entirety, tenancy in common

tenancy by entirety

General. A legal term for the ownership of property by a husband and wife as one. If either spouse dies, the property passes to the other spouse.

see: tenancy

tenancy in common

General. A legal term for the ownership of property by two or more individuals that do not have the right of survivorship. If one of these individuals (tenant) dies, the property passes to that individual's estate and not to the other property owner(s).

see: tenancy

ten day free look

Health/Regulation. Many state insurance departments require that a prospective insured have ten days to examine a health insurance policy. If the policy does not meet with the insured's satisfaction, the policy can be returned without any obligation.

tender

General. A formal offer or bid; to proffer or make available.

tender offer defense expense insurance

Casualty. A form of legal defense coverage that pays for the cost to defend a corporation from an unfriendly takeover attempt. This coverage is usually provided by the London market.

syn: takeover attempt insurance

tentative premium

General.

see: provisional premium

tentative rate

General.

see: provisional rate

ten year averaging

Employee Benefits. A tax provision that was repealed by the Tax Reform Act of 1986, which could be used to reduce income taxes on distributions from qualified pension or retirement plans, by allowing such payments to be averaged over ten years. Averaging is now limited to five years.

ten year vesting

Employee Benefits. A rule in the Employee Retirement Income Security Act of 1974 (ERISA) that allowed employers to require an employee to have ten years of service before being vested in a pension plan. The Tax Reform Act of 1986 reduced the vesting period to five years.

syn: cliff vesting; see: vesting

term

Insurer Operations. The length or period of time during which an insurance policy or bond is in force.

see: policy period; Fr: terme; Gr: Frist; Sp: período, vigencia

term health insurance

Health. A contract of health insurance that makes no provision for renewal or termination other than by expiration of the policy term.

terminal dividend

Life. An additional dividend paid to a life insurance policyholder when a policy terminates. Such a dividend is usually paid only after a minimum in-force period of 10 to 20 years.

terminal funding

Employee Benefits. The funding of a pension plan by an employer in a lump sum upon retirement of an employee. The Employee Retirement Income Security Act of 1974 (ERISA) eliminated this funding method for qualified pension plans and requires current funding of future pension liabilities.

see: Employee Retirement Income Security Act of 1974

terminal reserve

Life. A life insurance reserve which is established at the end of each life policy year.

compare: initial reserve, mean reserve; see: preliminary term

termination

Life. Ceasing coverage on a whole life insurance or endowment policy for nonpayment of premium prior to its expiration date.

see: lapse

Insurer Operations. The cancellation of an insurance policy by an insurer for nonpayment of premium.

see: cancellation

termination rate

Insurer Operations. A rate of cancellations and/or lapses of policies experienced by an insurer.

compare: persistency; see: lapse ratio

term life insurance

Life. Life insurance that is in effect for a specific limited length of time (i.e., 5 or 10 years). If the insured does not die within the period, the coverage

© 1991 NILS Publishing Company

term life insurance — continued
ceases. Unlike a whole life policy, this type of policy does not build up any cash or nonforfeiture values.
compare: life expectancy term insurance, permanent life insurance; see: automatically convertible term life insurance, decreasing term life insurance, extended term life insurance, level term life insurance, life expectancy term insurance, re-entry term life insurance, renewable term life insurance

term policy
Insurer Operations. An insurance contract written for a period of more than one year.

term rate
Insurer Operations. The rate for a term policy.
see: term rule

term rule
Insurer Operations. A rule found in rating manuals concerning discounts for policies that are issued for a period of time longer than one year.

territorial limitation
Insurer Operations.
see: geographical limitation

territorial rating
Insurer Operations. A method of using geographical areas to assist in the classification of risks and subsequent setting of rates. This process assumes geographical location is a significant factor in loss experience.

terrorist insurance
Property. Coverage that can be added to a worldwide property insurance program, to provide insurance against destruction of property by terrorists.

tertiary beneficiary
Life. The life insurance policy beneficiary that is named as the third person to receive policy proceeds or benefits. No benefits are payable to this beneficiary if either the first or second beneficiary is alive.
see: primary beneficiary, second beneficiary

testamentary trust
Financial Planning. A form of inter-vivos trust established by an individual through a will. The individual establishing the trust can change its provisions by changing the will, but when the individual dies, the testamentary trust becomes irrevocable.
see: inter-vivos trust, trust

testing and research laboratory errors & omissions insurance
Casualty. Errors and omissions coverage for laboratories involved in testing and research. Coverage is written subject to complete information on the nature of the testing and research performed.

testing exclusion
Property. A boiler and machinery policy exclusion, which suspends coverage during the period of time that a covered object is undergoing testing. Coverage remains in force prior to and after such testing.

Thalsol
Health/Life. The name of an ancient Greek benevolent society that is considered one of the foundations for modern life and health insurance.
see: insurance

theatrical property coverage
Inland Marine. Inland marine coverage for props, costumes, and other property that is used by a theatrical company or production. Generally such events are scheduled in the policy declarations. (*ISO Coverage Form CM 00 29.*)

theft
Crime. An act or instance of stealing. The taking or removal of property from its rightful owner. Theft encompasses both burglary and robbery.
see: pilferage; Fr: vol; Gr: Diebstahl; Sp: robo sin violencia

theft, disappearance and destruction of money and securities coverage form
Crime. A crime coverage form that covers loss by theft, disappearance, or destruction of the insured's money and securities inside the insured's premises as well as outside the insured's premises while in the custody of a messenger.
syn: crime coverage form C

theory of probability
Risk Management.
see: probability

third country national (TCN)
International. An employee who is a citizen of a first country employed in a second country by an employer domiciled in a third country.

third-party administrator (TPA)
Risk Management. A claims administrator or insurance company that pays claims on behalf of a self-insured organization. The services such a firm provides can include processing of claims, (including audits, adjusting and, often, negotiating and settlement) record keeping, self-insurance certification, and notification of excess insurers.
syn: administrative agent; see: benefits manager, deposit administration plan

© 1991 NILS Publishing Company

third-party administrators professional liability

Casualty. Liability coverage protecting third-party administrators against claims alleging negligent errors or omissions.

see: **third-party administrator**

third-party beneficiary

General. A legal term used to identify an individual or entity that is not a party to a contract, but possesses a legally enforceable right under it.

third-party liability

Casualty. Under a liability policy, an individual or entity that has been injured by or has otherwise incurred loss due to an act of the insured (the first party), is entitled to receive benefits from the insurer (the second party).

compare: **first-party insurance**

third-party liability insurance

Casualty. A term for liability insurance.

see: **third-party liability.**

third-party over suit

Casualty/Workers' Compensation. A suit involving an injured worker attempting to seek recovery from a third party (other than an employer) in the belief that the third party caused the injury. This situation usually arises when an injury is caused by a product or piece of equipment used by the worker in the scope of employment. Should the employee sue the manufacturer, the manufacturer may in turn sue the employer in the belief that the fault lies with the employer's use (or misuse) of the product or equipment. The manufacturer's suit against the employer is termed a "third-party over" suit and is covered under the employer's workers' compensation and the employer's liability policy.

syn: **liability over suit**

third-party payor

Health. A term signifying the insurance company that pays for services provided to a patient.

thirty and out

Employee Benefits. A pension plan option allowing a participant to retire after completing 30 years of credited service, regardless of age.

thirty-year cap

Employee Benefits. A pension plan provision which reaches maximum benefit or accumulation levels after 30 years of credited service.

three-D ("3-D") policy

Crime.

see: **dishonesty, disappearance and destruction policy**

three-fourths loss clause

Property/Ocean Marine. An obsolete clause once contained in property and marine policies, providing that an insurer's maximum loss would be three-fourths of the actual cash value of the property. In effect, this clause imposed a 25 percent deductible.

three percent rule

Employee Benefits. A rule used in vesting pension plan benefits. The participant's accrued benefit must be at least equal to three percent of the participant's normal projected retirement benefit for each year of participation, with a maximum of 100 percent after 33-1/3 years of participation.

see: **unit credit actuarial cost method**

threshold level

Automobile. A provision of some no-fault automobile insurance programs which allows an injured party to sue if a dollar or injury threshold is exceeded (such as $1,000 or disfigurement or death).

ticket policy

Health.

see: **travel accident insurance**

ticket reinsurance

Reinsurance. A method of indicating the placement of reinsurance on a policy, where a form is attached to the daily report indicating the details of any reinsurance that has been effected.

tickler

Agency/Insurer Operations. A system used by agents and underwriters to remind them of actions that must be taken.

see: **expiration card, expiration file**

tight market

Insurer Operations. A period of time during the underwriting cycle when there is little or no insurance capacity. It is distinguished from a hard market by a lack of policyholder surplus, as opposed to being created by that segment of the underwriting cycle when heavy losses and extreme price cutting create a lack of capacity. Occasionally, a tight market will occur toward the end of a calendar year when underwriters have used their allocated surplus, particularly as on the London market.

compare: **hard market, soft market;** see: **underwriting cycle**

time charter

Ocean Marine. The hiring of a ship with the vessel owner's crew managing and navigating the vessel, but its cargo capacity taken by the hirer for a specified period of time for carriage of goods or passengers. The vessel may be hired, or chartered, to sail anywhere in the world or anywhere within stipulated geographical

© 1991 NILS Publishing Company

time charter – continued
limits on as many voyages as can be fitted into the charter period.

see: **charter party**

time deposits

Financial Planning. Interest-bearing deposits with a financial institution that must remain on deposit for a specified period of time, in order that the deposits receive the full interest available. Early withdrawal can result in penalty provisions such as loss of some interest or payment of interest at a lower rate.

time element insurance

Property. Insurance which provides coverage when a direct property loss results in an indirect or consequential loss, such as loss of earnings or increased expenses. Coverage is usually tied to the loss of earnings or increased expenses over a specific period of time.

see: **business income coverage form, extra expense insurance**

time limit

General. The period of time in which a notice or proof of loss must be filed.

see: **notice of loss, proof of loss**

Health. A statutory provision in most states applying to individual health insurance policies. An insurer has a time limit (usually two or three years) to deny a claim on the basis of an adverse physical condition which existed at the time an insured completed the application, but which the insured did not include on the application.

syn: **certain defenses; see: material misrepresentation**

Insurer Operations. The period of time (90 to 120 days) allowed for a proof of loss or notice or claim to be completed.

syn: **certain defenses; see: proof of loss**

time-loss unit

Property. The amount of economic loss an insured would suffer for each unit of time that production was interrupted or curtailed. This concept must be a consideration in adjusting a business income loss.

syn: **rate of loss**

time value of money

Risk Management. The concept that an amount of money received now is worth more than the same amount of money received a year from now, because today's money can be invested and earn a return as the year elapses. Such value is calculated by use of a compound interest table which will indicate the value between two points in time.

see: **present value**

title

Title. A document that constitutes evidence of a legally exclusive possession of property.

see: **certificate of title, paper title**

title insurance

Title. An insurance policy indemnifying an owner of real estate for any loss sustained by reason of defects in the title obtained by the owner.

see: **title insurance company, Torrens System**

title insurance company

Title. An insurance company that is specifically chartered to write only title insurance policies. Historically these companies have operated in limited geographical areas because of the need to review documents at local halls of records.

see: **abstract of title, chain of title**

Title XIX Benefits
Health.
see: **Medicaid**

Title XVIII of Social Security Act
Health.
see: **Medicare**

tontine

Life. An early form of life insurance which is now illegal. It is named after the Italian, Lorenzo Tonti, who during the 17th century came up with the idea of establishing a state lottery to raise money for the French government, in which the oldest survivor would collect the money. It later developed into an agreement where several participants placed an amount of money in escrow, with the understanding that after an agreed period of time, survivors would share the accrued proceeds. Tontines are now illegal, as they had the unintended effect of encouraging participants to assure they were the surviving party by arranging to have the other participants murdered.

see: **insurance, joint life and survivor insurance**

top-heavy plan

Employee Benefits. An employee benefit plan that primarily benefits highly compensated employees, top executives or owners of a business. It is difficult for a top-heavy plan to qualify for favorable tax treatment.

see: **nonqualified plan**

tornado

Property. A whirling wind, accompanied by a funnel-shaped cloud, that is very violent and destructive and which travels in a narrow path.

see: **windstorm insurance**

Torrens System

Title. A form of title insurance where a county

© 1991 NILS Publishing Company

recorder or county clerk provides a written guarantee of clear title when a property is transferred. The guarantee is based on the fact that the county recorder registers the title and maintains the deed records. Under this system, a transfer fee is charged which includes a part of which is used to finance an insurance fund to pay damages in the event the county recorder makes an error.

see: title insurance

tort

General. A private, civil, noncontractual wrong for which a remedy through legal action may be sought. A tort can be either intentional or unintentional. Liability insurance responds principally to unintentional torts. Intentional torts (deliberate acts) are not usually covered by insurance.

see: intentional tort, tort feasor

tort feasor

General. A legal term for the individual who has committed a tort.

see: tort

total debt

Financial Planning. The sum of an organization's long-term debt and short-term debt.

see: long-term debt, short-term debt

total disability

Health/Workers' Compensation. A disability which prevents a worker from continuously performing any part of his or her occupation and that does not allow them to perform any other employment.

see: disability, partial disability, permanent partial disability, permanent total disability

total loss

Insurer Operations. A loss payment by an insurer which equals the maximum insurance policy limit.

see: actual total loss, constructive total loss

Property. The total destruction of an insured property at a location; nothing of value remains.

compare: partial loss

total loss only clause (TLO)

Ocean Marine. Ocean marine insurance that responds only if a vessel or cargo is a complete loss. Partial losses are not covered.

see: actual total loss, constructive total loss

towing and labor costs

Automobile. An optional automobile coverage that can be added to a policy's physical damage coverage, providing reimbursement up to a specified amount for towing or on-site labor costs, necessitated by a covered, disabled vehicle.

toxic

Loss Control. A substance that is poisonous to the human body. There are degrees of toxicity – from mildly toxic, to highly or deadly toxic.

trading partnership

General. A partnership in the business of buying and selling property.

see: partnership

trailer interchange agreement

Automobile. An agreement between two truckers allowing a trailer containing cargo to be transferred from one to the other for the continuation of a trip.

see: interchange insurance

trailer interchange insurance

Automobile.

see: interchange insurance, trailer interchange agreement

trailing dividend yield

Financial Planning. The total of the dividends declared over the last 12 months, divided by the recent price.

see: dividend yield

transacting insurance

Regulation. A term found in state insurance codes, which refers to the carrying on of the business of insurance. It is usually further defined as the solicitation, inducement, negotiation or advising of an individual concerning insurance.

transfer agents errors & omissions insurance

Casualty. Errors and omissions insurance for securities transfer agents. Includes coverage for securities forgery, erasure guaranty and voluntary destruction of stock records.

transfer of business

Insurer Operations. An arrangement by sale, reinsurance, merger, consolidation or assumption, under which the business of one insurer is transferred to another one.

transfer of coverage

Employee Benefits. Transfer of coverage under a group policy or benefit plan from one carrier to another, including transfer under an optional choice enrollment plan.

transfer of risk

Risk Management. The shifting of a risk to another person or organization. This transfer can be accomplished by subcontracting hazardous work, requiring

327

© 1991 NILS Publishing Company

transfer of risk — continued
hold harmless agreements or other contractual agreements or by purchasing insurance.
   see: avoidance, diversification, insurance, retention

transit insurance
Inland Marine. Insurance covering loss or damage to goods while they are being transported.
   see: cargo insurance, trip transit insurance

transition program
Insurer Operations. A program implemented in conjunction with the 1986 ISO Liability Rating Plan, to compensate for large premium differences on mercantile premises and operations coverages. Such coverages are now rated on gross sales. Formerly rated on square footage, the program set upper and lower amounts for premium changes caused solely by an exposure base change.

transportation expense coverage
Automobile. Coverage under an automobile policy's physical damage section, which pays for substitute transportation should a covered vehicle be stolen.
   see: rental reimbursement coverage, temporary substitute automobile

transportation facilities
Inland Marine. Facilities such as a bridges, piers, wharves, loading facilities, or pipelines which are covered by inland marine insurance.
   see: instrumentalities of transportation and communication

transportation insurance
Inland Marine/Ocean Marine. Insurance that covers merchandise or goods in the course of transit by air, rail, truck, barge or ship from a starting location to a final destination.
   see: cargo insurance, inland marine insurance, ocean marine insurance, transit insurance, trip transit insurance

transportation ticket insurance
Health.
   see: travel accident insurance

traumatic injury
Health. A physical or mental injury caused by an external force to an individual's body, as distinguished from a disease.

travel accident insurance
Health. A form of accidental death, dismemberment and disability insurance commonly sold at airports. Coverage is issued in conjunction with a common carrier (airline, train) ticket and is limited to travel periods during the trip. The term "transportation

ticket insurance" was once used to describe this insurance, because coverage was once provided in the form of an additional stub on the traveler's ticket.
   syn: ticket policy, transportation ticket insurance; see: air travel insurance, railroad travel policy

travel agents liability insurance
Casualty. Coverage for travel agents against claims arising out of negligent acts, errors and omissions committed by the insured, or persons for whose acts the insured is legally liable. Coverage usually extends to employees, tour guides and tour directors under contract. Coverage applies worldwide for accidents or occurrences such as cancelled hotel or tour reservations, lost luggage and misleading travel brochures.

treasurer
General. The executive financial officer of a business enterprise or organization entrusted with the receipt, care and disbursement of funds.
   compare: chief financial officer, controller

treasury stock
General. Shares of stock that were once issued and outstanding, but which have been reacquired by the corporation and held in its own treasury. Treasury shares are economically indistinguishable from authorized, but unissued shares. Historically, they have been treated as having an intermediate status. Many of the complexities created by treasury shares revolve around accounting concepts.
   see: authorized shares, issued stock, share of stock

treatment, storage and disposal facility
Casualty.
   see: closure and post-closure insurance

Treaty of Paris
Ocean Marine.
   see: enemy goods

treaty reinsurance
Reinsurance. An automatic reinsurance agreement between the ceding company and the reinsurer in which the reinsurer is bound to accept all risks ceded to it, usually for one year or longer.
   compare: facultative reinsurance; see: aggregate excess of loss reinsurance, automatic reinsurance, Carpenter Plan, catastrophe reinsurance, excess of loss reinsurance, omissions clause, quota share, special acceptance

trending
Risk Management. The necessary adjustment of historical statistics (both premiums and losses) to present levels or expected future levels, to reflect measurable changes in experience over time caused

© 1991 NILS Publishing Company

by dynamic economic and demographic forces, and to make such data useful for determining current and future expected cost levels.

see: **loss development, loss development factor, loss trends**

trespasser

General. An individual entering the property of another without permission. The property owner has little or no responsibility to a trespasser.

compare: **invitee, licensee; see: attractive nuisance doctrine, degree of care**

tribunalization

General. The process of approval at Lloyd's, by a committee of five individuals, of a correspondent (usually in the United States) who is sponsored by a Lloyd's broker. Once approved, the correspondent can bind coverage and issue certificates of coverage on behalf of Lloyd's.

see: **Lloyd's of London**

trick and device exclusion

Automobile. An exclusion in some automobile dealers' physical damage policies which eliminates coverage for losses due to fraudulent acts such as a customer stealing a car under the pretense of test-driving or paying for the auto with a bad check.

syn: **false pretense exclusion; see: conversion, embezzlement, or secretion exclusion; false pretense coverage**

trigger

Casualty.
see: **coverage trigger**

trip cancellation insurance

Casualty.
see: **charter fare protection insurance**

triple A

Organizations.
see: **American Automobile Association**

triple A tenant

Financial Planning. A prestigious and financially strong tenant, who will often act as an anchor tenant; a tenant which attracts other tenants of quality.

syn: **AAA Tenant; see: anchor tenant**

triple indemnity

Life.
see: **multiple indemnity**

triple protection policy

Life.
see: **double protection life insurance**

triple trigger theory

Casualty.
see: **Keene Doctrine**

trip transit insurance

Inland Marine. Insurance on a single shipment of property for a specific trip on a common carrier. Specifically excludes shipments via the U.S. Postal Service, since the USPS is not a common carrier.

syn: **single risk cargo insurance; compare: parcel post insurance**

trucker

Automobile. An individual or entity engaged in the business of transporting property by truck for hire.

see: **common carrier, contract carrier**

truckers coverage form

Automobile. A form of the business automobile policy designed to insure a trucker.

truckers down-time insurance

Automobile. A form of loss of earnings insurance for truckers that provides coverage when a tractor or trailer cannot be operated because of a collision, fire or other insured peril. The coverage has no daily limitation, and is an "actual loss sustained" form. Coverage can include payments on a financed unit and the cost to lease a replacement unit while a damaged one is being repaired.

truckers insurance

Automobile.
see: **endorsement, interchange insurance, Interstate Commerce Commission, motor truck cargo insurance, motor truck cargo radioactive contamination insurance, truckers coverage form, truckers down-time insurance, truckers legal liability insurance**

truckers legal liability insurance

Automobile. Coverage insuring a trucker against legal liability arising out of damage to cargo in his care, custody or control (i.e., while being transported in an insured vehicle).

true group insurance

Health/Life. An insurance program through an employer, union or association whereby all group members are accepted for coverage regardless of their physical condition. This generally results in a savings for employees, but the underwriter usually reserves the right to write some employees on a sub-standard basis.

compare: **fictitious group; see: discretionary groups, group health insurance, minimum group**

Automobile. An insurance program organized through an employer, union or association, offering all

true group insurance – continued
employees personal automobile insurance regardless
of their types of vehicles, or driving records. This can
result in a savings to employers, but the underwriter
will usually reserve the right to exclude a percentage
of bad drivers or to write them on a substandard basis.

trust

General. A legal agreement whereby legal title to
property is held by one person or entity (trustee) for
the benefit of another (beneficiary).

see: agent's trust, American Trust Fund, beneficiary of trust, inter-vivos trust, irrevocable
trust, life insurance trust, living trust, Lloyd's
Premium Trust Fund, medical expense reversionary trust, multiemployer welfare association, personal trust, qualified terminable interest property trust, short-term reversionary
trust, testamentary trust, trust agreement, voting trust

trust agreement

Financial Planning. The legal agreement which documents the rules that are to be followed by a trustee in
administering assets within a trust.
Life. A life insurance policy rider indicating how policy
proceeds are to be distributed.

trust and commission clause

Property. A provision contained in many property
insurance policies extending coverage to property of
others held by the insured in trust, on commission, for
storage, for repairs, or for other reasons.

see: care, custody or control

trust deed

Title. A deed of land to a trustee in trust, as security
for performance of an obligation. The trustee has the
power to sell the land on default of the obligation.

syn: deed of trust; see: deed

trust departments errors & omissions insurance

Casualty. Coverage for trust departments of banks
against any claims by clients alleging breach of duty in
the administration of estates or trusts or managing
real or personal property, caused by any negligent act,
error or omission in the scope of the trust department's duties.

see: fiduciary bond

trustee

General. A person or entity who holds the title to
property in trust for the benefit of another.

trusteed assets

General. Assets that have been placed in trust with a
financial institution for a specific purpose. *Example:*
An insurance agent's premium trust accounts.

trustee group

Employee Benefits. A group insured under a policy
issued to the trustees of a fund established by two or
more employers; one or more labor unions or a
combination of employers and labor unions.

trustees and fiduciaries errors & omissions insurance

Casualty. Errors and omissions coverage, permitted
under the Pension Reform Act of 1974, that protects
trustees and fiduciaries who directly or indirectly
exercise control over pensions or employee benefits
falling under the act. Such insurance may be purchased out of the assets of the plan or trust in order to
protect the plan and its fiduciaries.

tuition and fees insurance

Property. A form of loss of income insurance that
provides protection to a school, college or university
for the loss of tuition and fees caused by a direct loss
resulting from an insured peril.

see: business income coverage form

turnkey insurance

Casualty. A professional liability coverage designed to
protect general contractors and architects and/or
engineers involved with a specific construction project under 1) a turnkey construction contract; 2) a
design/build construction contract; or 3) a project
management team construction contract. Turnkey
insurance combines design error & omissions and
completed operations coverages.

see: completed operations coverage, design errors & omissions

turnover rate

Employee Benefits. A rate or frequency by which
employees terminate employment with an employer
for reasons other than death or retirement. The rate is
expressed as a percentage of those leaving to the total
number of those employed over a stated period of
time.

twisting

Regulation. An attempt by an agent or broker to
persuade a policyowner, through misrepresentation,
to cancel an existing policy and replace it with another
policy.

see: anti-coercion law

two-hand controls

Loss Control. Devices for a machine which require
simultaneous application of both hands to operate the
control, so that the operator's hands are kept out of
the point-of-operation area while the machine is
operating.

see: point of operation

© 1991 NILS Publishing Company

tying arrangement

Regulation. An agreement between a seller and a purchaser that a sale of a product to the latter is contingent upon the latter's purchase of another product or service of the seller. State insurance regulation generally prohibits tying the sale of insurance to any other product or service.

typhoon

Property.

see: hurricane

© 1991 NILS Publishing Company

U

uberrimae fidei

Insurer Operations/Reinsurance. A Latin legal term which translates to "utmost good faith." As respects insurance contracts, it is assumed both parties to the contract (insurer and insured, insurer and reinsurer) have entered into the contract in good faith and have disclosed all relevant facts with the intent to carry out their obligations. If a lack of such good faith is proven, an insurance contract may be declared null and void.

    syn: **utmost good faith;** see: **follow the fortunes**

"UL Approved"

Organizations.

    see: **Underwriters Laboratories, Inc.**

ultimate mortality table

Life. A mortality table based on the experience of a book of insurance policies that compensates for adverse selection by eliminating the experience of those policies that were issued within the past five to ten years.

    see: **adverse selection, mortality table**

ultimate net loss (UNL)

Insurer Operations. The sum of all costs that an insured and/or insurer is legally obligated to pay as the result of a claim including judgments or compromises, legal, medical and investigation expenses, less any salvage and subrogation and reinsurance.

    see: **net loss, net underwriting loss**

ultra vires

General. A Latin legal term which translates into "beyond power or authority." It is applied when a corporation exceeds its legal powers or its stated purpose. Modern courts, generally, will validate all corporate acts, even if they are ultra vires.

    compare: **intra vires**

umbrella liability insurance

Casualty. A special liability policy which serves three main functions: 1) Provides high excess coverage over a primary or underlying liability policy; 2) Provides broader coverages than the primary liability policy, usually excess of a self-insured retention; and 3) Provides a drop-down feature which automatically replaces coverage provided by underlying liability policies when they are reduced or exhausted by loss. Ordinarily used for commercial risks, umbrellas have also been developed for personal lines. The form was first introduced in the U.S. by Lloyd's around 1947, but umbrellas are currently offered by many American insurance companies writing liability insurance.

    compare: **bumbershoot, excess liability insurance, parasol policy;** see: **drop-down provision, personal umbrella, self-insured retention**

umpire

General. A term used in place of "arbitrator" in some contracts.

    see: **arbitrator**

unallocated benefit

Health. A health insurance policy provision which provides a maximum amount of reimbursement for the costs of all extra miscellaneous hospital services without specifying or scheduling the amount that will be paid for each type of service.

    compare: **schedule**

unallocated claim expense

Insurer Operations. An expense that cannot be assigned to and recorded with a specific claim. This includes claim department operating expenses such as rent, heat and electricty, and other overhead expenses.

syn: unallocated loss expense; compare: allocated claim expense; see: claim expense

unallocated funding agreement

Employee Benefits. An agreement found in a pension plan providing that money paid into the plan that is not currently allocated to purchase retirement benefits cannot be commingled with any other funds. Such funds are not allocated to a specfic plan participant, but can be used when a plan participant retires, to purchase an annuity policy for that individual or pay benefits directly to the participant.

unallocated loss expense

Insurer Operations.
see: unallocated claim expense

unauthorized insurance

Insurer Operations. Insurance written by an insurer not licensed by the country or state where the coverage is being provided.

compare: excess lines, surplus lines; see: unauthorized insurer

unauthorized insurer

Insurer Operations. An insurer not licensed, or a reinsurer neither licensed nor approved, in a designated jurisdiction.

compare: admitted insurer; see: nonadmitted insurer

unauthorized reinsurance

Insurer Operations/Reinsurance. Reinsurance placed with a reinsurer which does not have authorized status in the jurisdiction of the primary insurer.

compare: authorized reinsurance; see: nonadmitted reinsurance

unbundled services

Risk Management. Certain services, such as claims administration, claims adjusting and loss control are automatically included when an insurance policy is purchased. For large policyholders, some insurers will provide an insurance policy which excludes some or all of these services which are then either provided directly by the insured or contracted for from an outside vendor.

uncertainty

General.
see: risk

unconscionable contract

General. A contract in which one of the parties is placed in a position so one-sided, or a bargaining position so inferior as to be declared unenforceable.

see: contract

underground exclusion

Casualty. An exclusion under the 1973 ISO liability rating program which applied to businesses involved in operations like grading, paving, excavating, drilling, burrowing, filling, back-filling or pile driving. The exclusion denied coverage for property damage to underground wires, pipes, cables, sewers, etc., caused by such operations. The coverage could be purchased back for an additional premium.

see: blasting and explosion exclusion, collapse exclusion, XCU exclusions

underinsurance

Risk Management. The purchase of insurance with limits inadequate to meet policy coinsurance requirements, or the failure to purchase insurance in amounts sufficient to cover the amount of a large loss.

compare: noninsurance, overinsurance

underinsured motorist coverage

Automobile. Coverage which may be endorsed to an auto policy that pays damages for bodily injury to its own insured, in excess of the insurance of another motorist who is legally liable for such damages but who has inadequate liability coverage.

compare: uninsured motorists coverage

underlyer

Reinsurance.
see: underlying limits

underlying insurance

Insurer Operations.
see: primary insurance

underlying insurance policy

Insurer Operations. A policy providing coverage below an umbrella or excess policy in a layered program.

see: master insurance policy

Property. A policy required by mortgage holders which duplicates portions of the coverage provided by a master policy.

compare: single interest policy; see: certificate of insurance, layering, loss payable clause, master insurance policy

underlying limits

Insurer Operations. The limits of insurance or reinsurance in place before the next level or layer of insurance or reinsurance attaches.

syn: underlyer; see: layering

© 1991 NILS Publishing Company

underlying premium

Reinsurance.
see: subject premium

underwriter

Insurer Operations. An individual skilled in the process of selecting risks for an insurance company. The term originated in London at the Lloyd's Coffee House, where an individual wishing to provide insurance protection signed their name *below* a written description of the protection to be provided, and therefore became an underwriter.

see: Chartered Life Underwriter, Chartered Property and Casualty Underwriter, lay underwriter, lead underwriter, Lloyd's underwriter, risk appraiser, selection of risk, underwriting, underwriting department

Life. An individual who is a life insurance agent.
see: risk appraiser

underwriters fire patrol

Property. In the past, insurers had their own fire brigades or fire patrols which fought fires on their insured's properties. Insurers often competed for business on the basis of their fire patrols. A policyholder's property would display a fire mark to identify which patrol protected it. In some communities the insurers would join together to organize and maintain a single brigade or patrol, which would then protect the entire community.

syn: fire brigade; see: fire mark

Underwriters Laboratories, Inc. (UL)

Organizations. Members: A non-profit testing laboratory sponsored by the National Board of Fire Underwriters. *Objectives:* Testing various materials, products, and devices, such as appliances and electronic equipment to see whether they meet safety requirements. Those products certified by the Laboratories as meeting their standards are considered "UL Approved" and may bear a symbol indicating as much. *Founded:* 1894. *Headquarters:* Northbrook, IL.

Underwriters Laboratories of Canada (ULC)

Organizations. Members: Canadian insurance companies. *Objectives:* Maintains and operates laboratories and a certification service for examining, testing and classifying devices, construction materials and methods to determine their fire and safety characteristics. *Headquarters:* Scarborough, Ontario, Canada.

underwriting

Insurer Operations. The process of reviewing applications for coverage and the information contained therein. Those that are accepted must then be classified by the underwriter, according to the type and degree of risks, and the appropriate rates assigned for the exposure.

see: classification, mass underwriting, risk classification

underwriting cycle

Insurer Operations. An often-studied historical phenomenon in insurance, where rates and premiums (and therefore profits) rise and fall in sharp cycles, rather than growing in a smooth, slow pattern. The factors involved in creating the cycles are interest rate and stock market cycles; flow of excessive new capital into the insurance industry during profitable years; social and economic inflation; catastrophic losses and competition.

see: buyer's market, cash flow underwriting, hard market, soft market, tight market

underwriting department

Insurer Operations. The employees and operations of an insurance company that are responsible for evaluating applications submitted to the company and determining whether a policy should be issued, and if so, the terms, conditions and rates of that policy.

underwriting income

Insurer Operations. The gain or loss by an insurance company from the business of insurance. *Formula:* Underwriting Income = Insurer's Earned Premium, minus the sum of Incurred Losses and Loss Adjusting Costs, other Incurred Underwriting Expenses, and Policyholder Dividends.

compare: underwriting profit or loss; see: underwriting income per share

underwriting income per share

Insurer Operations. Statutory underwriting profit adjusted for the equity in the amount transferred to or from the unearned premium reserve divided by the number of common shares outstanding at year end.

underwriting margin

Insurer Operations. The difference between 100 percent and the sum of the loss and expense ratios in property/casualty underwriting. It may be either positive (indicating an underwriting profit) or negative (indicating an underwriting loss).

see: expense ratio, loss ratio

underwriting profit or loss

Insurer Operations. Money earned or lost by an insurer in its underwriting operations, as distinguished from money earned or lost in the investment of assets. *Formula:* Underwriting Profit or Loss = Earned Premiums less Losses, Loss Adjusting Expenses Incurred and other Underwriting Expenses Incurred.

compare: underwriting income; see: cash flow

© 1991 NILS Publishing Company

underwriting profit or loss — continued
underwriting, net underwriting loss, net underwriting profit

undesirable list
Insurer Operations.
see: prohibited list

unearned premium
Insurer Operations. The amount of premium remaining after deducting the earned premium from written premium. The amount of premium remaining on a policy for the remainder of its term.
compare: earned premium; see: premium

unearned premium reserve
Insurer Operations. The sum of all the premiums representing the unexpired portions of the policies or contracts which the insurer or reinsurer has on its "books" as of a specific point in time.
compare: earned premium; see: funding of reserves, premium, unearned premium

unearned reinsurance premium
Insurer Operations/Reinsurance. The amount of reinsurance premium remaining on a reinsurance contract for the period of time the policy must continue in force.
compare: earned reinsurance premium; see: premium

unemployment compensation
Employee Benefits. State and federal programs funded by payroll taxes which pay weekly income benefits to workers temporarily unemployed.

unemployment compensation disability insurance (UCD)
Health. State legislation imposing legal liability on all employers to provide weekly benefits to employees that sustain off-the-job accidents or sickness. If an employee receives workers' compensation benefits they are excluded from receiving the state-imposed disability benefits.
see: statutory disability income

unemployment insurance
Casualty. Federal legislation allows qualified nonprofit organizations to self-insure their unemployment compensation obligation. Some insurers provide coverage for this obligation on a stop loss or excess of loss basis.
see: unemployment compensation

unfair claims practice
Regulation. Deliberate action taken by an insurer to avoid paying claims to insureds. Many states have passed laws patterned after model legislation developed by the National Association of Insurance Commissioners (NAIC) in response to these actions requiring that insurance claims be handled fairly and that an open line of communication must exist between the insured and the insurer.
see: bad faith

unfair discrimination
Regulation. Offering a lower rate or broader coverage to one party, but not to another when both present the same underwriting considerations. This practice is prohibited by state insurance departments.
see: discrimination, equity, nondiscriminatory, rate discrimination, rate making, redlining

unfair labor practices
General. Tactics by an employer or a union which are legally prohibited.
see: Taft-Hartley Act

unfair trade practices
Insurer Operations/Regulation. With respect to insurers and their agents, the term "unfair trade practices" usually includes boycott, coercion, intimidation, dealing in bad faith, price-fixing and other noncompetitive actions, etc.
see: anti-coercion law, bad faith, unfair claims practice

unfired pressure vessel
Property.
see: pressure vessel

unfired vessels
Loss Control. Any vessel normally operated under pressure or vacuum, but not directly heated by fire or fuel gases. Electrically heated pressure vessels are classified as unfired vessels.

unfunded supplemental actuarial value
Employee Benefits. A pension plan's excess supplemental actuarial value over its actuarial asset value.

uniform bill-patient summary
Health. A written statement from a medical services provider documenting both the billing and medical information.

Uniform Commercial Code (UCC)
Regulation. A business code that has been adopted as statutory law in most states. The UCC governs commercial transactions (sale of goods, ownership) concerning personal property.

uniform forms
Insurer Operations. Insurance industry forms such

© 1991 NILS Publishing Company

as ACORD forms and ISO Policy forms developed by industry organizations for broad use.

see: ACORD forms, Insurance Services Office

uniform hospital discharge data set

Health. A recommended hospital discharge abstract, developed by the Uniform Hospital Abstract Subcommittee of the United States National Committee on Vital and Health Statistics.

Uniform Individual Accident and Sickness Policy Provisions Act

Health/Regulation. Model legislation developed by the National Association of Insurance Commissioners (NAIC) that has been adopted by all states. The Act requires certain provisions for all health insurance policies such as beneficiary changes, submission of proof of loss, policy reinstatement and a grace period.

uniform premium

Health/Life. A rating system used by life and health insurers which does not distinguish between applicants for such usual rating classifications as age, sex, or occupation. All applicants receive the same rates.

see: age discrimination, gender rating, occupational hazard

uniform provisions

Life. Life insurance policy provisions which are required by state law to be contained in all policies. Some latitude is usually allowed as to the exact wording, but the intent must be contained in the policy.

see: standard provisions

Health.

see: Uniform Individual Accident and Sickness Policy Provisions Act

uniform simultaneous death act

Life/Regulation. Legislation adopted in most states providing for the passage of benefits when an insured and the beneficiary of a life insurance policy both die simultaneously or within a short time of each other in a common accident where it cannot be determined who died first. In such cases, where such laws exist, it is presumed that the insured survived the beneficiary. Therefore, the policy benefits will be paid to a secondary beneficiary or, if not named, to the insured's estate.

see: second beneficiary

uniform straight bill of lading

Inland Marine/Ocean Marine.

see: waybill

unilateral contract

Insurer Operations. An insurance policy is a unilateral contract because only the insurer is involved in drafting the contract and making an enforceable offer.

The insured makes no promise, but rather pays a premium indicating acceptance of the offer.

see: contract of adhesion

uninsurable risk

Insurer Operations. A risk where there is no insurable interest. A risk where the potential for loss is so great it does not meet the definition of insurance. A risk where insurance is prohibited by public policy or is illegal.

syn: noninsurable risk; see: insurance, public policy, special risks, substandard risk

uninsured motorist law

Automobile. State legislation in most states requiring insurance companyies writing automobile insurance to offer all of their policyholders protection against uninsured motorists.

see: uninsured motorists coverage

uninsured motorists coverage

Automobile. Coverage that must be offered to insureds in many states and which, when added to an automobile policy, pays damages for bodily injury to its own insured for which an uninsured motorist is legally liable, but unable to pay.

syn: family protection endorsement; compare: unsatisfied judgment fund; see: underinsured motorist coverage, uninsured motorist law

union shop

Employee Benefits. A place of employment where the employer may hire non-union employees but after a short period of time, (usually thirty days), the new employees must become members of the union or be discharged.

unique impairment

Life. A life insurance underwriting term denoting substandard or uninsurable risks such as physical, moral or financial conditions that are below normal underwriting criteria.

unisex legislation

Regulation. Legislation which prohibits distinguishing between males and females in developing insurance rates or coverages. It requires that for a given class of insurance all individuals regardless of sex are to receive the same rates and coverages.

see: gender rating, sex discrimination, uniform premium

unit credit actuarial cost method

Employee Benefits. Calculating pension plan benefits, based on the accumulation of "benefit units." (Benefit units are themselves based on such things as salary and service years.) Under this method a plan's normal cost for a year is based on the sum of 1) the

© 1991 NILS Publishing Company

unit credit actuarial cost method — continued
present value of units accumulated by plan participants during the current year, and 2) the present value of accrued benefits credited to participants for service prior to the present year.

syn: accrued benefit cost method, accumulated benefit cost method; see: actuarial cost method

United States Government Life Insurance (USGLI)

Life.
see: National Service Life Insurance

United States Longshoremen's and Harbor Workers' Act of 1927 (USL & H)

Workers' Compensation.
see: Longshoremen's and Harbor Workers' Compensation Act

universal life insurance

Life. A form of life insurance in which the policyholder may periodically change the death benefit and modify the amount or timing of premium payments. The insurance company policy expenses and other charges are specifically disclosed to the policyholder and are deducted from the premium. The balance of the premium is used to pay mortality charges, and any remaining funds are credited to the policy and earn interest based on interest rates that usually are tied to U.S. Treasury issues or money market rates.

syn: flexible premium adjustable life insurance; compare: universal variable life insurance; see: accumulation value, additional deposit privilege, guideline premium, interest free loan, level death benefit option, statement of policy information, unscheduled premium payments

universal mercantile system

Property. A rating system for property insurance risks that is no longer in wide use. It has been replaced by a new system developed by the Insurance Services Office (ISO).

universal variable life insurance

Life. A form of life insurance that combines the features of universal life insurance and variable life insurance. Under this program, the policyholder can direct the insurer as to which investment vehicle excess premiums and interest are to be invested. These investment vehicles are separate accounts and may include equities, bonds, or real estate. This policy is considered a replacement for standard universal life insurance which ties investment income to U.S. Treasury issues and money market rates.

compare: universal life insurance

University Risk Management and Insurance Association (URMIA)

Organizations. Members: Colleges and universities with insurance and risk management offices. *Objectives:* Promote the exchange of ideas and information about sound insurance and risk management. *Founded:* 1966. *Headquarters:* Birmingham, AL.

unlevel commission

Agency/Insurer Operations. A commission system where agent commissions are higher the first year an insurance policy is written, and then reduced on anniversary or renewal billings. Designed to encourage the development of new business, this system has been criticized as encouraging unneeded replacement policies, particularly to the elderly with Medigap policies.

syn: graded commission; compare: level commission; see: agent's commission, first-year commission, renewal commission

unlimited reporting period

Casualty.
see: maxi tail

unlimited tail

Casualty.
see: maxi tail

unoccupied

Property. A building that is furnished, but in which nobody resides. Some property insurance policies suspend coverage if a building is unoccupied beyond a specific period of time, usually 60 or 90 days.

compare: vacant; see: vacancy or unoccupancy permit

unreported claims

Insurer Operations. A claim that has occurred, but has not yet been reported to the insurer. Insurers account for such claims by establishing an incurred but not reported (IBNR) reserve.

see: incurred but not reported

unsatisfied judgment fund (UJF)

Automobile. Funds established in some states to reimburse those injured in auto accidents, who have been unable to collect judgments against the individuals responsible for their losses and injuries.

compare: uninsured motorists coverage

unscheduled premium payments

Life. A universal life insurance policy provision that allows a policyholder to make additional, unscheduled premium payments at any time in order to build equity in the policy investment feature.

see: universal life insurance

338

© 1991 NILS Publishing Company

unscheduled property floater

Inland Marine. An inland marine policy that provides blanket coverage on all property of a specified classification, (such as "household furnishings" or "tourist luggage"), usually on an "all-risks" basis.

compare: **scheduled coverage**

unsecured bond

Financial Planning.
see: **debenture**

upper explosive level (UEL)

Loss Control.
see: **flammable limits**

uprising

Property. An insurrection, revolt or rebellion. Losses resulting from such an event are often excluded from property insurance policies.

see: **civil commotion, riot**

up-stream merger

Risk Management. A merger of a subsidiary corporation into its parent.

see: **merger**

Urban Development Act of 1970

Crime. An act passed by Congress in 1970 that established the Federal Crime Insurance Program, to provide coverage for business owners and residents located in high crime areas. The program is administered by private insurers under the direction of the Federal Insurance Administration.

see: **federal crime insurance program**

use and occupancy insurance (U & O)

Property. A term used to describe loss of income coverage under a boiler and machinery policy; also an obsolete term for business income insurance. Use and occupancy insurance covers an insured business for loss of use of equipment caused by an insured peril.

see: **business income coverage form**

use limitation

Aviation. An aircraft policy exclusion that excludes coverage if the aircraft is used for a purposes other than those indicated in the policy's purpose of use classification.

see: **business and pleasure, fixed base operators, flying clubs, general aviation, industrial aid operators**

usual, customary and reasonable fees (UCR)

Health. The prevailing fees charged by a physician for a particular procedure. It is based on fees charged by physicians with similar training and experience within a specific geographical area.

see: **schedule**

utilization review

Health. A review of the appropriateness and quality of care provided by a hospital to its patients.

utmost good faith

Insurer Operations/Reinsurance. The insurance contract is a personal contract between an insurer and insured where each party must be able to rely on the other for valid critical information.

syn: **uberrimae fidei**; see: **fiduciary**

© 1991 NILS Publishing Company

vacancy or unoccupancy permit

Property. A permit obtained by an insured from a fire underwriter to maintain coverage on a building that has been vacant or unoccupied beyond the limitation period (usually 90 days) specified in a policy. A charge is made if the vacant or unoccupied structure is in an unprotected area; usually, the permit is granted free of charge when the structure is in an area with satisfactory fire protection.

compare: change in occupancy or use; see: occupancy, unoccupied, vacant, "while" clauses

vacant

Property. A building in which no people have been living or working and no contents have been stored for at least the past 60 or 90 days. The standard fire policy prohibits vacancy after a certain amount of time.

compare: unoccupied; see: occupancy, vacancy or unoccupancy permit

validation period

Life. The length of time it takes a life insurer to amortize the expense of a new life insurance policy. Because expenses such as commissions, file setup, and medical examinations create higher first-year expenses than those for future years, these costs must be amortized over several years.

valid contract

General. An oral or written contract that complies with state laws and is therefore enforceable.

see: contract

valuable papers and records insurance

Inland Marine. An inland marine policy covering such property as blueprints, manuscripts, maps, historical documents, or everyday business records on an "all-risks" basis.

valuation

General. The act of assessing the value or worth of an article, usually by appraisal.

see: appraised value

Insurer Operations. The determination of insurance company claims reserves needed to pay future claims.

see: actuarial valuation

Property. The determination of property values to be insured under a property policy.

see: actual cash value, agreed value, appraised value, business interruption value, depreciated value, economic value, fair market value, functional replacement cost, insurance to value, market value, replacement cost, reproduction cost, tax-appraised value, valuation of loss, valuation of potential property loss

Life. The determination of a life insurance company's policy reserve.

see: asset share value, tabular value reserve method, valuation premium

Regulation.

see: valuation of assets

valuation method

Insurer Operations. The procedure used by claims adjusters in determining that a loss has occurred and in establishing the economic value of the loss. It involves a step-by-step procedure, starting with the filing of a claims, contact with the claimant, review of policy coverages, determination of value, and finally, payment of the claim.

see: valuation of loss

valuation of assets

Regulation. The assets of an insurance company are

341

© 1991 NILS Publishing Company

valuation of assets — continued
valued based upon rules promulgated by state insurance departments. These rules are based on guidelines developed by the National Association of Insurance Commissioners' Committee on Valuation of Securities. Valuation criteria dictate that an insurer's real estate is valued at book value, its common stock is valued at current market value, its quality bonds at amortized value, preferred stock at original cost and common stock at year-end price.

see : mandatory securities valuation reserve

valuation of loss
Insurer Operations. The procedure to be followed by an insured in order to establish the value of a property loss. Procedures include the filing of a claim, and a proof of loss supported by receipts, appraisals or other evidence of an asset's worth. The valuation of some losses requires subjective interpretation, as they involve partial damage or loss of numerous items for which valuation support is lacking or otherwise unavailable.

see: valuation method

valuation of potential property loss
Risk Management. A technique used in risk management involving the identification and valuation of property loss exposures. The dollar value assigned to each risk can be based on replacement cost; actual cash value (physical depreciation considered); original cost; depreciated value; market value; or tax appraised value – depending on its current use and the organization's financial structure. Once loss exposures are identified and valued, funding for a potential loss, including transfer of risk, can be developed.

see: actual cash value, depreciated value, fair market value, functional replacement cost, market value, replacement cost, reproduction cost, tax-appraised value, valuation, valuation method

valuation premium
Life. A rate for a life insurance policy which is based on the reserves an insurer must maintain to meet state insurance department standards. The reserves on a class of policies are valued so that there will be sufficient assets to pay all claims in full, and then a rate for the policies is developed based upon this value. Some insurers may deviate from the valuation premium rate based upon favorable experience or updated mortality tables. If this is done, an insurer must establish a deficiency reserve in the event the rate is inadequate.

see: deficiency reserve

valuation reserve
General. An accounting reserve established to anticipate a decrease in an asset's value; e.g., a depreciation reserve which would protect an insurer against wide swings in the price of securities.

see: reserve

value
General. A consideration sufficient to support a contract, a commitment to extend credit, or a past debt.

valued bill of lading
Ocean Marine. A bill of lading issued by the carrier, indicating the amount which the shipper has declared as the value of merchandise. The carrier will be held liable for the amount indicated if the carrier is found responsible for loss or damage to the shipment.

syn: ad valorem bill of lading; see: bill of lading

valued business interruption insurance
Property. Covers a stated amount of lost earnings for each day the insured incurs loss due to interruption of its business due to an insured peril.

compare: maximum period of indemnity, monthly limit of indemnity; see: business income coverage form

valued clause
Automobile/Property. A provision in some automobile and property insurance policies stating the value of each insured item.

see: stated amount

valued policy
Life. An insurance policy which pays a specified amount which is not directly related to the extent of loss. A life insurance policy is a valued policy, because it does not restore an insured to the same financial position as before the loss.

compare: indemnity agreement
Automobile/Property. An insurance policy which pays a specified amount for a covered item in the event of a total loss.

compare: nonvalued policy; see: limit of liability, stated amount

valued policy law
Regulation. A regulation adopted in some states to discourage insurers from selling more insurance than needed on a property. It requires that in the event of a total loss, all insurers must pay the face amount of the policy, regardless of the traditional role of indemnity – to restore on indemnitee to his or her original position – unless fraud or arson is involved.

see: overinsurance

value reporting form
Property.
see: reporting form

© 1991 NILS Publishing Company

values

Life. Shorthand for "nonforfeiture values" among life insurers.

vandalism

Property. A coverage included with malicious mischief insurance. It is the willful or malicious destruction or defacement of another's property.

see: vandalism and malicious mischief coverage

vandalism and malicious mischief coverage (V&MM)

Property. Insurance coverage which protects against loss due to vandalism and malicious mischief which is usually provided by an endorsement to a fire insurance policy. Basic homeowner's and commercial property insurance forms now include this coverage automatically.

see: malicious mischief, vandalism

vanishing premium

Life. A life insurance policy with large premium payments in its initial years which are used to quickly build up its cash value. After an adequate cash value is accumulated, remaining premium payments are made by borrowing against the policy's cash value.

syn: premium offset

variable

Risk Management. An actuarial term for a quantity that may assume any one of a set of values.

variable annuity

Life. An annuity where the accumulation and benefits are expressed as "benefit units" or "accumulation units," rather than in dollar amounts. Unit values may be based on a number of different factors, such as a specific portfolio of stocks, or the Consumer Price Index. When benefit payments begin, the accumulated units are converted into a fixed number of units upon which the monthly benefits will be based.

see: cost-of-living variable annuity plan, equity variable annuity plan, insured variable annuity plan

variable life insurance

Life. Life insurance with benefits tied to the return of a specific portfolio of securities. Often, the policyholder may select from several portfolios which have different investment objectives. The policy offers a fixed premium and a minimum death benefit. The better return the investments earn, the higher the benefit or surrender value of the policy.

compare: fixed annuity, universal life insurance, universal variable life insurance; see: indexed life insurance

variable premium life insurance

Life. A life insurance policy which allows the policyholder to vary the premium payments subject to certain prescribed limitations. The policy benefits and cash value accumulation will vary according to the size of the premium payments made. The most common form of variable premium life insurances is the universal life insurance policy.

compare: variable life insurance; see: universal life insurance, universal variable life insurance

variable rate mortgage

Financial Planning. A mortgage on which the interest rate charged by the lender may be adjusted in accordance with a stipulated cost-of-funds index (i.e., New York prime).

syn: adjustable rate mortgage

vault

Crime. A fortified room or compartment used for the safekeeping of valuable property (e.g., money, jewelry, valuable papers, etc.).

see: safe

vendee

General. An individual who buys property.

compare: vendor

vendor

General. An individual who sells property.

compare: vendee

vendor's endorsement

Casualty. An endorsement that extends a commercial general liability policy to cover designated vendors as additional insureds with respect to bodily injury or property damage arising out of the named insured's products.

venture

Ocean Marine. An undertaking, such as the voyage of a vessel.

see: adventure, common venture

verdict

General. A jury's finding of fact.

see: directed verdict

vertical merger

Risk Management. A merger between a firm and one of its major suppliers or customers.

see: merger

vested benefit

Employee Benefits. A benefit that has been fully credited to an employee without further requirements, including continued employment.

see: vesting

© 1991 NILS Publishing Company

vested commissions

Agency/Insurer Operations. Commissions due an insurance agent on renewal policies regardless of the agent's continued employment by the insurer or agency writing the business.

vesting

Employee Benefits. A pension plan participant's right to receive benefits from employer contributions to a plan even if the participant is no longer an employee of that employer. All employee contributions made to a plan are fully vested at the time they are made. Employer contributions are vested according to a schedule contained in the plan.

see: conditional vesting, deferred vesting, immediate vesting, vested benefit, vesting schedules

vesting schedules

Employee Benefits. The Tax Reform Act of 1986 established two minimum vesting schedules for pension plans: 1) One hundred percent vesting after a plan participant has completed five years of service, or 2) Twenty percent vesting after completing three years of service and 20 percent additional vesting each year thereafter with 100 percent vesting achieved within seven years.

see: ten year vesting, vested benefit, vesting

Veterans Administration (VA)

Organizations. A federal agency which administers various programs for individuals who served in the United States armed forces. These programs include life and health insurance as well as mortgage loans, educational loans and grants, and pension benefits.

see: Veterans Administration Hospital, Veterans Group Life Insurance

Veterans Administration Hospital

Health. A hospital operated by the Veterans Administration for individuals who served in the armed forces. Most health insurance policies exclude expenses in VA hospitals because they are provided without cost.

see: Veterans Administration

Veterans Group Life Insurance (VGLI)

Life. Life insurance offered to veterans that were covered by a Servicemen's Group Life Insurance policy during active duty. The coverage is a five-year nonrenewable term policy that can be converted to individual permanent life issued through an insurance company participating in the veterans program.

see: Servicemen's Group Life Insurance, Veterans Administration

veterinarian professional liability insurance

Casualty. Insurance that protects veterinarians from claims alleging injury resulting from malpractice, error or mistake in rendering or failure to render professional services.

see: pet insurance, pet salon liability coverage

vicarious liability

Casualty.
see: contingent liability

victim compensation

General. Legislation passed in some states which provides a fund to pay victims of certain types of crimes for their loss and/or suffering.

vision care insurance

Health. Health insurance coverage for eye examinations and eyeglass or contact lens prescriptions.

vis major

General. A Latin legal term which means "overpowering" force. It is used in reference to an accident that has occurred where no one is responsible.

see: act of God

void

General. A legal term signifying that a contract has no legal force or effect. Such a contract is treated as if it never existed.

see: public policy, unconscionable contract

voidable

General. A legal term for a contract that can be annulled at the option of one or more of its parties.

voidable preferences

General. A transfer of property that enables a creditor to obtain a greater percentage of debt than other creditors.

volcanic action

General. A violent explosion in a vent in the earth's crust from which molten or hot rock and steam issue. Volcanic action is an excluded peril from most property policies but coverage is included with earthquake insurance.

see: earthquake

voluntary compensation endorsement

Workers' Compensation. An endorsement to a workers' compensation policy which provides statutory coverage for employees who do not fall under a state's workers' compensation act, such as farm workers. This endorsement provides that the insurer will pay statutory benefits to the insured person in exchange for the injured worker releasing the employer and the insurer from further liability. If the employee does not sign the release, any further compensation under the endorsement ceases.

© 1991 NILS Publishing Company

voluntary employee contribution plan

Employee Benefits. A pension plan where participants may elect to make regular contributions to the plan by payroll deductions. Under most qualified plans, such employee contributions would be tax-deferred.

see: qualified plan

voluntary insurance

General. Insurance coverage that is not required to be purchased by law or in compliance with directives of a governmental agency and is available from a voluntary insurer.

compare: compulsory insurance

voluntary insurer

Insurer Operations. An insurer offering voluntary insurance, as opposed to social insurance (i.e., Social Security, unemployment compensation). Voluntary insurers include private insurers, cooperatives, governmental agencies and self-insurers who can offer a wide spectrum of insurance coverages.

voluntary plan termination

Employee Benefits. Ending a pension plan at the election of an employer or sponsor. The employer has the unilateral right to change or terminate a pension plan at any time. However, the termination must meet requirements set out by the Employee Retirement Income Security Act of 1974 (ERISA). Assets must be distributed to the participants according to federal guidelines.

see: Employee Retirement Income Security Act of 1974

voluntary reserve

Insurer Operations. A reserve established by an insurer from its policyholders surplus which is not required by statute. This reserve is often used for the payment of future policyholder dividends, or to indicate financial strength. Generally, such reserves will appear as a liability on the insurer's financial statement, but are not deductible for tax purposes.

compare: statutory reserve; see: balance sheet reserves, policy reserve

volunteer public safety officers

General. Members of volunteer fire departments, rescue squads or ambulance corps.

voting trust

General. A trust created by an agreement among shareholders to transfer legal title to their voting stock to a party (trustee) who is authorized to vote the stock as a unit.

compare: proxy

voyage

Ocean Marine. A vessel's complete journey, from home port through all of its ports-of-call back to home port. The journey of a cargo consignment, from its origin to the warehouse of its final destination.

see: venture, voyage charter, voyage clause

voyage charter

Ocean Marine. The hiring of a ship with the vessel owner's crew managing and navigating the vessel, but its cargo capacity taken by the hirer for a single voyage to move a shipload of cargo from one port to another.

compare: bareboat charter; see: charter party

voyage clause

Ocean Marine. A clause in some ocean marine policies which limits the period of coverage to the time it takes for a voyage. A voyage can be comprised of a single trip or a number of trips grouped together.

see: voyage charter

© 1991 NILS Publishing Company

wage index

Employee Benefits.
see: Social Security Wage Index

wage loss

Workers' Compensation. A workers' compensation concept initiated by Florida in 1979, which ties employee recoveries in permanent and partial disability claims to their actual economic loss, rather than to projections of such loss.

compare: reduced earnings

wages, maintenance and cure

Ocean Marine. An admiralty law provision indicating the care that an injured seaman is to receive. Wages are to continue during the seaman's injury or illness up to the time a voyage ends. For vessels operating year round and on inland waterways, wages are not to be paid beyond one year, the end of a contract or the period of illness – whichever is shortest. A lawsuit must be brought by the seaman to recover earnings beyond this period of time. The term "maintenance" means providing rehabilitation and a proper working environment to the seaman; while "cure" refers to medical treatment for injury from accident or illness, usually free of charge.

see: cure, Jones Act, maintenance, seaman's remedies

waiting period

Health. Under a disability policy, the period of time between the beginning of a policyholder's disability and the beginning of the policy's benefits.

syn: elimination period

Property. Under a boiler and machinery policy's loss of use coverage, the waiting period is a form of deductible and is usually specified in time (hours or days) before which the policy will not respond to a loss.

waiver

General. The intentional act of relinquishing a known right, claim or privilege.

syn: doctrine of waiver; Fr: renonciation; Gr: Verzicht; Sp: renuncia

Health/Life. A policy rider excluding coverage for specified disabilities or injuries that normally would be covered by the policy.

Insurer Operations. The relinquishing of an insurance policy's written terms or conditions by the actions or statements of an insurer's agent or employee upon which the insured relied.

see: acquiescence, estoppel, laches

waiver of inventory clause

Property. A clause found in many property insurance policies, which waives the requirement to provide an inventory of undamaged property when the loss is less than a specified amount (usually $10,000), or less than five percent of the amount insured.

waiver of premium

Health/Life. A provision found in some life insurance policies which forgives premium payments when the insured is disabled for more than six months.

waiver of restoration premium

Insurer Operations. A provision found primarily in policies issued in the London Market which provides for reinstatement of the face amount of the policy limits without payment of an additional premium, in the event a claim is paid.

Surety. A provision contained in a bond which automatically reinstates full coverage after payment of a loss without the payment of an additional premium.

© 1991 NILS Publishing Company

waiver of subrogation rights clause
Property/Casualty. An endorsement issued by an insurer that waives its right of subrogation against a third party. It is usually requested by an insured in conjunction with a lease.

wanton disregard
General. A legal term for the overwhelming lack of care for the rights or well-being of another party. In a negligence case, such lack of care is evidence of gross negligence.
see: degree of care, gross negligence

war clause
Health/Life. A clause included in life insurance policies which excludes coverage for death or injury caused by war. Some policies contain an absolute war exclusion applying to any insured, while others apply only to members of the armed forces while serving in a war zone.
see: military service exclusion, war risk accident insurance

war damage insurance corporation
Insurer Operations. A reinsurance program developed by the U.S. Government during World War II to cover private property in the United States from war damage.

warehouseman
Casualty/Surety. A person in the business of storing the goods of others for compensation.
see: warehousemen's bond, warehousemen's legal liability coverage

warehousemen's bond
Surety. A surety bond provided by a warehouseman that guarantees that goods stored in a warehouse will be delivered upon presentation of a receipt.
see: bond

warehousemen's legal liability coverage
Casualty. Coverage for a warehouseman or bailee which covers liability imposed by law for loss, destruction or damage to property contained in the insured's warehouse. A major exclusion to this coverage is a loss caused directly or indirectly by fire, which must be covered separately.
see: care, custody or control

warehouse receipt
Inland Marine. A document issued to a bailee by a warehouseman for goods stored in the warehouse. Regulated by the Uniform Commercial Code, such receipts have a degree of negotiability.

warehouse-to-warehouse coverage
Inland Marine/Ocean Marine. A clause that can be added to inland and ocean marine policies extending the policy to cover property in transit – goods from the shipper's warehouse to the consignee's warehouse.
see: cargo insurance, processing endorsement

warrant
Financial Planning. An option to buy a security, usually a common stock, at a set price (the exercise price) on an established future date. A warrant establishes no claim on either the equity or the profits of a company.
see: option

warranted no known or reported losses
Insurer Operations. A warranty provided to an insurance company as an inducement to back-date the effective date of coverage. It is provided by the insured so that unknown claims which surface after the effective date will be honored by the insurer.
see: antedate

warranties of insured
Insurer Operations. 1) Statements or promises made by the applicant when applying for insurance which the insured guarantees to be as stated and which, if false, will entitle the insurer to avoid the contract of insurance. This is termed an affirmative warranty. 2) A promise by an insured that certain conditions will be carried out during the term of the policy such as maintaining fire sprinklers or burglar alarms in working order. This is termed a promissory warranty.
see: affirmative warranty, implied warranty, representation

warranty
General. A statement to the insurer by the insured upon which the validity of the insurance policy depends. The insurance contract is not binding unless the warranty statement is literally true. *Example:* The insured states that a watchperson will make hourly rounds when the plant is closed.
see: express warranty, implied warranty

warranty company
Property.
see: warranty fire

warranty deed
Title. A deed that guarantees a freehold in writing by the grantor and the grantor's heirs or successors.
see: deed

warranty fire
Property. A type of insurance used for substandard and accommodation fire risks, where there is a capacity problem. Coverage is divided on a pro rata basis with a licensed domestic insurer and the London Market. The domestic company issues an insurance policy which contains all the terms and conditions of coverage and is known as a "warranty company." The

© 1991 NILS Publishing Company

London Market insurers agree to follow the terms and conditions of the warranty company.

warranty of authority

Agency/Insurer Operations. The implied warranty that an agent actually possesses the authority the agent purports to possess.

see: expressed authority, implied authority

war risk accident insurance

Health. Coverage for accidental death, dismemberment or disability for civilians going into areas of the world where there is conflict or risk of war.

war risks insurance

Ocean Marine. Coverage on ships or cargo against loss or damage by enemy action and against damages sustained in fighting such an action. The perils of war are excluded from most policies.

Warsaw Convention

Aviation. An international agreement, originally ratified by 42 countries in 1929, which defines the liabilities of airlines operating between countries, as well as over international waters. Since its initial ratification, many other countries have signed the agreement. The Warsaw limitations do not apply if it can be proven an accident was caused by "willful misconduct" on the part of the airline or its crew.

watchman warranty clause

Crime/Property.
see: watchperson warranty clause

watchperson

Loss Control. An individual retained by an organization to care for and have custody of property inside the organization's premises.

see: watchperson warranty clause

watchperson warranty clause

Crime/Property. A warranty clause which provides a rate credit on burglary and fire policies when the insured agrees to maintain a watchperson on duty at the insured premises.

syn: watchman warranty clause

watercraft endorsement

Casualty. An endorsement to a homeowner's or commercial general liability policy, that covers watercraft excluded by the watercraft exclusion.

see: watercraft exclusion

watercraft exclusion

Casualty. An exclusion found in homeowners and commercial liability policies which excludes coverage for watercraft which exceed a certain size (usually 26 feet or 50 horsepower).

see: watercraft endorsement

watercraft nonowned coverage

Casualty.
see: nonowned watercraft liability

water damage clause

Property. Coverage for the accidental discharge or overflow of water or steam from within a plumbing, heating, or air-conditioning system or domestic appliance, but only when such discharge or overflow is the direct result of breaking or cracking of any pipes, fittings, parts, or fixtures forming a part of such system or appliance. The cost of tearing out and replacing any part of the covered building(s) to make repairs to the system is also covered.

compare: sprinkler leakage coverage

water damage legal liability

Casualty/Property. A liability coverage which protects the insured from damage to rented or loaned premises resulting from leakage or overflow of water caused by the insured's negligence.

compare: sprinkler leakage legal liability insurance

watered stock

Risk Management. Corporate stock that has been reduced in value by the issuance of par value shares for less than their par value.

see: bonus shares

water exclusion clause

Property. A clause found in most property insurance policies, excluding loss resulting from flood, backup of sewers or drains, and underground water.

water pollution liability

Ocean Marine. A shipowner's obligation for any water pollution caused by its discharges of oil or other polluting or hazardous substances. The shipowner is responsible for cleanup, or paying for the cleanup.

see: Water Quality Improvement Act of 1970, Water Quality Insurance Syndicate

Water Quality Improvement Act of 1970

Ocean Marine/Regulation. Federal legislation adopted in 1970 that requires the owners of vessels to clean up or cover the cost of cleanup of waters polluted by discharges from their vessels.

see: water pollution liability, Water Quality Insurance Syndicate

Water Quality Insurance Syndicate

Ocean Marine. A marine syndicate established in 1971 to insure shipowners from liability for water pollution.

see: water pollution liability, Water Quality Improvement Act of 1970

© 1991 NILS Publishing Company

water resource insurance

Property. A form of loss of earnings coverage, designed for small hydroelectric power generating plants to reimburse insured plants in the event that daily water flow at the site is reduced by such occurrences as drought or natural disturbances.

see: rain insurance

wave damage insurance

Property. Insurance for property loss due to the perils of high waves or overflow from tides.

wave wash

Property. Property damage caused by the action of large waves.

see: wave damage insurance

waybill

Inland Marine/Ocean Marine. A bill of lading usually issued by airlines and trucking companies, indicating the merchandise to be transported, as well as shipping instructions.

see: air waybill, bill of lading, master air waybill

wear and tear exclusion

Inland Marine/Property. An exclusion contained in most property insurance policies, denying coverage for losses resulting from reduction in the value of property due to normal usage or operation.

see: deterioration

weather insurance

Property. Insurance which indemnifies the sponsor of an outside event, a resort operator or a manufacturer of a product that depends on a specific weather condition (rain, snow, freeze, sun) for sales. Coverage provided includes cancellation of outdoor concerts, carnivals, parades, sports events, skiing or reduced sales of certain products or services.

compare: entertainment insurance; see: rain insurance

wedding presents floater

Inland Marine. A property floater policy providing "all-risks" coverage on wedding presents before and after the wedding, but usually not for more than 90 days after the date of the wedding.

weekly compensation

Workers' Compensation.

see: average weekly benefits

weekly premium insurance

Life.

see: industrial life insurance

weight of ice, snow or sleet insurance

Property. Coverage for buildings and their contents from damage directly attributed to the weight of ice, snow or sleet on the structure.

welding screen

Loss Control. A portable screen made of fire resistant materials designed to control flying welding or metal cutting sparks and shield non-welders from the welding glare.

Welfare and Pension Plans Disclosure Act

Regulation. Federal legislation passed in 1958 which requires pension plan administrators to file a plan description with the Labor Department for all plans covering 25 or more participants. A description must be made available to plan participants and must include a benefit schedule; type of administration, and a copy of plan documents. An annual financial statement must be included for plans with more than 100 participants.

see: employee benefit plan, Employee Retirement Income Security Act of 1974

wet marine insurance

Ocean Marine. Ocean marine insurance which covers ships and their cargos.

see: ocean marine insurance

wet pipe sprinkler system

Loss Control. An automatic sprinkler system where all piping is filled with water under pressure and released by a fusible mechanism in the sprinkler head.

compare: dry pipe automatic sprinkler system; see: automatic sprinkler system

wharfingers liability insurance

Casualty. Special coverage for owners and operators of landings or wharves. The contract combines bailee protection and liability for damage to hulls and cargo in the custody of the wharf operator, with coverage against third party liability arising from damage by property in the custody of the wharf operator.

see: care, custody or control

what if

Surety.

see: as if

"while" clauses

Property. Coverage suspension provisions found in older property insurance policies such as "while" the property is vacant.

whole dollar premium

Insurer Operations. Rounding off of an insurance policy's premium to a whole dollar amount. Premium calculations of 50 cents or less are dropped, while premium calculations of 51 cents or more are rounded up to the next dollar.

see: premium

350

© 1991 NILS Publishing Company

whole life insurance

Life. Life insurance issued for the life of the insured (so long as premiums are paid), where the face value of the policy is payable to the beneficiary at the death of the insured. In most cases, no physical exam is required.

compare: endowment policy, term life insurance; see: limited payment life insurance, ordinary life insurance, permanent life insurance

wholesale group insurance

Life/Health.

see: franchise insurance

will

Financial Planning. A formal document by which a person provides for the disposition of their property ("estate"), to take effect upon their death. A formal document that appoints an executor to administer an estate.

see: intestate

willful injury

General.

see: intentional injury

windstorm

Property. A wind of velocity sufficient to damage buildings and structures. Areas subject to hurricanes and tornadoes present the greatest windstorm loss potential.

see: windstorm insurance; Fr: tempête; Gr: Sturm; Sp: vientos tempestuosos

windstorm insurance

Property. Coverage under a property policy for loss caused by tornadoes, hurricanes and high winds. Historically, this coverage has been part of the extended coverage endorsement, but now is frequently included as part of the basic coverages. In areas where windstorms are common (e.g., along the Gulf of Mexico, in the southwest U.S., and in the Great Plains states) such coverage may be excluded and only available for an additional premium.

Wisconsin Life Fund

Life. A unique system of life insurance, available only to residents of Wisconsin.

with average

Ocean Marine. Coverage which can be added to an ocean marine policy that is free from particular average conditions. Partial loss or damage to the property insured by the basic named perils is recoverable in full.

compare: with average if amounting to 3 percent; see: average

with average if amounting to 3 percent

Ocean Marine. Coverage which can be added to an ocean marine policy that, in addition to being free from particular average conditions, covers partial losses caused by the basic perils named in the policy, provided that the amount of the partial loss is equal to or exceeds 3 percent of the insured value of the property coverage.

compare: with average; see: average

without prejudice

General. Without detriment to the existing rights of the parties.

see: dismissal

with prejudice

General. With detriment to the rights of one or more parties to a legal proceeding.

see: dismissal

Women Leaders Round Table (WLRT)

Organizations. Members: Women life insurance agents who sell a specified amount of life insurance. *Objectives:* Recognizes women life insurance agents who meet specified annual premium volume requirements. *Headquarters:* Washington, D.C.

see: National Association of Life Underwriters

Women Life Underwriters Confederation (WLUC)

Organizations. Members: Life and health underwriters. *Objectives:* Developing educational opportunities; providing peer support and sales motivational techniques. *Founded:* 1987. *Headquarters:* Reston, VA.

work and materials clause

Property. A provision contained in many property insurance policies which allows an insured to maintain on the premises the work and materials usual to the operation of the insured's business. This clause prevents the policy from being voided under an increased hazard provision.

see: increased hazard

workers' compensation catastrophe policy

Reinsurance. A catastrophe excess of loss reinsurance policy purchased by a primary insurer to cover workers' compensation claims in excess of a retained limit.

see: excess of loss reinsurance

workers' compensation excess insurance

Workers' Compensation.

see: aggregate excess workers' compensation insurance, specific excess workers' compensation insurance

workers' compensation insurance (WC)

Workers' Compensation. Insurance which covers an

© 1991 NILS Publishing Company

WC — continued
employer's responsibilities for injuries, disability or death to persons in their employment, as prescribed by state workers' compensation law and other statutes. Historically, workers' compensation laws were intended to provide a mechanism by which workers could obtain medical treatment for injuries suffered while on the job site, and by which employers could know with certainty that by providing these benefits, their liability would be limited. Recently, however, workers have been successful in eroding this concept and bringing court suits against employers.

syn: coverage A; compare: nonoccupational policy; see: common law defense, deductible workers' compensation plans, dual capacity doctrine, employer's liability coverage, exclusive remedy, Federal Employees' Compensation Act, Federal Employers Liability Act, second injury fund; Fr: accidents du travail; Gr: Arbeitsunfallversicherung; Sp: compensación obrera o riesgos profesionales

workers' compensation law

Workers' Compensation. Legislation found in all states which requires employers to pay benefits to employees injured or who became ill during the course and scope of employment. Benefits are scheduled in the legislation and the legislation provides that an employee may not sue the employer for most common law damages.

compare: disability benefit law; see: domestic, workers' compensation insurance

working capital

Surety. Total current assets less total current liabilities. Working capital (or net current assets) includes such current assets as cash and government securities, receivables, and inventories, minus such current liabilities as accounts payable, current taxes, dividends payable, short-term bank notes, and the portion of long-term debt that comes due over the next 12 months.

syn: net current assets; see: internal financing

working cover

Reinsurance. An excess of loss reinsurance contract written directly over a policy with a low retention causing frequent penetration of limits.

syn: working layer; see: excess of loss reinsurance

working layer

Reinsurance.
see: working cover

work program clause

Reinsurance/Surety. A clause found in contractors bond reinsurance policies which provides that the primary carrier's retention is a specified level of an insured contractor's total volume of work, rather than an individual contract or bond amount.

world insurance

International. The scope and importance of insurance activities throughout the world. Insurance providing coverage worldwide.

Worldwide Assurance for Employees of Public Agencies (WAEPA)

Organizations. Members: Federal civilian employees. *Objectives:* Providing group life, accidental death and dismemberment and dependent group life insurance coverage to the federal civilian employees at reasonable costs. *Founded:* 1943. *Headquarters:* Falls Church, VA.

worldwide coverage

Casualty. An endorsement to liability policies that extends the policy territory to anywhere in the world. Some policies require that a suit against the insured must be brought in the United States or Canada.

see: geographical limitation

wrap-up

Casualty/Workers' Compensation. Insurance on large construction projects arranged by the owner or general contractor in such a way that all interests involved (such as the owner, general contractor, subcontractors, architect, engineer, and surveyors) are combined and insured under one policy with a single insurer. Occasionally, the wrap-up will only include workers' compensation insurance; generally, it includes both liability and workers' compensation insurance.

writ

General. A court order.
see: summons

write

Insurer Operations.
see: underwriting

written business

Insurer Operations. Insurance on which an application has been filed but for which a policy has not yet been delivered and/or the first premium has not yet been paid.

compare: delivered business, examined business, issued business, not taken, paid business, placed business

written premiums

Insurer Operations. The aggregate amount of premiums written by an insurer during a specified period of time, including both earned and unearned premiums.

compare: earned premium; see: premium, unearned premium

© 1991 NILS Publishing Company

wrong

General. The illegal invasion of another person's interest.

see: tort

wrongful abstraction

Crime. A term used in crime insurance policies meaning the illegal removal of property. Includes all types of burglary, robbery and theft.

wrongful act

Casualty. Coverage included in a directors & officers liability insurance policy which insures them for lawsuits for errors, misstatements or breach of duty.

see: directors & officers liability insurance

wrongful death

General. A legal term for a death caused by an individual or entity without legal justification. Such a death will often result in a suit against the responsible party on the basis of negligence or an intentional act.

see: tort

wrongful discharge or discrimination legal expense insurance

Casualty. Coverage that provides an employer reimbursement for legal expenses involved in defending against suits from employees alleging wrongful discharge, discrimination or sexual harassment.

see: discrimination, sexual harassment, unfair labor practices

© 1991 NILS Publishing Company

XCU exclusions

Casualty. The ISO rating program for the 1973 Comprehensive General Liability policy included classifications for organizations with operations particularly exposed to explosion (X), collapse (C), and underground (U) hazards. For such organizations, the classification code means that hazard is excluded from the policy unless the exclusion is deleted for an additional premium. The 1986 CGL program does not include these rating factors and the form has been revised to automatically cover the XCU exposure.

syn: **explosion, collapse, and underground exclusions; see: blasting and explosion exclusion, collapse exclusion, underground exclusion**

x table

General. A term referring to drafts of rate tables under development.

© 1991 NILS Publishing Company

yacht

Ocean Marine. A relatively small ocean going vessel, usually in excess of 26 feet, characterized by a sharp prow and graceful lines. It is primarily used for pleasure and may be propelled by means of sails, or by steam or motor power.

see: **watercraft exclusion, yacht insurance**

yacht insurance

Ocean Marine. A special policy insuring yachts, cabin cruisers, inboard motorboats and sailing ships. Most policies cover the hull, sails, fittings, furniture, provisions, machinery and equipment. The policy is valued, and full insurance to value is required. Usually written on an "all-risks" basis for hull coverage, named perils forms are also used.

yearly renewable term

Life. Term life insurance which may be renewed annually without evidence of insurability by acceptance of a premium for a new policy term.

syn: **annual renewal term**; see: **re-entry term life insurance, term life insurance**

years of service

Employee Benefits. A period of time credited to a pension plan participant for employment with the plan sponsor. Some plans require continuous employment, while others have specific rules in the event of breaks in employment.

see: **vesting**

York Antwerp Rules

Ocean Marine. A set of rules – initially agreed upon in 1890 and last revised in 1950 – by which ocean marine general average losses are adjusted.

see: **general average**

your product

Casualty. A term used in simplified language liability policies, which means manufactured goods or products sold, handled, distributed, or disposed of by the insured. It includes containers in which the product is shipped and warranties or representations made with respect to the product's fitness, quality, durability, or performance.

see: **products-completed operations insurance**

your work

Casualty. A term used in simplified language liability policies which means work or operations performed by, or on behalf, of the insured including materials, parts, or equipment furnished in connection with such work. It includes warranties or representations made with respect to its fitness, quality, durability, or performance.

see: **products-completed operations insurance**

© 1991 NILS Publishing Company

zone rating

Automobile. A rating method used to rate commercial auto policies, where units are larger than a light truck and are operated over 200 miles in distance from the garage location.

see: **long haul, radius of operation**

zone system

Regulation. A method for the triennial examination of insurers developed by the NAIC. Under this system, examination teams are assembled from the insurance departments located in a specified zone (i.e., region of the country), and the results of the audit are accepted by all insurance departments.

z table

Life. A life insurance mortality table developed from major life insurer experience from 1925 to 1934. This was the forerunner of the Commissioner's Standard Table of Mortality.

see: **mortality table**

ACRONYMS

The following chart lists, in alphabetical order, acronyms used in insurance and risk management. In most cases, you'll find full definitions and descriptions for these terms and organizations in the glossary text.

AAA . . . . .American Academy of Actuaries
. . . . American Agents Association
. . . . American Arbitration Association
. . . . .American Automobile Association
. . . . Association of Average Adjusters of the United States
AACI . . . . American Association of Crop Insurers
AADC . . . . American Association of Dental Consultants
AAI . . . . Alliance of American Insurers
AAIMC . . . . .American Association of Insurance Management Consultants
AAIS . . . . American Association of Insurance Services
AALU . . . . Association For Advanced Life Underwriting
AAMGA . . . . American Association of Managing General Agents
ABA . . . . American Bar Association
ABS . . . . American Bureau of Shipping
ABS Record . . . . American Bureau of Shipping Record
ACAS . . . . Associate of the Casualty Actuarial Society
ACCI . . . . .American Corporate Counsel Institute
ACLI . . . . American Council of Life Insurance
ACSC . . . . Association of Casualty and Surety Companies
ACV . . . . actual cash value
ACWRRE . . . . American Cargo War Risk Reinsurance Exchange
AD & D . . . . accidental death and dismemberment
ADR . . . . American Depository Receipt
ADS . . . . .American Depository Shares
ADTA .Association of Defense Trial Attorneys
AEIA . . . . American Excess Insurance Association
AFIA . . . . American Foreign Insurance Association
A & H . . . . accident and health insurance
AHIS . . . . .American Hull Insurance Syndicate
AIA . . . . .American Institute of Architects
. . . . American Insurance Association
. . . . .Association of Insurance Attorneys
AIDS . . . . acquired immune deficiency syndrome
AIHA . . . . American Industrial Hygiene Association
AIHSA . . . . American Insurers Highway Safety Alliance
AIME . . . . average indexed monthly earnings
AIMU . . . . American Institute of Marine Underwriters
AIP . . . . .annual implementation plan
AIPLU . . . . American Institute for Property and Liability Underwriters

AIRAC	All-Industry Research Advisory Council
AIRB	Aviation Insurance Rating Bureau
AISG	American Insurance Services Group
ALC	American Life Convention
ALIC	Association of Life Insurance Counsel
ALIMDA	Association of Life Insurance Medical Directors of America
ALOS	average length of stay
AMEMIC	Association of Mill and Elevator Mutual Insurance Companies
AMIC	American Marine Insurance Clearinghouse
AMIF	American Marine Insurance Forum
AMW	average monthly wage
ANI	American Nuclear Insurers
ANL	above-normal loss
ANSI	American National Standards Institute
AP	additional premium
APIW	Association of Professional Insurance Women
APS	attending physician's statement
ARIA	American Risk and Insurance Association
ARM	adjustable rate mortgage
	Associate in Risk Management
ARMI	Associated Risk Managers International
ASA	administrative services arrangement
	American Surety Association
	Associate in Society of Actuaries
ASCLU & ChFC	American Society of Chartered Life Underwriters and Chartered Financial Consultants
ASIS	American Society of Industrial Security
ASM	available seat miles
ASME	American Society of Mechanical Engineers, Inc.
ASO	administrative services only
ASPA	American Society of Pension Actuaries
ASSE	American Society of Safety Engineers
ATRA	American Tort Reform Association
BCBSA	Blue Cross and Blue Shield Association
BCSP	Board of Certified Safety Professionals
BFCGL	broad form comprehensive general liability
BFPD	broad form property damage
BI	bodily injury
B&M	boiler & machinery
BOP	business owners policy
CAPP	Conference of Actuaries in Public Practice
CARE	Concerned Alliance of Responsible Employers
CAS	Casualty Actuarial Society
CCIA	Consumer Credit Insurance Association

CCIC	Conference of Casualty Insurance Companies
CD	certificate of deposit
CDW	collision damage waiver
CEB	Council on Employee Benefits
CEBS	Certified Employee Benefit Specialist
CEO	chief executive officer
CERCLA	Comprehensive Environmental Response, Compensation and Liability Act
CFO	chief financial officer
CFP	Certified Financial Planner
CGL	commercial general liability
	comprehensive general liability
ChFC	Chartered Financial Consultant
CHIAA	Crop-Hail Insurance Actuarial Association
CICA	Captive Insurance Companies Association
CIRB	Crop Insurance Research Bureau
CLU	Chartered Life Underwriter
CNHI	Committee for National Health Insurance
COB	coordination of benefits
COBRA	Consolidated Omnibus Budget Reconciliation Act of 1985
COC	course of construction
COGSA	Carriage of Goods by Sea Act
COGWA	Carriage of Goods by Water Act
COO	chief operating officer
CPA	Certified Public Accountant
CPCU	Chartered Property and Casualty Underwriter
CPL	comprehensive personal liability
CPP	commercial package policy
CRA	Cargo Reinsurance Association
CSL	combined single limit
CSO Table	Commissioners Standard Ordinary Table
CSP	Certified Safety Professional
DAP	deposit administration plan
dB	decibel
DB & C	dwelling, buildings and contents
DCF	discounted cash flow techniques
DDD	dishonesty, disappearance and destruction
DI	double indemnity
DIC	difference in conditions
DITC	Disability Insurance Training Council
DMIC	Direct Marketing Insurance Council
D & O	directors & officers liability insurance
DOT	Department of Transportation
DPP	deferred premium payment plan

DR	daily report
DRG	diagnostic related group
EA	Enrolled Actuary
EAP	estimated annual premium
EBRI	Employee Benefit Research Institute
EC	extended coverages
ECC	Eastern Claims Conference
ECF	extended care facility
ECFC	Employers Council on Flexible Compensation
EEL	emergency exposure limit
EFT	electronic funds transfer
E & O	errors & omissions insurance
ERIC	ERISA Industry Committee
ERISA	Employee Retirement Income Security Act of 1974
ERP	extended reporting period
E & S	excess and surplus lines
ESOP	employee stock ownership plan
EXIM Bank	Export-Import Bank
FAA	Federal Aviation Administration
FAIR plans	Fair Access to Insurance Requirements
FAP	family automobile policy
FAR	Federal Aviation Regulations
FAS	free along side
FASB	Financial Accounting Standards Board
FCAS	Fellow of the Casualty Actuarial Society
FCIA	Foreign Credit Insurance Association
FCIC	Federal Crop Insurance Corporation
FCPL	farmers comprehensive personal liability
FC&S	free of capture and seizure
FDA	Food and Drug Administration
FDI	foreign direct investment
FDIC	Federal Deposit Insurance Corporation
FELA	Federal Employers Liability Act
FFMA	Fraternal Field Managers Association
FIA	Factory Insurance Association
	Federal Insurance Administration
	full interest admitted
FIC	Fraternal Insurance Counselor
FICA	Federal Insurance Contributions Act
FICC	Federation of Insurance and Corporate Counsel
FIFO	first in, first out
FIRM	flood insurance rate map
FLMI	Fellow of the Life Management Institute
FM	Factory Mutual System

FMV	fair market value
FOB	free on board
FOB Destination	free on board destination
FOC	Fire Office Committee Forms
FPA	free of particular average
FPAAC	free of particular average American conditions
FPAEC	free of particular average English conditions
FSA	Fellow of the Society of Actuaries
	funding standard account
FSLIC	Federal Savings and Loan Insurance Corporation
FSPA	Fellow of the Society of Pension Actuaries
FTC	Federal Trade Commission
FVD	full value declared
GA	general agent
	general average
GAAP	Generally Accepted Accounting Principles
GAMC-NALU	General Agents and Managers Conference of National Association of Life Underwriters
GASB	Governmental Accounting Standards Board
GCW	gross combination weight
GFCI	ground fault circuit interrupter
GIC	guaranteed investment contract
GKLL	garagekeepers legal liability insurance
GVW	gross vehicle weight
HFIE	Huebner Foundation for Insurance Education
HI	health insurance
HIAA	Health Insurance Association of America
HII	Health Insurance Institute
HLDI	Highway Loss Data Institute
HLV	human life value
HMO	health maintenance organization
HOLUA	Home Office Life Underwriters Association
HPR	highly protected risk
HSA	health systems agency
HSP	health systems plan
IADC	International Association of Defense Counsel
IAO	Insurers' Advisory Organization of Canada
IASA	Insurance Accounting and Systems Association
IBC	Insurance Bureau of Canada
IBNR	incurred but not reported
ICA	International Claim Association
ICC	Interstate Commerce Commission
ICEDS	Insurance Company Education Directors Society
ICP	Insurance Conference Planners

ICPA . . . . Insurance Conference Planners Association
ICPI . . . . Insurance Crime Prevention Institute
IEA . . . . Insurance Educational Association
IFEBP . . . . International Foundation of Employee Benefit Plans
IHOU . . . . Institute of Home Office Underwriters
IIA . . . . Insurance Institute of America
IIAA . . . . Independent Insurance Agents of America
IIAC . . . . International Insurance Advisory Council
IIC . . . . Insurance Institute of Canada
. . . . International Insurance Council
IIE . . . . Illinois Insurance Exchange
IIHS . . . . Insurance Institute for Highway Safety
III . . . . Insurance Information Institute
IIMA . . . . Insurance Industry Meetings Association
IIS . . . . International Insurance Seminars, Inc.
. . . . International Insurance Society
ILCA . . . . Insurance Loss Control Association
IMCA . . . . Insurance Marketing Communications Association
IMUA . . . . Inland Marine Underwriters Association
IPFA . . . . Insurance Premium Finance Association
IRA . . . . individual retirement account
IRES . . . . Insurance Regulatory Examiners Society
IRI . . . . Industrial Risk Insurers
IRIS . . . . Insurance Regulatory Information System
IRPM . . . . individual risk premium modification rating plan
IRR . . . . internal rate of return
ISCEBS . . . . International Society of Certified Employee Benefit Specialists
ISNY . . . . Insurance Society of New York
ISO . . . . Insurance Services Office
ITI . . . . Insurance Testing Institute
IVANS . . . . Insurance Value Added Network Services
JUA . . . . joint underwriting association
LASH . . . . lighter aboard ship
LCA . . . . Life Communicators Association
LCF . . . . loss conversion factor
LDF . . . . loss development factor
LDW . . . . limited damage waiver
LEA . . . . Loss Executives Association
LEL . . . . lower explosive level
LIAA . . . . Life Insurance Association of America
LIAMA . . . . Life Insurance Agency Management Association
LIC . . . . Life Insurers Conference
LIFO . . . . last in, first out
LIMRA . . . . Life Insurance Marketing and Research Association

LOC . . . . letter of credit
. . . . line of credit
LOMA . . . . Life Office Management Association
LPG . . . . liquefied petroleum gas
LPRT . . . . Leading Producers Round Table
LTD . . . . long term disability
LUPAC . . . . Life Underwriter Political Action Committee
LUTC . . . . Life Underwriting Training Council
MAC . . . . maximum allowable concentration
MAELU . . . . .Mutual Atomic Energy Liability Underwriters
MAPS . . . . .market assistance plans
M&C . . . . manufacturers and contractors liability insurance
MDO . . . . monthly debit ordinary life insurance
MDRT . . . . Million Dollar Round Table
MGA . . . . .managing general agent
MIB . . . . Medical Information Bureau
MICA . . . . Mortgage Insurance Companies of America
MMII . . . . Mass Marketing Insurance Institute
MNC . . . . .multinational corporation
MOP . . . . manufacturers output policy
MPCI . . . . .multi-peril crop insurance
MVR . . . . .motor vehicle record
NABRTI . . . . National Association of Bar-Related Title Insurers
NACA . . . . National Association of Catastrophe Adjusters
NACIA . . . . .National Association of Crop Insurance Agents
NACSA . . . . National Association of Casualty and Surety Agents
NACSE . . . . National Association of Casualty and Surety Executives
NAFI . . . . National Association of Fire Investigators
NAFIC . . . . .National Association of Fraternal Insurance Counselors
NAHU . . . . National Association of Health Underwriters
NAIA . . . . National Association of Insurance Agents, Inc.
NAIB . . . . National Association of Insurance Brokers, Inc.
NAIC . . . . National Association of Insurance Commissioners
NAII . . . . .National Association of Independent Insurers
NAIIA . . . . National Association of Independent Insurance Adjusters
NAILBA . . . . National Association of Independent Life
Brokerage Agencies
NAIW . . . . .National Association of Insurance Women
NALC . . . . National Association of Life Companies
NALU . . . . National Association of Life Underwriters
NAMIC . . . . .National Association of Mutual Insurance Companies
NAPIA . . . . .National Association of Public Insurance Adjusters
NAPSLO . . . . National Association of Professional Surplus Lines Offices
NASBP . . . . National Association of Surety Bond Producers

NASD	National Association of Securities Dealers
NATB	National Automobile Theft Bureau
NBFU	National Board of Fire Underwriters
NCCI	National Council on Compensation Insurance
NCCMP	National Coordinating Committee for Multiemployer Plans
NCIA	National Crop Insurance Association
NCIS	National Crop Insurance Services
NCOIL	National Conference of Insurance Legislators
NCPI	National Committee on Property Insurance
NCSI	National Council of Self-Insurers
NCUA	National Credit Union Administration
NEBI	National Employee Benefits Institute
NFCA	National Fraternal Congress of America
NFGMIC	National Federation of Grange Mutual Insurance Companies
NFIP	National Flood Insurance Program
NFPA	National Fire Protection Association
NHAFA	National Health Care Anti-Fraud Association
NIA	National Insurance Association
NICO	National Insurance Consumer Organization
NIDC	National Insurance Development Corporation
NIOSH	National Institute for Occupational Safety and Health
NIPA	National Institute of Pension Administrators
NOC	not otherwise classified
NPV	net present value method
NRC	Nuclear Regulatory Commission
NSC	National Safety Council
NSIPA	National Society of Insurance Premium Auditors
NSLI	National Service Life Insurance
OASDHI	Old Age, Survivors, Disability, and Health Insurance
OCP	owners and contractors protective liability
OD	occupational disease
OFA	Organized Flying Adjusters
OL&T	owners, landlords, and tenants liability insurance
OPIC	Overseas Private Investment Corporation
OSHA	Occupational Safety and Health Act
OTC	other-than-collision coverage
P/E	average annual price-earnings ratio
PAP	personal automobile policy
PARMA	Public Agency Risk Managers Association
PBGC	Pension Benefit Guaranty Corporation
P&I	protection & indemnity insurance
PI	personal injury liability
PIA	primary insurance amount
	Professional Insurance Agents

PICA . . . . Professional Insurance Communicators of America
PILR . . . . Property Insurance Loss Register
PIMA . . . . Professional Insurance Mass-Marketing Association
PIP . . . . .personal injury protection
PLIA . . . . Pollution Liability Insurance Association
PLRB . . . . Property Loss Research Bureau
PML . . . . probable maximum loss
PPF . . . . personal property floater
PPO . . . . .preferred provider organization
PRIMA . . . . Public Risk Management Association
PSRO . . . . Professional Standards Review Organization
Q TIP Trust . . . . qualified terminable interest property trust
QC . . . . quality control
RAA . . . . .Reinsurance Association of America
RAM . . . . reverse-annuity mortgage
RCRA . . . . Resource Conservation and Recovery Act of 1976
REIT . . . . real estate investment trust
RFP . . . . request for proposal
RIMS . . . . Risk and Insurance Management Society, Inc.
ROI . . . . return on investment
RP . . . . .return premium
RPG . . . . risk purchasing group
RRG . . . . risk retention group
RRSP . . . . registered retirement saving plan
SAA . . . . Surety Association of America
SAP . . . . Statutory Accounting Principles
SAWW . . . . statewide average weekly wage
SBLI . . . . savings bank life insurance
SCIC . . . . Society of Certified Insurance Counselors
SCPCU . . . . .Society of Chartered Property and Casualty Underwriters
SEC . . . . Securities and Exchange Commission
SEP . . . . simplified employee pension
SEUA . . . . South-Eastern Underwriters Association
SGLI . . . . .Servicemen's Group Life Insurance
SIA . . . . Society of Insurance Accountants
SIIA . . . . Self-Insurance Institute of America
SIPC . . . . Securities Investor Protection Corporation
SIR . . . . self-insured retention
. . . . .Society of Insurance Research
SITE . . . . Society of Insurance Trainers and Educators
SMP . . . . .special multi-peril program
SOA . . . . .Society of Actuaries
SPBA . . . . Society of Professional Benefit Administrators
SRA . . . . .Society for Risk Analysis

SR&CC	strikes, riots and civil commotions
SRMC	Society of Risk Management Consultants
STD	short-term disability
TCN	third country national
TDA	tax deferred annuity
TDB	temporary disability benefits
TEFRA	Tax Equity and Financial Responsibility Acts of 1982 and 1983
TLO	total loss only
TPA	third-party administrator
UCC	Uniform Commercial Code
UCD	unemployment compensation disability
UCR	usual, customary and reasonable
UEL	upper explosive level
UJF	unsatisfied judgment fund
UL	Underwriters Laboratories, Inc.
ULC	Underwriters Laboratories of Canada
UNL	ultimate net loss
U & O	use and occupancy
URMIA	University Risk Management and Insurance Association
USGLI	United States Government Life Insurance
USL & H	United States Longshoremen's and Harbor Workers' Act of 1927
VA	Veterans Administration
VGLI	Veterans Group Life Insurance
V&MM	vandalism and malicious mischief
WAEPA	Worldwide Assurance for Employees of Public Agencies
WC	workers' compensation
WLRT	Women Leaders Round Table
WLUC	Women Life Underwriters Confederation

FOREIGN INSURANCE TERMS

The following three tables list—in alphabetical order—French, German and Spanish insurance terms along with the corresponding English terms. The definitions for the English terms are found in the main text of the Glossary.

The foreign insurance terms appearing in this Glossary were derived from the "Foreign Insurance Words Dictionary" which appeared in the September/October 1989 issue of *Reinsurance Digest*, published by Reinsurance Communications Co., Inc. These were supplemented by the foreign term reviewers indicated in the acknowledgments.

French Insurance Terms

accident . . . . accident
accidents du travail . . . . occupational accident, workers' compensation
affaire . . . . business
arbitrage . . . . arbitration
assurance maritime . . . . ocean marine insurance
assuré . . . . insured
automobile . . . . automobile
avarie commune . . . . general average
avenant . . . . endorsement
bâtiment . . . . .building
blessure . . . . .injury
blessure corporelle . . . . bodily injury
cautionnement . . . . bonding
coassurance . . . . coinsurance
compagnie d'assurances . . . . insurance company
connaissement . . . . bill of lading
contrat . . . . contract
coque . . . . hull
courtier . . . . .broker
couverture provisoire . . . . binder
débit . . . . debit
décès . . . . death
déductible . . . . deductible
dépendant . . . . dependent
dépréciation . . . . .depreciation
devis estimatif . . . . appraisal
dommage causé par acte de malveillance . . . . malicous mischief
dommages éprouves par les
    (voitures or automobiles) . . . . physical damage (automobile)
durée de la police . . . . policy period
effets à recevoir . . . . .accounts receivable
émeute . . . . riot
énumeration des risques . . . . named perils

exclusion	exclusion
expertise	loss control
explosion	explosion
foudre	lightning
frais	expenses
franchise	deductible
garantie	surety
glissement de terrain	subsidence
grêle	hail
grève	strike
incapacité	disability
incendie	fire
indemnité	indemnity
inondation	flood
invalidité	disability
larcin	pilferage
lésion	injury
lieux	premises
locaux	premises
machinerie	machinery
marchandise	stock
mouvement populaire	civil commotion
mort	death
objet	object
obligataire	obligee
ouragan	hurricane
passager	passenger
perte	loss
petit vol	pilferage
police	policy
prime	premium
principal	principal
proposition	application
réclamation	claim
rémuneration	remuneration
renonciation	waiver
résiliation	cancellation
responsabilité avouée	admitted liability
responsabilité légale	legal liability
risque	exposure
risque assuré	peril (insured)
ristourne de prime	return premium
sauvetage	salvage
soumission	application, bid

subrogation . . . . subrogation
taux . . . . rate
tempête . . . . windstorm
terme . . . . term
transport . . . . inland marine
tremblement de terre . . . . earthquake
valeur à neuf . . . . replacement cost
ventes . . . . sales
vol . . . . theft, robbery
vol par effraction . . . . burglary

German Insurance Terms

Abschreibung (Herabsetzung) . . . . depreciation
anerkannte Haftpflicht . . . . admitted liability
Angebot . . . . bid
Angehörigen . . . . dependents
Anspruch . . . . claim
Antrag . . . . application
Arbeitsunfall . . . . occupational accident
Arbeitsunfallversicherung . . . . workers' compensation
Aufwendungen . . . . expenses
Aufruhr . . . . riot
Ausschlüsse . . . . exclusions
Beitrag . . . . premium
benannte Gefahren . . . . named perils
Bergung . . . . salvage
Binnentransport . . . . inland marine
Blitzschlag . . . . lightning
Böswilligkeit . . . . malicious mischief
Debit (Soll) . . . . debit
Diebstahl . . . . theft
Einbruchdiebstahl . . . . burglary
Entschädigung . . . . indemnity
Erdbeben . . . . earthquake
Ersatzwert . . . . replacement cost
Explosion . . . . explosion
Feuer . . . . fire
Forderungen Aussenstände . . . . accounts receivable
Frist . . . . term
Garantie . . . . surety
Garantieversicherung . . . . bonding
Gebäude . . . . building
Gefahrenumstand . . . . exposure

Foreign Insurance Terms

Gegenstand . . . . object
Geschäft . . . . business
gesetzliche Haftpflicht . . . . legal liability
Gläubiger . . . . obligee
grosse Havarie . . . . general average
Grundstück . . . . premises
Hagel . . . . hail
innere Unruhen . . . . civil commotion
Invalidität . . . . disability
Kasko . . . . hull
Kasko (Auto) . . . . physical damage (automobile)
Konnossement . . . . bill of lading
Kraftfahrzeug . . . . automobile
Kündigung . . . . cancellation
Lager . . . . stock
Makler . . . . broker
Maschinen . . . . machinery
Mitversicherung . . . . coinsurance
Nachtrag . . . . endorsement
Neuwert . . . . replacement cost
Objekt . . . . object
Offerte . . . . bid
Orkan . . . . hurricane
Passagier . . . . passenger
Personenschaden . . . . bodily injury
Plünderung . . . . pilferage
Police . . . . policy
Prämie . . . . premium
Prämiensatz . . . . rate
Prinzipal . . . . principal
Raub . . . . robbery
Regress . . . . subrogation
Rückvergütete Prämie . . . . return premium
Schadenkontrolle . . . . loss control
Schätzung . . . . appraisal
Schiedsverfahren . . . . arbitration
Seetransport Versicherung . . . . ocean marine insurance
Selbstbeteiligung . . . . deductible
Senkung . . . . subsidence
Storno . . . . cancellation
Streik . . . . strike
Sturm . . . . windstorm
Tod . . . . death
Ueberschwemmung . . . . flood

Umsatz . . . . sales
Unfall . . . . accident
Vergütung . . . . .remuneration
Versicherungsnehmer . . . . insured
Verletzung . . . . .injury
Verlust . . . . loss
versicherte Gefahren . . . . .peril
Versicherungsgesellschaft . . . . insurance company
Vertrag . . . . contract
Vertragsdauer . . . . policy period
Verzicht . . . . waiver
Vorläufige Deckungszusage . . . . binder
Vorräte . . . . .stock
Waren . . . . .cargo

Spanish Insurance Terms

accidente . . . . accident
accidentes de trabajo . . . . occupational accident
actos por personas mal intencionadas . . . . malicious mischief
alboroto popular . . . . riot
arbitraje . . . . arbitration
asegurado . . . . insured
automóvil . . . . .automobile
avalúo . . . . appraisal
avería gruesa . . . . general average
bonding . . . . bonding
cancelación . . . . cancellation
cargo . . . . debit
casco . . . . hull
coaseguro . . . . coinsurance
compañía de seguros . . . . insurance company
compensación obrera o riesgos
profesionales . . . . .workers' compensation
conmoción civil . . . . civil commotion
conocimiento de embarque . . . . bill of lading
contrato . . . . contract
control de pérdida . . . . .loss control
corredor . . . . .broker
costo de reposición . . . . .replacement cost
cuota . . . . rate
cubierta provisional . . . . binder
cuentas por cobrar . . . . accounts receivable
cuota . . . . rate

daño físico (automóvil) . . . . physical damage (automobile)
débito . . . . debit
deducible . . . . deductible
dependientes . . . . dependent
depreciación . . . . depreciation
desmoronamiento . . . . subsidence
edificio . . . . building
el que se beneficia . . . . obligee
empresa . . . . business
endoso . . . . endorsement
exclusión . . . . exclusion
existencias . . . . stock
explosión . . . . explosion
gastos . . . . expenses
granizo . . . . hail
huelga . . . . strike
hundimiento . . . . subsidence
huracan . . . . hurricane
hurto . . . . burglary
incapacidad . . . . disability
indemnización . . . . indemnity
incendio . . . . fire
inundación . . . . flood
lesión . . . . injury
lesiones corporales . . . . bodily injury
maquinaria . . . . machinery
muerte . . . . death
negocio . . . . business
objeto . . . . object
oferta . . . . bid
pasajero . . . . passenger
pérdida . . . . loss
período . . . . term
peritaje . . . . appraisal
poliza . . . . policy
predios . . . . premises
prima . . . . premium
prima de devolución . . . . return premium
principal . . . . principal
ratería . . . . pilferage
rayo . . . . lightning
reclamación . . . . claim
remuneración . . . . remuneration
renuncia . . . . waiver

responsabilidad admitida . . . . admitted liability
responsabilidad legal . . . . legal liability
riesgo . . . . .exposure
riesgo asegurado . . . . peril (insured)
riesgos especificados . . . . named perils
robo con violencia . . . . .robbery
robo sin violencia . . . . theft
salvamento . . . . salvage
seguro marítimo . . . . ocean marine insurance
seguro terrestre . . . . .inland marine
solicitud . . . . application
subrogación . . . . subrogation
tasación . . . . appraisal
terremoto . . . . .earthquake
terrestre . . . . .inland marine
tipo . . . . rate
valuación . . . . appraisal
ventas . . . . sales
vigencia . . . . term
vigencia de la póliza . . . . policy period
vientos tempestuosos . . . . windstorm

Also from NILS Publishing

■ **National Insurance Law Service** For over 40 years, this has been the industry's premier source of information on state insurance regulation. At over 185 looseleaf volumes, the National Insurance Law Service brings you the statutes, regulations and related regulatory materials with which insurers, reinsurers, agents and brokers must comply. Separate volumes are available for each U.S. state and possession, and each book features a detailed index. Revision services for each volume keep them up-to-date and accurate.

■ **National Indexes** Using the same terminology found in the National Insurance Law Service's back-of-the-book indexes, our National Indexes make multi-state (even 50-state) research quick, easy and comprehensive. These softbound indexes are re-issued annually, and separate National Indexes are available for Insurance Laws and Insurance Regulations. A third National Index—the National Index of Insurance Definitions—helps you locate definitions for significant terms in insurance statutes and regulations.

■ **National Insurance Law Review** A quarterly compilation of the most significant articles on insurance law, selected by the Editors of the National Insurance Law Service from among the nation's foremost university and independent law reviews. Save research time (and money) by turning to the industry's oldest and most respected law review: the National Insurance Law Review.

■ **Insurance & Liability Reporter** A twice-monthly newsletter, reporting on the most significant decisions in insurance and liability law. Using 64 on-the-spot contributors (the continent's most respected law firms in insurance and liability litigation)—at least one in each U.S. state and Canadian province—and online legal research facilities, the Reporter brings you decision summaries and analysis long before other newsletters. More importantly, it's the first and only newsletter to focus on *both* insurance *and* liability issues. Edited by Mark S. Rhodes, an author, contributor, and editor of such works as *Couch on Insurance* 2d (Rev. Ed.), *Comparative Negligence*, and *Long, Law of Liability Insurance.*

■ **Insurance Periodicals Index** A comprehensive index to the more than 15,000 articles that appear every year in over 35 magazines and journals in insurance. All the major publications are indexed—*Business Insurance, Best's Review* (Life/Health and Property/Casualty editions), *National Underwriter* (Life/Health and Property/Casualty editions)—as well as the more specialized publications—*Employee Benefits Journal, Risk Management* and *Life Insurance Selling.* With the *Insurance Periodicals Index*, you'll turn back-issues of these publications into a valuable research tool. Published annually in two softbound volumes.

■ **Reinsurance Law** A comprehensive survey of the significant decisions and events that have shaped the business of reinsurance. Special emphasis is given to the British experience in this single looseleaf volume. Regular updates bring you analysis of new developments, as well as an expansion of the book's discussion of the U.S. reinsurance market.

■ Captive Insurance Manual This two-volume, looseleaf reference is truly comprehensive: you not only benefit from expert analysis of every major U.S. & off-shore domicile's laws and regulations, you get the actual text of those laws and regulations. The domicile discussion also includes current information on political, social and economic situations. And, of course, you benefit from clear, practical treatments of U.S. tax implications, feasibility considerations, and captive formation and operation. Update service keeps you fully informed of amendments in laws and new tax decisions.

For details on these and other information services available from

NILS Publishing Company

Call TOLL-FREE

1-800-423-5910

Ask for the Telemarketing Department

TO THE READER

While we've made every possible effort to ensure that *Rupp's Insurance and Risk Management Glossary* is accurate, comprehensive and useful, it is inevitable that we've omitted some terms. Perhaps you believe a definition is not as clear as it could be. In either case, we would appreciate your suggestions for additions and corrections. Please send them to us by using photocopies of the following form.

Mail Your Comments To Us

NILS Publishing Company
ATTN: New Products Dept.
21625 Prairie Street
Chatsworth, CA 91311

Fax Your Comments To Us   (818) 718-8482

Please indicate "New Products Department" on your FAX Transmittal Form.

Call Us Toll Free   1-800-423-5910

Ask for the New Products Department.   or (818) 998-8830

Term:_____

Subject(s): _____

Definition/Comments:

_____
_____
_____
_____
_____
_____
_____
_____
_____
_____
_____
_____
_____
_____
_____
_____
_____

Cross References:_____

Thank y